INDEPENDENT
TELEVISION
IN BRITAIN

Volume 5

ITV and the IBA 1981–92: The Old Relationship Changes

Other volumes in the same work

Volume 1 ORIGIN AND FOUNDATION, 1946–62
(*by Bernard Sendall*)

Volume 2 EXPANSION AND CHANGE, 1958–68
(*by Bernard Sendall*)

Volume 3 POLITICS AND CONTROL, 1968–80
(*by Jeremy Potter*)

Volume 4 COMPANIES AND PROGRAMMES, 1968–80
(*by Jeremy Potter*)

INDEPENDENT
TELEVISION
IN BRITAIN

Volume 5

ITV and the IBA 1981–92:
The Old Relationship Changes

PAUL BONNER
with
LESLEY ASTON

First published 1998 by
MACMILLAN PRESS LTD
Houndmills, Basingstoke, Hampshire RG21 6XS
and London
Companies and representatives
throughout the world

ISBN 0–333–64773–4

A catalogue record for this book is available
from the British Library.

This book is printed on paper suitable for recycling
and made from fully managed and sustained forest sources.

10 9 8 7 6 5 4 3 2 1
07 06 05 04 03 02 01 00 99 98

Printed in Great Britain by
Antony Rowe Ltd, Chippenham, Wiltshire

CONTENTS

LIST OF PLATES

(The late) **Sir William (Bill) Brown** Scottish Television: Managing Director 1966–90, Chairman 1991–95. (Knighted 1996.)

Sir Alastair Burnet Independent Television News: Newscaster *News at Ten* 1967–90, Associate Editor and Director 1981–90. Knighted 1984).

Bryan Cowgill Thames Television: Managing Director 1977–85.

Richard Dunn Thames Television: Director of Production 1981–85, Managing Director (subsequently Chief Executive) 1985–95.

Greg Dyke London Weekend Television: Director of Programmes 1987–91, Managing Director (subsequently Group Chief Executive) 1990–94. (Previously TVS: Director of Programmes 1984–87 and before that TV-am: Editor-in-Chief 1983–84).

David Elstein Thames Television: Director of Programmes 1986–92. (Previously founded Brook Productions (an independent producer) 1982. Primetime Television (independent producer): Managing Director 1983–86.)

Sir Paul Fox Yorkshire Television: Director of Programmes 1973–84, Managing Director 1977–88. Director, Thames Television 1991–95 (Knighted 1991.)

James Gatward Television South (subsequently TVS Entertainment): Managing Director 1979–84. Chief Executive 1984–91. TVS Television: Chairman and Chief Executive 1984–90, Chairman 1990–91.

David Glencross Independent Broadcasting Authority: Deputy Director of Television 1977–83, Director of Television 1983–90. Independent Television Commission: Chief Executive Designate 1990, Chief Executive 1991–96.

Michael Green Carlton Communications: Chief Executive 1983–91, Chairman 1983–. Carlton Television: Chairman 1991–94.

Leslie Hill Central Independent Television: Managing Director 1987–91, Chairman and Chief Executive 1991–95.

Lord (Clive) Hollick MAI: Chief Executive 1974–. Meridian Broadcasting: Chairman 1992–96. (Life Peerage 1991.)

Lady (Shirley) Littler Independent Broadcasting Authority: Director of Administration 1983–86, Deputy Director General 1986–89, Acting Director General 1989–1990, Director General 1990. (Centre of picture; with Clare Mulholland, Deputy Director of Television, on right, and Barbara Hosking, Controller, Information Services.)

David McCall Anglia Television: Chief Executive 1976–96. Anglia Television Group: Chief Executive 1986–96.

Sir David Nicholas Independent Television News: Editor 1977–89, Chief Executive 1977–91, Chairman 1989–91. (Knighted 1989.)

Professor Sir Alan Peacock Committee on Financing the BBC: Chairman 1985–86. (Economist who has held many senior academic appointments – particularly relating to Public Finance – and governmental advisory roles. Knighted 1987.)

Marcus Plantin London Weekend Television: Director of Programmes 1991–92. ITV Network Centre: Network Director 1992–97.

David Plowright Granada Television: Managing Director 1981–87, Chairman 1987–92.

Stewart Purvis Independent Television News: Programme Editor *News at Ten* 1980–83, Editor *Channel Four News* 1983–86, Deputy Editor ITN 1986–89, Editor 1989–91, Editor-in-Chief 1991–.

Andrew Quinn Granada Television: Managing Director 1987–92, Chief Executive 1992. Independent Television Network Centre: Chief Executive 1992–95. (Previously Managing Director Granada Cable and Satellite 1983–87.)

Gerry Robinson Granada Group: Chief Executive 1991–96, Chairman 1996–.

Peter Rogers Independent Broadcasting Authority: Director of Finance 1982–90. Independent Television Commission: Deputy Chief Executive and Director of Finance 1991–96. Chief Executive 1996–.

Sir George Russell Independent Broadcasting Authority: Member 1979–86, Chairman 1988–90. Independent Television Commission: Chairman 1991–97. Independent Television News: Chairman 1988. (Knighted 1992.)

Brian Tesler London Weekend Television: Managing Director 1976–90, Deputy Chairman 1982–84, Chairman 1984–92. LWT (Holdings) plc: Deputy Chairman 1990–94.

Lord Thomson (of Monifieth) Independent Broadcasting Authority: Deputy Chairman 1980, Chairman 1981–88. (Life Peerage 1977.)

John Whitney Independent Broadcasting Authority: Director General 1982–89. (Pictured on left, at the IBA's farewell party for Lord Thomson in December 1988).

Lord Windlesham Author (with Richard Rampton) of Report of *Death on the Rock*. (Amongst previous roles was Minister of State at the Home Office 1970–72, Minister of State for Northern Ireland 1972–73 and Managing Director of ATV Network 1975–81).

Out with the IBA – in with the ITC

The high degree of regulatory continuity maintained across the changes brought about by the Broadcasting Act 1990 is visible by comparing the picture of the Members of the last Authority in 1990 and the first Commission in 1991.

LIST OF TABLES AND FIGURES

PREFACE AND ACKNOWLEDGEMENTS

This volume of *Independent Television in Britain* differs in form as well as content from its predecessors. It is a measure of the speed of change in British television in the last decade that the context of publication now offers a potentially broader-based readership than that for previous volumes.

There were only three channels of television available to British viewers at the start of the 1980s. Now there are five almost universally available from terrestrial transmitters and more than fifty beamed specifically at British audiences by satellite. Cable television was an infant industry in 1980, consisting of some sixteen operators. By 1997 there were 137 franchised cable operators, each offering up to fifty channels to subscribers (*ITC Factfile 1997*).

In production a whole new industry of some 600 companies was created during the decade as a result of the requirement that Channel Four should commission 'a substantial proportion' of its programmes from independent producers. Subsequently the other major broadcasters were required to commission 25 per cent or more of their programming from independent producers.

In education the number of universities and colleges offering undergraduate degree courses in Media Studies expanded from about a dozen in the early Eighties to 107 by 1997 and those institutions with postgraduate courses rose from a handful to sixty-seven in the same period (*Media Courses in the UK,* British Film Institute, 1997). A research project at Brunel University in 1996 calculated that there were then 32,000 media students in the UK (*Evening Standard*, 5 November 1997).

This book is therefore written in a style that assumes a wider audience than just the executives and producers of the old duopoly of the BBC and ITV, the staff of the latter's regulator, the IBA, and a limited academic readership. This volume could not take for granted a knowledge of the intricacies of the British independent television system.

The consequent explanations of the detail of its operations may irritate some insiders who know it all already but it is hoped that they will understand that such explanations are necessary to fulfil the book's function for its new audience. That

xi

hope is underlined by the fact that many senior figures in the old industry have contributed time and memory to give this book more authority than it might otherwise have had. My sincere thanks to all those who agreed to be interviewed (listed on pp. xiv–xviii) and to the even greater number of people from ITV's past and present who have provided specific information. In the case of regional matters this was often in writing. As well as Laurie Upshon (who is credited in the text) these 'correspondents' were Peter Moth, Mike McLintock and Donald Cullimore.

Particular thanks are due to those untiring archivists at the ITC and the ITV Network Centre, Miranda Parker and Andrew Read. Both made important contributions to the book but they also are responsible for the maintenance of a culture of orderly and economic preservation for which future writers and students of the Media will be grateful. The enlightened policy makers in both organisations who enable the support of this culture will doubtless only get their reward in some archival heaven, meanwhile they certainly have my gratitude! My thanks also go to Sara Winter at the ITC, whose contributions ranged from organisation of the complex interview schedule and the handling of all consequent correspondence, to the typing of research notes – with a thousand tasks in between – all this on top of her 'day job'. Her unflagging enthusiasm over the three years does her great credit. Credit for transcription of the interviews goes to Bill Bourne and his team at Bourne Associates.

In a sense *Independent Television in Britain* is an exercise in accountability by the ITC and ITV, who have supported the project financially as well as providing access to their documents. Written too close to the events it relates to allow of a true historical perspective, but more authoritative than the journalism contemporaneous with those events, this book should indeed be read as 'an account' of the key developments, issues and incidents that took place within Independent Television between 1981 and 1992 – with slight but relevant overlaps either side of those dates. This volume deals solely with ITV and the IBA (later the ITC). The next will cover the newly arriving competitors within the commercial television business: Channel Four, TV-am, BSB, Sky – and the fusion of the latter two.

Like its predecessors this volume takes themes, rather than chronology, as the basis for its structure. Within those themes there are accounts of events which serve to delineate the very considerable forces for change that impacted on the industry – both from outside and from within – during the period. Accounts of developments are placed in the book where they are most relevant. For example the Ministerial Direction restraining broadcasters from broadcasting direct statements made by representatives of Northern Ireland terrorist organisations is to be found immediately after the account of events surrounding the programme *Death on the Rock*.

In such a structure as that outlined above, the Bibliography and the Index play a vital part for readers. Credit for the effectiveness of these tools (and gratitude for his factual help with the book itself) goes to Barrie MacDonald, the Librarian of the ITC, who has provided this service now for three authors producing the five volumes of *Independent Television in Britain* published so far by Macmillan.

Finally, this volume owes a huge debt to Lesley Aston. She started as its diligent researcher facing quantities of material that would have overwhelmed others, but her rigour of thought and the clarity of her research notes as we progressed were to make her in effect the book's co-author. Lesley was also a supportive force in the sometimes lonely task of producing this type of book. We hope that you will find this an accessible, if inevitably somewhat eclectic, portrait of an extraordinarily eventful period in British commercial television.

Paul Bonner

LIST OF INTERVIEWEES AND THEIR PRINCIPAL RELEVANT POSITIONS HELD 1981–92

Andy Allan
Central Independent Television: Director of Programmes 1984–90. Central Broadcasting: Managing Director 1990–93. (Previously Tyne Tees Television: Director of Programmes 1978–83, Deputy Managing Director 1982–83, Managing Director 1983–84.)

Sir Brian Bailey
Television South West: Chairman 1980–93. (Knighted 1983.)

John Birt
London Weekend Television: Director of Programmes 1982–87.

Sir Christopher Bland
London Weekend Television: Chairman (of LWT (Holdings)) plc 1984–94. (Knighted 1993.)

Kenneth Blyth
Independent Broadcasting Authority: Chief Assistant to the Director General 1979–88, Secretary 1988–90. Independent Television Commission: Secretary 1991–93.

Melvyn Bragg
London Weekend Television: Head of Arts 1982–90. Controller of Arts 1990– . Border Television: Chairman 1990– .

(The late) **Sir William (Bill) Brown**
Scottish Television: Managing Director 1966–90, Chairman 1991–95. (Knighted 1996.)

(The late) **Frank Copplestone**
Westcountry: Deputy Chairman 1991 until his death in 1996. (Previously Southern Television: Managing Director 1976–88.)

Barry Cox
London Weekend Television Controller of Features and Current Affairs 1981–87, Director of Corporate Affairs 1987–94.

Huw Davies
HTV: Director of Television (of HTV Wales)

	1981–87, Chief Executive (of HTV Wales) 1987–91, Group Director of Television 1989–96.
Patrick Dromgoole	HTV: Assistant Managing Director and Programme Controller 1981–87, Managing Director 1987, Chief Executive (of HTV Group) 1988–91.
Richard Dunn	Thames Television: Director of Production 1981–85, Managing Director (subsequently Chief Executive) 1985–95.
Greg Dyke	London Weekend Television: Director of Programmes 1987–91, Managing Director (subsequently Group Chief Executive) 1990–94. (Previously TVS: Director of Programmes 1984–87 and before that TV-am: Editor in Chief 1983–84.)
David Elstein	Thames Television: Director of Programmes 1986–92. (Previously founded Brook Productions (an independent producer) 1982. Primetime Television (independent producer): Managing Director 1983–86.)
John Fairley	Yorkshire Television: Director of Programmes 1984–92.
Sir Denis Forman	Granada Television: Chairman 1974–87, Granada Group: Deputy Chairman 1984–90. (Knighted 1976.)
Dr John Forrest	Independent Broadcasting Authority: Director of Engineering 1986–90. National Trans-communications (NTL): Chief Executive 1991–94.
Robin Foster	National Economic Research Associates (NERA): Director and Head of London communications practice 1986–93.
Sir Paul Fox	Yorkshire Television: Director of Programmes 1973–84, Managing Director 1977–88. Thames Television: Director 1991–95. (Knighted 1991.)
James Gatward	Television South (subsequently TVS Entertainment): Managing Director 1979–84. Chief Executive 1984–91. TVS Television: Chairman and Chief Executive 1984–90, Chairman 1990–91.
David Glencross	Independent Broadcasting Authority: Deputy Director of Television 1977–83, Director of Television 1983–90. Independent Television Commission: Chief Executive Designate 1990,

	Chief Executive 1991–96.
James Graham	Border Television: Managing Director 1982–95 Deputy Chairman 1990–95 , Chairman and Chief Executive 1995– .
Michael Green	Carlton Communications: Chief Executive 1983–91, Chairman 1983– . Carlton Television: Chairman 1991–94.
John Henwood	Channel Television: Programme Controller 1983–86, Director of Programmes 1986–87, Managing Director CTV and Group Chief Executive 1987– .
Leslie Hill	Central Independent Television: Managing Director 1987–91, Chairman and Chief Executive 1991–95.
Lord (Clive) Hollick	MAI: Chief Executive 1974–. Meridian Broadcasting: Chairman 1992–96. (Life Peerage 1991.)
Barbara Hosking	Independent Broadcasting Authority: Controller, Information Services 1977–86. (Subsequently Westcountry Television: non-executive director 1992–97, Deputy Chairman 1997– .).
Roger Laughton	Meridian Broadcasting: Chief Executive 1991– . (In 1990 headed MAI Broadcasting – the precursor to Meridian.)
Lady (Shirley) Littler	Independent Broadcasting Authority: Director of Administration 1983–86, Deputy Director General 1986–89, Acting Director General 1989–1990, Director General 1990.
David McCall	Anglia Television: Chief Executive 1976–96. Anglia Television Group: Chief Executive 1986–96.
Gus Macdonald	Scottish Television: Director of Programmes 1986–90, Managing Director 1990–.
David Mellor	Home Office: Under-Secretary 1983–86, Minister of State 1986–87 and 1989–90. Department of National Heritage: Secretary of State 1992.
Sir David Nicholas	Independent Television News: Editor 1977–89, Chief Executive 1977–91, Chairman 1989–91. (Knighted 1989.)
Professor Sir Alan Peacock	Committee on Financing the BBC: Chairman 1985–86. (Economist who has held many senior academic appointments – particularly relating to Public Finance – and governmental advisory roles. Knighted 1987.)

Bob Phillis	Central Independent Television: Managing Director 1981–87. Carlton Communications: Group Managing Director 1987–91. Independent Television News: Chief Executive 1991–93.
David Plowright	Granada Television: Managing Director 1981–87, Chairman 1987–92.
Stuart Prebble	Granada Television: Producer 1983–87, Editor *World in Action* 1987–89, Head of Regional Programmes 1989–90. North East Television (Granada sponsored bid for licence for North-East region): Managing Director 1990–91. Granada Television: Head of Factual Programmes 1992. (Took a leading role in the Campaign for Quality Television 1989–90.)
Stewart Purvis	Independent Television News: Programme Editor *News at Ten* 1980–83, Editor *Channel Four News* 1983–86, Deputy Editor ITN 1986–89, Editor 1989–91, Editor-in-Chief 1991–.
Andrew Quinn	Granada Television: Managing Director 1987–92, Chief Executive 1992. Independent Television Network Centre: Chief Executive 1992–95. (Previously Managing Director Granada Cable and Satellite 1983–87.)
Stephen Redfarn	Westcountry Television: Chief Executive 1991–97. (Previously merchant banker. Consultant to Television South (TVS) 1980–90.)
Gerry Robinson	Granada Group: Chief Executive 1991–96, Chairman 1996– .
Peter Rogers	Independent Broadcasting Authority: Director of Finance 1982–90. Independent Television Commission: Deputy Chief Executive and Director of Finance 1991–96. Chief Executive 1996– .
Sir George Russell	Independent Broadcasting Authority: Member 1979–86, Chairman 1988–90. Independent Television Commission: Chairman 1991–97. Independent Television News: Chairman 1988. (Knighted 1992.)
Christopher Scoble	Home Office: Assistant Under-Secretary of State, Broadcasting Department 1988–91.
Colin Shaw	Independent Broadcasting Authority: Director of Television 1977–83. Independent Television Companies Association: Director Programme Planning Secretariat 1983–87. Broadcasting

	Standards Council: Director 1988–96.
Louis Sherwood	HTV Group: Chairman 1991– .
Desmond Smyth	Ulster Television: Financial Controller and Company Secretary 1976–83, Managing Director 1983– .
Paul Styles	Independent Programme Producers Association: Director 1987–91. KPMG Management Consulting: Head of Media Consulting 1991–95, Director 1995–, Head of Broadcasting Department 1996– .
Muir Sutherland	Thames Television: Director of Programmes 1982–86.
Brian Tesler	London Weekend Television: Managing Director 1976–90, Deputy Chairman 1982–84, Chairman 1984–92. LWT (Holdings) plc: Deputy Chairman 1990–94.
Quentin Thomas	Home Office: Head of Broadcasting Department 1984–88. (Life Peerage 1977)
Lord Thomson (of Monifieth)	Independent Broadcasting Authority: Deputy Chairman 1980, Chairman 1981–88.
Harry Turner	Television South West: Director of Marketing 1980–85, Managing Director 1985–92.
Donald Waters	Grampian Television: Director of Finance and Company Secretary 1976–87, Chief Executive 1987– . Deputy Chairman 1993– .
John Whitney	Independent Broadcasting Authority: Director General 1982–89.
Lord Windlesham	Author (with Richard Rampton) of Report of *Death on the Rock*. (Amongst previous roles was Minister of State at the Home Office 1970–72, Minister of State for Northern Ireland 1972–73 and Managing Director of ATV Network 1975–81).
John Wotton	Partner at Allen & Overy, legal advisers to the Independent Broadcasting Authority and to the Independent Television Commission.
Sir Brian Young	Independent Broadcasting Authority: Director General 1970–82. (Knighted 1976.)

Valuable help for this volume was also received from:

Bob Bairstow, Bob Burrows, Sir Ralph Carr-Ellison, Bryan Cowgill, Professor Andrew Ehrenberg, Nigel Hancock, Sandra Horne, Pat Mahoney, Sir Donald Maitland, John Marchant, Paul Mathews, Mike Scott and Ward Thomas.

INTRODUCTION:
THE IBA AND ITV – 'THE CURIOUS PARTNERSHIP'

... the curious partnership that has grown up over 25 years between a public authority established by Parliament and a handful of public limited companies, financed largely by advertising and answerable to their shareholders.

Lord Windlesham, *The Times*, 18 September 1981

That 'curious partnership', described by the departing Managing Director of ATV in a farewell critique of the Independent Broadcasting Authority's 1980 contract award system for Independent Television franchises, was to undergo greater change and expansion in the period 1981–92 than at any time since the founding of the original Independent Television Authority and the development of the ITV network between 1954 and 1962. The system was to be subject to greater political scrutiny and change by legislation than at any time in its history.

This volume deals with the achievements of those old partners, the IBA and the ITV contractors, the changes and the consequences of the changes for them as they were remoulded by a Broadcasting Act more controversial than any of its thirteen predecessors. Out of the legislative changes emerged the Independent Television Commission and C3 (ITV) licensees respectively, with a new, more distanced, relationship. This volume also describes, in some detail, the incidents and processes that brought first threat and then renewal to the major component parts of Independent Television in Britain.

Volume 6 will describe the expansion of British commercial broadcasting and the moves towards genuine competition for advertising revenue. This will include the development of the fourth channel, Breakfast TV, cable and satellite. 'Towards', because the era of true competition only really opened up as the period covered by these two volumes closed and new licences under the Broadcasting Act 1990 came into force on 1 January 1993. At that point Channel Four was required for the first time to compete head on with ITV for revenue from advertising, instead

1

of being financed by subscription from the ITV companies, in return for their being allowed to sell advertising on Channel Four in their particular franchise region.

During the decade covered by this book some degree of competition did become a reality for most ITV companies for the first time. Previously only the two London companies had competed in the same advertising market. The IBA under its legislative powers was able in 1980 to introduce a separate national Breakfast franchise on the ITV channel. And technical developments in satellite broadcasting, together with an entrepreneurship new to the industry (the former only dimly perceived at the start of the decade and the latter totally unforeseen), enabled further expansion of commercial broadcasting, financed primarily by subscription but also taking advertising revenue. Even this limited competition was to add to the normal strains between 'the curious partners'. A regulator well prepared for tensions with ITV over programme quality, advertising and so on was to find itself facing new responsibilities for judgement in areas of new technology, ownership and financial viability – much of this outside its previous remit and all carrying a seemingly new dimension of political sensitivity.

As will become apparent, by the middle of the Eighties the effects of even quasi-competition were to erode another relationship – Professor Alan Peacock was to call it 'The Comfortable Duopoly' – that had developed over the thirty years that Independent Broadcasting had co-existed with the only other television organisation authorised by Parliament to broadcast to the United Kingdom audience – the BBC. The loss of the cosy semi-monopoly was not much mourned by the new generation of broadcasting executives who were gradually replacing those they scorned as 'dinosaurs' but the destabilising effect threw up strains at a high level within the two organisations which were damaging both to the institutions and to individuals.

The story of this time of change in commercial broadcasting cannot be told chronologically for the most part. It is a narrative with themes and natural dramatic forms – the establishment of characters, a build-up of incident and tension leading to a dramatic climax followed by denouement. The themes relate to one another: The Discovery of the Real Cost of Programmes, The Need to Challenge the Broadcasting Unions, The Odium that Attaches to a Monopoly of Broadcast Advertising, The Power of the Views of Conviction Politicians and – above all – The Search for a Form of Public Service Broadcasting that can Survive the Market.

The Eighties, of course, saw both the apogee and perigee of that ultimate prime minister of conviction: Margaret Thatcher. However, although she did have some direct personal involvement in bringing about the radical changes that faced commercial broadcasters by the end of the decade, as will be seen, there were many other forces at work.

The decision of the electorate at the 1979 General Election to return a Conservative government with a powerful majority and a leader with a known preference for market economics might be seen as implying an instinctive understanding of the need for radical social and economic overhaul of Britain after the social, industrial and financial effects of the Socialism and so-called 'wet' Conservatism of the

Seventies. Whether or not that is true, a Prime Minister and government were elected, and then sustained in power for three terms, who pursued what they saw as a mandate for radical change with a vigour unseen since the 1945 Labour government. And many of the policies the government were to carry through – in trade union legislation, the adoption of market forces as a prime determinant for change, the challenging of bureaucracy and so on, were to have a crucial impact on many hitherto unchallenged institutions in Britain – from the Stock Exchange to the Greater London Council. Independent broadcasting could hardly have expected to be ignored; and yet many in the industry do appear to have been caught off guard when it was their turn to come under political scrutiny in the second half of the Eighties.

With the hindsight that is inevitable in any historical view, it is now possible to see that the fulcrum for the changes in commercial broadcasting was positioned a little after the report of the Peacock Committee in July 1986 (its title: *Report of the Committee on Financing the BBC* was given an ironic slant by subsequent events). The train of events that started with the publication of the report and which led to a wholly new approach to the disposal of the privileges and responsibilities of being a commercial broadcaster will be followed in detail in the later chapters of this volume.

For broadcasters and regulators there was a further force introducing change and competition which was to interact with the political forces already at work. This emanated from new developments in technology – in particular, developments in transmission technology. A television signal is complex and therefore 'wide' when compared with radio or telephony. Since the start of television in Britain, spectrum scarcity – the limited bandwidth available to carry the rather bulky television signal – had restricted the number of channels available. There is an interactive relationship between scarcity and regulation. The fewer the channels the greater the number of viewers per channel and the more power the people who provide the programmes are believed to hold. Orthodox political belief (on both sides of the House) has therefore always been that broadcasters must be highly regulated to prevent the abuse of this power.

As a result, though new transmission possibilities – first on UHF, then by satellite – were discovered by research and development engineers, the actual expansion of television broadcasting has always lagged well behind discovery. As the previous volumes of *Independent Television in Britain* have related, as every new opportunity became a technically available step, a new government Commission was convened to consider and recommend how it should be controlled. As most readers will know, the first channel (BBC) began television broadcasting ahead of the world in the Thirties. It restarted after the Second World War, the second (ITV) started in the Fifties, the third (BBC2) in the Sixties and now at last in the early Eighties there was to be a fourth channel. The start of Channel Four was just one event that was to throw more than a passing shadow over the old relationship between the IBA and ITV.

However, other clouds, unseen at the beginning of the decade, were darkly gathering above the IBA and all its responsibilities and relationships. These were indeed seeded by technological developments and the new political philosophies (some would say ideologies), but the prime factor in the breaching of transmission limitations to achieve market competition at last in Britain was to be entrepreneurship.

However people may regard the impact of his achievements, it cannot be denied that Rupert Murdoch is a media entrepreneur truly on a scale never before experienced. He is to the world what Randolph Hearst was to the United States or Lord Northcliffe to the United Kingdom. And he held a grudge against what he saw as the over-regulated British broadcasting system – and in particular the IBA.

Readers who come to this volume having read Jeremy Potter's riveting account in Volume 3 of *Independent Television in Britain* of events at London Weekend Television in the early months of 1971 will know the background to this. In effect Murdoch, who at that time owned only the *Sun* and *News of the World* newspapers in Britain, had bailed out a nearly bankrupt London Weekend by buying 36 per cent of the non-voting shares and underwriting a one-for-three rights issue needed to pay for the new LWT South Bank Television Centre. He and the majority of the Board found the senior management wanting and got rid of them. Murdoch then used his Australian television experience as a hands-on temporary Programme Controller to strengthen the network's weekend schedule.

This was welcomed by some of the other ITV companies but not by the (then) Independent Television Authority (ITA). The non-Murdoch newspapers had been quick to draw the Authority's attention to this control of television by the man whom they characterised as 'The Dirty Digger', because of the *Sun*'s predilection for titillating stories and pictures – Page Three Girls were new then. This self-serving guidance to the Authority could be ignored – up to a point. Murdoch's populist approach did indeed change the nature and, in particular, the public service performance promised by the company the regulator had contracted for the London Weekend role in 1967.

Under the legislation the Authority was required to act to ensure the original contract was maintained. It moved cautiously. It did not withdraw the contract and readvertise (which might have destabilised the entire ITV network) but it did require LWT to make a new submission for its own contract, including the nomination of a new managing director and a new programme controller, with Murdoch returning to a non-executive Board role. This became a very public matter and Murdoch was furious. He accused the ITA of character assassination by what he saw as their portrayal of him as a man unfit to control a public television station. There was a subsequent rapprochement with the ITA, stage managed by the new Chairman and Managing Director of LWT, John Freeman, and Brian Young the relatively new ITA Director General. But many believe that Rupert Murdoch neither forgot nor forgave.

This story is retold in some detail here because, although it does not belong in the narrative of this volume, it is germane to events in the latter half of the book

– in particular to those relating to Ownership in Chapter 7 and, in Chapter 9, to the position of the goverment *vis-à-vis* the IBA and ITV during the Battle of the Broadcasting Bill. Murdoch had an admirer in Margaret Thatcher and his thinking may well have influenced her government's policies. But he did not just keep his views privy to political insiders. In August 1989 he delivered them head-on to the elite from Britain's duopoly of broadcasting organisations:

> I start from a simple principle: In every area of economic activity in which competition is attainable, it is much to be preferred to monopoly. The reasons are set forth in every elementary economics text book, but the argument is best proved by experience rather than theory.
>
> Competition lets consumers decide what they want to buy; monopoly, or duopoly, forces them to take whatever the seller puts on offer. Competition forces suppliers to innovate continually, lest they lose business to rivals offering better, improved products; monopoly permits a seller to force outdated goods onto captive customers. Competition keeps prices low and quality high; monopoly does the opposite.
>
> Why should television be exempt from these laws of supply and demand, any more than newspapers, journals, magazines or books or feature films? I can see no reason, which is why I believe that a largely market-led television system, with viewers choosing from a wide variety of channels financed in various ways, will produce a television system better than today's. (MacTaggart Lecture, given by Rupert Murdoch at the Edinburgh International Television Festival 1989)

It was a text for the times. Even Murdoch's own manoeuvre just over a year later, when his Sky Television ambushed BSB to achieve a 'merger' to give him a virtual monopoly of satellite broadcasting in Britain during the regulatory confusion of the end of the IBA and its phoenix-like rebirth as the ITC, did not deny that. For ITV the writing was in the sky from the mid-Eighties.

Readers of the chapter in this book on Networking (Chapter 5), might feel that had ITV taken in the Murdoch message they might have acted differently in 1990/91. It was an irony that of the three companies (Thames, TSW and UTV) that did shrewdly invest in SES, the Luxembourg company that launched and owned the Astra satellites that were to be the vehicles of Murdoch's challenge, two failed to win a licence in 1991. Indeed Thames Television, despite that wise move and its successful 'management service' challenge to the unions (see Chapter 4), was to appear to become a sort of lightning conductor for the wrath of government with commercial television during the period.

Just as history always offers the opportunity for hindsight, so it often pinions the actions of people and institutions to their past. It can certainly be said that self-change within both ITV and the IBA would have given the government less justification for the radical and, as even some outside the industry argued, potentially damaging aspects of the Broadcasting Bill when it went before Parliament in 1989.

The Bill was much modified before it passed into law (see Chapter 9) but it was still significantly to change the role and even the title of commercial television's regulator and to result in the change not just of three of the companies that constituted ITV (that had happened before) but to change fundamentally the control and the economics of commercial broadcasting in Britain. The full consequences of those changes may not be visible until some time after this book is published. But the facts, eyewitness accounts and often conflicting views of the participants that are the body of the book will allow the reader to make his or her own judgement, as well as to gain some access to the drama that was played out in the Eighties within the enclosed world of the network of the ITV companies and their regulator.

1

HEADED FOR CHANGE: 1980–82

The IBA – The Search for 'a Better Way'

The phrase that was to echo down the decade for the IBA – 'There must be a better way' – spelt out the frustration of the man who had inherited responsibility for the turmoil in commercial television following the contract renewal process that had started in 1980, leading to the selection of companies to receive contracts for their regional franchise areas from 1982. The words were, surprisingly, not reliably attributed in writing until four and a half years after they were uttered. Then it was left to the man whose words they were to attribute them to himself.

The minutes of the meeting of the Members of the Authority (in effect the Board of the IBA) of 9 May 1986 record as follows:

> The Chairman said, however, that he had kept on saying that *there must be a better way* ...

That Chairman was Lord Thomson of Monifieth. Thomson had been nominated for the role by William Whitelaw after the Conservative victory in May 1979 had brought Margaret Thatcher to power as Prime Minister, with Whitelaw, her trusted 'elder statesman' and deputy leader, as Home Secretary. He had been his party's Home Affairs spokesman since 1975. The Home Office was responsible at that time for broadcasting (as it had been since 1974 and would be until 1992, when the new Department of National Heritage was established), and in 1979 broadcasting was unusually high on the incoming government's agenda.

In the Queen's Speech on 15 May 1979, which outlined the legislative priorities of the new government, a new Broadcasting Bill was promised that would end the uncertainty about the prospect of a fourth television channel in Britain by giving the Independent Broadcasting Authority responsibility for setting it up. In fact this was a continuation of decisions put in train by the previous administration, which had in April 1979 empowered the IBA to build transmitters for the new channel. Three Members and the Chairman of the Authority had served their time and replacements were required. Whitelaw and his civil servants needed to make the appointments quickly to ensure both continuity of development of the long-awaited new channel and rigorous supervision of the start of the new ITV contracts (including, for the first time, a national contract for television at breakfast time) to be advertised in January 1980. Lady Plowden, the outgoing Chairman, had served since 1975.

Thomson had been the Labour MP for Dundee East from 1952–72 and held senior posts throughout the 1964–70 Labour government, rising to Cabinet rank. His final role in government was as Secretary of State for Commonwealth Affairs. In 1973, when Britain joined what was then the European Economic Community, Thomson became one of the first of its Commissioners from the United Kingdom. He was made a Life Peer in 1977.

Though they were never particularly close, William Whitelaw had known George Thomson when they were on opposite benches in the Commons. Importantly, by 1980 Thomson had also had three years' regulatory experience as Chairman of the Advertising Standards Authority. Whitelaw's nomination of Thomson for Chairman of the IBA had to be approved by the Prime Minister. That approval having been received, there was some discussion on terms and conditions. Whitelaw proposed that Thomson should be appointed Deputy Chairman and Chairman Elect for 1980, taking over from Plowden on 1 January 1981 – after the new ITV contracts had been awarded but before the new contractors came on air a year later. In theory this provided a degree of continuity at the top of the IBA that had not been achieved previously. Lady Plowden wanted Thomson on board even earlier:

> I hope your approach to Lord Thomson will succeed and if so that he will be able to attend meetings by the early autumn when we have to take many decisions about new franchises for the television companies and for the organisation of Channel Four. (Letter Lady Plowden, Chairman of the IBA, to the Rt. Hon. William Whitelaw, Secretary of State for the Home Department, 5 July 1979)

In fact Thomson did not join the Authority until the beginning of 1980 but even a year of overlap turned out to be an uneasy affair. Lord Thomson recalled in an interview during the research for this volume:

> It wasn't a very clever formula because a Chairman Elect is an awkward thing for a chairman, breathing down their neck. We got on well together because I made a very positive effort about it and so did Biddy [Lady Plowden's Christian name, Bridget, was usually shortened to this form by friends and colleagues], she was wonderful in that way ... I went off and visited all the transmitter sites and the regional officers and tried to be as far away as possible. She was the Chairman and she had responsibility for these decisions (the contract awards). She asked my opinion about them as they were emerging, but they were her decisions, not mine. I, for instance would not have gone ahead with breakfast television at all, not on principle but in terms of timing. I thought the big change

of the whole franchise round and Channel Four was quite enough for us to digest. And I'd have left breakfast television over to mid-term or something like that. (Interview with Lord Thomson)

To many Home Secretaries broadcasting was an irritation amongst the more substantial elements of the portfolio: Police, Prisons, Immigration. But Whitelaw appeared rather to enjoy his responsibility for radio and television. Perhaps it was a leavening in the mix of his weightier responsibilities. He did regard British broadcasting as a national asset and was proud when he left office to be regarded as 'the father of Channel Four' – the first new British television channel for eighteen years when it was launched in 1982 – despite parliamentary difficulties that had attended the conception of its Welsh counterpart – Sianel Pedwar Cymru.

However in 1980 Willie Whitelaw had other difficulties with Independent Television. Home Secretaries were accustomed to being lobbied from time to time by ITV companies about the behaviour of their regulator, the IBA. Since the mass privatisation of the public utilities the tensions between the regulated and the regulators have become common currency in Parliament and in the press. But at the start of the Eighties such tensions and the consequent lobbying were a more private affair.

It is important to remember that the IBA, as the then regulator of commercial television, had powers verging on the draconian. No less than twenty-five clauses of Part 1 of the 1981 Broadcasting Act gave the Authority considerable discretion over the ITV companies and their affairs. Its ultimate power was the withdrawal of contract but the IBA also owned, operated and controlled the means by which the ITV companies reached their markets – the transmitters. It even controlled the lines bookings that gave access to the British Telecom circuits on which the ITV signal was distributed to the transmitters. In short the IBA was the broadcaster as well as the regulator.

The cost of the bureaucracy of regulation and the UK-wide technical operation of transmission was to rise from £30,243,000 in 1981 to a high of £74,919,000 in 1989. The vast majority of this was paid for by the ITV programme companies – the remainder by Independent Local Radio (ILR), until responsibility for commercial radio was removed from the Authority in 1990. This 150 per cent increase in the cost of the IBA in eight years should be seen against a background of increasing responsibilities during the period and against a rise in ITV revenue from around £600 million to £1,600 million in the same period. But the increasing cost of regulation was to be drawn to the attention of Whitehall and, more significantly, it was to catch the eye of the new breed of 'advisers' in Downing Street.

The ITV programme companies, though they had a monopoly of commercial access to the audience in their region under their contracts from the IBA, were in effect just what that name implies – producers of programmes to the IBA's broad specification under the legislation. These they then packaged with the advertisements they were licensed to sell to generate revenue and sent out of their buildings as an electronic signal to be broadcast by their regulator. Contentious programmes could be previewed and rejected for transmission (this saved the public embarrassment of the IBA 'pulling the plug' on a scheduled programme during transmission). As those who have read the first volumes of *Independent Television in Britain* will be aware, these elaborate precautions arose from Parliament's deep-seated fear in 1954 both of the arrival of commercial television on the American pattern to threaten the valued broadcasting ethos built up by the BBC and, more realistically, of the political power of the medium.

Thus, if the ITV companies had raised their concerns with the Director General or his staff, had put them to the Chairman and Authority Members, and were not satisfied with the response, faced with this very powerful control mechanism they fell into a pattern of privately lobbied 'appeals' to the Home Office Broadcasting Department. While the British broadcasting structure was a stable duopoly, the Department saw the protests for what they were and almost invariably supported the regulator and the status quo. But just occasionally the protests were seen to merit a touch on the tiller to vary the course ahead.

The first of those occasions in the Eighties came very early and was related to the need for 'a better way'. After ITV had suffered a ten-week strike in 1979 and a drop in revenue year on year from £363 million to just under £347 million, complaints focused on the unrealistic nature of the IBA's onerous conditions attached to the new contracts, including those for the financing of the new venture of which Whitelaw was so proud – Channel Four. These two aspects were crucially linked, since the ITV companies were called upon to fund the start-up of Channel Four out of revenue across the period of contract renewal or change. Previous experience had shown a dip in revenue at these times of change in the ITV system. In the two years after the 1968 round revenue dropped by just over £4 million which was, at the time, just over 4 per cent. This time the fall-off was expected to be greater.

Importantly, one of the most insistent critics of the Authority was the man who had been Minister of State for Northern Ireland during the difficult years 1972–73 (1972 was the year of the 'Bloody Sunday' shooting by British paratroopers of Catholic civil rights demonstrators in Londonderry) while Whitelaw had been Secretary of State for the province. This was Lord Windlesham, at this time the Managing Director of the Midlands ITV contractor, ATV Network.

ATV suffered a concatenation of financial, senior management and regional political difficulties during 1979–80, which have been described in detail in Chapter 23 of Volume 4 of *Independent Television in Britain,* but superimposed upon these (and interacting damagingly with them) were the demands of the IBA for a greater reflection under the new contract for the Midlands of the regional aspirations of the different sectors of that large and diverse part of Britain, the borders of which had originally been determined by the coverage of the BBC's television transmitters as they spread across the country in the late Forties and early Fifties.

There was a particular requirement to recognise the separate cultural and business patterns of Nottingham and the East Midlands in the structure of the company. When the contract was finally awarded there was also a requirement for ATV to change its identity and reduce the shareholding of its owners, ACC, to 51 per cent and to offer the remaining 49 per cent to aspirant shareholders in the Midlands – 'with special consideration for those who interested themselves in other groups bidding for this franchise'.

In the event none of the interests which had been participants in ATV's competitors, Midlands Television and Mercia Television, took up the offer and the major new shareholders turned out to have virtually no Midlands associations: Robert Maxwell, Sears, Ladbrokes and D.C. Thomson, the Dundee publisher of comic books and periodicals whose shareholding in Southern Television had been one aspect of the IBA's decision not to renew Southern's contract in 1980. Combined with conflicts with the IBA about limitations they imposed on his role in the new company, these events led to Lord Windlesham's resignation on 15 May 1981.

Fifteen years later, looking back, Lord Windlesham still saw the IBA's decisions as having been 'un-worldly' and 'unrealistic'. His judgement:

> The combination of the admirably high-minded and public-spirited Chairman, Bridget Plowden (Lady Plowden), and (Sir) Brian Young, with all his good qualities as Director General was, I think, an unfortunate one. They were too similar in outlook. Had there been a juxtaposition of, say, Bridget Plowden as Chairman and Bob Fraser, with his political skills and cunning as Director General, that would have been a very good partnership. Conversely had Brian Young been Director General with Charles Hill, with all his political skills and down-to-earth approach, as Chairman – again they would have had complementary qualities and the leadership of the Authority would have been far stronger and more rounded in its skills and abilities than was the case at the crucial moment of the franchise allocation. (Interview with Lord Windlesham)

Lord Windlesham is not alone in this view. Paul Fox (now Sir Paul), as Managing Director of Yorkshire Television (YTV), was left trying to find new local shareholders after the IBA had required YTV to demerge from its owners, Trident Television – thereby losing from ITV the financial skills and clout with the Conservative Party of James (now Lord) Hanson. How valuable his presence might have been in the later Eighties when ITV and the IBA were to be subject to the antipathetic scrutiny of Mrs Thatcher must be a matter for speculation. Sir Paul Fox recalls:

> If ever there was a man who was interested in television it was James, and James should have been embraced by the IBA. But it was Bridget (Lady Plowden) and Brian (Sir Brian Young) between them who were unbusinesslike and didn't know what life was about at the sharp end and thought, 'We don't want this buccaneer around the place'. In the light of what happened afterwards, how wrong they were. (Interview with Sir Paul Fox)

Sir Brian Young had come from running the Nuffield Foundation to the IBA to be Director General in 1970, in succession to Sir Robert Fraser. He had a formidable intellect – King's Scholar at Eton, a First in Classics at King's College, Cambridge – and a strength of character honed by four war-years as a Naval (RNVR) officer in destroyers. After the war he had returned to Eton as an assistant master and went on to become Headmaster of Charterhouse at the age of thirty. (ITV managing directors were to notice that Young, a tall man, had his desk raised up on blocks. This gave him more leg room but also had the effect that he appeared to loom large over those who sat facing him at meetings in his office. Some felt this contributed to his 'headmasterly' image as Director General of the IBA.)

Young had been recruited to the IBA by its then Chairman, Lord Aylestone, and served under him for the first five of his twelve years as DG. Aylestone brought to the partnership a sense of discipline (his war service had been as a Warrant Officer in the RAF) that matched Young's but also an acute political realism that came from fifteen years' service as a Whip in the Parliamentary Labour Party. It was a good partnership which only wobbled when Aylestone's political antennae were overly sensitive in areas not susceptible to Young's intellectual rigour – as in the case of Rupert Murdoch at London Weekend Television, referred to in the Introduction.

But when Aylestone was due to retire in 1975 the then Home Secretary, Roy Jenkins, brought the Deputy Chairman of the BBC, Lady Plowden, across to be Chairman of the IBA. This didn't quite have the impact on the ITV system that the move of Lord Hill from the Chairmanship of the (then) ITA to the BBC in 1967 had on that organisation. When, after his first few weeks at the BBC, Lord Hill met David Attenborough, the camaraderie that exists between popular performers allowed him to ask why nobody at the BBC seemed willing to talk to him. Attenborough paused only for a moment before replying that Hill needed to understand that his appointment was to BBC staff as the appointment of Rommel would have been to members of the Eighth Army.

To ITV, Lady Plowden's arrival in 1975 was perhaps more akin to Montgomery leading the Afrika Korps. The impact of the combination of her and Young on the business-driven culture of ITV caused one senior executive from that time to remember about his first meeting with them that 'You could smell education like embrocation in a rugby changing room.'

Perhaps the most clear expression of the best and worst effects of the Plowden and Young partnership was that they were at their best in generating the IBA's rigorously thought-through approach to the translation into a fine practical blueprint of the spirit of the best of the proposals for the fourth channel that had been put to the Annan Committee (side-stepping the worst aspects of the Committee's own conclusions). In this they had the very considerable help of their staff and in particular of the Director of Television, Colin Shaw, who had served under Plowden at the BBC as Secretary to the Board of Governors and who shared to a very considerable extent her concern to conserve the public service element in commercial broadcasting.

On the other hand lies the unworldly and apparently slipshod approach to the contract for ITV's Breakfast Television – over which the staff appear to have had rather less of a say – the consequences of which were to dog the Authority in one form or another for the next seven years.

However, in relation to the changes in the ITV contracts, it could be said that the companies protested too much. Colin Shaw feels that they sometimes mistook the leasehold nature of their contracts for a freehold:

> ... they'd been doing well, they'd been there for a period of time which made them feel that they belonged and the system belonged to them. And when we made changes they found it difficult to understand that we were doing something we were perfectly entitled to do. (Interview with Colin Shaw)

It was among the consequences of this combination, good and bad, that Lord Thomson took over as Chairman of the IBA on 1 January 1981. One of the most criticised aspects of the 1980 franchise process was that of the public meetings. Twenty-one Final Public Meetings, chaired by a member of the Authority with representatives of the applicant consortia present, were held up and down the United Kingdom in the six months between the submission of applications for ITV contracts on 9 May 1980 and the Authority's final decision-making meetings in the late autumn. Some 6,000 members of the public attended this last round of meetings but prior to those there had been 200 public meetings in the previous year, attended by nearly 15,000 people. No public consultation on such a scale had ever been undertaken by a public body in Britain before. The meetings were in general orderly and good humoured but the final round hardly tested the professional communicator applicants and the earlier consultations merely threw up grand themes, like the importance of regionalism. For Lord Thomson this part of the process contributed to his unease;

> I think one of the things that made me feel there must be a better way was basically the very cumbersome and to some extent cosmetic nature of the operation. As a working politician I had seen enough of public participation to have no particular illusions about it. (Interview with Lord Thomson)

His first public use of the phrase that was to have such a prolonged life and such political consequences was, as is often the way, very un-deliberated:

> It was at the Royal Television Society Conference at Cambridge, the first one I attended, in 1981. But it wasn't in a prepared speech, it was an ad lib ... a *cri de coeur*, and a very genuine one, but it wasn't thought out in advance. And at the time I uttered 'there must be a better way', I had no better way particularly in mind ... I then worked out a better way but it was greatly overtaken by events. (Interview with Lord Thomson)

The search for the grail of 'a better way' can be said to have been started in a paper (IBA 195(81)) produced by the Director General for discussion at the extended Authority meeting (525(81)) on 23/24 July 1981 in preparation for the public position that he and his new Chairman would be called upon to take when they appeared together on the platform at the Royal Television Society (RTS) Convention at Cambridge seven weeks later.

The paper is in three parts. The first deals with 'The Television Franchise Process considered as a whole'. Part II is 'Consultation with the Public' and, at fifty paragraphs, is twice as long as each of the other parts. Part III analyses 'Procedures within Brompton Road'. (70 Brompton Road, a large 1950s-style office building opposite Harrods, was the headquarters of the IBA at that time.) The paper stops short of being self-congratulatory. It notes that, after an initial positive reaction from the press applauding the Authority's 'having effected a greater degree of change than was generally expected, so displaying courage and imagination, as well as a reassuring confidence in the future of ITV ...', the press 'perhaps to some extent nurtured by the companies, adopted a severer tone'. The paper goes on to note criticisms that 'The franchise process is no better than a lottery; the Authority are a lay body passing judgement on professionals ... guilty of erratic judgements ... there is no means of the companies or ... public knowing the particular reasons in particular instances why the Authority chooses some applicants and rejects others.'

Discussion of the paper, as minuted, was not incisive. The suggestion that the lay members of the Authority might be strengthened by the co-opting of professionals at the time of a contract round was rejected – presumably because the IBA staff were deemed to have the necessary professional knowledge and input to the selection process in their advice to the Authority. It was, however, decided that the Authority would, in future, discuss the franchise process once a year and any change thought necessary as conditions in the industry changed could be reflected in an updating of the procedure. Significantly no one in discussion picked up the paper's reference to the fact that '... The *Daily Telegraph* ... strongly advocated putting the contracts out to tender and awarding them to the highest bidder.' Perhaps because Sir Brian Young's paper pre-empted discussion with the statement that 'operations of a public broadcasting service are not necessarily best conducted by those with the biggest purse ...' and a reference to 'acrimony' in Australia where such a system existed.

The Authority Members inherited by Lord Thomson from Lady Plowden on 1 January 1981 were of the calibre deemed by the Prime Minister's office (in consultation with the Home Office) to be appropriate at that time for the governance of public bodies in general. However the mix for broadcasting – and this applied also to the BBC Board of Governors, from whom the pattern was derived – varied only in reflecting one aspect of the specialism involved by the appointment of at least one person from a technical or scientific background and also, reflecting the nature of the social and industrial fabric of Britain at the time, a senior trade union official. In common with many bodies with UK-wide responsibilities there were (and are) representatives for each of the 'national regions', Scotland, Wales and Northern Ireland. The years that followed were to see the mix change by the inclusion of a member chosen to reflect the increasing ethnic diversity of Britain and later, reflecting a trend which was to have a major impact on ITV, the dropping of the trade union figure. But in 1981 the Members of the Authority were:

The Marchioness of Anglesey, CBE
Mr A.M.G. Christopher
Mrs J.D.M. Jowitt, JP
Mrs J. McIvor
Professor H. Morris-Jones
The Rev. Dr W.J. Morris, JP
Mr A.J.R. Purssell
Professor J. Ring
Mr G. Russell
Mrs Mary Warnock

The Deputy Chairman, newly appointed on Lord Thomson's accession to the Chair on 1 January 1981, was Sir John Riddell, Bt. He was a banker, Russell and Purssell were senior figures in industry, Ring was a scientist, Christopher the trade unionist, Warnock an academic, Anglesey served on the Arts Council. The representative for Scotland was Morris, a senior figure in the Church of Scotland, Wales was represented by Morris-Jones, an academic, and Northern Ireland had a legal academic representative in McIvor.

These were the men and women who now faced the complex consequences of the selection of companies for the ITV regional franchises that they had made the previous year under a different chairman. They also had the added responsibility of Channel Four and the new Breakfast Television franchise. And their load of responsibility for commercial radio grew by the month as new stations were advertised, applicants selected and broadcasts started. The years 1981–82 saw the number of Independent Local Radio stations increase from twenty-six to thirty-eight. By the time the Broadcasting Act of 1990 requirement that the IBA hand over responsibility for commercial radio to the Radio Authority was carried out on 1 January 1991, the number started had risen to seventy-eight (*Broadcasting in the United Kingdom* by Barrie MacDonald, Mansell 1993). But by that time some stations had failed, each failure (and a larger number of narrow escapes) bringing a need for further judgement and decision by Members of the Authority. There were normally between eight and ten members besides the Chairman and Deputy Chairman. Their average period of service on the Authority was seven years at this time. Four of the ten serving in 1981 were due to leave by the end of the year. Originally the Authority met only once a month but by 1980 the increasing workload had demanded a pattern of two meetings a month, usually on the first and third Thursday

– with a working dinner or an 'overspill' half-day meeting associated to meet the demands of the growing agenda. In preparation for these meetings Members were expected to read a dozen or more papers each time. These were prepared by the IBA staff and dealt with complex policy matters and strategy as well as the regular programme, technical and financial analyses.

For this the Members of the Authority had received £1,800 p.a., plus expenses in 1980. But in 1981 this was increased to £2,500 and increased in line with the retail price index for the rest of the decade. The Chairman's remuneration in 1981 was just under £20,000 plus expenses and by the time of his departure in 1988 had risen to just over £35,000. The Deputy Chairman received roughly a quarter of those amounts (IBA Annual Reports). The Chairman also had the use of a chauffeur-driven car and a penthouse apartment at the top of the IBA's headquarters at 70 Brompton Road.

Changes and Concerns at ITV

Issues, strategies and anxieties in independent television can range from the joint to the several: joint where the threat or opportunity can only be met by an overall 'ITV' response – conjoining the fifteen companies – and several where each company sees its interest as distinct from those of the others. Between those two poles lie a range of responses, most often those where subgroups of likeminded companies form. Usually the alliances are to do with scale. In 1982 the largest: Central, Granada, Thames, London Weekend and Yorkshire, had one community of interest as the major revenue earners and guarantors of programme provision to the fifteen-company network, where the other ten had another. Then there was a subset of differences between the smallest five companies (Border, Channel, Grampian, Ulster and – until the end of 1981 – Westward) and the middle five (Anglia, HTV, Scottish, Southern – again to the end of 1981 – and Tyne Tees).

Historically these communities of interest became reflected in the structure built up to manage the joint responsibilities of the companies. Increasingly in the Eighties the chairmen of key meetings in ITV, faced with intractable differences of view on items on the agenda where detail was important, would be forced to set up subgroups to consider the issue and report back in order that they could continue with the main business. In the generally good-natured atmosphere of ITV's meetings, executives, all too aware that a point of intractability was about to be reached, would chorus with the chairman: 'I feel a working party coming on'!

However, the scale of the bureaucratic ramifications of requirements for discussion, consensus and decision, as well as the co-ordination and control required for the operation of a broadcasting network by a federation of what became fifteen individual public companies of different sizes and cultures, itself became an issue for the companies in the 1980s.

The original companies had formed a trade association, the Television Programme Contractors Association in 1954, to deal with matters of common interest. By 1981 its name had become the Independent Television Contractors Association (ITCA) and its functions ranged from legal and copyright dealings on behalf of the network through marketing, network finance, industrial relations and (where objectives could be agreed upon) political lobbying at Westminster (and, increasingly, in Brussels) to Programme Planning and the contracting and arrangements for the coverage of sport and other major events by ITV.

The Association also had an important function in relation to the advertising ITV companies carry to achieve their revenue. Formally the regulation of advertising was the legal responsibility of the IBA but it held the ITV companies responsible for ensuring that all commercials that are broadcast conform to its Code of Advertising Standards and Practice. To achieve this the companies set up a self-regulation system at the Association. Advertisers had to submit their scripts and (usually) finished commercials to the Association's Copy Clearance procedure. The department that carried out this work was the largest of those that made up the Association. It is to the credit of those involved that, despite the inevitable tensions involved in such regulation, Copy Clearance, now at the Network Centre and retitled the Broadcasters Advertising Clearance Centre (BACC), is a function within ITV that commands continuing respect within the advertising industry.

In 1987 the Independent Television Contractors Association was to change its name again to the more readily intelligible one of the ITV Association (ITVA). The following year the purchase for the network of feature films and television programmes from overseas (previously undertaken by Granada) was added to the ITVA's responsibilities.

The senior ITV forum for discussion and, if agreement (or, more usually, consensus) was reached, decision, was and remains the Council of the Association. Council (no definite article is used) consists of the 'principal' of each of the ITV companies. Originally all of these took the title Managing Director but by the end of the Eighties the term Chief Executive was increasingly used. The Chairman of Council was at that time a member of Council elected by his peers for a two-year period.

A tradition had grown up that allowed one in three chairmen to be from the 'middle five' companies. In 1980 Bill Brown, the Managing Director of Scottish Television (STV), was succeeded as Chairman by Brian Tesler of London Weekend Television (LWT). Tesler brought to the role a background of successful programme making and scheduling as well as a keen understanding of finance and a natural diplomacy. He was to need all of these qualities in the difficult transition period of 1981/82 when two new companies, Television South West (TSW) and Television South (TVS), had to be inducted into the network and two other major players (Central and YTV) were struggling with the consequences of the IBA's requirements for their new contracts.

But the new contractors did not take their places at Council until they started broadcasting on 1 January 1982 . Therefore those who sat around the table at 2.30 p.m. on the second Monday of each month in the gloomy room on the second floor at the headquarters of the ITCA, Knighton House in Mortimer Street (just to the north-east of Oxford Circus), at the start of 1981 were:

David McCall (Anglia)
Lord Windlesham (ATV)
James Bredin (Border)
Ken Killip (Channel)
Alex Mair (Grampian)
David Plowright (Granada)
Ron Wordley (HTV)
Brian Tesler (LWT) – chairman
Bill Brown (Scottish)
Frank Copplestone (Southern)
Bryan Cowgill (Thames)
Peter Paine (Tyne Tees)
Brumwell ('Brum') Henderson (Ulster)
Peter Battle (Westward)
Paul Fox (Yorkshire)

Perhaps half a dozen of these men were of a level of ability that would have allowed them to run a complete television channel on their own. Indeed two had done so; both Fox and Cowgill had been Controllers of BBC1 and Fox was later to return to the BBC as Managing Director, Television. But there was also a sprinkling round the table of those seen by some as 'backwoodsmen'. These figures were sometimes effective enough in the context of a small company but not always able (or sometimes not willing) to act decisively on the broader stage. Given the federal nature of ITV, this meant that often it had to progress at the pace of the slowest. It is, incidentally, a melancholy fact that there was never a female member of Council during the whole period from 1955 to 1992.

Council had standing subcommittees on all the key joint interests: Finance, Marketing, Engineering, Legal and Industrial Relations which were usually chaired by a member of Council and were serviced by a secretariat from the ITCA. There were also ad hoc subcommittees like the Future Development Committee and the Channel Four Working Party. Frequently the subcommittees spawned further sub-workgroups to undertake specialist work for them.

Council members also chaired the Boards of enterprises set up to carry out operations for the network; teletext and subtitling, Oracle Ltd and the quality control and content checking of purchased material, the Independent Film Services Centre (later the ITFC). They were also present on the Board of Independent Television Publications, the wholly-owned subsidiary that published ITV's programme schedule magazine – *TV Times*. And, most importantly, the major companies and some other Council members were also members of the Board of the jointly-owned news provider for the ITV network, ITN.

At ITN Board meetings the IBA was represented by the Director General, as an observer, to see fair play in the inevitable struggles to reconcile the cost to the network on the one hand with the need for quality and breadth in its news coverage on the other. The IBA also had a right to be present at the second most senior ITV forum – the Network Programme Committee (NPC).This was the bi-monthly discussion of future network programme strategy and finance and consisted of Council and the five Network Controllers – the Directors of Programmes of the five major companies. The IBA was represented by the Director of Television – the IBA having the right of schedule approval. In timing, NPC was held on the Tuesday after Monday's Council and it preceded the formal interface meetings with the IBA, the Programme Policy Committee (PPC) and the Standing Consultative Committee (SCC). The latter dealt with business and political matters and was chaired by the Chairman of the Authority.

The detail of programme generation for, and the scheduling of, the hours that ITV transmitted synchronously as a network (at the start of the Eighties this was some fifty-two hours a week) were dealt with at a separate fortnightly Monday meeting – the Network Controllers Group (NCG). In essence NCG was a subcommittee of NPC, which amongst its other functions had the power of approval over the network programme budget for the year ahead, for formal recommendation to Council.

NCG (colloquially known as 'the Controllers Meeting' or just 'Controllers') was frequently and famously disputatious. After some of the earliest conflicts, of which there was never a record, NCG was felt to require an independent chairman and formal minute-taking and, once again, the IBA insisted upon the presence of its Director of Television – in this case primarily to ensure a balanced schedule of programmes and to see that the interests of the companies not represented there were not overlooked. From that time it was chaired by the Association's Director of the Programme Planning Secretariat. Of the four people who accepted to undertake this somewhat thankless role over the years, two were ex-IBA Directors of Television, one an ex -ITV Programme Controller (from a non-major company) and the fourth was the ex-Director of Programmes from Channel Four. This independent chairman attended Council for information purposes (as did the other ITCA departmental Directors) but was not a member. Other Programme Planning Secretariat staff undertook the demanding and crucial roles of chairing the network's Planning and Finance meetings that picked up the pieces after 'Controllers' and supplied a coherent version of the schedule and its financial accounts for implementation by all the companies.

The Planners in particular were crucial to the operation of the network. They fettled the raw outline schedule from the Controllers into a viable transmission schedule in which the uncomfortable realities of lengths of series, durations of programmes and – importantly – IBA scheduling requirements were reconciled and accommodated. The Planners were the Sergeant-Majors, bringing good order and military discipline to their Officer/Controllers orders. The Controllers' decisions were sometimes inspired but often impractical for what was the most complicated television system in Britain.

The Controllers were drawn from the brightest and the best in British broadcasting and much of their aggression stemmed from the complexities and limitations of the system that had been allowed to grow to control ITV programming. As one member of the group in the Eighties put it; 'it's like asking thoroughbreds to be harnessed to a creaking cart'. Miraculously, apart from a few stumbles in the early Eighties, the cart usually ran well ahead of the BBC (see Figure A, Share of Terrestrial Audience).

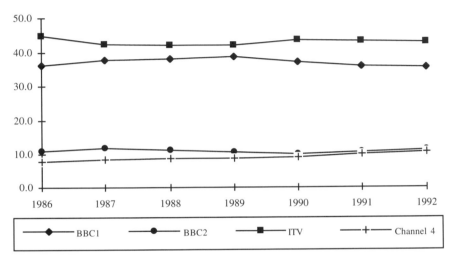

Source: ITC Research

Figure A   Percentage Share of Terrestrial Audience

The Directors and staff of the Association were the employees of the companies jointly but few had broadcasting experience and they were structured in a quaint manner in which no one had clear-cut executive responsibility – even for their own staff. The General Secretary (later Director) of the Association, whose role was to administer the Association on behalf of the Chairman of Council, depended on his colleagues to allow him to achieve even the position of *primus inter pares*. Not surprisingly, it was a difficult role to fill and when the first Secretary General, Mary Lund, retired in 1980, a man from the BBC's Secretariat was hired to replace her but after a sojourn of less than six months he returned to the better-defined structures of the BBC. When head-hunters were called in they could not find anyone in broadcasting who wanted the role and in the end recommended the General Secretary of the British Amateur Athletics Board, David Shaw, who was appointed towards the end of 1981.

The complexities of the ITV system and the ramifications of the Association were to grow even further during the decade. The resulting slowness of response of the system and the increase in costs 'at the centre' became a focus of frustration for the companies – to the point where, when consultants Coopers & Lybrand Deloitte were called in by Council in 1991, they identified 128 committees and subgroups organised by the Association on behalf of the companies. These were computed to absorb over 5,500 man days a year. Of those, over 4,000 involved ITV staff and the remainder Association staff. The cost of these meetings to ITV was £904,000 p.a. (C&LD report for Council, February 1992). Additionally the annual budget of the Association, including its staff and capital costs, rose from just over £2 million in the financial year 1981/82 to £12 million in 1992 (Annual Report to Council, July 1981 and C&LD, February 1992). By 1992 the search for 'another way' had spread well beyond the matter of the award of contracts for commercial television to the whole basis of the financing, the organisation and the technology of broadcasting in Britain.

Meanwhile, in 1981, the concerns around the ITCA Council table focused on the old and continuing headings of finance and industrial relations (programme supply was not an issue at that time – though it had been in the past and was to become one again all too soon). However, finance and industrial relations had now been given three added dimensions of difficulty:

1. The change of companies in the network with TVS, TSW and Central (the restructured ATV) preparing to broadcast from 1 January 1982.
2. Channel Four, which would come on air on 2 November 1982. (The month was chosen by the IBA because that was the time at which the progress of their massive transmitter building plan would ensure that the new channel could reach at least 80 per cent of the UK population; the day was chosen by Jeremy Isaacs, the channel's chief executive, in a typical gesture that some saw as *chutzpah* and others as hubris, because it was the anniversary of the BBC's first television broadcast in 1936.)
3. TV-am, the star-studded applicant group who had so impressed Lady Plowden and the Authority at interview the previous year that they won the Breakfast-time contract. The details of the birth and the history of the early years of these two new enterprises (along with BSB, Sky and Cable) will be the subject of Volume 6 of *Independent Television in Britain* but it is important here to relate the ways in which their advent was seen by ITV as a threat.

In the case of Channel Four the threat was financial but there was also a lingering sense of anger amongst some ITV managing directors at what they saw as a series of betrayals by the IBA. Even before the start of BBC2 in 1964 ITV had always sought channel parity with the BBC. Possible uses for the 'fourth channel' was one of the matters that the Labour government of 1974 was finally able to put to the Committee on the Future of Broadcasting, under the Chairmanship of the distinguished academic, Lord Annan. This had been set up by Labour in May 1970 but had then been set aside by the incoming Conservative government of that year. During the interregnum, in May 1971, the IBA had set up a joint working party with the companies to examine the practicalities of a second service to be supplied by the existing contractors and paid for out of advertising revenue collected by them.

Not surprisingly after such preparation, ITV's submission made a strong case for an ITV2 offering complementary programmes and scheduling in the manner of the BBC1 and BBC2 relationship. It argued convincingly that this would make better use of their resources. The submission was well written (as might be expected when its authors included Sir Denis Forman, John Freeman, Lord Windlesham and Jeremy Potter) but it could be described as imaginative in its style rather than its proposals:

> With ITV2 complementing it, the popular channel (ITV1) would no longer be hag-ridden by the notion that the virtue of its service is measurable by its deference to minority interests. There can be no justification for pleasing too few people at the expense of too many. Nobody would see much point in presenting a string quartet in an almost empty Albert Hall. A Wigmore Hall is what ITV now requires. (Paragraph 95, ITCA submission to the Annan Committee, 1975)

The IBA was supportive of a second independent channel but with a number of caveats that reflected on the one hand past criticism of the Authority for over-indulging ITV – particularly in the matter of profitability – and on the other the strength of the opinions on the subject that had been put forward during the prolonged public debate that increased in scope (and volume) over the four years of the Annan interregnum.

To get a perspective on the merits of ITV's case, it is worth tracing a brief outline of the events which led to the sense of outrage on the part of some in ITV. Groups with names like Free Communications and TV4 had been put together by programme makers and academics to offer ideas for alternative structures to run a fourth channel that would extend the range of programmes for the viewer and, significantly for programme makers in the future, also proposing alternative sources of programmes. The most important of these had been a proposal in 1972 by Anthony Smith, a fellow of St Anthony's College Oxford, who had been a television producer at the BBC during the Sixties and whose restless intellect had often put him in conflict with the powers that ran that institution. This proposal was for a new concept, a *publisher broadcaster*. He called it The National Television Foundation. Later that year it found an unexpected champion proposing an unexpected bedfellow for it on a surprising platform.

Since 1959 Granada Television had sponsored a series of lectures which covered arts, science, politics and the mass media. These took place at the Guildhall in the City of London and lecturers had included Lords Annan, Hunt, Scarman and

Windlesham. In 1972 Granada invited as speaker Sir Hugh Greene, who as Director General of the BBC for the ten years 1959–69, had engendered a unique atmosphere of creativity and broadcasting elan in the Corporation while presiding over the BBC's fight back against the 70:30 ratings lead that ITV had established by 1960. So when Sir Hugh said that, given the quality of programmes that ITV now produced, it was only fair that ITV should have a second channel but that they should not have all of it, perhaps they should share it with the National Television Foundation, both parties took heart from that endorsement. So in the ensuing five years before the wisdom of Annan was finally available (in the report of the Committee on the Future of Broadcasting), some in ITV allowed themselves to believe the argument was won. When Annan reported, proposing the creation of a new Open Broadcasting Authority to be responsible for the fourth channel and the rechristening of the IBA as the Regional Broadcasting Authority, and his proposals were widely criticised as structurally unworkable and financially non-viable, they came to believe again that they might get an ITV2, or something very like it.

But the IBA read the *realpolitik* of the situation better. The case against 'the straitjacket of duopoly', made so cogently by programme makers disenchanted by the constraints put upon enterprise and creative adventure in the broadcasting authorities, was now accepted as orthodoxy. The only questions were how far the straitjacket had to be loosened and how the new development could be reliably financed. Brian Young believed that even in a recession ITV was the only resilient source of finance available to start up the new channel, but he and Colin Shaw also knew that after the prolonged debate ITV2 would not be acceptable to Merlyn Rees, the Home Secretary. Young and Plowden had also been consulted by William Whitelaw as Shadow Home Affairs spokesman and they knew that the farthest he would go was a second commercial channel 'with safeguards' – effectively a channel paid for by ITV but with a guaranteed programme-making and scheduling independence from ITV and a 'distinctive' approach to programming.

What the Labour government would have decided we will never know because the party was dispatched into opposition by the General Election of May 1979. As the incoming Home Secretary, Whitelaw sensed that the fourth channel debate had gone on long enough and was in danger of becoming an embarrassment to the new administration. He wanted it speedily resolved and out of his in-tray. His Broadcasting Department officials opened up intensive discussions with the Authority's staff and the Authority retreated with its senior staff for a weekend of confidential discussions at a hotel in Egham, Surrey. They paid particular regard to the matter of advertisers' complaints about ITV's alleged abuse of its monopoly, which the Broadcasting Department had warned them that Sally Oppenheim, the Minister for Consumer Affairs, was pursuing vigorously in the Cabinet subcommittee. But the Authority could see no way of getting ITV to pay for an independent fourth channel if they were not allowed to sell advertising on it. In the end, it is said, Whitelaw managed to get this through the subcommittee by knowing the time of Mrs Oppenheim's hair appointment and slipping it through while she was at the hairdressers. Alas for history, nobody is – even now – prepared to confirm or deny this on the record. However the Home Secretary was able to announce in very broad terms plans for the new channel to the Royal Television Society (RTS) at Cambridge in September 1979 and this was followed by a statement from the IBA in November attempting to define the distinctive nature it had in mind for the new channel by indicating their view of proportions of types and sources of programmes they would wish to see on it.

In the sense that it was to be allowed to sell the new channel as well as its own, instead of having to face a competitor, ITV was not justified in feeling betrayed. But the 'pace of the slowest' factor told and they were always left playing off the back foot. Their expectation had been for at least *some* element of control. Even if the IBA had carried through its proposal for an Authority-employed scheduler or scheduling referee between the two channels they felt that the ground rules would have granted ITV the primacy enjoyed by BBC1 over BBC2. But in the rush of events in 1979–80 (when they were themselves involved in the demanding business of reapplying for their contracts) communications about the new channel somehow failed to the point where the radical nature of the implications behind the elegantly written policy statement published by the IBA in August 1980 took them by surprise. It was radical in the two worst dimensions for ITV – both, in their view, audience losers. First, it was to be alternative in the sense of being asked to cater for minority interests, to be 'innovative' (which they read as experimental); second, it was to take a substantial proportion of programmes from the hitherto largely untried independent production sector. Also – and this they saw as a final Plowden/Young touch – the channel would have to carry 15 per cent of educational programmes.

For the setting up of this project, wholly owned by the IBA with two £50 shares, the companies were going to have to find £18.2 million 'subscription' to cover the financial year 1981–82 and £85.4 million for 1982–83 – all this was to be 'pump priming' before any revenue that might be generated by such a channel began to flow. The money for building the transmitters for the fourth channel had been found by the IBA out of their 'rental' revenue – but of course that came from ITV as well.

ITV was, indeed, the financial locomotive that pulled the whole train of Independent Television. The locomotive was on overload in this period. Added to Channel Four which was to broadcast to English/Scottish/Northern Irish audiences there was Sianel Pedwar Cymru to broadcast to Wales in Welsh and to be controlled not by the IBA but by a new regulatory body – the Welsh Fourth Channel Authority and this completely new initiative was to cost ITV a further £20 million in 1981–82. So embarrassed was Whitelaw about having been politically cornered into this by the Welsh Nationalist MP Gwynfor Evans, that he persuaded the Treasury to raise the ITV companies' 'free slice' before they paid their special tax known as the Levy (see Chapter 7) from 2.0 per cent to 2.8 per cent of revenue or £650,000, whichever was the larger.

Sir Brian Young was able to pass this piece of better news to the companies in June 1981. It did little to mollify them. In July Brian Tesler wrote to Young on behalf of the companies to say that it was their view that if the IBA imposed too high a Fourth Channel Subscription some of them would not be viable and would seek to 'hand back their contracts'. The Authority considered this at its meeting of 23/24 July but was not of a mind to back down and instructed the Director General to inform ITV of this and announce the subscription 'without delay'. As a result of summer holidays and the pattern of monthly meetings Brian Young was not able to respond to Tesler until 27 August and his letter could not be discussed until the Council meeting of 9 September. At that meeting voices were raised in outrage. As Chairman of Council, Tesler responded on 15 September:

> I should be less than candid if I did not now tell you that your letter has been read by all managing directors with a great sense of dismay, partly because the problem which faces us seems as far from solution as ever, even more because we seem to be at loggerheads with the Authority to a degree which could become seriously damaging between colleagues. (Letter Chairman, ITCA, to Director General, IBA, 15 September 1981)

The letter went on to acknowledge the Authority's absolute right to decide the subscription and to assure the Authority that ITV wanted the fourth channel to be a success. But it then pointed out forcefully that the companies also had a legal duty to their shareholders. They were not 'in business to go out of business'.

Then, with the diplomatic skill for which he was renowned, Tesler continued:

> The companies, who have given anxious thought to the present unhappy situation, believe that a solution might be found which would safeguard the basic needs and rights of both parties ...

He went on to propose a 'yardstick' by which the Authority would assess the maximum level of finance to be made available from year to year to Channel Four. This could then be accepted and companies could plan ahead financially. In essence the letter was proposing something that had gained currency in those almost daily telephone conversations between the various managing directors that bind the ITV network together between meetings. The idea was that the 'yardstick' should be a known percentage of the Net Advertising Revenue (NAR). If the Authority could accept that, then further discussion could focus on what percentage could sustain the new channel on the one hand and allow the companies to remain viable on the other.

The Director General commended the proposal to the Authority as offering a way forward and by its meeting in October the Director General was able to report agreement by all parties to the principle.

In truth, some ITV companies did have real financial problems – ranging from the restructuring of ATV into Central Television and the further contractual requirement that the company relocate from Elstree to the Midlands and build a new studio centre at Nottingham at one end of the scale, to a damaging industrial relations position at Border Television that had led it to run up nearly a million pounds of debt (at a time when the value of the company was only £1.2 million) at the other. In the end the IBA borrowed £30 million to help the companies by allowing them to pay their fourth channel subscription by instalments. Also a band of indicative percentages of NAR were agreed (14–18 per cent) from within which the annual subscription rate would be chosen. Ultimately in 1985, to avoid an annual wrangle, it was agreed that the 17 per cent rate would operate each year from 1986, unless exceptional circumstances reduced ITV's revenue.

These financial tensions between the old partners did leave an indelible mark. Sir Brian Young was due to retire after twelve years at the helm at the end of 1982 and the search for a replacement was about to start. What the ITV companies believed they needed was someone in charge at the IBA who understood *business* ...

2

DOWN TO BUSINESS – NEW NAMES, NEW ROLES – AND POLITICAL SHADOWS ON THE WALL: 1982–84

New Recruit at the IBA

There had never been such a year for recruitment for high-level jobs in broadcasting as 1981. In that year the new Central Television was looking for a managing director to replace Lord Windlesham, London Weekend was to lose its Director of Programmes, Michael Grade, to America, the newly appointed ITV contractors, TVS and TSW were staffing up and Channel Four was looking for a Director of Finance (it was to find a managing director instead) and the new channel-to-be was also seeking a dozen of a new breed of broadcasting animal – the commissioning editor. At the highest level, the BBC advertised for a new Director General to replace Sir Ian Trethowan and the IBA announced that its Director General, Sir Brian Young, would be retiring at the end of 1982. Perhaps because of the range of other opportunities, the response to the advertisement for the IBA job when it appeared in January 1982 was not overwhelming.

However it did include an application from a man who had already spent six years as a regulator. Gordon Borrie was the Director General of the Office of Fair Trading. Borrie was a barrister but one who had developed management skills as well – he had been Dean of the Faculty of Law at Birmingham University prior to his OFT role. Another leading candidate from outside the organisation was Dennis Trevelyan. He had served at a senior level in the Broadcasting Department of the Home Office but had now been Director General of the Prison Service for four years.

Besides these two outsiders – both of whom could be regarded as having had relevant experience at a senior level – there were two internal candidates, also with considerable qualities and, of course, the most appropriate experience. These were John Thompson, the IBA's Director of Radio and Colin Shaw, the Director of Television. Thompson was a journalist who had spent a brief period at ITN as a newscaster/reporter but who was best known for his successful editorship of the *Observer* Colour Magazine in the Sixties. Shaw was particularly well qualified.

Having started as a regional drama producer with BBC radio in Leeds, he had read for a law degree in his spare time, become a Planner in the Television Service serving under one of the most significant figures in the development of BBC Television, Joanna Spicer, and ended up in the BBC as its Chief Secretary. It was from this position that he had followed Lady Plowden to the IBA in the new post of Director of Television, when Bernard Sendall, the Deputy Director General with reponsibility for programme services, retired in 1977.

At any previous time in the Authority's history any one of these four might have been deemed qualified to become the regulator in chief of commercial broadcasting. However, such had been the clamour in Lord Thomson's ear from the companies and from Westminster about the need for a DG who understood business and could find 'better ways' of realising the IBA's public service functions, that he had come to think that:

> ... a Director General, if I could find one, who combined the flair and experience of the business side of broadcasting, together with a sense of social responsibility in public service, would be a good formula. (Interview with Lord Thomson)

In February Lord Thomson was attending a Radio Conference in Monte Carlo. John Whitney, Managing Director of Capital Radio, the popular London radio station, was organising a dinner for some of his radio contractor colleagues. He thought it diplomatic to include the Chairman of their regulatory body amongst the guests. This was the first time Whitney had met Thomson. They got on well. Whitney is renowned for his courtesy and thoughtfulness for others in social situations and is an accomplished host but he was somewhat surprised upon returning to the UK to receive a call from Lord Thomson inviting him to the unlikely venue of the Strand Palace Hotel, opposite the more fashionable Savoy in the Strand – a place where they were highly unlikely to encounter colleagues.

Thomson had admired Whitney's style when they met in Monte Carlo but since then he had also studied his curriculum vitae. John Norton Braithwaite Whitney had been a successful independent radio producer thirty years before the breed became fashionable and multiplied. He had set up Ross Radio Productions in 1951 to make programmes for the off-shore commercial station Radio Luxembourg. Four years later – just as ITV was about to go on the air – he had the foresight to acquire the UK rights to one of the two successful US-patented script display systems off which television presenters could read their words without appearing to do so. It was called Autocue. And later Whitney had extended his activities to television programme making, usually in co-production with ITV companies: *The Flame Trees of Thika* with Thames Television and, most famously, *Upstairs, Downstairs* in partnership with John Hawksworth for London Weekend Television. Whitney had also chaired the Association of Independent Local Radio Contractors. Brought up a Quaker, he also had a track record of public service. Amongst other voluntary work he had founded Recidivists Anonymous, the self-help organisation for people coming out of prison. Whitney's 'profile', therefore, appeared to fit almost precisely Thomson's definition of a Director General for the IBA of the Eighties.

However, as Whitney entered the Strand Palace he had no idea of this. He was inclined to think that he was in for an informal warning about something to do with Capital Radio. Some of the station's 'socially useful' programming – particularly its phone-ins about medical and sexual problems – had caused complaints to the IBA he knew, but the Chairman ... and the Strand Palace?!

After the usual exchange of courteous enquiries while tea and watercress sandwiches arrived, as John Whitney recalls, Thomson delivered the bombshell:

> I think he said to me at that stage, if I were to be invited to come forward and stand as a candidate for the position of Director General, what would I feel about it? (Interview with John Whitney)

Whitney was stunned. Never in his wildest moments had he expected that anybody would add up what he himself considered to be something of a ragbag of experience and come up with the view that its total value qualified him for such a role. Also he was somewhat in awe of Sir Brian Young. He asked for time to consider.

Given the need for confidentiality, there were really only two people to whom he could turn for advice. One was his wife, Roma; the other was his chairman at Capital, Sir Richard Attenborough, the actor and film director, whom Whitney felt bound to inform of the approach and whose opinion he valued. Attenborough was also Deputy Chairman of the embryo Channel Four which was due to go on air for the first time later in the year. He was a man whose warm personality and track record of shrewd decisions in the entertainment business led many to seek his advice.

At home, discussion centred on money (Whitney would have to sell his shares in Capital and in his television company, Consolidated, if he took the job and he might reasonably have expected a higher salary elsewhere than the £40,000 on offer from the IBA) balanced against the honour:

> I thought at the time, and I still do feel to this day, that to put back something into a system that had given me a lot of pleasure and reward was something that was an honour ... something which I could be privileged to do. (Interview with John Whitney)

So when the matter of the succession to Sir Brian Young reached the Authority's agenda for its meeting on 14/15 April the Chairman had been able to put forward Whitney as an addition to the shortlist of interviewees. The minute of that meeting simply records:

> After a lengthy discussion, a clear consensus emerged in favour of Mr Whitney's candidature. (Minute of Authority meeting 542)

In fact Lord Thomson had to use all his skills as chairman to get that result. Both Colin Shaw and John Thompson had strong support.

The press was a little grudging in its response to the appointment, as it often is when confidentiality has been totally observed and newspapers have been forced into guesses well wide of the mark. But the *Daily Telegraph* got to the heart of the matter:

> The appointment was generally well received in independent broadcasting circles ... Mr Whitney ... is recognised as a man who plainly runs a very successful operation. (*Daily Telegraph*, 21 April 1982)

Indeed the ITV managing directors were pleased to have a businessman at Brompton Road at last but they too were surprised by the choice and instructed their ITCA spokesman to refer to the appointment as 'interesting and imaginative'. But it was Lord Thomson himself who was perceptive about internal IBA reaction. He said in his press statement; 'We had to disappoint some very good people.' That disappointment was not going to make the new DG's life easy.

New Recruits – ITV

The two new faces who joined the ITV Council table after their companies started to broadcast in January 1982 had, of course, been selected not by their Boards – indeed, they had selected their Board members for the most part – but by the elaborate and much-criticised IBA contract renewal process referred to in the previous chapter. By definition they had both run highly successful campaigns to achieve their new position but neither fitted naturally into the 'gruff, bluff, tough' atmosphere of debate generated by, say, Fox, Cowgill and Plowright (YTV, Thames and Granada) nor did they have much in common with some of their regional company colleagues like 'Brum' Henderson (Ulster) or Ron Wordley (HTV).

This difference of cultures was to lead one of the new managing directors to hand over his seat at Council first to a joint MD, whom the company had been required by the IBA to appoint, and then, within months, to his Chairman (a move that was itself controversial: traditionally ITV company chairmen were above the shot and shell of network debate and the MDs preferred it that way). The second new Managing Director was later crucially to misread his company's opportunities within the network (see Chapter 5).

Kevin Goldstein-Jackson was the Managing Director, and founder, of the new contract holder for the South-West, Television South West (TSW). He was christened Kevin Grierson Jackson but was said to have adopted the name Goldstein as a gesture of solidarity with the beleaguered Israelis at the time of the Yom Kippur War. Thin-faced, tieless and carrying papers for meetings in a supermarket plastic bag, Jackson's very appearance ran counter to the ethos of ITV, where a suit- and tie-wearing tradition had been generated by the pioneers in the earliest days by the need to build confidence in commercial television amongst the establishment in Britain.

In fact Jackson was highly educated (degrees in philosophy, law and sociology) as well as having experience as a programme maker within three regional ITV companies. He had devised a brilliant strategy to wrest the contract for the South West from Westward Television which would, even if that company had not scored the spectacular 'own goals' described in Chapter 10 of Volume 4 of *Independent Television in Britain*, almost certainly have succeeded. He 'nursed' the contract area for four years before making the application and recruited a Board-in-waiting of professionally able people, as well as of the traditional 'great and good'. The non-executives included two lawyers, an accountant and an engineer as well as three Deputy Lieutenants of the counties covered in the franchise. Significantly it also included a prominent trade union official from the region who was to become Chairman in a somewhat unusual manner. At the rehearsal in the Hyde Park Hotel prior to the Authority interview round the corner in Brompton Road the nominated chairman, Sir John Colfox, had not been so fluent and effective as his deputy Brian Bailey of NALGO and between rehearsal and interview it was agreed that their roles should be reversed – it is said that this restructuring took place on the pedestrian crossing between Bowater House and the Scotch Wool Shop.

Jackson had run a very effective campaign which had included taking the Board members away for weekends and teaching them about television. He had then been able to involve all of them in the franchise application process, so that when they came before the Authority at interview they were the best informed and had the most coherent approach of all the new applicant groups.

However, in the end not only did Jackson's talents remain untapped by the ITV network but his own company found it more and more difficult to contain his restless pursuit of new ideas and enterprises. He had a disputatious relationship with Peter Battle, the joint MD, whose appointment the IBA – concerned at Jackson's lack of experience at the senior level of management – had made a condition of the contract. Battle left in July 1982, only six months after the station went on the air, with consequent embarrassment for the company.

On the programme side, an adventure by Jackson into major film drama intended by him for network transmission, *Where There's a Will* with Patrick MacNee, cost £750,000 but under the regional access networking arrangements operating at the time could only recoup £25,000. His public criticism of Granada's programme purchasing policy on behalf of the network brought not only a stinging rebuke from David Plowright, Granada's Managing Director, but also a threat to cut TSW off from the supply of cinema films and US and Australian programmes, on which ITV companies are dependent for the economic viability of their programme schedules. A public attack by Jackson on Channel Four's programme policy was embarrassingly countered by commentators noting that one of the channel's series most reviled by critics was made at TSW under Jackson's personal production supervision: the aptly named *Cut Price Comedy Show*.

By 1984 such events, and the increasing amounts of time Jackson was spending on projects in the Middle and Far East, led the TSW Board reluctantly to take the view that he should move on. By the end of January 1985 the founder was gone and TSW was under the managing directorship of the colourful Harry Turner who had been Sales Director for Westward before continuing that role for TSW.

The other new face at the ITCA Council table in January 1982 was that of James Gatward. Though new to Council, as a freelance drama producer Gatward had worked for a number of ITV companies, as well as the BBC, and had a good reputation as a producer – particularly of children's drama production. Competition for the South and South East franchise had been intense and children's programming had been one of the points of appeal in his consortium's application.

The IBA under Lady Plowden and Sir Brian Young had always sought to redress what they saw as the tendency of commercial television schedules to migrate to the populist end of the programme mix. And quality children's programmes were for them a touchstone. Indeed the Authority had expressed concern about the quality of ITV children's programmes in annual reports. Gatward had not only his own reputation to offer but he had persuaded one of the best BBC children's producers, Anna Home, to join him. He also offered other counters to the perceived populist tendency of ITV by recruiting a Programme Controller who was a distinguished documentary maker and BBC science and industry programme editor, Michael Blakstad, as well as Herbert Chappell from the BBC as Head of Arts and a Head of Education (John Miller) from the Open University.

Gatward also had a businesslike Board under a chairman, Lord Boston, who had been a BBC radio current affairs producer. But it was Gatward's executives who appeared to the Authority to be what would now be called 'a dream team'.

However as the Eighties progressed it became apparent that Gatward's colleagues around the Council table, more experienced in commercial television, did not see it that way. James Gatward brought to the table powerful ambitions but his company's fortunes were to describe an almost perfect arc of rise and fall through the contract years to 1992 and he was to remain something of an outsider.

There was a third new face at Council at the start of 1982 who had been appointed only a few weeks before the turn of the year. When Lord Windlesham had resigned at the ATV Midlands Board meeting of 5 May 1981 in disillusion at what he saw as the disastrous requirements imposed by the IBA for the restructuring of his company as a condition for the retention of the Midlands contract, he had agreed to continue to serve until the end of the year in order to allow a successor to be found. He was asked by his Board for suggestions and himself sought advice from a few trusted network managing director colleagues. One in particular, the previous Chairman of Council, Bill Brown of STV, was firm in his recommendation of the Managing Director of Independent Television Publications (ITP), the ITV network subsidiary which published *TV Times*, Bob Phillis.

Phillis was indeed well qualified for the job. He had read Industrial Economics at Nottingham University and thus combined a business qualification (rare in broadcasting at that time) with at least a connection with the Midlands. More importantly, he had ten years' direct experience at various levels of that then seething cauldron of industrial relations difficulties, the printing industry, and had lectured on industrial relations at Edinburgh University for four years in the early Seventies. Given the already apparent adverse trade union response to certain of the IBA conditions, like the requirement to move from the Elstree studios to a complex to be built at Nottingham, that experience was likely to prove invaluable.

Meanwhile the company had employed a firm of head-hunters, Goddard Kay Rogers and Associates (GKR), to find a successor to Windlesham. Phillis was high on their list. After initially rejecting an approach by Roy Goddard, one of the founder partners of GKR (who later became a member of the Authority and then the Commission), Phillis revised his decision and, in the absence abroad of the new Chairman (Gordon Hobday, the Chairman of Boots the Chemists), was interviewed by two members of the old ACC Board, Ellis Birk and Sir Leo Pliatzky. Phillis was appointed in September but was unable to take up his new role full time until 1 January 1982.

While still in charge at ITP, Phillis faced formidable tasks on behalf of his new company. In the final three months of 1981 he had to place 49 per cent of the company's equity and (as described in Chapter 1) it was an IBA requirement that this should be with Midlands-based investors. With the help of the Deputy Director General, Anthony Pragnell (whose pragmatic intercessions between the more unrealistic demands of the outgoing Chairman and DG and the companies during this crucial period are felt by many who were involved to deserve greater recognition), the local investment ambition was allowed to remain a theoretical aim but was abandoned in practice.

The difficulties of such a share placement were exacerbated by the need to reach agreement, so that a prospectus could be produced, on the division of the assets of the old company and its subsidiaries – the Elstree and Birmingham studios, the various pension funds and so on – with the 51 per cent shareholder ACC, which was itself in financial difficulty as a result of the cost of one of Sir Lew Grade's few feature film failures, *Raise the Titanic* ('It would have been cheaper to have lowered the Atlantic' was his characteristic conclusion) ... The placement was finally achieved on 15 December – only eight working days (because of the Christmas holidays) before the deadline of 31 December 1981.

Amongst a welter of other lesser problems one was particularly irritating. The restructured company needed a new name but an alert Midlands entrepreneur had already registered every conceivable name for a Midlands franchise holder – from 'Albion Television' to 'Hearts of Oak' and including Central Television – with the objective of holding the winning applicant company to ransom. Phillis and the able and creative Director of Programmes whom he had inherited from Windlesham,

Charles Denton, outmanoeuvred the entrepreneur by a clever counter-ploy. They registered the company as Central *Independent* Television.

Business Matters – Little and Large

As Phillis joined ITV's Council further problems lay ahead for his company: notably the building and manning of the major new studio centre at Nottingham required by the IBA contract and the looming threat of takeover bids for the tottering ACC. But now he had also to turn his mind to the concerns facing ITV companies jointly as a network.

The ten-week strike in 1979 had cast a long shadow over the Council table and the minutes for the first months of 1982 show a wide range of agenda items as being seen to have industrial relations implications. The build-up to the launch of Channel Four, with its new forms of programme generation and particularly its distribution through the ITV companies for the insertion of the advertisements, gave great scope for the trade unions to raise bargaining points about new working practices. Issues ranging from the coverage of the World Cup football in Spain to the attempts by ITN to catch up with the rest of the world's television news providers by moving from film to electronic cameras – particularly important at this time of the Falklands War – were being used by the relevant trade unions (usually the Association of Cinematograph, Television and Allied Technicians – ACTT – but sometimes also the Electrical, Electronic, Telecommunications and Plumbing Union – EETPU) to lever 'new money' out of what they recognised as strong bargaining positions within a cash-rich industry. Industrial relations in ITV during the Eighties are dealt with in detail in Chapter 4 later in this volume but it is possible from newspapers as well as the minutes of Council to see how Phillis came to undergo nervous questioning by Council colleagues after a *Daily Telegraph* headline on 2 January 1982:

PAY DISPUTE HALTS STUDIO AS NEW TV STATIONS GO ON AIR

This was above an article which revealed that although Television South, Television South West and Central Independent Television had started broadcasting in place of their predecessors, a pay dispute with electricians had kept the temporary East Midlands local programmes studio in a converted sweet factory on the Giltbrook Estate in Nottingham off the air and with it the new local news for that area. The concern of Phillis' colleagues was: would the contagion spread as a result of sympathetic action (legal in those days before the Thatcher government's industrial relations legislation outlawed it) around the network? The electricians' claim would have raised their average take-home pay from £20,000 to nearly £27,000. The action did not in the event receive support from electricians in other ITV companies but the sweet factory studio never did get on the air – though every night a team of journalists and presenters prepared a bulletin for broadcast – and East

Midlands viewers had to wait eighteen months, until the new East Midlands Television Centre opened in September 1983, to see news entirely dedicated to events in their area.

While industrial relations were almost permanently at the forefront of the minds of Council in the first years of the decade, the agendas and minutes for the period show that the business of the network's subsidiaries tended to take an amount of time inversely proportional to their financial benefit to the companies. Thus Independent Television Publications (ITP) Ltd, the highly profitable publisher subsidiary with monopoly rights to the ITV schedule for the publication of *TV Times* received scant attention in the early years, except for a brief period when Channel Four (ever anxious to question all assumptions made about it by ITV) appeared not to be willing to grant the copyright in its schedule to the publication. However, after negotiations had brought the new channel certain guarantees about the extent and character of the intended coverage of their programmes a licence was granted for the use of the C4 schedule.

All then was to go quiet on the ITP front at Council until much later. In 1988, *Time Out* magazine initiated a campaign to free the TV schedule listings from the exclusive copyright granted to BBC Enterprises' *Radio Times* for BBC programmes and ITP's *TV Times* for ITV and C4 programmes. As the campaign grew, it became clear that, despite a finding by the Monopolies and Mergers Commission in 1985 that was favourable to the broadcasters, their monopoly might be ended by the 1990 Broadcasting Act. A decision in principle was taken to sell ITP. However, it was a decision which would have complicated consequences in terms of Levy and Capital Gains Tax implications. Also publication of a listings journal was a requirement in each ITV company's contract with the IBA. Nevertheless the Authority agreed the sale of ITP at their meeting of 12 January 1989 and a buyer – the Reed-IPC Group – was found. The sale price was £113 million. ITV also received £28 million in respect of the royalties for the listings copyright assigned up until the end of December 1992 (C4 received £3.19 million for this) and a dividend of £10 million just before completion of the sale. The money was divided amongst the companies on a 'latest NAR share' basis (IBA Information Paper 104(89), 19 July 1989).

One of the subsidiaries that lost money at that time and received a considerable amount of Council's attention had, by an irony, arisen from an earlier ITV triumph. In the early Seventies the IBA Engineering researchers, the ITCA Engineering Department, BBC Engineering research and BREMA (the television set manufacturers' trade association) were jointly examining a possibility that had arisen from research into television transmission by digitally encoded signals to achieve better quality and more economic use of the frequencies allotted for broadcasting. As a by-product of this research they discovered that by encoding some of the 625 lines that lay outside the TV picture area (the Vertical Blanking Interval – VBI – lines) messages in text could be carried along on the back of the normal picture and sound signal without interfering with reception. A decoder on home sets would then be able to disentangle the text from the rest of the signal and print the messages on viewers' screens. Thus was 'teletext' born.

With television-set manufacturers keen to market another facility as the impact on sales of the availability of colour pictures diminished, some ITV companies were able to launch a service of news, weather and schedule information in text which they called ORACLE (as was later to become the custom, a memorable acronym was devised and fitting words – Optional Reception of Announcements by Coded Line Electronics – arrived at to describe the function). The BBC came up with their less memorably titled, but equally effective, CEEFAX service a year later.

Concern at Council in early 1982 was not with the teletext 'pages', which could carry advertisements and would ultimately allow the service to pay for itself (or 'wash its face' in the jargon of Council at that time). The problem was with an ancillary use of the system devised by ITCA and IBA engineers which allowed lines of text to appear at the bottom of the TV picture in sequence and which could be used, with careful (and costly) preparation, for subtitling films and plays for the deaf and hard of hearing. Once ITV had developed it and started a trial service, the most popular part of which was the subtitling of the two half-hour episodes of *Coronation Street* each week, the IBA saw this as a particularly important development for the service of a section of the public (which it estimated at up to eight million people) that had hitherto felt excluded from full access to television.

This constituency soon developed a powerful 'deaf lobby' which battered on the doors of MPs, the press and the IBA and BBC seeking extension of the service. By 1982 the Authority was demanding that ITV subtitle five hours of programmes a week in peak time by the end of 1983 with a progressive escalation towards a target of all major productions being subtitled by the mid-Nineties (Letter DDG, IBA, to Chairman, ITCA, 25 March 1982). Council regarded the latter demand, with its estimated cost of £500,000 p.a. as 'unrealistic' but were faced with the immediate requirement for an extra £73,746 for the current budget with increased cost to companies on top of that as regional services extended. At Council Paul Fox summed up the situation as he saw it: prospective returns were minimal and immediate outlays considerable. A strategy was devised to ask the IBA to delay the expansion of hours until after research commissioned from the University of Southampton on techniques and the usefulness of the service to the target audience was available. Meanwhile ITV agreed to extend the service geographically to include the London companies for the first time and Council agreed that the ORACLE service should receive more on-screen promotion to try to increase revenue from it. The battle over the amount of the subtitling provision by ITV was to continue but it was in essence about the costs and timetable for expansion. There was never any doubt about its value to its audience – or the negative public relations effect of not extending the service. By the end of the contract period (1992) the vast majority of peak-time programmes were subtitled for the deaf and hard of hearing, including the important but difficult and expensive process of subtitling the news.

The whole business of the 'promotion' of ITV programmes, its other services and, importantly, the opportunities it offered advertisers, was felt by Council to be particularly crucial in 1982, when ITV would be required to underline its strengths and distinguish them from the opportunities offered by new Channel Four – even though it was also to sell C4 airtime. ITV companies (who each sold the advertising slots for their areas at that time) were aware that TV-am would be a real competitor for revenue once it was on the air early the following year. And figures for the previous year had revealed that another new competitor, Independent Local Radio, had burst through the £50 million revenue mark from a standing start seven years earlier.

Traditionally the companies promoted themselves and 'their' programmes to their regional audiences – even if many of those programmes were made by other companies and broadcast as part of the network programme supply – rather than promoting ITV as a network. Therefore viewers in, say, the north-west identified with Granada rather than ITV, in central Scotland with STV, in the south-west with TSW and so on. As a consequence awareness of ITV in the public mind was fragmented and confused compared to that of the monolith of the BBC. Also one of the many complaints of the advertising industry (see Chapter 7, Section I, 'Advertising') was that they could not buy ITV at a 'one stop shop' but had to deal with fourteen different sellers if they wanted a commercial to be viewed throughout the United Kingdom. So when, in May 1982, the Chairman of the Marketing Committee (Clive Leach, the Sales Director of YTV) put his annual budget for central promotions (that is the promotion of *ITV* and its programmes) he was able to argue successfully for a 50 per cent increase of budget for the year ahead. However the arguments about the need to build ITV as a 'brand' were to continue through most of the contract period – reaching a climax in 1988.

These were, however, small financial items compared with the annual Network Programme Budget (which was approaching the £200 million mark in 1982 and was to rise to over £500 million in the following ten years). Agreement on this, the largest sum expended jointly by the ITV network companies, actually took place not at Council but at Network Programme Committee, where carefully prepared detailed drafts of the Budget were presented by the members of the Network Controllers Group to the managing directors in that forum dedicated to programme policy and finance matters. The proposals were then taken away for scrutiny by company finance directors, discussed with fellow managing directors (usually in the 'peer' groups of small, middle and major companies), sent back for revision where necessary before final agreement at NPC. Council would sometimes subsequently ask for revisions to deal with exceptional circumstances – sudden downturns of advertising business, industrial disputes and so on.

As well as network finance, Council increasingly during the Eighties was to deal with political matters, where ITV was required to put forward a united view in response to questions from ministries or matters arising in Parliament. 1982 was a politically sensitive year. The early months were the key period of the Falklands War with a prime minister deeply critical of media coverage of events. Her harshest criticism was reserved for the BBC but ITV companies were well aware that any restraint on the extra finance required for coverage by its subsidiary ITN would be viewed with disfavour. In their role as the ITN Board the companies found the extra – believed to be £1.8 million. Approximate figures only are available (see Chapter 6).

During the spring the managing directors in their various phone calls to one another and dinners together began their biennial discussion of who should succeed as Chairman of Council. On some occasions this could require the reconciliation of diverse views making the process as controversial and as time-consuming as the election of a pope. But this time in the light of the emergence of a prime minister with superstrong convictions about everything, including television, there was little doubt in anybody's mind.

Paul Fox had shown both subtlety and strength in dealing with politicians as Head of Current Affairs for BBC Television and when he arrived in ITV in 1973, he had very soon found himself at home amongst the politically adept senior figures of the network – John Freeman, Lord Windlesham and Denis Forman. Now the first was coming up to retirement at LWT, the second had resigned and the third had stepped back from Council and was engaged in the production of what turned out to be one of the finest flowerings of television drama of the decade on any channel – *The Jewel in the Crown.* Fox was to work hard to get Lord Harlech, the well-connected founder Chairman of HTV – as David Ormsby Gore MP, he had risen to ministerial office in the Macmillan Conservative government – involved in the representation of ITV's cause at senior political levels but Harlech was to die in a car crash in January 1985, just before the period of the fiercest political pressures that ITV had ever faced.

So Fox it was who was elected Chairman of Council at the meeting on 7 June 1982. As was the custom he would not take up his role until 1 August. He was able to persuade his colleagues, against normal practice, to allow him to remain YTV's representative at the Network Controllers Group throughout the period of his Chairmanship of Council.

The Politics and the Business of New Technologies – The Hunt Committee

One of the potentially most important items of 1982 in the political dimension of Council's agenda was the need to give evidence to the Hunt Committee. The Home Office, faced, as so often, with the Department of Industry's pressure at Cabinet to be allowed to take the initiative in driving forward the twin new technologies of cable and satellite transmission of television, responded by setting up a Committee of Inquiry into Cable Expansion and Broadcasting Policy under Lord Hunt of Tanworth, who as Sir John Hunt had been Secretary of the Cabinet from 1973–79. Its remit was:

To take as its frame of reference the Government's wish to secure the benefits for the United Kingdom which cable technology can offer and its willingness to consider an expansion of cable systems which would permit cable to carry a wider range of entertainment and other services (including, when available services of direct broadcasting by satellite) ...; to consider the questions affecting broadcasting policy which would arise from such an expansion, including in particular the supervisory framework. (*Report in the Inquiry into Cable Expansion and Broadcasting Policy* (Cmnd 8679) HMSO, 1982)

Noting the implications for itself, and for ITV, of the second part of Hunt's remit, and alarmed by a statement by the Home Secretary that the first Direct Broadcasting by Satellite (DBS) channels would be controlled by the BBC, the IBA had been quick to consider its position and submit evidence right at the start of 1982. In summary, it supported the expansion of cable development, provided public service broadcasting available to all was preserved, saw subscription as 'the most appropriate source of finance for cable services', made a plea for a 'must carry' rule for BBC, ITV and C4 on all cable stations and for the protection of the public from cable buying up exclusive rights to major events and restricting their availability. Finally it made a strong case for a 'pragmatic approach' to the supervision of cable, recognising 'the need to encourage investors' and concluded 'The Authority looks forward to playing a similar role in the development of cable services' to that which the Annan Committee had recognised it had done in 'organising commercial broadcasting' in the UK (Summary IBA evidence to Hunt Committee, 1982).

So effective was the IBA's response that by the May meeting of the Authority the Chairman was able to report that the Authority had been praised by Hunt 'for the speed and clarity' of its evidence (Minutes of Authority meeting 544 (82)). But this was not to bring the IBA reward in the short term.

Meanwhile ITV, its pace of response bedevilled as ever by its federal nature, set a deadline at April 1982 Council for its Future Development Committee (FDC) to provide a submission by June. At May Council the Chairman of the FDC, Bryan Cowgill, promised circulation of a draft in time for discussion at a special Council meeting on 18 May. Following this the Secretary of the ITCA would 'synthesise' comments and circulate a revised draft.

The meeting on 18 May supported key elements of the draft. Like the IBA, ITV sought a 'must carry' BBC, ITV and C4 rule for cable stations. However, an amendment was proposed by Peter Battle – still at TSW at this time – which sought to require that the ITV signal carried in any area must be the local station only and not one from elsewhere in the UK. Battle's background was in the sale of advertising for various ITV companies and from numerous skirmishes in the 'overlap areas' on transmission boundaries (where viewers could tune to two or more ITV stations) he was particularly well aware of the dangers to any company's revenue of cable carrying a rival company into a major town or city in its region. Council had no difficulty in agreeing this amendment to the ITV submission.

ITV also proposed that great sporting and other national events must continue to be available to the full national audience. It believed that cable should be regulated but at a level less than that exercised by the IBA/BBC. The draft did not specify the IBA as the regulator for cable but, as an amendment, 'Brum' Henderson of Ulster Television (who received a great deal of support and understanding from the IBA about the difficulties of broadcasting in Northern Ireland in the Seventies) got the meeting to agree that the decision on a national licensing body 'should not explicitly exclude the IBA'.

ITV's real concerns about cable, however, were financial. A draft paragraph on the possible impact of advertising on cable was strengthened to recommend a separate inquiry into the matter. And ITV was fascinated by the revenue possibilities of subscription on cable. Subscription would make no impact on advertising revenue and it was 'new money' into the business. ITV therefore recommended that they should be permitted to participate in both programme provision and investment in cable. It was agreed to pursue the possibility of a potential for the re-engineering of the old VHF 405-line television transmission system for an ITV off-air subscription service separately. The submission reached Hunt just before the June deadline and ITV was called to give oral evidence on 10 June.

When the Hunt Report was published four months later, ITV and the IBA were both pleased to see that Paragraph 24 of Hunt's Summary of Conclusions did propose a 'must carry' rule. However, buried in the body of the full report, Paragraph 61 shows that although ITV won the Peter Battle point about carrying the local ITV franchise holder only, Hunt hankered after a possibility that Scots exiled in London should be able to watch STV on local cable (oddly, the Committee seemed to assume that Welsh exiles would want to see the Welsh fourth channel rather than HTV Wales.). Paragraph 9 did allow ITV (and newspapers and radio) to invest in cable but not to have a controlling interest. Paragraph 29 did propose to prevent rights to the transmission of national events becoming exclusive to cable but ITV was discomforted to find virtually no restrictions on advertising time on cable.

The IBA, however, was deeply disappointed to find that Paragraph 46 recommended the setting up of a new Cable Authority 'for awarding franchises and monitoring performance'. It continued to lobby the Home Office on the need for unified regulatory standards. However, the Cable and Broadcasting Act 1984 was framed to set up a separate Cable Authority. Responsibility for cable did finally devolve upon the IBA's successor, the ITC, as a result of the Broadcasting Act 1990 (see Chapter 9). But the implications of new technological developments – particularly satellite – were to haunt the IBA during the period.

The Broader Political Scene – Prime Minister's Visits

It was in his second year as Chairman that Paul Fox was to face a crucial test of his political skills. The Prime Minister had accepted an invitation to lunch with

Council that Fox had managed to ease into her full diary with the help of his old friend from the *Yorkshire Post*, Bernard Ingham, now Mrs Thatcher's press adviser. Wednesday 15 February 1984 appeared to be an almost ideal moment for such an event. ITV was basking in the warm critical and public acclaim for *The Jewel in the Crown*, Granada's serial dramatisation of Paul Scott's quartet of novels about the British in India. The seventh episode (out of fourteen) was to be transmitted on Tuesday 14 February, the eve of the Prime Minister's visit. But Mrs Thatcher (like most MPs) saw little television except on Saturdays – not a good night by which to judge any television channel. If the programme context was propitious but ignored, the physical context for the lunch at Mortimer Street was, as Bill Brown, Managing Director of STV and a previous Chairman of Council, remembered:

> Awful, terrible. It was in the Conference Room, which was a bad room, badly lit. And she obviously felt she was in the lions' den, she felt very uncomfortable. It was the wrong shape. Not only could we not have private conversations until the end of lunch, we were all so close together that we were all hanging on the conversation between her and Paul ... we were all trying to chip in and have our say. It was really awful. We raised a number of things that she just absolutely squashed ... I made the great mistake of thinking she might have a sense of humour. She said, the only night I ever watch television is Saturday and Saturday night television is appalling. There is nothing to watch. Why don't you do some decent concerts or operas on a Saturday night? And I said, well, you could always watch *Union World* on Channel Four, Prime Minister, thinking she'd laugh. But I got the treatment, the full laser treatment for about half a minute on the iniquities of ITV's labour relations. (Interview with Bill Brown)

Paul Fox, the Chairman, himself took a similar view of the event. But for him the trouble started as he greeted the Prime Minister at the door. Mortimer Street is situated in the heart of London's fashion design area:

> ... clearly people had got to hear that she was coming so people in the fashion world and everybody else were standing in the street and she played to the crowds first of all and then flushed with the fact that the populace had turned out to cheer, she came up and launched into us ... It was a deeply uncomfortable lunch. The mistake was it was too big ... too many people sitting there, too many people ... thought it was not good politics to speak. (Interview with Sir Paul Fox)

Only David Plowright of Granada is remembered as having put ITV's point of view cogently and firmly but Mrs Thatcher was not to be swayed. The meeting did no noticeable damage to individual reputations. Paul Fox was made a CBE the following year but he concluded: 'It was an occasion that did the ITV companies no good at all.' ITV was not to be allowed to make any positive impact on the political agenda for broadcasting for the remainder of the decade.

A lunch three months earlier with the Authority, in their dining-room overlooking Harrods, had been better organised and had, on the surface, appeared to have gone better. But the Prime Minister seemed to feel uncomfortable in a situation that tended to reveal the ignorance that lay behind her convictions about broadcasting matters.

To any prime minister broadcasting is inevitably low in priority when set against the major parameters of the state of the nation – finance, crime, employment, defence, the state of the party and so on. (Indeed only when broadcasting impinges critically on any of these does the leader seek to scrutinise broadcasting.) Attempts to remedy the ignorance by providing the necessary information tended to appear patronising or partisan, or both. But Authority members and staff sought to explain ITV's finances, the regulation of violence in programmes and the IBA's powers to, as she put it, 'take away' franchises. The Prime Minister expressed particular concern that the shareholders lost everything as 'a result of the IBA's arbitrary judgement'. Apparently another seeker after a better way, she seemed at this point to support the idea of longer contract periods and even the idea of so-called 'rolling contracts' (renewals at the IBA's discretion, without readvertisement). But her level of perception of broadcasting matters was revealed by a parting remark that it appeared that broadcasters who supported her election campaign subsequently found it difficult to get, or to keep, employment in broadcasting. It transpired that she was referring to Hughie Green and Pete Murray.

So before the Eighties had reached their half-way mark, events were already moving towards making 'the curious partnership' of the IBA and ITV vulnerable to the ideas of the 'Tory think tanks'. These – the Institute of Economic Affairs, the Centre for Policy Studies, the Adam Smith Institute – together with the Prime Minister's advisers, the Secretary of State for Trade and Industry (Lord Young), Sir Jeffrey Sterling, Professor Brian Griffiths, combined to fill her personal broadcasting policy vacuum with ideas that were polemical rather than practical.

3

PROGRAMMES

SECTION I: PROGRAMMES MADE BY ITV COMPANIES

The last years of the ITV companies as contractors (survivors of the 1991 bid process became *licensees*) were a remarkably creative and successful period of programme making for commercial television – as the awards showered on their programme makers (see Tables A and B) during the period demonstrate. Given the adverse factors in the industrial and political climate described elsewhere in this volume, this must redound to the credit of all involved – management as well as production people.

It might be expected that ITV would perform well in the field of light entertainment but to win the *Rose d'Or* at the International Festival of Light Entertainment Television at Montreux for three years running (1989–91) is a feat unmatched before or since by any other broadcasting organisation in the world. And ITV's winning of seven awards at the Prix Italia between 1982 and 1991 demonstrates an unusual degree of success at the highest international level of competition for drama and the arts.

To uncover the background to these programme strengths, it is necessary to look beyond the central bureaucracy of the ITCA and IBA, with which this volume has largely been dealing so far, and move out to the fifteen network companies – where programme making was nurtured in a quite different way from the BBC. It was less centralised and sometimes (though by no means always) better financed and, above all, more internally competitive than the BBC. The IBA had an important role in setting and monitoring standards for quality and range of programmes made but the viewer-winning strength of ITV was always refined in the furnace of inter-company competition.

Competition between the network's major programme supplying companies – Central, Granada, London Weekend, Thames and Yorkshire – was limited by 'the guarantee'. This was an agreement whereby those companies supplied programmes for fifty peak-time transmission hours a week, each approximately in proportion to its percentage of Net Advertising Revenue (NAR), in return for guaranteeing the ten other companies that they would always be supplied with the minimum mix of programmes required by the IBA in the terms of their contracts. There was

Table A   International Awards

Year	Award	Category	Programme	Channel
1982	Golden Rose	Rose d'Or	Dizzy Feet	Central TV
1982	Prix Italia	Prix Italia for Drama	Cream in my Coffee	LWT
1982	Prix Jeunesse	Story Telling	The Pied Piper of Hamelin	Thames TV
1983	Golden Rose	Prix spécial de la Ville de Montreux	It's your Move	Thames TV
1984	Golden Rose	Prix spécial de la Ville de Montreux	The Benny Hill Show	Thames TV
1984	Prix Italia	Prize of the Regione, Venezia Fruili for music	Ralph Vaughan Williams – Symphonic Portrait	LWT
1984	Prix Italia	Prix Italia for Drama	Made in Britain	Central TV
1985	Golden Rose	Rose de bronze	Spitting Image	Central TV
1986	Prix Jeunesse	Prix Jeunesse independent from the categories	Look at Me	Central TV
1986	Prix Jeunesse	Special Prize in the name of UNICEF	Look at Me	Central TV
1987	Golden Rose	Rose de bronze	Torvill and Dean's Fire and Ice	LWT
1987	Prix Italia	RAI Prize for fiction	Scab	Yorkshire TV
1988	Prix Jeunesse	Special Prize in the name of UNICEF	A Couple of Charlies	Central TV
1989	Golden Rose	Rose d'Or/Prix de la presse	Hale & Pace	LWT
1990	Golden Rose	Rose d'Or/Prix Special de la Ville de Montreux/ Prix de la presse	Mr Bean	Thames TV
1990	Prix Italia	Prix Italia for documentaries	Hello. Did you hear us? Red Hot	Central TV
1990	Prix Italia	Hegione Sicilia Prize for Ecology Programme	Can Polar Bears Tread Water?	Central TV
1991	Golden Rose	Rose d'Or	A night on Mount Edna	LWT
1991	Prix Italia	Prix Italia for credits and title sequences	The South Bank Show	LWT

Source: Prix Italia and Golden Rose of Montreux Archives.

Table B   Domestic Awards

Year	Award	Category	Winner	Channel
1982	BAFTA	Documentary Programme	Laurence Olivier – A Life	LWT
1982	RTS Programme Awards	Original Programme	Whoops Apocalypse	LWT
1982	RTS Programme Awards	Regional Programme	Recipe for Disaster	TSW
1982	RTS Journalism Awards	TV Reporter	Michael Nicholson	ITN
1982	RTS Journalism Awards	News International	ITN News 'El Salvador: Shoot out on Polling Day'	ITN
1982	RTS Journalism Awards	Current Affairs International	World in Action 'The Mystery of Flight 163'	Granada TV
1982	RTS Journalism Awards	Home News	ITN News 'Canberra Homecoming'	ITN
1983	BAFTA	Drama Series/Serials	Kennedy	Central TV
1983	BAFTA	Actuality Coverage	ITN Coverage of the Lebanon Crisis	ITN
1983	RTS Journalism Awards	Daily News Magazine	Coast to Coast	TVS
1983	RTS Journalism Awards	Foreign News	David Smith 'Beirut, the British Under Fire'	ITN
1983	RTS Journalism Awards	Home Current Affairs	TV Eye 'Here Comes Cruise'	Thames TV
1984	BAFTA	Drama Series/Serials	The Jewel in the Crown	Granada TV
1984	BAFTA	Light Entertainment Programme	Another Audience with Dame Edna Everage	LWT
1984	RTS Programme Awards	Original Programme	Skin Horse	Central TV (for C4)
1984	RTS Programme Awards	Regional Programme	I Can Hear you Smile	Scottish TV
1984	RTS Journalism Awards	Cameraman of the Year	Nigel Thomson	ITN
1984	RTS Journalism Awards	Regional Daily News	Calendar	Yorkshire TV
1984	RTS Journalism Awards	Home Current Affairs	World In Action 'The Honourable Member for Belfast West'	Granada TV
1985	RTS Programme Awards	Original Programme	28 Up	Granada TV
1985	RTS Journalism Awards	Journalist of the Year	Ken Rees	ITN

continued

Table B   continued

Year	Award	Category	Winner	Channel
1985	RTS Journalism Awards	Cameraman of the Year	Sebastian Rich	ITN
1985	RTS Journalism Awards	Regional Current Affairs	London Programme 'Southwark'	LWT
1985	RTS Journalism Awards	Special Commendation	Bradford City Football Ground	Yorkshire TV
1985	RTS Journalism Awards	Home News	The Tottenham Riots	ITN
1985	RTS Journalism Awards	Special Commendation	OB Team Live coverage of the Bradford City Football Stadium Fire	Yorkshire TV
1986	BAFTA	Factual Series	World in Action	Granada TV
1986	RTS Programme Awards	Children's Programme	Look at Me	Central TV
1986	RTS Journalism Awards	Journalist of the Year	John Suchet	ITN
1986	RTS Journalism Awards	Cameraman of the Year	Mike Inglis	ITN
1986	RTS Journalism Awards	Regional News Magazine	Granada Reports	Granada TV
1986	RTS Journalism Awards	Regional Current Affairs	London Programme 'Death of a Black Hell's Angel'	LWT
1986	RTS Journalism Awards	Home News	'Evelyn Glenholmes – Britain's most wanted woman'	ITN
1986	RTS Journalism Awards	Special Commendation	David Glencorse	STV
1987	RTS Journalism Awards	TV Journalist of the Year	Desmond Hamill	ITN
1987	RTS Journalism Awards	TV Cameraman of the Year	Philip Bye	ITN
1987	RTS Journalism Awards	International News	'Inside the Bourj Al-Barajneh Camps'	ITN
1987	RTS Journalism Awards	Special Commendation	Luke Casey	Tyne Tees TV
1988	RTS Programme Awards	Single Documentary	Afghantsi	Yorkshire TV

continued

Table B   continued

Year	Award	Category	Winner	Channel
1988	RTS Programme Awards	Regional Programme	The Calendar Fashion Show	Yorkshire TV
1988	RTS Journalism Awards	Regional Current Affairs	London Programme 'The Wall of Silence'	LWT
1988	RTS Journalism Awards	Home Current Affairs	Crying in the Dark	Tyne Tees TV
1988	RTS Journalism Awards	International Current Affairs	Afghantsi	Yorkshire TV
1988	RTS Journalism Awards	Home News	Soldiers Lynched	ITN
1988	RTS Journalism Awards	Special Commendation	Special Report, Lockerbie	ITN
1989	RTS Programme Awards	Drama Series	A Bit of a Do	Yorkshire TV
1989	RTS Programme Awards	Single Documentary	Four Hours in My Lai	Yorkshire TV
1989	RTS Programme Awards	Regional Programme	Charlie Wing	TVS
1989	RTS Journalism Awards	TV Journalist of the Year	Paul Davies	ITN
1989	RTS Journalism Awards	Regional Daily News Magazine	Coast to Coast (South)	TVS
1989	RTS Journalism Awards	News Home	Kegworth Air Crash	ITN
1989	RTS Journalism Awards	News International	Bucharest	ITN
1990	BAFTA	Comedy Series	The New Statesman	Yorkshire TV
1990	BAFTA	Children's Programme	Press Gang	Central TV
1990	RTS Programme Awards	Children's Award – Drama and Light Entertainment	Press Gang	Central TV
1990	RTS Programme Awards	Single Drama	Shoot to Kill	Yorkshire TV
1990	RTS Programme Awards	Drama Series	Inspector Morse	Central TV
1990	RTS Programme Awards	Single Documentary	Red Hot	Central TV
1990	RTS Journalism Awards	TV Cameraman of the Year	Eugene Campbell	ITN
1990	RTS Journalism Awards	Judges Award	Sir David Nicholas, CBE, Chairman	ITN
1991	BAFTA	Drama Serial	Prime Suspect	Granada TV
1991	BAFTA	Drama Series	Inspector Morse	Central TV

continued

Table B   continued

Year	Award	Category	Winner	Channel
1991	BAFTA	Actuality Coverage	Coverage of the Gulf War	ITN
1991	RTS Programme Awards	Single Drama	Prime Suspect	Granada TV
1991	RTS Programme Awards	Regional Documentary	Summer on the Estate	LWT
1991	RTS Journalism Awards	TV Journalist of the Year	Michael Nicholson, OBE	ITN
1991	RTS Journalism Awards	TV Cameraman of the Year	Nigel Thomson	ITN
1991	RTS Journalism Awards	Regional Daily News Magazine	Coast to Coast (South)	TVS
1991	RTS Journalism Awards	News International	News at Ten 'Flight from Saddam Hussein'	ITN
1992	BAFTA	Drama Series	Inspector Morse	Central TV
1992	BAFTA	Drama Serial	Anglo-Saxon Attitudes	Thames TV
1992	RTS Programme Awards	Single Documentary	Katie and Eilish – Siamese Twins	Yorkshire TV
1992	RTS Programme Awards	Regional Documentary	Tuesday Special Caution – Our Hands are Tied	Central TV
1992	RTS Journalism Awards	TV Cameraman of the Year	Ian Robbie	ITN
1992	RTS Journalism Awards	Regional Daily News Magazine	Central News West	Central TV
1992	RTS Journalism Awards	Regional Current Affairs	The Candidates News at Ten	Yorkshire TV
1992	RTS Journalism Awards	News International	'Discovery of the Serb Camps'	ITN
1992	RTS Journalism Awards	Project Award	First Tuesday 'Cold Blood, The Massacre of East Timor'	Yorkshire TV
1992	RTS Journalism Awards	Sports News	Olympic Drug Scandal	ITN

Source: RTS and BAFTA Archives.

a further mechanism that had grown up over the years that allowed some of the 'middle five', Anglia and STV, in particular, a small measure (just ten to twelve hours a year) of guaranteed access for drama (see Chapter 5).

In theory each major company could make whatever it wanted in its guaranteed hours and thrust it on the rest of the network. However, part of the friction at the Programme Controllers Group meetings was caused by the antidote to this. Anyone who tried to supply unsuitable programmes under the guarantee, to the detriment of the network's performance, had a very hard time indeed from the other companies' Controllers. One aspect of internal competition, therefore, was the professional judgement of peers. Another driving force was company pride in each company's own programme-making ethos. This lay behind the excellence of *The Jewel in the Crown* (Granada) and *Anglo-Saxon Attitudes* (Thames). Equally, the quality of the more popular drama, like the pioneering hour-long comedy drama series *A Bit of a Do* (Yorkshire) or the polished period detective series *Poirot* (London Weekend), came from the same equivalent of the Army's regimental pride. That pride was in part related to the desire to associate the company's name with quality in the public mind but more specifically it was to demonstrate to the regulator, the Authority, that not only the word but the spirit of the company's contract was being fulfilled.

Pride was not only about quality, it was also about quantity – the number of viewers watching. The ultimate driving force behind ITV's programme success was, and remains, the fight for advertising revenue. Again, because the companies sold their own advertising, that was a matter of company pride and helped to shape the culture of each company in a particular way.

It was these competitive forces – for a company's programme quality to be seen in the best context in the ITV schedule and for that schedule to allow the company to derive strong revenue from its advertising (objectives which themselves often pulled in different directions) – that were the main factors in the cauldron of dispute that was the Programme Controllers Group (PCG – later to be renamed Network Controllers Group, NCG).

A Little Difficulty at the Weekend

London Weekend Television's ethos was driven by the fact that the company had only a two and a half day contract with three periods of peak-time earning power (Friday to Sunday) when the other London company, Thames, had four and a half days with four peak-time periods (Monday to Thursday). The other companies had seven-day contracts but the old ITA had decided during its discussions on the restructuring of the ITV network in the run-up to the 1967–68 franchise round (see *Independent Television in Britain,* Volume 2) that the London area was by then sufficiently prosperous to support two stand-alone franchises, rather than the previous complex system of a London Weekend contractor also holding a weekday contract elsewhere in the UK. This also helped to avoid too great a domination of the network by London in a different way.

ATV had broadcast to London at weekends and the Midlands during the week. From 1968 it gained a seven-day Midlands contract – a change that was ultimately to lead to the trauma (described in Chapter 2) arising from the IBA requirement that Central move from Elstree, just north of London, to a new studio centre in the East Midlands. In the same restructuring, Granada had its region cut in half with the prosperity of Leeds, Bradford, Sheffield and the surrounding shires going to a new company, Yorkshire Television. These changes were, perhaps, not unrelated to tensions that grew up between Granada and London Weekend in the Seventies and were to continue throughout the period covered by this volume (and which, arguably, only ended with the takeover of LWT by Granada in 1994).

The weekend in London is attractive to advertisers – it has a high proportion of top classification (ABC1) male high spenders with availability to view – but in the early Eighties LWT faced two severe difficulties: firstly, BBC1, headed initially by Bill Cotton, BBC Television's ex-Head of Light Entertainment who had generated much of the product, and then by Alan Hart, their ex-Head of Sport, who was particularly determined to beat the competition at weekends to enhance the viewing figures for the BBC's increasingly expensive sports contracts, was able to schedule particularly strongly at the weekends at this time. With series like *The Two Ronnies, All Creatures Great and Small* and *Howards Way* all at the top of their form, it was not unknown for the BBC to take a 70–80 per cent share of the weekend peak-time audience. Advertisers grew noisy in their complaints and even Ron Miller, LWT's legendarily successful Sales Director, found it difficult to increase revenue.

The second difficulty for the weekend contractor was that under the networking arrangements (and also for economic reasons) it had to broadcast a proportion of the other major companies' productions. These were often devised and delivered by companies with a programme ethos that was not subject to the same competitive pressures. John Birt (an ex-Granada man, now the Director General of the BBC), who took over from Michael Grade as LWT's Director of Programmes in 1982, remembered:

> The London [split] – which nobody ever writes about – is absolutely critical to an understanding of ITV of that period, and probably still is. Whereas your share of audience didn't matter anywhere else, it did matter in London. There was a clear correlation in London between your share of audience and your share of revenue. And that's why both Thames and LWT were so sharp about the strength of the schedule and had a different attitude from the rest of the system. LWT felt very much like the David in the system; you faced the Goliath of the BBC at the weekend and the Goliath of the rest of ITV not wanting to help you. With the monopoly of the sale of advertising in their areas, ratings in a sense did not much matter to the seven-day companies: they were going to make the money

anyway – that's certainly how they behaved. And (therefore) they were programme led, not schedule led ... One has to be fair, why were they that way? Because the strength of the schedule didn't matter to them financially and, secondly, because we were in a system where you got your franchise back by making good programmes, and we all worked in an environment where we were all driven by a culture not that different from the BBC's; where we were all driven by the ethics and concerns and attitudes of the producer group in television. Plainly that was not a culture that was commercially driven in terms of the needs of the audience. And I think all this had a big impact on LWT culture. You felt like the Israelis, you had to be good. And I think that's why LWT was a very, very sharp company as a result, because it had to be. (Interview with John Birt)

Brian Tesler was Managing Director of London Weekend Television for fourteen years from 1976 and he saw LWT's normally exposed position made more difficult by the financial effects of the advent of Channel Four superimposed on the recession of the early Eighties:

The decline in revenue was partly because of Channel Four. We paid a subscription ... in order to earn the right to earn revenue from Channel Four ... the money going out for subscription (was) in no way matched by the money coming in from Channel Four, selling airtime on Channel Four, nor even from selling programmes to Channel Four ... the weekend company was selling a lot of programmes to Channel Four but not at any great prices. It wasn't that we had a shortfall in revenue, but the further complication was that the entire industry was experiencing the same kind of decline, they were pulling in their horns. They were all seven-day or weekday contractors ... And what they lost at the weekend against strong BBC competition they could make up during the week, when BBC competition was not so strong. And so they tended to put their strongest programmes in the weekdays. So we suddenly found ourselves in the most extraordinarily weak position. (Interview with Brian Tesler)

Ultimately out of that weak position was to emerge a more rigorous approach to programme costs and planning (see Chapter 5), a new bond with another company and a new form of programme.

Meanwhile Tesler and Birt undertook a whistlestop tour of the major companies and some of the 'middle five' to try to create a greater understanding of the weekend's needs and, indeed, of the network's need of a strong weekend against the BBC. They argued, with some justification, that the advertisers' view of the weekend decline of audiences tended to affect their view of ITV as a whole. The meeting with Granada was not a happy one. One aspect of tension, Tesler remembers, centred on an old sore in the relations between southern and northern ITV companies – the sharp difference of taste in entertainment:

John (Birt) and I saw David Plowright (MD of Granada) and Mike Scott (Director of Programmes) at Golden Square (Granada's London headquarters). And I actually said, 'Look David, we need good programmes from Granada and one of the things we need is good light entertainment programmes, and frankly David your head of light entertainment programmes ... He's a very, very nice guy, terrific guy, but ... he is *Wheeltappers and Shunters Social Club* and *The Comedians*. And they are good programmes but everything he's done since has been ... becoming more parochial.' David, to give him his due didn't throw us out of his office ... (but) he didn't do anything about it either. (Interview with Brian Tesler)

David Plowright, born and bred in the north-west, had made a considerable contribution to the development of investigative television journalism in the UK in the Sixties and was a Granada man to his boots. He was also a veteran of the Monday morning confrontations at Controllers meeting and scheduling tensions with LWT – most recently with John Birt's predecessor, Michael Grade, over the placing of *Brideshead Revisited.* Plowright had believed, with some justification, that *Brideshead* was ideal for Sunday night. It ended up playing on Monday. He recalls both mild ire and a specific irony from the meeting:

I do remember getting a little cross with John Birt because he, like a number of Granada youngsters used to spend a lot of time at programme committee meetings and dinners I used to have ... saying why the hell do you tolerate the schedule being dominated by light entertainment? We really must find better slots for our distinguished output. So it was quite amusing when John rather diffidently suggested that Granada's offerings for the Sunday schedule might be a little more popular in their appeal. And I do recall saying to him that I didn't feel inclined to change the character of the company for his particular needs. (Interview with David Plowright)

Of the major companies, only Yorkshire Television, the smallest, where Paul Fox and his (largely ex-BBC) senior programme staff had maintained an awareness of southern tastes, responded positively to LWT's call. The larger regionals were keen to contribute programmes for the weekend but a combination of restrictive networking arrangements and LWT's financial position precluded this, at least initially.

That financial position required a radical approach from Birt in his first year as Director of Programmes:

Our adverse financial position meant that I had to pull back on our transmission budget, and therefore ... I had to put a lot of programming into stock and transmit from stock over quite a long period of time. It was basically a two-year period of severe disruption to the LWT production cycle, which was not good for my reputation within the company. We'd just had a Director of

Programmes who'd been able to spend, spend, spend and then we had a new Director of Programmes cutting production. Moreover, in order to get maximum value, not only did we have to cut production but we had to try to do it in a way which had the least impact on the transmission schedule, where we were unaided, as we felt, by other companies. So we resolved on a strategy of maximising the number of popular entertainment shows in the schedule. So I was cutting back on production in general but increasing the volume of shows which would give high rating delivery. So it was not a happy period within the company. (Interview with John Birt)

Outside the company there was some scepticism as to whether the financial situation was as serious as LWT said it was. And nowhere was there greater scrutiny of LWT's finances than at the IBA, which had to agree to any schedule change that affected the company's contractual obligations. And not only were LWT holding over drama and situation comedy and replacing it with entertainment shows, they wanted to reduce the run of *Weekend World*, the LWT-produced network political and economic affairs flagship programme (of which Birt himself had been editor), and cancel a number of local programmes.

Local programmes for London had always been a focus of contention between the London companies and the IBA. Perhaps London is too highly populated and amorphous for the audience to relate to specific items in programmes for the area but, whatever the reason, such programmes have seldom found favour with the audience. Over the years IBA staff have tended to take the view that this is because the contractors concerned haven't put enough effort into them. And here was a London contractor trying to wriggle out of producing them. Brian Tesler chose the day before Christmas Eve 1982 to break the news, in writing, to the new DG, John Whitney.

Tesler, whose sense of timing was renowned, appears to have carefully chosen his moment. Not because it was the eve of the holiday but because of the IBA's agenda. He knew that the Authority was as concerned as he was about the impact on ITV of the IPA/Equity dispute (see Chapter 4) and, as we have seen, the Authority was also seeking the enfranchisement of all companies' shares. But in almost every case problems arose. Arising out of the December Authority meeting concern was registered that voting shares in LWT (even within the company's then 12 per cent limit for any single shareholder) should not fall into the hands of shareholders 'unacceptable to the Authority'. Ten years after the Murdoch affair with LWT (see Introduction) and under another chairman and a new DG, some tribal memory within the IBA caused the issue to be raised specifically in respect of LWT.

Tesler received an informal warning from the IBA's new Director of Finance, Peter Rogers, while they were together as fellow Channel Four directors at a working weekend on 29/30 January 1983, that the IBA could not appear to respond sympathetically to one company when all ITV companies were suffering financially. An IBA acceptance of the LWT case would lead to a queue of others asking to off-load their local programme obligations.

But by March the Authority had given LWT much of the easement they had asked for – a particular exception being the cutting back of *Weekend World*. How was this achieved? Certainly Tesler had argued the special circumstances of his company well but the minutes of the Authority meeting on 2 March 1983 reveal that LWT had also threatened to sell unspecified 'investments' to raise cash if contractual obligations were not temporarily relaxed to meet their difficulties. Such a gesture might have had an adverse impact on the city's view of LWT and therefore on the IBA-required enfranchisement.

The effects of Birt's radical rethink brought about the development of a new programme genre – the 'people programme'. In 1980 the Controller of Entertainment at LWT, David Bell, was finally able to lure away from the BBC a fellow Scot, Alan Boyd. Boyd was trained as a scientist but had gone into television and had turned the art of game shows on television into a mystique, if not exactly a science. He had been responsible for the BBC's hugely successful *Blankety Blank*. He wanted to develop his game show theories further on screen but ran up against a propensity in his boss at the BBC, Bill Cotton, for wanting to wring the last drop of ratings benefit out of hard-won success rather than divert energy into new developments.

So Boyd went to LWT and developed a new dimension of the game show – a dimension that owed something to the Theatre of Embarrassment. It was called *Game for a Laugh*. When Birt inherited it in his schedule he realised it and programmes like it could fulfil his need for comparatively low-cost shows with 'high ratings delivery'. But Birt's predecessor, Michael Grade, whose stint as Controller BBC1 later in the Eighties showed him to be a superb scheduler, had put *Game* in the Saturday night schedule alongside action drama – like *The Professionals*, with young male appeal – where its young presenters (Jeremy Beadle, Sarah Kennedy, Henry Kelly and Matthew Kelly) and their energetic style and sometimes humiliating tricks on members of the audience were well appreciated as a form of entertainment.

Birt, having taken over, commissioned volumes of demographic audience research on weekend viewing patterns. (His nickname at Controllers was 'Mainframe'. This sobriquet had the ambivalence favoured by clever minds seeking relief from the alternating tensions and tedium of the meetings. It could be taken as referring to Birt's passion for the detail of computer-based research – or to his own computer-like apparent inflexibility of thought. It was not long, however, before demographic research was to become an increasingly significant factor in ITV's scheduling decisions.) Birt took the view that *Game* was just the ratings winning support that his flagging Sunday night needed. He was right. The move raised the ratings for the programme from eleven to fourteen million. However, the Sunday slot exposed it to the gaze of an older, more critically demanding segment of the audience who tuned to ITV on Sunday evenings to see drama and LWT's arts flagship for the network, *The South Bank Show*. And, as the ideas for 'laughs' that were both funny and acceptable began to dry up, there were complaints from this minority and there was a hot blast of criticism in the press and some expressions of concern from the IBA. *Game* was taken out of the schedule. But Boyd had more than one barrel to his people-show gun – and he had spare ammunition too.

The harnessing for LWT of the talents of the Liverpool pop singer of the Sixties, Cilla Black, to become presenter/host to this new genre of programme must be attributed to John Birt. His own Liverpool background gave him credibility when he sought to persuade the performer that such a step was for her a positive one (see *Running the Show: 21 Years of London Weekend Television,* by David Docherty, Boxtree, 1990).

It was before the demise of *Game for a Laugh* that, while the voluble Boyd was explaining to Black the format for the next people-show he had in mind, the words *Surprise, Surprise!* seemed to sum up the new show. It became her catchphrase and the title of a show which is still running as this is written, fourteen years after its birth, and which has regularly beaten the BBC1 opposition. It attracted nearly sixteen million viewers at the peak of its popularity.

The early success of *Surprise* encouraged Birt and Boyd to look to Black when the pilot programme for the replacement for *Game* caused Birt – who by 1985 was steering LWT's programmes towards the IBA's mid-contract review scrutiny – some anxiety. The pilot was for a show adapted from a US show called *Blind Date*. There were various options for diminishing the potential for voyeurism and embarrassment in this formula for the televisual exploitation of the oldest urge. The one that Boyd took successfully was to follow through the selection of boy by girl and vice versa and their departure together to tourist destination 'romance' with separate interviews with each partner and to show the face of the other while each interview was being played. The other decision was to try to fend off any tendency for the audience to perceive the formula as a serious mating game, rather than a light-hearted romp, by having a 'camp' presenter. This was a trick that had worked elsewhere but here it simply added to the potential for trouble with the IBA. Cilla Black would superimpose a clean, almost matronly dimension without spoiling the fun. Fortunately Black had seen and enjoyed the Australian version of the show – *Perfect Match* – and was keen to take the role. And, after a few requirements from the IBA, including chaperoning on location, had been met, *Blind Date* became another LWT Saturday night saviour and something of an institution for the nation at large.

But by 1985 a downside to this success began to appear. LWT's quality entertainment star of the Seventies, Stanley Baxter, and a new young talent, Russ Abbott, went unused, because of the expense of production, and were thrown into the open arms of the BBC's Head of Light Entertainment, James Moir. And Birt lost two of his own Heads in quick succession; Humphrey Barclay, Head of Comedy and David Bell, Head of Entertainment (and talented producer of *The Stanley Baxter Show*). Boyd, the game- and people-show king, inherited the LWT entertainment earth until his appointment as Director of Programmes at TVS two years later when Birt moved to the BBC.

For some it may be tempting to try to find in these events a moment of significant change in ITV's approach to programmes but in truth ITV companies have always cut their programme cloth according to the needs of their revenue stream at any moment in time. When revenue picks up, company pride and the desire to impress the regulator again become paramount – all other factors being equal. And as the Eighties progressed very few factors were to stay the same for any ITV company. Perhaps the greatest change affecting companies' programme production was the emergence of the independent producer with the arrival of C4 and the mandated use of the new breed by ITV as a result of the Peacock Report (see Chapters 5 and 8).

For LWT the people-show developed out of a sudden need for retrenchment but its success with viewers allowed it to live on alongside the restarting of drama production, which included such widely praised and successful ventures as *London's Burning*, originally a two-hour special about a London Fire Brigade crew written by Jack Rosenthal but developed into a long-running series. This amongst other successes, like *The Charmer, Wish Me Luck* and, later in the period, the stylish *Poirot*, were amongst productions that lifted the company's drama output from an all-time low of only seventeen hours in 1983/84 to twenty-seven hours by 1986/87. (It should be noted that ten years earlier LWT had been contributing over sixty-five hours of drama to the network.) There had always been shows on television that involved ordinary people but it was the commercial pressures of the weekend schedule that gave rise to the the Eighties explosion of such a specific form of highly developed people-show.

Satire on Sunday – Innovation from the Fens, via Central

10.00 p.m. on Sunday 26 February 1984 saw the first transmission of a series that was innovative and controversial and, as the weeks went by, increasingly funny and popular. It was the sort of bold, risk-taking adventure that might have been expected from Channel Four but not from ITV. It was called *Spitting Image* and it was to become the first successful satirical comedy series since *That Was the Week, That Was* et al. on the BBC in the early Sixties. It was to become something of a national talisman during the Thatcher years.

Spitting Image came to the network from Central Television. Central's Director of Programmes at that time was Charles Denton – a man prepared to try to move television forward and face the inevitable trouble involved in so doing, provided the talent was worth it. The history of how the series reached Denton is important to relate because it perhaps helps to explain why the normally cautious John Birt was willing to see such a risky venture scheduled at the weekend.

The story starts with a London Weekend graphics designer called Martin Lambie-Nairn, one of whose tasks in the Seventies was to work at weekends on *Weekend World* when John Birt was its editor. He listened to the radio while working and became particularly addicted to the topical satirical Radio 4 programme *Week Ending*. He also met senior politicians in the hospitality room after they had appeared on

Weekend World. As an artist observer, rather than a hard-bitten current affairs producer directly involved in the series, Lambie-Nairn became fascinated with the distinction between the real person behind the public figure and how that person wished to be perceived – the very stuff of satire.

In 1981 Lambie-Nairn left LWT to go freelance. One of his early commissions was to create an identity for the new Channel Four. His multi-coloured '4' symbol made an immediate impact and his company, Robinson, Lambie-Nairn, was soon much in demand and financially secure. The idea of a visual *graphic* satire never left him. A colleague put him in touch with two artists who had built something of a reputation for themselves by producing three-dimensional caricatures of public figures which were then photographed to illustrate articles in the newspaper colour supplements that boomed in the Sixties and Seventies. The artists were called Peter Fluck and Roger Law. They had met at Cambridge Art School at the age of sixteen under the tutelage of Paul Hogarth, who was to the left politically and had been a man of action (in the Spanish Civil War and elsewhere), as well as being an artist. He had taught Fluck and Law the concept of 'the artist reporter'.

Lambie-Nairn and they were totally different in character but found common ground in the concept of an animated graphic form of satire for TV – a sort of *Muppets* with a current affairs cutting edge. Lambie-Nairn's company financed the initial developments but a Cambridge connection achieved funding from the inventor/industrialist Clive Sinclair (who was a great supporter of British film animation) for the first pilot.

For cheapness, this ten-minute show was shot on a home video camera in a photographer's studio in Camden but with the first versions of the Michael Foot puppet (getting hopelessly entangled in some curtains) and the cowboy version of Ronald Reagan with a script by the ex-*Not the Nine O'Clock News* producer, John Lloyd (who had been brought in by Lambie-Nairn as the producer) and satire writer and stand-up comedian Ben Elton, it was good enough to persuade Denton that this was something worth developing further. This was just as well, since Clive Sinclair withdrew his support soon afterwards.

The marriage of Fluck and Law and John Lloyd and their other producer, Jon Blair, to Central should have been made in heaven. Denton admired Lloyd's work. Lloyd now commanded the (sometimes grudging) respect of Fluck and Law and they all knew they needed Blair to run the show. (Lambie-Nairn had taken a back seat by this time.)

Although Central had inherited some of the people who had worked for the company's predecessor, ATV, on *The Muppets*, that series had been made at Elstree and this was to be made in Birmingham. As some of the Elstree expertise had stayed in London rather than move to the Midlands the morale of the others was not high (see Chapter 2). Also, though Denton had alerted the IBA to the nature of the project and he had reported it to his Board, he had, wisely perhaps, not communicated fully the degree of potential offence that the satire might cause. If he had, the forces of opposition which any such venture faces might have triumphed and *Spitting Image* might have been still-born.

Difficulties with the studio direction side of the production were ironed out by the use of Peter Harris, an old *Muppets* hand, much liked by the studio crew, who according to Lewis Chester's book on *Spitting Image* (*Tooth and Claw*, Faber & Faber, 1986), tended to view the puppet of the Queen as 'our Miss Piggy'. But the Central Board were a different matter. The Duke of Edinburgh was due to open Central's new Nottingham studios the week after the first programme. As a consequence despite Denton's fierce defence – and the acceptance of the material by Stephen Murphy of the IBA's Programme Division – the Board required that all references to the Royal Family in that first episode be deleted. The series more than made up for that later but the relationship between the creative team and Central remained an edgy one.

The programme won the Bronze Rose at the Montreux International Light Entertainment Television Festival in 1985 and many other prizes. There was never a season in its twelve-year lifespan when the series didn't cause outrage to someone while making millions laugh. Denton's successor as Director of Programmes at Central, Andy Allan, took responsiblity for the series for over ten years. Renowned himself for his wit, he was powerfully protective of the talent:

> Well it made life fun. I don't regard these things as headaches. I mean I think being rung at 8 o'clock on a Sunday night by a distraught lawyer asking if you think it's within the bounds of good taste and decency to show a puppet of the Queen's bottom, then that's when you know you're alive. But wish you were dead! (Interview with Andy Allan)

Dramatic Developments

As has been indicated earlier, the one other company that had been more consistently understanding of the needs and importance of the weekend schedule than others was Yorkshire Television. And it was that company that gave rise to another significant entertainment development later in the Eighties.

One reason for Yorkshire's interest in the weekend was that, as the winner of a completely new franchise (previously included in the Granada/ABC area) in the 1968 contractual upheaval, they had always had to fight the more established companies for programme space in the network schedule. After initial difficulties in 'selling' to the network, the company began to establish a reputation for good, writer-led drama and powerful documentary making. But it was not until the managing director, Ward Thomas, brought Paul Fox across from being Controller of BBC1 to replace Donald Baverstock as Director of Programmes in 1973 that Yorkshire began to gain any reputation for light entertainment programme making. Paul Fox, aware of the entertainment weakness, had cannily induced the BBC's Head of Comedy, Duncan Wood to move across with him. Wood had been a virtuoso producer/director at the BBC, with *Hancock's Half Hour* and *Steptoe and Son* amongst other successes to his credit.

At Yorkshire he set up a strong team which included a talented younger colleague from the BBC, Vernon Lawrence. They produced a number of hit comedies, including *Only When I Laugh* with Richard Wilson, James Bolam and Peter Bowles and the endearing (and enduring – repeats were still pulling in more than a million viewers on C4 in 1996) *Rising Damp*, written by Eric Chappell and starring the ineffable partnership of the late Leonard Rossiter and Frances de la Tour.

The comedy writers with whom Wood and Lawrence worked often chafed at the twenty-three-minute running time allowed by the advertisements on ITV for 'half-hour' comedy compared to the twenty-eight minutes allowed by the licence-financed BBC. (Allowing for applause and opening and closing credits, this reduced further to some twenty-one and twenty-six minutes respectively.) This is still a matter on which there are a number of opinions but writers who had worked for both organisations took the view that the missing five minutes limited both character and plot development. Comedy denouements on ITV tended to lack the subtlety of those on the BBC. Some executives from a programme background believe that these factors even had an impact on the image of ITV as a network.

The appeal of the comedy elements in such drama series as *Auf Weidersehen Pet* (Central) and *Minder* (Thames) led the way but it was Lawrence with writer David Nobbs who first tried the first full-blooded comedy 'hour'. They took the risk of not having studio audience applause, which gave them a running time of about three-quarters of the hour slot. To their own talents were added the proven comic ability of actor David Jason and the less familiar but equally effective comedy playing skills of Nicola Pagett. The comedy drama *A Bit of a Do* was born.

Yorkshire's Director of Programmes, John Fairley – unlike some of his Controllers Group colleagues – had developed a good relationship with Greg Dyke (who had succeeded John Birt at LWT in 1987) and was able to convey the potential of the series for Dyke's campaign to strengthen the weekend schedule and the series ran at 9.00 p.m. on Friday nights in January and February1989 to audiences which reached fifteen million. A further series was commissioned and these successes led to other variants of the new form – like *The Darling Buds of May*, adaptations by (initially) Bob Larby of the H.E. Bates short stories published under that name. So successful was this that it can be said without exaggeration that a whole new generation took the amoral but hilarious doings of Pa and Ma Larkin and their ever-extending brood to their hearts. The presence of David Jason in the cast (again), location filming in the best summer for thirteen years and a certain relevance to Thatcher's Britain helped but it was the comedy skills in writing and production that sought, found and conveyed the comic heart of the stories to create a 'feelgood' hour on Sunday evenings in the spring of 1991. *The Darling Buds of May* had a pleasurable impact on the national psyche probably unmatched by any other entertainment programme during the period. The hour-long comedy series was here to stay.

However the one-off drama – the single play, so beloved by critics and regulators but less and less secure in the affections of viewers – was an ITV casualty towards the end of the period. The genre was a long time a-dying. The Authority at its annual meeting with Controllers in the summer of 1986, sought to give the single play the kiss of life. But in the end single plays were losers on three counts: firstly, they were unpredictable in appeal to the audience. Secondly, they were uneconomic – series and serials were cheaper with repeated use of sets or locations and casts on long-term contracts. Their third adversity related to a much broader swing in British culture that was to lead to a parallel impact on West End theatre, where the newly written play was increasingly displaced by revivals and a flood of musicals. Britain in the Eighties was turning from drama (perhaps too often associated in the minds of the public in the past with the adjective 'harrowing') to entertainment.

The entertainment end of the drama spectrum was inhabited by what Granada liked to dignify with the cumbersome description 'bi-weekly serial drama' but everyone else called 'soaps'. Celebrating both its twenty-fifth and thirtieth anniversaries during the period, *Coronation Street* was, and remains, a unique blend of the serious and the comic, retained from its roots in the north-west of England. All objective data show it to be the brand leader amongst UK soap operas – staying ahead of a strong new contender, *Eastenders* (BBC), and remaining unthreatened by a strengthened *Emmerdale* (YTV) or the soap commissioned by Channel Four in 1982, *Brookside*.

For most of the period *Coronation Street*, or *Cor'n St* as it was known by the network's planners, was what they referred to as a weekday 'property', that is, it was shown in London by Thames. But when Greg Dyke took over as Director of Programmes at LWT in May 1987 he eyed the sixteen to eighteen million audience that it commanded before satellite and cable competition was serious, with envy. He and the new Granada Director of Programmes, Steve Morrison, did not see eye to eye. Their altercations at Controllers Group were said to be worse than those between their predecessors, John Birt and Mike Scott, but one who had witnessed both recalled that: 'At least with John and Mike there were long silences.'

But Greg Dyke had, at ITV strategy conferences and other industry meetings, struck up a genuine friendship with the man who became David Plowright's successor as Managing Director at Granada in the same year that Dyke took control of programmes at LWT, the shrewd, businesslike and affable Andrew Quinn. There had been attempts to get a Sunday afternoon 'omnibus' version of the Monday and Wednesday *Coronation Street*s networked but these had always foundered on the companies' local programming scheduled at that time. Dyke did not have much difficulty persuading Quinn of the virtues of a third episode of *Coronation Street* on a Friday – though it threw up some writing and production problems, it would increase both the advertising and programme revenue streams – but Thames had the right to block the move of a weekday series into their London rival's airtime. David Elstein at Thames enjoyed wheeling and dealing as much as Dyke and a complex set of trade-offs was arrived at that allowed Elstein to accept the logic of a Monday, Wednesday, Friday *Coronation Street.* The first Friday edition appeared on 3 October 1989.

David Elstein himself had been responsible for developing *The Bill* from a one-hour police series into a popular twice-weekly serial. (It too eventually was to develop a Friday episode in 1993.) All in all the period was a boom time for soap operas on television – and for writers, actors and producers working in the genre. The peak-time single play may have died during the period but popular drama on television had never been more alive.

Outside peak time, *Dramarama*, on Children's ITV (an umbrella title introduced in January 1983 to help promote ITV's output for children) did preserve twelve episodes a year of the single drama species throughout the period. Television for children targeted by ITV at the 4.00 p.m.–5.15 p.m. slot on weekdays and on weekend mornings was of a generally very high standard and at the start of the Eighties there was a feeling at the IBA and in the network that the quality was underestimated by parents, who had often been devotees of BBC radio or television programmes for children when they were the only ones available, before ITV started up.

A new policy for an expanded (by fifteen minutes a day) and properly promoted output for children emerged from an IBA Consultation on Children's Programmes at Cambridge in July 1981. Quality was maintained by the Children's Committee. Technically this was a subcommittee of the Network Controllers Group. In fact the group was made up of able and very competitive children's programme specialists from the network, under the chairmanship of a Controller. The man who led the group at the time of the expansion was Charles Denton, the Director of Programmes at Central. He was succeeded in the chair of the group by his successor at Central, Andy Allan. In 1988 Gus Macdonald of STV took over the responsibility and gained the network's gratitude for cutting costs by a third without perceptibly sacrificing quality.

Notable Children's ITV popular drama series from the period include: *Educating Marmalade* (Thames), *Supergran* (Tyne Tees), *Press Gang* and *Woof* (Central). In factual programmes *The Book Tower* (YTV) won acclaim (and a BAFTA award) for succeeding in using television to introduce young people to literature. The irreverent *Your Mother Wouldn't Like It* (Central) used the young talents found by an innovative community project – the Junior Television Workshop – set up by Central's Head of Children's Programmes, Lewis Rudd.

Fact + Fiction = Friction

The equation above was derived by a Human Sciences academic at Brunel University, Julian Petley, as a title for an essay in the publication *Media, Culture & Society* (Volume 18, Number 1, January 1996, Sage). Both title and work attempt a description of the cause and effect that gave rise to one of the major battles between broadcasters and politicians in the Eighties.

In fact the causes of friction are more complex than most people (including academics and politicians) realise. The dramatised documentary has been a source of controversy ever since it was introduced to television by BBC producers in the Fifties. By definition a bastard form, it had its genesis in both the work of BBC Radio Features in the Forties and the documentary work for the cinema of Flaherty and Grierson between the wars. This cinematic form reached a functional apotheosis in its use by the Crown Film Unit's works of exhortation and education during the Second World War.

There is one key factor that cannot be extended to the form's use on television; that was that the viewers of those Crown Films were aware that they were part of the war effort, they were 'on our side'. They were clearly labelled as a partial view of the world. The problem for broadcasters was that they were by law required to be impartial. And there were problems with labelling also. The BBC unwisely labelled its memorable 1966 production by Ken Loach and Tony Garnett, *Cathy Come Home*, as 'semi-documentary' in *Radio Times* and were roundly chastised for so doing by their ex-Head of Talks and Documentaries, the formidable Mrs Grace Wyndham Goldie, in the following terms:

> ... such a description surely means that we are being offered a production which the BBC accepts as a style, and which deliberately blurs the distinction between fact and fiction. Viewers are entitled to know whether what they are being offered is real or invented. (*Sunday Telegraph*, 8 January 1967)

'Real or invented' – both words tend to over-simplify the issue by ignoring factors like audience expectation and conditioning, style of writing and direction, the strength and credibility of performance and so on. *Cathy* was, of course, entirely fictional in its portrayal of a young woman's descent into the vortex of the Kafkaesque bureaucracy that faced the homeless mother and child. It was transmitted in a drama 'slot' in the BBC schedule but it dealt with a situation all too real for some viewers and Loach used all his undoubted skills to achieve realism on the screen.

Some of the controversies arising from successors to *Cathy*, like *The Monocled Mutineer* or *Bomber Harris* or programmes like *Who Sank the Lusitania?* were really about interpretations of fact in relation to history (though many of the protaganists would claim they were arguing for that seductively unattainable goal 'the truth') and the closer the situation portrayed was to the present, the greater the controversy. Even the distant past, in such generally lauded series as Christopher Ralling's *The Search for the Nile, The Fight Against Slavery* and *The Voyage of Charles Darwin,* gave rise to the odd flutter in history faculty dovecotes.

But more controversial even than matters of fact were the portrayals of events for the purposes of verisimilitude. Similar events *might* have taken place but what was seen on screen was the product of the imagination of writers as an interpretation of history. In the Eighties this became known by a new definition of the word 'faction' – this one word both being and standing for an elision of fact and fiction.

ITV's dramatised documentaries at this time were almost always about contemporary or recent events because the greater part of them stemmed from the network's current affairs programmes. For instance Granada had added a strong realistic documentary element to its traditions when in the mid-Sixties it tempted Dennis Mitchell away from BBC London and back to his northern roots (where ten years earlier he had made a film version of his radio documentary *Morning in the Streets* for BBC North Region) to work alongside the development of investigative journalism in *World in Action,* which had started in 1963. *World in Action*'s first editor was the combative, hard-driving Australian journalist, Tim Hewat. The series continued under David Plowright and a roll-call of able editors, employing a huge range of talent, the diaspora of which was later to colonise large areas of the upper reaches of British broadcasting. Most had journalistic backgrounds and instincts. Some, like Derek Granger, Leslie Woodhead and Michael Apted had instincts (and skills and ambitions) that related more to the drama of the narrative form that is the stuff of television. It was, with hindsight, inevitable that, as government and other authorities, never very open in the UK, became agressively less accessible to the media in the Eighties, these diverse traditions and ambitions would come together to produce the 'dramatised investigative documentary' form.

This fusion obviously had a particular potential for explosions when dealing with difficult contemporary issues like Northern Ireland and the police. *World in Action* had a track record of confrontation with authority on contemporary issues that went back to its first edition in March 1963 when a programme on defence spending was cancelled because Hewat, backed by Granada's Chairman, would not agree to make the cuts in the programme required by the old ITA before transmission.

Subsequent chairmen and managing directors of Granada Television stood firm behind subsequent editors whose often exclusive investigative stories led to no less than sixty rows that reached the public prints in the years to 1990. Many more programmes were subject to formal but unreported discussion between Granada and the IBA before broadcast.

World in Action took on everything from police corruption to homosexuality in the Girl Guides and from torture in Turkey to starving Brooke Bond tea workers in Sri Lanka. Some of *WIA*'s outstanding 'battle honours', like the programme on British Steel in 1980 and aspects of the Poulson Affair in the mid-Seventies, were won in the High Court; others, like the *WIA* on Barratt Houses in 1984, were kept out of the courts and press but went before the then new Broadcasting Complaints Commission, which had been set up under the 1980 Broadcasting Act and created in 1981 to consider and adjudicate on complaints of unjust or unfair treatment or unwarranted infringements of privacy. Initially it was chaired by Lady Pike and the legal status of some of its procedures was open to question. At that time they were referred to by one executive who had appeared before the Commision as being like those of the 'Court of Star Chamber'.

Sir Denis Forman, who was Chairman of Granada Television and a resolute supporter of *WIA* throughout what may now be seen as its most rigorous and fearless period, recalls the scale of investment required to stand up to such scrutiny:

> To reach a high standard in *World in Action* you had to 'spike' maybe two (programmes) out of five, and the other three would come good ... and I can remember facing the Board to tell them that we had written off a huge sum of money – a million pounds or whatever – I would say that although substantial it was not enough. One way of measuring the quality of programming is by the amount you spend on programmes that *don't* go on the screen, even though it appears to be extravagant. Your write-off expenditure is a very small proportion of your total programme budget. The Finance Director did not always share the enthusiasm for writing things off, but it is one of the aspects of good broadcasting. (Interview with Sir Denis Forman)

But, however good the research, it had to be comprehensible on the screen and, if possible, the principals involved in the story must be given the chance to respond on screen. Increasingly during the Eighties people or institutions faced with revelations about their activities refused to respond on screen, often seeking injunctions to prevent the broadcast. Producers got round the non-appearance of principals by 'balancing' the commentary with the statements that had or might have been offered in refutation. But this process often over-simplified and sometimes misrepresented the arguments and by the dullness of its form often lost viewers to more palatable alternatives.

Two solutions were arrived at. In one Granada borrowed a formula developed at Harvard University and used in military and management training called a Hypothetical – in which high-level people with relevant experience representing the protagonists of both (or all) parties were brought together with an interlocutor to explore what might lie behind actions in such a situation. This was not ideal for investigation of the particular but was a valuable form for unravelling motives and interests in otherwise impenetrable scenarios relating to policing, defence, business and so on.

The other form, shared with all other broadcasters but finding a particular style through *World in Action*, was the dramatised investigative documentary. Granada's style can be said to have derived from the reporting style of *WIA* on the one hand and the tough realism that tended to permeate even the company's period fiction on the other. It may be significant that several senior figures in Granada had worked in both drama and factual programmes within the company during their careers.

The specific genesis of this genre lay in *WIA*'s approach to the reporting of major events behind the Iron Curtain. Leslie Woodhead, in particular, had pioneered a technique in which eyewitness accounts of key meetings and events were obtained from 'dissidents' and dramatised – memorable programmes like *Three Days in Szczecin* (1976) were the result. One of the most powerful and effective of this genre was to reach the ITV screen in 1990 – *Who Bombed Birmingham?* This was based on the account by the Labour MP, Chris Mullin, of the wrongful arrest and conviction of six people for the bombing of a Birmingham pub. They were subsequently released.

Meanwhile, by 1988, after political rows over the BBC's 'faction' drama production *Tumbledown* (vividly portraying the chaos and trauma of the Falklands War seen from the soldiers' point of view), new concerns about the genre began to surface.

At the IBA, which had responsibilities under the Broadcasting Act to ensure that 'due impartiality is preserved' in 'matters of political or industrial controversy or relating to current public policy', this was seen as having some implications for faction as well as conventional current affairs and staff arranged a presentation to members of the Authority on Due Impartiality in relation to all types of programmes. In fact it was political reaction to the current affairs report *Death on the Rock*, which had been transmitted on ITV earlier in the year – see below – that gave rise to the presentation but in it the IBA's Director of Television, David Glencross, identified the issues arising for the regulator (and broadcaster) from the faction genre. They were, he said:

1. Historical accuracy – if it is a work of imagination based loosely on facts, don't pretend, as the BBC did with *The Monocled Mutineer* that it is a work of historical record. Mind you who agrees on the historical record, still less on the interpretation of it? But that's another debate.
2. Second, is the programme fair to individuals, alive, or whose relatives may still be alive? Should individuals, even if fairly represented, be dragged into the public gaze if they are only minor characters in the events described – an issue which arose in *Tumbledown*.
3. Thirdly, is the programme impartial? We do have guidelines on impartiality in drama, though they relate principally to dramas, faction or not, dealing with political issues at the time of an election or during events of national importance – the Falklands, Suez, the miners strike for example. (Annexe to minutes of Authority meeting 675 (88))

In the discussion that followed Sir Michael Caine, one of the more rigorous minds on the Authority, was recorded as saying that:

one could not expect to achieve a political balance in art or drama. Artists tended to be at the radical end of society. No programme could be truly impartial. It needed to be a mixture of partialities. It was important that news and current affairs should be accurate but there was too much concern about the form of presentation. (Annexe to minutes of Authority meeting 675 (88))

This rather relaxed statement seems to sum up the Authority's view on faction and impartiality in 1988. But the controversies surrounding the genre were soon to reach a crescendo. A number of non-programme events contributed to this. The most important was the debate arising from the Broadcasting Bill (see Chapter 9). But another factor was a change at the Authority. In 1989 Sir Donald Maitland, the tireless and perceptive Deputy Chairman, had retired and been replaced in April the following year by Lord Chalfont.

Chalfont, who as Alun Gwynne Jones had followed a distinguished war in Burma and anti-communist guerrilla action in Malaya with intelligence staff appointments, had in 1961 been made an offer to continue his military career by other means – as the Defence Correspondent of *The Times*. In this role he was frequently asked to appear on television, where his fluency and authority on defence and foreign affairs led to a retained role with the BBC. Success on screen undoubtedly helped to launch a political career. Harold Wilson gave him a Life Peerage in 1964 in order to make him Minister of State at the Foreign and Commonwealth Office. This appointment was said to have brought some comfort to those in the security establishment whose concerns about Labour governments of the period have been well-chronicled elsewhere (Wilson's *Final Term: Labour Government, 1974–76*, George Wigg's book *George Wigg* and so on). Mrs Thatcher was known to seek a similar sort of comfort in her 'one of us' appointments to the media – first her Finchley friend Stuart Young as Chairman of the BBC (sadly to die after only two years in office at the age of fifty-two and be replaced by the indestructible Marmaduke Hussey) and now Chalfont as Deputy Chairman of the IBA – an organisation she was becoming as doubtful about by the late Eighties as she had been about the BBC earlier in the decade.

During the Seventies Chalfont's politics had moved overtly to the right. Though this only took him to the cross benches in the Lords and not to the Tory side, he was known to have sympathy with aspects of Mrs Thatcher's politics and he became associated with the so-called Media Monitoring Unit which fed Conservative Central Office examples of what it regarded as 'left-wing bias' on television. Consequently he came to be seen as something of a bogeyman by media liberals.

At Authority meetings Chalfont was certainly trenchant on the subject of impartiality. However at a seminar on Drama-documentary, jointly organised by the IBA and the British Film Institute, held in October 1990 (after the transmission of *Who Bombed Birmingham?* and just before the 1990 Broadcasting Act was to receive Royal Assent, this was at a time when fellow members of the Lords were still fighting a rearguard action for impartiality to be written in terms on the face of the Act) he was firm but restrained:

> The great majority of people in this country believe that the great majority of television is fair, objective, decent, accurate and excellent. The great majority of people in this country also believe that a small minority of television is none of those things; and I believe that sensible, flexible, effective regulation is

necessary to ensure that that remains a small minority – indeed if it is not eliminated altogether.

... on the other side of the spectrum are the people who argue that the only way to get this right is to have a code of behaviour which has the force of law. At the moment, of course, neither the BBC's guidelines nor the IBA's code of conduct has the force of law. It only has the force of the regulator and the sanctions that are available to the regulator. So what they want to do is either to have the whole of the code of impartiality on the face of the Act, or at the very least they want the code to be endorsed by Parliament and in that way to achieve the force of law.

I believe, as I think most of us who have anything to do with the business of communications agree, that would be a most undesirable state of affairs. (Transcript of IBA/BFI seminar on Drama-documentary, 1990)

And indeed, despite the efforts of Lords Wyatt and Orr-Ewing, the legal requirements on impartiality remained much the same as they had been in the 1981 Broadcasting Act. However the ITC was now required to explain in detail aspects of its code, such as the definition of 'major matters', what constituted a series, and 'personal view' programmes.

But specifically on faction Chalfont had this to say:

I think that in the case of the drama documentary I would suggest that one of the requirements should be ... that dramatic representation of contemporary or recent events must not be allowed to suggest conclusions which would not be sustainable in a current affairs programme. (Ibid.)

In fact *Who Bombed Birmingham?* was made with the forensic rigour of the best of current affairs practice and, significantly, its allegation that the police knew the real identity of the bombers soon after the conviction of the innocent people whose appalling treatment by police and prison staff the programme so graphically portrayed, caused little press outcry. To the surprise of some, the most adverse comments came from Chris Mullin (the MP on whose researches the programme was in large part based – and who was the subject of a stunning performance by John Hurt in it) and others whose concerns were that if ever those named in the film were captured their chances of a fair trial would be slim – an accusation that could have been made when three of the suspects had been named in a non-drama *World in Action* in October 1989.

As a result of the regulatory restructuring brought about in the 1990 Broadcasting Act (see Chapter 9) there was to be a new separate Radio Authority and Lord Chalfont was to become Chairman. But after such a year, 1990 had also seen the transmission of Yorkshire Television's faction *Shoot To Kill* – a programme which had brought the wrath of one of the most respected television reporters on Northern Irish affairs, Peter Taylor, down upon the head of the film's director, Peter Kosminsky, at that year's Edinburgh Television Festival for 'fabrication' in an area where the truth was already difficult enough to ascertain and convey, the regulation of faction could not remain as relaxed as when David Glencross had described it to Authority members only two years earlier. At that time the relevant section of the IBA's Television Guidelines had read:

> It is not unusual for plays and films on television to be concerned with matters of political or industrial controversy or with current public policy, and therefore to fall within the requirements of due impartiality. Problems are most likely to occur in connection with dramatised documentaries, when it may seem that dramatic devices are being used to convince viewers not merely of the factual accuracy of the actions portrayed but of the validity of a particular point of view or a particular explanation and interpretation of society or recent history ... The due impartiality required of a play by an independent dramatist *is not identical to that required of a current affairs programme* ... (Paragraph 6.2, IBA Television Guidelines, April 1985)

After a sharpening of the wording (and the production of a draft for discussion within the industry by the new ITC in February 1991), the ITC Programme Code reads:

> a clear distinction should be drawn between plays based on fact and dramatised documentaries which seek to reconstruct actual events. Much confusion may be avoided if plays based on current or very recent events are carefully labelled as such, so that fictional elements are not misleadingly presented as fact ...
>
> The dramatised documentary which lays claim to be a factual reconstruction of a controversial event covered by the Act *is bound by the same standards of fairness and impartiality as those that apply to factual programmes in general.* It is inevitable that the creative realisation of some elements (such as characterisation, dialogue and atmosphere) will introduce a fictional dimension, but this should not be allowed to distort the facts.
>
> ... Care should be taken in scheduling drama and drama-documentary programmes portraying controversial matters covered by the Act. Impartiality may need to be secured by providing an opportunity for opposing viewpoints to be expressed. This might take the form of a studio discussion following the drama itself or a separate programme providing a right to reply within a reasonable period. (Paragraph 3.7, ITC Programme Code, January 1993)

Thus was 'faction', and the new genre of the dramatised investigative documentary, tamed. However, the programme event that had given rise to the presentation on impartiality to the Authority in the autumn of 1988, and arguably had more of an impact on the political relations of ITV and the IBA than any new programme genre, was in fact a production in a traditional current affairs slot.

The Government versus Thames Television and the IBA:
This Week – Death on the Rock:

Thames Television's *This Week* had been one of the twin pillars of ITV's current affairs coverage (along with *World in Action*) for over thirty years. Its name had been changed to *TV Eye* in 1978 to go with an attempt at a more populist approach but it was changed back to *This Week* when a previous editor of the programme, David Elstein, returned to Thames as its Director of Programmes in 1986. More flexible in format than *WIA*, the *This Week* slot could contain a live studio interview with the Prime Minister one week and a filmed report on dangerous toys the next. The series had a good reputation within the television industry for its coverage of Northern Ireland.

The edition of *This Week* broadcast at 9.00 p.m. on Thursday 28 April 1988 was about an incident in Gibraltar on Sunday 6 March that year in which two men and a woman, admitted almost immediately by the IRA to be a unit 'on active service', were shot dead by men acknowleged the following day by the Foreign Secretary in the House of Commons to have been members of the British security services.

The programme itself and the events that preceded and followed its transmission have given rise to more newspaper references than any other ITV programme of the period. Although this chapter contains an outline summary of the programme and the contentions arising from it, as always detail is crucial to any considered judgement and serious students of this event in British political history (and, indeed, in the history of Independent Television) should refer to these sources – in particular the report of the inquiry into the making of the programme carried out at the behest of the Board of Thames, with the agreement of the IBA, by Lord Windlesham and Richard Rampton QC. Although dismissed by leading government figures on its publication at the end of January 1989, the report's factual accuracy has never been successfully challenged. For those unable to obtain a tape of the programme, the report does also contain a transcript, with annotations of the relevant visuals.

For politicians (and broadcasters) Northern Irish matters are always a sensitive area. Defence issues related to Northern Ireland raise the sensitivity quotient still further.

In the House of Commons it was the Foreign Secretary, Sir Geoffrey Howe – calm and statesmanlike (to the point of tedium, some MPs believed) – rather than the Secretary of State for Northern Ireland, the explosive Tom King or the Minister of Defence, George Younger – who was empowered by the Prime Minister to make the statement that, in the event, was to give rise to the programme. Speaking of the shooting of the IRA trio he is recorded in Hansard as saying:

On their way towards the border, they were challenged by the security forces. When challenged, they made movements which led the military personnel, operating in support of the Gibraltar police, to conclude that their own lives and the lives of others were under threat. In the light of this response they were shot. Those killed were subsequently found not to have been carrying arms. (Hansard, 7 March 1988)

Sir Geoffrey also referred to a car parked in the vicinity of the ceremonial guard changing (by, at that time, troops of the Anglian Regiment) which was always watched by a crowd of locals and tourists. Of the IRA group he added that:

Their presence and actions near the parked Renault car gave rise to the strong suspicion that it contained a bomb, which appeared to be corroborated by a rapid technical examination of the car. (Ibid.)

He then dropped his own metaphorical bombshell by revealing that it had subsequently been discovered that there was no bomb in the car, or anywhere else on the Rock.

Roger Bolton, the editor of *This Week* (and prior to that of the BBC's major current affairs vehicle, *Panorama*), and no stranger to the sensitivities surrounding events connected to Northern Ireland, read the statement on teletext in his office and recognised the contradictions inherent in the Minister's statement. Bolton has recorded his reaction to the statement in his book, also called *Death on the Rock*:

It seemed to me that this incident was now certain to become extremely controversial and to be used by all sides in the Irish Question to their own advantage. It would clearly be seen by many people as an example of the alleged 'shoot to kill policy' operated by the British Government, and it took no great insight to realise that within a few days a madonna-like painting of Mairead Farrell (the female member of the IRA unit) would adorn the sides of houses in West Belfast, or that a Roman Catholic priest would refer to her as a martyr. The incident also appeared to indicate, despite the absence of a bomb, that the IRA had conveniently forgotten about what its political arm, Sinn Fein, had called 'the disaster' of Enniskillen. (*Death on the Rock and Other Stories* by Roger Bolton, W.H. Allen, 1990)

Enniskillen was the town in Northern Ireland where, during the previous year's November Remembrance Day parade, the IRA had exploded a bomb that had killed eleven people and wounded over sixty – mostly civilians.

Bolton continued:

... I had decided long ago that I had to judge a story by its importance, not by the political fall-out one might face.

But it was not until after eight days' preliminary research both in London and Gibraltar by the producer allocated to the potential programme, Chris Oxley, and reporter

Julian Manyon, and by researchers in Northern Ireland, as well as calls by Bolton himself to the Ministry of Defence and Downing Street, that he and his head of department, Barrie Sales (also an ex-BBC current affairs veteran) decided that there was sufficient previously unrevealed relevant material to justify the mounting of an investigative programme, even if the British government was not prepared to take part.

The reason given for this failure of the government to contribute its point of view to the programme is given in his memoirs by Sir Geoffrey Howe (Lord Howe by the time they were published in 1994):

> That was quite simply because neither government nor SAS soldiers were in a position to give evidence to any *pre*-inquest television programme, for so long as the soldiers faced a possible verdict of unlawful killing and the consequent risk of prosecution for murder. (Chapter 36, *Conflict of Loyalty* by Geoffrey Howe, Macmillan, 1994)

Up to the week of transmission attempts were continued by the *This Week* team to obtain participation or statements from the government. The further research, filming in Spain, Gibraltar and Northern Ireland as well as London, editing and commentary preparation took another five weeks.

Viewed nearly ten years after transmission, the programme itself (which was granted a special forty-five-minute slot by the Controllers Group, to allow it to carry sufficient detail to help the audience to understand the complexity of the issues) appears painstakingly researched, clearly presented and as balanced an investigation as would be likely to be possible without the cooperation of the key control agency behind the events in Gibraltar on 6 March 1988 – the Ministry of Defence. Certainly the IBA programme staff took that view when they previewed the programme on Wednesday 27 April, the day before transmission. They sought only minor commentary changes relating to an implication in the draft commentary that the Gibraltar inquest on the deaths would be unlikely to be able to establish the truth. The Director of Programmes at Thames, David Elstein, previewed the programme that evening and was also satisfied. Such viewings were routine and would have taken place before the transmission of any current affairs programme dealing with Northern Irish affairs. But in this case the IBA was under unusual pressure.

On the evening of Tuesday 26 April Lord Thomson had received a telephone call from Sir Geoffrey Howe asking whether the IBA was aware of the programme – to which the answer was 'yes' – and then whether Thomson was aware that it was the government's view that such a programme would be prejudicial to the inquest. Thomson replied that IBA staff would be viewing the programme and taking any necessary legal advice prior to agreeing transmission. He also undertook to let Sir Geoffrey know their final decision.

The IBA's Director of Television, David Glencross, showed the programme to leading counsel, seeking guidance on both the inquest concern and the matter of whether the programme was duly impartial. On the latter counsel was satisfied and on the subject of the inquest he took the general view that because the inquest would be held in Gibraltar at some future time (no date had been fixed) the transmission would be unlikely to 'contaminate' the proceedings. But counsel recommended that, because the programme raised public policy issues, the Authority's Chairman should be aware of these before transmission was finally agreed. In the event the Chairman did view the programme but because he was not available that evening he left a note for the Director General, John Whitney (who also viewed the programme later that day) saying that it should be transmitted and the Foreign Secretary's office should be informed of the decision, as Howe had requested. The Deputy Chairman, Sir Donald Maitland, was not consulted – as he related in his memoirs:

> In the course of 27 April the programme – *Death on the Rock* – was seen by the staff of the IBA, by the director general and by George Thomson. *Although I was at Brompton Road on that day, I was not made aware of the problem and did not see the programme in advance.* (*Diverse Times, Sundry Places* by Donald Maitland, p. 277, Alpha Press, 1996)

Given Maitland's distinguished thirty-year Foreign Office career, this was a curious omission.

Whitney delegated the task of informing the Foreign Secretary of the IBA's decision to David Glencross, who contacted the relevant civil servant at the Foreign Office early on Thursday, the day of transmission. After telling him that the decision was to transmit the programme as scheduled it became clear that Sir Geoffrey would wish to speak to Lord Thomson again at midday. At that time the Chairman would still be uncontactable because he was en route back to London, so, as had been agreed with the FO, the handling of the call fell again to the Director of Television.

Howe was a former Solicitor-General and had, as a young Queen's Counsel, represented a number of Coal Board officials at the inquiry into the Aberfan disaster in 1967, when a coal pit slag heap that had been loosened by torrential rain, avalanched over a school with horrific loss of young lives – about which the tabloid newspapers made comments which were felt to have prejudiced the inquiry. He made a number of points to Glencross about the danger of such a broadcast to the inquest, referring in particular to the guidelines drawn up by Mr (later Lord) Justice Salmon in a report to the government on the subject in 1969. Glencross noted the points and said he would take further legal advice. Together again with counsel they scrutinised the Salmon Report in relation to the programme.

Paragraph 159 of the *Windlesham/Rampton Report* gives eight reasons why they and the Chairman, on his return to Brompton Road, finally considered that the Foreign Secretary's arguments ought not to prevail:

(i) The programme had produced new witnesses for the inquest who might not otherwise have been available.

(ii) The programme did not set itself up as an alternative inquest or inquiry. It had volunteered all its information to the Gibraltar coroner.

(iii) At the time of the programme, no date for the inquest had been set.

(iv) It was clear that the broadcast of the programme in the United Kingdom would not constitute a contempt under the existing law.

(v) The effect of the Salmon Committee's recommendation was that any extension of the law of contempt should be limited to interviews or other material obtained or published with the deliberate intent or obvious likelihood of causing any relevant evidence to be altered, distorted, destroyed or withheld. The IBA's considered view was that the interviews with witnesses in *Death on the Rock* did not fall into that category.

(vi) The Salmon Committee's recommendation was made in 1969. Under the Contempt of Court Act 1981, a publication can only incur strict liability for contempt if it creates 'a substantial risk that the course of justice ... will be seriously impeded or prejudiced.' In the IBA's opinion, the programme did not fall within that definition.

(vii) Because Gibraltar is a small community, the shootings were already likely to have been the subject of much public comment and discussion, even without the benefit of press and broadcasting coverage. There had been a great deal of local coverage in the Gibraltar press and on television, including eyewitness accounts, in the weeks between the shootings and the Thames programme. The Gibraltar authorities had made no move to prevent this. There had also been extensive coverage in the UK press, without comment from government or the law officers.

(viii) The programme was a legitimate piece of journalistic activity. It was not designed to usurp the function of the inquest, nor was it trying to set itself up as a quasi-legal process.

And so the broadcast went ahead as billed in *TV Times*, at 9.00 p.m. on Thursday 28 April 1988. Unusually for a current affairs programme, which – because of their last-minute nature – normally only have generic title billings, the subject and scope of the programme had actually been given in *TV Times* when it was distributed the previous week. This gives rise to the legitimate question as to why Sir Geoffrey waited until two days before transmission before intervening. And it should be remembered that the government did have powers under the Broadcasting Act 1981 (Section 29(3)) actually to prohibit the broadcast – which it used only seven months later to ban the broadcasting of the voices of those representing proscribed organisations like Sinn Fein and the UDA – rather than just getting a minister to 'lean' on the regulator.

Surprisingly, the IBA did not tell Thames Television of the Foreign Secretary's intervention or their assessment of the situation before the broadcast. This was something that, when discovered, deeply upset the new Chairman of Thames, Sir Ian Trethowan. As an ex-Director General of the BBC and one-time political correspondent for the *News Chronicle* and ITN, Sir Ian had, not unreasonably, expected that Lord Thomson should at least have taken him into his confidence on the matter. It was not a happy start to an important new relationship. At Thames only Roger Bolton, fielding a last-minute check from Peter Ashforth of the IBA's Television Department about the legal advice Thames had received, suspected that the IBA might be under pressure.

Among the Authority too there was some concern at the lack of consultation. On 12 May, at their first meeting after the transmission of *Death on the Rock*, members were generally supportive of the Chairman's actions but some, Sir Michael Caine in particular, believed that members should have been invited to join him at his preview of the programme.

What was it about this programme that led to such high-level pre-broadcast intervention and rage that led the Prime Minister to tell a group of visiting Japanese journalists (before she or the nation had seen the programme) that it was trial by television and that her response was 'deeper' than fury?

Perhaps it was the fact that overall the description on events leading up to the killings only allowed of two explanations – cock-up or conspiracy – and that the witnesses found by Thames graphically described the shooting of the unarmed IRA members at close range in a manner that made it clear that no attempt was made to wound and arrest rather than kill.

On the other hand, seen from the government's point of view, there can be little doubt now that the security services had become aware of a newly planned IRA campaign against British targets outside the UK (British service personnel were killed in Holland in May and in Germany subsequently) and, given the likely damage to Britain's standing abroad as well as to human life, the Prime Minister and her relevant ministerial colleagues were determined to snuff this out before it began. Any implication that success in this had been tainted by mistakes or illegal actions was bound to generate a powerful abreaction.

In terms of illegality all turned on the rules of engagement relating to the IRA issued to the commander of the operation on the ground. These were revealed at the inquest as saying that the SAS were allowed to shoot to kill, without challenge 'if the giving of a warning or any delay in firing could lead to death or injury to you or any other person, or if the giving of a warning is clearly impracticable'. These rules were in line with known military practice in Northern Ireland. But because of the failure of the Ministry of Defence or the government to brief the programme, even 'off the record', as to the facts, the programme makers were forced to speculate about the SAS actions. One of the programme's questions was that, as it had become apparent at the first moment of confrontation that the IRA were unarmed, had the 'movements' of the IRA personnel been interpreted by the SAS as movements to reach a radio remote trigger for the bomb which was believed to exist? Even if the Renault car parked near the parade square was believed to contain a bomb (the explosive for which was subsequently discovered to have still been in Spain at the time), there was no record of the IRA triggering a bomb from a position out of line of sight and at the range of over a mile and a half. The programme also stated that, since British intelligence with Spanish security help knew precisely when the IRA group was going to cross into Gibraltar they could have been arrested at the border with less apparent threat to civilians. Were the IRA deliberately led into a trap?

There was, of course, much more detail to the programme – both in analysis and evidence. There may have been clear explanations and answers to all these questions but, oddly, after the Foreign Secretary had failed to have the programme banned, the government chose not to make any statement but to use 'disinformation' to discredit key witnesses who had described the killings in the programme, or to fabricate inconsistencies between what the programme showed and witnesses' subsequent accounts.

Andrew Neil was by this time Editor of Rupert Murdoch's *Sunday Times* but in the early Seventies had been *The Economist* correspondent on Northern Ireland, where he had made contacts with MoD personnel that were sufficiently good that he was subsequently invited to participate in at least one high-level MoD seminar. Neil's journalistic integrity would have resisted any use of this connection by the MoD. However, a review of the newspaper coverage of the time does show the *Sunday Times* as the most aggressively critical of *Death on the Rock* of all the papers. The paper also appears to have had exclusive sources of information that supported the MoD's version of events. After the broadcast some of Neil's editorial acolytes appeared to take this 'disinformation' material at its face value. One reporter who had worked for them on the story subsequently wrote to the *UK Press Gazette*:

> After the programme I interviewed two witnesses to the shootings of the three IRA terrorists in Gibraltar who appeared on the programme – Josie Celecia and Stephen Bullock.
>
> The account of my interviews with them was inaccurate in the *Sunday Times* and had the effect of discrediting parts of the documentary and the evidence of another witness, Carmen Proetta. (Letter Rosie Waterhouse to *UK Press Gazette*, 2 January 1989)

Carmen Proetta suffered the worst at the keyboards of the British press and subsequently won apologies and damages for libel from a number of national papers – including the *Sunday Times*, from which she received £150,000 and her costs in March 1991. Roger Bolton, the editor of the programme, received a settlement from the *Daily Mail* which published a retraction and apology for implying that Bolton had cooperated or had secret dealings with terrorists in the past.

Were none of the criticisms of the programme by politicians and journalists justified? Lord Windlesham and Richard Rampton QC in their inquiry did sustain, in part, criticism of the way the evidence of one witness was deployed in the programme. Kenneth Asquez was a nineteen-year-old bank employee who, in conversation with his colleagues at the Algemene Bank had claimed to have seen the shootings from a passing car. A Major Randall, late of the Gibraltar Regiment, who had taken a video of the scene soon after the shooting, which was used both by news broadcasts at the time and later in the *This Week* programme, knew Asquez and his parents slightly and he also banked at the Algemene. He joined in a conversation between Asquez and his friends and subsequently passed the information that Asquez had witnessed the shootings to the Thames team. When approached, Asquez was unwilling to be filmed. But he did provide Randall with a handwritten account of the shooting. This gave the most graphic account of any of the witnesses to which the production team had access, of the shooting of one of the IRA men at point blank range while he was lying on the ground and the SAS soldier had his foot on his chest. Thames got a local lawyer to interview Asquez and draft a deposition for him to swear and sign, with the understanding that it would be used anonymously in the programme in place of filmed testimony. Asquez went to the lawyer's office and agreed a statement which bore a close resemblance to the account he had given Randall (which the Thames team had deliberately not passed to the lawyer, as a form of check on Asquez' veracity) but Asquez was not prepared to swear to the statement or sign it – though he did agree to its use in the programme.

Asquez may have been a witness whose account of what he had seen was reliable but, with hindsight, he should perhaps have been recognised as a less than wholly reliable personality. He retracted parts of his statement at the inquest on the deaths in September, saying that he had been harassed by Randall. This claim is denied by Randall, whose denial is supported by the Windlesham Report.

Windlesham and Rampton (who took evidence, in confidence, from the MoD as well as the witnesses and programme makers) were not critical of the use of the seventy-two words from Asquez' unsigned statement in the programme but of the lack of detail about their provenance:

> We think it would have been preferable to have given a fuller account of the circumstances in which such an unusual piece of evidence had been obtained and of the reasons for its inclusion in the programme. (Paragraph 111, Chapter 7, *Windlesham/Rampton Report on 'Death on the Rock'*, Faber & Faber, 29 January 1989)

Windlesham and Rampton also supported to some degree criticisms of another aspect of the programme. This was the commentary introduction to the witnesses on film where the degree of condensation in the 'pointer', used to indicate to the audience what to listen for, was felt to be too great adequately to convey the substance of the evidence that the programme makers had gathered. Bolton, Manyon and the production team disputed this but Windlesham and Rampton concluded:

Ordinary viewers of television programmes do not stop to consider whether the clear implications of the commentary are strictly supported by the evidence which is laid out in the programme. They do not have the advantage of a written transcript, nor do they have the time or inclination to formulate reasoned arguments why this or that statement by the commentator may not stand up to close examination. (Paragraph 119, Chapter 8 ibid.)

While seeking to establish the facts central to the programme and its role in Independent Television's history, it is perhaps important also to scythe through some of the mythological undergrowth that has grown up around it. In case the use of the word 'myth' is thought to be prejudicial, perhaps the most effectively neutral way of referring to this penumbra surrounding *Death on the Rock* is to record that a number of hypotheses have arisen, without readily apparent factual support. Those most often heard include:

1. *The Rock* sank the 'flagship' ITV company Thames' chances of success with its application in 1991 for a licence to continue as weekday broadcaster for London.
2. The IBA's credibility with the government was finally destroyed by its behaviour over *the Rock*.

The first of these is the most serious because, since neither the regulator at the time nor the Windlesham Report found any serious fault with the company's performance in relation to the programme or its current affairs output as a whole, it would imply that the ITC's process for dealing with the bids for licences was not objective – taking account of 'what the government might think', rather than the merits of the application and the level of the bid.

The analysis of the bid process in Chapter 10 of this volume demonstrates clearly that the assessment by the ITC of the Thames application and bid could not have been affected by subjective judgements, even subliminally. However, it should be recorded that, from interviews undertaken for this volume, it is clear that a number of senior figures in the industry at the time do still believe *the Rock* incident must have had *some* effect on the Thames decision.

On the second hypothesis, it is true that the Home Affairs Committee Report recommending the abolition of the IBA and its replacement by a new Commercial Television Authority was published two months after the transmission of *Death on the Rock*. In fact, the committee had been sitting for a year by the time the controversy arose and its conclusions were effectively framed by then. Also, the committee's (self-appointed) remit was:

To inquire into the implications for the regulation of broadcasting of Direct Broadcasting by Satellite and Cable Television, the future of public service broadcasting in an increasingly deregulated broadcasting industry; and the potential of subscription as a means of broadcasting finance. (Paragraph 1, Volume 1, Home Affairs Committee, Third Report, 22 June 1988)

The apparent last words on the *Death on the Rock* affair go to the Chairman of the IBA:

> Sir Geoffrey Howe did his duty and I did mine, and if you do not like that sort of conflict of duty between Government and broadcaster, then you should not be chairman of an independent broadcasting authority. (Article by Lord Thomson in the *Daily Telegraph* of 28 December 1988, a valedictory upon his retirement at the end of that year as the IBA was about to be replaced by the 'shadow' Independent Television Commission under George Russell)

But it is necessary to ask where the minister responsible for broadcasting, the Home Secretary, stood in this confrontation between broadcasters and government. He is not recorded in the press or Hansard as expressing any view. But Richard Dunn, in a speech to the Royal Society of Arts in November 1994, revealed:

> There is one aspect to this story that has not been told before, and I think that it is time to do so because it helps to underline the differences of opinion in Cabinet that were to lead, in my opinion, to such deep flaws in the 1990 Broadcasting Act. On the night before *Death on the Rock* was transmitted, Ian Trethowan and I had dinner with Douglas Hurd, the Home Secretary. It was a private occasion, so we did not refer to it in the ensuing storm. Over dinner, which had been arranged some weeks earlier to discuss the forthcoming White Paper (on broadcasting), the Home Secretary told us he had been telephoned the previous day by the Foreign Secretary. Sir Geoffrey had explained the programme being planned by Thames and had urged Douglas Hurd to ask the Chairman of the IBA to postpone its transmission until after the inquest (for which, incidentally, no date had been set, and wasn't for some months).
>
> Douglas Hurd said he had told Geoffrey Howe that he would not call the Chairman of the IBA, and said he did not think it was right for the Government to interfere in programme decisions that were clearly the responsibility of the IBA. He asked us if the Authority had been fully and properly consulted, and whether they had previewed the film. When I explained that the IBA Director of Programmes (sic) and the Director-General had already viewed it, and the Chairman of the IBA would see it later that evening, he was content. Thames was willing to abide by the decision of the IBA. So was the Home Secretary.
>
> I am certain he was right, and in taking this line, he was in step with his predecessor, Lord Whitelaw, who once said 'the first principle of broadcasting must be to defend the independence of the authorities from Government and Parliament'. I am sure Douglas Hurd shared this view and I recall him saying, 'Government have their concerns; television and the press have theirs.' In other

words, our interests were different, and bound to be in conflict from time to time
... (The Peter Le Neve Foster Lecture at the Royal Society of Arts, 16 November
1994 – *The 1990 Broadcasting Act: a benefit or disaster?*, given by Richard Dunn)

So the Home Secretary's view was in accord with the traditions of liberal and constitutional conservatism. It is perhaps not surprising to find Mrs Thatcher writing
in her memoirs:

... the idea that a small clique of broadcasting professionals always knew what
was best and they should be more or less immune from criticism or competition
was not one I could accept. Unfortunately, in the Home Office the broadcasters
often found a ready advocate. (*The Downing Street Years* by Margaret Thatcher,
HarperCollins, 1993)

Through the Home Office the broadcasters were made to bow to the Iron Lady's
will in the matter of 'the oxygen of publicity' for terrorists, however, only six months
after *Death on the Rock* was transmitted. A Direction from the Home Secretary
arrived at the BBC and the IBA on 19 October 1988, made under the Licence and
Agreement and Section 29(3) of the Broadcasting Act of 1981, placing restrictions
on broadcasters reporting on terrorism in Northern Ireland by requiring them to
refrain from broadcasting in interviews direct statements by members of such
proscribed organisations as Sinn Fein, or by their supporters. Broadcasters reached
common cause in defiance of this act of censorship, however, and brought in actors
to read the on-camera statements of leaders like Gerry Adams. The actors became
so adept at timing their reading to synchronise with the speaking lips that in time
audience ridicule was more effective than political protest. The government under
Mrs Thatcher's successor, John Major, was somewhat relieved when the ceasefire
of 1995 in Northern Ireland gave them the opportunity to rescind the direction.

SECTION II: PROGRAMMES ACQUIRED BY ITV

Whose Dallas is it Anyway? – The Battle for Southfork

Death on the Rock may have achieved the distinction of the largest number of
newspaper references to any ITV programme during the period covered by this
book, but it was a very different title, *Dallas*, that, three years earlier, had set the
previous record for column inches. And it only *nearly* became an ITV-scheduled
programme. The destructive impact of that 'near miss' on ITV was such that it requires
the history of it to be set out in some detail.

The reason for the huge press interest was two-fold. First, this was a series which
was followed by the majority of readers of the popular papers. Second, as the saga

about the fight for the series between the BBC and ITV unfolded, it had more than a touch of soap opera about it itself.

Dallas was one of the most successful 'soaps' of all time. First broadcast in the US (on the CBS network) on 2 April 1978, it ran for thirteen years until 3 May 1991. Its plot lines have been summarised as follows: 'A wealthy Texan oil family indulge in sexual and commercial intrigues in a bid to unsettle their rivals and each other' (*The Guinness Television Encyclopaedia*, Guinness Publishing, 1995).

The *Dallas* affair was a convulsive incident in Independent Television on such a scale that it set company against company, the IBA and ITV against the BBC, all three against a major US distributor and it was ultimately to give rise to a new management team at Thames of Richard Dunn, as Managing Director, and David Elstein, as Director of Programmes, who were responsible for the company at the time of *Death on the Rock* three years later.

But at the start of 1985 the Managing Director at Thames was still Bryan Cowgill – a role he had held since he was recruited from the BBC in 1977. Cowgill was a highly competitive individual. Commissioned from the ranks in the Royal Marine Commandos during the Second World War, he had returned to start at the bottom in journalism as a copy boy on a Lancashire regional newspaper before rising to editor of his local paper, joining the BBC in 1955 and rising again through BBC Television Sport (where his colourful language on the 'talkback' communications circuits to remote locations on the Saturday afternoon *Grandstand* multi-outside broadcast sports programme was the stuff of legend) to become the Channel Controller of BBC1 in 1974. There 'Ginger' Cowgill's competitive approach to scheduling commanded respect amongst his rivals around the ITV Controllers table. This was one of the elements in the Thames Board's decision to poach him from the BBC.

As has been explained earlier, the only real competition in ITV at this time was between the two contractors who shared the London television advertising market – each fighting to maximise revenue in their sector of the week. Each felt particularly vulnerable to individual BBC successes in their 'patch'. *Dallas* was originally turned down on behalf of ITV on the annual autumn buying trip to Los Angeles in 1978 by Paul Fox (as Chairman of the network's Film Purchase Group) and Leslie Halliwell, the respected authority on films who, though he remained a Granada employee, bought overseas material on behalf of the network. The pilot had been shown to them just before they were due to fly back to London – and after they had completed all the purchases that their budget allowed. It was immediately snapped up for the BBC by Bill Cotton and the BBC's Head of Acquisitions, Gunnar Ruggheimer, whose buying trip was a day or two longer.

The series became a phenomenal success in the UK. Watched by an average of thirteen million, it was transmitted by BBC1 right in the middle of ITV network's potentially most valuable peak-time slots – initially at the weekend, later in midweek.

Episode 1 – 1981

Only one fact is absolutely certain about the events surrounding the renewal of the contract for the UK rights to *Dallas* in 1981. That is that there *was* an attempt to transfer those rights from the BBC to ITV. In an official account of events, written four years later, the man responsible for the purchase of cinema films and foreign television productions for ITV, Leslie Halliwell recorded that:

> ... we did not try to steal *Dallas*; on the contrary Worldvision (the distributors of the series) tried very hard to make us an offer, and the BBC was fully aware of the situation. (Paper for Film Purchase Group, ITV Network, 15 July 1985)

However, Halliwell goes on to say that a Worldvision employee had told him that:

> ... even before the Hollywood trip of 1981, Thames had made it plain to him that they alone would buy *Dallas* given the chance. (Ibid.)

Thames Managing Director, Bryan Cowgill knew that the traditional 'gentlemen's agreement' between the BBC and the ITV companies (and supported as a matter of public service principle by the IBA) to avoid competition over the renewal of purchase contracts so as to prevent unnecessary demands on the BBC licence fee or ITV revenue, would mean that, unless he could find a way to intervene, the series would be renewed by the BBC for another three years. There was no formal way to fight back. Film Purchase Group (FPG) reported to the Network Programme Committee (NPC), on which the IBA was represented.

Cowgill instinctively distrusted the collective nature of the purchasing role of FPG. Like all the network activities of ITV, it was inclined to move at the pace of its less adventurous members. Also, Thames' representative on the Group was the Director of Programmes, Nigel Ryan (an ex-ITN Editor), not Cowgill. Ryan was a man of great ability and charm but not as competitive as Cowgill. Cowgill always felt that Ryan had been thrust upon him as a result of IBA pressure on the Thames Board after the departure of Jeremy Isaacs from the role.

The IBA had firm views that the jobs of managing director and controller of programmes (increasingly around the network called 'director' in recognition of the controllers being granted seats on their Boards) should be separate functions. Cowgill believed that as an expert scheduler he should have the dual role, in the way that his old colleague from BBC days, Paul Fox, had been allowed to do. But Fox had only been granted this privilege because of the IBA's concern about the possible conflicts of interest for Ward Thomas, the founding MD of Yorkshire, when he became Managing Director of Trident Television, the holding company who also owned Tyne Tees Television in the unique pre-1982 ownership situation at Yorkshire which so infuriated the IBA (see Chapter 2).

Ironically, Thomas and Fox had approached Cowgill to be Director of Programmes at Yorkshire just prior to the Thames offer of the managing directorship. And when Cowgill turned them down, Fox, who was also an able scheduler, fought to keep both jobs. He was finally forced to relinquish the controller role in 1984. There was also felt to be some tension between the two because Fox, though something of an elder statesman in the network, ran the smallest of the major companies while Cowgill, who had been his studio director at the BBC, ran the largest.

Fox was, in Cowgill's view, unlikely to be supportive in any plan he initiated to prize *Dallas* away from the BBC. However, Cowgill had been Chairman of ITV Sport in the autumn of 1978 when Michael Grade, as Director of Programmes at LWT had brought off a spectacular competitive coup against the BBC. As the weekend network 'nominated contractor' (designated by the network to undertake programme planning and operations for the weekend network schedule), LWT was the home of ITV Sport's production *World of Sport*, planning and linking the various contributions by other members of the network as well as their own Saturday afternoon coverage of sport.

Grade, like all LWT Programme Directors before him, resented the BBC's contractual right to share coverage of Football League fixtures, which gave them what was then a pillar of their Saturday night schedule – *Match of the Day*. So, in secret negotiations through a Labour MP who was also a member of the Football League's management committee, Grade secured a three-year *exclusive* contract for League coverage costing twice what ITV and the BBC had previously paid jointly. The press christened Grade's coup 'Snatch of the Day'. The BBC professed outrage but public, press and Parliament were, in truth, tired of the BBC's intransigent refusal to alternate major sports coverage – like the soccer World Cup and FA Cup Finals, as well as the Olympic Games events – with the consequence that viewers had the same sport on two television channels. Importantly, on that occasion the IBA had seen the public interest as best served by the principle of alternation and, having had their intervention on ITV's (and the viewers') behalf rejected sharply by the BBC, it was privately not displeased by LWT's initiative. Ultimately, however, BBC pressure achieved a settlement that allowed it a share of the League's matches at a higher price – a result that might have given Cowgill cause for thought.

When the *Dallas* contract was due for renewal in 1981, Cowgill turned to Grade, amongst others, for support. Besides Grade's natural competitiveness there was another reason for looking to the other London company for support. At that time the BBC was transmitting *Dallas* in weekend peak time – on Saturdays in January to May and Sundays in October 1981. LWT would benefit by the removal of the series from the weekend and Thames by its presence in the weekday schedule. There was also the possibility of weekend repeats in the summer.

It was clear to both that FPG might resist a network purchase, not just because of the scrutiny of the IBA, who were unlikely to see higher ratings as a justification for the risk of an all-out purchased programmes and films war that could have an impact on the licence fee – or, at least, be made out by the BBC to have done so

– but also because some ITV companies would also be concerned about a rise in programme purchase prices.

It has been said in the press and elsewhere that the FPG purchasing executive, Leslie Halliwell, was bound by an unwritten agreement with the BBC not to 'poach' series on renewal. In fact there was a *written* agreement (by yet another irony in this saga, it was drawn up between ITV and the BBC as a Concordat in an attempt to avoid contract-grabbing chaos in the aftermath of the 'Snatch of the Day' affair) which the ITCA took the trouble to register with the Office of Fair Trading under the Restrictive Trading Practices Act – a wise move as it turned out four years later. It declared:

> The only understanding we have with the BBC is that once a series has been acquired by one organisation, that organisation is offered the first option for renewal of a second series. (Memorandum RS 406, Film Purchase, Registered by ITCA with OFT on 4 October 1978)

Meanwhile the Cowgill/Grade alliance looked to a joint campaign at the Film Purchase Committee to persuade others to counterbid against the BBC for *Dallas*. As rumours of tensions between Worldvision and the BBC over the price for renewal began to circulate during the summer, Thames' experienced film and programme buyer, Pat Mahoney, made an approach to establish the position. He casually raised the possibility of an interest in a call to Worldvision's Colin Campbell (who was ultimately to lose his job over the *Dallas* affair). Campbell was not entirely surprised by the approach. Mahoney had talked before of Thames 'going it alone' to get *Dallas* – but that had been at an industry party and Campbell had put it down to Mahoney's occasionally somewhat 'macho' approach to purchasing. He agreed to meet Mahoney at a Park Lane hotel but felt honour-bound to inform his BBC client of the approach. Gunnar Ruggheimer, a splenetic but canny Swede who had run television networks in Canada and Ireland before joining the BBC, was not amused. When threats failed to dissuade Campbell from meeting Mahoney, Ruggheimer fixed to meet Campbell at the hotel immediately after Mahoney. From this point the BBC was aware it was likely to have to pay a great deal more per episode for renewal than it had intended. Cowgill and Grade sensed that there was a possibility of outbidding the BBC and even if they failed to persuade their colleagues at least the extra money the ploy had induced the BBC to pay could not now be spent on improving the BBC's ratings in other ways.

Halliwell knew of the Cowgill/Grade interest in the series, but when he was in Los Angeles a few weeks later, in May 1981, just after the arrival of FPG members for the first of their buying trips that year (in the less cost-conscious early Eighties there was enough interest in US programmes, as well as film, for it to be felt necessary for both ITV and the BBC to send groups consisting of managing directors, programme controllers and buying executives to California twice a year to see pilots and early episodes of new series) he was surprised by a phone call while they were viewing at MGM. It was from Colin Campbell of Worldvision, whose scheduled meeting with the group was due to be at 7.30 that evening. Halliwell recalled the contents of the call four years after the event:

> Campbell ... said that negotiations with the BBC over *Dallas* had broken down, that the show was therefore on the open market, and that he would like us to think about our attitude before the meeting that evening. His suggested price was 40,000 dollars for two runs, and he inferred that the BBC had made a derisory offer for only one run. I immediately informed the group ... What we did not know until later was that Kevin O'Sullivan (Chief Executive Officer of Worldvision) had given Colin Campbell a firm instruction that he was to get the record fee of 40,000 dollars for *Dallas* in the UK. During the day Colin had further talks with Gunnar/Alan (Ruggheimer and Howden, the BBC purchasing team), who knew that the show was now considered by Worldvision to be on the open market and that they had offered it to us. This seems to have induced them to go to 35,000 dollars for two runs, and Gunnar threatened to withdraw even that at 7.30 that evening. I therefore received another urgent request from Colin to bring our meeting forward to 7.00 p.m.
>
> I went on ahead (of the group) at this time and conveyed the ITV view that we were sorry that the subject of *Dallas* had come up again in this way, but since it had, *and since some of our members were interested*, and on the assumption that the BBC knew we were involved, we might put forward a bid on certain conditions but it would not exceed 35,000 dollars, possibly 36,000 dollars given time for some members to call London. Colin said that this would not be enough.
> (Paper for Film Purchase Group, ITV Network, by Leslie Halliwell, 15 July 1985)

At this point the FPG chairman, Paul Fox, caught up with Halliwell at the meeting and confirmed that ITV would not pay more than had already been offered. Campbell then rang the BBC team and told them that on a first refusal basis they had a deal at $35,000. Ruggheimer agreed the deal. When O'Sullivan heard about it he was furious that he hadn't got the $40,000 he had told his men to get. He abrogated the deal and fired Colin Campbell. Ruggheimer then got the BBC to sue Worldvision for breach of contract and O'Sullivan responded by countersuing the BBC for restraint of trade. Writs flew back and forth throughout the summer. ITV's interest was sustained by the minority at Film Purchase Committee but minutes for its meeting of 24 June noted tersely: 'We feel the BBC really did have a deal, and that we should not exacerbate the situation, especially since there are so many complications' (Minutes of ITV FPC, 24 June 1981).

Two months later Halliwell was instructed to: '...indicate to Worldvision that in view of the prevalence of law suits and solicitors threats, any enthusiasm we may have had for continuing discussions is waning' (Ibid., 17 August 1981). Whether this was a triumph of the timid, or of the 'gentlemen', or simply a sensible strategy in the circumstances is not entirely clear, but by the autumn of 1981 a settlement was reached and the BBC had secured the series once more.

Soon afterwards Grade left LWT for Hollywood. By the time *Dallas* was up for renewal again he was back in the UK – as the Controller of BBC1. Cowgill, however, was still at Thames and not about to give up.

Episode 2 – 1985

In late November 1984 on the fourth floor of the Euston Tower building that was Thames' central London headquarters (the company's main studios were on a stretch of the riverbank at Teddington), Bryan Cowgill was conducting his annual review of the successes and failures of the past year's schedule with his Director of Programmes, now Muir Sutherland, and the Head of Planning and Presentation, Tim Riordan. With them was Pat Mahoney. By this time the BBC had moved *Dallas* out of the weekend into the heart of Thames' territory: Wednesday. Cowgill's ire at the BBC's consequent success with the audience on Wednesdays was palpable. Mahoney proposed that, if he was so concerned about *Dallas*, why not try again to acquire it when the contract was due for renewal early the following year?

Cowgill asked what it would cost to be sure of taking the series from the BBC. Mahoney proposed that they should offer double what the BBC was paying and that they should also offer to buy a new series on offer from Worldvision – *Highway to Heaven*. Not surprisingly, he believed Worldvision would find such a deal difficult to resist. Cowgill knew the people at Worldvision and knew very well that they would do such a deal if it were offered. But there were difficulties. He didn't have a network ally, as he had in Michael Grade in 1981, and the old problem of the 'gentlemen's agreement' still stood in his path. But his instinct was that the BBC was growing more competitive rather than less and that, as the weekday company, Thames would bear the brunt of the fight. Christmas came and went. Then one morning early in the New Year, Muir Sutherland asked Mahoney what he had done about *Dallas*. Mahoney said that since there had been no positive response to his idea at the planning session, he had done nothing. Sutherland said that Cowgill was 'very keen' on the proposal. Sutherland, as Director of Programmes was also a director of the company but, given the likely sensitivities in this case, Mahoney felt he should seek a clear instruction from Cowgill himself. Cowgill saw Mahoney immediately and confirmed that he was interested in *Dallas* on the terms in which he believed he had indicated interest when Mahoney had made his proposal in November.

Mahoney raised the question of the likely reaction of ITV colleagues – in particular the chairman of the Film Purchase Group, Paul Fox. Cowgill indicated that he would take the responsibility for handling any reaction from that quarter. But Mahoney left the office still feeling the position remained partially unresolved – he had not had a clear instruction to do the deal. In the afternoon Muir Sutherland came into his office again and asked Mahoney what he was going to do. Mahoney said that because it was likely that the new Head of Acquisitions at the BBC, Alan Howden, would seek to renew with Worldvision during his annual trip to the

National Association of TV Program Executives (NATPE) conference and programme market in San Francisco from 10 to 14 January, he would need to go immediately to New York to see Bert Cohen, the Vice President at Worldvision in charge of foreign sales, to demonstrate the serious nature of Thames' offer. Cowgill at first agreed this plan but at the last minute queried the need to go to New York. On hearing from Mahoney that he had already fixed to see Cohen in New York the following day, he confirmed his agreement to the trip.

New York was icy, the pound was down – as near to parity with the dollar as it has ever come – and it was Mahoney's first visit to the city. Thames had an agent for its US sales in New York, Don Taffner, who was a very able salesman (his popularisation of *The Benny Hill Show* made Thames many dollars and his sale of and publicity support for series like *World at War* earned it kudos – at least amongst Americans sufficiently sophisticated in their knowlege of Britain to understand that serious programmes were made by ITV companies as well as the BBC). Mahoney was able to base himself at Taffner's offices in the heart of Manhattan.

The morning after he arrived he went to see Bert Cohen and put to him the 'difficult to resist' offer: Thames would pay $60,000 an episode for *Dallas* for that year (the BBC was paying $35,000 under the existing contract and hoped to get the renewal for $44,000) and they would buy it for all time with a 7 per cent inflator each year and in addition they would take *Highway to Heaven* for all time at $30,000 with a 5 per cent inflator. Cohen's response was to ask to have those terms in writing. Mahoney said he could but added that he'd need to talk to London to arrange it. He returned to Taffner's offices and after a call to Muir Sutherland in London and with some help from Taffner, a wording was reached outlining the offer, which Mahoney then signed on behalf of Thames and took to Worldvision. Cohen took him to see his boss, Kevin O'Sullivan, whom he had known for some years. O'Sullivan remarked on the generosity of the offer and said that Worldvision would give him an answer by that evening. Clearly the BBC had to be given the chance to counter the offer. It took until the following day before Mahoney had a call from Cohen to say that the deal was agreed. He flew back to London vaguely expecting to receive a hero's welcome. Instead he found a call from Bill Peck, who had replaced Colin Campbell as Worldvision's man in London, to say that he was on his way round to Euston with a proper contract for signature by either Mahoney or a director of the company. Mahoney found it was surprisingly difficult to get an appointment to see Cowgill.

After explaining to Cowgill's PA that Peck was now in reception with the contract for signature, he was allowed to join Sutherland and Cowgill in Cowgill's office. With the need for secrecy uppermost in his mind, the Managing Director had not sought the prior agreement of the Board. Normally, film or programme purchases along with the company's plans for major productions were reported in routine paperwork to the Board. Some exceptional items were raised by the executive directors in advance but in general the Thames ethos was that once the Board had approved the year's budget, their executives got on with the job. Matters that affected revenue – like industrial relations disputes or a downturn in the advertising market – were in general of more concern than expenditure within budget. The contract for *Dallas* was for £1.16 million for the first year. It was open-ended, with annual rises, but Cowgill believed it could be accommodated within his overall budget, even if other companies didn't show it. And he was sure they would.

With hindsight it might be thought that it would have been advisable to warn the Board of the sensitivities of the other parties involved – Thames' network colleagues and the IBA, as well as the likely reaction of the BBC. But to Cowgill at the time these were not insuperable hurdles. Anyway, the next Board meeting was not for a fortnight and here was a man at their door demanding a signature on a contract and his company was already in possession of a piece of paper that was probably legally binding. In the end it was Muir Sutherland who signed the full contract.

They had not expected events to move so fast. Deals for bought-in series often took months between initial agreement and the signature of a contract. But this one was different.There was much at stake for the seller as well as the buyer.

If Worldvision, with this deal, could break what the US distributors regarded as a cartel between the only two buyers in the UK market, then the organisation would enhance not only its revenue but also its reputation amongst its peers. Both buyer and seller wanted the deal for competitive reasons – but the seller's priority was speed and telling the world, while the buyer's was the need for a cautious, step by step approach to breaking the news. Cowgill sought a special meeting of the Thames Board. But before it could take place the word was out – within broadcasting circles if not yet on the street. The BBC had digested the news from Alan Howden of his conversation with Bert Cohen and on Saturday 12 January Paul Fox was telephoned by Michael Grade – back from the US but now on the opposite side of the fence as Controller BBC1.

When Grade told him that Cowgill had made a bid for *Dallas*, Fox's reaction was that Cowgill had made the move without the authority of the Film Purchase Committee of which his company was a member and that he believed that ITV would not support the deal. He then rang David Plowright, Granada's Managing Director, who was also the ITCA Council Chairman. Plowright agreed: the integrity of the network and its relations with other distributors and the BBC were at stake.

On the following Monday, 14 January, managing directors gathered at Knighton House for the first Council of the New Year. Film purchase was normally a matter for Network Programme Committee, not Council. However, as well as the urgency of the issue, Council was, as we have seen, the only senior forum in ITV at which the IBA was not represented. The minutes of Council did not go to the IBA either, and, possibly for reasons of security but more likely because the matter was not official Council business, the *Dallas* discussion was not minuted. But those involved remember that Fox and Plowright confronted their friend and colleague. Cowgill was far from apologetic. He had brought off a major competitive coup for ITV. All the other companies could transmit the series, paid for on the normal

NAR share basis. Fox and Plowright were now joined by Bob Phillis of Central in their declared intention not to show a series bought outside the agreed negotiating system, at a price that was higher than they would have sanctioned and which set an unfortunate precedent for future deals. Though some of the smaller regional contractors might not have minded transmitting the series at their reduced version of NAR share, the consensus was that companies would not show a series bought in this manner.

On this occasion the discussion at Council may have remained secure but with knowlege of the affair spreading within the BBC and ITV it was only a matter of time before the news got out. The time it actually took was three days. On Thursday these headlines appeared:

BIG SOAP WAR BUBBLES OVER
Sun – Thursday 17 January 1985

COWBOY COWGILL
Thames TV Boss Outguns the Beeb
Daily Star – Thursday 17 January 1985

BBC LOSES DALLAS WAR WITH THAMES
Daily Telegraph – Thursday 17 January 1985

THAMES 'POACHES' DALLAS
Financial Times – Thursday 17 January 1985

This was the first intimation that the IBA had of Cowgill's coup. The Director General, John Whitney, summoned Bryan Cowgill to his office immediately. Having established that the reports were based on fact and that the contract had been signed, Whitney recalls that he:

> ... reminded Cowgill that the Authority approved the schedules and could stop *Dallas* being broadcast if it considered that by broadcasting the series the wider interests of broadcasting policy were being harmed, as would be the case if a number of companies refused to broadcast, as some had already indicated. Quite apart from this factor, I wondered how Thames could justify their action at a time when so much attention was focused on BBC and ITV funding and resources. [Note: this conversation took place the day after the Chairman of ITV's Council had led a group of MDs – including Cowgill – to the IBA to lobby for a reduction in the proposed C4 subscription. It was also during the run-up to the appointment of the Committee on Financing the BBC under Professor Alan Peacock two months later, in March 1985] ... I told Cowgill that he should hand the series back to the BBC on the grounds that he'd been overenthusiastic in his desire to acquire the series, and that since other ITV companies were not

prepared to transmit the programmes, we, the ITV companies and the IBA, would be seen as responsible for preventing viewers from enjoying a popular programme. (Interview – during which John Whitney was able to refer to his diary notes of the period)

Cowgill found this position difficult to comprehend. Surely, both for the public good and the financial health of the commercial television network, the regulator should be doing its best to ensure the whole nation had access to *Dallas* by mandating, or at least encouraging, the other companies to show it – not asking Thames to hand it back to the opposition? But, conscious that the specially summoned Thames Board meeting would not take place until the following day, he said he would need to consult before making any formal reponse to the Director General's proposals.

Cowgill immediately contacted his Chairman, Hugh Dundas, to tell him of the IBA's demand that Thames hand back the series to the BBC. Dundas, whose slight build and courteous but self-deprecating manner led people to be surprised to learn that he had won a Distinguished Flying Cross for bravery in the Battle of Britain and was twice awarded the Distinguished Service Order in the North African and Italian campaigns later in the Second World War, admired Cowgill's competitive spirit and is said to have been on the point of nominating him as his successor as Chairman when the *Dallas* affair arose. He was inclined to believe Cowgill when he told him that it was likely that, given time, all the companies would fall in line and take the series.

They agreed that before the full Board met the following day, they should discuss the matter with the Deputy Chairman, Sir John Read and another non-executive director, John Davey. They could then formulate a response to the IBA that they would propose to the Board. These two were important because they represented what were at that time the only shareholders in Thames – Thorn EMI and BET respectively.

Sir John Read was by now Chairman of the Trustee Savings Bank, but the major part of his career had been at Electrical and Musical Industries Ltd (EMI) where he had risen to Chief Executive and then Chairman. EMI had acquired control of ABC television just after the ITA-induced merger between ABC and Rediffusion to create Thames in 1968. Read had been kept off the Thames Board by the ITA until 1973 as part of the delicate balancing act that it then had to do to sustain the goodwill of the other major shareholder, Rediffusion's owner British Electric Traction (BET). (See *Independent Television in Britain*, Volume 4, Chapter 4.) John Davey had been a senior finance executive at Rediffusion and might have expected to be Director of Finance at Thames but instead received the consolation of representing his old company (and its owners) on the Thames Board from its inception. As we shall see later (Chapter 7, Section II 'Ownership'), both Thorn EMI and BET had, for reasons of their own separate financial strategies, decided to divest themselves of their shareholdings in Thames and were already in discussions with a potential buyer.

At that meeting, which the Director of Programmes, Muir Sutherland, also attended, it was agreed that the proposal to the Board should be to fight back against what was felt to be a precipitate and wrongheaded intervention by the IBA and to try to win over their ITV network colleagues. But they also decided that Dundas and Cowgill should go together that evening to Brompton Road to see the Director General to ask whether he would reconsider the IBA's position before the Thames Board meeting the following morning. But Whitney, who had by now consulted the Chairman, remained adamant. If ITV was not going to network the series, then it must be returned to the BBC. That was where the public service interest lay – and in not raising programme purchase costs unnecessarily for either the BBC or ITV.

Dundas duly reported this at the specially convened Board meeting at Euston on the morning of 18 January. Cowgill reported that he had had a call from Whitney that morning saying that if Thames were to offer the series back to the BBC and the Corporation were to turn it down, that might alter the Authority's position. Cowgill then explained to the Board that:

> had he consulted the Film Purchase Committee or the Authority neither would have supported the acquisition of the series and he had concluded the deal as he saw it to be in Thames' best interests financially (even if only screened in the London area) and in audience terms. The price for the 1985/86 season was £53,000 per episode for 22 episodes. (Minutes of Thames board meeting, 18 January 1985)

At this point came the first warning shot. John Davey is recorded as saying that:

> he did not accept that Thames would necessarily benefit financially on (sic) the deal and that an acquisition of this nature should not have proceeded without prior consideration by the Board. (Ibid.)

But, after discussion of both the Worldvision contract and Thames' contract with the Authority, it was agreed to:

> Try and gain through discussions at Chairman and Managing Director level an acceptance of the series by other ITV companies. The main dangers of this course were the inevitable bad relationship with the Authority and the possible longer term consequences attached thereto. (Ibid.)

However, at the normal Board meeting, which fell less than a week later, on 24 January, the Chairman had to report that his contacts at chairman level did not lead him to be optimistic about the likelihood that other companies would transmit *Dallas* and that, at an ITN Board meeting the Managing Director had attended on the Monday of that week, the other ITV managing directors had emphatically confirmed their position to him but had added that:

> he would have their support in any negotiations that would enable Thames to offer the series to the BBC with the network contributing to any shortfall in the sale price to the BBC. (Minutes of Thames Board meeting, 24 January 1985)

The Chairman also reported that on Wednesday he had met Lord Thomson who had told him that, at a special meeting the previous day, the Authority had taken the view that:

> it was impossible to over-emphasise the seriousness of what had been done. (Ibid.)

Thomson had also said that the Authority had formally decided that it would not mandate the other network companies to screen *Dallas* if they did not wish to do so but that the Authority had deferred any decision that it might reach if Thames did decide to transmit the series without the rest of the network doing so.

In fact the minutes of the Authority meeting on 22 January are rather less draconian in tone than the account of the conversation with Lord Thomson that Hugh Dundas gave to the Thames Board. The Resolution of the Authority meeting supports the proposals of the Chairman and Director General and authorises the Chairman to:

> let Mr Dundas know that, in the Authority's view, it might be in the best interests of ITV and of UK public service broadcasting, if Thames felt able to explore the possibility of returning *Dallas* to the BBC. It should be emphasised that, in the particular circumstances, this was a matter on which Thames themselves must make their own decision. Mr Dundas should also be told that, if Thames decided to retain the series, the Authority would not be prepared to mandate its showing across the ITV network. (Minutes of Authority meeting 601 (85), 22 January 1985)

Nowhere in the minutes of the Authority meeting is there reference to the impossibility of over-emphasising 'the seriousness of what had been done'. This could just be a difference of minuting style but, in the light of subsequent events, it is possible to take the view that either Thomson was overstating the Authority's view in his conversation with Dundas or that Dundas exaggerated in his account of that conversation to his Board, or that both these things took place. In any event the Thames Board:

> agreed that an essential first step was to talk to Worldvision, to discuss the problems with them in the light of the ITV network's reaction, and to obtain the reaction

of the distributor to these new circumstances. (Minutes of Thames Board meeting, 24 January 1985)

Cowgill agreed to see O'Sullivan of Worldvision when he was in the US the following week. Kevin O'Sullivan was a first generation Irish-American whose father had fought against the British in the Troubles but had lost out in the subsequent internal struggles within the Republican movement and had chosen to leave the new republic for the New World. The young Kevin was not brought up to have an instinctive trust of the British. Cowgill and Muir Sutherland met O'Sullivan on Monday 4 February. Aware of Worldvision's penchant for litigation as well as of O'Sullivan's personality, Cowgill reported to the Thames Board meeting two days later, that he had told O'Sullivan:

> ... Thames had no wish to break the contract for *Dallas* but was concerned at the prospect of the televising of a series being restricted in the UK due to the violent antipathy of some of the ITV companies (Yorkshire and Granada in particular) to the deal. Given these circumstances, he had to consider with Mr O'Sullivan whether the series should be offered to the BBC on the clear understanding that Worldvision would still receive the full licence fee. (Minutes of Thames Board meeting, 6 February 1985)

O'Sullivan's response was uncompromising:

> Mr O'Sullivan said that the BBC had declined to take the series after weeks of negotiations and he was not prepared to consider it again being offered to the BBC. (Ibid.)

There was more. Cowgill reported that O'Sullivan had inveighed at length against the anti-trust aspects of the 'gentlemen's agreement' between ITV and the BBC. It appeared that in a conversation with Michael Grade at the BBC, Grade had mentioned Paul Fox's response on being told by Grade of the Thames initiative. O'Sullivan had emphasised to Cowgill 'that Worldvision would not be an accessory to any such arrangements'.

Cowgill also reported that O'Sullivan had contacted him after the meeting to ask about the IBA's position (Dundas had asked Cowgill not to refer to the IBA's views at the meeting with O'Sullivan) and had said that if the IBA should ban transmission then the contract would be void. On being told that the IBA had not so far said they would ban transmissions, O'Sullivan said, ominously, that if they did then the US film industry business association, the MPA, would be asking 'in very public terms' why they had done so.

After Cowgill's report the Chairman, Dundas, is recorded as saying:

that Mr O'Sullivan's views made the resolution of the problem very difficult and while it was unfortunate that Thames should be in the position it was now in, the main objective was to seek a solution in the very best way that could be found. (Ibid.)

The resolution of the meeting reads:

> With the importance of longer-term relationships with the Authority in mind, it was agreed on the necessity to convince the Authority that Thames had tried hard to vary the present arrangements with Worldvision but this had proved impracticable. Thames was anxious to work out with the Authority the best solution to the problem. It was agreed that the Chairman and Managing Director proceed on this basis and report to the Board before any final action was taken. (Ibid.)

That mission was to destroy the good working relationship between Chairman and Managing Director and cast the Authority in a difficult role. Dundas and Cowgill went to see Thomson and Whitney at the IBA on the following Monday, 11 February. Despite their receiving a graphic account of O'Sullivan's position and being aware from the Authority's Secretary, Bryan Rook, who had scrutinised the contract, that the series could not legally be reassigned, the IBA pair still insisted that the series must be returned to the BBC.

Dundas summoned a special meeting of the Thames Board for the Friday of that week. He spelled out to the meeting the alternative courses of action the company could take. In essence (though he didn't say this) the first was Cowgill's course and the second was his own.

Either Thames could, since the contract did not contain a right of assignment, hang on until January 1986, when the programmes became available to Thames, and use the time to persuade the other companies that it was in their best interests to transmit the series. If the majority agreed to do so then the IBA was unlikely to intervene further. Or:

> the company could decide that having, without the Board's authority, acquired a property the possession of which was in the event doing us nothing but damage, we should make further determined efforts to find some way of dispossessing ourselves of it. Furthermore, the company should do so even though the chances of succeeding were not good and even though if we did succeed we would be seen publicly to have suffered a defeat. (Minutes of Thames Board special meeting, 15 February 1985)

Dundas commended the second course to the Board, saying that he disliked succumbing to pressure as much as the next man but that as Chairman of Thames his one overriding responsibility was 'to protect our franchise' and that 'the adoption of the "digging in" alternative would actually quite seriously count against the company with those who ... would decide on the issue of our next contract'. He then said that 'it was a matter of deep regret that he had not been able to see eye to eye with the Managing Director over this issue'.

In the ensuing debate Cowgill fought his corner effectively. First he fairly reported the dialogue at NPC where Granada and Yorkshire had maintained their positions, but Paul Fox had offered to resign as chairman of the Film Purchase Group. He then went on to spell out the dangers to the company's sovereignty in future of giving way to unreasonable pressure from other companies. As far as the IBA were concerned, there was nothing about the series or the obtaining of it that offended under the Broadcasting Act and their attitude was unjustifiable. This was underlined by their unwillingness to take any action – either against or for Thames. Worldvision was immovable on the matter of assignment to the BBC, but even if it wasn't Cowgill was deeply concerned about the matters of principle involved in giving way to the pressures resulting from the properly competitive acquisition of a commercially beneficial property like *Dallas*.

In this Cowgill was supported by several of the non-executive directors and all the executives. Sutherland was particularly strong on the potentially disastrous impact on advertisers of handing back such a successful series to the BBC. But the Chairman and, significantly, the representatives of the major shareholders, were firmly against Cowgill. In the end a last-minute agreement was reached to establish formally, by letter, which companies would, and which would not, show the series before taking a final decision between the two courses of action open to the Board.

The results of this poll are not extant – indeed some of the companies may not have replied or may have replied equivocally – but from other evidence it seems unlikely that in February 1985 the major companies would have shifted their ground. 1985 was, after all, the period of the IBA's mid-term review of their contractors' performance. But would they have done so by January the following year? Even at the end of January 1985 *Marketing Week* had published figures which showed that the ITV network could take £1 million in revenue for each episode of *Dallas* shown. The network's relations with advertisers were never good because of ITV's monopoly of television advertising but they were to hit a new low in 1986/87 and the *Dallas* affair was not going to help.

At the IBA, the Authority minutes show that in February and March, though *Dallas* was on the agenda, on each occasion the Chairman said that there was nothing further to report. At first sight this may appear odd, but the Authority could reasonably be said to have put the ball firmly in Thames' court by the resolution at its January meeting, and its Chairman and Director General had maintained that position in subsequent meetings with Dundas and Cowgill.

Also there were more pressing matters facing the Authority. Channel Four was now a success but it was at its most controversial – with its *20/20 Vision* programme on MI5 and its 'instant replay' of the trial of civil servant Clive Ponting on Official Secrets Act charges. IBA staff recommendations about those had to be discussed and upheld, or not. TV-am's financial structure was still giving concern and its programmes, though felt to be much improved, were still subject to scrutiny. And in the ITV sector the companies' continuing concerns about the C4 subscription, the consequences of the resignation of Kevin Goldstein-Jackson at TSW, changes of shareholding at Tyne Tees and the appearance of a six-year-old girl telling an 'offensive' story in *Game for a Laugh* all vied for the Authority's attention at this time.

But most significantly at this period, the heaviest burden of the Authority's business related to Direct Broadcasting by Satellite (DBS) in the proposals for which the IBA were linked with the BBC in the 'Club of 21' to plan the provision of services for the broadcast satellites being built at the government's behest by British Aerospace.

The saga of DBS will be dealt with fully in Volume 6 of *Independent Television in Britain*. It is sufficient to say here that the diplomatic complexities of the relationship between the IBA and the BBC over DBS meant that the chairmen of the two organisations, Lord Thomson and Stuart Young, had been in frequent and increasingly close contact since 1983. Previously, relationships between the chairmen of the two organisations had usually been somewhat distant and confined to formal meetings once or twice a year. The development of the Thomson–Young axis was one of the dimensions of the *Dallas* affair that contributed to an inevitability more commonly associated with Greek drama than with soap opera.

At the March Thames Board it was apparent that Dundas was now meeting Lord Thomson without Cowgill present. Though this meeting had been officially only to tell Thomson about the letters of inquiry to the other companies, Thomson had become, *de facto*, a chairman-level link between the rivals for the *Dallas* rights.

By the April meeting a non-executive director, Gary Dartnell, the head of Thorn EMI's Screen Entertainment Division, had visited O'Sullivan, whom he knew, while he was on a business trip to America. He reported that the meeting was cordial but O'Sullivan unmovable. At this point Dundas appears to have supported his managing director's plan that in June Thames should put a formal proposal to each company for participation in the transmission of *Dallas* paid for on the normal NAR share basis.

But by 4 June Dundas was reporting that a legal opinion from a leading New York attorney had said that the contract was assignable and that he had met the Chairman of the BBC and the Managing Director of BBC Television, Bill Cotton, to ascertain whether they would be willing to accept an assignment. What he didn't say, but is evident from a letter from Dundas to Thomson of the same day, 4 June, is that Lord Thomson brought the three of them together at the IBA. The BBC, not surprisingly, were willing to take the series back but only on the basis that they paid no more for it than they would have done in the course of normal renewal negotiations with Worldvision. Cotton, who had sometimes been in conflict with Cowgill at the BBC when Cowgill had been Controller of BBC1 and he had been Head of Light Entertainment, perhaps sensing a split between Dundas and his managing director, lost no time in exploiting the position by relating the implication, taken from Grade's account of his conversation with Paul Fox, that Cowgill had misled Dundas as to the likelihood of the other ITV companies taking the series.

On 12 June the show business paper *Variety* broke the news (clearly leaked by someone at Worldvision) that the Chairman and MD of Thames had met O'Sullivan in New York on 10 June seeking to assign the series to the BBC and that he had turned them down but had offered to meet the Chairman of the IBA to seek his help in getting the series onto the entire ITV network. The article referred to O'Sullivan's strong views on the anti-trust (monopoly) implications of the relationship between ITV and the BBC.

Dundas hastily called another special meeting of his Board on Friday 14 June at which he reported on the meeting with O'Sullivan, who had been as intransigent as ever on the matter of assignment to the BBC. Dundas also reported that he had a conversation with the President of Worldvision's owners, Taft Television, who had encouraged him to try to set up the meeting between O'Sullivan and Thomson. By now the New York lawyer was advising that Thames could assign without Worldvision's agreement. But British counsel's opinion on the competition law aspect of the matter had advised that it would be unwise to do so.

In the last week of June, O'Sullivan arrived in Britain and completed a whirlwind sequence of meetings not only with Lord Thomson at the IBA but also with David Plowright at Granada, Brian Tesler at LWT, Bob Phillis at Central and, as an ominous grace note, he also went to see the Office of Fair Trading before a final meeting with Dundas and Cowgill.

As Dundas was to report to his Board at their meeting on 3 July, O'Sullivan told the Thames pair that:

> as a result of what he had heard at those meetings, he now understood and accepted the fact that the other ITV majors were really determined not to screen *Dallas* in their areas. He now, therefore, for the first time, fully understood Thames' dilemma, as well as Worldvision's and had offered to re-open negotiations with the BBC, as if the contract with Thames did not exist. (Minutes of Thames Board meeting, 3 July 1985)

The degree of split between chairman and managing director by this point is evident from the fact that Cowgill felt it important to tell the Board that he had met O'Sullivan on his visit prior to the joint meeting and that O'Sullivan had told him that:

> if he (Cowgill), as Managing Director, did not wish to see the series passed to the BBC, then Worldvision would honour the deal. He (O'Sullivan) had asked for a meeting with the Managing Director and the Chairman to get a clear statement on Thames' position.

Cowgill went on to say that, despite his strong personal views, he recognised that:

> as Managing Director he had clear obligations to the shareholders and had accordingly arranged the meeting. He said that he, personally, was opposed to the series going to the BBC, but given the clear views of the owners of Thames, he could not go against them. He believed the deal made commercial sense but had become the subject of accommodation. (Ibid.)

The battle was over. There were a few more skirmishes but now it was a matter of identifying the dead and wounded – and counting the cost. On the evening of Friday 12 July *News at Ten* announced:

> The Managing Director of Thames Television, Mr Bryan Cowgill, said today that he had resigned because of the row over his purchase of *Dallas*, the American television series and to protest against interference by the Independent Broadcasting Authority.

The newsreader went on to outline Cowgill's achievements, which included persuading Morecambe and Wise and Mike Yarwood to make shows for Thames rather than the BBC and building up Thames' overseas sales into a multi-million pound business which had won the Queen's Award for Industry. The item concluded with a brief interview with Bryan Cowgill, in which his closing words were:

> I do recall that ITV was set up to compete with the BBC and not to proceed along a relationship of cosy and, I believe, dangerous accommodation. (Transcript, *News at Ten*, 12 July 1985)

Two days later Hugh Dundas was also interviewed by ITN:

> What went wrong simply was that Thames, unilaterally, without consulting the other people who have got to show it and pay for it and who have ... a well established (programme buying) mechanism, went ahead and said 'Now I have got it you chaps come in'.
>
> Why did he do that I shall never know. I have told Bryan time and time again that he is a very intelligent man, and he is one of the most intelligent men I know. How could he have momentarily exercised such misjudgement, because he must have known that all hell would break loose. (Transcript, ITN Saturday 8.45 p.m. News, 14 July 1985)

At the Authority meeting on 31 July 1985 the Chairman thought fit to remind members of the reasons for the IBA's involvement. The regulator had a responsibility to the public. The public interest in this case was that a popular television series should remain available to all those who had been regular viewers up to now.

It was also not in the public interest to encourage a programme buying free-for-all which would inevitably inflate costs. Lord Thomson also noted with satisfaction that the Chairman of Thames had issued a statement saying that at no point had the IBA threatened to take their licence away. It is at least possible to argue that during the year of the IBA's mid-term review of their contractors' performance, they did not need to.

The view of public service broadcasting that Lord Thomson so staunchly represented ran counter to the government's view of the world and, in the same sense, it also ran against the spirit of the times. That, and the fact that the IBA in 1985 was not as good at explaining itself as it was later to become, were not good auguries for the future of the Authority.

Thames did eventually have to pay the BBC £300,000 of the £500,000 the Corporation required to subvent the return of *Dallas* at Worldvision's new price. The remainder of the money was collected and paid over by the ITCA from those companies who had refused the series. The fact that the long and irritable negotiations over the handback of *Dallas* to the BBC often seemed to be conducted in public and overlapped with the refusal by the IBA to allow Michael Green's Carlton Communications' bid to buy Thames to go ahead (see Chapter 7, Section II, 'Ownership') hardly helped the IBA. The 'dry' (that is, right-wing) elements around the Prime Minister viewed the defeat of entrepreneurial initiative by what they saw as old-fashioned collectivism as something that must and could be changed. And the destruction of the career of Cowgill, one of the senior executives in ITV best equipped for the business of the now inevitably increasing competition in broadcasting, did not do the ITV network itself any favours either.

A footnote: The Office of Fair Trading did not intervene in programme purchasing – despite the visit of Mr O'Sullivan and despite a question in the House of Commons. On 21 October a Conservative with an interest in media and communications matters, Mr John Gorst, was prompted to ask what the Department of Trade and Industry was doing to ensure that the purchasing arrangements of the broadcasters were not 'in contravention of the provisions of the Restrictive Trade Practices Act'. He was given a typically equivocal answer by the then junior minister at the DTI, Michael Howard, who merely said that the broadcasters had 'denied the existence of arrangements concerning the purchase of film or other programme material which might require registration under the Restrictive Trades Practices Act 1976' (Hansard, 21 October 1985).

However, the truth was that the limited formal agreement between ITV and the BBC about first refusal at renewal had been registered with the OFT under the Act in an explanatory memorandum (RS 406) in October 1978. This had been confirmed in correspondence between David Shaw, General Secretary of the ITCA and Mr J.C. Octon, Assistant Director of the Competition Policy Division of the OFT as recently as 13 September 1985 – a fact which would have been available to the DTI civil servants preparing Mr Howard's answer. The original memorandum had explained that there was and had always been competitive bidding for new series and cinema films, though the winner was to have first option for the renewal of rights to broadcast. This had been accepted by the OFT. Mr Howard did not make that clear to the House, doubtless pleasing the Prime Minister by leaving another stick around with which government might beat the broadcasters.

Sins

By pure coincidence it was another imported programme purchased from Worldvision that was to cause ITV and the IBA difficulty, this time as a result of public reaction and political consequences, in that *annus horribilis* for the two organisations: 1987.

At 7.45 p.m. on the evening of Sunday 6 September the first segment of a three-part mini-series called *Sins* was transmitted. *Sins* had been made and shown in the US in three two-hour segments. In the mid-Eighties ITV's Controllers had devised a pre-autumn scheduling ploy to carry the strong Sunday night audience over to the less strong first weekdays by scheduling mini-series of three two-hour episodes across Sunday, Monday and Tuesday. On the Sunday, in order to maintain the News within peak time, as required by the IBA, a two-hour mini-series episode needed a start time well before the agreed 'watershed' of 9.00 p.m. (the time by which parents were assumed to be responsible for what their children were allowed to see).

The production starred Joan Collins, with Gene Kelly taking a (non-dancing) cameo role. With its customary concision *The Guinness Encyclopaedia of Television* describes the plot thus: 'An ambitious woman builds the world's most successful magazine empire.'

TV Times put Joan Collins on its cover that week and was less succinct than *The Guinness Encyclopaedia* but its implications were equally innocuous. What neither reveal is that the series started with black and white flashbacks to the childhood of the heroine in wartime Europe. These included the beating up of a young pregnant woman by SS men in front of her terrified children (one of whom was to grow up to be the heroine) and subsequently the rape – implied, rather than seen on screen – of the heroine as a teenager. Revenge for those incidents was an important part of the storyline running through the episodes.

Programme Controllers, in their Film Purchase Group role, had actually viewed these scenes nearly two years earlier when the series was screened for them, prior to purchase, by the distributors, New World Television, at a screening in Granada's viewing theatre in Golden Square in February 1986. However, because of a legal wrangle over ownership of the right to sell the series between New World and Worldvision (distributors of *Dallas*), the membership of the Group had changed between viewing and transmission. In fact only two Controllers remained: Andy Allan (Central) and John Fairley (YTV). John Birt, the Programme Controller of LWT, the company that was to play out the first episode of *Sins*, had departed to the BBC in the interim and been replaced by Greg Dyke.

The IBA was later to write that 'the Film Purchase Group had clearly identified the need for editing' (Letter John Whitney to Brian Tesler, 18 September 1987). In fact the minute of the February 1986 viewing session simply records that, in a flashback, '(the heroine) sees her pregnant mother killed, shoots two Germans, takes refuge in a brothel, and is raped en route for St Lazaire' (Minute of Film Purchase Group meeting, 3/4 February 1986). It is also true to say that Controllers, both old and new, were normally reliant for such matters upon the safety-net of ITV's Film Clearance Committee (FCC) function in place beneath them in the network hierarchy.

The function of FCC was to scrutinise purchased films and – occasionally – programmes, to ensure that they conformed to the IBA guidelines and to supervise editing where it was required. The Committee, which was chaired by Pat Mahoney of Thames, was made up of film purchase and programme planning (scheduling) staff from around the network – all experienced at what is now called 'compliance'. They were expert in what scenes and shots could or could not be transmitted at particular times in the schedule and programmes and films were 'certified' as suitable for transmission at any time, or with restrictions resulting from the IBA's Family Viewing Policy (that is, the 9.00 p.m. 'watershed' and so on.) or subject to editing, or both. The Committee obviously could not all view everything bought by ITV, so it shared out work between members, who only brought difficult judgements back for the whole committee to view. Occasionally, after consultation with Controllers and IBA programme staff, whole films were rejected for purchase as too difficult to transmit. In the Eighties these included *Straw Dogs, Last Tango in Paris* and *The Exorcist*.

Some members of FCC saw *Sins* at a screening in Monte Carlo and agreed that, with some edits to the flashback scenes, the mini-series was suitable for showing at any time after 7.30 p.m. (There is no formal record of that agreement but it was reported to NPC on 8 September, the day after transmission, by Greg Dyke and is confirmed in his later, written, report.)

Though members of FCC were experienced at making judgements on taste, decency and violence, their role was to *recommend* – the final decision to transmit, or not, was the responsibility of the Programme Controller of the company that would be 'playing out' the film from its telecine or videotape machine for transmission by the rest of the network. That Controller, usually guided by his planner, would withdraw a film from transmission to avoid audience offence after news of any major tragedy coincident with the film's plot. For instance, the comedy *Airplane* might well be withdrawn if scheduled on the night on which a major air disaster was reported on the news. Normally such an embargo was only considered necessary for a few days or even hours after the event.

At the end of the third week of August a deranged man called Michael Ryan ran armed to the hilt round a quiet town called Hungerford, in Berkshire, and killed sixteen people. The scenes from Hungerford shown on the news made a major impact on the national psyche of Britain. Tragically, there have since been other events of this type in the UK, but at that time it was felt that mass murders were horrors that took place in other countries – particularly in America. A link was made in newspapers and Parliament between Hungerford and television violence and in particular violence in films and imported material shown on television.

On 25 August the IBA had issued a news release. Its first two paragraphs read:

> The IBA and the Independent Television companies are continuing to take the fullest care about any programmes in the current schedules which could be seen as offensive or emotionally distressing in the aftermath of the Hungerford tragedy.
>
> More generally, all programmes continue to be scheduled in the light of the IBA's guidelines on the portrayal of violence on television and its family viewing policy, and of the requirement that, so far as possible, nothing is included which offends against taste and decency, or is likely to incite crime or to be offensive to public feeling. (IBA News Release, 25 August 1987)

The following week the IBA rammed its message home with a further news release, the first paragraph of which reads:

> In the light of public concern following the Hungerford tragedy, the Independent Broadcasting Authority today reviewed once again its arrangements for dealing with television programmes containing violence. (IBA News Release, 3 September 1987)

Three days later ITV transmitted *Sins*. The flashbacks to the war were on the screen well before 'the watershed'. The scene was not directly relevant to the carnage at Hungerford but clearly the IBA guidelines on what could be shown before 9.00 p.m. had been breached at the most sensitive of times for public feeling – and for government feeling. Mrs Thatcher had been to Hungerford the day after the tragedy and the following week called in the Home Secretary to discuss measures to protect the public. Violence on television was high on their agenda, alongside the restriction of firearms.

The post-transmission inquiry within ITV was immediate and thorough. It so happened that there was a Controllers Group meeting the morning after the 7.45 p.m. Sunday transmission of the first episode. Some controllers were aware of complaints by viewers registered by their duty officers' telephone logs, but the IBA still had a representative at NCG at this time (they ceased to attend six months later) and the IBA's Director of Television, David Glencross, raised the matter at the start of the meeting. Controllers agreed with him that, in the version transmitted, the early scenes were not suitable for pre-9.00 p.m. showing. Greg Dyke was already seeking information within LWT and would report to NPC the following day. The minute also records that 'Mr Glencross was obliged to state that the Programme

Controllers, the IBA felt, could not delegate these responsibilities to others but must assume them personally' (Minutes of NCG, 7 September 1987).

It turned out that Dyke's report to NPC was necessarily of an interim nature because the person at LWT who had been responsible for viewing and editing *Sins* prior to transmission, Margaret Walker, had gone on leave just before transmission. He was anxious that she should not be made a scapegoat in her absence. He accepted responsibility for the transmission but believed that the network system had failed to provide adequate information to the company playing out the episode on the network's behalf. David Elstein, whose company had played out the two weekday episodes, reported that in light of the reponse to the first episode, Thames had reviewed those episodes (both scheduled for an 8.00 p.m. transmission) and taken twenty seconds of a sequence involving a gun out of the final ten minutes of the series.

The Chairman of NPC at that time was the Managing Director of LWT, Brian Tesler. He asked the Secretary to the Committee, who as Director of the Programme Planning Secretariat at the ITVA was independent of any company, to investigate, uncover any failures of the system and recommend how it could be made more secure. In the meantime the version of any mini-series for network transmission would have to have the personal approval of the Programme Controller of the originating company and that of another member of the Controllers Group.

At SCC later that morning the Director General, John Whitney, is minuted as saying that:

> Given the importance of the series to the success of ITV's autumn schedule launch, and the publicity given to it, it was astonishing that nobody at a very senior level in the companies appeared to have questioned its suitability for showing at the time in question. This indicated a weakness in procedures of serious magnitude. He required an assurance that there would be no repeat occurence ... Managing Directors should take a personal interest in the programmes for which they were responsible. (Minute of SCC, 8 September 1987)

Both Richard Dunn and David McCall said that while they shared the Authority's concern, and accepted responsibility for the general nature of the programmes originated by their companies, they hoped that the Authority would accept that managing directors could not be expected personally to scrutinise every programme that went out on their transmitters. Brian Tesler reported the protections and investigation that had been put in place at NPC. Privately, several managing directors thought that John Whitney had been 'over the top' in his reaction to *Sins*. Three years earlier, when he was new to the job, Whitney had himself viewed and approved a violent film portrayal of life in a 'borstal' institution for young offenders, called *Scum*, to be transmitted on C4. Subsquently the IBA had been taken to Judicial Review by Mrs Mary Whitehouse on behalf of her National Viewers and Listeners Association for allegedly breaching Section 4 of the Broadcasting Act. The Court found that the IBA was not in breach but the judges were critical of Whitney for not referring the film to the Authority Members for decision and the Authority for not instructing him to do so. Though this was reversed a year later at the Court of Appeal, sensitivities at the IBA remained high.

A week after the transmission of *Sins* Greg Dyke was able, with the help of his Planner, Warren Breach and Margaret Walker (now returned from leave), to complete his internal LWT investigation and hand his report to Brian Tesler, his managing director. Tesler immediately passed it to John Whitney at the IBA. After recounting the history of ITV's purchase and delayed showing of the series, Dyke quoted Warren Breach's private note made after the Monte Carlo viewing in February 1986:

> Viewed 4½ hours of *Sins*, which is ideal for the Autumn. Very glossy, very Joan Collins (even has Nazis). Margaret Walker viewed on a different day and says that the pregnant woman sequence and the rape can both be heavily edited to make the series suitable for 19.45.

Dyke went on to give an account of Walker's judgements and actions in relation to the first episode which was to be transmitted by LWT:

> Margaret took the view that only 12 seconds needed to be removed from the print she received. She considered the scene in question harrowing but acceptable by the criteria of 31 years' experience in these matters. In particular she took account of the fact that the scenes accurately reflected many of the acts which were committed by the Nazis in France during the Second World War.
>
> Some weeks later, but still pre-Hungerford, Margaret decided to take a second look at the newly edited version. She still considered it suitable for transmission post 19.30. She did not regard it necessary to refer the decision to the Controller of Programme Planning (Warren Breach), which is the customary procedure when she has any doubts. In the past, she has taken very strong stands on what she has regarded as unsuitable material and even forced late changes in the schedule ... In the case of *Sins* she had no doubts. (LWT memo from Greg Dyke to Brian Tesler, 14 September 1987)

After saying that 'The mistake was one of human judgement', Dyke went on:

> As a result we can no longer leave ... decisions of this kind to the judgement of just one person. There must be a second opinion and, if there is any doubt, the Director of Programmes of one or more ITV companies must be referred to. (Ibid.)

The memo omits to question why, after the Hungerford massacre and in the absence of Walker, Breach – the only other person in the company to have viewed the episode – did not seek his Controller's advice as to whether the series should be postponed.

Two weeks after the transmission of *Sins*, at the next meeting of the Authority, it was the members who resolved to reprimand the companies as a whole over the affair. Accordingly, Whitney sent a letter to Brian Tesler, in his capacity as Chairman of NPC, registering the Authority Members'

> strong dissatisfaction with what had occurred, in particular that no Controller or Managing Director had seen fit to satisfy himself about the suitability of *Sins* knowing that the Film Purchase Group had clearly identified the need for editing. (Letter DG, IBA, to Chairman, NPC, 18 September 1987)

As has already been shown, the word 'clearly' is hardly an accurate description of the FPG minute. Whitney compounded the severity of his interpretation of the Authority's requirement for a reprimand to the companies by accepting the advice of his new Controller of Information Services, Colette Bowe, to issue an IBA News Release giving the text of the letter.

At the NPC meeting on 13 October, the report by the Director of the Programme Planning Secretariat revealed that FCC had not previously been required to certify mini-series and recommended that the network should now require the Committee to view and report on all mini-series that had been purchased, but not yet transmitted, and that all edits required would be carried out by the transmitting company's staff and reviewed by the Programme Controller. Thereafter mini-series would join films on the certification sheets from which Planners made up the schedule to be approved by Controllers. Any series requiring editing which remained untransmitted for six months would be reviewed before scheduling. These proposals were accepted by NPC and by the IBA. Whitney wrote to Tesler:

> We accept these (procedures) as a sensible response to the need for a more rigorous system of clearing acquired material and I am grateful to you for ensuring that all the relevant industry groups have been involved in contributing to these proposals.
>
> The new system offers important safeguards for the future. I know the members of the Authority will be encouraged, as I am, by the speed and thoroughness with which the review has been conducted. (Letter DG, IBA, to Chairman NPC, 11 November 1987)

But tighter precautions could not undo the damage. The error of judgement over *Sins* was to count against ITV and the IBA with the Prime Minister – and it was to face the Director General of the IBA with an almost insuperable task later in the month of transmission when he came to make his presentation at her seminar at 10 Downing Street (see Chapter 8).

Violence on Television – the Research

Although the IBA Television Programme Code had always warned producers on the possible dangers of copycat effects and advised 'if in doubt, cut', the existence of a direct causal link between television and social violence had always been resisted. Despite the report from the US National Institute for Mental Health in May 1982 which linked television violence to aggressive behaviour in young people, an inquiry by William Belson into *Television Violence and the Adolescent Boy* (Saxon House, 1978) fuelled by several articles by the journalist Milton Shulman and dubious monitoring studies by the National Viewers and Listeners' Association, the IBA continued to quote its evidence from the 'Attitudes to Broadcasting' annual survey which repeatedly showed that only a tiny proportion of viewers were offended by violence on television (which was far less of a concern than 'bad language') and that it figured far less in viewers' complaints than, for instance, scheduling, especially the number of repeats on television.

In 1985, the IBA published *Dimensions of Television Violence* by Dr Barrie Gunter (Gower, 1985), who was later appointed Head of IBA Research. He queried the crude use of the term 'violence' and argued that most audiences are discerning and perceive so-called 'violent' incidents in different ways, according to whether the incident is fact or fiction. Viewers were capable of making subtle and complex judgements about what they had seen according to context and circumstance. The research showed the difficulty of attempting to study this area by simple counts of the number of violent incidents independent of their content and meaning. These views were summarised in a illuminating article 'Plenty of evidence; very little proof' (*The Listener*, 23 January 1986, by Dr Barrie Gunter).

Nevertheless, after the Hungerford massacre in August 1987, the government failed to be persuaded by such arguments and promises were exacted from the IBA, after meetings at Downing Street, that monitoring on television violence would be extended. Disquiet was confirmed by the establishment of the Broadcasting Standards Council in October 1987 with a remit (among other matters) to consider complaints about violence on television and radio, as well as drawing up a code and commissioning research on the issue.

ITV Saves *Baywatch* for the World

The Saturday 5.30 p.m. slot is crucial to ITV – particularly in the autumn and winter schedules. It is the time when the family assembles around the television set after shopping or playing sport (or watching sport on television) and in effect it is the start of Saturday peak-time programming. In the Eighties, viewer choice at the time was often the determining factor of channel choice for the evening, or at least a substantial part of it.

ITV had traditionally filled its Saturday teatime slot at 5.30 p.m. with adventure series aimed at the whole family. Often these were acquired from overseas. Some, like HTV's *Robin of Sherwood* were British but made with the overseas market in mind. From 1984 an American series called *The A-Team* filled the role admirably. For those not familiar with the nature of the series it is perhaps worth quoting a letter from the IBA to a viewer concerned with the apparent violence in the series in which the 'team', led by 'Hannibal' (played with an astonishingly straight face by George Peppard) and including 'Mr T', whose mohican hairstyle became a fashion note for British male youths – pursued 'baddies' with gunfire and explosions but no blood:

> ... the programme is tongue-in-cheek throughout. It is very much in the vein of *Tom and Jerry*, Punch and Judy and the Keystone Cops and silent movies generally ... a research survey of parents who had watched *The A-Team* with their young children revealed that the great majority of them found it quite harmless, and simply entertaining. (Letter Robin Duval, Chief Assistant, Television, IBA, to a viewer in Clapton, East London, 24 April 1986)

However, after the Hungerford shootings in the summer of 1987 the series inevitably came under scrutiny again. This time it was LWT itself, in its new post-*Sins* film clearance routines, which paid particular attention to the *A-Team*'s content.

A carefully edited *A-Team* did continue to appear on ITV that autumn. However, viewers began to complain about what was done to the series rather than what was done on screen. A viewer from West Yorkshire wrote to the IBA:

> *The A-Team* is a forty-eight minute programme and has of late been chopped by the TV companies to roughly forty-two minutes. To lose six minutes is bad enough, but tonight's episode was a mere *thirty-nine* minutes long ... Butchery IN a TV programme I can understand being censored (and this programme has never been guilty of such sequences), but butchery OF a TV series is unacceptable. (Letter to IBA, 12 September 1987)

Robin Duval at the IBA had watched the episode concerned himself and replied 'I would agree that the plot was a little difficult to follow' as a result of the cuts and that he would pass the viewer's letter to LWT for comment.

But worse was to follow for LWT and the network. NBC had in fact cancelled its contract for the series that year, after a five-year run. So the hunt was now on for a replacement for *The A-Team* anyway. Another import, *Beverly Hills 90210*, was tried in the slot but dealt with themes that were rather too serious for the audience at that time. A sixth edition of Central's weeknight *Blockbusters* was tried in the autumn 1988 schedule but did not hold the audience as well as it did in its weekday slots and for autumn 1989 the network had to resort to *A-Team* repeats.

However, in the network's film-buying trip to Los Angeles that autumn the ITV Controllers saw a new series, again commissioned by NBC, about 'the diverse lifestyles and adventures of a group of Southern California lifeguards both on the beach and at home' (*BIB Television Source Books*: 1996–97). The prospect of handsome, well-built young Americans courageously saving lives in many different ways and contexts, but with no guns and little violence, proved irresistible to ITV's Controllers, Film Purchase executives and Planners. David Hasselhoff and Pamela Anderson were set to rescue the Saturday 5.30 p.m. slot on ITV as well as those drowning off Santa Monica.

Rescue it they did. When the series came to British screens on 6 November 1990 it was a hit – with an audience reaching nearly thirteen million when the first series was transmitted in January 1990. While ITV was happy; the IBA was still uneasy:

> The content of the *Baywatch* series was at times questionable in the earlier part of Saturday evening. Its images of buxom female life-guards and sun lovers on Malibu Beach attracted both a large following amongst younger viewers and criticism from others who found its fleshy emphasis sometimes gratuitous. (IBA Annual Report, 1990)

However, before the IBA could pursue its concerns further, disaster struck the Saturday slot from another direction. NBC, dissatisfied with its ratings in the US, cancelled the series after one season. *Baywatch* itself now had to be rescued.

ITV, knowing from previous experience that it would be difficult to find a replacement, got together with the Fremantle Corporation of Australia, and other satisfied buyers and distributors – TF1 of France, Beta Film of Germany and Retaitalia of Italy to pre-finance further series from the production company, in return for distribution rights or a share of the take. The 'fleshy emphasis' was slightly modified in the UK version to ease the IBA/ITC's anxiety. By the mid-Nineties the series was dubbed into Chinese and Greek as well as French, German and Italian and shown in 142 of the world's 189 countries. In the way of investment in production, ITV did not receive a great financial return – but the series did solve the channel's Saturday 5.30 p.m. slot problem for six years.

SECTION III: NETWORK SCHEDULE DEVELOPMENTS

Sport – Win Some ... Lose More

An area of programming where the increasing competition between broadcasters during the Eighties brought about battles that were often a paradigm of those of its subject, was that of sports coverage. The battles were not just between the major broadcasters. In ITV there was internecine strife between the companies and in some sports there was deadly rivalry between two or more ruling bodies.

The appeal of sport for television had originally been two-fold. It filled hours of transmission cheaply and it attracted a large audience. For ITV there was a third benefit: sport attracted a male audience that included the young and, for some sports, had a reasonably even spread across the socio-economic categories. At the start of the Eighties advertising industry research showed that males still made most of the decisions on major household expenditure and young (sixteen- to twenty-four-year-old) males had, since the Sixties, gained increasing spending power of their own outside the family. Sports coverage was potentially a great revenue earner. However, at the start of the period the cost of sports contracts was going up and the audience for some forms of sport was diminishing. It is against this background that a quite radical change of strategy by ITV in the mid-Eighties should be seen.

The network had not convened a Sports Working Party since 1969 and by 1981, when sports rights costs to ITV were to rise above £4 million in the following year for the first time, it considered that another review of sport was becoming an urgent requirement. Not only were audiences and costs causing concern but with Channel Four about to go on the air, it was thought that better economic use of existing sports rights could be made by sharing some coverage with the new channel.

The Chairman of this Sports Working Party was David Plowright, Managing Director of Granada, in his role as Chairman of NPC. It consisted of Paul Fox, Michael Grade, David McCall, Managing Director of Anglia, and Ron Wordley, Managing Director of HTV, represented the interests of the 'regionals' (the non-major companies). Wordley's company had an agreement with the Welsh Rugby Union by which, under the banner of its national region's culture, it showed Welsh club rugby live – the only Rugby Union games transmitted anywhere on ITV. (Some northern companies showed Rugby League locally.) It was always the hope of Fox and some other managing directors that one day this connection might be used to bring all the Home Unions' matches (now the Five Nations tournament) across from the BBC to the ITV network. Also a member of the group was Jeremy Isaacs, the Chief Executive of Channel Four, who would determine which sports might be shared with ITV while still maintaining C4 remit's requirement to be distinctive. Guarding the network's financial sensitivities was Tony Brook, the Director of Finance of TVS. TVS was new to the network but Brook was not – he'd served with the IBA and then Central before James Gatward had lured him to the new franchise holder for the south and south-east.

In attendance at the Working Party were the 'sports experts', John Bromley, Controller of Sport at LWT and responsible for the ITV network's Saturday afternoon flagship sports programme, *World of Sport*. Bromley was Chairman of the network's Sports Experts Group, the *de facto* Head of ITV Sport, though, for reasons of companies' sovereignty, there was no such title. Other experts were Ronald Allison of Thames and Adrian Metcalfe, previously at LWT but by this time C4's Commissioning Editor for Sport.

This powerful team somehow failed to tackle the various factors which were beginning to affect ITV's sports coverage. They gave *World of Sport*, which was viewed by 2.6 million on average while the BBC's *Grandstand* had an audience of 3.6 million, a clean bill of health. They paused only to consider whether wrestling (seen by many as a branch of entertainment rather than sport) was a desirable component of the programme. Given that it was usually the highest rating part of the afternoon – reaching a peak of 5.5 million – they left it there, despite the fact that the various sporting bodies with whom they negotiated rights saw the transmission of wrestling as betraying a lack of seriousness in ITV's approach to sport.

The group did also think about abrogating the National Events Agreement by which the BBC and ITV both had the right of live broadcast access to the major sporting events like the FA Cup Final, the Grand National steeplechase, the Derby flat race, Wimbledon tennis and so on. When ITV did show these head to head with the BBC, as they did with the Cup Final and the Derby, it usually achieved an audience of less than half that of the BBC. But, in the end, the desirable objective of gaining exclusive rights to some of the key events, which would mean having to overcome the adverse responses from the IBA and the Home Office – let alone the inevitable outcry in Parliament that would be stirred up by the BBC (see Section II, *Dallas*, 'Episode 1', above) – was discarded as too difficult.

Of the group's final recommendations only one had any bite. To control the unpredictable flow of unbudgeted money spent on the opportunist buying of rights to events which then displaced programmes from the schedule that had often already been paid for, they sought 'To change the current special event procedure for sport to an annual sports budget ... with the (network) Finance Committee overseeing all expenditure' (Report of the Sports Working Party, 22 January 1982).

The lack of radical recommendations for change was a demonstration in miniature of ills that were to afflict ITV's responses to a changing world over a wide variety of issues, many more important than sport, in the years ahead. The prime obstacle to change was the interlocking balance of self-interest between the sovereign companies in a system where any change had to be agreed by all. But it has to be said that the complacency of a monopoly of television advertising revenue also militated against any real motivation for change at this time.

By 1983 the slide of ratings for sport in general on ITV, and in particular the Saturday afternoon *World of Sport*, had finally become so serious that, at the insistence of Paul Fox and Bryan Cowgill, managing directors of YTV and Thames respectively (who twenty-five years earlier had helped to found the BBC's *Grandstand* – the model for *World of Sport*), not one but *two* working parties were set up that autumn to devise new strategies for ITV sport.

One group was at Controller level. Chaired by Colin Shaw, at this time Director of the Programme Planning Secretariat at the ITCA, it consisted of John Birt, who had just taken over from Michael Grade at LWT, and Mike Scott of Granada, representing the major companies, Philip Garner of Anglia represented the medium and small regional companies and there was also a representative from Channel Four.

The second group was the committee of companies' Heads of Sport, known collectively as The Sports Experts Group (SEG). Their advice was to feed into the Controllers Group through the attendance of the Chairman and Deputy Chairman of SEG, John Bromley and Ronald Allison. Several of the members of SEG, Paul

Doherty of Granada in particular, were antipathetic towards Bromley and the London-based determination of ITV's policy on sport but there was also strong feeling amongst the group that the Controllers did not appreciate sport and were always trying to limit its presence in the schedules. Controllers for their part saw many sports as unpredictable in ratings performance with a tendency to occupy too much airtime with too little benefit. As a result different ITV company regions would 'opt-out' of, say, snooker at a wide variety of different times – sometimes to accommodate their required regional programmes but often simply to get a movie on the air as early as possible. In these circumstances it was hardly surprising that the introduction to the SEG report made dour reading:

> ITV Sport needs reviewing and reviving, of that there can be no doubt. Disenchantment among some Controllers, disputes over scheduling and disappointing ratings in some areas are outweighing the undoubted success stories in others.
> ITV has never broken free of its 'Racing and Wrestling' image and the available evidence indicates that it is the BBC which is recognised by the majority of viewers as the *Sports* channel ('Sport on ITV and Channel Four: The Next Five Years', Paper by ITV's Sports Experts Group, 28 October 1983)

However, the SEG's recommendations were aggressively radical:

1. The dismantling of *World of Sport* in its present form, substituting major event coverage, live wherever possible, from 1500–1640. This would allow alternative programming from 1300–1500.
2. The dropping of Wrestling.
3. Moving Horse Racing (Midweek and Saturday) and Golf (excluding Saturdays) to Channel 4.
4. To obtain two of the major television sports contracts presently held by the BBC – the World Snooker Championships and British Athletics.
5. Discarding our present joint contracts with the BBC to the Football League and the Football Association in favour of unilateral bids for the exclusive rights to (a) The Milk Cup Competition and (b) the FA Cup Competition (except the Final which, of course, remains a non-exclusive 'national' event).
6. Long-term exclusive contracts with Top American Boxing promoters and a major UK involvement. (Ibid.)

A further radical proposal was structural. With refreshing frankness the group described the current situation of sport within ITV as: '... diffused, uneconomic and inevitably political' and recommended:

> The creation of a central base for ITV Sport – independent of any single Company – would be the logical final step in the plan for the future and remove

the biggest single handicap ITV Sport presently has in competing with the BBC. (Ibid.)

This was not the first (or last time) that a sports equivalent to ITN had been proposed within ITV and the report argued cogently that the proposal would provide:

(a) Quicker decision, more efficient and competitive.
(b) One overall budget would reduce the need to refer.
(c) Centralised budgeting and costing would be simpler and more efficient.
(d) Sports and sponsors would have one reference point. (Ibid.)

These were all objective reasons but they ran counter to the structural culture of ITV. Also, with Michael Grade's departure to America in 1981, Bromley had now lost the support of someone who was a powerful friend, not just his Director of Programmes, at LWT. Some years earlier, at the *Daily Mirror* sports desk, Bromley had been Grade's unofficial tutor in sports journalism.

Now at LWT sport was as subject to Birt's financial stringency measures as the output of other programme departments. However, the events Bromley handled for the network were not subject to these exigencies and a well-funded Independent Television Sport (ITS) away from any ITV company must have held a strong appeal. Equally, some of his colleagues may have seen the setting up of such a unit as a chance to replace him themselves.

The Controllers Group Working Party's report weighed up the arguments for and against the ITS proposal and found them:

> ... finely balanced, but (it) believes that the proposal should be given further study, with particular reference to accommodation, staffing, the relationship of executive producers to their own companies and to the network, and to the devising and administration of a budget. (Report of Controllers Group Working Party on Two-Channel Sports Coverage, 17 May 1984)

Thus the ITS proposal was politely kicked into touch. The truth was that although some Controllers saw virtue in the idea, the majority were forcefully against another autonomous power base within ITV. One, in the shape of ITN, was enough, they felt – as did their managing directors (see Chapter 6).

However, the senior group did support most of the other recommendations of SEG – in particular that ITV's guiding principle for sports coverage in future should be; 'live, high quality and exclusive' (Ibid.).

After a thorough sifting at the Network Strategy Conference at Lainston House, near Winchester in October, the proposals were ratified by NPC on 11 December 1984, with a three-tiered executive structure (Sports Management Group – chaired by a controller, an executive committee and the Sports Experts Group) controlling network sport, in place of an ITS. Under the banner of 'live and exclusive' *World of Sport* was dismantled and the new Saturday and Sunday schedule pattern put in place in early autumn 1985 – with wrestling as a separate programme and the football results provided by ITN.

By now the Football League had finally capitulated to the broadcasters' financial blandishments and the first ever *live* League matches began to appear on ITV and BBC1 in the autumn of 1985. ITV Sport had begun to turn the corner and achieve its goals. Two other key victories were involved. The previous year the Amateur Athletics Association had finally been convinced that ITV could do justice to its sport in quality of coverage – and in payment. When the agreement was reached the AAA's income from television was £750,00 per year. By 1989 it was to reach £5 million.

In 1988 ITV reached the peak of its sporting ambitions when a brilliant campaign by the new young Directors of Programmes at LWT and Thames, Greg Dyke and David Elstein, beat the new-born but ill-fated British Satellite Broadcasting and the BBC to gain the exclusive live coverage of Football League matches for the following four years at the previously unheard of price of £11 million a year. It made sense in revenue terms but in feeding the greed of the League, ITV was to sow the seeds of its own sporting downfall in the longer term. The following year was to see another contractual triumph for ITV – though when the actual contracted event took place two years later it was to be at a bitter-sweet moment in the network's history.

For more than a decade ITV had sought to prise international rugby away from the BBC. Again and again the stumbling block had been the ruling bodies' view of ITV's competence and motivation. The English Rugby Football Union, in particular, believed the BBC's coverage of rugby to be the acme of broadcast sports coverage and was concerned at the possible impact on the image of the game of commercials played before the kick-off, at half-time and after full-time. The Welsh Union was more open-minded on the subject, having seen live club rugby coverage by HTV that was every bit as competent as that of the BBC and unbesmirched, in the view of the majority of its members, by the playing of commercials at appropriate moments. This stance was certainly not harmed by the presence on the main Board of HTV of the great Welsh and British Lions wing-threequarter, Gerald Davies.

But when it came to the contract for coverage of the 1991 Rugby World Cup, for which Britain was to be host nation, the joint Rugby Union World Cup Committee appointed the Keith Prowse Agency to handle the broadcast, sponsorship and other rights associated with the tournament. Once the leading theatrical, concert and sporting ticket agency in Britain, KPA had been through difficult times before a rebirth. KPA in turn employed a dynamic ex-pop music entrepreneur, Alan Callan and his company, CPMA, to handle the negotiations. Callan talked ITV's language, or at least that of its younger, more thrusting, executives: the language of marketing and sponsorship deals, exploitation of rights, and so on.

As important to ITV – if not more so – was the composition of the World Cup Committee's panel responsible for co-ordinating the broadcasting coverage worldwide. This was chaired by an ex-Fleet Air Arm pilot from Cornwall, the West of England stronghold of rugby, who had gone on to become the greatest England Rugby wing-forward (a position now known as flanker) of the post-Second World War period, John Kendal-Carpenter. Kendal-Carpenter was by now the headmaster of Wellington School, also in the West Country. He was perhaps the most open-minded member of the English Rugby Football Union. Also on the panel were Keith Rowland of the Welsh Union and Marcel Martin of France. The panel was to be joined before the final decision on who should be the host broadcaster by a representative of the New Zealand Union. Their professional advisers were Callan and an independent producer specialising in sport, Mike Murphy, whose company, TSL, had produced programmes for both Channel Four and ITV.

ITV's Chairman of Sport (the Controller nominated by his peers to be responsible for sport), Greg Dyke, was away at Harvard Business School – in preparation for his elevation to Managing Director at LWT the following year. The ITV group was led instead by Thames' Director of Programmes, David Elstein – Dyke's predecessor in the Chairman of Sport role. They assembled at Kendal-Carpenter's club, the East India in St James' Square, on the afternoon of Friday 20 October 1989, to negotiate on what turned out to be the first ever level playing field for ITV versus the BBC on international rugby rights.

Elstein had with him his Head of Sport, Bob Burrows, who had now succeeded John Bromley as Chairman of the ITV Network Sports Committee but, because yet another scrutiny of the ITV Sports unit idea was taking place, Burrows was only nominated as the Acting Head of ITV Sport. Also on the ITV team was an experienced and imaginative sports producer/director from Thames, John Watts. Thames would be the 'lead' company for ITV, with support from other companies from the network – in particular HTV and STV. French coverage for the World Cup matches, in locations that ranged from Grenoble through Toulouse to Paris, was to be by TF1.

The final member of the commercial television group was Mike Miller, Channel Four's Commissioning Editor for Sport, who had taken over from Adrian Metcalfe. Channel Four's support with airtime was crucial to the bid because only by joint scheduling between ITV and C4 could the coverage offered by BBC1 and BBC2 be matched.

The ITV presentation went well. Elstein's charm and flair for salesmanship were well supported by Burrows' solid practical approach to the demanding logistics of televising of thirty-two matches in twenty different stadiums in five countries. And John Watts' innovative plans for coverage, which included hand-held radio cameras roaming the touch line to bring detail of lineouts, rucks and penalties, seemed to meet with approval. On the all-important matter of finance, the usual intelligence sources of both broadcasters had ensured that the bids were very close – at just above £2 million.

In a confidential report of the meeting to the NPC Chairman, Leslie Hill and the controllers, Burrows wrote that:

> If there is only a marginal difference between us and the BBC, then the Rugby people are unlikely to 'change sides'. However if we were this week to guarantee a rights figure of £3 million, I get the impression that this would put the issue beyond doubt ... (Paper, 'Rugby World Cup – Latest Position', 23 October 1989)

Since the cost of the crews and equipment to cover the matches would add another £2.38 million to the rights cost, this proposal was not likely to be popular with the network. But Leslie Hill had nominated three managing directors to whom the Chairman of the Controllers Group could refer on the bid price, provided the Controllers agreed the scheduling modifications requested by the World Cup body. The young Controllers Group of this time worked more closely with their companies' Marketing Directors than their predecessors had done, on matters like audience research and promotion. They readily recognised the possibilities for rugby on ITV, not only for revenue but to help attract a younger, more upmarket, audience to the network. They saw the Rugby World Cup as an investment in the future of the channel. ITV was developing a worrying tendency to attract more older and downmarket viewers than the BBC. This potential for the recapture of younger male viewers overcame the Controllers' normal suspicion that sport occupied too many hours and commanded too small an audience and they agreed the scheduling extensions and supported the increase in rights fee.

A flurry of phone calls and hectic shuttle diplomacy to meet the final bid deadline two days later wrung an agreement out of the 'three wise men' to the extra £800,000 – with the severe proviso that it was at no extra cash cost to ITV. This meant, in effect, that sponsorship, plus a slight increase in C4's contribution (the channel had only offered £400,000 for a dozen or so matches at this point), were required to fill the gap. The Chairman of the Network Sponsorship Working Party was Granada's able Marketing Director, Malcolm Wall, who was still young enough to be playing rugby for the Harlequins club at this time, and he undertook to handle the network's sponsorship for the World Cup. He called in John Marchant, a sponsorship specialist in Granada's Sales Department. They were aware that Frank Willis, the IBA's Director of Advertising, and Clare Mullholland, the Deputy Director of Television, were working towards a liberalisation of the guidelines – as far as was allowed by the 1980 Broadcasting Act.

New guidance on programmes funded by non-broadcasters, issued by the IBA in November 1989, started the process of public consultation which was to lead to the acceptance of sponsorship for certain categories of programme in the ITC Code of Programme Sponsorship published on 10 January, 1991. As early as the spring of 1989, after consultation with Willis, Marchant had been able to negotiate sponsorship for the new network weather forecast (see below) and he and Wall felt able to assure the nominated managing directors that the money could be found.

Finding it was another matter. There had been no market for sponsorship up to this point and therefore there was no crowd of clients at the door. Also there were two key sensitivities. One was that the subject was under scrutiny at the IBA – any mistake could set the potential enhancement of revenue by sponsorship back to the dark ages. The other was the response of the rugby authorities. They were lining up sponsors for the Rugby World Cup event itself – who would have to be offered first refusal of the broadcast sponsorship. In the event Air New Zealand, Famous Grouse whisky, Fuji film and the others did not see any advantage to adding on-screen logos to their advertisements at the ground, in literature and so on. This was to turn out to be a short-sighted view but it freed Marchant to find a sponsor who would be dedicated to the broadcasts and be as interested in publicising them as ITV was itself.

An advertising business contact led him to Sony Broadcast UK Ltd, suppliers of broadcast equipment to the industry. They were enthusiastic about the idea of sponsoring the World Cup but did not have the scale of marketing budget required. They directed him to the domestic equipment side of Sony. There Marchant made contact with one of the new breed of young, positive marketing heads, Brenda Jones. As with Alan Callan, she talked ITV's language and, after a presentation by Burrows and John Taylor (a former Welsh international and commentator) she saw clearly the potential for Sony. With Marchant, she fought off the doubts of the media department of Sony's advertising agency (Bartle, Bogle, Hegarty) and with their creative people designed a memorable opening sequence in which the camera appeared to be in the ball – to tie in with the slogan 'ITV's World Cup, with Sony – for a better view'. Early versions of this had favoured Sony at the expense of ITV. That had brought ITV's Controllers into play. They were the guardians of what was to appear on the ITV screen and they did not want to trigger a regulatory landmine by the overexposure of a sponsor. They were also concerned that ITV might be giving away too much screen time to Sony for the £1.3 million that they were receiving from the sponsorship.

The Chairman of the fledgling Broadcast Board, which was to take over from NPC in the post-1990 Broadcasting Act era, Andrew Quinn, was called in. Now Managing Director of Granada, he adjudicated with typical dexterity between the sponsorship executives acting for the network, who happened to be from his own company, and the network Controllers, who nominated John Fairley of YTV to be responsible for arriving at a solution acceptable to NCG. Sizes of Sony logos and their times on screen were reduced, as was the number of trailers carrying the Sony logo, which, due to a misunderstanding, initially appeared to have been agreed by the ITV Sport sponsorship negotiators at 150. It came down to 30, but Sony still received value for money. In research into the effectiveness of the sponsorship after the event, qualitative groups were questioned to discover the degree of awareness of the sponsor:

Sony was the first name mentioned – spontaneously – every time. In some cases it was the only name mentioned. Sony was seen as the main sponsor of the event itself and was thought to have made the greatest financial contribution to the whole event. (RBL (Research International) report for ITV, 31 January 1992)

This result can hardly have pleased the event's actual sponsors – like Famous Grouse, Air New Zealand and Fuji – who had been offered the opportunity of sponsoring the television coverage and had declined it. Such success was to lead to a whole crop of sponsored programmes, and slots – like the Coca-Cola-sponsored film *Premiere* – on ITV in the late Eighties and early Nineties. However, despite the visibility on screen, sponsorship was never to account for more than 1 per cent of ITV's annual revenue during this period.

One factor in the success of the rugby sponsorship, which seemed of little importance at the time but which was later to assume a significance far beyond its origins, was the choice of the music to go with the ITV/Sony opening titles played before each afternoon's coverage. As always, there was a race against time to achieve agreement between the parties and there was no time to create original music. Instead the producer, John Wood, and his music consultant, Rick Blasky, chose a section of *Jupiter*, from Gustav Holst's *Planets* suite, and wrote some stirring words in praise of sporting achievement. This, when sung in the final version by the New Zealand opera star, Dame Kiri Te Kanawa, reached the popular music charts (while the official Rugby World Cup song sank without trace) and became the official theme for the subsequent World Cup in South Africa in 1995.

By the time the 1991 Rugby World Cup was played, two years after the original contractual negotiations with the broadcasters, Burrows and his seventy ITV sports specialists, mostly from Thames but also recruited from across the network, had honed their expertise and teamwork with the outside broadcast crews to a fine pitch. And, as well as the addition of lightweight radio cameras roving the touch line, Burrows and his team brought in a further innovation. Referees agreed, for the first time in Britain, to carry tiny transmitters to communicate their on-field decisions to the commentators, ensuring that the audience received a more authoritative account of the game than ever before. At the end of the tournament it was acknowleged that ITV had raised standards of coverage of the game:

ITV's coverage undoubtedly lifted the televising of the game to a new plane. Dressing-room interviews and the wealth of cameras and fresh camera angles made it look a much more professional exercise. As in football, ITV's obsession with close-ups and action replays interrupting live play irritated, but overall there could be nothing but admiration for the coverage, which grew in authority. (*The Times*, 8 November 1991)

Also the foreign broadcasters – some of whom had been concerned that the facilities they required from the host broadcaster might not be as good as those they were used to from the BBC – were satisfied by the quality of the coverage that they took as a multilateral feed and also with the facilities provided by the able engineer in charge, Roger Philcox, and his technical team as well as the liaison, accreditation and other services supplied by the ITVA's tiny Sports Unit, led by the formidable Patricia Gregory.

By the time the tournament was under way, however, the 1990 Broadcasting Act was about to have its major impact in ITV. On the day the commentary and unilateral coverage team travelled to Paris for the France–England quarter-final match the newspapers handed to them by the cabin staff read:

THAMES AND TV-am LOSE LICENCES
(The Times, 17 October 1991)

TIDE TURNS ON THAMES
(Guardian, 17 October 1991)

STUNNED THAMES STAFF FACE UNCERTAIN FUTURE
(Independent, 17 October 1991)

The team had learnt at Teddington the previous day that the company was one of the four that had failed to gain a licence to continue broadcasting beyond the end of 1992. The activity and adrenalin flow of covering the tournament was to suppress the true impact for those involved. But as some of them gathered outside the ITV office in the West Stand Car Park for drinks a fortnight later after the final, in which Australia had beaten England twelve points to six, the truth began to sink in. They might be out of work in just over a year's time. At dusk a drizzle started to fall and, in the sodium floodlights, faces that would normally have been relaxed and cheerful after a job well done, were tired and grim as well as damp. At a party for all the technicians and contributors back in the Thames studios at Teddington later that evening spirits did briefly begin to rise again, but the sense of the irony of the ultimate defeat having been thrust upon Thames during such a time of professional triumph will live in the memories of those who were there for a very long time.

The quality of ITV's coverage of the Rugby World Cup would undoubtedly have made it a more threatening competitor against the BBC for the Five Nations rugby rights had the negotiations for that competition's contract renewal fallen after and not, as they did, just prior to the World Cup. But there was considerable consolation in the subsequent gaining of the UK rights and consultancy to the SABC for the 1995 World Cup, as well as rights to the Rugby Seven-a-side World Cup and a number of internationals to be played in the southern hemisphere – although, as before, not all the network applauded the latter.

Rugby Union Football can be seen as the icing on ITV Sport's cake. The working ingredients of substance were Association Football (soccer) and boxing. (The fact that 'football' in network discussions and schedules is always a reference to soccer serves to demonstrate, perhaps, the peripheral position of rugby for ITV.) But ITV's grip on the rights to key boxing and football contracts was to be loosened by two legal hammer blows in 1989 and 1991 respectively.

The size of audience for major boxing contests on television tends to vary in proportion to the size of the boxers involved. Therefore the rights for the coverage of heavyweight fights are the most important and, with rare exceptions, the most expensive. The tradition of the limited competition of the duopoly broadcasters had become one in which the promoters or distributors of the various 'world title' fights played the two UK broadcasters off against one another where they could, but almost invariably ended up with the one with the most money to invest – ITV. There were no other considerations to favour the BBC in this case. It was ITV which nurtured young British boxing talent in its midweek fights. But by 1989 the UK broadcasting horizon was changing.

The long-delayed launch of a British satellite service (BSB) was to take place before the end of the year and, more significantly as it was to turn out, the newspaper proprietor who had such an unhappy experience of the British television regulatory system (see Introduction), Rupert Murdoch, had acquired a little-watched European satellite channel, Sky, and was about to relaunch it on the new Astra satellite (these developments will be covered in detail in Volume 6 of *Independent Television in Britain*), the reception area 'footprint' of which covered the UK. Importantly, it was to have a strength of signal that, contrary to expert opinion at the IBA and elsewhere, turned out to be strong enough for direct reception in the home, rather than just via cable.

While broadcasting was changing, so was boxing. A proliferation of Heavyweight titles had been thrown up as a result of more than one body claiming to be the authority controlling 'World' titles. But by 1987 the World Heavyweight Champion accepted by most authorities was a tough, ruthless but skilled young black American fighter called Mike Tyson. Towards the end of 1987, ITV's then Head of Sport, John Bromley, after meeting Tyson's co-managers, Bill Cayton and Jim Jacobs at the Trump Plaza Hotel in Atlantic City, was assured by Cayton that the Tyson fights could be delivered to ITV (including the one with the popular British champion Frank Bruno in London) by negotiation, either with the co-managers or with the man they referred to as 'their promoter', Don King.

ITV had a good relationship with King and, on one of the promoter's visits to London, an agreement in principle was reached with him for a deal involving four fights by Mike Tyson for a total of £2 million. As was usual, at the point when the agreement was made not all opponents were known (although Michael Spinks and Tony Tubbs looked likely) and dates were approximate.

A certain mythology has grown up around the evening at a rather raffish club, called the Riffifi, in Hay Hill, off Berkeley Square in London's West End, where Bromley and King reached this agreement on 28 October 1987. It is true that Bromley made notes of the amounts to be paid for each of the fights on a napkin as an *aide*

-*mémoire* but it is not true that this was ever regarded as a contract. Indeed, the minutes of the subsequent Controllers' Sports Sub-Committee make it clear that 'Mr Bromley reported the verbal agreement of Don King to ITV's four-fight Tyson bid. No written agreement was possible until some legal points had been clarified' (ITVA minutes, Controllers' Sports Sub-Committee, 17 December 1987).

By the following year it was apparent that, because of the British interest, the Tyson v. Frank Bruno fight was going to attract Rupert Murdoch as a possible 'dish-driver'; that is, if Sky had the fight live and exclusive, it would sell subscriptions to the channel and the necessary receiving equipment in greater numbers than any mix of films or programmes on the new Sky channels ever could. There was also a complication resulting from the fight being mounted at Wembley.

Tyson's manager, Bill Cayton, had, it began to appear, vested the UK broadcast rights jointly in Jarvis Astaire, the vice-chairman of the company controlling the venue for the fight, Wembley Stadium, and the British boxing promoter Mickey Duff. Astaire, a property developer and himself a promoter of sports events, was an astute businessman who had frequent business contacts with the BBC.

Nevertheless the ITVA Sports Unit's Legal Executive – who had confirmed the deal by fax to King and Cayton and had sent a draft contract – felt confident enough at the first meeting of the new enlarged Sports Sub Group, chaired by Greg Dyke, to assure members that, despite the fact that the contract was unsigned, 'its terms were binding under British Law because two (of the) fights had already been relayed (by ITV)' (ITVA minutes, meeting of Sports Sub Group, 14 April 1988). In fact many sporting and other contracts in broadcasting do remain unsigned as a result of continuing legal wrangles until after the programme has been transmitted. However, payment for the third fight (Tyson v. Spinks in June 1988) was made not to Don King but to Big Fights Inc – a Cayton company – apparently with Don King's agreement. This was to prove more significant than anyone in ITV realised.

As the result of a car crash, in which Tyson was injured, the Tyson v. Bruno fight was delayed until the end of February 1989. In August 1988, Bromley flew out to New York to confirm with Cayton that ITV had the rights under the four-fight contract negotiated with Don King with Cayton's and Jacobs' full knowlege and approval. Cayton claimed that Astaire and Duff as the local promoters had insisted on controlling the UK TV rights as part of the deal. He said that there was never a four-fight contract for Tyson because no contract was ever signed and no confirming telex ever sent because ITV's telex contained terms that were unacceptable. Bromley warned Cayton that ITV would be prepared to take legal action against both the local promoters and Cayton to preserve their rights. He then returned to London.

Murdoch was due to launch his first four Sky channels on Astra on 5 February. On Wednesday 4 January he called a press conference at the Grosvenor House Hotel in Park Lane, London, to announce that Sky Television plc had acquired rights to transmit coverage of the Tyson/Bruno fight live in the UK. He pre-empted the public interest lobby by allowing the BBC rights to the recording for later transmission.

Murdoch is said to have paid over £1 million for the fight – vastly more than its then audience of a few thousand was worth to him – but it secured a coup that was of huge value in the marketing of Sky.

ITV, having sought counsel's opinion from David Eady QC soon after hearing that Astaire was saying that ITV did not have the rights to the fight, and prior to Bromley's trip to confront Cayton in New York, felt confident enough to mount a last-minute legal challenge to this arrangement.

But when the the companies jointly went before Mr Justice Hirst from 8 to 15 February against Cayton (who had agreed to accept the jurisdiction of the British Courts), Sky, the BBC and Bruno and his manager, to seek confirmation of their contractual entitlement, ITV as plaintiffs made something of a sorry sight in court, where the defendants' barristers made much of their executives' apparent reliance on napkin notes and faxes in support of their claim of contract.

There were a number of absentees from the court. Astaire had refused to be conjoined in the action but had agreed to abide by its outcome. Jacobs was too ill to travel to London (he died during the course of the hearing). But the most notable absentee was Don King, who had refused to support either side. As a consquence of his absence in particular there were inevitable conflicts of evidence. When these arose the judge preferred the evidence of Mr Cayton, whom he described as 'a wholly admirable witness'. Others may have taken a different view but this remark must have appeared to Cayton amply to justify his decision to accept British jurisdiction. Of John Bromley and his ITV Sport colleagues the judge said that although they had been 'doing their best in the witness box to give an accurate account of all the matters to which they referred, their evidence throughout was, however, strongly tinged with wishful thinking ...'.

The judge found that on the evidence 'any suggestion that a binding contract was concluded at any time up to and including the draft (unsigned contract) was completely unsustainable' (Judgment, quoted in the report for ITV by their solicitors, Goodman Derrick & Co., 22 February 1989).

On the second issue of whether there was a contract implied by the conduct of the defendants:

> Mr Justice Hirst preferred the arguments of the Defendants that ITV's case had to fail since ITV relied on two different offers (the telex and the draft contract) and it was impossible to say which of the two was available for acceptance. (Ibid.)

This result was a humiliation for ITV. Not only did they lose the rights to a fight which would have been a major earner for the network companies but they were jointly saddled with legal costs estimated at £300,000. A seven-point plan to prevent such a contractual disaster occurring again was adopted by NPC in April 1989, but the strongest boxing event of the year in Britain had got away from ITV – it was a sign of things to come.

In June 1989 John Bromley resigned. There was no causal relationship between the Bruno/Tyson affair and this resignation, which was a consequence of the restructuring both of LWT and ITV Sport by Greg Dyke, but the year was a dark one for the man who had led ITV Sport in its strongest days in the Seventies and early Eighties.

The second legal blow to fall on ITV Sport came in early 1992. The network, led by Greg Dyke, now Chairman of Council as well as of Sport, had sought jointly with some First Division Clubs to follow the Football League contract that expired at the end of the 1991/92 season with one for a smaller 'Super League' which would guarantee viewers quality football, the broadcaster large audiences and the clubs more money for fewer games. In short it was the sort of 'everybody wins' contract that Dyke's recent course at Harvard Business School must have taught as a best practice objective. ITV also sought regional rights to matches between at least some of the clubs that remained as the detritus of the old First Division.

By this time Murdoch's Sky had swallowed its direct-to-home broadcast rival BSB but was still losing money and was now hungry to guarantee a surplus of subscription revenue over expenditure – an operating profit – as early as possible. To the dismay of the middle-class audience Murdoch captured the Cricket World Cup in March 1992. At the same time his lieutenant in London, a small, dynamic New Zealander called Sam Chisholm, was secretly negotiating with the top clubs that would make up what was now to be called the Premier League.

Chisholm had an ally on the inside. Alan Sugar was an entrepreneur whose electronics empire, Amstrad, had been built on the burgeoning market for cheap personal computers. With brilliant timing he had diversified into satellite receivers for the launch of that market and had originally taken a small shareholding in BSB but sold it before the Sky-BSB merger. Sugar was also the Chairman of Tottenham Hotspur Football Club – one of the intended Premier League Clubs.

In the formal offer made to Sir John Quinton, the Chairman of the Premier League, by Greg Dyke (by now the Managing Director of LWT but retaining his role as Chairman of ITV Sport) on behalf of ITV on 12 February 1992, ITV was to pay £18 million for thirty matches a year. As Dyke's letter made clear, though ITV required the UK exclusive live coverage rights for this, the network was prepared to let the League sell the recorded rights to the BBC, for their Saturday night *Match of the Day*, and the European live satellite rights to the European Sports Network (formerly Screensport), as well as to allow – for the first time in Britain – the new revenue enhancing (but audience distracting) revolving advertising boards in the grounds. ITV computed that the League would derive at least £40 million a year from this bundle of rights. A fortnight later a not wildly inaccurate version of the ITV bid ('£80 million over four years') appeared in the press. Clearly ITV had nothing to gain by this leak which gave BSkyB a valuable target above which to aim.

Three months later there had been no formal response from the League to ITV's offer, but plentiful rumours of a higher bid by BSkyB had led Dyke to sound out other managing directors in his routine phone calls to them about preparing a higher bid. The Premier League also had much to discuss. Its twenty-two clubs had even more of a communications problem than the fifteen ITV companies and the League also had smaller groupings within itself. For instance six clubs, led by Arsenal, were so strongly in favour of ITV that there was, briefly, talk of a further breakaway group if the League were to take the satellite route. In truth there were real problems, particularly with sponsors, if satellite were the only live outlet. ITV's audience for a strong match would have been twelve to fifteen million, BSkyB's between two and three million. How much money would be lost in sponsorship by this loss of exposure? What premium should the League seek by way of compensation? These were the sort of questions being faced for the first time by clubs, the management ability of most of which was not their strongest suit.

The final decision on the bids was to be taken at a meeting of the chairmen of the clubs on 18 May and ITV were prepared to counter BSkyB, with a bid that was not as high but which would more than match the Sky bid after allowing for the greater revenue that the larger terrestrial audience could generate for the League. That offer, submitted on the day of the meeting, was for a total of £200 million over four years – well over twice as much as the ITV's original bid.

However, the arrival at a final decision by the League can certainly be said to have been controversial in a number of ways. There had never been a formal closing time for bids. It was assumed that the start of the 18 May meeting was a *de facto* closing point but much depended on the Chairman of the League, Sir John Quinton, and his chief negotiator (and Chief Executive designate), Rick Parry. ITV certainly believed that Parry had set the deadline for 10.00 a.m. Accordingly the bid was delivered to Parry's hotel room at 8.20 a.m. by Trevor East, ITV's Deputy Head of Sport, who had a special responsibility for football. East went on to hand out copies of the bid outside the meeting room as the chairmen assembled. It was from this vantage point that East thought he heard Alan Sugar on the telephone in the anteroom revealing ITV's final bid to BSkyB. In the *Financial Times* three days later East was quoted on what he had heard Sugar say:

> He was very excited. He was saying things like: 'Don't you understand? You don't seem to have taken it in. These are the figures. You've got to get something moving quickly.' According to Mr East, the Amstrad Chairman concluded by saying: 'Blow them out of the water.' (*Financial Times*, 22 May 1992)

In fact, as a press release speedily issued on Sugar's behalf on the day of the *Financial Times* article stated, it was Rick Parry, still acting in his role as negotiator, who had an hour and a half earlier offered Sam Chisholm a final chance to rebid. Chisholm had phoned Murdoch and roused him from his sleep in New York at around 3.30 a.m. He came back to Parry with a bid that was, in effect, worth £10 million a year more than ITV's.

The League accepted the BSkyB bid – by fourteen votes to six, with two clubs abstaining. In the end the decisive factor was probably the fact of the BBC's willingness to join BSkyB in the contract and show recorded highlights to a size of audience which when added to the live satellite viewers could reach six to eight million, rather than the £306 million of the combined bid. Some who were involved believe that the BBC's 'defection' was brought about by pressure from Rupert Murdoch on 'Duke' Hussey, the BBC's Chairman, who had been retained as a consultant by Murdoch after he took over the *Sunday Times* in 1980. But given that Murdoch had played the 'let the BBC show the recording' public access card previously for the Tyson v. Bruno fight, perhaps nobody should have been surprised that it was played again.

But Dyke, who on 19 May had sent a rather gracious note to Chisholm congratulating him on his victory – 'It was a fair and open battle and your millions were simply too much for us' – by the 21st had come to see the battle as something less than fair. He wrote to Quinton pointing out that Parry had not come back to the ITV representatives outside the meeting to tell them of Chisholm's final bid and offer them the opportunity of matching or bettering the new BSkyB offer:

> We believe this chain of events leaves you no option but to start the process again. We would ask that both BSkyB and ITV be allowed to submit sealed bids to an independent arbitrator. We would also ask that the BBC and ITV be asked to bid separately for the Saturday night highlights package. The bids should be opened at a meeting of all twenty-two clubs, and the representatives of all three broadcasters should be allowed to make presentations to the clubs, as we have requested on many occasions. (Letter Greg Dyke, Chairman, ITV Sport, to Sir John Quinton, Chairman, FA Premier League, 21 May 1992)

Quinton's response sought to defend the apparently somewhat casual approach to procedure and went on indirectly to attack ITV for the leak of the network's bid and the fall-back plan for a six-club league:

> ... the Premier League deliberately attached virtually no conditions to the bidding process in the interest of obtaining the offer most beneficial to the Premier League. The one (informal) requirement we did lay down was that the bids were to be kept private and that the bidders were not to negotiate direct with any of the Premier League Clubs. (Letter Sir John Quinton, Chairman, FA Premier League to Greg Dyke, Chairman, ITV Sport, 22 May 1992)

Quinton then referred to Dyke's 'fair and open battle' acknowledgement to Chisholm – the letter had somehow found its way on to the pages of the *Sun* newspaper – before concluding:

There is no question of the bidding process being reopened. This matter is concluded and ... we hope the clubs can now be left to concentrate on the Premier League itself. (Ibid.)

Dyke was furious at this response. He was by now Chairman of ITV's Council and his network colleagues were supportive when he sought their agreement to the ITVA and LWT jointly taking Counsel's Opinion and if this were favourable, seeking an injunction on the basis that the terms of ITV's offer had been confidential but had been revealed to the competing bidder. However, when the matter came before Mr Justice Ferris on 26 May, he had a sworn affidavit before him in which Rick Parry testified that:

I telephoned Sam Chisholm and said that I had had another offer from ITV. I did not tell him the amount of it but told him it was still below BSkyB's offer although it was very close and if he wanted to feel confident that my recommendation to the clubs would be approved by them he should seek a more significant safety margin. (Note of Judgment of Mr Justice Ferris – ITVA Ltd & LWT (Holdings) Ltd and The Football Association Ltd & Southampton Football Club Ltd, 26 May 1992)

Mr Justice Ferris refused to grant an injunction and legally and officially that was the end of the matter. BSkyB and the Premier League were to become almost synonymous. ITV was left with other English League Football and, increasingly, European contests like the UEFA Cup. Dyke still believes that ITV was not fairly treated over the Premier League but now sees other factors to have been at work behind the denial of live showings of the best of British football to the mass audience via the public service broadcasters:

... what we all didn't see at the time was that in the end pay television was such a massive force that you couldn't overcome it unless you got political support, and unfortunately, we were living with the ... Thatcherites who believed that money was everything. (Interview with Greg Dyke)

Significantly perhaps, during the period that this is being written, in the second half of the Nineties, ITV, now primarily under the ownership of three men – Michael Green, Gerry Robinson and Lord Hollick – who, if not all Thatcher admirers, certainly see money as the most effective determinant of any business, including television, is fighting back and has just captured from the BBC the FA Cup and Formula One motor racing contracts for record amounts of money. But success against the old enemy of the terrestrial wars cannot be a guarantee of victory on the new fronts that have opened up against foes in space and underground.

The Sunday Break

An ITV/IBA ritual that continued through the Eighties but ceased with the advent of the ITC in January1991, was that of the annual meeting between the Network Controllers Group and the Chairman and members of the Authority. This exercise in access by the regulated to the ultimate regulators took place just before the summer holiday period and there was usually something of an end-of-term feel about the affair. However, it was regarded with disfavour by the programme staff of the IBA, who believed, sometimes correctly, that the Controllers would use the occasion to appeal over their heads on matters like scheduling policy. Precautions were taken to ensure that the members were briefed never to answer definitively questions or proposals relating to regulatory policy and the Controllers were set rather anodyne questions to which to respond. However, occasionally, either by blunt bludgeon or subtle knife-thrust by the controllers, or by free-spirited initiative on the part of members, reality was allowed to intrude.

One of the issues least related to reality was the scheduling of religion on ITV. Since 1956 in the slot from 6.15 p.m. to 7.30 p.m. both BBC and ITV had carried religion. In ITV's case this was entertainment flavoured with religion – approved by the IBA as a 'musical act of (religious) reassurance' (Letter Colin Shaw, IBA, to Berkeley Smith, ITCA, 1 June 1983). This same head-to-head scheduling would have been the subject of regulatory disapproval if it had been applied to, say, football but this lack of an alternative for viewers seeking secular fare had the blessing of the Central Religious Advisory Committee (CRAC). CRAC was instituted in 1923 as the first of Reith's BBC advisory bodies (see *The History of Broadcasting in the United Kingdom*, Volume II, Chapter II, Part 5). At the foundation of ITV in 1955 Sir Kenneth Clark as the first Chairman of the then ITA had agreed that, to avoid duplication of religious advice, CRAC should advise the Authority also. The irony that this body should then recommend that the old Sunday evening blank screen 'Closed Period' – itself a device to avoid accusations of the BBC seducing congregations away from Evensong – be filled with religion on both channels seems not to have aroused comment. The Sunday Break (there was actually a series called *Sunday Break* made by Penry Jones at ABC in the late Fifties), as the Closed Period came to be known when occupied by religious programmes, remained unchallenged – until an initiative on the part of BBC2.

In 1972, Christopher Chataway, as Minister of Posts and Telecommunications lifted all restrictions on the number of hours that television could be broadcast. The then Director of Programmes, Television, at the BBC, David Attenborough, cast around for suitable but inexpensive ways of filling BBC2's hitherto vacant daytime hours. As a result of legislation in the Sixties, some professional sports could, for the first time, be played on Sundays. (Football and cricket were allowed – horse racing had to wait another twenty-five years.) Professional county cricket matches in Britain had traditionally occupied three days, or, in the case of international 'Test' matches, five days. None of these were played on Sundays.

Attenborough and BBC Television Sport approached the cricket authorities with the idea of a one-day contest between county teams. Many negotiations had to take place – with players, potential sponsors for a trophy and so on. But, from the broadcasters' point of view the most delicate of these was with CRAC.

The one-day matches had to offer a set number of 'overs' to each side. (An over provides six opportunities for a batsman to score 'runs' by striking a ball bowled to him and, simultaneously, provides the opposing team's bowler with six opportunities to dismiss the batsman from his role in a number of different ways.) The problem was that different bowler/batsman combinations in cricket can cause overs to take more or less time. Though the pious hope was for matches to finish by 6.00 p.m. and the programme to end by 6.15 p.m., the unpredictable time factor posed the threat that the sanctified time of the Sunday Break might itself be broken. 6.30 p.m. was a more realistic finishing time – and then there was the possibility of extra overs to avoid a 'tie' ...

The story of how the BBC persuaded CRAC to allow cricket to breach the Sunday Break may be apocryphal. It is said that Attenborough turned for advice to his boss, and friend, Huw Wheldon, then the Managing Director of BBC Television. Wheldon knew his cricket – and the church. The glamorous new young (forty-three) Bishop of Woolwich had just been made a member of CRAC. His name was David Sheppard. Not only had he played cricket for the Sussex county team for fifteen years but he had played twenty-two times for England. Wheldon took Attenborough to the next meeting of CRAC. His eloquent advocacy of the need to use the changing nature of the British sabbath to positive advantage by encouraging the interest of youth in traditional British sport and its values was underlined by Sheppard's presence and overwhelmed objections of principle from some members of CRAC. The Break was breached.

Ten years after that breach John Birt went in to bat on the subject of the Sunday Break – against the Chairman and Members of the Authority.

His brief ranged much wider than just religion. In a presentation called 'Competition and Change' he presented a number of proposals to focus programme expenditure where it could be most competitively effective in a schedule which itself should, he suggested, be less bound by regulatory obligation. Many of the ideas in Birt's presentation were to be accepted by the end of the decade but at the time the IBA took the view that arguments for greater investment in peak time were a ploy to extract more revenue from the system and – given the easement of LWT's regulatory burden earlier that year (see the beginning of this chapter) – they were regarded with disfavour verging on outrage. A memorandum by Television Division sent to Authority Members four months after their meeting with the Controllers concluded:

LWT's own peculiar difficulties lie at the heart of the Birt thesis. When examined in detail, neither his general argument nor the figures on which it is based carry conviction ... And his general thesis about narrowing the range of ITV's output is extremely dubious. (IBA Paper 174(83), 10 November 1983)

In fact the only point on which Birt did gain any ground at the time was religious programming. Because earlier in the year the BBC had moved their serious religious series, *Everyman*, out of the Sunday Break to a post-10.00 p.m. slot, Colin Shaw, still at that point the IBA's Director of Television, went before CRAC to argue that in fairness ITV should be allowed to move their equivalent programme, *Credo*, also. The difficulty was that the BBC was cannily placing its programme opposite the highly regarded, but relatively low rating, *South Bank Show* and ITV could not place *Credo* after *SBS* without being accused of requiring viewers seeking serious coverage of religion also to be insomniacs. While Shaw accepted that placing *Credo* before the *South Bank Show* would leave ITV in general, and LWT in particular, dangerously uncompetitive, when he went before CRAC on 21 June the committee was not impressed by the argument that as a consequence *Credo* should be moved to lunchtime.

Despite the IBA's dismissal of Birt's proposals, with the funding of C4 now depending on it besides their own, the competitive health of the ITV system as a whole was becoming a paramount consideration for the Authority. It ignored CRAC's position and, at its meeting on 20 July, agreed that *Credo* could be moved to lunchtime on Sunday. It was not a major concession – after all the more competitive *Highway* (presented by Harry Secombe and produced by the redoubtable Bill Ward, the former Programme Controller at ATV, whose career started with BBC television's first broadcast in 1936) was still to be broadcast opposite the BBC's *Songs of Praise* in the Sunday Break – but it was a significant pointer to the direction in which television was to move in the next decade.

It was Birt's successor at LWT, Greg Dyke, who was to attempt, five years later, to break the remaining roadblock for viewers of simultaneous religion on Sunday evenings on both the major UK channels.

Once again the opportunity was the ritual annual meeting of the Controllers with the Authority. On 30 June 1988, following a typically sharp analysis by David Elstein of Thames of the threats to ITV from a reinvigorated BBC1 – whose new soap, *Eastenders*, was accumulating ratings as fast. Dyke gave a vigorous presentation on the competitive weakness that resulted from the current Sunday schedule.

His proposal was to replace the remaining evening religion (*Highway*) at 6.00 p.m. in autumn and winter with a popular current affairs series based on the American CBS network's *60 Minutes* formula. This would have had the triple benefit of strengthening the schedule at that time, replacing the old current affairs warhorse *Weekend World* with a more popular style of programme (but one which would still satisfy the IBA's contractual requirement for weekend current affairs), and allowing a religious magazine to follow the morning service instead of it continuing to occupy the 2.00 p.m. slot and consequently delaying the start of ITV's films and other popular programmes in the increasingly important ratings battleground of Sunday afternoon. As a sop to CRAC, *Highway* would stay at 6.00 p.m. in the spring and summer.

Powerfully persuasive though Dyke sought to be, Lord Thomson, who had been in the chair for seven of these rituals previously and who had been carefully briefed by the IBA's programme staff, was his usual canny self in response:

> The Chairman said the presentation had been very useful in clearly setting out the choices. He explained that the Authority had a statutory duty under the Broadcasting Act to consult its religious advisers. (Annexe to minutes of Authority meeting 673 (88), 30 June 1988)

By 'religious advisers' in this context, Thomson meant primarily the panel of advisers that the old ITA had found that it needed to deal in sufficient detail, and in confidence, with ITV's religious programming; a task for which CRAC, as a large joint body advising both British broadcasters, was not constructed. Originally there were just three ITA religious advisers and no permanent staff but by 1988 the IBA panel consisted of seven and there was also a Religious Broadcasting Officer and assistant. The expansion was in part an easing of the grip of the traditional British churches on broadcast religion to reflect the broadening ethno-religious base within Britain's culture but the membership also now demonstrated changes within the traditional churches. During the Eighties the panel came to include a rabbi, a Moslem scholar, and an Anglican headmistress, alongside clerics from the Catholic and United Reformed churches as well as those from the Churches of England, Scotland and Ireland.

But Lord Thomson had gone on to warn the Controllers that he 'felt it had been unwise to give advance publicity to these proposals as it had generated much concern amongst various religious bodies' (Ibid.). This was a reference to an unattributable briefing to the press from LWT which had brought headlines in *The Times* and *Daily Telegraph* on 1 June which in turn generated an on-the-record response from the IBA that was uncompromising:

> If proposals are forthcoming from ITV companies to alter the nature and timing of religious broadcasting, the Authority would take advice from its religious advisers and the Central Religious Advisory Committee. (*The Times*, 1 June 1988, quoting an IBA spokeswoman)

In fact the IBA's own religious advisers had considered ITV's proposals for Sunday religious programmes at their meeting a fortnight earlier than the Controllers, working on intelligence gathered after the press leak had alerted staff to the fact that ITV planned to move religion out of Sunday evening. Despite their disparate backgrounds, the advisers' response was united:

The Panel expressed their concern at the marginalisation of religious programmes implied by the suggested changes ... The panel affirmed the principle that religious programmes should be scheduled at times when they are accessible to major audiences. (Minutes of meeting of the IBA's Panel of Religious Advisers, 15 June 1988)

The IBA had a duty to consult the advisers, as the Chairman had told Controllers, but it was not compelled to accept their advice. However, CRAC was another matter. It had a public profile and issued press statements of its own when it saw fit. It was an eighteen-strong body, with members of the IBA Panel amongst them. It was chaired by an Anglican bishop – the Rt. Rev. and Rt. Hon. Graham Leonard, Bishop of London. Leonard was an influential writer on theology and other aspects of church affairs. In short, not a man to be ridden over roughshod by ITV Controllers with ideas that might appear to sacrifice God for the sake of Mammon.

Controllers were not unaware of the sensitivities involved and did not ask Greg Dyke to repeat his presentation before CRAC. Instead they despatched their Chairman, the Director of the Programme Planning Secretariat to make the same presentation, supported by Steve Morrison, Granada's Director of Programmes, whose persistence in negotiation and Jewish faith were felt to be assets in this context. Also attending was a posse of seven of the IBA's programme and other staff, who brought to the meeting their own attitudes to the issue. They were asked by the Chairman to deliver these prior to the arrival of the ITV pair. After the IBA Religious Broadcasting Officer, the Reverend Eric Shegog, had outlined the changes proposed by ITV he 'asked members to note the significance for religious broadcasting of this meeting of CRAC' (Minutes of the 55th IBA meeting of CRAC, 22 September 1988).

He hardly needed to remind them. Every week at this time newspapers were speculating about the content of the government's White Paper on Broadcasting, which was due for publication in the autumn. This speculation included the possible abolition of the IBA (which had been proposed by the Home Affairs Select Committee in July). This looked the more likely as the Gibraltar inquest on the death of the IRA personnel gave Tory papers a peg upon which to hang further antipathy to the Authority. (See *Death on the Rock*, pp. 69–79.) Taken with the changes proposed by Professor Peacock's Committee two years earlier, this gave rise to a view amongst many of the intelligentsia in Britain that public service broadcasting was mortally wounded. Seven days after the CRAC meeting a group of Granada producers founded the Campaign for Quality Television (see Chapter 9).

It was against this background that the Very Reverend John Harley Lang, Dean of Lichfield, brought his broadcasting expertise, gained as Head of Religious Broadcasting at the BBC from 1971–80, to bear on the matter of *Highway*'s replacement in the autumn and winter months by current affairs and the move of serious religious programming (Central's *Encounter* had now replaced LWT's *Credo*) from 2.00 p.m. to 12.00 midday, with *Highway* back in spring and summer together with some documentaries on religious subjects in the late evening. He was implacably opposed to these moves:

> CRAC had before it the most radical proposal ever to marginalise religious television. It would reduce the total number of people watching and put the programmes into unsocial hours. He added that, faced with the possible demise of the IBA, it was a mistake to anticipate that public service broadcasting was therefore at stake. The assumption that a current affairs programme would get a bigger audience than *Highway* could only be based on a personality-based trivi- alisation of current affairs. (Ibid.)

Irked by the fact that their prime opponent appeared to be the 'man from the BBC', the two ITV representatives pointed out that the proposals found slots for religion less exposed to increasing competition and might increase the availability of televised religion to those who actually wanted to view it, but they were fighting a battle already lost.

After the ITV men had left the meeting, the Committee listened to IBA research that told them that the loss of *Highway* in winter would lose about 60 per cent of the ITV audience for religious programmes but there was already no doubt about their advice to the IBA. The minutes of the meeting show that CRAC members were unanimous in their opposition to ITV's proposals, even before hearing the research. A few days later the Authority accepted CRAC's advice and rejected the reduction in numbers of *Highway* programmes and its move to the afternoon but accepted ITV's move of serious religion to midday.

The epilogue to this determined attempt by CRAC to stem one small trickle of the tide of free market social change in the Eighties may be seen as a parable for the wider scene in Britain. By January the following year *Encounter* had been moved from 2.00 p.m. to midday, and by January 1993, in one of the first schedule changes made by the new ITV Network Centre's Director of Programmes after the 1990 Broadcasting Act's changes were in place, religion on commercial television was removed from the Sunday Break period altogether.

Daytime and Night-time ... but First the Weather

That ITV should not have had a national weather forecast until 13 February 1989 – nearly thirty-four years after the network first went on air – may be seen by those new to the history of British commercial television as a matter for astonishment. However there were a number reasons for this delay. One was that the BBC had a long-standing monopoly of the services of the Meteorological Office, which itself was owned by the Ministry of Defence. None of the parties saw any reason to breach this agreement voluntarily. And no government had seen it as necessary to legislate that they should do so.

The second reason was that, although the IBA's regional contracts contained a requirement for the provision of a local weather forecast there was no requirement for a national service. Perhaps the overriding factor was that, until the Eighties and the arrival of more accurate weather forecasting, as a result of computer and satellite weather monitoring developments, the regional forecasts – usually obtained from local naval or air force stations and presented by one of the familiar local news team – were more accurate and more user-friendly than the Met. Office national forecasts on the BBC. The latter were often viewed with ridicule and were, and to some extent remain, fodder for comedians and satirists.

However, with the commercialisation of the Met. Office, an opportunity arose that ITV's Controllers discussed in 1988 and put in hand with International Weather Productions, a commercial off-shoot of the Met. Office, through a rather reluctant ITN. ITN believed it was in the business of hard news and tended to regard forecasting as speculation and outside its remit. Also, Controllers were anxious to put the forecast within the news transmission slot which ITN had always fought to protect. In the end negotiation achieved a clear demarcation between news and weather forecast and a sharing of the transmission time of two minutes after the lunchtime and evening news and ninety seconds after *News at Ten*, between the news slot and the network's time.

Allowance for possible sponsorship was made in the initial contract and, as mentioned earlier, the ITV National Weather became, in September 1989, the first ITV network-sponsored programme. The sponsor, paying £1.75 million pounds for the first year's sponsorship, was PowerGen, one of the two power generating companies privatised out of the old Central Electricity Board. Similar contracts with the same body have followed that first initiative.

Daytime

The daytime schedule changes during the period relate to the morning rather than the afternoon. Though the latter came to be scheduled more competitively – and in the case of Children's ITV, commissioned more relevantly for the audience – the major new market lay in the morning where, despite its problems, TV-am had created a sales beachhead. But before the opportunity could be exploited a contentious structural change across the two IBA channels was required – the transfer of Schools programmes to Channel Four.

This proposal arose at the ITV Strategy Conference held at Selsdon Park in April 1983 in discussions arising from the threat posed by the BBC's decision to transfer their Schools programmes from BBC1 to BBC2, to allow a more entertainment-led morning schedule after *Breakfast Time*. As was customary in ITV, a working party was set up under the chairmanship of Bryan Cowgill. It costed the project and concluded that it would need the IBA to approve an increase in advertising minutage and a relaxation of the foreign quota rules to be viable.

The IBA was supportive in principle of proposals to strengthen the ITV morning schedule. Such moves could help both the revenue of the financial locomotive of the independent system, ITV, and the viewership of its still not entirely secure offspring, TV-am. However, the Authority would face criticism if it agreed to the clearance of the ITV morning schedule for commercial use by the transfer of Schools programmes to Channel Four before that channel was universally available in schools all over the country. There were still significant gaps in coverage in 1983. The IBA therefore proposed that the transfer be deferred until the autumn of 1984. They were then second-guessed by their own Education Advisory Council, which recommended deferment until 1985.

By 1984 the position *vis-à-vis* the BBC had changed. The Corporation was in financial difficulty and could not afford a truly competitive morning schedule on BBC1, and ITV's audience share and revenue had improved. Early in 1985 it became clear that the BBC would not be able to introduce a strong morning schedule until 1986 at the earliest. At NPC on 16 April, the Chairman, Bob Phillis, revealed to David Glencross that the companies were split on the issue of the transfer of Schools to achieve a stronger morning schedule. The majors and TVS (and Channel 4) wanted the transfer to take place in 1986, after the necessary year's notice. But HTV, TSW and Grampian were against any transfer at present – Grampian vehemently so, on the basis that the cost would exceed the revenue. The national agreements with the unions were still in place (see next chapter) and the opening up of a full morning schedule could lead to claims that would cost them more than they would earn. The other companies felt that in the light of the current economic position there should be a further year's delay. Glencross pointed out that with the need for consultation and at least a year's notice to the schools, the IBA was put in a difficult position by ITV's split views. He gave the network until July to reach an agreed position. At a special Council meeting held in May the companies reached a compromise and finally agreed to the change taking place in autumn 1987.

By 1987, C4 coverage was 99.2 per cent of the UK and a plan was drawn up whereby ITV would pay for the distribution of the programmes on video cassette to the schools in those few areas that still could not receive C4. However, C4 had its own tentative plans for morning television. And there was the matter of the channel's *amour propre*. For reasons of continuity of identification, these programmes were still to be called 'ITV Schools', even on the C4 screen. Then there was the matter of the regional schools programmes for Scotland and Northern Ireland schools only. (Welsh Schools programmes were to transfer to the separate Welsh-language channel, Sianel Pedwar Cymru – S4C.) At that time there were no regional opt-outs on Channel Four – its founding fathers had ensured (with the agreement of the IBA) that, although the channel's signal passed through the local ITV company's control room for the purposes of injecting the advertisements that the company had sold, each company could be bypassed by remote control (the so-called 'black box' mechanism) from C4's HQ in Charlotte Street. This was primarily to protect the sovereignty of C4's signal from the effects of local ITV disputes (which was why the black boxes were fought against so bitterly by the unions – see Volume 6 of *Independent Television in Britain*) but in relation to the Schools transfer it meant that the matter had to be negotiated sensitively with the channel by the IBA. Though the Authority was both owner and regulator of C4, the channel's concerns that regional Schools programmes might just turn out to be the nose of a Trojan Horse had to be assuaged. And then there was the matter of money.

C4 wanted to be paid for carrying the service and freeing ITV to make more money. The IBA would not agree this; but the contract between ITV and C4 for the transfer was required to ensure that C4 did not lose money. Although this negotiation took time, with the IBA's backing it probably could have been speeded up to allow the transfer to take place in 1986 – had ITV been united in pressing for it.

It was not until the autumn term of 1987 that Schools programmes finally appeared on Channel Four, after an intensive publicity campaign by the ITVA and the companies aimed at Local Educational Authorities and the 28,500 schools themselves (IBA *Television and Radio Yearbook*, 1987).

The final agreement with the channel ensured that the first year's programmes were commissioned and paid for by ITV and the 'packaging' (editing all the programmes together on one tape, with the necessary graphics, for transmission) continued to be carried out by the ITV company which had done it for the network, Central Television. The commissioning and packaging were phased over to Channel Four in subsequent years and ITV's payment for the programmes ceased with the end of the contract period on 31 December 1992. Thereafter C4 was selling its own advertising. The IBA did not permit advertising around or between Schools programmes but C4 was allowed, as ITV had been, to transfer advertising time elsewhere in the non-peak schedule to recoup the 'lost' revenue. (In fact C4 was allowed to go rather too far in this direction by transferring 100 per cent of the notional Schools minutage. In November 1993 the channel was required by the IBA to transfer only 60 per cent (ITC News Release, 23 November 1993).

In the second week of September 1987, ITV was at last able to launch its new morning schedule. But the delay had been damaging. The BBC had been able to start a full daytime service a year earlier in October 1986. ITV's programmes consisted of a game show – originally *Chain Letters* with the ubiquitous Jeremy Beadle – following on from TV-am at 9.25 a.m, then a US soap, *Santa Barbara*, before the major new programme series at 10.30 a.m, a studio discussion programme, *The Time ... the Place* (later found to sit better in the schedule at 10.00 a.m. and also, incidentally, to gain more favour with newspaper sub-editors if written with a comma instead of the full stops!) ... This had a format based loosely on the American *Phil Donahue* series which followed the breakfast time *Today* show on NBC.

The Time, the Place had a core production team which travelled round the regional companies' studios with the host companies' staff working on the show. The presenter was Mike Scott, who until a few weeks before the first broadcast had been sitting at the ITV Network Controllers Group table as Granada's Director of Programmes. Scott, like many from the Granada 'school', had accumulated a wide range of experience during his career – cameraman, reporter, programme editor and, importantly, he had been the anchorman on the *Granada 500* series of live studio discussions which ITV networked in pre-General Election periods. He was well suited to the job. He and the producer, Mary McAnally, worked together with the regional staff – most of whom responded very positively to the chance to work on a network programme. It brought about a degree of cooperation between the sovereign companies of ITV which was normally only achieved during a *Telethon* or a General Election.

The only critic to write seriously about the new daytime schedule, Chris Dunkley of the *Financial Times*, gave the first programmes of the new series a somewhat crusty welcome:

> In the event *The Time ... The Place* has proved so far to be less than sparkling. The discussion on marriage, held near Gretna Green, consisted of a plod round the predictable bases, and the programmes on meningitis and test tube babies were little better. Only the genuinely topical discussion about the Dewsbury school row came alive ... (Christopher Dunkley, *Financial Times*, 16 September 1987)

However, the series was soon a success with the audience (it was seen by over one million daily after the first three months). It forced the BBC to step up their competitive reponse. They did so with *Kilroy*. However, the eponymous ex-MP never quite captured the robust, down-to-earth credibility of debate on public issues that Scott brought to *The Time, the Place* at its best and by 1989 it was watched by one and a half million against *Kilroy*'s one million.

Scott's move enabled broader benefits for the network too. The Controllers' table also lost John Birt (to the BBC) in 1987 and, as referred to earlier in the chapter, was refreshed by Greg Dyke, taking over as LWT's Director of Programmes. Steve Morrison took over the Granada Controller's chair from Scott. One of the first graduates of Colin Young's National Film School, Morrison had taken several roles at Granada – most notably as producer of the Oscar-nominated feature film *My Left Foot*. David Elstein had taken over at Thames the previous year and John Fairley of YTV and Andy Allan, of Central, had both joined the group in the early Eighties. It was now a youthful group. Only their new chairman, Paul Bonner, had yet reached the age of fifty. Despite continuing confrontations between LWT and Granada, it was this highly competitive team who were to take ITV's viewing ratio against BBC1 to the highest level since the days of Fox, Grade and Denton in the late Seventies.

Night-time

Night-time – expansion of the broadcasting schedule into the hours between midnight and 6.00 a.m., to provide a twenty-four-hour ITV service – was to prove even more contentious than the strengthening of daytime. It was to become a political battleground.

The Peacock Committee, reporting in July 1986, had, in its Recommendation 9, drawn attention to what it called 'the non-occupied night-time hours (1.00 a.m. to 6.00 a.m.) of the BBC and ITV television wavelengths' and had concluded that they 'should be sold for broadcasting purposes'. This was at one with the Committee's proposal that was to have such an impact on ITV – Recommendation 10 that 'Franchise contracts for ITV contractors should be put to competitive tender'. The two recommendations, taken together, were exactly what Mrs Thatcher's 'think tank' at 10 Downing Street, Professor Brian Griffiths, Jeffrey Sterling, and her political staff, headed by David Wolfson, wanted to hear. And because they had a considerable influence on the Secretary of State for Trade and Industry, Lord Young, the issue of selling off unused airtime – even before a new Broadcasting Act was in place – became one of the pressure points at which the Department of Trade and Industry could harry the Home Office, as it often did at this period, to be more agressively market-minded. Douglas Hurd, the Home Secretary, was not a man to be harried (see Chapter 8). Nevertheless he referred in a speech to the ITV companies exercising 'squatters' rights' in the limited use of night-time that they were making and his civil servants indicated to the IBA that it should examine carefully whether ITV's night-time hours, if they remained unused, should not be sold to the highest bidder for the period of the extended contract, 1990–92. The IBA in turn warned the companies that this was a matter they should take seriously.

In July 1987 the IBA itself began negotiations with BETA, the union which represented its transmitter engineers and was able to reach agreement for a viable manning pattern for a year's experiment in all-night broadcasting – which had maintenance as well as pay consequences for the system.

The situation by the beginning of 1988 was that only the two London companies and Anglia were broadcasting right through the night. Granada, Central, YTV were to start six weeks after the turn of the year. TVS was broadcasting until 4.00 a.m. on Friday and Saturday and up to 2.30 a.m. for the rest of the week. HTV were on the air until 2.30 a.m. from Thursday to Saturday.

Each company made up its own schedule; though a 'northern alliance', Granada, Central and STV shared many programmes (Yorkshire went its own way) and there was a southern equivalent with Anglia and TVS taking LWT's 'Night Network' at weekends and Anglia taking some Thames programmes on weekdays. There were some socially useful night-time programmes – *Jobfinder* provided help for the unemployed, giving regional job opportunities in each of the areas of Granada, Central and Yorkshire and ITN provided an hour-long News at 5.00 a.m., just before TV-am came on air, which was taken by all the companies that broadcast through the night. Initially the remaining smaller companies were not able to mount such a service. All in all, though the night-time hours were beginning to be used, it all looked very uncoordinated – and it was certainly uneconomic.

At its meeting on 21 January 1988 the Authority decided to put its foot down:

(The Authority) wants the ITV companies to develop proposals as early as possible, and not later than mid-summer this year, which would enable viewers in all parts of the country to have night-time service in the 1990–92 period, and preferably before then.

This could take the form of a sustaining network service with opportunities for regional opt-outs as desired, a system that would parallel arrangements in the existing transmission hours ...

The IBA understands that a number of regional companies have so far not developed night-time services ... because they have judged it uneconomic ... The anticipated advertising revenue is for these companies held to be below the cost of providing the service, the costs including not only the programme costs but the costs of selling the advertising and overnight manning costs in transmission control. (Letter Director General, IBA, to Chairman, ITV Association Council, 4 February 1988)

The IBA knew that transmission costs were becoming more negotiable (see Chapter 4) and the programme costs were for the companies to hold down but on the costs of advertising sales it had something new to offer that was to gain in significance over time:

... the IBA would be prepared, if necessary, to see advertising sold for one company by another, or by an agent selling on behalf of a number of companies. (Ibid.)

Meanwhile the Deputy Director General, the redoubtable Shirley Littler, was bringing the accumulated strengths of her thirty years in the Civil Service to a robust defence on the other front. She wrote to the Head of the Broadcasting Department at the Home Office, Quentin Thomas:

There is probably no need to labour the points that: under the present contracts the ITV contractors have the right to broadcast in all the hours on the ITV channel not occupied by TV-am; the decision about what happens in the period to the end of 1992 is a matter for the Authority; and that in proposing the three year extension enacted in the Broadcasting Act 1987, the Government accepted that any legislative changes which it might want to introduce would be directed to the new contract period starting on 1st January 1993.

... I have confirmed that the Authority is not attracted by the idea ... of a separate night time contract starting in 1990 ... (Letter Deputy Director General, IBA, to Head of Broadcasting Department, Home Office, 16 February 1988)

To be successful this robust defence on behalf of the ITV companies required them to be seen to move fast in the provision of an attractive night-time service. In fact it took ITV nearly five months to agree on a network service. In a paper written for the increasingly impatient Authority Members at their meeting on 21 July, the IBA programme staff reported:

> After some initial confusion among the companies about how they should present plans for a night time service in the extended contract period, they have produced a coordinated proposal which appears practical and shows signs of fresh thinking. Granada Television is to act as 'the co-ordinating contractor' for the new service, to be known as Night Time Network. (IBA Paper 102(88))

But there was a last-minute hitch. The Finance Director of the IBA, Peter Rogers, had also put his staff to work checking out the viability of the proposal. In her researches, his assistant, Sheila Cassells, had spotted a flaw in the financial arrangements that lay behind a system that would charge the network £8,000 per hour for the thirty-seven-hours-a-week service but also allow companies to opt in and out of the service to suit their own viewers' tastes. The old North–South divide was rearing its head again. She concluded:

> Two points need to be emphasised. First the cost to an individual company of any one programme will depend on the number and NAR shares of companies taking a particular programme. In other words, the reflexed (Note: 'reflexed' means the cost redistributed in NAR shares adjusted to the number and NARs of the companies taking the programme.) NAR shares will be calculated for *each* programme. Granada has not yet considered how to perform the accounting function.
>
> Secondly, the attached schedule shows the companies 'committed' to particular original programmes. However, the commitment does not extend beyond a verbal undertaking and I do not think we should place too much reliance on the schedule.
>
> ... I would find it difficult to give the night time network a seal of approval. (IBA internal memo, Miss Cassells to Mr Rogers, 8 July 1988)

The IBA's Director of Television, David Glencross, felt it necessary to seek assurance from ITV that the service was, in fact, financially underwritten by all companies. In truth part of the ITV delay had been the result of the companies' own suspicions of Granada's motivation. Ever territorially ambitious, Granada did believe that the new IBA dispensation for night-time – allowing one company to act as a sales house for others – could be made to work to its financial advantage in the longer term. In the end the fact that the limited size of any financial advantage that could accrue to Granada, and the pressure of time, probably did more to secure agreement than the company's attempts to reassure the network. But it was not until the end of the summer break that the Director of the Programme Planning Secretariat at the ITVA was finally able to respond to the IBA on the network's behalf:

> ... it should be clearly understood by the Authority that, for the period of the existing and extended franchise term, the Network guarantees to sustain the full night-time service across the entire ITV system. (Letter Director of Programme Planning, ITVA, to Director of Television, IBA, 31 August 1988)

Seven days later the IBA felt secure enough to announce:

> The IBA has approved the proposals which were submitted by the ITV companies for a night-time television service. All ITV regions will have programmes through the night by October 3. ITV and TV-am together will be providing Britain's first 24-hour television channel. (IBA News Release, 7 September 1988)

The service was of some benefit to the sleepless, the unemployed and, with its 5.00 a.m. ITN News, to growing numbers of people who, in an increasingly competitive jobs market, found they had to get up at that time to travel and be at work by 7.30–8.00 a.m. But it was not a service that was ever justified for ITV by the revenue it attracted and the government's threat to legislate for an auction of the night hours to a separate contractor would appear not to have been viable on a self-sustaining basis.

However, entrepreneurs with broadcasting ambitions, like Richard Branson of Virgin or Michael Green of Carlton Communications, might have been prepared to carry the loss on the margins of their other enterprises to gain a toe-hold in commercial television ahead of the new licensing system for ITV and, importantly, the advertising industry, with its bitter dislike of ITV's monopoly position, might well have been prepared to pay a premium price to a competitor – as it was to do when Channel Four was allowed to sell its own advertising four years later. So perhaps the threat had not been entirely without substance after all.

Charity Begins ... and Ends

One new programme development that was uniquely ITV's had a life that precisely spanned the period covered by this volume. It was the use of television for charity fund-raising, called *Telethon*, that had been effective in North America and Australia. The first British *Telethon* was on 3 October 1980 and the last on 18/19 July 1992. Started originally as a local programme at Thames Television by Simon Buxton of their social action *Help!* programme but developed into its network form by veteran producer, Diana Potter, it was later hosted by London Weekend Television, with contributions, as well as opt-outs by all the other companies in the network. *Telethon* was broadcast continuously for up to thirty-six hours – using a gamut of devices from sponsored climbs up the exteriors of tall office buildings, through celebrity guest performances and appeals to moving short video or film inserts demonstrating the real needs of the sick or disadvantaged or disabled, to get viewers to 'pledge' money to be distributed to charities.

During *Telethon*'s twelve-year lifespan, the five broadcasts raised £66 million, for causes ranging from Housing Associations catering specifically for disabled people to charities providing relief for the 'carers' of chronically sick patients.

The distribution of the money raised some practical and ethical difficulties at first but a well-administered Independent Television Telethon Trust (ITTT) was set up – drawing, in part, from the experience of Granada's *Reports Action* and Thames' *Help!* programmes in working with volunteer agencies. The ITTT Board had charities and independent regional trusts represented on it, as well as executives from the bank, the accountants and telephone company that supplied their services to the project without charge.

In the end a belief arose amongst some militant disabled people that the programmes 'demeaned' and 'stereotyped' them and there were demonstrations outside LWT's building before and during the programmes. There were scuffles with artists and staff arriving for the programme, with resultant adverse publicity. In fact, by the 1992 *Telethon*, all fifteen ITV companies had held disability awareness workshops for their staff and the programme held consultations with groups of disabled people to arrive at guidelines ranging from language ('never use the words "handicapped", "victim" or "afflicted by"') to how to interview a person in a wheelchair.

After the changes in ITV wrought as a result of the 1990 Broadcasting Act, the network consensus turned against continuing what had been a praiseworthy attempt to cater for the increasing desire on the part of viewers to respond to the needs of those shown by television to be less fortunate than themselves.

SECTION IV: ITV'S REGIONAL PROGRAMMES

The regional dimension to ITV's programming has been one of its most positive factors, culturally, commercially and politically, since its inception in 1955. There were, and remain, a number of reasons for this. Although regional advertising does not provide a very large proportion of any ITV company's revenue, each company has always needed to achieve a strong sense of its presence in its area as part of its individual 'brand' identity nationally, as well as to fulfil the terms of its contract (now its licence) with the IBA (now ITC). The two aims coincide most strongly in the provision of local news and weather.

In 1990 the IBA published a research paper *Mapping Regional Views* which confirmed that the majority of viewers valued their ITV regional service and particularly their local news. Over 60 per cent of ITV's regional output is news, news magazines and weather – an overall quantity that by the end of the Eighties was approaching 3,000 hours a year. The increase on previous periods was in part to do with efforts to target audiences more effectively with news that was relevant to them. It is an old journalistic truism that to be effective local news must make its audience feel they may see coverage that includes people and places they know personally. However, the companies' regional areas had been defined at their foundation by the coverage of the VHF transmitters for the old 405-line black and white service of the Fifties and early Sixties. The coverage areas were mostly too large to allow the separation of one set of community interests from another. With the coming of UHF transmissions covering smaller areas, separation became possible. In the Eighties, with the encouragement of the IBA, it became a reality.

By 1988 the fifteen ITV companies were providing separate local news broadcasts to twenty-one different areas. An example of the benefits of this fruitful fragmentation was the improvement of service achieved by Tyne Tees Television. The region contained the two distinct communities reflected in the company's name. The people of Newcastle-upon-Tyne, Jarrow and South Shields and the other Tyneside communities have different historical loyalties and cultural identities from those of the towns along the Tees: Middlesbrough, Stockton and, on the coast, the Hartlepools.

The company's regional news programme *Northern Life* faced particularly strong competition from BBC Newcastle, where the Regional Television Manager (Head of Programmes), Jim Graham (later the Managing Director of Border Television), had built up a strong team of editorial staff and presenters for the BBC's Regional News from the mid-Seventies.

Under its then Director of Programmes (subsequently Managing Director), Andy Allan, Tyne Tees began to provide a separate news service for the Teesside communities and the cathedral city of Durham, fed through the transmitter at Bilsdale that covered the southern half of the region. Allan, aware that improvements of service are of little use if they go unnoticed, combined this move with a schedule change by which he time-shifted the then still popular motel-based network 'soap', *Crossroads* (a series for the termination of which he was later to be responsible, when Director of Programmes at Central), to a slot opposite the BBC's Regional News. The combined moves put *Northern Life* firmly back into the region's weekly top ten programmes after some years of BBC domination.

Other companies met this need for a better focused local service with different types of initiative. Anglia Television, with its large regional area, stretching from Great Yarmouth in the east to Peterborough and Northampton over one hundred and twenty miles to the west and from King's Lynn in the north to Ipswich and Chelmsford sixty or so miles to the south, adopted a different approach. When the IBA's Chairman, Lord Thomson, was asked in April 1982 to open Anglia's new studio complex, with its permanent studio for *About Anglia*, the programme was able to call on local news centres with reporters and camera crews permanently based in Peterborough, Northampton, Luton, Chelmsford and King's Lynn. The following year the King's Lynn centre fell victim to Yorkshire Television's increasing competition from that company's separate news service dedicated to the area and radiated from the Belmont transmitter for the east and south-east of Yorkshire's region. Increasingly in a number of regions the better service of the public was to become a tool for expansion of viewership and thus of revenue. By mid-1990 YTV was producing three different local editions of its news programme, *Calendar,* and Anglia had formally moved to the production of separate news services for Anglia East and Anglia West.

One region had always been designated as 'split' in the company's contract with the IBA. Harlech Television (later HTV), with its franchise to cover Wales and the West of England was required to reflect the full culture of Wales – including the language – and to provide a completely separate programme service, including a separate regional news bulletin, for the West of England. On 1 November 1982 HTV was relieved of the requirement to transmit a regional news in the Welsh language (*Y Dydd*) by the arrival on air of a complete channel in Welsh: Sianel Pedwar Cymru – Channel Four Wales (S4C). Many of the new channel's current affairs programmes were provided by HTV under contract (its news being provided by the BBC). HTV was then able also to provide a fuller news and current affairs service for its English-speaking audience. (Note: the commitment of STV and Grampian to carry a small proportion of programmes in Gaelic, to help sustain that language culture in Scotland, continued through the period. Channel Television, ITV's smallest company, also provided for its minority culture with *Les Français Chez Vous* and amongst the major companies Central, Granada and YTV made increasing provision for Hindi, Urdu and other Asian-language speakers in their regions.)

Besides Wales and the West, the IBA had created in 1982 two other formal 'dual regions': East and West Midlands, under the Central Television contract, and South and South East, under that of TVS. The start of Central's East Midlands service was delayed by industrial disputes (see Chapter 2) until the autumn of 1983. Duality in the South of England did not have an easy birth either – as the man who had been Features Editor for the outgoing contractor and became the Senior Producer for the new South East news operation recalled:

One of the major tasks facing the newly formed company was the planning and construction of the new TVS headquarters in the South-East ... at Vintners Park just south of Maidstone. However, that building was not going to be ready until the middle of 1982 and negotiations secured the continued use of Southern's small studio in Russell Street at Dover ... It was by no means large enough to accommodate the thirty-plus team of journalists, technicians and support staff that had been assembled to start operating the South East news service. Extra accommodation was found further along the road above the workshop of a fast tyre and exhaust fitter. (Written contribution by Laurie Upshon)

TVS' Controller of News and Current Affairs, Bob Southgate, initially judged that the scale of expansion of the news to cover the dual region effectively required an increase of news crews from Southern's three (with some 'stringer' support) to fourteen. In the end the company settled on nine – still a three-fold expansion. Initially too the programme structure of the 'dual' news was expansive (if complicated) and is worth detailing here – in part for the light it may shed on TVS Managing Director James Gatward's view of ITN in relation to his company (see Chapter 6).

> Southgate had proposed a complex structure for the nightly news programme. It would straddle the hour between 5.30 and 6.30, hammocking the ITN news bulletin. The first segment of the news programme before ITN would be purely local, concentrating on stories from each of the parts of the region. The editorial team devised a process by which they were able to take off the ITN titles and end credits – running them on the monitor behind the presenter – and introduce the national and international news from their London studios.
>
> The middle segment of the programme was designed to reflect the whole region. It would take the best stories from the South and South East and run them in a 20 minute segment. That was to be produced on alternate nights by the South and South East teams. The final segment of the programme, lasting for another 10 minutes, would revert to a more localised service.
>
> The system worked badly – it provided no clear vision for the programme and created technical problems in trafficking material. It became obvious that when there was a major story in the region that was also of national interest, there would be considerable duplication ... within a short time it was decided to run the two programmes separately and abandon the early start. (Ibid.)

By October 1982 the new Maidstone studios were ready for use and thereafter the IBA noted that '*Coast to Coast* for the South and *Coast to Coast* for the South East became quite distinct with their own teams of reporters and presenters and different styles which appealed to the two areas' (IBA Annual Report, 1982/83).

Twice during the period smaller regional companies were called upon to provide ITV's initial response to major disasters. In 1988 Grampian Television won great praise for its coverage response to the massive explosion and fire on the North Sea oil rig Piper Alpha. As well as news coverage, this included the instant mounting of a special – *The Time ... The Place* – for the network the following morning.

Just before Christmas the following year another horrific event, causing a double devastation, took place just to the north of the Solway Firth. A Pan American Airways Boeing 747 exploded in mid-air and major portions of the plane crashed on a little town called Lockerbie in the early evening. The tragic loss of both passengers and townspeople, and the likelihood of terrorist involvement, drew media attention from around the world. Border Television's studios were only twenty minutes' drive from the site. Staff were attending their Christmas party at the time of the crash and arrived at the location and provided the first reports still in party clothes. The rapid response meant that coverage by the tiny company provided 80 per cent of the material for the ITN Special on the tragedy.

Perhaps uniquely, the small size of the Border area's population allowed the company to cooperate with the emergency services in summoning off-duty medical staff to the local hospitals by superimposing captions over the normal programme service. Local news updates were inserted between programmes and carried appeals to people not to make unnecessary telephone calls. Border went on to win a special award from the Royal Television Society for its journalistic work that night and in the ensuing days. The company also provided live coverage for the network of the memorial service held at Lockerbie early in the New Year. The sensitivity of Border's handling of the story on behalf of ITV, in comparison with that of other organisations, also drew praise from local residents.

Amongst the major companies, Granada was able to open its new Liverpool news studio – required by the IBA – early in 1982. However, use of the Electronic News Gathering (ENG) equipment – on which the full operation of the new system depended – was held up by an industrial dispute until the autumn.

Central, having finally started their East Midlands news in 1983, were criticised by viewers in the south of their large region who felt that they were not properly served by Birmingham. Concerned that, whatever system was arrived at for renewal of franchises, this would count against them with the regulator, the company took the advice of Bob Southgate (who had been recruited from TVS by Central's new Director of Programmes, Andy Allan in 1984 to be Central's Controller of News and Current Affairs) to open up a Central South news operation for the Ridge Hill and Oxford transmitters – covering an area stretching from Milton Keynes in the east to Monmouth in the west, and the southern Cotswolds in the north to Swindon in the south.

The capital cost would be £3 million but the operation was to be one of the first in ITV to benefit from post-industrial relations legislation management thinking, where five people would do the work that would previously have required twenty-five, with slimline annual running costs of £2 million as a result. This slimming down was to be achieved by the use of a fully computerised newsroom. The computer would control the videotape machines, caption and the newsreaders' teleprompt equipment. Directors using remote controlled cameras would do their own vision-mixing and there was to be no floor manager. Work started on the conversion of an industrial unit at Abingdon, to the south of Oxford on 5 September 1988. Just over four months later – 9 January 1989 – *Central News South* was launched. Laurie Upshon, who had followed Southgate from TVS to Central and been one of the planning team, remembers it well:

> The opening night was a shambles. The control systems between the computer and the automated tape player seized up just as the programme went on the air. None of the location reports compiled during the day were available and the presenters were left wondering whether they were rehearsing for *It'll Be Alright*

On The Night. Only the presence of ski-jumper Eddie 'The Eagle' Edwards, a local hero, as a live guest stopped the programme becoming a total disaster.

The launch party became a wake and Edwards was invited back the following night – just in case. This time the computer worked and the programme was transmitted to double the previous night's audience – an audience anticipating a repeat performance of the opening night. They were disappointed by the outcome, but not by the programme. In the ensuing 12 months *Central News South* achieved audience shares of up to 50% of the total television viewing. The sales team attracted 50 new advertisers in the first year, bringing in an additional £1 million in revenue. (Written contribution by Laurie Upshon)

For the London companies local news was an IBA requirement, as elsewhere. However, it had to overcome a double difficulty not faced by ITV companies serving other regions. The first is demographic. London, as a cosmopolitan capital city, is populated only in part by people born and bred there. And, paradoxically, native-born Londoners seldom identify with London as a whole. They may have local loyalties – sometimes fierce – but these tend to be to a particular territory in the city.

The other major part of the capital's population are transients – people who have come to the capital only to pursue their careers. Some may settle and bring up families in London but their identification with their locality is often slight, their sense of 'home' lying more with their place of upbringing – a city, town or village perhaps hundreds of miles from London. These peculiarities face London television news editors with a very distinctive task. Unlike the London evening newspaper they do not have a captive audience of train and bus passengers, neither can they provide a hard copy events guide to be kept for reference. In consequence, much of their news agenda is made up of crime, local politics and transport breakdowns – not a mix generally calculated to bring a warm glow to hearth and home.

The second, more particular, difficulty for the London companies' provision of local news was the London split. The weekday contractor, Thames, produced a nightly *Thames News* for the area. This was presented for the fourteen years up to 1991 by the ex-ITN newscaster (and successful novelist), Andrew Gardner. Its editorial and reporting team was of such a high quality that it frequently lost staff to more senior roles in other companies. Towards the end of the period the company created a number of local news bureaux around the region. Thames public relations staff found it easy to remember the initial three as 'all the fords – Dartford, Watford and Guildford'. The biggest London regional live event coverage during the period was the three-hour Thames' special *Safe from the Sea,* on the opening of the new Thames flood barrier by the Queen in 1985.

The London Weekend contract up until 1981 had required the company to start broadcasting at 7.00 p.m. on Fridays. In the new contract for 1982 onwards the start time was brought forward to 5.15 p.m. This change brought with it a potential revenue benefit, for which LWT had lobbied, but if the company had been asked to set up a full news operation much of the benefit would have been expended on that. The IBA settled upon a less than happy compromise by which there was a half length *Thames News* prior to LWT's taking over with their new *The 6 0'Clock Show*. This was edited initially by Greg Dyke and introduced by Michael Aspel and Janet Street-Porter. Its mix of local reporting, chat and entertainment, produced to national network standards, did a great deal to anchor the majority audience to ITV in London on Friday evenings. However, the IBA remained critical of the London news situation throughout the Eighties, seeking a more cooperative effort between the two London companies. It was not until the new licence period, when Carlton and LWT fused their news provision into a joint company, London News Network, which provides bulletins across the whole seven days, that this criticism was answered.

Friday night was (and still is) a key night for regional programmes. The network schedule ceased at the end of *News at Ten* and the regions went their different ways. Some, like Granada and STV ran previews of regional sport during the autumn and winter, LWT used the period to carry its weekly *The London Programme* covering regional current affairs. One of the more audacious offerings was Central's live *Central Weekend*, billed as 'The programme that takes sides on issues and puts them before special guests and an audience, live – anything can happen.' 'Anything' not infrequently required presenters Andy Craig and Sue Jay to physically restrain participants from coming to blows with their opponents. Its presence on Central's screens owed something to Tyne Tees' *Friday Live* and Andy Allan's move from that company to Central. Viewers in the Midlands found the formula compulsive viewing.

Another perhaps even bolder Friday night venture was started in the late Eighties across the water in Ulster. *Kelly's People* was (and still is) primarily an entertainment talk show but in it presenter Gerry Kelly does not shrink from confronting his audience with the difficult issues of the region – not so much sectarian issues as those for the whole community that are not usually dealt with by UTV's current affairs programmes – matters like the growing drugs problem in Ulster, the extraordinarily high level of homophobia in the province and scandals in the Catholic Church. In eight years *Kelly's People* has become a Friday night institution in Northern Ireland and commands a larger viewing share than any of the other ITV regional programmes in that slot.

On Friday nights most of the 'seven day' companies also carried programmes offering some form of a platform on which local Members of Parliament (and, later in the period, MEPs) could face questions on local issues. At Anglia the rather staid *Members Only* gave way to *Cross Question*, Border had *Question Time*, Grampian *Crossfire*, Granada *Under Fire*, STV *Ways and Means*, TVS *Agenda* (on Sunday at lunchtime), TSW *Politics South West*, YTV *Calendar Commentary*, and Channel Television had *Report Politics*, dealing with the politics of the Islands' States. Other companies chose to deal with politics in their general current affairs programmes.

These local platforms had an important further purpose for the companies. The hospitality after the programme was an ideal moment for the company's managing director to raise his company's concerns about the government's media or financial policies. These opportunities were much used after the Peacock Report and right through to the passing of the Broadcasting Act in 1990.

Grampian Television was particularly effective in getting the MPs from its remote region interested enough in its ideas for three of them, one from each party, to put themselves forward for involvement in the Committee Stage of the Broadcasting Bill. These were Robert Maclennan, the Liberal Democrat member for Caithness and Sutherland, John McAllion, the Labour MP for Dundee East and the Rt. Hon. Alick Buchanan-Smith, the Conservative MP for Angus and Mearns. Robert Maclennan became a key figure on the Committee.

However, such fragmentation of lobbying, however valuable to ITV companies on specific issues like ownership, did not help to create a clear image of the views of Independent Television as a whole – a factor which allowed (and required) the IBA to make much of the running with proposals for amendments during the debate on the Broadcasting Bill.

Besides the 60 per cent of news and current affairs there was, and is, a wealth of regional programming in the other 40 per cent. These other programmes include arts, health in many regions, farming in all except London, and, in every region, social action and religion. Two significant developments in most regions in the later Eighties, reflecting the times, were local programmes dealing with unemployment (usually under the title *Jobline*) and those seeking public cooperation on behalf of the police. (STV's *Crime Desk* and LWT's veteran *Police Five* were precursors of a new series *Crimestoppers*. Co-commissioned by Thames and LWT from an independent producer this was a series in which several other regions joined.) And from 1986 another social concern arose in which ITV's regional dimension was to prove valuable:

> All the ITV companies supplemented the national coverage given to the AIDS problem with their own local programmes, which were able to consider the subject as it applied specifically to their own region. One particular benefit was that such programmes were able to join forces with local organisations and agencies in offering advice and help to viewers. (IBA Annual Report, 1986/87)

Finally, several companies made drama and entertainment programmes for regional audiences. STV's *Take the High Road* was a twice-weekly soap opera of Scottish country life which was originally run at particular times of the year, but by 1986 its popularity led the company to make it a year-round feature of its regional schedule. It was also a valuable training ground for staff for STV's network drama output. Granada used some of its regional slots for entertainment. Some of this, like *Multi-Million Viewer Audition, Off Peak* and *The Every McGann Show* was also helpful for the development of talent and formats for later sale to the network (or C4). Strength in regional programmes was, and remains, an important factor both for the company concerned and its relationships with its audience and the IBA, but it is also the foundation upon which the network itself is built. Even in the competitive Nineties which might be thought to be an adverse climate there is growth in regional programming. In 1993 all the ITV companies exceeded the number of hours of regional programming required in their licences (the requirements being a reflection of what had been promised in their applications). A total of 163 hours 3 minutes per week was required and an average of 180 hours 22 minutes was achieved. Some companies exceeded their requirement quite considerably; LWT was required to transmit 3 hours 31 minutes of local programmes and actually transmitted 5 hours 20 minutes a week on average. Central's figures were 15 hours and 21 minutes and 19 hours 26 minutes respectively. Other companies, like Yorkshire, Meridian and Westcountry, broadcast up to half an hour more a week than their requirement (*ITC Notes*, No. 21, September 1994).

One final note on regional developments. For economic and, to a lesser extent, demographic reasons, collaboration between companies became more frequent in some areas of regional programming. Joint transmission between regions had always existed for non-networked football matches but now collaboration in production spread to other programme areas like farming and the arts. Later the IBA felt it necessary formally to redefine regional programming to validate this development:

> ... Certain co-productions (or co-commissions) between not more than three regional C3 licensees may also be counted as regional programmes by each of those licensees, provided each programme contains material of particular interest to the regions concerned. (*ITC Notes*, No. 21, September 1994)

Viewer Consultative Councils (VCCs)

Towards the end of the period the IBA's monitoring of companies' programmes by its network of National and Regional Officers was given an additional dimension. Since 1970, the IBA had carried out a major annual survey to track public attitudes. Initially entitled *Attitudes to Broadcasting*, it was later renamed *Television: the Public's View*. In addition to core questions, repeated annually, thus providing valuable opinion trends, the survey was adapted to cover topical issues although it related mainly to the IBA's responsibilities for consumer protection (for example, taste, decency, offence and impartiality) and programme standards. In the 1980s this systematic measurement of public opinion based on statistically representative samples of the viewing population was complemented by feedback from the General Advisory Council, a large, rather cumbersome national committee which tended to be skewed towards older, middle-class viewers, which had been set up in 1964.

In 1990, a decision was taken to set up ten Viewer Consultative Councils (VCCs) based in Wales, Northern Ireland, Scotland and seven in England. VCC members were specifically recruited to represent the UK population in terms of age, gender, geographical location, ethnic origin and occupation. Their function was to discuss and advise on television services within each of the Channel 3 regions. Quarterly meetings were generally attended by a Commission member and by the relevant Regional Officer. One of their first jobs was to comment on the applications for the Channel 3 licences although this was supplemented by a wider public consultation when the applications (minus the confidential business plans) were made available for scrutiny in all major UK libraries.

4

INDUSTRIAL RELATIONS, INDEPENDENT PRODUCTION AND THE COST OF PROGRAMMES – ITV THE 'LAST BASTION'?

Mrs Thatcher twice sounded the warning note to existing companies, that 'television is the last bastion of restrictive practices'. Her vehemence on industrial relations at one point bracketed ITV with the English National Opera and Covent Garden – causing Mr Jeremy Isaacs, chief executive of Channel Four, who is about to take over as administrator of the Royal Opera House, to protest that he had often been chastised for things that he had done but never for things he hadn't yet got to. (Peter Fiddick, writing in the *Guardian*, 22 September 1987, about a seminar Mrs Thatcher held at 10 Downing Street the previous day with broadcasting industry leaders)

ITV's then Chairman of Council, David McCall, who was present at the Downing Street seminar, was to tell an audience of ITV trade unionists a month later that 'The Prime Minister's remark ... covered not only ITV but the BBC.' However, the concept of ITV as 'the last bastion of restrictive practices' was not one that many people – even in ITV – would have sought to challenge in 1982 or even in early 1984. But, as was so often the case, the Prime Minister's conviction had by this time outlasted its relevance.

Though ITV was not formally to abandon national negotiations with the broadcasting unions entirely until the beginning of 1989, by 1987 most ITV companies were facing up to their industrial relations problems and beginning to use the government's trade union legislation, the Employment Acts of 1980, 1982 and 1984, as one tool in the process. Of particular relevance were those parts of the latter two Acts that ended the 'closed shop' and secondary strike action.

An important tool it was to be. The events that led up to the1979 ten-week national strike that blacked out the ITV network had demonstrated how easy it was for the 'craft', or 'staff', unions (the Association of Cinematograph, Television and Allied

Technicians – ACTT, the National Association of Theatrical, Television and Kine Employees – NATTKE (note: after merging with the BBC/IBA 'house' union in 1984 NATTKE became the Broadcasting and Entertainment Trades Alliance – BETA) and the Electrical, Electronic, Telecommunications and Plumbing Union – EETPU) to work effectively together to spread disputes from production to broadcast transmission and from region to region. This could now be prevented.

An additional lever available to ITV managements by 1987 was the success, expansion, cost effectiveness and increasing political clout of the independent producers, spawned by the requirement in the Broadcasting Act of 1980 (Section 4(3)(b)) that Channel Four must obtain 'a substantial proportion' of its programmes from independents. There was now an alternative to in-house production. On the broadcast side, as simpler and more automated transmission equipment became available even unskilled members of management could operate it. And, importantly, managements were now increasingly determined to emerge from the long shadow of 1979 and all that.

These factors were to prove decisive in the industrial relations battles in ITV in the second half of the Eighties. But at the start of the period the longest-running dispute to hit ITV and its new stablemates C4 and TV-am was, strangely, one in which neither those organisations nor the craft unions were involved.

Actors versus Advertisers

The 'performance', or 'talent', unions (the British Actors' Equity Association – Equity – and the Musicians' Union) wielded a different sort of power in broadcasting. Giving artistic performances in small groups, or sometimes alone, actors and musicians were (and are) indeed vulnerable to exploitation by employers. And, over the years, the performance unions built up formidable rules and sanctions to protect their members.

However, television is also vulnerable. Without actors, comedy performers and musicians an entertainment medium cannot function. (Of course writers are also important to that function but, lacking the possibility of a 'closed shop' policy they do not – to the chagrin of some – wield such power.)

In commercial television, performer power extends beyond the making of programmes to the making of money. It is possible to make television advertisements without actors but advertising industry experience was that for many products the dramatised form is the most effective.

So, when the advertising industry's negotiating trade association, the Institute of Practitioners in Advertising – IPA – wrote to Equity on 9 March 1982 to propose fees and residuals to be paid for performances in advertisements to be broadcast on the new stations Channel Four and TV-am, they appeared to have misjudged the strength of their position when they proposed that payments be related to audience size. The Basic Studio Fee (BSF) for actors appearing in commercials was a relatively small component of what they were paid; the residual fees paid for each showing provided the major part of their earnings. It was the latter that the advertisers proposed to link to audience numbers. Keeping the BSF at the same level would allow them to show the advertisements on any channel, simply adjusting the residuals as required. Even by the most optimistic projections for C4 and TV-am, the earnings of actors appearing on the new outlets would only be about 25 per cent of what they received for an ITV showing.

Equity was prepared to acknowledge that there should be some relationship of performers' earnings from commercials to the earning power of the advertisements but were looking for a figure of about 75 per cent of the ITV level. To outsiders the gap looked susceptible to a negotiated settlement. But to take that view was to ignore the volatility of Equity's Council (their elected executive committee) on the one hand and the hubris of the advertising industry on the other.

Talks between the two sides during the summer and autumn of 1982 broke down and on 2 October Equity instructed its 30,000 members not to work on commercials for C4 unless paid the rates that applied to ITV. This was precisely a month before Channel Four was due to go on the air. Oddly, when the new channel started up on time on 2 November, the fact that there were no advertisements shown in the Granada, Scottish and Ulster areas was due to local ACTT disputes (see below) and not to the IPA/Equity stand-off. Commercials were shown on C4 in other regions and, to get round the Equity rules, they were usually made with film or stills of the product with music, text and sometimes non-union voice-overs. They were few in number and, for the most part, not strong on impact. Now the start of the second new opportunity for advertising on British television, Breakfast Television, to be provided for the first time on ITV by a new and separate ITV contractor, TV-am, though delayed from the autumn to allow C4 to establish itself, was looming.

The Independent Broadcasting Authority had no official standing in the dispute between the actors and the advertisers but it did have very particular responsibilities for ensuring that the new television services were started and continued to broadcast. The IBA was, therefore, inevitably drawn into taking a role in the dispute. And in Lord Thomson, ex-Chairman of the Advertising Standards Authority, and John Whitney with his knowledge of both the acting and advertising worlds from his days as a programme maker and then a commercial radio executive, the IBA had a high-level team well qualified to act as peacemakers. Also in Peter Rogers and his finance department they had the means to project the results of all the possible options in the complex formulae put forward by both sides.

At the Authority meeting of 2 December 1982, Thomson sought and received support for an initiative by his Director General to try to resolve the dispute. By the final meeting of the year, on 15 December, the view on the eighth floor of Brompton Road was optimistic:

> The Director General said that TV-am were hopeful of concluding a satisfactory arrangement with the parties based on a new formula related to a system of royalty payments and the value of advertising campaigns. If successfully concluded it

might be possible to translate the arrangement to ... Channel Four. If, however, the Channel Four situation remained deadlocked, arbitration had not been ruled out but it was not being considered at this stage for fear of further entrenching attitudes. (Minutes of Authority meeting 559, 15 December 1982)

It was a few days later that Brian Tesler chose to send his *cri de coeur* seeking to reduce LWT's programme commitments because of the impact of the dispute on the company's projected earnings from C4 (see Chapter 3).

But, despite a New Year's Eve intervention by Lord Thomson to set up an IBA chaired working party in an attempt to facilitate the reaching of an interim agreement, a fortnight before TV-am was due to start on 1 February 1983, talks between the IPA and Equity broke down once again.

For TV-am this was disaster. Unlike C4, which received a guaranteed revenue (the Fourth Channel Subscription) from ITV in return for ITV selling the new channel's airtime, TV-am was to sell its own airtime, like any other contractor, and live off the proceeds. However, TV-am had an additional problem. As the company approached the end of 1982 it was still some £7.5 million short of the £15.5 million capital it needed. Potential investors were clearly likely to be frightened off by any threat to revenue. And if the limited advertising on C4 was anything to go by, then the IPA/Equity dispute would strangle TV-am at birth. (The full story of TV-am will be told in Volume 6 of *Independent Television in Britain*.)

The publicly visible opposing personalities in the dispute were Peter Plouviez, General Secretary of Equity and David Wheeler, Director of the IPA. Plouviez had spent twenty-seven years as a professional trade union executive. Although never an actor, he had a genuine empathy with his members and a shrewdly political intellect. Wheeler did have a background in marketing and advertising but had been a trades association executive for only four years. Unlike some negotiators, their relationship never became close. Also they each had distinctly unusual bodies to whom they reported.

The Equity Council was elected by the membership; the more influential Executive Committee was elected by the Council from its own ranks. The active (that is, vocal) membership was at this time dominated by the left. But despite that, the bulk of members voted with caution and no hard-left candidates like the Redgraves or de la Tours were elected to the Council. Miriam Margolyes appears to have been the most radical of those elected in June 1982. However successive Councils, led by John Barron and Hugh Manning, were responsive to their members' views and took a hard-line approach. Prosperous advertising and television industries should be made to pay as much as could be negotiated for their members. Activists' lobbying of the Council and Executive was to add a certain volatility to the union's policy decision making.

The IPA membership was primarily composed of advertising agencies. The advertisers' association was the Incorporated Society of British Advertisers (ISBA). But the IPA was the negotiating body and through it the interests of the advertisers were also represented. Advertisers and agencies had somewhat different priorities. In principle both were concerned to keep the already high cost of commercials down in any way they could; but most agencies' fees were linked to the total cost of any campaign and they were generally more concerned with what they saw as ITV's tendency to abuse its monopoly to drive up airtime costs. This limited the number of advertisers who were able to afford to advertise on television – the medium from which the agencies received the highest fees. It could be said, therefore, that the IPA members were more concerned to 'punish' ITV by a prolonged dispute and ISBA members the more truly desirous to keep the cost of commercials down by confronting Equity.

There were other factors of particular difficulty in the negotiations. A proposal that based its calculations for payment on audience size immediately called into question the accuracy of the existing audience measurement systems.

The new Broadcasters' Audience Research Board (BARB) had arisen out of the painful forced union of the old ITV Joint Industry Committee for Television Advertising Research (JICTAR) and the BBC's Audience Research Department. The methodology (and, usually the results) of those two organisations had differed. Each had produced figures that had tended to favour its owner. It had taken the Annan Committee to point out that a joint venture with more objective results would be preferable. But the joint venture, BARB, had only started functioning in August 1981 and Equity was well aware that a year later the audience figures it produced were still a matter of controversy between the television and advertising industries. It was a weakness upon which the union was able to play heavily in the coming months.

Meanwhile, TV-am was not alone in feeling victimised by the dispute. At the end of February the annual *Marketing Week* Conference took place in Monte Carlo. Traditionally this was a battleground for grudge fights between Directors of Advertising and ITV Sales Directors during the day's proceedings followed by *bonhomie* together in the evening. Key speakers were usually able to take a lofty strategic view. But when Paul Fox, as Chairman of ITV's Council, stood up to address the conference he was his usual gruff self – but he chose to wear the network's heart on his sleeve:

> ... we are in the midst of a traumatic dispute; a dispute in which we, the ITV companies, are not involved – and yet we are the chief victims. ITV is suffering; Channel 4, for which we pay, is bleeding. That is the message which on the eve of this conference I have tried to put across to our advertisers. You should know that I have written to fifty top advertisers to say so. The independent television industry is being damaged – and whatever fine words may be uttered here today and tomorrow, that is the overriding message of this conference: ITV is suffering. And if this dispute goes on, there won't be a conference in two years time.
>
> These are no idle words. They will, I hope, be heard here, and in Belgrave Square (the offices of the IPA) and in Harley Street (Equity), because if I may

say so, enough is enough. (Speech by Paul Fox to *Marketing Week* Conference, Monte Carlo, 24 February 1983)

Some advertisers in his audience saw this as hyperbole and few were moved. They knew that in January ITV had asked the IBA to let them sell more than the normal limit of six minutes an hour average of advertising time. The IBA had not been willing to go that far but they had allowed ITV to 'redistribute' two minutes an hour extra into peak time from less lucrative parts of the schedule. A typical reaction to Paul Fox's speech was sent to him at ITCA:

> From our standpoint, it seems just another example of contractors wishing to exploit irresponsibly their monopoly selling position in the hope that cost increases for television advertising will have a fair chance of simply being passed on, to first the advertiser and then the consumer.
>
> I can assure you, however, that in the case of this Company any serious escalation in actors' costs will not be funded by increases in the total advertising appropriation but by reduction in the media budget. Furthermore this Equity threat and your attitude to it are just further factors, on top of the appalling decline in TV-AM ratings and value which are causing us, seriously and actively, to consider moving money from television to other media. (Letter Managing Director, Pedigree Petfoods, to Chairman, ITCA, 28 March 1983)

Of course there was posturing on both sides of this argument. Each knew that it needed the other. But clearly at this point, as far as the advertisers were concerned, there was not going to be a speedy conclusion to the dispute. And the actors had little to gain by giving ground. They would not even accept arbitration by ACAS – though that organisation did supply some conciliation services during the dispute – which was to last another twenty long months.

In fact it was the IBA, rather than ACAS, which by March was looking to provide a conciliator role. Lord Thomson wrote to both the protagonists in the middle of the month to propose a Commission of Enquiry, serviced by the IBA but with an independent chairman. The IPA responded positively to the idea but, as recorded in the minutes of the Authority meeting of 23 March:

> Mr Plouviez had stated that the Council of Equity did not believe that the setting up of an independent inquiry would lead to the settlement of the dispute. (Minutes of Authority meeting 563, 23 March 1983)

This was not the last time that the Equity Council was to reject a proposal offering a way forward. But the IBA was now to find itself increasingly centre stage in the dispute. Its most senior figures understood the business, they had the back-up to calculate the consequences of the various options for both sides and they had a motivation which was transparent to all and unbiased as between the parties. The

IBA simply wanted properly to nourish their new television services and sustain their old one. Though for reasons of commercial sensitivity they kept the desperate state of TV-am's finances from the parties.

By now new 'stars' were arising from advertisers' attempts to circumvent the Equity ban. The most unlikely of these was Ian Melrose, the sales and marketing director of Wall's Meat. Unlike the Freddie Lakers and Bernard Matthews of this world, Melrose was a reluctant performer whose slightly truculent attitude to being on screen but visible relish for his company's sausages seemed to his advertising agency to be right for the job. Other products turned to non-Equity celebrities. Barbara Woodhouse (the BBC's dog training lady, of 'Staaay!' fame) sold eggs to go with Mr Melrose's sausages, for instance. But many advertisers were reluctant to buy airtime on the new channels in these circumstances. The resulting scramble for airtime on ITV inflated prices and increased the already high tension in relations between the ITV companies and the advertisers. And fewer and fewer actors were being employed in commercials. Torin Douglas, an authoritative commentator on the advertising industry, in an article for the *Sunday Times* on 6 February 1983, charted a drop of the use of actors from 2.54 per commercial in 1981 down to 1.91 in 1982. (That was partly because of an increase in repeat fees for commercials on ITV which started operating in 1981 but the dispute was sharpening the decline.) Clearly by the summer of 1983 everybody was beginning to lose out. Pressure increased for a settlement.

In June John Whitney wrote to both sides proposing a joint IPA/Equity working party with an independent chairman and independent researchers to provide accurate and neutral data to both sides. The Equity Council welcomed the data supply but rejected the joint working party idea. They said they had new proposals to put to the IPA.

In September the negotiators of both sides had agreed a complex interim agreement. It had supplementary payments for low-paid performers (a key consideration for Equity), an 'access fee' of 100 per cent of the BSF when the commercial was first played on C4 or TV-am and thereafter a 'tapering' reduction of 'use fees' (residual payments) the more the commercial was played. These reduced from 55 per cent of the ITV rate to 20 per cent on C4 and 37 per cent to 13 per cent on TV-am. This was more than IPA members had hoped for but they were prepared to accept it. But when Plouviez put it to his Council it was rejected. The IPA was outraged:

The IPA is astounded by the decision of Equity's Council to reject the terms of an Interim Agreement on repeat fees for Channel Four and TV-am which had been jointly arrived at with the Equity negotiators. Four weeks earlier the Equity Council had recommended a similar agreement to their members for acceptance ...

The IPA is, therefore, now forced to the conclusion that it is impossible to negotiate meaningfully with Equity and that many weeks of apparently successful negotiation have proved worthless. (IPA Press Statement, 20 September 1983)

By October TV-am, eight months after it went on air, was on the point of financial collapse. Its new Chief Executive, the Conservative MP Jonathan Aitken, (the presence of a sitting MP as the Chief Executive of an independent television company was a result of one of the many 'needs must' temporary relaxations of the normal rules by the IBA in respect of TV-am during this period) wrote to the Home Secretary, the Chancellor of the Exchequer and the Minister for Arts, seeking their intervention in the dispute, claiming that the company was losing £500,000 a month and that 'If this haemorrhage of income continues much longer we will almost certainly be forced to go into liquidation' (Letter from Jonathan Aitken MP to Douglas Hurd, Home Secretary, 6 October 1983). Hurd replied on behalf of the other addressees. He was sympathetic to Aitken's frustration that TV-am was in a third-party position and unable to influence the resolution of the dispute, he praised the work of the IBA (and John Whitney in particular) but he concluded 'I do not believe that Government can or should intervene directly, but we will do what we can to encourage the peacemakers' (Letter Douglas Hurd, Home Secretary, to Jonathan Aitken MP, 26 October 1983).

There then followed a nine-month stalemate quite unprecedented in even the industrial relations of British commercial television. TV-am continued to be the hardest hit by the dispute but a combination of financial restructuring and populist on-screen initiatives driven by the company's young and dynamic Director of Programmes, Greg Dyke (the puppet character Roland Rat being the most memorable), both somewhat reluctantly agreed by the IBA on an interim basis, allowed the company to survive.

The financial restructuring of TV-am in the spring of 1984 (making available a crucial extra £4 million) had enlarged the shareholding of the Australian financier Kerry Packer, whose company, Consolidated, was now to be represented on the TV-am Board by someone who was not unfamiliar with the ITV system.

He was Bruce Gyngell, whose background was as a reporter and commentator in Australia, where he achieved no little renown. But he had surprised everyone by moving in 1972 to Britain to become Lew Grade's right-hand man at ATV after an attempted 'coup' to oust Grade from day-to-day control of the company by his New Zealander predecessor, Robin Gill. He stayed at ATV until he returned to Australia in 1975.

At the beginning of May 1984 Gyngell took over the running of TV-am from the controversial Jonathan Aitken, with the title Managing Director. He was an unconventional leader but his experience and determination stabilised the company – though he lost it the services of Greg Dyke and later he was to lead it into its own distinctive confrontation with unions (see Volume 6, *Independent Television in Britain*).

Meanwhile, the following month the annual elections for Equity's Council and Executive swept away the previous intransigence of the left majority. Activists, Miriam Margolyes amongst others, were voted out, and from the more pragmatic new members, Derek Bond was elected as President. This opened the way for new talks between Equity and the IPA. The two sides met, under the chairmanship of

John Whitney, on 23 July and again on 10 August. By 18 September agreement was reached. The low pay supplements remained but the complex 'tapering' of residuals over the number of showings was abandoned in favour of a straight 55 per cent of the ITV rate for showings on Channel Four and 37 per cent for those on TV-am. The IPA had won on the matter of principle of not paying ITV rates for the new, and smaller audienced, outlets. Equity had got almost double what they had originally been offered.

Thus, after almost two years, ended the longest-running dispute to affect independent broadcasting in Britain.

The Managers versus the Technicians

An indication of the potential abilities available in the active membership of the broadcasting unions was that there were no less than two elected ACTT officials in major ITV companies who later became members of their company's Board. One was David Elstein at Thames. The other was Greg Dyke at London Weekend.

Elstein, after four years as an independent producer, returned to the London weekday contractor as Director of Programmes in January 1986. He remembers the impact on him of returning to the industrial relations of an ITV company:

> It felt like stepping back into a time warp. Virtually the first thing I stepped into was a PAs (Production Assistants') dispute. One of those regular ACTT issues of ... the '60s and '70s, and there it was still in the '80s. And it felt so alien. After four years of working in an environment where those things just didn't happen, you just got on and made programmes, it was really hard to cope with ... And it was very painful as well, because I knew most of the PAs personally, having worked with a lot of them. And it was quite hard to say to them 'look, your jobs are coming to an end. For most of you there is no need for you any longer at Thames. There is no need for PAs to go on locations. The only PAs that are strictly needed are in the studio for live shows.' Which most of them were not qualified to do ... And we reduced rapidly down to 30–20, and eventually less than 10, because that was all we needed. But it was quite shocking to come back to a company which was embroiled in such a minute issue, which was virtually able to paralyse the whole business. (Interview with David Elstein)

This was in a company which to all outward appearances had faced down the unions two years earlier when a long summer of disputes about new rosters to minimise the overtime paid to transmission staff and the use of the new video camera and editing technology led to blank screens on 17 October. The Managing Director, Bryan Cowgill, accepted a plan put to him by the Director of Production, Richard Dunn. It was a plan that proposed the unthinkable: the management would operate the station.

It was an arcane fact, largely unknown to outsiders, that ITV managements usually tried to raise controversial issues with the unions at the beginning of the summer, so that any consequent industrial action affecting transmission fell during the period of the year with the lowest revenue. Conversely the unions would seek, by prevarication, to extend discussions until 'Week 40' at the beginning of October, when the all-important autumn schedule properly got underway and their actions would have a maximum impact on the company's revenue.

It is a valid question to ask how a sophisticated and well-paid workforce could behave in such a self-defeating manner. It is equally relevant to ask how, up until this point, managements had let them continue to do so. It is true that in the early days of television staff had been required to work long hours, often in what would now be regarded as unhealthy conditions. This had given rise to legitimate union representations. It is also true that the ACTT, the union that, for historical reasons, came to represent most employees in ITV, carried from its origins in the cinema film production industry a particular mind set that might be described as 'no exploitation without compensation'. But by the Eighties new technology that actually made the job concerned *easier* was likely to be met with a demand for premium payments – and premium payments for the largest possible number. An outside observer might identify greed, syndicalism and a tendency to short-term expediency as key elements involved on both sides. However, it was also true that government incomes policies – 'wage freezes' – in the 1970s had meant that 'new technology' claims were often the only way that workers could increase their income.

It was the entrenchment of precisely those elements in industrial Britain as a whole that the Prime Minister felt that she had been elected to challenge, and vanquish, at the end of the Seventies. It cannot have helped ITV's cause with the PM that current affairs programmes of the period presented themselves at Downing Street for interviews with up to five times the number of technicians and production staff as foreign broadcasters (she could not be expected to distinguish between news and currents affairs crewing) and more even than the reviled BBC. The 'last bastion' comment should be seen in this context.

But, as was indicated at the beginning of the chapter, a number of ITV company managements were already taking various types and degrees of action. Thames had a particular need to be seen to make a publicly visible stand against the unions. In the covering letter sent with their new contract in 1981, the IBA Chairman, Lady Plowden, had written to the then Thames Chairman, Lord Barnetson:

> We touched at interview on the question of the level of costs generally in Independent Television at the moment, and on the inescapable fact that Thames's practices affect the whole system. I know you are well seized of the need to control costs in present circumstances, but it would be right for me to record here our continuing concern. (Letter, Chairman, IBA, to Chairman, Thames, 28 December 1980)

That letter was seen by Thames as an implied threat in relation to their next contract. The letter also called for 'the possibility of enabling the public to buy some shares in Thames Television'. Richard Dunn, who was Director of Production at this time, recalls the effect of the letter's contents on the company's approach to the dispute with their ACTT transmission staff.

> These were two very important matters because clearly they could be taken in evidence against us in eight years' time if we hadn't done anything ... and that was a significant spur to the action that we took in 1984. (Interview with Richard Dunn)

Dunn also believed that it was crucially important for management to be seen to manage. The heart of any television station is its Central Transmission Facility (CTF), which presents and transmits the programmes and, in commercial television, the revenue-earning advertisements. For historical reasons, up until this time Thames CTF staff had been self-rostering. The unions wanted thirty-two staff, all to be paid at six times the normal hourly rate (the industry term for this was 'golden hours'), to run a night-time service, an expansion of operation favoured by the IBA (see Chapter 3).

The management developed a roster by which the night service could be run by six people on time-and-a-half rates. Dunn received support from Cowgill and the Board when he sought to impose the new roster. The ACTT called a strike (at Thames only, but the rest of the network felt some unease that the confrontation might spread) which, with consequent blank ITV screens in London on weekdays, lasted from 27 August to 3 September while both sides attended ACAS to seek an agreement. The union negotiators settled on terms a great deal closer to the Thames management proposals than the rank and file thought desirable. By mid-October (at the height of the autumn schedule battle for ratings and revenue) another dispute had been constructed by the union around extra payments for the use of electronic Portable Single Cameras (PSC), rather than film cameras, for Electronic News Gathering (ENG).

While Dunn was at ACAS, Fred Atkinson, a wise and able engineer, who was in charge of operations at both the transmission centre at Euston Road and the outside broadcast centre at Hanworth and was Dunn's right-hand man, worked out a roster of managers to run the station. These included a backbone of managers of the key transmission, videotape and telecine (film transmission) areas. But the remainder of the forty-five or so people necessary to keep the station on the air were hastily trained finance, personnel and other members of the non-broadcast aspects of management. Dunn proposed the plan to Cowgill, who backed it. Fred Atkinson on the operations side and Barrie Sales on the programme schedule side (the Director of Programmes, Muir Sutherland was on Thames business in Australia) were to implement it.

The PSC dispute started at Euston on Thursday 18 October and Thames was blacked out again. On Friday evening LWT took over the London screen as usual until Sunday night. But the familiar Thames logo flickered to life again on London screens on Monday 22 October. The Thames management service was up and running. The effects of the second strike of 1984 had been limited effectively to a day and a half off the air.

At the start there were, inevitably, visible 'glitches' in the service but viewers over the years have proved remarkably tolerant of, even amused by, the occasional error on screen. It is persistent interference with the picture or sound to which they object most strongly. As the days went by the service became more confident. Originally it was confined to films and old programmes. This limited service had been approved in advance by the IBA's Television Division as 'an emergency service' but with the usual admonition that the service must return to normality as quickly as circumstances allowed.

With the NUJ Euston chapel on strike in sympathy with their colleagues of the ACTT shop, it was Thames' corporate affairs department that rose to the challenge of restoring a local news service. This was memorably presented on screen by the rubicund face and full figure of the Director of Public Relations, Donald Cullimore with contributions from his colleague Ronald Allison, Thames' Head of Sport. Cullimore had been ITN's Lobby Correspondent and Allison had been a BBC News reporter before moving to Buckingham Palace Press Office and then Thames. The media world much enjoyed their contributions. The 'Peterborough' column of the *Daily Telegraph* even found a pleasurable nostalgia in the fact that, since the autocue operators were on strike, the two men had reverted to the 'head down with an occasional glance up to the camera' newsreading technique of the Fifties. The London *Evening Standard* was less supportive, believing, not entirely without justification, that a number of stories each night were culled from that paper's early editions.

Though the NUJ stayed 'solid' with the ACTT, NATTKE did not. The sight of their members crossing picket lines to what the unions called 'the black network' was to cause lingering bad blood, both between ACTT and NATTKE and, on an individual basis, between members of NATTKE who had followed the official union policy and crossed the picket line and those who, out of personal sympathy with their ACTT workmates at Thames, had simply stayed away.

Meanwhile Richard Dunn was at ACAS again. And this time he had a fair wind behind him. The management service was not just filling the screens, it was being watched. The London weekday ITV share of viewing during the period of the service in October 1984 only went down to 46 per cent compared to 48 per cent in the same month the previous year.

The attitude of the rest of the ITV network company managements began to change from apprehension to approbation. Mrs Thatcher asked Bernard Ingham to phone Bryan Cowgill indicating her support. By the end of the second week of the service a deal was reached that included some stipulations about training for operators of the new PSC cameras but no premium payments for their use. However it was to be a further two years before agreement was reached on the use of PSCs for programmes other than news. Dunn was careful not to claim a 'victory' but the outcome of the Thames management service was clearly seen by others as precisely that. When a year later the *Dallas* affair unseated Cowgill, it was not surprising that the Board of Thames should turn to Richard Dunn to be their next managing director.

The Thames example had the effect that Lady Plowden's letter to Lord Barnetson had sought. Its impact on the rest of the network was that those companies that did not already have plans for such a response to industrial action quickly devised them. Knowledge of this by the unions acted as something of a deterrent and only one other company needed to put is plans into effect.

Ulster Television was rightly proud of its record of impartial and often courageous coverage of events in its troubled territory. But when, in 1983, Desmond Smyth took over from 'Brum' Henderson as Managing Director he felt less happy about the company's industrial relations record. Given the difficulties and dangers of reporting the Troubles – and even, on some days, of getting to work, the union could legitimately claim to have more than the usual concerns on behalf of its members. UTV's very active ACTT shop was led by a shop steward with a national role in the union, Jim Bell. And at a national level a certain competitive element had, historically, spread new claims and disputes, particularly on working hours and premium payments, from company to company. But now it was management initiatives that were spreading and evolving. Smyth noted the success of the Thames management service in facing down the unions and took the precaution of sending his non-broadcast related managers on technical operations courses at Ravensbourne College (a television training establishment in Kent supported by the ITVA to the tune of £324,500 per year by 1990).

Bell's actual job was as an engineer in the transmission control area. But he also owned a pub. In most ITV companies there were engineers and operations staff who had second careers during this period. Their union-negotiated overtime rates and shift patterns in ITV left them with either money to invest in a business, or time to run one – or both.

Bell's absences on union business in London were tolerated by the company but records also showed a high level of absence for sickness. The stress of some aspects of life in Belfast gave rise to an understanding of the need for time off. But this ill health seemed to have no consistent pattern – either medical or incident related. A preliminary investigation showed that disciplinary action would be required. For this to be effective, the evidence had to be unchallengeably objective. So when, one day in the spring of 1987, Bell's wife rang in to say he was sick again, a private investigator was sent later that day to the pub. He sat there for several hours while Bell served at the bar and lifted barrels – apparently in good health. Bell was confronted with the evidence and procedures for dismissal started. The ACTT shop staff walked out on 10 April.

When, by 15 April, it was clear that there would not be a quick resumption of normal working, the management moved into the technical areas and ran a service, consisting mostly of films, from 5.00 p.m. to midnight each day. Legislation since 1984 meant that the NUJ shop could not take sympathetic action, so, importantly for Ulster, a daily news service was included in the schedule. It was a limited affair read from the presentation studio but it did add to the credibility of the service with viewers. However this management service was particularly successful with the local audience because amongst the films shown were a high proportion of Westerns. Psychologists (and historians) can make of it what they will but it is a firm UTV belief that Western films are more popular in Ulster than elsewhere in the UK. The use of the genre combined with comedy in the film *Support Your Local Sheriff*, with James Garner and Walter Brennan, received a particularly positive response. A man from Cookstown rang in to the UTV studios at Havelock House to express the appreciation of everybody in his street for the film. He ended the conversation with the hope that the strike continued for a long time.

This success with the people of the communities amongst whom they lived – taken with hardship amongst the lower paid – had a demoralising effect on the strikers. The management had calculated that the strike might last three months. It collapsed after two weeks.

There followed a period of some difficulty with anonymous letters to members of management and a further dismissal but, like Richard Dunn at Thames, Desmond Smyth was careful not to claim 'victory'. Unlike Thames, however, UTV used this lowest moment in management/staff relations as a launch platform for a fundamental change in the relationship:

We set about a transformation at that time. It took two to three years. We introduced profit-sharing; we introduced savings-related share option schemes; we introduced teams around the building – generally a more participative type of style, and gradually that really started to work. By 1990 ... it was a totally different situation ... the management was thinking about the future, thinking about the contracting process, thinking about strategy, policy and so on, and planning the programmes ahead up to the end of the following calendar year. So it was a complete turnaround, and we were in good shape in 1990 going forward for the licence, in good shape to face competition. (Interview with Desmond Smyth)

The staff embraced new technologies instead of delaying their introduction by demands for premium payments and although the reduction of employees at UTV was relatively small – from 304 in 1987 to 293 in 1990, the overall effect of the changes that followed the management service was to provide a more competitive stance for UTV in the face of the new process of bidding for licences.

The concept of the viable management service in ITV was to become the equivalent of the nuclear deterrent – used twice, with a devastating effect on the unions' dominance, it never needed to be used again. At LWT, where, in the early Eighties, the traditional working agreements in a company that broadcast at the weekend meant overtime working to the point where a videotape editor was said, in one year, to have taken home more pay than the managing director, the weapon was to prove crucial. The management – Brian Tesler as Managing Director and Greg Dyke as Programme Director – decided that the best way to change the working practices was to have a confrontation with all the unions at one time. This 'big bang' strategy required the existence of a plan for a management service to be known to the staff. The strategy had a uniquely LWT dimension to it. Greg Dyke remembers:

> We had all the tapes taken out of the building ... hidden in garages and elsewhere. We had an alternative broadcast centre set up. We all walked around with teach-yourself-Dutch books so that they would think it was in Holland – but actually I think it was in Holland Park! (Interview with Greg Dyke)

Beyond the lighter aspects the overall strategy was more far-reaching than anywhere else in the network at the time:

> ... once you'd got rid of the unions, it was a real challenge then to manage the company, because the unions had managed the company up till then, and suddenly you had to manage the company, keep people motivated ... And, in a way, with management that had never done it. Half of them we had to get rid of. What was interesting was to watch ordinary, quite average, people become very good, given their heads and allowed to get on with managing. (Ibid.)

The first casualty on the management side was the industrial relations department. And over the following five years LWT's staff was reduced from around 1,465 to 723 between 1986 and 1991, without any industrial action. The losses on the production facilities division were reduced from over £22 million to £2 million in the same period. The resulting increase in company profits not only was to stand it in good stead for the licence process but also was to prove very valuable for senior managers and directors in an innovative piece of company financial restructuring that is described in Chapter 7.

A few years earlier than LWT's identification of industrial relations managers as part of the problem, Border Television had taken a different but equally radical course. In the midst of an ACTT strike in the autumn of 1982, which blacked out the station for a month, the Board of Border had brought in as Managing Director a local man who had run BBC North-East, before being sucked down to London in the classic BBC manner to obtain experience of the more rarified levels of the Corporation's Secretariat. James Graham had been a good 'man manager' at the BBC in Newcastle and he relished the challenge of running the smallest mainland ITV station – even though he knew it had problems. It may have been a small company but the crisis was massive:£1 million of debt, shares at 12 pence, the station off the air, and industrial relations that appeared intractable. Graham resolved the ACTT dispute but almost immediately had a run-in with the EETPU. After a torrid confrontation with the tough area secretary of the union, Eddie Brennan (with whom the young Jim Graham had played football when they were at school), poacher was persuaded to become gamekeeper. With Brennan as Head of Industrial Relations, more efficient working practices were introduced, but, importantly, Graham also reduced management numbers, brought in creative executives he had trained in his BBC Newcastle days and also used plant and staff more cost effectively by attracting commissions from Channel Four and making regular series of young people's and religious programmes for the new channel. With these measures, and with the help of the programme supply and transmission cost subventions that the small companies received from the larger companies, Border returned to profit.

All the companies found different routes to the improvement of their industrial relations position and improving their competitiveness during the Eighties. Some went further in this than others and, as will become clear in later chapters, some did not go far enough. But the companies' ever more widely differing approaches were to put the collective network agreements with the unions at national level under increasing strain.

The National Agreements

When the dam did break, it was sudden:

> On 11 April 1988, Tyne Tees Television is informing ACTT, BETA, EEPTU and NUJ that the company is withdrawing from the ITV National Agreements. (Memo from Chris Stoddart, Director of Resources, Tyne Tees Television to his colleagues on the network's Industrial Relations Sub-Committee (Staff) – of which he was Chairman, 11 April 1988)

This unilateral move took colleagues by surprise:

> Both the decision itself and its timing are potentially damaging to the credibility and public standing of the other ITV companies. The implication of Tyne Tees' decision is that the other ITV companies are handling their collective industrial relations so ineffectively, and the progress being made towards the achievement of the companies' objectives in relation to the staff unions is so inadequate, that Tyne Tees can no longer afford to accept the constraints that other companies are prepared to accept. The corollary of this is that the companies which remain 'members of the club' are somehow less determined to be effective than Tyne Tees. (Briefing note from John Calvert, ITVA Director of Industrial Relations to the Chairman of the ITVA Council, David McCall, 14 April 1988)

The thunderous tone adopted by Calvert (who, ironically was later to become Managing Director of Tyne Tees) was not entirely unjustified. Only five months earlier, in November 1987, at an industrial relations conference held at Thames, the network had unanimously rejected the suggestion that, from an agreed date, individual companies could withdraw from the National Agreements as and when they judged that they were ready to do so. Instead a proposal to enable companies to have some local negotiating options was before the Council meeting on the very day that Tyne Tees made its announcement. Tyne Tees had been party to that proposal but both they and LWT had warned at the November conference that they felt severely constrained by the terms of the National Agreements.

In fact the Tyne Tees move had grown out of a dispute about who should charge some batteries at the station. But David Reay, the Managing Director of Tyne Tees, who had a background in broadcast engineering, had clearly signalled his intentions in a note to all his staff nine months earlier. He told them he was looking for savings in staff costs, which had risen to 60 per cent of the total costs over which the company had control (that is, costs other than ITVA, IBA, C4, ITN, and so on, charges). He went on:

At present there are too many lines of demarcation, not just in the classic sense between unions, but between sections and even between grades within sections. Many of our practices go back years and are no longer appropriate to the present pace and style of production. And many practices date back to old technology which is no longer used. The Independent production units are starting with virtually a clean sheet by not being hidebound by old practices. This means that the main principle we should apply is not how we have done things but how we can do things, reasonably and cost effectively ... This way we can meet and beat the competition. (Management notice to staff, 'Tyne Tees Television – Changes Ahead', 17 July 1987)

The company's position could not have been spelled out more clearly. A copy of that notice, with its clear implication of the need to negotiate locally, did go to the Industrial Relations Secretariat at the ITVA. But it was the timing of Tyne Tees' move that rankled.

Given the terms of Reay's note – which applied to all ITV companies, to a lesser or greater extent – it might be asked why the National Agreements had lasted so long. The final statement of justification for them can be found in the notes of a meeting held as late as February 1987. There it was said that:

The main reason for having a National Agreement was the degree of centralisation of the unions, particularly the ACTT, and the fear that smaller companies would be 'picked off'. Managing Directors were more anxious to preserve a national structure than many of their managers. The companies had enough in common to maintain a national system but great difficulty in uniting around common policies, e.g. few companies would spend half a per cent (of the salary bill) to 'buy out' golden hours.

... Although the companies had different arrangements in relation to pay and grading structure, the National Agreements were more or less followed in other respects. Earnings, however, were more the result of local management decisions. Because of the difficulty in uniting companies on specific objectives, it was probably unrealistic to envisage negotiating out clauses from the National Agreements. (Note of a special meeting of Industrial Relations managers (the Staff Work Group), held at The Bear Inn, Woodstock, Oxfordshire, 5 February 1987)

The second of those paragraphs clearly defines both ITV's greatest difficulty in working collectively as a network – that it must always move at the pace of the least progressive – and the reason why one or more of the companies with a need or strategy to become more competitive would, sooner or later, have to abrogate the National Agreements. It may be tempting to see the first paragraph as demonstrating the degree to which senior industrial relations staff were out of touch with the thinking of their managing directors, but events, both inside and outside ITV, were moving fast at this time; Professor Peacock had reported only seven months earlier and the implications of his report for ITV (see Chapter 8) were still being digested, the Tyne Tees notice to staff appeared five months later, the Downing Street seminar was held eight months later and the abrogation just over a year after the Woodstock meeting. ITV's industrial relations, like its advertising sales techniques and, to a large extent, its production, had been relatively unchanged for thirty years before that.

When the National Agreements were formally ended by ITV in April 1988, the unions were also required to devise new strategies and negotiating processes for the new era. By this time NATTKE had merged with the so-called BBC 'house' union (actually also the union of some IBA staff), the Association of Broadcasting Staffs (ABS) to form the Broadcasting and Entertainment Trades Alliance (BETA). When the end of the National Agreements faced the unions with having to negotiate separately with each ITV company (a process familiar to the trade union movement as 'plant bargaining'), further unity seemed to offer greater strength. Merger talks took place between BETA and ACTT. These were not to bear fruit until 1991, when BECTU was formed, but in 1988 the unions negotiated at each company side by side.

Initially many of these local agreements were very similar in terms to the National Agreements (even at Tyne Tees) but quite soon these were to begin to change radically. That working in ITV was a well-paid job for life was an assumption that was to disappear in the next four years.

ITV was now to change faster than it had at any time since the 1950s. And those changes that were not politically imposed were driven, not by competing broadcasters, who had yet to arrive with any force, but by the threat of such competition and, more immediately, changes in the world of production – driven by the twin motors of the growth and requirement for a minimum 'quota' of independent production in ITV transmissions and the erosion of the old 'guarantee' system of production in ITV (see next chapter).

Independent Production and the Cost of Programmes

The industry's need to achieve political credibility in the face of a known timetable of broadcasting legislation under a government with a free market philosophy and anti-union tendencies, was certainly one motivation behind ITV's confrontations with the unions in the Eighties. However, the main driving force was the need to keep programme costs down.

It is fair to say that the precise cost of individual programmes was not a matter that concerned ITV companies until 1980. The cost of the network's annual programme plan was agreed by NPC on behalf of Council and, in a bad year for revenue, possibly adjusted downwards subsequently. Medium and small companies were really only concerned about the contribution each had to pay for their supply of network programmes under the Live Network Agreement (see Chapter 5) and the Majors traded programmes on a 'points' basis in a mechanism one of the objects of which was to ensure that the system was 'revenue neutral' and that no major cash settlements between companies were required. This system also served to keep secure the actual cost of any one company's programmes from the others. This lack of outside scrutiny had the effect of allowing each company to account for programmes in a different way. It was not conducive to financial rigour.

Two things happened to focus managing directors' attention on the cost of individual programmes. One resulted from an unusual chance impact of words uttered by someone from the BBC. In the manner of an asteroid crashing into a planet, there were to be reverberations from the impact and, after a pause, a quite dramatic change of climate.

Perhaps not surprisingly, the man whose words had such impact later became Director General of the BBC, but in November 1980 he was the Corporation's Controller of Television Planning and Resource Management. Michael Checkland had a history degree from Oxford, as well as having qualified as an Associate of the Institute of Cost and Management Accountants, and had spent five years as an accountant in industry before joining the BBC in 1964. He was highly regarded by producers, as well as management, for his financial rigour tempered by an understanding of the needs of the creative process. But at the time he was largely unknown outside the Corporation.

The venue for Checkland's speech was the Southampton studio centre of Southern Television. As part of its campaign to retain its contract in the 1980 franchise round, the company had offered to host a Royal Television Society conference called *The Production Explosion*. The intention was to explore how the extra production required by C4, TV-am and expansion of the hours transmitted by existing channels would be made (or acquired) and paid for. By the time such programmes came to be transmitted Southern Television had lost its contract (many thought unfairly) and ceased to broadcast.

At 9.15 a.m. on Saturday 1 November Checkland stood up to speak. His contribution was called 'Harsh Realities of Production Cost'. He broke down BBC Television's expenditure as 10 per cent on new equipment and building costs, 30 per cent programme costs – 'including actors, writers, news agencies, purchased programmes, sporting contracts, film stock, design materials, etc.' and 60 per cent to pay and house staff. It was this latter proportion upon which Checkland focused:

> ... I believe the key to our ability to handle the production explosion lies in the 60 per cent we spend on staff.
>
> How often, in order to keep the screen alight, have all sections of television broadcasting in this country agreed to manning arrangements which later they have lived to regret?

Memories of the settlement terms of recent disputes caused the ITV members of his audience – who had expected the speech to be primarily relevant to the BBC – to pay closer attention to what Checkland was saying:

> Let me suggest some areas we have to examine.
> 1. Have our manning arrangements kept in line with changing production methods? Take the studios: has the adoption of rehearse/record techniques with two and sometimes only one camera shooting (instead of six) been accompanied by appropriate reductions in technical crew levels?
> 2. Have we adjusted our recruitment policies and qualification levels in line with new technology? As new equipment becomes more reliable and operationally simpler, do we need the level of skill we required to operate earlier generations of production equipment? Are some of the industrial relations problems in television related to an over-qualified staff who are in no way stretched by the nature of the tasks they now have to undertake?
> 3. Can we afford to continue with some of our demarcation problems and those cosy standby arrangements we have created?' (RTS Journal *Television*, January/February 1981)

These questions were seen as having a universal pertinence but it was the spelling out by Checkland of average BBC programme costs that really caused alarm. The cost of BBC drama was given as £112,000 per hour. ITV executives in the audience knew that their 1980/81 'tariff' drama rate, by which programmes were traded in the network, was £76,000 per hour. They all knew that figure was imprecise but the 33 per cent difference took them by surprise. The BBC could not be that much more inefficient at production than ITV – particularly since the BBC was known to pay about a third *less* to its staff than ITV. The BBC also had the advantage of a largely centralised production facility in London with concomitantly more efficient use of plant, as well as lower artists' expenses, than the regionally-based ITV. Something was wrong somewhere.

John Birt, as the new Director of Programmes at LWT in 1982, was faced with the other incentive to scrutinise the cost of producing programmes in ITV – the need to arrive at a price at which to sell programmes to Channel Four. Finding no system of accounting for many parameters of the production process, Birt, with the help of Chris Turner a finance executive, set about analysing the real costs of production. Some of what he discovered said more about management slackness than about accounting methods or industrial relations practices.

For instance programmes like *The London Programme* and *The South Bank Show* booked a complete studio for a whole day to record links between items in the shows that could amount to as little as three minutes of the finished programme.

> We quite quickly stopped doing it that way ... We'd always operated under the assumption that it was more expensive, because the marginal cost was more expensive, to make (programmes) outside, that somehow or other cheaper equalled studio, and we came to understand that studio wasn't cheap at all, that it was a highly labour intensive activity ...
>
> ... We moved a very large number of our factual programmes out of the studio and indeed had a much higher production value in the process ... and we came to understand that we were all kidding ourselves about what the total real cost of those programmes was, and that ITV's tariff system was not actually reflecting real value and real cost. (Interview with John Birt)

The Birt/Turner analysis of total production costs at LWT did help to allow the company to address its financial problems. This meant casualties amongst their productions for ITV (see Chapter 3) but it also meant sales to C4 that were negotiated with a knowledge of total costs. This led to LWT, with programme contributions to C4 that ranged from light entertainment through young people's and ethnic programmes to religion, initially having a higher level of recoupment of costs in sales to C4 than most other companies. Across the network others were following suit. And, as we have seen, this was the start of a continuum that was to lead from better accounting practices to more efficient production and then challenges to the unions on working practices and overtime.

By the time that ITV was facing up to the Peacock Committee in 1985 it felt confident enough to commission a report from Peat Marwick, the accountants, comparing ITV costs with those of the BBC. In fact Peacock's assessment was to be critical of both broadcasters' programme costs but it carried an understanding of the background out of which the costs arose, for which, typically, he found a suitable historical analogy from what might be expected to be a favourite source:

... there is suggestive evidence that BBC costs are higher at least in some cases than those of the small independent producers (allowing as best we can for non-comparable elements) and that ITV costs are higher than those of the BBC. (Like all generalisations this one is subject to many exceptions.) The reasons for the tendency to high costs ... arise not from easily rectifiable personal failings, but from the nature of what we have called ... 'The Comfortable Duopoly'. We would echo the words of Adam Smith about the officials of the East India Company when they had a virtual monopoly of trade in India: 'It is the system of government, the situation in which they are placed, that I mean to censure; not the character of those who have acted in it. They acted as their situation naturally directed, and they who have clamoured loudest against them would, probably, not have acted better themselves.' (Paragraph 645, *Report of the Committee on Financing the BBC*, HMSO, July 1986)

Peacock's Recommendation 10, that 'Franchise contracts for ITV contractors should be put to competitive tender' was the radical attempt to change 'the system' out of which high programme costs arose which was to have such a shattering impact on Independent Television (see Chapters 8–11). Meanwhile, it was not until after the process of reforming ITV's networking system, which included an attempt to create a genuine internal market for programmes, got underway in October 1987 that even a unified total costing system could be agreed by all the companies.

5

NETWORKING: THE SUM OF ITV'S PARTS – OR CARTEL?

Critics Within

Like many internal business arrangements that are exclusive in their effects, the complex networking system that had grown up in ITV over the years was always bound to be subject to criticism from those who were excluded. At the start of the Eighties this criticism was largely internal, with the small and medium companies as critics of the effects of the major companies' dominant role in networking. By the end of the period the true outsiders – the independent producers – were to put the matter of ITV's networking arrangements on the national political agenda.

By the time of the publication of the Broadcasting Bill in late 1989 (see Chapter 9) the controversy appeared to have had the effect of removing any reference to the need for a regulated network for what, for a brief period, became known to politicians (if not to the public) as 'Channel 3', rather than ITV.

The document that christened ITV as Channel 3 was the government's White Paper, rather grandly entitled *Broadcasting in the '90s: Competition, Choice and Quality*, published (complete with annual-report-type glossy colour pictures of the industry) in November 1988. On networking it said 'It should be for the operators (licensees) ... to decide on commercial grounds on any arrangements for networking or syndicating programmes among themselves' (Paragraph 6.15, White Paper, *Broadcasting in the '90s*, 1988).

The IBA's folk memory scented possible anarchy on the air if networking and its regulation were not clearly defined in the Act. It was moved ultimately to provide, in one of its early background briefing papers for MPs and others, a *raison d'être* for networking which stands as the clearest statement of the necessity of a network for a federal regional broadcaster in the then thirty-three-year history of independent broadcasting. Had it been produced even three years earlier it might have saved a great deal of trouble:

Networking of programmes, so that they are seen in every Channel 3 region, is crucial for the following reasons.
– the costs of production can be spread over the whole system in proportion to each licensee's advertising revenue. This enables higher production values providing greater viewer satisfaction.
– a comprehensive and wide-ranging service can be offered to satisfy the wide variety of tastes and interests which the Bill requires of Channel 3. [Previous Broadcasting Acts had referred to a 'proper balance and wide range' in the subject matter of programmes.]
– the resulting service will be more attractive to advertisers, thus generating more revenue for the programme service.
– the requirement of 25 per cent of independent production can be met more effectively from the independents' point of view if there is a network in place.
– the absence of a Channel 3 network would give the BBC an enormous competitive advantage. The BBC could negotiate for artists and writers and producers in the knowledge that, unlike Channel 3, they could guarantee national exposure. (IBA Background Paper No. 3, 19 January 1990)

It is true to say that this explanation was still seen as specious by the more hard-line independent producers and some of their political allies, who believed that without statutory regulation the companies would have reached an agreement amongst themselves that would have suited them. Those who have read the two Chapters 33 of Volumes 1 and 2 of *Independent Television in Britain*, 'The Network Carve-Up' and 'The Networking Tangle', may indeed doubt whether a networking system organised by the companies would have been fair to all the companies – let alone independent producers – without the intervention of a regulator.

The Live Network Agreement (LNA), devised between the companies and the ITA in 1963 to put an end to the 'Carve-Up' accusations was, when taken with its later modification, so complex that more than one ITV managing director during the discussions on networking reforms in the mid-Eighties likened it to a Victorian statesman's view of the Schleswig-Holstein question: 'Only three men understood it and one is dead, the second mad and I'm the third and I have forgotten it.' (Note the actual quotation, attributed to Lord Palmerston by R.W. Seton-Watson in *Britain in Europe 1789–1914*, is that 'only three men in Europe had ever understood the Schleswig-Holstein question, and of these the Prince Consort was dead, a Danish statesman – unnamed – was in an asylum, and he himself had forgotten it' (*Oxford Dictionary of Quotations*, 4th Edition, Oxford University Press, 1992). The first to use the quotation about ITV's LNA system was almost certainly the late Bill Brown. He had the most legitimate claim to its use, since he joined Scottish Television in 1958 and was the company's Deputy Managing Director at the time of the original LNA negotiations in 1963, Managing Director from 1966 to 1990 and Chairman from 1991 to 1995 – not quite the equal of the fifty-year span of the great Victorian's active political life, but the nearest approximation achieved within ITV.

In effect at the start of the Eighties there were five dimensions in which programmes were sold or exchanged between ITV programme contractors:

1. Between the five major companies.
2. From one of the five Majors to any one or all of the ten others (the 'regionals').
3. Between the ten regionals.
4. From a regional to all the other companies.
5. Between all companies – this for Special Events like the Cup Final, the Olympic Games, a General Election or a Royal Wedding.

The LNA was the agreement that governed the first of these. Under it the regionals did not pay for the programmes they took from the Majors (the network supply) on the basis of actual cost. In that way no regional company could say it was deterred from showing a network production by the price. This was achieved by fixing an hourly rate for each regional contractor related to its Net Advertising Revenue.

The rate was a sliding scale that, in the second half of 1981 for instance, started at 0.399 per cent for a company with a NAR share of £100,000 ranging up to 1.3385 per cent for a company with a NAR of £8,000,000. A company in receipt of £3,250,000 revenue would in theory, therefore, pay an hourly rate of 1.038 per cent of that figure, that is, £337.00 per hour. But the payment system was further complicated by the fact that over the years negotiations between the different sets of companies had produced further refinements that meant that the regionals paid 112 per cent of the scale rate for the first twenty-five hours in any week, 40 per cent for the next ten hours and 15 per cent for the remainder – except for Schools programmes and Adult Education repeats, which were charged at 10 per cent. The very smallest companies, Border and Channel, received a further discount negotiated on an ability-to-pay basis.

These abstruse equations should not be allowed to hide the importance to both parties of the agreement. For the regionals it guaranteed fifty hours a week of audience-attracting programmes of a quality and mix approved by the Authority for a discount price. For the Majors it guaranteed fifty hours of production shared between them with at least some return on their production investment. Although that return seldom amounted to more than 10 per cent of the total cost, it was the second half of the mutual guarantee on which the claims of unfairness and demands for reform were to focus during the decade. When the cry of 'Abolish the Guarantee' went up – first from the regional companies and then the independent producers – it was for access to the network as programme suppliers. It was not about the other half of the guarantee – the obligation to keep smaller companies supplied with network material in all circumstances at a cost that they could afford. The five Majors themselves, as we have seen in the previous chapter, traded on an exchange basis with a tariff value that was supposed to approximate to cost but, at the start of the period at least, was actually more like one half to two-thirds of the cost. The total of the tariff for each contractor's output as a proportion of the total output by the five was intended to be equal to that company's share of the national Net Advertising Revenue.

Amongst those of the larger regional companies that had held contracts since the late Fifties or early Sixties, and had been parties to the original Live Network Agreement in 1963, there was an acceptance – however grudging – of this system. Anglia and STV, in particular, had long ago negotiated a position with the Majors in which they supplied a limited amount (the total for all the large regionals was some forty hours a year) of drama and some other programmes, such as Anglia's long-running, and award-winning, natural history series, *Survival*, to the network. All the companies were compelled by the terms of their IBA contracts to employ skilled staff and maintain expensive studios at their provincial bases. The 'non-Majors' would have liked to have produced more and been better paid for it. Above all they would have liked to get rid of the rather demeaning 'regional offers' process whereby they had to go cap-in-hand to a subcommittee of the Network Controllers Group to 'sell' their offers.

HTV, a later comer to ITV than Anglia and Scottish, had, in Patrick Dromgoole, a Programme Controller (later Managing Director) whose earlier career as a theatre, film and television director had enabled him to build up a range of international co-production arrangements that allowed him to 'sell' to ITV at attractively low prices to try to push up the margin of the regional quota. Tyne Tees found a niche market in the supply of children's programmes. But when the new TVS company took over the wealthy South and South East franchise (now further enriched by the transfer of the Bluebell Hill and Tunbridge Wells transmitter areas from the London franchise) from Southern in 1982, its Managing Director, James Gatward, did not like what he found in the networking arrangements:

> ... we were the equal third largest company in the land, and we were not having any of the privileges of the other five. I lobbied everybody. We had two famous dinners ... the five old warhorses and me ... Cowgill and Plowright and Tesler, Fox and Bob Phillis. No way were they going to give an inch. (Interview with James Gatward)

One of the 'old warhorses', Yorkshire Television's Paul Fox, remembers the occasion well:

> James said, 'And just before dinner I'd just like to make you a little presentation.' And for 45 minutes he made a presentation, basically showing that TVS were earning greater revenue than Yorkshire; were almost as big as LWT; and that, as a result they felt they ought to be at least a sixth major, but possibly really ought to replace Yorkshire in the total of five. And didn't exactly win my

goodwill. It was not a way to bring me round to his way of thinking. (Interview with Sir Paul Fox)

However, one in the room took a more pragmatic view of the proceedings. The needs of the weekend schedule were never far from the forefront of Brian Tesler's mind. Part of Gatward's presentation suggested that 'We already produce on an *ad hoc* basis the bulk of our network output for the weekend. Major status would enable us to rationalise this output and to develop strands and programme teams' (TVS Presentation). Tesler knew that Major status was not an option. For one thing the IBA would have to rewrite not only the contract of TVS but those of all the rest of the network would require modifications that were likely to be controversial – to say the least. As he was to write to Gatward subsequently in response to continued lobbying by TVS for a modified form of Major status:

> ... the change you propose would require the formal consent of the other Majors – and probably the other regionals too, since every company would be affected by it in one way or another. I cannot see Granada and Yorkshire going to the Authority in enthusiastic support; can you? (Letter Brian Tesler to James Gatward, 6 January 1986)

However Tesler had seen at the original presentation that an informal 'guarantee' by LWT to get mutually-agreed amounts of TVS production onto the network through the weekend schedule might serve both parties well. There was one difficulty. The weekend schedule, as has been described in Chapter 3, required programmes of an intensely popular character. The Director of Programmes at TVS, Michael Blakstad, was an accomplished documentary maker and had edited Science and Industrial programmes with great skill but he was not strong on popular drama. There was more than a little tension between him and Gatward, who, as an ex-drama director, tended to try to keep control of the drama himself. TVS productions were not always well regarded by the network. And neither of them had the light entertainment experience that contributions to the weekend schedule would demand. But Tesler had a plan.

Greg Dyke had been one of LWT's most promising young producers when he left in 1983 to become TV-am's Editor-in-Chief and help rescue the IBA's chosen breakfast contractor from the oblivion towards which it was headed in its first year. (The full history of TV-am's painful birth will be told in Volume 6 of *Independent Television in Britain*.) By the following year Dyke had been instrumental in achieving an audience for TV-am that was large enough to generate revenue on a scale that made the company viable. But now he was in conflict with his new Managing Director, Bruce Gyngell, the Australian broadcaster who had served ITV in Lord Grade's colours in the Seventies, about the future direction of the company. Tesler knew this and he and his Controller, John Birt, agreed that it would provide both quality control at TVS for the output that LWT was to guarantee to take and a safe haven for Dyke in a position where he was with them rather than using his talents against them. Knowing of Gatward's dissatisfaction with Blakstad, Tesler contrived a walk alone with Gatward at an industry conference to draw to his attention Dyke's potential for generating programmes that would be better received by the network than those produced by TVS hitherto. It must be said at this point that Gatward is adamant that he chose Dyke on his merits from a number of possible candidates and there was no 'You take Greg and we'll network your programmes' deal. However, the LWT team's accounts demonstrate an implied, if not explicit, deal. Brian Tesler remembers telling Gatward at the conference:

> ... it's very important that we keep people like this in the system and that they don't go to the BBC ... Not only that, he knows the sort of things we want at the weekend. He could help you make the programmes that we could then put into the weekend schedule. (Interview with Brian Tesler)

John Birt took the view that the regional companies' aspirations to provide programmes for the network offered an opportunity to LWT:

> We saw TVS as a company with an awful lot of money which it didn't know how to spend. And we were very keen to see, if I put this at its most tactful, a popular programme controller at TVS. (Interview with John Birt)

Greg Dyke, characteristically, puts it more directly:

> I was put into TVS by LWT ... basically London Weekend said, look, we'd like to take some more programmes ... and James was keen for that, particularly entertainment, because he had studios sitting empty. But, they said you've got to get a new Director of Programmes, and what about this bloke? And at that stage I was just in the middle of falling out with Gyngell, and got a call from Gatward and I went to meet him and said, yeah, I'll go. (Interview with Greg Dyke)

Once at TVS Dyke quickly gathered around him a new team able to deliver to network standards: John Kaye Cooper for light entertainment, Graham Benson for drama, Clive Jones for news. Mike Southgate joined them to organise the more effective use of the lavish production facilities at Southampton and Maidstone. In drama *The Ruth Rendell Mysteries* became a staple of the Sunday night network schedule. In entertainment TVS were the first to discover and use the talents of the comedian Bobby Davro for the network and also moved into the highly competitive field of game shows with *Catchphrase* amongst others. The drive to get quality TVS programmes seen nationally on the ITV network was a success.

Greg Dyke also put his considerable energies behind Gatward's continuing campaign to get TVS proper major company status.

On 23 October 1985 they were to go to Brompton Road with Tony Brook and John Fox (the TVS Sales Director) to put to Director General Whitney and his staff a carefully modified version of the original proposal. A fortnight before the meeting Whitney wrote to Gatward saying 'It could well make our discussion more constructive if you could put your arguments on paper in advance of the meeting ...' (Letter, Director General, IBA, to Chief Executive, TVS, 10 October 1985). Whitney's letter then asked a number of quite penetrating questions: whether TVS wanted to be a full Major, at the Controllers' table, or simply to have a guaranteed number of hours of programmes on the network; what would be the effect on the Majors and on the other regionals; how would TVS' greater contribution strengthen the network programme output 'on the basis of your own track record 1982–85'?

It was clear to the TVS team from these questions that the IBA programme and financial staff were standing ready to go through any written proposal with a fine-tooth comb and to have counter-arguments ready before TVS were across the threshold of John Whitney's office – that was the regulatory tendency. Other managing directors might have sent the data; it was, after all, the IBA's right to demand it. It was perhaps typical of James Gatward's approach to life that, just over a week later, he coolly replied:

> ... we will not be supplying a paper ahead of our presentation but will be leaving behind full documentation for your consideration once the presentation has been made. (Letter, Chief Executive, TVS, to DG, IBA, 21 October 1985)

The presentation, with accompanying slides, took nearly half an hour. It started by describing the need for change in ITV:

> We believe the ITV schedule is vulnerable, particularly at weekends. There is an inherent structural weakness in the system because it relies so heavily on one major company – LWT – for both the quantity and quality of programmes for the weekend schedule. We are not saying that the three 7 day Majors do not produce programmes of sufficient quality and quantity, but that these companies traditionally prefer to see them used to maintain the strength of the weekday schedule. What is needed is an increase in the amount of domestic peak time quality available, not only to keep the weekday schedule fully competitive, but also and more importantly to improve the weekend offering. (TVS Paper presented to the IBA, 23 October 1985)

The paper went on to make a far-sighted point about the vulnerability of US material on ITV once satellite broadcasters, who would initially only be able to afford such material, had satiated whatever audience taste there still was for it in the UK. It made the arguments that the TVS Dual Region – with major studios in both Southampton and Maidstone – had the production capacity and that (quoting the Henley Centre for Forecasting) in the South the per household income and spending that lay behind TVS' already healthy revenue, was set to grow faster than in the rest of the country. The company saw its change to Major status as a two-stage mechanism. It should immediately become a Major company at weekends, remaining a regional during the week. At the next contract round the franchise should be for a seven-day Major but still with an obligation to produce the majority of its product for the weekend.

On the matter of the effect on the other companies, TVS believed the changes could be made with no adverse impact on its fellow regionals. The Majors would, for TVS' first stage of elevation to join them, continue to receive 59 per cent of the LNA payment which would continue to be paid for the weekday network programme supply. The loss of LNA payment for the weekend TVS estimated at £5 million per year. The more severe impact of a sixth Major on a seven-day contract could be adjusted in the terms of the next set of IBA contracts. The remainder of the paper described TVS' programme successes – emphasising not only Drama but also the quality of those categories known to be dear to the regulator's heart – Documentary and Children's programmes.

After questions, Whitney thanked Gatward and his colleagues for their presentation and promised to respond in due course, but the TVS team sensed a rather negative attitude – fuelled perhaps by consideration of the likely response of the other Majors, as Tesler was to confirm in the letter to Gatward quoted at the start of this section. Though the paper put to the IBA was clearly informed by LWT thinking, that thinking was about the weekend contractor's needs – and these stopped short of a ringing endorsement of TVS' desire for Major status. Therefore Gatward had provided a similar, but differently angled, presentation to Tesler and Birt. It argued simply for:

> ... the creation of a second category A Major supplying material at the weekend ... Our belief is that TVS has the resources, and financial stability to develop the talents required to provide the strength and variety necessary to produce a more stable schedule ... (as) a Dual Region with Network Production centres in Southampton, Maidstone and Gillingham we already produce on an *ad hoc* basis the bulk of our network output for the weekend. Major status would enable us to rationalise this output and to develop strands and programme teams. ('TVS – *The Second Weekend Major?*', Paper by TVS, October 1985)

The paper also sought to put and answer an obvious question:

> Why is it necessary for TVS to have Major status ...?
> ... the price we receive for our Network Output is crucial. We already make a substantial loss 'above the line' on material we supply ... the Maximum Hourly

Rate barely covers 50 per cent of the direct costs on Drama and quality Entertainment.

The pricing and selection process (of regional company offers), with its submission of programme ideas, costs of which are inevitably cut back, often below cash expenditure, its pilots paid for by the company, and finally its selection and possible rejection by a Committee, does not encourage either quality or quantity of production. (Ibid.)

That was the nub of the matter. Gatward and Dyke were neither of them the type to accept the status quo without questioning it – even to their allies. They, in their newcomer regional company, saw the major companies sitting at the Controllers' table and exchanging the majority of the network's programme opportunities between themselves without the scrutiny of price and quality to which the regionals were subject, as an unfair and uneconomic system – but one which they wished to join. The fact that the system guaranteed a network programme supply was irrelevant to a region as wealthy as TVS. Other large regions felt a similar frustration with the process and were critical of it but only TVS sought to elbow its way on to the Controllers' table as a solution. In the short term they failed. As we've seen above, even their ally at LWT, Brian Tesler, believed that the immediate opposition of other Majors would be too great to be overcome.

But that failure did not mean that TVS did not have an impact on ITV's networking system. The company's campaign impinged to a quite significant degree on the IBA's thinking about the need for reforms to the networking system. David Glencross recalls the IBA's response to Gatward's ambitions:

He wanted to become a sixth Major. And the five majors resisted. And we didn't support it either ... That wasn't the basis on which the 1980 contracts had been awarded. But nonetheless we were conscious of the pressure from TVS, who came to see us on more than one occasion ... And we did believe that the Controllers Group, with these guarantees and the regional companies in the role of supplicants, really looked very odd ... It might have been all right when the system first started, when the four big companies, as they then were, were really much bigger than the rest. But now there had been some equalising up in revenues and in terms of production base ... it was (now) a system, which at least logically, was very difficult to defend ... (Interview with David Glencross)

And it was a system that was increasingly under attack. Gatward, his Chairman, Lord Boston, and other members of the board, lobbied tirelessly at Westminster and Whitehall as the government started to prepare its White Paper on broadcasting. And , in the minds of some of those being lobbied, TVS' criticisms of the ITV system seemed to link up with those from another quarter.

Critics Without

The independent producers, who had sprung up around the foundation of the channel that was required to obtain 'a substantial proportion' of its programmes from independents (that is, producers who were not also broadcasters), Channel Four, were able lobbyists. Many of them had cut their lobbying teeth gaining the requirement for the channel to use them as producers. Now they were turning upon the other broadcasters, which, with large staffs of their own, were not inclined to take productions from outside unless there was some attractive and exclusive element involved that they could not obtain in any other way.

By 1985, when the Peacock Committee was set up, the independents' unique combination of trade association and trade union – the Independent Programme Producers Association – was led by a chairman who was far from the stereotype 'media man' that Peacock and some members of his Committee might have been expecting. Michael Darlow (another product of Granada, able to turn his hand to more than one task in broadcasting) was as intellectually rigorous as he was persistent and he had a strongly moral attitude that may have appealed when set against some of the others who were to give evidence to the Committee. Certainly nobody reading the preamble to Recommendation 8 of the Peacock Report (note: Recommendation 8 stated that the BBC and ITV should be required to take 40 per cent of programmes from independents by the end of a ten-year period) could doubt the degree of rapport that Darlow, his Director Paul Styles and their team reached with the committee.

In August 1986, the month after Peacock reported, the independents set up a lobbying group, the 25% Campaign, to follow through their success. The Campaign's committee contained some of the brightest and best connected names from the independent production world. Along with Darlow were Phillip Whitehead, an ex-BBC producer, who had been Labour MP for Derby North up until the previous General Election (and was a former member of the Annan Committee), David Graham, who had a good relationship with Downing Street, Michael Jackson, who had been one of the successful lobbyists for Channel Four's independent production requirement, John Wyver, Lavinia Warner, John Ellis and others. They tempered Peacock's 40 per cent over ten years to the more realistic – and realisable – target of 25 per cent of independent production in each broadcaster's schedule each year at the end of a five-year period.

Their campaign was very effective. It offered a government dedicated to an enterprise culture (but which had initially distanced itself from Peacock's proposals – because of what the Prime Minister, at least, saw as their failure 'to tackle the BBC') a stick with which to beat the broadcasters, which the broadcasters would find difficult to show to be too severe.

In early December the Home Secretary, Douglas Hurd, summoned both the BBC and the IBA chairmen, their Directors General and a top aide each, to meet himself and his Secretary of State, David Mellor, and their senior civil servants to discuss the 'government suggested' figure of 25 per cent of independent production. In fact Hurd was summoned to Downing Street and Mellor conducted the meeting. Thomson was ready with three strong defences of ITV. It was already making a major contribution to independents through the Fourth Channel Subscription. ITV was, by Parliament's design, a regional network and most independents were in London. Also the ITV companies were five years into eight-year contracts which had required some, like Central, Granada and TVS, to spend enormous sums on new production facilities and staffing. Mellor was in listening mode and at his most diplomatic in response. However, David Glencross, in his account of the meeting, noted:

> In brief private conversations with Home Office officials it was clear that the broadcasters would have to do something which would 'satisfy ministers' (and by implication the Prime Minister herself) but that Home Office officials themselves were aware of the practical difficulties faced by the broadcasters ... (IBA Notes of meeting at the Home Office, Friday 5 December to discuss independent production on ITV and the BBC, dated 10 December 1986)

The Home Secretary's follow-up letter arrived at the IBA a week after the meeting:

> We should like to move towards a position where, on the ITV system independent productions took up around 25 per cent of the air time devoted to originally produced material. We also believe it to be right if independent productions came to claim a similar share of the production budget: ... we quite understand that it may take some time to build up a share of that kind. But I hope an early start can be made and that we can look forward to a target of this kind being achieved in four years. (Letter Home Secretary, Douglas Hurd, to Chairman of the IBA, Lord Thomson, 11 December 1986)

Clearly Glencross' assessment had been correct. 'Four years' was to establish a strong negotiating position (and satisfy Number 10) and 'move towards a position' and 'a target of this kind' gave the ITV system some room to manoeuvre – but not much.

The IPPA team, with colleagues from the British Film and Television Producers Association (BFTPA) and the Association of Independent Producers (AIP), was to set up a forum called the Independent Access Steering Committee (IASC). It was headed by Darlow and its representatives were to meet both the BBC and ITV in separate bilateral discussions. However, for the independents the most important discussions were the tripartite meeting between the IASC, ITV and the IBA. These were chaired by the Director General of the IBA, John Whitney – himself a former independent producer who had some insight into the angst of the independent. As a result, though the atmosphere at the meetings is not generally remembered as one of rapport, John Whitney was praised by all parties for his contribution. Paul Styles recalls:

John Whitney really acted as trying to guide this thing through. There was a series of incremental steps set by benchmarks of 500 hours in year one, rising to a fairly disputed figure of somewhere between 1200 and 1500 hours (in year five).

In retrospect I think the independents always had a dilemma ... it was possible to get 25 per cent of the hours but only be worth 10 per cent of the value. So one of our more subtle arguments was (for) parity across the schedule areas. (Interview with Paul Styles)

The other key figure was Michael Darlow, who brought the same degree of mature political skill to his relationship with Whitney as he had to that with Peacock and, to some extent, set the agenda during the meetings of spring and summer 1987. He was able to do so because after the first two tripartite meetings he had seen the need to set up a secretariat at the 25% Campaign to provide an information power base for selecting and briefing those who would contribute to or take part in the negotiations. This would be financed for six months by IPPA and BFTPA/AIP and run by the Campaign's Administrator, an able and dedicated young man called John Woodward. The Campaign had already commissioned a paper from Jonathan Davis, an independent consultant, which had proved an invaluable objective briefing on the issues involved in the negotiations, for both ITV and the independents. It concluded:

> Negotiation between the ITV companies and the independents should be governed by three overarching considerations: the efficiency and viability of the ITV companies is to be maintained and, where possible, enhanced; the integrity of the independents must be guaranteed; and whatever approaches are adopted to the commissioning process, they should bolster programme quality and diversity. (Briefing Document on Independent Production and the ITV Companies, prepared on behalf of the 25% Campaign by Jonathan Davis, March 1987)

Had ITV been aware of the document and the considerable understanding of ITV's difficulties in adapting to independent production that it contained, the network might have been more positively responsive in negotiation. However, it was only sent to the Home Office and the DTI, and shown to selected journalists in July. By then the campaign was becoming a blitzkrieg, – with two or three letters a week from Darlow, Woodward or Styles to all levels within the two ministries.

The independents' prime objectives at this time were:

1. Proportion of hours and money spent on independent production across all parts of the ITV schedule to be 25 per cent by the end of five years.
2. Fair Terms of Trade with ITV – to be standard across the network.
3. Definition of an Independent to be a production company not owned wholly or in part by an ITV company.

4. An effective and transparent system of monitoring of independent production percentage to be set up by the IBA.

They had the support now of government on the first of these and by mid-May the IBA had given assurances at a further meeting at the Home Office that, despite what it saw as valid ITV concerns about costs, impact on revenue and regional availability, it would ensure that ITV delivered to indicative figures that would be set in annual steps to meet the final 25 per cent target. The proportion would be entailed in the ITV companies' extensions of contract to cover the years 1991–92, if required. The last item was in the IBA's own hands but would still need acceptance by the other parties.

The definition of an independent was to prove highly contentious. The minutes of the tripartite meeting of 8 April 1987 show the ITV representatives – some of whose companies had, for historical reasons relating to the beneficial trade union agreements available for film production, wholly owned subsidiary 'independent' production companies, like Central's Zenith and Thames' Euston Films – looking for the possibility of continuing broadcaster investment up to 25 per cent. The IBA (and John Whitney in particular) was clearly genuinely mystified as to why the independents were rejecting the possibility of substantial injections of capital into their businesses. The old accusation that independent production was 'not so much a business, more a way of life' apparently still rankled and Darlow felt it necessary to clarify their position to Whitney after the meeting:

> ... I thought it might be helpful if I wrote to you with a little more background information on our thinking about one issue which has to date led to failure to agree – Definition of Independents.
>
> ... The reasoning behind our position is three-fold. Crossholding between ITV companies, their subsidiaries or owners, and independents must by its nature be in conflict with the government policy objective of fostering a third force to compete in the supply of programmes which is genuinely independent of the existing broadcasters. The same objection would obviously apply to ITV companies being allowed to appoint directors.
>
> The provision of substantial amounts of capital, such as the ITV companies appear to envisage, is not in our experience the most fundamental necessity in the establishment of viable independent production companies. Production companies, as opposed to facility companies, are not particularly capital intensive. Commitment to a sufficient volume of work is more necessary. Armed with such a commitment a producer usually has little trouble finding capital, co-investors or a line of credit.
>
> ... I hope this may set your mind at rest as regards any attribution to us of 'taking a bloody-minded attitude'. (Letter, Michael Darlow Head of Negotiations, IASC, to John Whitney, DG, IBA, 15 June 1987)

This issue was soon to be resolved in favour of the independents. But it was only possible to agree a set of guidelines towards Terms of Trade before the deadline of the IBA's meeting to report to the Home Secretary on 6 August. The actual Terms were to be argued over for a further eight months.

But by 7 August the *Financial Times* was able to report that:

> Independent Television Producers yesterday gave a qualified welcome to plans announced by the Independent Broadcasting Authority to give them greater access to the ITV system ... This should lead to the transmission in 1989 of between 175 and 225 hours of new (independently produced) networked material and between 200 and 400 hours of new regional material ...

Michael Darlow had had to resign from the chairmanship of IPPA to lead the Campaign and the IASC and had been replaced by a young National Film School graduate producer called Sophie Balhatchet. Perhaps anxious to make her mark, she was less than generous in her quoted response to the deal; saying only that 'there was just enough in the document to set the agenda for further talks'. David McCall, responding for ITV as chairman of Council, said that the IBA statement 'safeguarded the inherent rights of both the independent producer and the funding company'. This more statesmanlike response barely cloaked the fact that he and his colleagues were mightily relieved not to have had much more demanding indicative figures for independent production thrust upon them, which would have required widespread redundancies and might, they felt, have simultaneously weakened the schedule, with a consequent downturn in revenue.

But negotiations on the outstanding issue of Terms of Trade were to rumble on until the end of the year when the independents' patience ran out:

> Dear Home Secretary
>
> I enclose a copy of a letter I have today sent on behalf of my Committee to David Shaw, Director of the ITV Association, breaking off negotiations between us on the means of implementation of the Government's 25% Independent Access policy.
>
> ... On 19th October, in a desperate attempt to break the log jam we offered the most conciliatory set of Guideline proposals we could responsibly devise. These have now been comprehensively rejected in almost every important respect by ITV. The rejection includes the deletion of a number of points made in the IBA's 6th August Policy Statement. It is in this context that we have felt forced to break off negotiations. We now seem to have no alternative but to seek outside intervention to ensure that, in the Director General of the IBA's phrase, there is 'a level playing field'.
>
> I am writing a similar letter to Lord Young. (Letter Michael Darlow, Head of Negotiations, IASC, to the Rt. Hon. Douglas Hurd, Home Secretary, 8 December 1987)

Darlow overstated his case. There were limits to how far the ITV companies could move to meet the independents in the matter of direct access and central financing with a network that consisted of companies with separate and individual contracts with the IBA determining their responsibilities. This was a contentious difficulty that was only to be resolved four years later by the Monopolies and Mergers Commission. But the companies were made to look to government as though they were deliberately dragging their feet. They had no lobbyist as effective as Darlow to state the network's case.

The Reformation

Even at the start of 1987 the old ITV networking system was clearly under pressure from all sides to reform – from ITV's own larger regional companies (particularly TVS), and from the independents who, post-Peacock, were obviously going to continue their campaign for better access, and were, as we've seen, about to turn their critical attentions to the structure and practices of both the network and the companies. The ITV regionals were also lobbying government which, in turn was pressing the IBA for change. The IBA wrote to the companies:

> The Authority is seeking, in spite of the additional complications of independent access, to loosen up the arrangements for ITV in regard to programme exchange between the majors, the supply of programmes to the network by the ten regional companies, and the exchange of programmes between the weekday and the weekend. This would involve a reduction in the network pool in order to reduce the degree to which the make-up of the Schedules is determined by revenue shares. (Letter Director of Television, IBA, David Glencross, to Chairman of NPC, Brian Tesler, and Chairman of Regional Principals, David Reay, 14 May 1987)

ITV's annual Strategy Conference was to be held in Jersey that autumn. It was here that the crucial agreements to reform the system had to be forged. However, as the managing directors and programme controllers of all the companies flew in to the island on 28 October, through a haze of smoke from the burning of the trees brought down in the hurricane that had struck northern France and southern Britain two weeks earlier, they were feeling relatively relaxed. They had a plan.

Discussions during the summer between all companies at both controller and managing director level had produced an eight-point outline proposal for:

1. A basic network schedule allowing room for regional identity.
2. A Controllers' Group augmented by Regional Representation.
3. A system of common tariffs, but, as always, protection for the smallest Regionals.
4. A reduction in the majors' guaranteed hours, starting at 35 hours and progressively reducing further.

5. A 'flexi-pool' operated by the enlarged Controllers' Group, via the relevant specialist Sub-Groups.
6. A guarantee of 50 hours per year of drama for the Regionals.
7. Access for Independents via individual contractors.
8. Annual financial limits set for the value of the reduced guaranteed supply from the Majors and the new 'flexi-pool'. (Programme Planning Secretariat report of ITV Strategy Conference, October 1987)

A word of explanation is required about the so-called 'flexi-pool'. It was a term coined by Steve Morrison of Granada in a paper for the conference, to describe the hours of network programming, freed up by the reduction in guarantee, for which all companies would now compete. The pool would respond to the schedule's needs with specialist subgroups of expert producers in the different genres – drama, light entertainment, factual – each chaired by one of the Controllers Group, selecting the best of the programme proposals on offer, from whatever source. In industrial management terms these were to be 'quality circles', where the pooled expertise of the network would be able to push up standards and reduce costs. In practice they were to prove to be too slow in process to respond effectively to the schedule's (and the producers') needs and, worse, to continue to be subject to the Majors' dominance. 'Flexi-pool' was to become a term of abuse – fodder for critics of ITV's attempts at reform.

At Jersey there was general consensus for the eight objectives. Discussion centred mainly on finance and timing. Richard Dunn of Thames was anxious to see a sound financial infrastructure in place to support the new system before it started to operate. If it started in 1988, there was a danger of it 'going off at half-cock'. Andrew Quinn of Granada thought that the danger of going off at half-cock was less than the danger of not being seen to be achieving reform of the system quickly. Paul Fox, now very much the elder statesman amongst the managing directors, reminded the meeting of the recession. The new system would cost more. If the revenue was not there, goodwill was no use. It was, he said, no concern of government how the network was run.

Indeed finance was to prove to be the nub of difficulty in reaching agreement. But a compromise was reached of a quintessentially ITV nature. The eight proposals (which had now been elevated to the stature of principles) were agreed but two workgroups would be set up – one financial and one organisational – which would report to NPC by the end of the year on 'the precise mechanics and timing of the implementation of these principles' (ITV Press Release, 30 October 1987).

In truth the financial consequences of the proposals were horrendous; involving, as they did, a further move towards real total costing for programmes ('Tarriff C'), with a consequent dramatic increase to the LNA payments. Proposals for systems of 'capping', to limit the regionals' net exposure, a rebate from the Majors and a discount ('assistance mechanism') for the smaller companies were devised by the Finance Work Group under Derek Hunt, the Finance Director of Thames, but had to be agreed by all parties. A series of meetings as confrontational as any seen in ITV during the period took place between the Major companies and the two groups of regionals to set the levels of capping, rebate and discount. It took until July 1988 to reach even a one year only agreement, which was to run from 1 September 1988 to 31 August 1989.

The other post-Jersey workgroup, dealing with organisation, was able to move faster. The problems it faced were less intractable, since they did not directly address matters of finance. Also the group consisted of the network controllers, chaired by their usual neutral chairman, who was able to take soundings from around the network as decisions in sensitive areas were reached. The group was able to have its proposals approved by the first NPC meeting in 1988. In summary, these were:

That the seven hours reduction of the majors guarantee from 42 to 35 hours a week would come from 4 hours of general programming and 3 hours of sport. [Note: The Controllers had seized the opportunity of 'getting a grip' of the tendency of the less viewed sports to creep into the schedule, keeping out programming that performed better.]

The Programme Controllers Group would be enhanced by two controllers from the regional companies – Gus Macdonald of STV and Alan Boyd of TVS . The Group was formally renamed The Network Controllers Group.

The flexi-pool Sub Groups and their Chairmen would be:

> Andy Allan – Drama
> Alan Boyd – Daytime
> Greg Dyke – Sport
> David Elstein – Finance
> John Fairley – Entertainment
> Gus Macdonald – Children's
> Steve Morrison – Factual, including Education and Religion

The planners of STV and TVS would join the Network Planners. Both they and the two regional controllers would brief their regional colleagues on scheduling developments. (Minutes of NCG, 9 February 1988)

This last proposal was the most contentious. A direct quotation from the minutes of the meeting shows the Majors' concern to 'ring fence' the group's deliberations, for reasons of security, if for no other:

... for NCG to continue to discuss frankly, and in confidence, issues of policy and practice, and to formulate (and maintain) in necessary security forward schedules, there were some limits to any NCG member's freedom to divulge information outside the Group. (Ibid.)

And so the process of the reform to ITV's networking arrangements slowly advanced. Jersey, Turnberry, Brocket Hall ... the names of the ITV Strategy Conferences which chart the progressive reform of the network read like the names of battles. Critics certainly saw them as rearguard actions seeking to delay the advance of change. To ITV this was an honourable objective. The companies feared that too much change too fast might destroy both their business and a service to the public.

Turnberry came a year after Jersey and then, six months after that, in April 1989, Brocket Hall. And between these there were also the skirmishes conducted by the commandos of the Controllers Group at Eastwell Manor and the Hampshire Hotel. As the proposals to meet the IBA's requirements for progress in reform became more radical, agreement became harder to achieve. By the autumn of 1988 the government's White Paper on Broadcasting was to bring another whip to the network's back. In a paragraph entitled *The Government's approach* it said:

> The IBA and the ITV companies have been making efforts to bring greater efficiency and competition into the system, including greater use of independent producers. The Government believes that a more radical approach is needed. (Paragraph 4.10, White Paper, *Broadcasting in the '90s*, November 1988)

Government impatience was not surprising. But the IBA, having only received the proposed interim reforms to the financial side of networking for approval two months before they were due to operate, and itself under threat as a result of the Home Affairs Committee's report, *The Future of Broadcasting* (1988) (see Chapter 8), was also impatient. However it shared the companies' concerns that too much change too fast in ITV could damage all the broadcast systems for which the Authority was responsible. So when the Director General put a paper to the managing directors at the Standing Consultative Committee in September 1988, it contained radical proposals but offered 'softer' options as well. The paper required them to consider 'The abolition of *all* guarantees, including the regional drama guarantee.' But it also offered the alternative option of: '... a further and significant reduction in the guarantee whilst retaining some residual guarantees'.

On the organisational reforms, a radical solution that had been discussed and discarded many times over the years, but which was gaining currency again amongst critics of the system, was offered tentatively: '... there is a desire within the Authority to investigate ... the idea of a single commissioner and scheduler with a small central supporting unit ... jointly owned and funded, with an annual budget provided by all ITV companies'. But again the door to a less radical alternative was left open: 'The new process now in train needs time to demonstrate its effectiveness and general acceptability' (SCC Paper 16(88), 21 September 1988).

Not surprisingly, when only a month before the publication of the White Paper the managing directors, controllers, ITN, IBA and ITVA executives had gathered at the Turnberry hotel, high above the twin golf courses beside the Irish Sea, the network was not in a mood immediately to embrace the radical alternatives proffered by Whitney – though in the longer term they were to become the solutions imposed by the Broadcasting Act 1990.

In fact at this point the network was in something like disarray. As the new Chairman of NPC, Leslie Hill, opened the meeting, a blizzard of unofficial conference papers was being distributed to join the sixteen official ones – one of which was Whitney's SCC paper for further consideration. The most trenchant of the samizdat papers was, not unexpectedly, from TVS:

> The new networking arrangements were born out of good intentions and sensible compromise and have singularly failed to meet their potential in the first period ... Changes must be introduced to reach the objectives effectively. We have a 'well-intentioned cock-up' on our hands and the sooner we get rid of it the better. (TVS Paper on Networking Arrangements, 21 October 1988)

And when the various Controllers had reported, favourably by and large, on the work of their flexi-pool subgroups under the new networking arrangements, it was James Gatward who led the critics of the new system's slowness and lack of transparency. He was joined by Patrick Dromgoole of HTV and even by one of the Controllers, Greg Dyke, who was concerned about the impact that the system's apparent inadequacies and unfairness was having on the wider creative community of writers, freelance and independent producers on whose loyalty ITV depended.

But it was left to the well-respected regional ex-Chairman of Council, David McCall of Anglia, to make perhaps the most damaging attack on the new system. It was, he said, being manipulated by the major companies so that their best programme proposals were put forward for competition in the flexi-pool while their less strong programmes were made and screened under the guarantee – thereby increasing their production output beyond their NAR share. His Controller, Philip Garner (who was not a member of the Controllers Group) called this 'dumping'. The solution, it was proposed, was better 'scrutiny' by Controllers to achieve fair selection on the basis of the same standards of quality for both the guarantee proportion of the schedule and the flexi-pool.

Though the regional controllers from TVS and STV, nominated for NCG after Jersey, reported back regularly to their regional controller colleagues who were not, there was some feeling that their loyalties were being distorted by their continuous presence at the network table. A proposal for the rotation of regional controllers at NCG was floated – as was the idea of a ten-person NCG with all the large regions present.

Other flaws emerged in debate. If a programme series from the flexi-pool turned out to be a success with the audience, Controllers not unnaturally sought to renew or extend it. However, this 'committed' an increasing proportion of the flexi-pool money and meant there was an ever-reducing pool of opportunities for new programmes from the regions. Finally, it was an open secret before the conference that the Majors had not fulfilled the requirements, post Jersey, to reduce their output under guarantee for the year by the agreed 16.67 per cent – a reduction of seven hours from forty-two to thirty-five hours a week.

At Turnberry Brian Tesler, giving 'a view' from the major companies, made it clear that in reality the figure had been 6.67 per cent, or a reduction of less than three hours. This had been because of programmes already in the pipeline – a factor that had been left out of account at the time. It was this type of error that played into the hands of the ever-eager critics of ITV's management abilities. Tesler proposed that the 16.67 per cent reduction should now become the target for 1989/90 and 26.67 per cent for 1990/91 which would reduce the guarantee to twenty-eight hours and bring the flexi-pool up to twenty-one. The regional Drama Guarantee should remain at fifty hours for 1989/90 and reduce by 26.67 per cent the following year.

The Chairman, Leslie Hill, was new to the ITV system. He had been head-hunted to take over at Central when Bob Phillis had gone to work for Michael Green at Carlton Communications the previous year. At the age of fifty, Hill had run businesses ranging from office cleaning contractors, plant hire and building maintenance companies, to the largest UK and European Music business, EMI Records. Later he was to recall the impact ITV made on him:

> I was immediately struck by the fact that this was a very civilised industry, this was a very gentlemanly club, (with a) very high level of intelligence and very pleasant people ... so it was very good to come to that. But of course at the same time one was amazed that these people didn't seem to operate on normal business principles. I mean they were professional broadcasters and they were very good at what they had done, but they didn't seem to regard it as a business. (Interview with Leslie Hill)

Indeed Hill initially attracted some good-natured ridicule for his tendency to quote John Harvey-Jones, the ex-Chairman of ICI turned management expert, in his introductions to meetings. After his statutory JH-J quote (about seizing the initiative in competition) at Turnberry, Hill went on:

> I'm sure some of you are saying to yourselves: 'What the hell does John Harvey-Jones know about broadcasting? It's different.' Every business I've been in is different. And in every one they say, 'Leslie, you'll never understand, it's different from everything else' ... Clearly broadcasting is in many ways a very special kind of business, with all sorts of things about it which should not be looked at in the light of a normal commercial operation. But when you have a situation which is to do with getting people to do things and it's to do with money and making profit and then finally it is also about competition, the similarities between businesses are greater than the differences. (Verbatim transcript of ITV Strategy Conference, Turnberry, 24 October 1988)

With hindsight it is not surprising that when ITV networking plans under the new Broadcasting Act came to be rejected by the Office of Fair Trading, the network turned to Leslie Hill to lead the (successful) appeal to the Monopolies and Mergers Commission (see Chapter 11). It is also perhaps not surprising that in 1991 he was the Chief Executive who was able to calculate that his company could bid £2,000 and win the seven-day licence for the Midlands, while Carlton (a Central shareholder with a member on the Board) bid £43 million to gain the weekday London licence (see Chapter 10).

Turnberry may have been too early in Hill's career with ITV to benefit from his style of leadership and radical approach. In any event the agreement achieved at Turnberry for changes to the system for 1989/90 hardly met even the softer of the options in Whitney's paper for the September SCC. It could properly be described as minimalist. The Majors' guarantee was reduced from its notional thirty-two hours to thirty by enlarging the flexi-pool finance from £84.742 million to £110.742 million, while keeping the network programme budget the same as the previous year and programme prices the same. The regional drama guarantee remained the same.

On the organisational side the single-scheduler idea again received short shrift. It was agreed that the Network Controllers Group should remain the same size with the same membership (though the idea of rotating the regionals on NCG was retained in principle and there would be two informational meetings a year involving all fifteen companies' controllers). The flexi-pool Subgroups were to remain in place but their functioning would be reviewed in October 1989. The principle of 'scrutiny' of programmes put forward under guarantee to prevent 'dumping' by the Majors was accepted.

Concerned though it was to maintain stability in the system, the IBA was somewhat underwhelmed by this limited approach to change. The Authority was closer to the *realpolitik* of the situation and, after its November meeting, David Glencross wrote to Hill suggesting that the Majors' guarantee should be reduced to twenty-six hours rather than thirty, that the interim tariff system should make its final transition to total costing not later than 1990/91 and that the single network scheduler proposal be further considered. Glencross also sought that 'scrutiny' be rigorously applied and that the subgroups be more precisely briefed on the network schedule's requirements by NCG. After consulting colleagues, Hill replied accepting the last two points but pointing out that it would be better to wait for the publication of the White Paper, which was imminent, before deciding on further changes. But he agreed that a further Strategy Conference should take place when the White Paper's implications for ITV had been digested.

When the White Paper was eventually published in mid-November (see Chapter 8), it was clear about what government wanted to see in relation to networking – but that, as it turned out, was not a great deal of help:

Nor was it helpful that because of the Christmas break and commitments to business trips abroad, the next Strategy Conference could not be fixed before April. One of these unbreakable fixtures was the annual visit of controllers and some managing directors in their Film Purchase Group mode for the annual screening and buying trip to Los Angeles. It was there that an idea that was to throw the network into further disarray was born in the classic manner – in the bath.

More specifically it was in a jacuzzi in the Beverly Wilshire hotel. There Greg Dyke of LWT and his fellow controller and ally at YTV, John Fairley, had retired at the end of a long day of viewing and thinking up different ways of turning down new American series with sufficient diplomacy to retain good relations with the distributor while not having a 'no' mistaken for a 'maybe'. Dyke always found diplomacy a strain and he was a highly competitive scheduler, so he relieved his feelings on what he saw as the cumbersome inadequacies of the ITV networking system. Why not use the government's promise of 'lighter touch' regulation to end one of the drag factors on ITV's speed of decision taking – the need to go through the 'neutral' forum and bureaucracy of the Planning Secretariat? The schedule was already drafted by the planners of the Nominated Contractors, Thames and LWT, who also ran the network's operations, through the Network Operations Sub-Committee (NOSC), why shouldn't those companies present their schedules and make commissioning plans directly to the other companies with a programme interest in that segment of the schedule, with no guarantees for anyone? The IBA presence at Controllers, to see 'fair play', had been withdrawn earlier in 1988 and the view from the jacuzzi was that neutral chairmanship and centralised schedule publication would no longer be required under the lighter-touch regulation foreseen in the White Paper.

To consider what they would recommend, Controllers retreated to a hotel, Eastwell Manor in mid-Kent, favoured by LWT for strategic planning meetings. (It was known by that company's executives as 'Eat well Manor' – so lavish was the hotel's hospitality.) There, in a confidential debate between controllers only, it became apparent that the proposal – now known as Networking by Consent – was in fact likely to split the network. Fairley continued to support the Dyke plan and Andy Allan, of Central, saw the advantage of a voluntary networking system. However, David Elstein, while confident that Thames could work with either the proposed system or the current one, warned that 'consent' meant that the plan had to be acceptable to all companies in the network. He doubted that it would be. Steve Morrison of Granada was concerned that London would become even more dominant in the proposed system. The two regional representatives, whose companies (TVS and STV) were large enough to gain places at the network table, reserved the position of the regions as a whole until further consultation. Privately the frustrated Dyke threatened that, if there was no agreement, LWT might 'go it alone' and see who followed.

When David Glencross joined the meeting the following day he was aware of the Networking by Consent proposal though he, like the controllers, had not seen any paper detailing the proposals. He refused to be drawn on his views on what he'd heard. It was, he supposed, another option for consideration. But he added that he believed that networking would go on after 1992 and, he said, 'the ITC would be given the power to effect this if necessary' (Minutes of Controllers Meeting, Eastwell Manor, 22 February 1989).

In early December 1988 George Russell had been appointed Chairman of the IBA, and Chairman designate of the ITC, and had negotiated its transition into the proposed ITC. Russell was trusted by the Prime Minister and Glencross knew that not only the Home Office officials but also their ministers were now likely to accept that, whatever the White Paper (heavily influenced by Downing Street, Treasury and DTI thinking) had stated on the subject, changes to ITV's networking system would need to be approved by the IBA/ITC to ensure continuing programme quality through a stable and fair transfer of the system to the new licences in 1993. He promised a paper of the Authority's views for the Strategy Conference at Brocket Hall in April.

Greg Dyke and Brian Tesler consulted and lobbied further during the seven weeks before the conference and produced a revised proposal on paper. This stated that the weekend and weekday networks would consist of 'partners': Anglia, Central, LWT, TVS and YTV for the weekend, with the weekday group presumed by LWT to be: Central, Granada, STV, Thames and YTV. The partners would receive production contracts (but not guarantees) based on a combination of NAR share, output record and level of production resources. Tariffs would also be abandoned and programme prices would be decided by negotiation. Non-partners would be granted a 15 per cent (later increased to 20 per cent) reduction in their payment for being supplied with programmes from the two networks. The paper foresaw in this:

> a much reduced role for the regulatory authority and the ITVA. The companies in the two separate groups would not need a referee because they would have a written contract between themselves. (Paper for ITV Strategy Conference, 'Networking by Consent', by Greg Dyke and Brian Tesler, 3 April 1989)

In effect these proposals would have reduced the smaller ITV companies to the status of what are known in the US as affiliates – stations with assured discounted programme supply but no say in the control of the network. Given the requirements of their contracts with the IBA, at this point the writing was on the wall, rather than paper, for Brocket Hall.

At the conference there was, yet again, also a paper by TVS. It can perhaps most fairly be described as trying to combine elements of which the company approved, from both the existing system and the LWT proposal, to arrive at what it saw as an ideal networking arrangement. Its view of the ideal however, did not bow to the realities of the balance of power within the network.

The most thorough and authoritative analysis of the networking options available to ITV was provided in the paper for the conference by David Glencross. It warned of the danger of a repeat of the disruption after the major contract changes in 1968 which, he reminded his readers, had been brought about, in part, by LWT's attempts then 'effectively to go it alone' and which had ended up by reducing ITV's share of the audience in the autumn by 12 per cent and damaging LWT more than any other company (see Introduction).

Glencross went on to give a ('non-exclusive') list of the options. They had to be radical, he said, because the status quo was not an option – and neither was mere tinkering with the current system:

1. Guarantees for all companies. This would abandon the distinction between major and regional companies and give a production guarantee to each of the fifteen companies related to its NARAL – i.e. NAR with allowance for the new revenue component on the Levy (tax on ITV companies) that had been added to the profits element in the Budget just before the Conference.
2. An Expanded NCG. This was the Turnberry proposal for a Controllers Group of 11 companies.
3. Weekend/Weekday Scheduling and Commissioning Groups. The LWT proposal.
4. A Network Scheduling Company. This was the central scheduler idea, but with as much independence as possible for a wholly-owned subsidiary of the ITV companies. (Synopsis of IBA Networking Paper for Brocket Hall conference, 13 April 1989)

A central scheduler would, in theory at least, resolve the conflicts of interest inherent in a system where the network's programmes were selected by Controllers who were representing their companies as both producers and broadcasters – the 'buyer/seller' conflict that lay at the heart of all criticism of ITV's Networking Arrangements.

Had those at Brocket Hall paused to ponder the implications of the detail of thought and the amount of space in the paper devoted by the IBA to the central scheduler proposal, they might have taken the hint as to the Authority's preferred way forward. As far as the Majors (and, indeed, now TVS and STV) were concerned, the old saying about turkeys not voting for Christmas might be thought to apply. In fact the reason that the prime proposal in the Glencross paper was rejected almost out of hand may also have been that the minds of all arriving for the conference were now preoccupied with the LWT proposal.

Despite revision of the more contentious aspects of that proposal and the power of Brian Tesler's advocacy, the network remained divided on the matter. Most crucially it split the Thames representatives – Richard Dunn, the Managing Director, who had to go suddenly to Moscow before the conference and his Director of Programmes, David Elstein, who felt compelled to let it be known that his own supportive view of 'Networking by Consent' was not necessarily his company's view. Since several companies had made their support for the proposal contingent upon Thames organising the weekday network with the same dedication as LWT would devote to the weekend, unambiguous support by Thames was essential for agreement of the proposal.

After two days of discussion there was no agreement. However Controllers were required to establish the actual Thames position and, if possible, take discussions as far in the direction of the LWT idea as possible. If that were not possible, then what was known as the Brocket Hall fall-back position would be adopted. This required further progress in the direction set by Jersey and Turnberry, with another review after the Broadcasting Bill had been published.

At Council on 23 May 1989, under the chairmanship of Richard Dunn, it was reported that at the Controllers meeting the previous week:

> ... there were key issues over which Controllers disagreed: The membership of the proposed weekday/weekend groups; the size of guarantees; the degree – if at all – to which discounts should be part of the structure; and, to a lesser extent, the question of sub-groups and programme pricing arrangements. (ITVA minutes of special meeting of Council, 23 May 1989)

The minutes continue:

> The Chairman suggested that NCG had had time enough to reach a common view. Council had agreed to examine a 'fall-back' position and should now do that. Any such agreement was, in fact in line with the Jersey accord which called for a progressive yearly reduction in guarantees and the development of a freer programme market place by 1992.

Once again there was delay. Though the networking arrangements for 1990/91 were agreed on those terms in principle, members of Council wished to see the detail of this – including the plans for proper 'scrutiny' of all programme ideas by Controllers before commissioning – presented to NPC in June before final agreement. The slowness of ITV's cumbersome structure for decision taking once again drew criticism both from within and without. Increasingly, minds were to turn towards the single scheduler idea as the way forward.

As the Eighties drew to their close, particularly after the publication of the White Paper, most ITV companies, free now from the industrial relations shackles of the earlier years, were rationalising their financial and operational structures to improve competitiveness against the new broadcasters – and to allow them to make the highest possible bid under the 'auction' licence proposal.

For most of the Majors this meant creating separate production and broadcasting divisions (and in some cases, like LWT, Granada and Central, separate production facilities also) and setting them targets for profitability. With 'sellers' and 'buyers' split in this way in the companies, it was a logical step for network 'buying' to be centralised – provided the central figure could provide a network schedule which would maximise profits while still honouring the terms of the companies' contracts with the IBA.

The new Chairman of the IBA, George Russell, registered his concern at the Authority's August 1989 meeting about the uncertainty over networking and its effect on judgements about quality:

> ... that it was still unclear how the ITC would be able to offer a licence based on quality if a major proportion of the licensees' output would be supplied through a network, the existence of which had still to be determined at the date of the award. (Minute of Authority meeting 692 (89), 17 August 1989)

For those other interested critics of ITV's networking system – the independent producers – central scheduling was also seen as a way forward. But for them the proviso was that they had to be able to sell their programmes to the centre direct, not through their competitors, the companies.

So, when, in February 1991, the ITC issued the final version of its *Invitation to Apply for Regional Channel 3 Licences*, all eyes were on Section A.11 – Networking Arrangements. A.11 itself turned out to be a brief paragraph asking that:

> ... the applicant should state what kind of commercial arrangements for networking he (sic) would like to see, and how he would want to participate in networking arrangements with other Channel 3 regional licensees. (Paragraph A.11, p. 61, The ITC's *Invitation to Apply for Regional Channel 3 Licences,* 15 February 1991)

But prior to doing so the applicant was asked to note the twenty-one paragraphs of 'guidance' (113–34) earlier in the *Invitation to Apply* and a five-page Annexe (E) at the end if it. Ironically these guidance paragraphs were to be the mechanism that enabled the lighter-touch ITC to bring about the radical reformation of networking arrangements that had always somehow eluded the old heavier-touch IBA.

The paragraphs began with an assurance that the ITC had consulted the Director General of Fair Trading (DGFT) of their guidance notes, as they were required to do by the Broadcasting Act, and 'the guidance is acceptable to him'. As the successful applicants were to find out, the guidance may have been acceptable to him but the sum of their answers was not to prove acceptable to his staff (see Chapter 11). Meanwhile, Paragraphs 117–19 required that while:

> All regional Channel 3 licensees must have the opportunity to participate in the formulation of broad policy in relation to networking ... The executive decisions must not be taken by Channel 3 licensees or their employees, but by appropriately skilled and qualified staff employed specifically for the purpose. The reason for this separation is to avoid conflict of interest ...
>
> A possible organisational structure would be for the regional Channel 3 licensees to deal with the networking arrangements through a company wholly owned by them and established for the purpose ...

The ITC would not, however, insist upon a corporate structure. Other arrangements ... would be acceptable so long as the guidelines were observed and this was seen to be the case, e.g., there was a separate commissioning and scheduling staff (employed, for example, by a trade association) so that there was clearly not a conflict of interest between programme commissioning or acquisition, and programme supply.

So there it was: the newly licensed companies would be able to decide to have either a centrally scheduling ITV Ltd or an independent scheduler at the ITVA, or almost any structure between those two – provided there was clear blue water between the business of programme provision and that of broadcasting. This satisfied the large regionals; the Majors could live with an independent central scheduler, provided it was something short of an ITV Ltd. Typically the old 'contractors' set up a work group, the Netco Central Scheduling Blueprint Work Group. (The word Netco, which was to reappear in other contexts during the transitional period, did not indicate any commitment to a corporate entity at the centre. It was simply used to as a title for the handling of central broadcast management matters relating to the transition.) The group was to be chaired, not by the new Chairman of Council, Greg Dyke, but by Andrew Quinn, the Managing Director of Granada, a man with a strong track record in the management of change and who genuinely believed that a central scheduling system could allow the companies to be more competitive. Richard Dunn had nominated Quinn during his six-months' extension of chairmanship of Council as the member to handle all network matters relating to the transition from the requirements of the 1980/81 Broadcasting Acts to those of the 1990 Act.

At its inaugural meeting on the morning of Monday 10 June 1991 the group's first action was to shorten its title to the less cumbersome one of the A.11 Work Group. Its remit was to decide the structure and functions of the centre that the companies would propose for approval by the ITC and how that centre would reconcile the programme proposals of licensees into a network schedule that allowed them all to fulfil the terms of their individual licences, which were, in essence, a 'playback' of what they had proposed to the ITC in their applications. The *Invitation to Apply*'s guidance had covered most of the eventualities, but the reconciliation of programme promises into a network schedule 'matrix' was to prove to be its Achilles' heel, with promised Arts and other serious series having to be 'got away' (in Planners' argot) at 2.00 or 3.00 a.m.

Though TVS and HTV, two of the leading insider critics of the old networking arrangements, were somewhat preoccupied at this time with their own management and financial difficulties respectively (see Chapter 7), they appear to have been relatively satisfied with the changes required by the ITC post-1992. But what of the outsiders – the independent producers? The *Invitation to Apply*'s guidance appeared to take their aspirations extremely seriously. But at the heart of a genuinely open access approach lay a catch:

An independent programme maker should be free to put network programme proposals either to any of the regional Channel 3 licensees or directly to the central executive responsible for commissioning network programmes. Nevertheless, the ITC must be satisfied that it has the means to ensure compliance with the Broadcasting Act. If and when breaches occur the ITC must be able to apply effectively the sanctions which are available to it under the Act. (Paragraph 122, *Invitation to Apply*)

Compliance was to prove to be the worm in the bud. The ITC only had legal sanctions over the licensees, not the Centre with whom it had no contractual relationship. Therefore the compliance (legal scrutiny and checks that programmes conformed to the ITC's Programme Guidelines) had to be carried out by a licensee. The ITV companies – and later the new licensees – were to argue strongly that compliance was not a one-off event, like a health check, but demanded constant supervision throughout the production, from original specification at commissioning through to final editing and transmission. The only way to ensure this was for the independent production to be commissioned by a licensee – who would then accept the responsibility for compliance on behalf of the network.

Outraged by this denial of access to the centre of the type that they had at Channel Four, the independents argued that the compliance issue was an artificial barrier set up by the companies to stop their own production being undercut by the independent producer. They pointed to the fact that ITV had for many years entrusted the compliance of their films and other purchased material to a wholly-owned subsidiary, Independent Television Facilities Centre (ITFC) as evidence that compliance was 'assignable'. It was an issue that was to remain unresolved throughout the licence awards period in 1991 and was to come to a crunch in 1992, when the independents (who had now renamed their trade association as the Producers Alliance for Cinema and Television – PACT) turned to the Office of Fair Trading, claiming, amongst other objections to the networking arrangements, that compliance administered in this way was anti-competitive (see below and Chapter 11).

For ITV, during the last summer days of the old network, prior to the licence awards in October 1991, one of the tasks of the A.11 Work Group was to devise a transitional mechanism ('interim arrangements') for networking that could smooth out the potentially catastrophic leap from the old Controllers system to the unknown territory of a central scheduler.

In July the Group retreated from the barrage of headlines guessing at the size of their bids for licences (and, unnervingly, those of their opponents) to a hotel beside the Thames near Windsor. Its brooding Gothic style seemed somehow apposite. The building had been used in the past as the location for the *St Trinian's* series of British comedy films. That might, to some of ITV's critics, have appeared appropriate.

When, to relax at the end of a hard day's discussion, the Group took to the river in an Edwardian vintage motor boat it promptly broke down, leaving ITV's

Chairman of Council, two other managing directors and two controllers drifting out of control towards a weir. They were rescued by holidaymakers in a hired-by-the-week motor cruiser. What the newspapers might have made of the symbolism of both the location and that incident, had they ever found out, must remain conjecture.

Back on land the details for the management of the transition had begun to be agreed by the group, which had all the other companies' answers to Section A.11 of the *Invitation to Apply* available to it:

Programme commissioning and scheduling. To avoid a potentially catastrophic moment of change from the old to the new at the start of 1993, the Controllers Group (now retitled, in its new post-Brocket Hall eleven-person form, as the Network Scheduling Group – NSG) would commission and schedule up to the autumn 1993 schedule on the same financial and proportional basis as for 1991/92. During that period the new Central Scheduler would be commissioning and scheduling from autumn onwards under the new financial arrangement of negotiated prices.

Management Structure. Network programme policy and finance questions would be dealt with during the transition by a Netco Board, which would replace NPC and which would transmute to become the Broadcast Board in January 1993 – with the full requirements of the *Invitation*'s guidance paragraphs 116 and 117, that it be attended only by representatives who spoke for their companies' broadcast functions and not those of programme production. [This was to prove impossible for the smallest companies, who were unable to divide these functions while maintaining an efficient scale of management.]

The Central Scheduling Organisation. A structure for the CSO was to be proposed by the A.11 group to Council on the basis of the companies' A.11 replies and the study that Council had commissioned from Coopers & Lybrand Deloitte on how the CSO might relate to a new more efficient trade association over which Council would also preside. The job of devising and costing a CSO was delegated in the first instance to the Director of the Programme Planning Secretariat, on the basis that as chairman of NSG he was aware of all the functions that had to find a place in the new set-up. [This was to give rise to rumours that he himself was to become the central scheduler but that was never the intention. When he sought the advice of the group on the type of person required for the job, its advice – as minuted – was that what was needed was 'a Saint at the Centre'! However, it was always clear that what would actually be required was a highly competitive scheduler with ITV major company experience.]

The 'London Split'. A proportional division of the programme budget between weekday and weekend was to be worked out between the two London companies and proposed for agreement by the seven-day Majors. (Author's synopsis of ITVA Notes of Netco A.11 Work Group meetings June and July 1991)

These decisions, and the many that followed, all required the approval of the ITC. This was a very real sanction. The Commission was empowered under Section 39 of the Broadcasting Act 1990 to draw up and impose networking arrangements of their own if they were not satisfied with what was proposed by the 'Channel 3 licensees'. (Note: the Act followed the White paper in its use of this terminology for those companies, old or new, which would succeed in the bid process for licences to broadcast as 'ITV' from 1 January 1993. This was done in order to distinguish them from the licensees that would run Channel 4 and Channel 5 – it was not, as some thought at the time of the White Paper, an act of political spite, to wipe the independent broadcasting slate clean of the letters IBA and ITV at the same time.)

The ITC had a number of concerns about the proposed arrangements. The 'broadcast subgroup' representing all the companies, was to be the guarantor of the independence of the Central Scheduler and, as such it must only have representatives of the companies' broadcasting divisions on it. Representatives of the production divisions might be said to put pressure on the scheduler to take their companies' programmes, rather than those of independent producers. This was a problem for those companies that did not see a need for separation between the two functions. And, indeed, for the smallest companies it would have been uneconomic to provide two separate staffs.

A compromise was reached. The larger companies, which would seek to provide the majority of programming, must divide their functions; those who could only supply the occasional programme or series must be monitored to ensure that they did not pressure the Centre. There was some talk of an independent chairman for the group (which was ultimately to be called 'The Broadcast Board'), as there had been for NCG, but it was finally agreed that the presence of the Network Centre's Chief Executive on the Board would guarantee its independence from production pressure.

The ITC's other main concern was compliance. In a climate of political sensitivity about balance, violence, sex and bad language in programmes, effective compliance mechanisms were of paramount importance to the ITC. This was understood and accepted by the companies – who also saw it as a reason for not letting the Centre commission programmes directly with independents. This was to bring both organisations into conflict not just with the independents but also with another regulator.

Section 39 further required that the networking arrangements be approved by the Director General of Fair Trading, even though he had already approved the ITC's guidance to applicants on the matter. On the matter of compliance the A.11 Group's decision had been confident and clear-cut:

Compliance on matters like EC quota and proportion of independent production transmission would be the responsibility of the Centre. Compliance with ITC Codes would be (the) responsibility of the licensees as broadcasters and commissioners. (ITVA Note of meeting of the Netco A.11 Work Group, Oakley Court, Windsor, 3–4 July 1991)

During the eight months between that original decision and the submission to the ITC by ITV of their 'Principles' for networking there was an informal dialogue between the two organisations that modified many of the positions originally taken by ITV. Often these modifications did seek to level the playing field between independent and ITV production. For instance the ITC insisted that information on the schedule's requirements be issued *pari passu* by the Centre. But the ITC-approved section on compliance and independent production was, if anything, hardened:

Since the obligation laid upon the Independent Television Commission (ITC) under Section 14 (regional basis of service) and Sections 6 and 7 (compliance) of the Broadcasting Act can only be achieved by the ITC's relationship with licensees, the ITV Network Centre will not be able to contract programmes independently of the licensees. (*Channel 3 Networking Arrangements, Statement of Principles – as approved by the Independent Television Commission,* April 1992, published by the ITC on 14 May 1992)

It was this uncompromising attitude to the compliance question, with its implication that all commissioning – including independent production – would remain with the companies, that was the prime cause of outrage amongst independent producers. But they also had cause, they believed, to take a formal complaint to the OFT in ITV's decision to use the old system to commission the first two-thirds of 1993, rather than letting the Central Scheduler commission all programmes from 1 January 1993.

By May 1992 that transitional arrangement had been accepted by the ITC, mindful once again of the near disaster of the effects of sudden change on revenue at the time of the contract round of 1968. On compliance, though the ITC evidently accepted the legal basis of the need for that procedure to lie with the companies, there is some evidence that it would still have liked to have found a way – without jeopardising the compliance process – in which the sort of mechanism that it had proposed in paragraph 123 of the *Invitation to Apply* guidance section, for the Centre to 'commend' independent productions that it wanted to ITV companies for commissioning, could work.

However the ITC accepted the rejection of the 'commending' idea by the companies as unworkable because compliance had to be built into production from the original idea onwards right through production and that there was no way that the companies could accept 'commendations' for fully developed production commissions without making compliance less secure. It was necessary for the companies to bring productions to the Centre, their own and those of independents, and not vice versa.

The arguments on this with the independents – frequently in the public prints – were assuming an almost theological intensity at this point, but the die was cast. ITV's networking arrangements were finally submitted four months late to the ITC and agreed by the Commission in May. The ITC had justified its support for a closely supervised version of the ITV proposals at a meeting with the Director General of the Office of Fair Trading, Sir Gordon Borrie, and felt that its case had been accepted. The formal referral to the OFT was made on 15 May and the OFT Notice of Reference, asking for interested parties to make submissions by 2 July, was published on 4 June 1993.

Borrie was coming to the end of his term as Director General. He was replaced in May 1992 by the tough regulator from the Telecommunications watchdog, OFTEL, Sir Bryan Carsberg. (Borrie had held the post for sixteen years; Carsberg was to leave after only three – for the less public but better paid role of Secretary-General of the International Accounting Standards Committee.) The ITV networking arrangements were to be scrutinised by the new DG.

In July 1992 PACT, the independents' trade association, having taken Counsel's opinion, wrote to the OFT regretting that:

> ... the ITC lends its name to arrangements that singularly fail 'to ensure fair and effective competition in the provision of such services and services connected with them' (note: this is a quote from Section 2 (2) (a) (ii) of the Broadcasting Act referring to the ITC's responsibilities in the regulation of the provision of television services) (Submission to OFT by PACT, 8 July 1992)

The independent producers, the ITC and ITV were now on course for a collision at the OFT. That organisation, delayed by its need to brief a new Director General for his first really prominent referral, as well as by ITV's delay in getting the arrangements agreed by the ITC, took from July until December – the month before the date when the new arrangements would have to operate – to come up with its conclusions and requirements for 'modifications' to the networking arrangements. On the competition tests that the OFT were required to apply to the application of the provisions of the networking section (39) of the Broadcasting Act 1990 (contained in Schedule 4 at the end of the Act), the Director General said in the Report's summary:

> I have concluded that the arrangements are intended and likely to have the effect of restricting and distorting competition in connections with business activities in the United Kingdom and that they therefore fail the first part of the competition test, set out in paragraph 2(1)(a) of Schedule 4 of the (Broadcasting) Act.
>
> I have concluded that the networking arrangements as a whole contribute to improving the production of services, thus meeting the first criterion; allow consumers a fair share of the resulting benefit, meeting the second criterion; and do not afford the possibility of eliminating competition in respect of a substantial

part of the products in question, meeting the fourth criterion. I have also concluded, however, that the anti-competitive provisions are not indispensable, as would be necessary to meet the third criterion. The arrangements therefore fail the competition test. (Paragraphs 1.4 and 1.7 of the DGFT's Report *Channel 3 Networking Arrangements*, OFT, 3 December 1992)

In laymen's terms, ITV had passed three competition tests and failed one. However that one – the third criterion – was crucial to the matter of compliance and commissioning from the Centre. As Carsberg himself put it:

I have reached this conclusion chiefly because I am satisfied that it is possible to arrange matters so that the contract with an independent producer to supply a programme to the network could be made with the Network Centre (Paragraph 1.8, ibid.)

Carsberg then underwrote that assertion with a requirement to modify the arrangements:

I have therefore specified that the arrangements must be modified to allow independent producers to contract with the Network Centre for the supply of programmes, and that the Network Centre should be able to fund programmes not only at the time of delivery but, like licensees, also during their production, and that there should be a separate, identifiable compliance fee for all new programmes contracted for by the Network Centre. (Paragraph 1.11, ibid.)

No set of conclusions could have caused more affront to ITV, or have been received with greater satisfaction by the independent producers. However, as always the devil was in the detail of how the required modifications to the system might operate, and here the OFT's staff work let their Director General down – despite their having researched other broadcasting systems that commissioned independent productions in both Canada and America and their having hired a consultant who had been a senior executive both at one ITV company and at the ITVA.

The Report's detailed description of what should be done to achieve the modification included a proposal for pairs of contracts for compliance and supply and production and broadcasting which had a pleasingly logical symmetry but which betrayed – involving, as it did, four separate new forms of contract applicable to all programmes or series on the network, whether made by licensees or independents (Section 12, ibid.) – an ignorance of the practicalities of broadcasting.

In the body of the Report the OFT was severe, but not without some justification, about the rights demanded by ITV when contracting independent productions:

I conclude that the standard contractual terms in the Programme Licence, whereby the Channel 3 licensees seek UK transmission rights for 10 years with an option for a further 5 years and the additional rights, and in the 100 per cent Guidelines whereby the licensees seek perpetual rights, are intended and are likely to have anti-competitive effects on both programme production and on revenue generation. I therefore conclude that in this respect also the arrangements fail the first element of the competition test. (Paragraph 11.46, ibid.,)

There was much more: changes were required in the networking Principles, the Network Supply Contract, the Terms of Trade agreements and the Licence. Many of these requirements were flawed and failed to satisfy any of the parties. People involved at ITV began to feel that they had gained an insight into how some of the less fathomable of the OFT's pronouncements on other industries had been arrived at.

It was also the case that ITV, in the midst of the greatest upheaval in its history, did not explain its case to the OFT as effectively as it might have done. Several of those involved now feel there was also a certain degree of arrogance in their approach that was counterproductive.

ITV, the ITC and the interim arrangements could only be rescued by making a formal appeal to the Monopolies and Mergers Commission, which took until April 1993 to be heard and concluded (see Chapter 11). However, the existence of the appeal lifted any threat of a prosecution under Fair Trading legislation and the ITV network was able to carry through the transition period as planned.

The people involved in that transition were both at the Centre and in the companies and both had crucial parts to play in managing massive changes in networking procedures while maintaining quality on screen.

Greg Dyke had emerged, in that consensus of early morning calls, corridor and dinner conversations between managing directors that did duty as democratic process in the network, as the Chairman of Council to replace Richard Dunn in the summer of 1991. There were some foot-draggers in the eventual consensus. Dyke had been a controversial figure ever since he had emerged on the public stage as Editor-in-Chief at the beleaguered TV-am in 1983. He was thought not to be well regarded at the IBA/ITC. He was known to detest the organisation of which Council was legally the governing body, the ITV Association. But Dyke was also recognised as fearless and decisive and the network was, by now, beginning to grasp the need for these qualities. At Council, Richard Dunn, in his hand-over speech, praised Greg Dyke as 'a shaker and a mover'. The old network, already shaken by the legislative upheaval, needed to be moved on with confidence. Dyke was to be the man for the job.

He moved quickly. At the A.11 Group he had played a major part in determining the shape of the new Centre. He admired the professional qualities of Andrew Quinn, its chairman, who had also become something of a confidant. In fact Dyke wanted Quinn to become the Chief Executive of the new ITV Network Centre, with its scheduler and fifty or so planning, commissioning, finance and contractual staff.

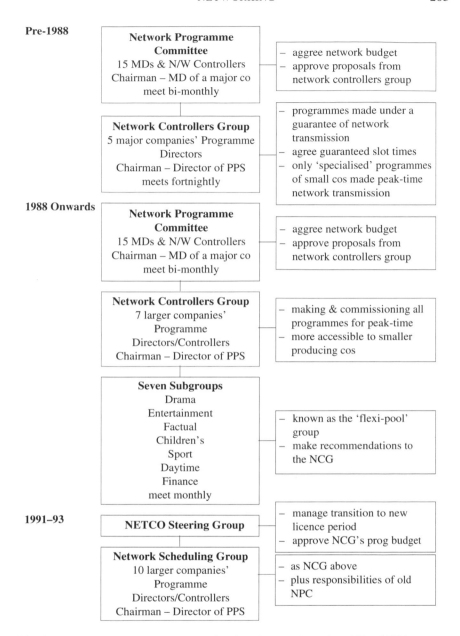

Pre-1988

Network Programme Committee
15 MDs & N/W Controllers
Chairman – MD of a major co
meet bi-monthly

– aggree network budget
– approve proposals from
network controllers group

Network Controllers Group
5 major companies' Programme Directors
Chairman – Director of PPS
meets fortnightly

– programmes made under a guarantee of network transmission
– agree guaranteed slot times
– only 'specialised' programmes of small cos made peak-time network transmission

1988 Onwards

Network Programme Committee
15 MDs & N/W Controllers
Chairman – MD of a major co
meet bi-monthly

– aggree network budget
– approve proposals from network controllers group

Network Controllers Group
7 larger companies' Programme Directors/Controllers
Chairman – Director of PPS

– making & commissioning all programmes for peak-time
– more accessible to smaller producing cos

Seven Subgroups
Drama
Entertainment
Factual
Children's
Sport
Daytime
Finance
meet monthly

– known as the 'flexi-pool' group
– make recommendations to the NCG

1991–93

NETCO Steering Group

– manage transition to new licence period
– approve NCG's prog budget

Network Scheduling Group
10 larger companies' Programme Directors/Controllers
Chairman – Director of PPS

– as NCG above
– plus responsibilities of old NPC

The 'Guaranteed Hours' were progressively phased out between November 1987 and 1991.
The Programme Planning Secretariat (PPS) was a department of the ITVA reporting to the NPC. It had no direct broadcast operational role. Its function was to derive a schedule for ITV and administer the schedule's financial and other consequences.

Figure B   Network Scheduling – the transition towards Central Scheduling.

However, events at Quinn's company, Granada, following the confrontation between the chairman of Granada Television, David Plowright and the new Group Chairman, Gerry Robinson, meant that such a move for Quinn, which would probably have affected Granada's share price as well as staff morale, was not possible. Head-hunters were put to the task of finding an alternative.

Meanwhile Dyke, who was well aware that even if decisions have to be made fast, an ITV Council Chairman cannot act on his own, had set up a group to which he could refer and which would have delegated powers from Council. Its composition had to be broader than the normal Chairman's Committee because all three size groups of companies had to be represented. And so the last Council working party of the old system was set up. It was called the Transitional Working Party and consisted of Andrew Quinn, David McCall and, representing the smallest companies, Donald Waters of Grampian, as well as Dyke. Inevitably, perhaps, the group became known as 'The Four Wise Men'. They were to prove to be a stabilising influence on a necessary sequence of difficult decisions that, in the heat of the pressure for change (and given Dyke's mercurial style), could have brought chaos to the network.

With their agreement, Dyke set about dismantling the old ITVA Central Secretariat that he so despised. The Director, David Shaw, and some 120 of the staff of the Association were made redundant. Shaw was a sincere and hardworking but undynamic man and he was not from a television background. His performance depended very much on his relationship with the Council Chairman. His most successful period on behalf of the network was at the time of the Peacock Committee (see Chapter 8), when he was working for David McCall, whose confidence he enjoyed. His relationship with Dunn, during the period of the White Paper and the Bill (Chapter 9), was not so positive and the ITVA was certainly less successful in presenting its case at that crucial time. And when Dyke became Shaw's Chairman there was virtually no common ground between the two.

Generally the staff recruited by the Association were intensely loyal to ITV but were seldom of a quality that people in the programme companies respected (or, if they were, they had been 'poached' by them or by other broadcasters). The companies themselves had all cut the size of their staffs dramatically (in the case of LWT by nearly half). They expected similar reductions to be made at the ITVA (and indeed, at the IBA, whose staff were paid for by the 'rental' from ITV, as it was transmogrified into the ITC).

Key staff in Programme Planning were spared to run the interim networking arrangements but it was made very clear to them that their futures would lie in the hands of the new Chief Executive and the central scheduler (now to be known as the Network Director). Here there were some planning and finance staff with knowledge of television, most of whom, when finally made redundant, quickly found berths with broadcasters – among them was the formidable Sports Executive, Patricia Gregory, who returned to BBC Television Sport at a senior level. Less fortunate was Ros Long, the dedicated Head of Planning, upon whose distillation of decisions out of the sometimes less than clear debate at Controllers and NPC meetings, and upon whose chairmanship of the bruising Planners meetings the network had depended since 1983. She was unable to find a further role in broadcasting. Planning was still a key function of the Centre but its form was to be radically different. Scheduling by committee was at last at an end. Now there could be unitary control by the Network Director and this required the sort of approach to planning that had hitherto lain in the companies rather than the Centre. The Film Purchase Department functions were to be retained at the Centre but also with new management. Also the European Liaison function was to be retained.

Europe had loomed ever larger in the affairs of Independent Television during the Eighties. The stream of Directives and Green Papers from the European Community relevant to broadcasting had increased in the second half of the decade and ITV was particularly concerned about restrictive European legislation on advertising (see Chapter 7) copyright and on sports rights and live transmissions of soccer. There was also a desire to ensure that satellite broadcasting was not allowed to escape the 'foreign quota' limitations which applied to terrestrial broadcasters. The prime burden of responding to draft legislation and for lobbying at Brussels and Strasbourg on behalf of the network was Sue Eustace, Head of European Affairs. She was well regarded by the network and amongst European broadcasters and was Secretary to the European Group of Television Advertising (EGTA).

Liaison with the European Broadcasting Union was carried out by the Director of Programme Planning Secretariat at the ITVA, alongside the Director of Television from the IBA (until 1 January 1991, when the IBA ceased to exist – the ITC was not 'a broadcaster' and so did not qualify as an EBU member). ITV was becoming increasingly resentful of the bureaucracy and cost of the EBU's Geneva headquarters. When a meeting to address this problem was finally convened in April 1990 at Marina outside Rome, the ITV/IBA representatives resisted the lobbying of the EBU's permanent staff but found themselves at the vote to be the only broadcasters in support of a plan to reform the EBU – the newly commercial TF1 of France having backed away from reform at the last minute. However, ITV did not give up and in 1993, with the support of the BBC, S4C and German, French and Scandinavian broadcasters, a management consultant, Nicholas Hayek (the man widely credited with the revival of the Swiss watch industry that allowed it to withstand the intense competition from the Japanese), was brought in to the EBU. His more radical proposals were ultimately watered down but a small saving on staff costs was achieved. But meanwhile ITV had become a founder member of the Association of Commercial Television in Europe (ACT) alongside TF1, RTL the German Kirch Group and Signor Berlusconi's Italian television empire. ACT later expanded to embrace Sky and other satellite broadcasters. Despite some criticism from other members of the EBU, ITV, RTL and TF1 were able to retain membership of the Union as well as the Association. This was important for continued access to the sports (including the Soccer World Cup) for which the EBU held contracts on behalf of its members.

Two other ITVA departments were retained because their functions were required by the terms of the companies' licences, as they had been in the old contracts. The Copy Clearance Department, whose judgement on whether advertisements conformed to the various Codes was accepted by the ITC as well as by the companies, was retained as the Broadcast Advertising Clearance Centre (BACC) and the Engineering Department became the Network Technology Centre. The Marketing function at the Centre was also going to have to change but there was less clarity of thought about the form it should take and it was to change shape (and personnel) several times during and after the transitional period.

The person selected from the head-hunters' shortlist for the role of Chief Executive was David Arculus. An extremely tall, thoughtful man, Arculus had been a BBC producer after he left Oxford in the late Sixties but then moved to magazine publishing with the expanding EMAP Group, becoming its Managing Director in 1989. In 1991 his company had been part of a consortium bidding for an ITV licence. It was Three-East Ltd, which passed the quality threshold but failed to oust Anglia in the bidding by just under £4 million. Arculus had not been closely involved in the bid but the broadcasting business interested him and at forty-five he was at an age when a move to a different business was worth considering seriously. So when Jill Carrick, the then fashionable hunter of media heads at the recruitment agency GKR (one of whose founder partners, Roy Goddard, was by this time a Commission member at the ITC), contacted him he was happy to discuss the role.

He was invited to dinner with 'The Four Wise Men'. They got on well and shortly afterwards negotiations for a contract as ITV's first Network Centre Chief Executive commenced. These were delegated by Dyke to Quinn. However, during his sequence of conversations with Quinn, Arculus became aware of the likely frustrations inherent in the complexity of decision taking in ITV and the relative powerlessness of the head of its trade association compared to the job of running a plc. At the last moment a difficulty over the contract arose and he took the opportunity to withdraw.

It was by now July 1992. The new Network Centre had to be in place by 1 January 1993, to meet the terms of the successful bidders' licences, but Dyke did not panic on losing Arculus. He had a plan. He knew that Quinn had done a very effective job of quickly restabilising Granada Television as its Chief Executive after the potentially damaging departure of David Plowright and that he was still as interested in the concept of a Network Centre as he had always been. As Quinn recalled:

> ... one of the very first reasons I became interested in a network centre was not just that I believed the focus was going to be necessary for ITV as a whole to compete against unitary structures who were out to steal our market, I always believed it would be a good thing for Granada because we could do better than our guarantees, we could grow our output. (Interview with Andrew Quinn)

Dyke knew that there was unanimous support for Quinn at Council and that Quinn now positively wanted the role. The necessarily attractive terms to compensate him for the move (Granada, once renowned as the pay miser of the network, had become more generous by the end of the Eighties) were quickly agreed. The appointment was announced on the last day of July 1992 and, perhaps because the government – and independent producers – had focused the media spotlight on ITV networking, the story expanded over the following week with interviews and features:

MR BIG SURVEYS HIS COMMERCIAL EMPIRE
The Times, 4 August 1992

QUINN ESSENTIAL
Media Week, 7 August 1992

Quinn himself now had to move fast. He and Dyke first settled the matter of finding someone who could take the difficult and exposed role of Network Director. The person must first and foremost be a strong ITV-style scheduler with a good understanding of programme finance; they must also be communicative, tough in defence of their decisions but diplomatic and flexible as well. This 'Saint at the Centre', as the A.11 Group had put it, was, some thought, not going to be easy to find. But, as usual, Dyke had an idea. He knew, from personal experience, that the weekend was the toughest, most competitive part of the schedule. His successor as Director of Programmes at LWT, selected by Brian Tesler and himself, had been Marcus Plantin, the Controller of Light Entertainment at LWT.

Plantin had shown an immediate grasp of the job that had surprised many. He had also shown, during his two years at the Network Controllers table, that he could 'tough it out' with the best of them but was also capable of arriving at compromise where it was genuinely required and was generally well regarded by his peers.

However, Network Director would be a high-profile role and Plantin was little known outside a tight group of television entertainment artists, producers and controllers. Also some in the network were suspicious of Dyke's motives for putting his own man forward. But Andrew Quinn was able to reassure these critics by pointing out that the Network Director would be answerable to the new Broadcast Board on which all companies would be represented. Predictably perhaps, Plantin's appointment was greeted outside ITV with something less than excitement:

GREY MAN OF TELEVISION REACHES FOR THE CONTROLS
Daily Telegraph, 2 October 1992

ITV NAMES MAN TO HEAD ADVERT-LED STRATEGY
Guardian, 1 October 1992

Within a very few months both those inside ITV and interested parties outside came to realise Plantin's merits – he was the right man at a crucial time. An examination of ITV's audience figures for 1992–94, the period of the transition, show no sign of the upheaval that was taking place in the network.

Meanwhile, Quinn, Plantin and the author, who as the now redundant Chairman of Controllers was retained by Quinn to help achieve continuity during the change, set about building the rest of the Centre. The first network commissioning editors were appointed. (Confusingly for readers of this book, they were given the title of Controller, which had become the currency in ITV for departmental heads now that all former Controllers of Programmes had become Directors.) It says a lot for Plantin that he sought out some of the most highly regarded production executives in the network and was able to persuade them to leave their companies (and in some cases move their homes) to take part in that leap in the dark – the new Network Centre. The first appointments were:

Controller, Network Drama and Entertainment – Vernon Lawrence
Controller, Network Documentary and Factual Programmes – Stuart Prebble
Controller, Children's ITV – Dawn Airey
Controller, Film Purchase – Pat Mahoney

Lawrence, from Yorkshire Television, had been responsible for the development of the new fusion of entertainment with drama that had been so successful for ITV in the Eighties (see Chapter 3). Prebble was an accomplished broadcasting journalist who had edited *World in Action* amongst other roles at Granada and had been one of the two driving forces behind the Campaign for Quality Television at the time of the Broadcasting Bill (see Chapter 9).

Airey was running the Planning and Presentation operation at Central when she was recruited and was widely regarded in the network as a rising young talent who could probably turn her hand successfully to almost any role in TV. Her subsequent career – commissioning editor at Channel Four and Director of Programmes for Channel 5 – has validated those opinions. Mahoney was the man at Thames who had snatched *Dallas* from the arms of the BBC – only to see it returned to them by his superiors in the network and at the IBA (see Chapter 3).

Andrew Quinn took one look at the financial systems at the ITVA, which, though not lacking in probity, were highly idiosyncratic and incapable of producing the management information necessary, and hired a tough Finance Director from TV-am, Stratis Zographos. Andrew Chowns from TVS joined a little later to handle the contractual business of the new Centre. Through the autumn this management team set about all the tasks that had to be achieved by the time that the requirements of the companies' new licences came into force – 1 January 1993. The first ever network contract with ITN was being drawn up by the inevitable working party but it had to be negotiated with ITN and agreed by the companies, including the new licensees – who knew little of the background. Access to the network's film rights had to be negotiated for the new licensees, with the Centre, as the reversionary rights holder, having in some cases to arbitrate between the outgoing and incoming companies.

Above all the contractual documents so crucial to the new operation of the network – the Network Supply Contract (between the licensees and the Centre, to ensure the supply of programmes), the Network Programmes Licence (between each programme supplier, ITV or independent, and the Centre), as well as the Letter of Intent, the Deal Letter (both of which were important for independent producers to raise money for production), the Production Contract and the ITV General Terms and Conditions Applicable to Production and Licence Contract – all had to be drafted and redrafted as the OFT reported and the MMC appeal went ahead. In this Quinn and his staff had valuable support from Leslie Hill, who had been delegated by Council to lead the appeal team, and ITV's legal adviser, Patrick Swaffer of Goodman, Derrick. The empowering of Hill in that role was to turn out to be one of Council's wiser decisions.

There was also the in-house task of making large numbers of staff redundant and, worse, having to keep others uncertain of their futures until some dimensions of the Centre's role under the legislation became clear in practice. The time taken by the OFT in its deliberations and the subsequent appeal to the MMC tended to delay this process – with adverse effects on staff morale.

There was also the matter of where the Centre should be housed. The ITVA had been due to move out of Mortimer Street to escape a massive rent rise in any event and a building nearby in Foley Street, which had previously housed ATV's London Presentation operation and then the television news agency WTN, looked to be the best move. However, the companies, as owners of ITN, were now the landlords of the new ITN HQ at 200 Gray's Inn Road with office space to be let (see Chapter 6). Quinn responded to the business needs of his colleagues but, typically, negotiated very favourable terms. The Network Centre moved into architect Norman Foster's total reworking of the old *Sunday Times* building on 1 June 1993. The Copy Clearance teams moved with the Centre but the engineers were housed with LWT on the South Bank. Other than Copy Clearance members, of the other old ITVA staff, less than twenty made the move to Gray's Inn Road. Two years later only four remained. The reform of ITV's networking arrangements was complete.

Andy Allan (now Director of Programmes at Carlton Television) probably had the greatest all-round experience at a senior level in the ITV system of the Eighties. He started the decade as Director of Programmes at Tyne Tees Television and became the Managing Director of that smallest of the 'middle five' companies in 1983. In the following year he joined the network Controllers table as Director of Programmes for Central. He became Managing Director of the broadcasting division of Central in 1990 and of Central as a whole in 1993 (Leslie Hill had become Executive Chairman) and, on the 'non-hostile' takeover of that company the following year, he became Chief Executive of Carlton UK Television. He put what many saw as

his much-needed talents back to the programming side of the company as Director
of Programmes in 1996. Allan's unique all-round view of the networking system
during the period provides an apt summary with which to conclude this chapter:

> It was a fascinating time because the absolute supremacy of the Controllers Group
> in ITV was starting to come into question. There were stresses and strains –
> particularly from TVS – and with Channel 4 you started to hear the mutterings
> from an independent production sector. And you felt this tide was starting to
> build. And I also think the managing directors started to get a bit fed up. People
> were saying this is not the BBC with adverts, this is a commercial business, with
> commercial business interests and the chief executive ought to be the guy in charge
> and yet all this power is ceded to these directors of programmes and you had a
> new breed of MD coming in who probably hadn't been a programme controller
> and therefore was a bit fed up at this notion that they weren't the stars and the
> programme controllers were the stars. (Interview with Andy Allan)

6

INDEPENDENT TELEVISION NEWS

The years 1980–92 at Independent Television News can truly be described as tumultuous. Events to be covered by ITN during the period included two wars in which Britain was a primary combatant nation; the momentous social, political, economic and defence consequences of the collapse of the Iron Curtain between East and West after forty years; the last, dangerously unpredictable, writhings of the apartheid regime in South Africa, as well as the continuance of the United Kingdom's own 300-year-old running sore in Northern Ireland.

Additionally there were the consequences of the greatest period of change in British politics since 1945. These had to be handled firmly, fairly but sensitively, in the face of a government whose view of broadcasting in general, and news in particular, sometimes appeared to verge on the paranoid. Events like the miners' strike in 1984 and, two years later, the bombing of Libya by American planes flying from bases in Britain were to prove particularly tender areas for coverage.

The immediacy of coverage and speed of intake of news material increased hugely during the period, with the development of ever lighter, and more light-sensitive, cameras and the means of transmission back to base by mobile satellite links from anywhere in the world. These developments put new strains on editorial decision taking as well as on reporters and camera, sound and technical staff. The list of ITN's awards in Table B (pp. 45–8) demonstrates how effectively people at ITN adapted to these new challenges while maintaining the high standards of journalism which ITN had set in its earlier years.

Both these technical developments and the change in British politics were to have particular impacts on ITN's finances and the organisation's relationship with its funders and owners, the ITV companies, and were to test ITN's management to, and sometimes beyond, its capacity.

The full story of ITN in the Eighties could, and perhaps one day will, take up an entire volume. This chapter must necessarily limit itself to an account of the growth of ITN during the period, within the business and legislative context of Independent Broadcasting in Britain during the period. The continuing achievements of journalists, camera crews and editors on-screen daily have spoken, and continue to speak, for themselves.

Within the context described, two relationships continued to determine the organisation's ability fully to perform its role as the news provider, initially to ITV and later also to other independent broadcasting channels.

The first of those determining relationships was that with its owner/funder/clients, the ITV companies. The second was that required to see fair play in the tug-of-war between the inevitably conflicting interests involved in the first relationship and to ensure the maintenance of standards. This responsibility had lain with the Authority since it had authorised the original ITV companies to set up 'a specialist subsidiary' for news in January 1955 and had insisted on a senior presence on the Board and right of prior approval of the person selected by the Board to be Editor.

The key figures in these relationships were the Chairman, the Editor and, in a slightly different dimension, the Director General of the IBA.

Chairmen, Editors and the ITN Culture

The job of chairman at the Board of ITN Ltd was different from that of the chairman of any normal limited liability company. There was a series of conflicts of interest involved. The main one was between the shareholders' roles as clients and as funders. Wanting to see the best news service at the lowest cost was not of itself a bad thing but it tended to create tensions that distorted the shareholders' perceptions of ITN's function. James Gatward once famously remarked at a Board meeting that his view of ITN was that it was simply the international newsroom of TVS. That was clearly not how the Editor – or the IBA – saw it.

The Chairman had to support the editor sufficiently to safeguard the companies' contractual interests but to support the ITV shareholders in controlling the financial impact on them of the Editor's natural ambition to run the best television news operation in the world. To do this the Chairman had to try to raise the level of debate above that of an extension of ITV's Council, to which it tended to descend. It was seen as a task demanding of intellect, judgement, a strong but diplomatic personality, patience, an understanding of journalism and of business and, above all, a knowledge of the ITV network system. Surprisingly, perhaps, most of ITN's chairmen during the period had most of these qualities. The man who saw in the decade had all of them.

The Chairman of ITN from 1976 to 1981 was the Chairman of London Weekend Television, the Rt. Hon. John Freeman. Freeman had been a junior minister in the post-war Labour government, Editor of the *New Statesman*, British High Commissioner in India and Ambassador to Washington. He had a broad experience of television. He and the BBC producer, Hugh Burnett, had created a personal interview series, *Face to Face*, in the late 1950s and early Sixties which had demonstrated the art of making the serious (Jung, Reith) popular and the popular (Gilbert Harding) serious. And when, in 1971, Freeman had been brought in to LWT as Chairman and Chief Executive, and had restored order after the chaos of the opening years of that company, his management skills had impressed many.

As a result, and above all from ITN's point of view, he commanded the respect of the ITV managing directors at Council and of the Director General and successive chairmen of the IBA. Even his most distinguished successors would have to agree that ITN was not to have a chairman of such stature for the remainder of the period.

Importantly, Freeman had presided over the selection of David Nicholas to succeed Nigel Ryan as Editor in 1977 and been there to support him for the following four years. Nicholas was to provide a continuity of ITN's culture and standards for a further ten years under chairmen who varied considerably in knowledge, experience and understanding of journalism and business.

When Freeman announced that he was standing down at the end of 1980, the Board and the IBA were agreed that the then Chairman of Thames Television, Lord Barnetson, a journalist-turned-businessman who was also Chairman of Reuters news agency, should take over. Ill-health prevented him from doing so and ITN was steered through the next four months by a combination of Freeman and the Deputy Chairman, the legendary founding father of ITV and successful novelist, Norman Collins.

Collins had in his time been Editor of the now defunct national daily newspaper of the centre-left, the *News Chronicle*, the Deputy Chairman to Victor Gollancz at the eponymous publishers and he had been the BBC's first post-war Controller of Television, resigning in 1950 to become the foremost of those who lobbied for commercial television in the UK. Having succeeded in that aim he became a director of one of the first ITV contractors, ATV. He might have qualified as a successor to Freeman but for his age; he was seventy-four and due to retire himself at the end of the year.

Freeman had then earmarked Lord Harlech, the founder Chairman of Harlech Television (which became HTV in 1968) to take over from him at ITN. As Sir David Ormsby Gore, Harlech had been one of Freeman's predecessors as British Ambassador in Washington, having previously been Minister of State for Foreign Affairs in the Conservative government under Macmillan. There were others in ITV who wanted to see David Harlech bring his political skills and experience to bear on the network's affairs – and where better to engage them than at ITN? But Harlech already led a very full life. His roles outside HTV included that of President of the British Board of Film Classification, adviser to the Victoria and Albert Museum, a Trustee of the Tate Gallery, as well as maintaining his transatlantic ties with chairmanships of the Kennedy and Pilgrim Trusts. He also held numerous company directorships. He wrote to Freeman regretting that he would not be able to devote enough time to do justice to what he regarded as a very important task.

The Board finally settled on a wildlife film producer as their candidate for Chairman of ITN. This was not as surprising as it might at first appear. Lord Buxton had indeed been an award-winning wildlife film producer and, as plain Aubrey Buxton, had been a founder member of the group that had won the ITV contract for the East of England in 1958. Their company was Anglia Television , of which Buxton became, and remained, a director.

A Norfolk landowner with a genuine interest in natural history, Buxton had set up the wildlife film unit promised in the franchise application to make the *Survival* series, which was to rival, and at times to surpass, the BBC's natural history programme quality during the 1960s. He was always popular with the IBA and had become one of that informal group of senior figures within ITV who were seen as 'elder statesmen'. He proved a fiercely loyal ITN chairman. He understood television and his connections at Westminster, in Whitehall and at Buckingham Palace (the wildlife connection brought him close to the Duke of Edinburgh) were valuable. However he was neither a businessman in the professional sense nor a journalist – and he did not have a seat on the ITV Council.

Buxton stepped down in 1986, after five years, to become Chairman of Anglia. Had he gone earlier there might have been a contest for the role between the two ex-journalist, ex-BBC, rivals on the Board, Bryan Cowgill and Paul Fox. However 1985 was the year of the *Dallas* affair. Cowgill had resigned as Managing Director of Thames and therefore his seat on the ITN Board, in July (see Chapter 3), and the unanimous choice as Buxton's successor was Paul Fox, who had been on the ITN Board since 1980.

Fox had started in television as a scriptwriter for the old BBC Television Newsreel. He had risen through the editorship of *Sportsview* to that of *Panorama* and thence through the headship of BBC Current Affairs to be Controller BBC1, before leaving the BBC to become the Managing Director of Yorkshire Television and a respected figure at ITV's Council. But when, after eight years on the ITN Board, two of them as Chairman, Fox returned to the BBC in 1988 as Managing Director of Television, the search had to start again.

This time the complication was that, from their various sources, the interested parties, ITN itself, ITV and the IBA, all knew that the much delayed White Paper on Broadcasting was likely to require ITV's news organisation to have a proportion of shareholders other than the ITV companies, after 1992. The question was: what proportion?

ITN, or at least some of its component parts, like the newscaster Alastair Burnet, a former editor of *The Economist* who had become a member of the Board in 1982, actually wanted greater independence for ITN and thought that a broader ownership base, ideally with total financial independence from ITV, would achieve it. Indeed he had used his close relationship with Downing Street to advocate such a move.

The ITV companies, not surprisingly, were vehemently against diluting their ownership with other investors whose interests might run counter to their own. They were certainly against outside investors having control of their news service.

The IBA suspected that ITN aspirations went much further, as a February 1989 Authority paper by the Deputy Director General, Shirley Littler, during the process of codifying the IBA's Authority's responses to questions arising from the Broadcasting White Paper, reveals: 'ITN may be coming forward with proposals for privatisation, possibly through the route of becoming an ITC subsidiary for a while' (IBA Paper 31(89), Part I, Section IV, last paragraph). Matters never quite went that far but this concern about the future ownership inevitably caused difficulty when it came to the appointment of a new Chairman. What was not predicable was that it would cause difficulty for the next *two* chairmen's appointments.

The Board, under Deputy Chairman Richard Dunn, agreed that in the circumstances it might be wiser if the Chairman did not come from any of the ITV companies. It was David Nicholas who came up with the name of George Russell.

Russell was a genuine industrialist. A graduate of the ICI management hothouse, he had gone on to become Managing Director of Alcan and then Chief Executive of Marley. He also held numerous non-executive directorships. Along the way his introduction to broadcasting had been as a member of the Authority from 1979 – 86. Soon after that he was appointed Deputy Chairman of Channel Four, where his counsel was very highly valued during the potentially volatile period of the transition from Jeremy Isaacs to Michael Grade in the role of Chief Executive and from Edmund Dell to Sir Richard Attenborough as Chairman.

Russell arrived at ITN just when his business ability was most needed, only to be snatched away after less than a year to apply his talents to a place of even greater need as Chairman of the IBA, guiding its transition to become the new regulator of ITV, the ITC. He had first impressed Mrs Thatcher when he had been to see her about the future of ITN, accompanied by Burnet (because Nicholas was away on holiday in America). His contact with Downing Street prior to that had tended to be through his old friend Bernard Ingham. But now he had caught the Prime Minister's eye directly.

Ironically, Russell was summoned to see the Home Secretary to be offered the ITC chairmanship while he was actually chairing an ITN Board meeting. His appointment to the ITC was widely applauded. Even the Board of ITN, though disappointed to lose a chairman of such quality, recognised the value of the appointment – though they were unaware of its particular future value to them at the time.

As an outsider, Russell had viewed the Board's voting structure with some surprise – even alarm. Neither the Chairman nor any executive director had a vote. Only the shareholders, who were, of course, also the clients, had votes. And these were proportional to the shareholding, which was on a NAR share basis. Therefore, once again, the major companies had control. Russell saw the consequence as being 'like chairing an annual general meeting every month', but the experience was to stand him and ITN in good stead during the debate over the Broadcasting Bill – where the ownership of the news provider for C3 (ITV) was to remain a contentious matter until the very last moment.

However Russell's departure at the end of 1988, after only six months, did leave the ITN Board with a real problem. How could they find a new chairman who was independent and upon whom they could all agree? Once again Dunn, as Deputy Chairman, had taken the helm – at a time of what were increasing financial difficulties for ITN. The Board all admired David Nicholas as a brilliant editor, who inspired his staff to his own high journalistic standards. This was crucial in the competition with the BBC for speed and quality of coverage. But some were less certain about his qualities as Chief Executive, a role he had also held since taking over as Editor in 1977.

The usual ITV network telephonic caucus reached agreement – not without dissent – that the only person who could be trusted to chair ITN during this interim period, until the final form of ownership was known, was Nicholas. His previous job would be split between an editor and a new chief executive with business experience and management skills. When Dunn put this to Nicholas he was initially concerned. But he came to accept the idea in principle, subject to his approval of the person appointed – to which as Chairman he was entitled. There was no problem filling the editor role. Stewart Purvis, the man who had taken charge of *Channel Four News* in 1983 and turned it from zero ratings into 'the thinking person's early evening news', had been made Deputy Editor of ITN in 1986 and now acceded to the full title. But agreeing on, and then recruiting, the right person as Chief Executive took what seemed to some members an unconscionable time.

Nicholas took over as Chairman at the February 1989 meeting of the ITN Board. In the Queen's Birthday honours of that year his twelve years as Editor were recognised with a knighthood. On the matter of the appointment of a Chief Executive, though head-hunters had been set to work, he and Dunn had reached an understanding that the ideal – and, indeed, in their minds the only possible – candidate was Bob Phillis, the ex-Managing Director at Central Television. Phillis' widely admired management expertise was now at the service of Michael Green as Group Managing Director of his Carlton Communications organisation.

Dunn knew that Green and Phillis did not always see eye to eye on that company's development and he and Nicholas set about prizing him away. It was to take them over a year to do so. Bob Phillis was finally able to join ITN in February 1991 – a month after the ITC had formally nominated ITN as the news provider for ITV after 1992. Nevertheless, as it was to turn out, Phillis arrived not a moment too soon.

Wars and Rumours of Overspends

War demands news coverage and it is generally the most expensive subject that any news organisation has to cover. The two major conflicts in the period – the Falklands in 1982 and the Gulf War in 1991 were ultimately to conform to that axiom. The Editor wrote:

> Midway through what was in any event a busy month the Falkland Island invasion took place. The resulting build-up has caused one of the biggest deployments in ITN's history and for what promises to be the longest time. At this moment there are seven staff reporters in the Southern Hemisphere and four staff camera crews.

I have to warn the Board that the order of costs involved in the first two weeks of the crisis is considerable and at the time of writing appears likely to continue for some weeks. It is the gravest story of its kind since Suez and ITN cannot but meet its responsibilities to the public and to ITV as the service to watch during times of national crisis. (Editor's Report to the ITN Board, April 1982)

As we approach the end of the fifth week of the Falklands crisis the overspending caused by our heavy outlay on deployment and satellites is of the order of £600,000. (Editor's Report to the ITN Board, May 1982)

The Falklands was an operation the news coverage costs of which would be, in theory, limited, as wars go. The battleground was a small group of islands far away and as a consequence of this isolation the Ministry of Defence had a stranglehold on news access. This appears to have been part practicality but primarily policy. The Ministry's PR department, perhaps with the Vietnam model in mind, advised the Minister, John Nott, of the dangers to the morale of the nation – and service families in particular – of allowing blanket coverage. The service chiefs at their Northwood HQ were anyway insistent that all satellite capacity was needed for military data transmission. They were also, of course, concerned for security. Joint BBC and ITN representations overcame MoD reluctance to have any reporters with the force at all. Mrs Thatcher in *The Downing Street Years* records that she believed that service chiefs were not concerned enough about the information Argentine agents might glean from the British media and gave way too easily.

ITN won the toss for the one television reporter allowed on the first ship going south. 'Tails' meant that Jeremy Hands of ITN went rather than Kate Adie. Because the massive bandwidth required to transmit moving pictures on the ships' satellite systems could have interrupted vital incoming defence data, coverage was initially limited to sound-only reports of the early naval and air force action. This also applied to the pool of one reporter each from BBC News, ITN and the Press Association on the flagship HMS *Hermes*. Their reports had to be sent back via tiny slots in the military message traffic on the satellite. They were therefore entirely under the control of the military.

The only other source of information in the early stages was the MoD spokesman in the UK, Ian Macdonald, whose sepulchral tones embedded themselves in the national consciousness (he was known at ITN as 'Macdalek'), carefully vetted still photographs of the action and, from foreign sources, some footage of the Argentine forces.

Michael Nicholson was ITN's reporter on *Hermes* and Brian Hanrahan the BBC's. Though Hanrahan's 'I counted them out and I counted them all back' phrase to emphasise the nil loss of Harrier aircraft in one action is remembered by many, Nicholson's word picture of the first reconnaissance photograph after the bombing of the runway at Port Stanley and his thoughtful *reporting* on the morale of the service personnel were journalism of a high order in difficult circumstances – and a counter to the propaganda of the Argentine junta that might have been expected to be appreciated by government. But conditions did not change, despite a deputation of editors (including David Nicholas) going to see John Nott personally to make representations for better access, until after the British landings on the islands. Even then the visual coverage was sparse and erratic.

To achieve broader coverage money had to be spent on the deployment of teams elsewhere. ITN's Chief News Editor, Nigel Hancock, sent Jon Snow and a crew to Tierra del Fuego, in Chile. (There Snow, with Brian Barron of the BBC, made plans to hire executive jets to achieve Falklands coverage. These had to be abandoned as the war in the air became one of such attrition as to make it unlikely that even a neutral civilian aircraft would survive in the area). Tim Ewart was sent to Uruguay and a team with Irish passports, including reporter Desmond Hamill, got into Argentina itself. Despite (or because of) the limited access to the theatre of war the coverage costs rose to heights never previously experienced.

The need to make news bricks without the straw of access, in order to fulfil a public demand for information led, unusually, to an agreement by the ITV Controllers for extra airtime after *News at Ten* to provide expert military analysis of the facts that were available and to reflect the political divides about the conflict. This series of nightly fifteen-minute specials was produced by ITN under the title *Falklands Extra*. And after Argentina surrendered, ITN produced a commercial video telling the whole story and including hitherto unseen footage of the war. The video was a profitable venture in itself but that profit could only make a tiny dent in ITN's massive expenditure on the war. The cost of covering the four-month conflict was eventually found to be more than triple Nicholas' initial estimate of £600,000.

Such overcosts were usually invoiced to the ITV companies in the proportions for which they normally paid for ITN. Coming at this time they would have been additional to the demands on the companies for the Fourth Channel Subscription about which the companies had already protested to the IBA (see Chapter 1). In June the Board approved the immediate payment of £1 million by their companies. In July it approved a further £500,000 payment. But to provide greater financial resource without such sudden recourse to the companies, it also authorised bank borrowing of £2.8 million to purchase the freehold of ITN House, which stood on a valuable site in Wells Street just north of Oxford Street. It was then possible, with the necessary guarantees from the ITV companies, for ITN to borrow up to a further £4 million to ease short-term demands on ITV. ITN was to remain in debt for the next ten years. But the purchase of Wells Street was to turn out to be an extraordinarily good investment.

The consequences of one particular undeclared set of hostilities were to prove as expensive as any actual war. The end of forty-five years of the Cold War and its consquences in 1990, and the dramatic social and political turmoil that led to it, demanded prolonged coverage in nine countries in eastern Europe, as well as in Moscow and Washington and, most memorably perhaps, Berlin. One of ITN's greatest successes during this period, a three-day lead and graphic coverage of the downfall of the corrupt communist regime in Romania, cost £500,000 alone. The overspend attributed by the Editor to 'the collapse of Communism in Eastern Europe' at the March 1990 Board meeting was £1.5 million. On hearing this, Richard Dunn spoke of the shareholders' 'fear of another Romania'.

New Technology – New Reach – New Costs

As well as the sheer number of international news events that demanded coverage, the nature of the coverage of the fall of communism, and, earlier, of the world's many distant bleeding sores of the period, Afghanistan, Beirut, Georgia, was changing – and that was adding to costs.

News in the 1980s became much more graphic than ever before as a result of two factors. One was the development of more visually aware journalistic skills in reporters, camera and soundmen. Alongside their traditional qualities of competitive enterprise, courage and persistence this interacted with that alluded to at the beginning of this chapter, the opportunities opened up by the new technologies of electronic and satellite newsgathering (ENG and SNG).

ITN started to introduce ENG cameras in place of film in 1980. This was earlier than the ITV companies, but because of union demands for extra payments for its use it was later than the management had wanted – as the minute of the Editor's report at the first Board meeting after the introduction mordantly recorded: 'Since Wednesday 10 September, ITN had two operational ENG units deployed for news coverage: four full years after the Board had authorised the purchase of the first ENG equipment' (ITN Board minute 3373, 15 September 1980).

Four years later ITN acquired its first transportable satellite ground station for SNG. Together these two developments made possible pictures from the heart of the news action, often in low light, and instantaneous transmission back to London from anywhere in the world. But that was only part of the new opportunities. Ever smaller widths of recording tape in the cameras and a miniaturisation of components brought lightweight editing equipment which allowed editing and dubbing on site. More reliable sound systems and really lightweight portable satellite gear made possible live two-way updates with the newscaster in the studio. This all added to immediacy – but also to cost. But there were some bulletins when it all seemed worth it – nights when ITV viewers saw history in the making:

I'll never forget the night that the Red Army withdrew in defeat from Kabul, we had a correspondent on the troop train who was able to go live from the bridge when they crossed into Russia. We had same day coverage from Kabul with a correspondent in the city, and from a Mujaheddin camp fire, outside Kabul, Sandy Gall live with a portable (SNG) dish. We did fifteen minutes live in the *News at Ten* recording the defeat of the Red Army pulling out ... I had to pinch myself ... (Interview with Sir David Nicholas)

A weird footnote to that extraordinary coverage: to get those signals back on the only available satellite, one intended for marine transmissions, ITN had to register Sandy Gall as a ship!

The cost of equipment for the new technologies and of personnel could be budgeted, but, with so many teams on the move around the world and an increase in bureaux in major foreign capitals, management supervision of all this expansion and the control of its costs was to become a major problem for ITN.

The climax of financial difficulty was associated with – but not caused by – the Gulf War. This war required an even more massive deployment of crews than for the Falklands. A more open approach on the part of the MoD offered the opportunity, for the first time, of frontline coverage relayed almost instantly from FTUs (Forward Transmission Units). This meant that some crews had to be trained and kitted out for frontline action. There was also deployment to the United Arab Emirates, Jordan (the staging post for Baghdad), to Bahrain and Saudi Arabia (Riyadh and Dhahran), and a strengthening of ITN's presence in Israel as well. ITN did get into Iraq through Jordan, obtaining memorable reports by Brent Sadler of US cruise missiles landing in Baghdad.

As the war progressed further memorable reporting was contributed by ITN: the pictures from the Royal Navy ships and helicopters in the Gulf approaches to Kuwait by cameraman Eugene Campbell, who was awarded an MBE for his work; the first reports from Iraqi-occupied Kuwait from Sandy Gall; the first broadcast from Kuwait City by Alistair Stewart.

Despite the likely massive cost of all this, when David Nicholas outlined ITN's plans for coverage of the Gulf War at the Board on 21 January 1991, the shareholders agreed that ITV would not seek a scaling down. Companies would also be invoiced for the costs of extra programmes, subject only to the agreement of the Network Controllers Group.

This meeting happened to be the first that Bob Phillis, the long-sought Chief Executive, attended. By the May meeting he and Stewart Purvis had to report that ITN's 'estimating processes had proved inadequate in a number of respects'. The costs of covering the Gulf War were ultimately to rise to an estimated £9 million – six times the cost of the Falklands. But between the two meetings financial problems had been uncovered at ITN that were far more grave.

Business, the Building – and the 'Black Hole'

I question whether a business system which was thought appropriate when it was founded in 1955 can possibly stand up to the shifting circumstances and requirements of the future. ITN is already a very different animal, on a level with the BBC and the three American networks, and to prosper it must develop and expand, and when necessary acquire new businesses like BASYS. It seems to me that thought must be given to the inevitability of ITN becoming commercial.

(Chairman's (Lord Buxton) memorandum to fellow ITN directors, 1984. Buxton quoted the passage again in a further note to directors, 4 March 1986)

The expansion of news coverage ran parallel to an expansion of business opportunities that were opened up by ITN in the wake of their journalistic activities. Between 1982 and 1992 ITN started to supply news for a second terrestrial channel, two satellite channels (for parts of the period), radio stations, a teletext service and an airline. It saw what had been its news film syndication agency grow, first as UPITN and then as WTN, into a global electronic information communication business. As early as 1983 ITN also acquired 51 per cent of BASYS Inc. of Mountain View, California, a provider of computerised newsroom systems, with whom its personnel had worked to adapt the BASYS system for ITN's needs. Finally ITV demanded a twenty-four-hour news service as it developed its night-time hours (see Chapter 3). However, for most of the period ITN's management remained what had been required to run television news provision for a single UK TV channel which broadcast for not more than fourteen hours a day.

Perhaps it was inevitable that, unless it was directed to change, the culture of ITN and the ethos of its management should remain a proudly journalistic one – as it had been under Nicholas' predecessors, Aidan Crawley, Geoffrey Cox and Nigel Ryan. And perhaps it was just as inevitable that a Board consisting of managing directors of companies whose businesses benefited from the luxury of monopoly should not recognise, until they themselves were under threat, that both ethos and management did need radical change. With hindsight, it is possible to see that these two factors, combined with the development of the businesses outlined above, were likely to lead to a management failure of one sort or another. What is surprising perhaps, is that so much expansion at ITN was managed with apparent competence for so long.

When Paul Fox took over as Chairman in 1986 the Board initiated a report by consultants Deloitte (later merged with Coopers & Lybrand) on options for the future, particularly in relation to funding and management. They reported in March the following year. Fox sought a view on the report from the IBA. The Director General, John Whitney, sought the advice of his Director of Finance, Peter Rogers. That turned out to be a very fortunate piece of delegation. Rogers' 'glosses' (as he put it) on the report remain perhaps the clearest summary of ITN's management difficulties in the Eighties and led to a clearer understanding on the part of the Authority of what, because of the conflicting interests involved, was to become one of the thorniest problems facing the IBA/ITC:

(i)   ITN was set up as a mutual company, i.e. one in which the investors and the customers are the same people.

(ii) The ITN business is now developing rapidly so that there is no longer an identity between investors and customers. The customers are being drawn from an increasingly wide circle, and by 1990 the ITV/Channel 4 news service might account for barely more than half (55%) of the business.

(iii) The present structure of ITN is wholly unsuited to the scale and diversity of the development referred to at (ii) above, because this structure:
  – provides an inadequate capital base
  – increases the exposure of ITV contractors to a range of business risks which do not arise out of the provision of the ITV/Channel 4 news services
  – generates inadequate commercial incentive and motivation within ITN
  – has produced an ITN management which on the business side, is not in my view fully up to the much larger, more difficult and more diverse tasks envisaged
  – has produced an ITN Board of Directors in which the main interest and expertise of the very powerful non-executive Directors (each one of them representing an investment stake) is focused in just one part of the ITN business. Moreover this is the part in which substantial growth is not anticipated.

Rogers took a far-sighted, and rather unbureaucratic, view of the future options for ITN:

(iv) If we retain the present structure then we should press for ITN to draw in its horns and focus almost exclusively on the provision of ITV/Channel 4 news services. Despite the difficulties which stand in the way of alternative courses of action, I would regard retrenchment of this kind as a dreary and unadventurous solution.

(v) If, on the other hand, we accept the expansion and diversification of ITN, then we shall have to come to terms with a new structure involving:
  – a wider shareholding
  – public flotation
  – substantially upgraded business management
  – the provision of the ITV/Channel 4 news services on a profit-making basis, with all shareholders benefiting from the profitability of these services

(vi) If the ITV/Channel 4 news services are to be supplied profitably by a restructured ITN, I see no reason why this should not be done on the basis of a negotiated service contract between ITN and ITV/Channel 4.

On a scheme that was close to the hearts of some of the senior management at ITN, Rogers was damning:

(vii) I mistrust ITN's desire to take a share of NAR in exchange for the provision of an ITV/Channel 4 news service. In my view, they just want to hitch themselves to a magnitude which they believe will grow rapidly in real terms

and give themselves an easy ride in terms of cost control. Nice work if you can get it, but they would not get it out of me. Additional points are:
  – a NAR basis breaks the link between the service provided and the cost of providing it. This reduces the customer's ability to mount a challenge on the basis of poor value for money.
  – ITN would almost certainly (as Deloitte say) seek escape clauses in case NAR actually falls, i.e. if the coin comes down heads, then ITN wins, if tails then ITV loses ... (IBA Memo from Peter Rogers, Director of Finance, to John Whitney, Director General, 2 April 1987)

By the autumn of 1987 Rogers had distilled his thoughts down to two options in a paper prepared for an Authority discussion on the future of ITN at the first of its two October meetings:

(i)   that ITN should be required to limit its horizons to the provision of news services to ITV, Channel 4, BSB and possibly Independent Radio. In this case there need be no major structural reform, although some limited but worthwhile changes might be made in the composition of the ITN Board and the approach to business planning generally;

(ii)   accept the desirability of a growth and diversification strategy. If, however, this wider remit is to be successful, then there will have to be changes in the ownership, corporate structure, funding and management of ITN. (IBA Paper 136(87))

At the end of the paper Rogers expanded on the changes that would be necessary:

The restructuring would involve additional equity, new shareholders from outside ITV, a reconstituted Board, service contracts including a profit margin for the ITV and Channel 4 news, improved strategic and financial planning, and probably a management shake up of some kind below Board level. This approach should help maximise the prospects of success in the new, larger and more diverse business. (Ibid.)

The staff recommendation was for the second, more adventurous, approach and this was accepted by the Authority. The idea of broadening ITN's shareholder base was therefore considered with approval within the IBA, where there was concern about the programme dimension as well as the financial aspects of ITN's future, well before the *realpolitik* that was to become apparent a year later, when the White Paper *Broadcasting in the '90s* was published:

... whereas at present all ITN shares are held by ITV contractors, under the new provision some shares would be held externally, by bodies without licences on any television channel. Eventually a majority of shares should be held by non-licensees. (White Paper, *Broadcasting in the '90s: Competition, Choice and Quality*, Section 6, Paragraph 13, November 1988)

A more extreme version of the idea had originally been promoted by Alastair Burnet and Whitney asked Rogers to meet Nicholas for discussions early in 1988. An ITVA-commissioned report by NERA had dealt with the possibility of a flotation for ITN. This report had angered ITN by 'its characterisation as an inefficient chattel of ITV' (Note of Rogers/Nicholas meeting, 17 March 1988). The meeting produced 'a ready meeting of minds' (Rogers' report of meeting to Whitney, 29 March 1988), Rogers foresaw 'two substantial obstacles in the path of ... an expanded and diversified ITN':

(i)   The management of ITN (including David Nicholas and Sir Alastair Burnet as executive directors) seem keen to pursue an expansionist policy, but the rest of the Board do not. This raises a difficult and sensitive problem of handling, ie., making common cause with the management of a company on a really major issue in the circumstances where the company's owners are known to take a different view ... shades of encouraging mutiny etc.

(ii) It is not easy to see how we could fulfil our statutory duty (under Section 22 of the Act) to ensure that ITN is properly equipped and funded if ITN were neither directly our contractor, nor indirectly subject to our influence because it was owned by ITV companies who were under contract to us ... (Ibid.)

He concluded:

I think there are two things that we could do to turn push into shove, viz:

(i)   Tell the ITV companies that we no longer find satisfactory the deficit funding approach to the financing of ITN. From the start of the extended contracts in January 1990 we would therefore like to see ITN established as a profit centre – still within ITV ownership – but providing news services to ITV, Channel 4, BSB, Superchannel, etc., on the basis of formal customer/contractor relationships using medium term service agreements and including profit margins or production fees ...

(ii) We need to undertake a thorough review of independent news provision, but one which is under our own leadership instead of finding ourselves constantly in the more restrictive position of commenting on consultants' reports for which the ITN Board are the client, and therefore in the driving seat. ... (Ibid.)

In the very one of those reports that had set Rogers thinking a year earlier, some of the Deloittes thinking had been about 'divisionalising' ITN's management of its different activities. This proposal had been seriously discussed at ITN as early as 1987 and later there had been some executive changes but full-scale division-alisation was later rejected as inappropriate for ITN.

Perhaps the most important promotion had occurred the previous year when Stewart Purvis was made Deputy Editor. Purvis, a reporter-turned-editor, had made his name when Nicholas appointed him to rescue *Channel Four News* from its early zero-rating failure. Within a year of his appointment in 1983 it had been christened by the *Independent* 'the thinking person's early evening news'. From 1987 Purvis was asked to attend Board meetings and quickly became a significant contributor to the policy debate within ITN.

However it was not until February 1990 that under the chairmanship of the now Sir David Nicholas, and with the help this time of the consultants McKinsey, a five-year Business Plan and structure was at last produced which, despite the unknown status at that stage of the Broadcasting Bill's proposals for shareholding divestment by ITV companies to less than 50 per cent, commanded broad support at the Board. Richard Dunn described it as: '... an intelligent and well argued summary of the kind that the Board had been looking towards for some years' (ITN Board minute 3788, 19 February 1990).

As Deputy Chairman, Dunn was becoming increasingly involved in the complex changes required at ITN. Subsequent events led to him assuming the role of Chairman. Previously, however, he had responsibility, as Chairman of the New Building subcommittee, over one of the most vexatious issues that even these tangled times were to throw up. The expansion of ITN had given rise to the biggest capital project in the organisation's history.

The need for a new ITN HQ was first put to the Board in July 1983. The pressures on space at Wells Street brought about by the development of *Channel Four News* alone were recognised by the Board as serious and a subcommittee was set up, originally under Bryan Cowgill. Its members then were the finance directors of Thames, LWT and Central. The experience of the Granada Group in handling property problems from cinemas to motorway service areas was recognised by the inclusion of their estates manager. Although there were financial inducements on offer for sites away from the centre of London, David Nicholas was adamant:

I thought we had a great asset in being in Central London in touch with the people who made news – in flesh touch ... lots of MPs and big people were in and out of the ITN building all the time. They'd have a drink with young journalists in the Green Room or go across to the wine bar. And I always felt that was a terribly important way, especially for young journalists, to keep contact. Whereas the BBC moving out to White City was remote ... I fought very hard to keep ITN in a W1 complex, though there were incentives to go to Docklands. (Interview with Sir David Nicholas)

The search for the right size of building in the right place at the right price, however, proved to be a long one. The old Bedford College building in Regents Park was one of the first stops, but the Crown Commissioners, who were the landlords, did not feel able to approve the changes to the building that were required. Then there was Triton Place – a grand-sounding name for a small close behind the then Thames building in the Euston Road – convenient but costly. The search continued and ranged from the old Royal Mint site near Tower Bridge, through Bankside power station to an old London Rubber Company condom factory between Stockwell and Brixton.

The latter site gave rise to some ribald comments. The fact was that in the post-pill, pre-AIDs era the London Rubber Company was forced to reduce production of its Durex condoms and needed to sell its least cost-effective factory. Nicholas relates, with relish, that his office would have been the retort room for the latex rubber production. He might then have been said to have been the best protected editor in British television.

Finally, in 1986, when Rupert Murdoch had broken his newspapers free of the traditional print union practices and made money by moving them to Docklands, accepting the financial incentives and selling his high-value Fleet Street and other sites, one of these became the focus of the ITN New Building subcommittee's attention.

200 Gray's Inn Road had been purpose-built for the *Sunday Times*, as Thomson House, in 1962. The relationship between ITN and this site was to become a saga of epic proportions. (The ownership changes at ITN related at the close of this chapter and the fact that the building is a realisable asset may indicate that it is a saga that has not ended even as this is written.)

GIR, as it became known, was first discussed as an option at the end of 1986. It was put to the Board as the preferred choice of the subcommittee in February 1987. The building was massive – offering some 180,000 square feet of usable space – it had housed the printing as well as the editorial operations of the paper. It would not be easy to convert to other uses and was therefore going at a bargain price. The vendor's representative turned out to be Rupert Murdoch in person on the phone – to the surprise of Paul Mathews, ITN's Deputy Chief Executive, who was handling the New Building project. However, he was not so startled as to forget to negotiate the asking price downwards – he got it down from £8 million to £7 million.

By this time ITN had a contract to provide news for Superchannel (the satellite initiative of an ITV consortium, see below) and there were negotiations to provide news for British Satellite Broadcasting's factual channel, so it appeared likely that more than half of the space would actually be required by ITN. The remainder would be let – to other broadcast industry tenants, it was hoped. Dunn and the executives of ITN were very keen on GIR. David Plowright believed that Docklands or some other more financially beneficial site should be considered. Some other ITV directors wanted to know the full costs of conversion before deciding. However at the Board meeting on 16 March 1987 they agreed the purchase price of £7 million for the building, subject to planning permission being available from the local authority for the conversion.

Camden Council was an old-fashioned Labour Party stronghold. In the conflict between the print unions and Mr Murdoch there was no doubt whose side they were on. They could not keep his business in their borough but they could make it difficult to sell the building, causing him financial loss. There was also, perhaps, a genuine concern about the effect of the move to Wapping on the longstanding local print and graphical community, many of whom lived as well as worked in the area. Whatever the motivation, the council appeared determined to make the sale difficult. An attempt to use the change-of-use regulations to restrict the building to use as a printers failed. But the council then sought a 'voluntary donation' to a trust to help unemployed printers and their families. Initially this was set at £1.5 million. But when that was rejected by ITN's negotiator, in this case the Company Secretary, David Roycroft, it was reduced to £700,000.

At its meeting in April 1987 the Board was split on this issue. Most seemed prepared to take a pragmatic view and were not against the donation in principle. But Paul McKee, formerly a respected ITN executive, now Deputy Managing Director of Yorkshire Television and representing that company on the Board, and Alex Mair, the Managing Director of Grampian Television, were very concerned about the implications both moral and legal of being required to pay for planning consent in this way. The Board agreed to seek counsel's opinion.

The May meeting was attended by Sir Frank Layfield QC, whose opinion had been obtained. His written opinion had concentrated on Camden's legal position but members were anxious to hear about their own legal position. Sir Frank was able to reassure them that such a donation would not be a criminal act on their part. However:

> The unlawfulness of the proposal stemmed from the fact that Camden Council would be acting *ultra vires*. This in turn would make any (planning) consent vulnerable to challenge ... e.g. from a disgruntled Camden rate payer. (ITN Board minute 3418, May 1987)

Asked by the Chairman, Paul Fox, what practical course he would recommend:

> Sir Frank said that his advice would be that in view of the urgent needs of ITN and the timetable involved, the best course of action would be to go ahead and pay the sum to Camden under the best arrangements that could be made. ITN should make it clear in the documentation their reasons for accepting the agreement. ITN should attach to the documents a valuation of the cost of not receiving planning permission. This was best set down before concluding the agreement rather than afterwards. As a re-insurance, assuming ITN had received its permission as a result of this agreement, it would be wise for ITN to make

a new application with some limited technical variation. This would mean that a new planning consent would be obtained which would be completely untainted. (Ibid.)

Paul Fox asked the chairman of the New Building subcommittee, Richard Dunn, for his views:

> Mr Dunn said that it had been the view of the building sub-committee that it was of paramount importance for ITN to find a new building quickly. This had been the basis on which the sub-committee had been working and care had been taken to seek legal advice and the advice of experts on the proposed deal with Camden. At no stage had it been suggested that what was being advocated would mean that ITN would be acting illegally. What had to be weighed up was the potential damage to ITN of any delay. It seemed clear that ITN would not be able to find another building for £7 million. (Ibid.)

But by now Granada's member of the Board had joined the voices of concern at the prospect of payment:

> Mr Plowright said that his concern would be for the credibility of ITN if it entered into a deal which could undermine its editorial integrity. How would ITN be able to face up, for example, to an investigation by a programme like *World in Action*? (Ibid.)

At this his fellow director, the face and voice of *News at Ten*, Sir Alastair Burnet commented that it was clear that such payments were not uncommon. (Subsequently ITN were to discover that Granada had entered a not dissimilar agreement with Liverpool Council for their new building in that city.)
    But the dissent was now a chorus. McKee said:

> ... he was not interested in ways of circumventing what was essentially an unlawful action ... In his view, any agreement with Camden was out of the question. (Ibid.)

Mair remained firmly against. James Gatward declared himself for purchasing the building without planning consent and then going to appeal. This was to become the prevailing view, despite a formidable rearguard action by David Nicholas:

> The Editor said that he totally rejected some of the rhetoric used during the discussion. Sir Frank's final advice took into account all factors including the welfare of the staff. The Editor added that he saw no harm in any agreement with Camden being made public.

He was satisfied that there was nothing to be ashamed of and he was concerned with the greater good of the company. The conditions under which staff were now being expected to work were intolerable. (Ibid.)

But it was no use. The shareholder members of the Board – the only ones with votes – had swung against his view:

After discussion, the Chairman said that it was the unanimous view of the Board that the building should be purchased; at a cost of £7 million and that no agreement such as had been proposed should be entered into. If Camden Council refused planning permission their refusal should be taken to appeal. (Ibid.)

After this decision Richard Dunn felt that he should resign as chairman of the sub-committee and he was replaced by LWT's Finance Director, Peter McNally. But calling Camden Council's bluff proved to have been the correct course. Though the council tried further blocking tactics – like seeking to apply restrictive clauses, on sub-letting and selling, to the permission which they eventually granted in October 1987 – the way was now clear for ITN.

By February 1988 an ingenious plan for development that satisfied the Board's concern about costs had been approved in principle. ITN would sell the building to a property developer, Stuart Lipton, whose company Stanhope properties would convert GIR for office use and then lease it back, with ITN taking responsibility for the internal fitting out and, importantly, for letting the space that it was not going to use – several complete floors. This looked a good deal in 1987 but the planning delay of eighteen months was to prove damaging.

When the plan for funding and development of the building was finally formally proposed to the Board by the subcommittee in March 1988 it must have seemed something of an anti-climax. In a paper which reiterated the arguments that the cost savings sought by the Board could not be achieved without new automated technology and that such technology could not be accommodated in the Wells Street building, figures were given that sought to demonstrate that, while the standing costs of GIR would be almost double those of Wells Street the operating costs after rental income would actually be slightly lower.

The Board approved the deal for the development and marketing of 200 Gray's Inn Road and, in effect, ITN became at this point a property company as well as a news provider. Paul Mathews duly celebrated the fact the following year by arranging the sale of Wells Street to the property company Speyhawk Mount Row for £24 million, just before the collapse of the property market that was to put Speyhawk into receivership.

Stanhope had chosen Norman Foster as the architect and eighteen months later, in the autumn of 1990, 200 Gray's Inn stood splendidly converted and ready for occupation. In December the staff of ITN moved in. The first news was broadcast from there as the shadow of the Gulf War loomed. However the ITN staff were alone in the building. The London property boom was over and the computer company to whom it had been hoped to let the remainder of the building had withdrawn. ITN itself was now burdened with the rent for the entire building – £5.5 million a year. For this and other reasons ITN had come to the brink of a crisis that was ultimately to lead to the verge of insolvency.

In a sense most of the major projects that expanded ITN in the 1980s were grafted-on rather than generic developments. ITN's core role as news provider to ITV did evolve, with requirements to provide night-time news, a newsflash service and open-ended major news events coverage – as election and other major event coverage had evolved in earlier decades. But developments like *Channel Four News* and options like Superchannel and BSB had to be planned growths outside the core function. As with all grafts there was always the risk of failure.

If ITN had had its way, news provision for C4 would not have been a very different variant from the ITV news service – a little more depth, a slightly broader agenda; in essence an upmarket version of, but subordinate to, the flagship *News at Ten*. Indeed, Alastair Burnet continued to take that view until he left ITN in 1991. But C4 believed that the channel's remit required a distinctive news with an innovative approach. (Full details of the Channel Four–ITN relationship will be covered in Volume 6 of *Independent Television in Britain*.)

The different approach to news content and treatment for C4 meant that ITN would have to base the pricing of their first major outside contract on costings that were to a degree hypothetical. There is some evidence that in negotiations with C4, ITN allowed themselves to be negotiated from an original asking price, which would have given them a handsome profit, down to a figure which did not actually cover their costs. News costs are dependent on the breadth of the content and, to a degree, the style, more than depth of coverage. C4 had no one with national television news experience amongst its senior executives – though the Senior Commissioning Editor for Factual Programmes, under whose aegis news fell, Liz Forgan, had previously been a journalist on the *Guardian*. She and Jeremy Isaacs had created the specification for C4's news but in the pressure to get the channel on air the negotiations were largely left to the man who had responsibility for the business affairs of the new channel, Justin Dukes. Dukes had no previous experience of television but he knew something of journalism – he had occupied a senior position at the *Financial Times* for a period. He was to prove a tough negotiator.

By September 1981 ITN's asking price was down to £6,166,000 per year – more or less the cost of C4 news as it was then specified. But Dukes sought reduction by a further million. ITN resisted but at the Board meeting of 20 October 1981 the Director General of the IBA, Sir Brian Young, and David McCall, the Managing Director of Anglia, who was on the C4 Board, urged their colleagues on the Board not to resist further reasonable reduction because 'the board of C4 were not all for ITN'. Whether C4 could have commissioned a quality news service from any other organisation at that time probably looks more doubtful now, after the experience of TV-am, than it did then. Also Brian Tesler (another member of both Boards) was later to reveal that C4's Chairman, Edmund Dell, had 'let it be known that he did not feel the channel needed a news programme' (Private note of the full discussion of *Channel Four News* at ITN Board, 17 October 1983). In any event the ITN Board approved a further reduction to £5,427,000. This did not prevent a challenge by C4 to the agreement in 1983. But that it was a rock-bottom, if not loss-making, figure that was agreed may be judged by the fact that five years after C4 had gone on the air, detailed costings by accountants of both parties led to a mutually agreed price of £11,022,000.

By that time (1987) ITN had more experience of pricing contracts. As early as July 1981 Granada had signalled a special interest in satellite broadcasting when at ITV's Council David Plowright had reported that his company would respond to a Home Office request for broadcasters' views on the subject separately from the network's joint response through the ITV Association. This pioneering interest of Granada's was to endure through early disappointments to ultimate success by the end of the decade. The company detached Andrew Quinn to work on the government-encouraged Direct Broadcasting by Satellite (DBS) initiative.

It was his report to Council at the beginning of 1985 that demonstrated that the project as proposed by the Department of Trade and Industry was an expensive way of propping up the British aerospace industry rather than a cost-effective opportunity for broadcasters. Quinn's boss at Granada, David Plowright, was Chairman of Council at this time and under his leadership less costly alternatives were explored. One of these was to use a cheaper French satellite that was already in position, TDF 1, to broadcast British programmes (BBC as well as ITV) to Europe, on a channel that would be paid for by advertising. It was to carry the ambitious title, Superchannel.

Over the years 1985–89 Superchannel was to take up more ITN Board discussion time that any other subject except the new building. The Board itself had examined satellite options – one was to take a cheap UK-based channel broadcasting to Europe which was up for sale and mount a twenty-four-hour news service. The channel broadcast under the name Sky. The idea was rejected on cost grounds. The eventual purchaser of the channel was Rupert Murdoch. It was the first step in his rise to dominance of the UK subscription broadcasting market by the end of the decade – by-passing on the way the British regulatory regime that he so despised (see Introduction).

The story of Superchannel itself will be found in *Independent Television in Britain*, Volume 6, but two factors in the channel's unhappy history affected ITN particularly. One was that Plowright did not obtain support for the initiative from all the ITV companies. Thames was to stand aside, preferring instead to join the European consortium, Société Europeene des Satellites (SES) investing in the hardware that was to become the Astra satellite system – now carrying the Murdoch BSkyB channels and many others. Thames' interests at the ITN Board were from that moment of decision inevitably going to be in conflict with the interests of the other ITN shareholders who had invested in Superchannel.

Ironically it had been Bryan Cowgill's report, as chairman of Council's Cable and Satellite Working Party which had originally given rise to the suggestion in June 1985 that 'a cheaper medium-powered satellite, with a wider footprint, to deliver services to all of Europe, with such services supported by advertising rather than subscription ...' was a better commercial prospect than UK DBS. A month later Cowgill was swept from the managing directorship of Thames in the aftermath of the *Dallas* debacle. His successor took the medium-powered satellite route – but with hardware rather than a programme service. (Anglia and TSW were also founder investors in Astra but did join the Superchannel consortium. Yorkshire initially stayed out of Superchannel and did not invest in Astra either.)

The second Superchannel factor that at first appeared likely to affect ITN was a decision that the channel would carry BBC programmes as well as ITV's – including BBC Television's news. Indeed Alasdair Milne, the BBC's Director General, appeared at one time to make the presence of BBC programmes on the channel conditional upon its showing BBC News. However, the BBC discovered that those were rights difficulties involved in the proposal to transmit their programmes by satellite. Seen as 'perfidious Albion' by the ITV companies concerned, the Corporation finally failed to make any programmes available to Superchannel and ITN had full running rights to news on the channel.

Plowright proposed that ITN invest in Superchannel as well as provide news for it. ITN's management supported the idea but the proposal was blocked by the 'outsiders', Thames and Yorkshire. If that investment had gone ahead it would surely have added to the sum of ITN's increasing financial difficulty. The Superchannel investment gap was filled by Richard Branson.

Meanwhile Peter McNally, the Financial Director of LWT had spotted another problem:

> Mr McNally noted that the cost per hour of the ITN proposal was well in excess of ... what could be afforded by Superchannel. He suggested that a half or even a quarter of the amount ... was all that could be met in the initial years. (ITN Board minute 3889, January 1986)

It subsequently transpired that the gap between what the news for Superchannel would cost ITN to make and what the channel was prepared to pay was £400,000 a year – the channel in fact being able to pay some 80 per cent of the cost. It was then agreed to explore a three-year contract with a first-year price of £2 million (that is, what the channel could afford at start up instead of the true cost of £2.5 million) with rises to compensate in the following years, breaking even at the end of the third year.

Even that somewhat commercially risky generosity of approach proved unacceptable to Superchannel. As might be expected with a number of directors being common to both the channel's Board and that of ITN, the negotiations became circular in character and rumbled on through most of 1986 – with the directors who were not party to both organisations becoming increasingly critical. By January 1987 Richard Dunn was requiring it to be minuted that:

> It remained the view of the Board of Thames Television that ITN should either be paid £2.5 million or have a fourth year management fee of 20%. ITN should not be obliged to accept both £2 million and 12.5% ... (ITN Board minute 3985, 19 January 1987)

He believed that his colleagues needed to look to their fiduciary duties as directors of ITN.

The matter was further complicated by Superchannel seeking the exclusive rights to ITN news within their satellite 'footprint' (coverage area) until 1990. ITN was by this time also in negotiation with British Satellite Broadcasting (BSB) whose DBS coverage did fall within that of the low-powered satellite that Superchannel would be using. BSB was also seeking certain services to be supplied on an exclusive basis to their proposed NOW channel. As Dunn is recorded as understatedly remarking, 'the Board had some difficult judgements to make' (ITN Board minute 3480, 18 November 1986).

Friday 30 January 1987 was a date that carried more than one portent for British broadcasting. Superchannel finally went on the air on that day and it was also the day that the new Chairman of the BBC, 'Duke' Hussey, ousted Alasdair Milne from his post as the Director General – with indelible consequences for the internal culture of the Corporation. ITN's bulletin on Superchannel carried the news to glittering celebratory gatherings, one including Margaret Thatcher (Superchannel being one of the few endeavours by ITV of which she is on record as approving) in the production facility at Limehouse and at the British Embassy in Paris.

By September the following year *Media Week* was reporting: 'Eighteen months after the launch, the cumulative deficit is heading rapidly towards £60 million and losses are still running at £1 million a month' (Article by Raymond Snoddy of the *Financial Times* in *Media Week*, 9 September 1988).

ITN's Superchannel news was watched by a mere 100,000 across Europe. The ITV investors decided to cut their losses. In May 1988 Central and LWT refused to put any more money into the channel. TVS, Anglia and YTV did increase their investment, as did Richard Branson, with Virgin taking a further £10 million share of the company. The original Managing Director, Richard Hooper, was replaced by a Virgin executive, Richard Devereux. Subsequently LWT sold its stake to Virgin. Granada sold its shares to Virgin and TVS. But even Branson's multi-faceted expertise could not bring Superchannel into profit. By August 1988 the channel was up for sale. It was even offered to ITN for a nominal £1 in early October. Wisely, ITN did not take up that particular opportunity for expansion.

In the autumn of 1988 the remaining investors rejected bids from Robert Maxwell and United Cable to sell the channel to the only financially acceptable buyer that could be found – a small Italian company supplying a pop music channel to cable companies based outside Lucca and owned by the Marcucci family, called Beta TV.

In the midst of this upheaval ITN remained unpaid by Superchannel. By November the company was owed £320,000 and on 11 November it withdrew its news service from the channel. The money was subsequently recouped but the outcome of this and other ITN enterprises of the period was the lack of confidence in ITN's commercial and financial abilities that was so graphically portrayed in Peter Rogers' analysis of ITN's position for the Authority. It was not until 1992, when NBC bought Superchannel as an outlet for their programmes in Europe and contracted ITN to make the channel's European and World News bulletins, that the Superchannel connection really paid off – leading to contracts for the ITN World News on PBS in America, Channel 9 in Australia, NHK in Japan and TV New Zealand.

Meanwhile, at the end of the Eighties all appeared well in the short term. The operating budget of £48,412,000 for 1989/90 was presented to the Board in June – the month that its new, and first internal, Chairman, David Nicholas, received his Knighthood in the Queen's Birthday honours – by a new young finance head, Penny Bickerstaff. Brian Tesler described this budget as 'the best he had seen from ITN in addressing the control of costs'. In fact, under the pressure of the demands of the coverage of the end of the Cold War, the new ITN building and the organisation's many new enterprises, ITN's financial control systems were beginning to buckle. At this point the affairs of ITN entered a downward vortex of forces, some of which lay within what should have been its ambit of control; many though lay outside.

By March 1990 the Board, now at the height of its internal conflicts over the position it should take on ITN's future ownership in the lobbying over the Broadcasting Bill, was told by Stewart Purvis that coverage of the collapse of communism had resulted in an overspend of £1.5 million. It is probable that by this stage nobody knew the precise figure. Penny Bickerstaff had left, suffering from exhaustion.

Sir Alastair Burnet had resigned from the Board in February on the ownership issue – though he continued to present *News at Ten* until August 1991. He had sought that ITN should have a majority of independent (that is, non-customer) shareholders and it is said that it was largely his lobbying of the Prime Minister that ultimately achieved Paragraph (9)(b) in Section 32 of the Broadcasting Act, in which C3 (ITV) licence holders were prevented from holding a majority stake in ITN from 1993 onwards. He had written to Whitney at the IBA in 1988 proposing a separate news and current affairs franchise, financed by the advertising revenue from the commercial slots around and in the programme – a possibility in which at one time David Nicholas also appeared to believe.

Burnet's farewell speech to the February 1990 Board managed to range over the history of ITV and at the same time be gnomic. The Bill was still in draft at that time and the sections dealing with news were then numbered 29 and 30:

... to my mind, clauses 29 and 30 are expertly and fairly drawn in the service of the government's competitive policy. ITN is given the chance (after 35 years) to react to new circumstances and stimuli as a free-standing company.

... I do not wish the perception of ITN ... to be the creature of an evident, cartel, the sole relic of the pre-1993 system, and the target of any easy political or commercial campaign against what will be called a stitch-up. I am also sceptical of getting the right sort of investment interest in ITN's development outside its Channel 3 contract if the company is seen to be so wholly subservient to the Channel 3 licensees, and their cost-centre way of financing it. (ITN copy of Sir Alastair Burnet's speech to the Board, 19 February 1990)

Burnet had served ITN as its Political Editor in 1963–64 before becoming Editor of *The Economist* in 1965. He became a newscaster with the very first edition of *News at Ten* on 3 July 1967. Remarkably he had managed to present the programme alongside Andrew Gardner for three nights a week while also still editing *The Economist* (on the other two nights Gardner's partner was the late Reginald Bosanquet). Later he became the permanent feature of the two-presenter format that then characterised ITV's main news bulletin and had been ITN's anchor presenter for General Elections and other national events coverage. Burnet's combination of journalistic sagacity and *gravitas* on air contributed importantly to the respect in which ITN was held – both by the public and by politicians. With his departure from the screen in 1991 a major change in format was thought necessary. A single presenter in a new, more sombre, setting emerged as a result of discussions. Trevor McDonald, a popular and respected ITN reporter was chosen for the new role.

In March 1990, at the first meeting after Burnet resigned from ITN's Board, David Nicholas reported on a meeting with the Home Office Minister of State responsible for guiding the Bill through Parliament, David Mellor. The requirement that the ITV shareholders should dispose of 51 per cent of their holding in ITN was not, it appeared, negotiable. It was implied that this was a result of Mrs Thatcher's special interest in news.

The key problem of any disposal of ITN shares was their valuation. The ITV companies wanted to see a value reflecting at least part of their thirty-five years of investment. But, as Andrew Quinn dourly observed, the value at that point was, in effect, nil. The companies needed time and calm conditions to let a value be developed. They hadn't got either.

Schemes for a news service company in which outsiders might hold 51 per cent, which could be separate from an assets holding company retained by ITV, were examined but rejected. Pelion was heaped upon Ossa as the shareholders were asked to provide guarantee for the borrowing of £17 million over September and October 1990 in respect of GIR. Greg Dyke and David Reay said that they believed ITN's costs to be 'out of control' but the Board 'reluctantly agreed the extra expenditure incurred' (ITN Board minutes, September 1990).

By October the GIR cost had grown to £18 million. There was difficulty arranging the borrowing and shareholders were also being asked to pay a deficit of £2.9 million on 1989/90 and £4.9 million of 'one-off costs'.

Three days before the October Board meeting a copy of a confidential letter from David Nicholas to the Home Secretary, telling him of ITN's financial plight and referring to the ITV companies' unwillingness to invest in the company when the Bill required them to become minority shareholders, found its way to the *Guardian*. Georgina Henry did not quote anybody but appeared to have been well briefed on the background to the letter. By the day of the meeting Sir David Nicholas was on the record for *The Times*:

> There is no question of going off the air or not paying wages ... Even if the worst came to the worst and the ITV companies refused to provide the £6.5 million, it would become a matter for the IBA, which under the 1981 (broadcasting) act, has a duty to see that ITV has an adequately financed and adequately equipped news service. (Article by Melinda Wittstock, *The Times*, 12 October 1990)

There was now real anger amongst the shareholders. They suspected the leak was deliberate and an attempt by ITN to force them to pay up, rather than to get the terms of the Bill changed. The new Finance Director, Clive Timms, who had come from managing the finances of News and Current Affairs at the BBC, must have wondered what he had got himself into. His new company was facing genuine insolvency, as he reported at the Board:

> The Secretary read out figures of the estimated overdraft position over the next six weeks and confirmed that if the shareholders now pay that part of the £4.9 million already invoiced, the £2.9 million deficit and the sums now due on the normal cash call, that the company could manage through to the end of October without either of the £9 million GIR funding amounts being in place. If at the end of October those funds were confirmed as available, but delayed for finalising of formalities, an early drawdown of the November cash call (from the companies) on 1 November would enable the company to continue until 22 November.
>
> If the £18 million GIR funding was secured by that date the company would then be adequately financed until March 1991, when if no income stream from the tenants was in position the company would again face a cash flow problem. (ITN Board minute 3859, 15 October 1990)

Shirley Littler, who had been confirmed as the Director General of the IBA/ITC at the beginning of the year, felt constrained to warn the companies formally of their responsibilities under the 1981 Broadcasting Act and pointed out that 'there would be a similar obligation under the 1990 Act (Section 32(12)) regarding the nominated news provider'. ITN had not at this time been nominated but she said that the decision on the nomination of the news provider would be known in December. A statement of intent from ITN's owners agreeing to disposal of their shares would be required. Timing of disposal would be open to discussion. This statement did at least prevent a circular – no investment without nomination, no nomination without investment – argument arising. A bad-tempered meeting ended in an agreement to have an extra meeting the following week, on 22 October, before which detailed cash flows would be made available to the companies, who would examine their own financial potential against a background of an advertising recession.

At that meeting firm commitments were made by the companies in return for assurances that ITN would make the real cuts in personnel and capital costs necessary to stay within budget. At the following meeting Nicholas was authorised to write to Shirley Littler that the Board had resolved to:

> recommend to the shareholders of ITN that they agree to use their best endeavours to fulfil the ownership provisions of the Act (as they apply to the nominated news provider) within the timescale laid down by the ITC. (Letter Chairman, ITN, to DG, IBA, 26 November 1990)

ITN was duly nominated as the sole news provider for C3, for the first five years, but not before an even darker hour for ITN. The Board saw the arrival at last of Bob Phillis, in January 1991, in the role of Chief Executive, as solving their problems. But even as he was taking over, the depth of these problems was revealed. A 'Black Hole' had opened up in the finances of ITN.

> I asked questions of the auditors and Clive Timms, and Clive came to me and said, 'Look, this is not the most auspicious of starts for you but I have to tell you that there is a serious problem. We cannot account for –' and at this stage it looked as if it might have been as high as 15 or 16 million pounds ... it hadn't been misappropriated or stolen, what had happened is that expenditure hadn't been accounted for. (Interview with Bob Phillis)

Clive Timms had only been Financial Director at ITN for four months and he had not had any overlap with his predecessor, who had left five months before he arrived. What he had discovered, just as Phillis was taking over as Chief Executive, was that items of expenditure, particularly satellite charges (which were substantial sums at this time because of the historic international events of the period), had not been processed and allocated to the profit and loss account, income and expenditure. They had been held in a suspense account to be dealt with later.

There was a second aspect to the problem. In the management accounts coverage costs were estimated each month from activity logs maintained by the newsrooms. Because of the overload on the accounting staff at this time, a significant time lag had built up before the estimates were reconciled with invoices, expense claims and so on. Hence the financial accounts only reflected estimated costs and, as is usual with estimates, the actual coverage costs were much higher.

Phillis had to move fast. He asked Timms to strengthen the financial staff by recruiting two qualified accountants and a qualified expenses controller. As importantly, he and Stewart Purvis devised a system whereby accounting staff became an integral part of the news teams. He is recorded in the minutes of the May 1991 Board as saying that he had 'some serious doubts about the adequacy of Coopers & Lybrand Deloitte as the company's auditors' and asked the Board's new Audit Committee to 'consider the desirability of a change in audit firm'. In September Coopers & Lybrand Deloitte were replaced by Arthur Andersen as auditors.

At the same meeting he outlined his cost-cutting plans, which involved the redundancy of over a hundred staff and no pay increase in 1991. The Board supported this and confirmed to Stewart Purvis that if industrial action arose as a result, the ITV network would accept a management service news. (Perhaps it should not come as a surprise at this point in the story to discover that there are no totally reliable figures for the number of people employed by ITN in the Eighties. The peak is believed to have been around 1200. By 1992 the figures are clear and show a reduction to 735. This fell by a further 150 over the next three years.)

At the following meeting on 17 June, Sir David Nicholas made a statement from the chair that he had 'come to the conclusion that it might be appropriate for him to bring forward his retirement as Chairman to October'.

The departure of first Burnet and then Nicholas in 1991 marked a watershed in the evolution of ITN from personal to professional management. Given the changes in society at large during the Eighties, it was perhaps inevitable. There was loss and there was gain for ITN in the change. But it was certainly part of the end of an era in the culture of independent broadcasting in Britain. Nicholas, like his predecessors, had sought to command all the news ground on behalf of ITN. He would often personally direct his troops to what needed to be covered. It was, he sometimes appeared to feel, his duty to rise above the mundane commercial concerns of his shareholders to achieve the greater journalistic good. He was a brilliant instinctive editor, to whom the audience owed much. ITN's coverage of the extraordinary events of the Eighties, outlined at the start of this chapter, can truly be said to have been an educational force – benefiting in particular that part of the ITV audience that had had less chance of formal education, many of whom seldom chose to watch the BBC. His was an achievement in accord with the educational traditions of his Welsh blood and upbringing. That was not diminished, only tarnished, by the events of his three years as Chairman – which many of his colleagues feel, with the benefit of hindsight, was a role too far.

New Tasks – New Ownership

Meanwhile, Phillis and Purvis, and Richard Dunn as their Chairman, had a great deal to do in the eighteen months before the terms of the new Broadcasting Act came fully into force.

There was the contract – for the first time – to be reached with the new ITV licensees. That took nearly two years and went right to the wire. At £53.6 million per year for a five-year term, Meridian, one of the new licensees, was unhappy about the price to the last. Roger Laughton, their Director of Programmes, finally signed, adding an 'under duress' caveat, on New Year's Eve of 1992 – only hours before it was due to come into force. If Meridian had failed to sign and as a result not been supplied with news, they would have been the first programme company in the history of the network to contravene the terms of their legal agreement with the regulator before they even went on air.

Then there was the matter of ownership. In September 1991 the ITV companies reallocated their 400,000 shares in ITN to reflect their proportion of NAR over the three years to July 1991 in preparation for the divestment of 51 per cent of their holdings. Phillis and his newly hired Director of Marketing, Dick Emery (who had been his Marketing Director at Central Television), and Stewart Purvis, met all the US networks, seeking a relevant new owner to join Reuters, whom they had already sought out through Lehmann Brothers (their chosen merchant bankers for the divestment) as a potential shareholder.

Reuters had bought the old Visnews television news agency some years earlier and appeared a very suitable shareholder. However the approach triggered the reappearance in Phillis' professional life of a figure who had been one of the reasons he had moved to ITN. Michael Green, the owner of Carlton Communications, was a non-executive Director of Reuters.

There were two other triggers to what became, in October 1992, a formal offer for the ITN shares by a consortium led by Carlton. Greg Dyke, who had been increasingly critical of ITN's management over the years he was on the Board, had, to some people's surprise, continued his criticism after the arrival of Phillis. In February 1992 Dyke resigned from the ITN Board in protest at its approval of ITN bidding for the teletext licence against the ITV-owned incumbent, Oracle Ltd. He was Chairman of ITV's Council at the time but his letter to Chairman Dunn made it clear that he was acting on behalf of LWT as a shareholder in protest at what he and the Board of LWT believed was 'unethical' behaviour.

Dyke, in one of his 'let's go round all the options' sessions (which always included what others would have classified as unthinkable) with the LWT Chairman, Christopher Bland, raised the idea of buying ITN with a ready-made consortium of the necessary proportions of ITV and non-ITV shareholders. Bland, who knew Michael Green well, tried the idea out on him. Green, whose company had won the London licence but was not yet on the air, had already focused on the possibilities of ITN.

Lord Sharp of Grimsdyke was the first independent non-executive member of the Carlton Board. He had been introduced to Green by Lord Young (the former Secretary of State for Trade and Industry, who was a cousin of Green's first wife's family – the Wolfsons). Sharp, who had been Young's predecessor as Executive Chairman at Cable and Wireless, was also on the Board of Stanhope, the property company owned by Green's old friend Stuart Lipton, the developers of GIR – ITN's headquarters. And the failure of ITN to find tenants for most of the 154,000 square feet of the building that it was not occupying was causing Lipton concern.

Green, a natural deal maker, put together a consortium initially consisting of Carlton, LWT, Central and Reuters but to which Granada was added, with Anglia and STV as 5 per cent shareholders. Thames, TVS and TSW had lost their licences and were paid off at £14 a share (which netted Thames over a million pounds). The other ITV companies who did not wish to be in the consortium were paid back their original £1 per share – though they were given a first-year discount on their news contract payments. Michael Green also successfully negotiated a tough deal with Lipton which, in effect, transformed GIR from being a liability to becoming an asset for ITN.

Michael Green took over from Richard Dunn as Chairman. Phillis, for whom Green's arrival to be his boss for a second time was not a welcome development, resigned in January 1992 to become Deputy Director General of the BBC. Green found a new Chief Executive in David Gordon of *The Economist* – who was to come into conflict with the ITV network, and his chairman, within six months. That is a subject for a later volume in this series.

Throughout all this turmoil Stewart Purvis and his journalists, camera crews and editors continued to apply their professionalism, casting light on the wounds of the world – from Belfast to Bosnia and Rwanda to Chechnya – and relating events taking place in Westminster, Washington, Brussels, Moscow and around the globe to the lives of ordinary viewers.

ITN and the Televising of Parliament

A significant broadcasting development of the Eighties in which ITN played a role (with the IBA and the ITVA's Programme Planning Department as participants, as well as the BBC) was the facilitating of television coverage of the proceedings of the Houses of Parliament for the first time.

Proceedings of both chambers of Parliament had been made available to broadcasters in sound only from April 1978. Its primary use had been on radio but ITN and BBC News had used extracts of the sound-only feeds, with appropriate still photographs or graphics, for coverage of important debates or significant statements. One of the disadvantages – for MPs more than broadcasters – of sound-only coverage was that the Commons, with its constant barrage of interruptions and cries of 'Order!' from the Speaker, sometimes sounded more like a bear garden than the Mother of Parliaments. Opinion in the House was split between those who thought that pictures would explain the sounds and those who thought that the problem would be exacerbated by visual portrayal of proceedings. In a series of votes in the House of Commons over the twenty-two years from 1966 to 1988 the latter were always in the majority.

Possibly because their proceedings were more calm and measured, the House of Lords was the more enlightened of the two chambers about making pictures of their debates available to the public. Their Lordships had actually voted in favour of televising their proceedings for an experimental period as early as 15 June 1966 – a full ten years before regular sound-only broadcasting began. But even in the upper House events moved at a stately pace. There was a closed-circuit experiment in 1968 but it was a further two years before there was a House of Lords Select Committee recommendation for a one-year experimental transmission and not until January 1985 that the first pictures (other than those of the ceremonial of the State Opening of Parliament) emerged from the Palace of Westminster.

The long-awaited pictures came from an ITN mobile control room (MCR) placed – after much negotiation – in the garden of the major-domo of the Palace, Black Rod. Crews from ITN and the BBC alternated in manning cameras placed behind their Lordships' seats and in the galleries above. Extra lighting was needed and its heat was considered a problem on some summer days. When the Commons finally voted in favour of the televising of their chamber on 9 February 1988 the resulting Select Committee was almost as much concerned with the technicalities: the need for low lighting levels, remote-controlled cameras and the minimal use of space at the Palace of Westminster, as it was with a code for the responsible coverage of debate. Having employed a consultant (John Grist, founder producer in 1959 of BBC Television's first programme totally devoted to politics, *Gallery* and later its Head of Current Affairs), questioned relevant witnesses from the British broadcasters and been to Canada to study the televising of the Ottawa parliament, the Select Committee on the Televising of the Proceedings of the House reported in May 1989. Its report was approved a month later. Grist was appointed an Officer of the House, as Supervisor of Broadcasting, and an experimental period of a year's broadcasting would take place before a review that would lead to the permanent broadcasting of Parliament. A Lords Select Committee agreed that arrangements for the coverage of their chamber should be conjoined in the same organisation as that of the Commons.

This now put the pressure on the broadcasters. In essence they had the summer parliamentary recess of four months to set up coverage of the two Houses of Parliament, which would start officially from the State Opening on 21 November 1989. The earlier autumn debates would be used for non-transmitted rehearsal. The broadcasters (initially the BBC, represented by the Chief Assistant to the Director General, the IBA – still technically at that stage the 'broadcaster' of ITV – represented by an ex-ITN member of their programme staff, Robert Hargreaves, and the ITV companies, represented by their Association's Director of Programme Planning, who also undertook a watching brief for C4) set up an ad hoc committee. This then recruited advisers: the ex-Controller of Engineering from BBC Television, Bob Longman, and Paul Mathews, lately ITN's Deputy Chief Executive, one of whose many responsibilities had been the broadcasting of the House of Lords. Grist,

Mathews and Longman set up the political, legal and technical structures for a joint company of broadcasters and Parliament to put a contract for the broadcasts out to tender. The company, the House of Commons Broadcasting Unit Ltd (HOCBUL), was set up by ITN's lawyers, Biddle and Co. with one of their partners, Hugh Johnson as Company Secretary and the Deputy Speaker of the House of Commons, the Rt. Hon. Harold Walker MP, as Chairman. The Board consisted of representatives of the broadcasters from the ad hoc group and delegated members of the Select Committee. The company was unique in that only the broadcaster members of the Board could accept any financial responsibility, Parliament being barred from conducting business activities. The company's authorised share capital of £100 was divided equally between the BBC and the IBA.

The Department of the Environment's Parliamentary Works Office organised and paid for the structural changes to make a control room available above the Lobby of the House of Commons while the broadcasters paid for the leasing of technical equipment (from ITN) and for its installation, at a cost of just under £400,000 (HOCBUL Budget 1989/90).

The cameras were wall-mounted and operated by remote control from the control room – with a consequent saving of space in the chamber and cost of operation. The service was paid for by a subscription of £384,245, divided between the broadcasters on a 'per channel' basis – the BBC paying two parts, ITV one and C4 one. Other 'sales' of the feed of the House of Commons pictures and sound – to foreign broadcasters, cable television and so on – raised £288,050 (Ibid.).

The tender process to select the operator for these facilities was won by an independent producer, Michael Braham and his company Broadcast Communications plc, who specialised in business programmes. Towards the end of the summer the broadcasters became aware that separate arrangements would be needed for coverage of Select and Standing Committees.

A further ad hoc group, under the chairmanship of the ITVA's Director of Programme Planning and now including C4, quickly put together a consortium of an independent producer (Barraclough-Carey) and a facilities company (Walshy's – founded by an ex-ITN cameraman), who recruited retired BBC and ITN cameramen to cover the Committees of the House for the period of the experiment. The joint organisation was called Commons Committee Television. Because this extra facility was not part of the HOCBUL operation it was not included in the subscription but paid for on a bespoke basis – any organisation requesting coverage of a committee paid a fee for that coverage, though the fee could be split with any others using the material.

Committee coverage was often relevant to ITV companies' local news broadcasts and pre-editing was required to save the prohibitive British Telecom lines costs that would have been involved in getting raw material back to, say, Aberdeen or Plymouth newsrooms during the late afternoon parliamentary news 'rush-hour'. This meant that an editing facility in Westminster was required. TVS came to the rescue of the other ITV companies by enlarging an editing and play-out facility it had set up at the Queen Elizabeth II Conference Centre (where Walshy's had their base) and making it available to the other companies.

Rules of coverage, of the House of Commons in particular, caused the only real friction between broadcasters and parliamentarians. The Select Committee Report had made detailed recommendations on how coverage was to be conducted, requiring that directors and producers of programmes should have 'regard to the dignity of the House and its function as a working body rather than as a place of entertainment'. The main restrictions to cause concern amongst the broadcasters were the prohibition of reaction shots and the requirement to stay on a shot of the Speaker during times of 'grave disorder'. After two months of the experiment the Select Committee agreed to a trial of certain modifications which permitted reaction shots of members referred to in debate – though this freedom did not extend to Prime Minister's Question Time or Ministerial Statements. The Committee also agreed 'to the use of group shots, midway between the standard head and shoulders shot and the wide angle shot, as well as to zoom shots to show a member in relation to colleagues in his or her vicinity' (Factsheet No. 40, House of Commons Public Information Office, May 1992).

When the year-long experiment ended there was a review. In general both Parliament and broadcasters were satisfied with the results. There was not time to set up a permanent system after the House had approved this in principle in July 1990. Both parties therefore agreed an extension of the existing arrangements for a further year to allow the new set-up – which was to integrate coverage and control of both chambers and of committees. A new company was formed to take over from the experiment's HOCBUL organisation.

This company was (and is) known as the Parliamentary Broadcasting Unit Ltd. (PARBUL). Its fourteen directors are drawn from both Houses (three from the Commons and three from the Lords, plus the Supervisor of Broadcasting) and from the broadcasters a further seven – including C4 and BSkyB. The company's function is defined as:

> ... to finance the staff and equipment for the television coverage of both Houses on the basis of the shareholdings taken by the participating broadcasting organisations and any revenue from the sale of the signal. (Factsheet No. 40, House of Commons Public Information Office, May 1992)

PARBUL short-listed five bidders for the coverage contract. They included the two companies involved in the experiment, Broadcast Communications plc, and the committee coverage consortium, now called CCT Productions Ltd. George Carey's CCT Productions won the contract and now operate from a purpose-built operations centre alongside the BBC and ITN's Parliamentary Units at 4 Millbank, across the road from the Palace of Westminster.

The coverage is extensively used by ITN and other broadcasters' news operations. The BBC frequently also broadcasts Prime Minister's Question Time live. The Select Committee also solicited applications to transmit continuous live coverage by cable. Three companies applied and the Committee selected United Artists Programming, which began broadcasting the *Parliamentary Channel* on 13 January 1992.

7

THE COMMERCIAL IMPERATIVE

SECTION I: ADVERTISING

Revenue from advertising is the lifeblood of any commercial television system. When the UK's first commercial channel opened up in 1955 as ITV its blood was pretty thin. The print mass media had over half a century's start and a firm grip on the market and Parliament, though anxious to see competition for the licence fee-funded BBC had legislated more checks than balances for the new channel. Partly this was to do with maintaining the values of what Americans told MPs was 'the best television in the world', partly it was to ease in the new medium without too much damage to the old. No politician wants to be blamed for a newspaper going out of business. Even the least-read paper is some voters' favourite. Ultimately two national newspapers, the *News Chronicle* and the *Daily Sketch* did die but there were many factors involved other than simply the arrival of the opportunity for the newspapers' advertising to move over to television. And many advertisers themselves were cautious about making such a move.

In fact it was the lack of advertiser support in 1956 that brought about the first agreement to network programmes between companies to save money. The original agreement was between Granada in the north and Associated Rediffusion in London. Other companies joined subsequently (see Chapter 5). In ITV the folk memory of thin times was maintained long after times had changed to fat. In 1986 ITV's revenue passed £1 billion for the first time. Advertisers came to feel that, like a wife married for her money, they were courted with some little grace but then, squeezed for every penny. Criticism of ITV by the advertisers became endemic. Perhaps this was inevitable in a system where one broadcaster had a monopoly of television advertising opportunities.

This criticism was to rise to a howling crescendo during the Eighties. Attempts to break the monopoly started even before the decade began. And as usual the IBA occupied a key role – as the regulator of advertising quantity and content, as arbitrator between the warring parties, and now, as regulator – and owner – of the second UK commercial channel.

Who Sells the New Channel?

When IBA Members met in Egham in Surrey, in October 1979, to discuss their strategy and future policy for the new fourth channel, they were faced with strong criticism from both the advertisers (ISBA – the Incorporated Society of British Advertisers) and advertising agencies (IPA – the Institute of Practitioners in Advertising). These stemmed from what the advertisers saw as a lack of real competition in airtime sales as a result of the ITV contractors' monopoly. The companies always maintained that they were in competition with each other but in practice every company, except those in London, had a monopoly sales position in its own region.

An IPA paper (10 October 1979) recommended a separate sales organisation for the fourth channel and outlined a possible organisational structure to provide competition in the sale of airtime alongside the complementarity of programming. The criticism of ITV was hard-hitting. The IPA regarded competition as necessary because advertising agencies had 'suffered from the systematic exploitation of their monopoly of the sale of television airtime'. They expressed concern that if ITV (it was called 'ITV1' in many of the papers to distinguish it from the fourth channel, which was seen by ITV and advertisers alike at that time as 'ITV2') was given the control of the sales of the fourth channel, these monopoly practices would be extended to the continuing detriment of advertisers and their advertising agencies. They claimed that the programme companies saw agencies and advertisers merely as guaranteed sources of revenue and not as customers warranting normal commercial consideration.

Nevertheless in response to Egham Paper 3 'Selling time on the Fourth Channel', Members of the Authority agreed that advertising time on the fourth channel should be sold by the ITV companies along the same lines as on ITV but 'subject to safeguards'. For instance, there should be no discounting for the time bought on the two channels unless discussed with the advertisers before final decisions were taken. This stance was broadly in line with the ITV companies' views which were set out in the memo 'ITV2 – the Fourth Channel' which argued that the best way of selling time on Channel 4 would be with their own sales forces in their regions and that a separate Channel 4 sales force would be wasteful of resources.

The ITV contractors also contended that in the exercise of their functions in obtaining the revenue for the Independent Television services they must be free to determine their own marketing and sales policies.

These recommendations were incorporated in the Authority's proposals for the Fourth Channel which were published in November 1979. As a result ITV was to sell Channel Four's airtime for the first ten years of the channel's existence. This increase in the scale of the monopoly certainly increased the level of criticism of ITV from the advertising industry but the IBA did not have any alternative. It had to fund from somewhere the channel that it was required by government to start. The regulator had no money of its own. The IBA could see no real alternative, at that stage, to the idea of letting ITV sell the airtime in return for paying a subscription upon which C4 could be founded and run. Indeed it was thought by many to be a rather elegant solution to the problem. (This did not, as we've seen in Chapter 2, prevent ITV from criticising the level of subscription.)

Objectionable Sales Practices

The advertising agencies' dissatisfaction with the ITV companies was reinforced by the advertisers. ISBA's objections to current sales practices were summarised in IBA Papers 281, 282 and 297 (1979). A letter from Ken Miles (Director of ISBA) set out 'some of the practices which we find objectionable on ITV1 and some suggestions for ways in which the position could be improved in the new contract period'. ISBA claimed that the main reason for these practices on ITV1 arose from lack of competition; in thirteen out of fourteen commercial television areas, the ITV contractor enjoyed a perfect selling monopoly within the television medium. This led to the contractors working as a *de facto* cartel which was organised to the disadvantage of its customers, the advertisers.

The main monopoly abuses in the current system were listed. These included the restriction of advertising time, or the number of programme hours, in order to push up prices artificially; the differential rates for advertising lengths and arrangements for the cancellation of airtime bookings. ISBA was also concerned by the 'marked lack of consultation' with advertisers by contractors before major changes were announced.

Recommendations by ISBA included three competing suppliers in London and a return to split weekly franchises for the major regions; the establishment of a permanent ITV users' liaison committee, operating under the auspices of the IBA (not ITCA), so that advertisers and contractors could meet on equal terms; a new approach to airtime cancellations and the banning by the IBA of the circulation of rate card changes between contractors before publication.

Faced with such a barrage of criticism, IBA Members expressed concern about the misunderstandings and relationships between the companies and advertisers and agreed that discussions should take place as soon as possible with the intention of establishing a consultative committee chaired by a representative of the Authority. The committee's terms of reference should cover both ITV and the fourth channel and should provide a forum for frank and open consultation at the top level rather than providing Authority arbitration on unresolved points of difference.

In 1980, the Advertising Liaison Committee (ALC) was established and held its first meeting on 27 June 1980 under the chairmanship of Lord Thomson, then IBA Deputy Chairman. Other IBA representatives were George Russell (a member of the Authority), the Director General and the Head of Advertising Control. ITCA, ISBA and the IPA were all represented at a senior level.

Broadcasting Bill (1980) Debate

Parliamentary debate on the patterns of advertising on the fourth channel was continued during the passage of the Broadcasting Bill. In the seventh sitting of Standing Committee E on the Broadcasting Bill (1 April 1980) Charles Morris MP claimed that:

> the contracting television companies have a monopoly and the laws of supply and demand do not operate in that area. Therefore, we should look at the interesting relationship between the television contracting companies and advertisers, and how it has operated in recent times. The IBA policy of distancing itself from the revenue-raising arrangements between the two has encouraged some of the independent companies to behave with arrogance in their relationship with advertising agencies. That cannot be justified. I have no natural sympathy for advertising agencies as such. Most can look after themselves. But in a state-established enterprise, we are entitled to expect higher standards than those in the commercial jungle. (Hansard Column 322, Standing Committee E, Broadcasting Bill, 1 April 1980)

Leon Brittan, Minister of State for Broadcasting at the Home Office, concluded the debate by saying that 'The Government have not sought to put into the bill anything that would restrict the type of advertising on Channel 4. In fact the position is quite the reverse. There is nothing to stop block advertising' (Hansard Column 345). He also referred to the setting up of the new Advertising Liaison Committee in the face of objectionable sales practices and wished that committee 'a fair wind' and hoped that the 'ill-feeling ... that has arisen over certain matters can be considered there and its causes resolved' (Hansard Column 362).

The Peacock Committee (1985)

Nevertheless, the frustration and dissatisfaction of the advertisers continued. When the Peacock Committee was set up in March 1985 to consider possible options for financing the BBC, Donald McLure (ISBA president) was reported in the *Guardian* (8 July 1985) as saying that 'The advertiser's view is quite straightforward. He's sick to death of having to pay more and more for his television airtime. He's fed up with being taken to the cleaners and will look sympathetically at any and all solutions which would promise even a minor ruffle of competition among the airwaves.' He confirmed that ISBA would be sending the Peacock Committee 'a strong submission' proposing a phased introduction of advertising on the BBC over a number of years.

Television 87 at Copenhagen: A New Low for ITV in Advertiser Relations

It is a matter of record, rather than hyperbole, to describe ITV's conference in Copenhagen at the end of April 1987 – attended by some 250 directors and senior executives of its advertising and agency clients and potential clients, as well as by other advertising-related business people and journalists – as a disaster:

> ... the real problems, voiced by all advertisers from Roger Humm [note: Humm was Managing Director of the Ford Motor Company – a speaker on the first day of the conference] onwards, were hardly addressed and certainly not answered. We all expected a fully interactive session, but it just did not happen.
>
> I don't want to go on reciting our criticisms, which we expressed strongly enough at the IBA Advertising Liaison Committee, but you should know that advertisers were certainly not satisfied or reassured by what they heard in Copenhagen, and are likely to go on saying so loud and clear. (Letter Ken Miles, Director of the Incorporated Society of British Advertisers Ltd, to David McCall, Managing Director, Anglia Television and, at this time, Chairman of the ITCA Council, 5 May 1987).

Indeed the advertisers had already talked loud and clear to the press:

> It would be hard to overstate the anger of many advertisers following the conference's disastrously ill-judged final session – an anger that grew as the evening progressed and clients had a chance to share their feelings.
>
> With ITV managing directors privately describing the session as embarrassing, clients describing it as arrogant and insulting, with one (ITV) sales director telling anyone who would listen that he would personally be writing to every delegate dissociating himself from the session, the conference was brought to an electrifying finale – and the scorch marks will be visible for some time to come. (Article by Torin Douglas, *Marketing Week*, 8 May 1987)

The initial disappointment of the advertisers when the Peacock Committee in 1986 failed to recommend advertising on the BBC was intensified by the rising cost of advertising. Torin Douglas was (and is) an authoritative commentator on advertising and the media, widely respected by both industries. He gave his view of the problem at *Television 87* in the *Observer* the day after the conference ended:

> Television advertisers have looked on ruefully as a succession of ITV companies have declared booming profits, largely fuelled by the recent dramatic increase in advertising revenue. Alarmed by the 25 per cent rise in airtime costs last year and frustrated by the failure of their campaign to get advertisements on the BBC and the refusal of the IBA to increase the number of advertisements in peak-

time, advertisers are also having to come to terms with a 10 per cent drop in the audience. (Torin Douglas, *Observer*, 2 May 1987)

The advertisers' attack was spearheaded by Roger Humm, Managing Director of the Ford Motor Co., who told the audience of advertisers and their agencies, that although Ford was committed to television advertising, the high costs were causing it to reconsider that commitment; since the launch of the Ford Granada two years ago he alleged that the cost of television advertising had risen by 40 per cent. His claims were backed by David Hearn, Managing Director of Smith's Crisps, who warned that media inflation and the failure to deliver audiences would force many advertisers to examine more creative ways to spend their budgets.

On the first day also, Brian Jacobs of the Leo Burnett agency had – with ITV's agreement – distributed a paper aggressively critical of ITV's 'unscientific scheduling' and its 25 per cent rise in airtime prices over the previous eighteen months. Interestingly the paper also proposed a central scheduler as part of the cure for ITV's 'failure':

> In particular, it seems to us that there is a need for someone to take an overall look at ITV schedules – without having to worry about the parochial and (often) political needs of the 'Big 5', and indeed of the other ITV companies. (Paper, 'ITV Scheduling: Time for a Change' by Leo Burnett, 30 April 1987)

The central scheduler idea was, as has been shown in Chapter 5, a little ahead of ITV's thinking (if not the IBA's) at that time. The paper was also ahead of its time in questioning whether ITV's main News bulletin really needed to be at 10.00 p.m. Should it not be at 8.30 p.m. to avoid the breaking of feature films of an adult nature (an increasing proportion of films at this time) at their half-way point for the news – in consequence losing up to half the audience thereafter, the paper asked. (This matter was to come to a head a year into the post-1992 Licence period – see Chapter 11.) Some ITV programme people themselves had long thought such a move would improve the schedule but they knew that the IBA, supporting the view at ITN, would not allow such a move. The fact that the advertisers appeared not to understand the regulatory situation only added to the rift between the two parties. As a headline put it at the time:

TROUBLED MINDS THAT DIDN'T MEET
Marketing Week on ITV's Copenhagen conference, 8 May 1987

As well as the Leo Burnett paper, advertisers and agency personnel had raised other serious questions about ITV's performance both from the floor and during a session on the platform on the second morning, chaired by Torin Douglas himself. So all were expecting answers from the ITV sales directors in the final session.

Instead they got a barrage of criticism of themselves, dolled up in a sort of mock TV business programme. The format was a mistake in Douglas' view, but, he said, it was the content that angered the advertisers. The sales directors were saying that:

... the main reason costs were going up was that advertisers and agencies weren't targeting their programmes properly and were insisting on discounts on station average price.

Toy commercials were shown in *Weekend World* and sanpro [sanitary protection] ads in *The Big Match* to illustrate how foolish advertisers could be.

One sales director described as 'madness' the practice of an advertiser preferring to pay £9 per thousand (viewers) provided it was a 25 per cent discount on station average (price), rather than £4.50 per thousand if it were only a 10 per cent discount. He omitted to mention that contractors often treat advertisers in exactly the same way, apparently preferring to take a high share of a small budget than a low share of a high one.

Another sales director endeared himself to his audience of 400 potential advertisers and agencies by describing their TV buying as O-level standard ...

Not a word was said about pre-emption [note; the practice of allowing an advertiser to push another out of a prime slot by paying a higher price – often done at the last minute], which often prevents advertisers getting the targeted slots they would like. Neither was anything said about the impression held by many advertisers that as soon as they express an interest in a particular target group the contractor will immediately charge a hefty premium. (Torin Douglas, 'How ITV failed at the last', *Marketing Week*, 8 May 1987)

Feona McEwan in the *Financial Times* (7 May 1987) commented that 'this was more than the familiar advertisers' whinge. For once that worn-out line that pips were squeaking was for real. Everyone, contractors included, was concerned.'

ITV was not entirely unresponsive in the face of the hail of critical fire. Speaking at the conference, Richard Dunn, Managing Director of Thames TV, had admitted the programme schedules had been inadequate but also attributed the change to the way the television audience was measured and the better weather for the decline in the number of viewers. Paul Fox, Managing Director of Yorkshire TV, who had become a sort of bulwark for ITV in the face of advertiser hostility (see Chapter 4), was reported as saying about the drop in ratings, '... it's happened before and we'll win back'.

The ITV company sales directors appear initially to have been more concerned with the causes of the failure of that fatal last session than the criticisms of ITV's business relations with its advertiser customers generally. On 7 May Jonathan Shier, the Director of Sales and Marketing at Thames, wrote to his colleague at Central, Dick Emery, who was Chairman of the network's Marketing Committee: 'The presentation was patronising, superficial, and for many of our customers downright insulting.' He then went on to say that it did not reflect 'the style and tone' of the draft script for the session that had been seen and agreed by the committee on 9 April.

A post mortem on 8 May, attended by ten out of the fifteen members of the Marketing Committee, concluded:

1. The format was unmanageable and should not be tried again ...
2. Sales Directors speaking collectively on behalf of ITV encounter hostility which is not present when they speak as individual brands (companies).
3. The presentation was over-ambitious, both in structure and in the number of messages it tried to convey.

The second of those conclusions reached some way towards the heart of the matter. Each of the companies' sales directors worked hard to to achieve good relations with clients and potential clients – none more so that those of the two London companies, who were competing for the same clients on the same territory – but, as in many aspects of ITV's relations with the outside world, the result was that each company's image was more significant, and usually better appreciated, than that of the network as a whole.

After the impact of Copenhagen had sunk in, it was decided that something had to be done about that factor – and fast. The usual working party approach was by-passed and Jonathan Shier, as Chairman-elect of the Marketing Committee, led a successful bid to Council for a budget to hire an advertising agency to promote the ITV brand.

By the autumn of 1987 three agencies had pitched for the role and, to the surprise of some, the rather traditional agency, J. Walter Thompson came out the winner. With a budget of £1.5 million, the business of producing 'commercials' for ITV was started and one of the most talented graphic design groups, English Markell Pockett was chosen to redesign the ITV logo, which had remained untouched by the design revolution of the Sixties and Seventies.

On 28 September 1987 the opportunity was also taken to change the confusing ITCA (Independent Television Companies Association) initials that had been applied to every joint network body, from Council downwards, to the clearer, and more ITV brand-friendly, ITVA (Independent Television Association). At the same time the trade union-like title of General Secretary of the Association was changed to Director.

The new 'commercials' for ITV started to be shown on 19 October 1987 with a research 'tracking study' set up to register any improvement in the ITV image. Some improvement – particularly in relation to ITV's reputation for drama – was recorded but the study was cancelled after the first year, apparently for financial reasons. ITV was, at subsequent times of advertiser pressure in the early Nineties, to wish that a constant record of the esteem in which the brand-image was held was still available to it.

Sir William (Bill) Brown

Sir Alastair Burnet

Bryan Cowgill

Richard Dunn

Greg Dyke

David Elstein

Sir Paul Fox

James Gatward

David Glencross

Michael Green

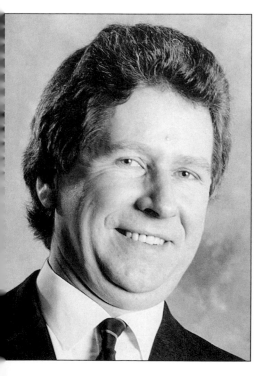

Leslie Hill

Lord (Clive) Hollick

Lady (Shirley) Littler, centre, with Clare Mulholland, right, and Barbara Hosking

David McCall

Sir David Nicholas

Professor Sir Alan Peacock

Marcus Plantin

David Plowright

Stewart Purvis

Andrew Quinn

Gerry Robinson

Peter Rogers

Sir George Russell

Brian Tesler

Lord Thomson (of Monifieth)

John Whitney

Lord Windlesham

Out with the IBA – in with the ITC
The high degree of regulatory continuity maintained across the changes brought about
by the Broadcasting Act 1990 is visible by comparing the picture of the Members of
the last Authority in 1990 (above) with the first Commission in 1991 (below).

The White Paper (1988)

The White Paper on broadcasting, published in November 1988, while following the Peacock Committee's recommendation not to allow advertising on the BBC, did envisage that the ITC would have a duty to draw up and enforce a code or codes on advertising and sponsorship which

> should allow more flexible regulation of advertising and sponsorship than is now possible under the Broadcasting Act 1981. The Government in particular favours liberalising the restrictions deriving from the 1981 Act on sponsorship, provided adequate safeguards are built in for editorial independence and transparency for the viewer (Paragraph 6.47, White Paper, *Broadcasting in the '90s*, November 1988)

The ITC remit would also include consumer protection for satellite services uplinked from the UK, such as Sky. The White Paper provided for advertising regulation to be carried out with a lighter touch. The IBA, in its response to the White Paper, confirmed that it would be 'inappropriate' for the ITC to pre-vet advertisements, but the licensees, as part of their licence conditions, would have to operate satisfactory arrangements to ensure that copy clearance was in line with ITC advertising codes. Severe sanctions were available if licence conditions were breached. The ITC would, however, remain accessible to the ITV companies at the pre-production stage for guidance on controversial proposals in order to minimise the need for expensive post hoc intervention. One area where the IBA was critical related to the recommendation to give the proposed Broadcasting Standards Council (BSC) the right to consider complaints on advertisements as well as programmes. The IBA felt strongly that advertisements should not be part of the BSC's remit since they did not have any understanding of this area and that it would be confusing for viewers to have two separate bodies investigating complaints about the same advertisements. One alarming (to the IBA) proposal which had been included in the White Paper (Paragraph 6.47) was that any maximum limits on advertising minutage should be subject to government approval and that the government should take powers to adjust this limit after consultation with the ITC. It was noted by the Chairman (George Russell), with relief, in ALC minutes 34(90) that this proposal had not appeared in the Broadcasting Bill.

In the Report stage of the Broadcasting Bill in the House of Lords (16 October 1990) Lord McGregor, Chairman of the Advertising Standards Authority, introduced an amendment to remove the BSC's power to deal with complaints about television advertising which, he claimed, would lead to 'further fragmentation' of the regulatory bodies dealing with advertising and would introduce 'new confusion and further muddle'. Despite support from Lords Plowden, Boston and Colwyn, the amendment was defeated by thirty-two votes.

European Developments

Lord Thomson, former EC commissioner, addressing a television and radio conference in February 1981, criticised (as did the British government) proposals for statutory controls on advertising. He believed that the Community 'ought not to be dissipating its energies in seeking to ensure that advertisements from Greenland's icy mountains to Sicily's golden strand conform to the same framework of control' (*The Times*, 12 February 1981).

When the Commission of the European Communities (CEC) published in 1984 the Green Paper 'Television without Frontiers' on the Establishment of the Common Market for Broadcasting, especially by satellite and cable, Harry Theobalds, the IBA Controller of Advertising referred to it in *Television Today* (9 August 1984) as 'a book consisting of 367 pages and the cover is lavender in colour'. He expressed strong opposition to any supranational legislation which might weaken the UK advertising control system. He also questioned the Green Paper suggestion that a maximum advertising time of 20 per cent of the total daily limit could be justified as an upper limit. He pointed out that 10 per cent of television broadcasting 'is not unduly intrusive' and he feared the danger that the maximum could become the norm.

When the EC draft directive on broadcasting was adopted by the European Commission in March 1986 it was proposed that a maximum of 15 per cent of airtime should be allocated to advertising rather than the 20 per cent envisaged by the Green Paper. The IBA, commenting in its 1986/87 annual report, was less defensive and thought that this amendment 'might be beneficial to Independent Broadcasting'. The draft directive, however, also contained proposals for a minimum programme quota of Community production and of production by independent producers which were not contained in the Green Paper. In its response to the Home Office on the draft directive the IBA, while appreciating the 'wish of the Commission to avoid opening up the European market to non-European marketing organisations' it also argued that 'the promotion of European culture should not be at the expense of the individual culture of the member states'. The IBA was also opposed to numerical limits or quotas on programmes.

The EC Directive on 'Television without Frontiers' and the Council of Europe Convention on Broadcasting were finally adopted on 3 October 1989. Both agreements were to be implemented in the UK by the Broadcasting Act 1990. One of the most immediate and visible signs of the EC Directive's provisions was the disappearance of the television advertisement for Hamlet cigars (together with its Bach musical accompaniment). The Directive prohibited the advertising of all tobacco products; although cigarettes and cigarette tobacco had been banned in the UK, pipe tobacco and cigars had, until then, been allowed.

Advertising Controllers

The Controller of Advertising at the IBA (later in the decade called Director of Advertising and Sponsorship) had always wielded power with a considerable financial consequence in what became a £billion-a-year industry during the Eighties. As well as firmness and diplomacy, the task required sufficient intellect to make sound case law – sometimes on the hoof.

In 1981, Harry Theobalds succeeded Peter Woodhouse, a former lawyer, as IBA Controller of Advertising. Torin Douglas, the media correspondent welcomed his appointment:

> Despite the fact that he has been at the IBA for 19 years and was deputy head of advertising control for nine of those years, Theobalds is almost certain to change the approach of the division, largely because his personality is very different from that of his predecessor, Peter Woodhouse. I predict that we shall be seeing far more of him than the public does of most IBA officials simply because he believes in being open with people and because, when asked to appear on a platform or give an interview, his natural inclination is to say yes. He is quite prepared to explain and defend any decision he has taken, to admit that a case has been a borderline one or that a decision might have been wrong, and he is known to talk regularly to agency media people to make sure he knows what is going on in the market place. Such an attitude is, I sense, totally in keeping with that of the IBA chairman, Lord Thomson, who also has more than his fair share of advertising contacts, through his chairmanship of the Advertising Standards Authority. (*Marketing Week*, 21 August 1981)

Frank Willis succeeded Harry Theobalds in 1987 as Controller of Advertising, and subsequently, Director of Advertising and Sponsorship. He came from the Department of Trade and Industry where he had been an Assistant Secretary. His criterion for exercising the controls at his disposal tended to focus on 'why not?' rather than 'why?'

Frank Willis outlined his philosophy of advertising regulation in an ITC publication in 1992. He summarised the new era of 'lighter touch' advertising regulation compared with the stringent control operated in the post-Pilkington period of the 1960s and 1970s. Looking back at the start of ITV in 1955 he wrote that:

> control of advertising standards was left very much to the ITV companies themselves. It was they who, through their central Copy Clearance Secretariat, vetted commercials and negotiated with advertising agencies. The Independent Television Authority had no specialised staff on advertising matters; instead no less a personage than the Secretary to the Authority himself cast an avuncular eye over the advertising output; but only from time to time and when *he* had time.
>
> In 1962 the Pilkington Committee blew a loud whistle. As far as it was concerned the whole advertising business had got out of hand; standards were sloppy, advertisers were getting away with murder, and the solution was for the Authority to take charge of what was being broadcast in its name. The Authority accordingly recruited its first Head of Advertising Control, the late Archie

Graham, and for nearly 30 years he and his successors held advertising within an iron grip. The ITV companies carried on their vetting work but the ITA (and subsequently the IBA) sat firmly on their back. Every script – even for the most tedious carpet sale – arrived for additional careful scrutiny in Brompton Road. At 9.45 a.m. every working morning Authority staff viewed a closed circuit transmission of new commercials and none was approved for broadcast until the ITA had given clearance. When complaints arrived – and complaints, like the poor, have always been with us – the Authority's instinct was to spring to the defence; after all the complaints were about its own decisions and it was not in the business of making mistakes. Indeed, in fairness, it appears to have made very few.

Looking forward to the new era of 'light touch' regulation in the 1990s Willis wrote that:

> ... the position will look very different. In fact it started to change a few years ago when the IBA took a policy decision to begin a process of managed transition towards the post-1992 'steady state'. In the Brave New World the emphasis will be firmly away from hands-on paternalism (some would say grandmaternalism) and much more on responsible self-regulation by the broadcasters. The ITC will not be agonising in advance over acceptable and unacceptable ways of referring to lavatories or whether the time has come to risk a ferret-down-the-trousers joke post 9 p.m. The decision whether or not to broadcast advertising will be for the broadcaster alone. There will be no ITC 'clearance' or 'approval'; and no prior veto. So what will the ITC be doing? Essentially three things – setting the standards by keeping the advertising code up to date, providing guidance to broadcasters on code application, and intervening where necessary to ensure that the code is respected.
>   ... the rough-tough martinet approach to regulation is not the recipe for success. The martinet rapidly forfeits respect and cooperation and is liable to find that the dividing line between black and white is defined by where he can make his writ stick in the face of legal challenge. The chief advantage of code-based systems of regulation is that they can aim for higher standards than, for example, those of criminal law. It is true that they can also provide cover for very low standards. This depends on the culture within which they operate and who is calling the final shots.

Willis concluded that:

> ... there is no question of returning to pre-Pilkington days. The wheel has not really come full circle. What we now have is a system which gives wider opportunity than ever before to commercial initiative and judgement balanced by a lean but, we hope, very effective regulator in the modern mould, to protect

the public interest. That the relationship between regulator and broadcaster is less umbilical than in the past is a strength rather than a weakness. (*Spectrum*, Winter 1992)

Liaison with the Advertising Industry – the Establishment and Work of the ALC

Sir Brian Young, in a letter in March 1980 to Ken Miles (Director of ISBA) on the setting up of the ALC, claimed that the 'strength of the committee will be in the fact that grievances can be aired without creating the atmosphere of a tribunal'.

The terms of reference for the ALC were settled at the first meeting in June 1980. These were:

> To consider matters of principle relating to commercial relationships which may be raised by the participating bodies;
> to improve liaison and communications on advertising matters between advertisers, agencies, the ITV programme companies and the IBA;
> to examine ways in which outstanding differences might be resolved;
> and to provide any guidance, advice and information which it may consider helpful to all involved in the Committee.

Issues were only to be referred to the ALC if it was not possible to resolve them within the industry and then only if a principle was involved. Lord Thomson, the Chairman, stressed that it would be inappropriate to discuss programme schedules.

Principles for Selling TV Airtime

The Committee began immediate consideration of a number of issues affecting the selling of airtime on both ITV and Channel 4. ISBA proposed that a Code for the sale of television airtime should be prepared. Specific issues for discussion were pre-emption, share discount schemes and cancellation clauses in rate cards. Although ISBA and IPA were not opposed in principle to the system of selling airtime which allowed one advertiser to lose commercial spots to another advertiser prepared to pay a higher published rate (pre-emption), disquiet was expressed that advertising spots could be pre-empted at any time up to the time of transmission and that the first advertiser did not normally have the option to match the bid. The ITV programme companies, however, contended that the system of pre-emption allowed advertising to find its right market price.

After extended discussion at the ALC a series of *Principles governing the sale and purchase of television airtime* were agreed and published on 5 January 1982 by which the ITV contractors undertook to:

Use their best endeavours to sell the maximum permitted amount of airtime irrespective of the rate involved.

Define cut-off points after which spots would no longer be liable to be pre-empted.

Give reasons in writing when cancellations were refused.

Give more advance information to enable advertisers and agencies to judge the probable state of the airtime market. [The contractors, however, declined to publish their past monthly revenues on a station-by-station basis, which was the guide to the level of demand which advertisers wanted.]

Provide more information in advance of any changes being made in terms and conditions or in the structure of their rate cards. (IBA News Release, 5 January 1982)

Brian Henry, editor of *British Television Advertising: The First 30 years*, commented that:

The Principles Governing the Sale of Airtime, like many other 'Heads of Agreement', concealed in their somewhat bland and nebulous simplicity years of acrimony and misunderstanding. Yet the new rules were far from innocuous and represented a real step forward in the relationships between the contractors and their customers. As in most prolonged negotiations, there had been concessions on both sides. All present at the ALC recognised that the Principles, like the rules governing the content of television advertisements, were not immutable. They were expected to become more specific especially after Channel Four and the new breakfast-time service had come on the air.

Torin Douglas in *Marketing Week* (8 January 1982) welcomed the document and thought 'it has been worth waiting for, not only for the principles it establishes but also for what it represents. It is nothing less than the first official declaration by the IBA that advertisers have rights in their dealings with ITV companies, just as viewers do.' Ken Miles (Director of ISBA) commented that 'We now have a set of principles against which particular complaints and criticisms can be judged.'

Following the publication of the Principles, the IBA stated in its Annual Report 1982/83 that no complaints had been received about the operation of the pre-empt system. Items for discussion during the four meetings of the ALC in 1982/83 included the regional share and parity discount schemes introduced by the regional companies as an incentive to advertisers to spend a greater share of national television expenditure in the region. ISBA and IPA were split on the validity of such schemes. Whereas ISBA opposed the schemes in principle because they inhibited an advertiser's freedom to allocate budgets in accordance with his own marketing policy, the IPA recognised that they had a place in programme rate cards provided that there was no penalty on the quality of time bought by non-participants in share schemes. The IBA noted that complaints had been received from some advertisers that without a share agreement they were unreasonably penalised in the allocation of airtime outside the share scheme. The Authority reminded the programme companies that there must be no unreasonable discrimination in the allocation of advertising time and an advertiser's inability to participate in a share scheme must not inhibit him in negotiating, within the published terms of rate cards, for a reasonable share of available time.

There was disquiet, too, about the Authority's decision to allow television contractors to aggregate an advertiser's total expenditure with a company, irrespective of how it was spent on ITV or Channel 4, for the purposes of share/parity schemes. The advertising industry alleged that the linked discount for share/parity schemes would lead to conditional selling, despite the assurances obtained from the ITV contractors that advertisers could not be forced to buy across both channels. The Authority assured them that any complaint about conditional selling relating to ITV and Channel 4 would be closely investigated.

Another area of discussion was the subject of PI (per item) rates available in some ITV regions to direct-response advertisers. The system, which allowed for an initial low entry rate, provided for the final payment to be determined by viewer response. Advertisers and agencies took the view that the rate was inherently discriminatory and its use (particularly in peak time) tended to harden the market for other television advertisers. After discussions at the ALC, full agreement was reached between the ITV companies, ISBA and IPA to exclude PI advertising from peak-time viewing as from September 1983. The agreement was registered by ITCA with the Office of Fair Trading.

The OFT and Competition Policy

During the early 1980s, the ALC had not been working in a vacuum in relation to wider competition and fair trading legislation. In the passage of the Broadcasting Bill in 1980 Leon Brittan had fired a warning shot in Standing Committee E (Column 363) about the danger of the 'conflict of bifurcation' of powers between the Office of Fair Trading (OFT) and the IBA. On 29 February 1980, Gordon Borrie, the Director General of the Office, had written to Peter Woodhouse, the IBA Head of Advertising, reminding him that 'any agreements between all members of the ALC would be subject to registration if they gave rise to matters specified in the Restrictive Trade Practices Act'. The publication of the Principles of airtime sales was promptly followed by a letter from Gordon Borrie to Lord Thomson pointing out the 'real danger of the Principles being developed to the point where he would have to consider them under restrictive trade practices legislation'.

Thames TV, JWT and the OFT

In July 1982, J. Walter Thompson, one of the leading advertising agencies, formally complained to the OFT, under the Competition Act 1980, about the operation of an incentive-discount scheme by Thames Television (TTV). This scheme gave an agency which guaranteed a predetermined proportion of its television expenditure to Thames Television the facility of buying airtime at one level below the customary rate. The OFT initially referred the matter to the IBA which issued a carefully worded reprimand based mainly on the fact that the Thames incentive scheme had not been disclosed in the company's rate card. The IBA said that future agreements between Thames TV and agencies and advertisers would have to comply with published tariffs agreed with the IBA, thus avoiding 'unreasonable discrimination', which was not acceptable under the Broadcasting Act 1981.

On 17 February 1983 the OFT announced that 'it has appeared to the Director General of Fair Trading (now Sir Gordon Borrie), that Thames Television has been or is pursuing a course of conduct which may amount to an anti-competitive practice'. He proposed to carry out an investigation under Section 3 of the Competition Act 1980 with a view to establishing whether Thames had been or was pursuing a course of conduct which did amount to an anti-competitive practice. The matters to be investigated were policies and practices applied to Thames in deciding whether to grant favourable terms and conditions to any person committing or agreeing to commit any proportion, level or amount of expenditure on television advertising time to the purchase of such time from Thames, and whether the application of such policies and practices was a course of conduct which amounted to anti-competitive practice.

On 23 February 1983, however, the terms of reference were amended so that under Section 3 of the Competition Act 1980 'The services to which the investigation is to relate are the supply of television advertising time and the provision of advertising agency services in relation to television.'

At the next meeting of the ALC the Chairman, Lord Thomson, said that the dispute had serious implications for all the organisations represented at the ALC and for the ALC itself. JWT had chosen to refer the matter to the OFT rather than use the disputes procedure established by the ALC. JWT had referred the dispute neither to the IBA nor to the IPA before making its reference to the OFT although the IBA had decided to investigate the sales practices of Thames Television after certain facts had been brought to its notice.

Unreasonable Discrimination

The OFT report on Thames Television Ltd, published in February 1984, concluded that Thames' share deals were not strictly anti-competitive under the Competition Act 1980 because the unique duopoly in London offered an alternative to advertisers and agencies dissatisfied with one or other contractor. Although the OFT decision was seen as a 'vindication of our integrity' as a company by Thames Managing Director Bryan Cowgill, the Director General of Fair Trading, Sir Gordon Borrie, added his own, less complacent conclusion: 'A practice which is not anti-competitive in terms of the Competition Act may nevertheless be discriminatory. The Thames share-deal system clearly discriminates between advertisers and between agencies.'

The IBA was upbraided over the operation of its responsibilities in the Broadcasting Act 1981:

> This report draws attention to the duty of the IBA to secure compliance with certain statutory rules as to advertisements, including a rule against 'unreasonable discrimination either against or in favour of any particular advertiser' and a rule about publication by contractors of their charges. The Authority has hitherto refrained from pronouncing on the principle of share-deal schemes. I propose to bring this to the Authority's attention. (OFT Report on Thames Television, February 1984)

Following the publication of the OFT report, ISBA director, Ken Miles, was quoted in *Marketing Week* (24 December 1984) as saying that 'We shall be pressing the IBA to ban share schemes or at least to set a date by which they will cease to be permitted.' Clive Leach, Chairman of the ITV companies' marketing committee, was vigorous in response: 'I don't see what grounds ISBA has. Share schemes are a perfectly legitimate part of normal trading.'

A series of bilateral meetings was held with organisations represented on the ALC during 1983 and 1984. The Authority was anxious to arrive at a 'firm position', bearing in mind its statutory duty to ensure no unreasonable discrimination. The outcome was that on 22 May 1984 the IBA published a statement saying that the ITV companies might continue to offer share and parity schemes in their published rate cards, subject to certain conditions. The IBA accepted that such schemes did discriminate between advertisers but, provided the basic conditions were met, they did not constitute 'unreasonable discrimination' since discounts and special terms were part of normal business practice.

Still dissatisfied, a possible referral to the OFT was threatened by ISBA in 1987. An ALC working party had also been set up to report on share schemes to the Authority. At an ALC meeting in July 1987, the Chairman, Lord Thomson, regretted the fact that the ISBA Council 'had felt obliged to make a formal reference to the OFT and this presented the ALC with a problem since it would be rather difficult for participating members to work in a frank and open way when an OFT reference was also under way'. Ken Miles of ISBA replied that it was because the ALC had not made sufficient progress on share and parity schemes that the ISBA Council had decided to follow legal advice to approach the OFT (ALC minutes 26(87)) and that since the IBA apparently had no power to ban such schemes outright, all the work that had been done failed to address the central principle. At this ALC meeting Lord Thomson requested that ISBA should withhold formal reference to the OFT until after the working party proposals had been referred to the Authority. After withdrawing from the meeting, Ken Miles returned and said that he believed that there were sufficient grounds to ask the ISBA Council to reconsider the position in the light of the proposed ALC working party (ALC minutes 26(87)).

In October 1987, possibly provoked by the stinging criticisms at the Copenhagen Conference in May 1987, the escalating costs of advertising airtime, and the threat of a further OFT enquiry, the Authority finally acceded to the ALC working party recommendation that the IBA 'should seek the removal from ratecards of regional share schemes which offer discounts to advertisers who undertake to spend a specified proportion of their network television advertising budget with an ITV contractor' as from 1 January 1988, on the grounds that the ALC contested that the share schemes acted as an artificially rigid framework for negotiation.

Satellite Services Advertising

The issue of 'unreasonable discrimination' was tested further in another context in 1988. This arose specifically from the question of the right, which had been fiercely resisted by some ITV contractors, of the new satellite services to advertise on ITV.

The IBA told the ITV Association in 1988 that a blanket refusal to carry advertisements for the new satellite services would be considered as 'unreasonable discrimination' under the Broadcasting Act. On 12 January 1989, the IBA issued a news release confirming that it would be likely to regard a refusal by an ITV contractor to accept advertisements for such a service as unreasonable discrimination against the advertiser concerned, although the IBA conceded that it did not think it would be reasonable for ITV companies to be obliged to carry advertising denigrating ITV programmes or seeking to persuade viewers to watch programmes at specific times on the new services. TVS, however, was reported in the *Financial Times* (13 January 1989) as intending to defy the IBA and refuse to take television advertising from competing satellite TV channels.

The opposition of ITV sales directors to IBA guidance was intensified after the Sky/BSB merger in November 1990. A fierce row broke out on 9 September 1991 between ITV and BSkyB when a satellite TV advertising campaign was due to be launched with the slogan 'Sky: see what you've been missing'. Some companies, including Thames TV, threatened to block the advertisement. After consultation in July 1992, the ITC issued a statement (17 December 1992) on whether it was permissible for ITV companies to refuse to accept advertisements for competing services considered also in relation to provisions of the Broadcasting Act 1990 (Section 2(2)) which refers to the duty of the ITC to discharge their functions in the manner which they consider best calculated to ensure 'fair and effective competition'. It confirmed again that ITC would be likely to regard a refusal to accept advertising of a generic kind from competing broadcasters as unreasonable discrimination, providing it complied with the ITC Code and was not denigratory, but that the ITC also considered that it would not be unreasonable for ITC licensees to refuse advertising promoting particular programmes at particular times on the competing services.

A summary of the ITC's consultation on this issue was presented to ALC in November 1992. The OFT's position was that they would be concerned if Channel

3 companies banned satellite advertising and if they did so by agreement this would probably lead the OFT to consider the matter under the Restrictive Trade Practices Act; on competition grounds there seemed to be no case for permitting bans in any circumstances. The OFT was applauded by both BSkyB and advertisers.

Joint Sales Arrangements

During 1989, a number of proposals were made to the IBA to combine the sales operations of two (or more) ITV companies in order to achieve economies of scale in the increasingly competitive market place. In November 1989, after lengthy discussion at ALC, the IBA issued guidelines for such arrangements designed to prevent them being operated anti-competitively. Two arrangements (one involving Central, Anglia and Border and the other HTV and Grampian) were implemented during the year, and a third involving LWT and TVS was announced in May 1990.

While the IBA accepted that it was legitimate for ITV companies to seek ways of improving the efficiency of all their operations, including airtime sales, as they prepared for a more competitive environment in the future, it was also concerned that while the ITV companies continued to dominate the airtime sales market, new formations for the sale of TV advertising should not lend themselves to abuses of market power, most notably through 'conditional selling'. The main recommendation was that no formations would be permitted which at the time of approval would account for 25 per cent or more of UK television advertising revenue.

Supply of Advertising – Minutage

The issues on the ALC agenda described so far related mainly to the demand for and selling of television advertising. The other side of the coin in this allegedly monopolistic situation was the supply of advertising which was controlled by the minutage allowed by the IBA.

There had been a longstanding rule, introduced at the start of ITV, that the amount of advertising on ITV should be not more than six minutes per hour averaged over the broadcasting day, with a maximum of seven minutes in any one clock hour.

The first dent in this rule was initiated by the IPA/Equity dispute. In January 1983, the IBA agreed that the ITV companies could redistribute two minutes of television advertising airtime into peak time. This followed a request from the ITV companies who claimed that they were beginning to suffer from the effects of the IPA/Equity dispute over repeat fees for advertisements on Channel 4. The concession was to prevail for the duration of the dispute. In effect, it meant that there was a temporary reallocation of two additional minutes of television advertising in peak time. This minutage was transferred to peak time without any complaints from viewers.

Despite lobbying from the advertisers, the IBA had announced on 19 February 1987 that it had decided that it would make no change to the maximum permitted amount of television advertising (seven minutes) normally allowed in any single clock hour. In July 1987, an ALC working party was set up with a brief, among others, to consider the implications of and assess the case for changes in permissible peak-time minutage. In October 1987, the ALC recommended that the IBA should consider a proposal to increase the maximum permissible advertising minutage, in the interest of moderating the continued upward pressure on airtime costs. The proposed increase was from seven to seven and a half minutes in a clock hour in peak time, although the overall amount of advertising permitted would remain unchanged at an average of seven minutes per hour. Responding with surprising alacrity, the IBA issued a press release (27 October 1987) stating that it had authorised (with effect from 16 November) this recommendation. Lord Thomson conceded that 'the IBA is conscious of the problems being experienced by advertisers as a result of the continuing increases in the real price of airtime, and was satisfied that a limited increase on the scale proposed could be achieved without adverse effect on programme quality and enjoyment'. In the longer run the IBA believed that advertising opportunities would be changed by developments in broadcasting, such as DBS.

What then caused this change of mind? According to an editorial in *Media Week*:

> ... the ITV companies have had their minds forcefully concentrated, first by the Government's movement towards a free market, and second by the extremely adverse client reactions to the Copenhagen conference. As a result, to protect their existing client base, they decided to get properly onside with agencies and clients. The IBA, which has usually ignored the views of the people who pay its salaries (advertisers), couldn't remain deaf to the lobbying of its own companies. (*Media Week*, 6 November 1987)

An Assessment of the ALC

What measure of success can be attributed to the ALC in dealing with the problems which led to its establishment? Three years after it was set up, Harry Theobalds, Controller of Advertising, wrote:

> During the past 12 months or so there has been a noticeable improvement in the relationship between advertisers and agencies and the ITV programme companies, and evidence of a greater willingness on both sides to see the other point of view. The committee has attracted some criticism in the trade press for its lack of teeth, but this indicates a lack of understanding and appreciation of the function of the committee. It was never intended to be a decision-making body, indeed, it has no statutory powers, and was formed to provide a forum for discussion and resolution of problems by common consent and agreement. (*Campaign*, 30 September 1983)

Theobalds saw the most controversial matters which the committee had considered were the operation of the pre-empt system of time-buying, regional share and parity schemes, and PI (per item) direct-response rates. But he thought that the most significant development had been the adoption of the set of principles governing the sale of television airtime which each ITV company had adopted.

A year later (15 August 1984) Lord Thomson wrote to Leon Brittan (then Home Secretary) recounting some of the achievements of the ALC He stated that: 'Without wishing in any way to overstate the progress the ALC has made, the views expressed at our last meeting by advertisers, agencies and television companies, indicated satisfaction with the way in which the very genuine conflicts of interest were being reconciled.' Leon Brittan acknowledged Lord Thomson's letter on 28 August 1984, referring to the fact that when the committee was established 'we all recognised that there were a number of problems, and a good deal of unhappiness about the relationship between the buyers and sellers of advertising time'. He wrote 'I am grateful to you and the Authority for the lead you have given, and I would ask you to pass on my appreciation to all the Members of the ALC for the positive and successful work they have put in over the past four years.'

Peter Rennie (Granada Sales Director), however, writing in *British Television Advertising: The First 30 years* (edited by Brian Henry) was less flattering. He recounted that the ALC had 'been described by a wag as a game played by dissenting adults. In reality the debate only flows in one direction, since the chair is held by the IBA who have a direct lien over ITCA but none over the other parties at the feast.'

Credit for the establishment of a forum to discuss contentious issues of mutual interest to both the ITV companies and the advertisers may be given to the IBA but when JWT referred their complaint about Thames TV to the OFT in 1982, the ALC Brompton Road machinery was simply by-passed and on the thorny question of share schemes and the rising costs of television airtime, action was probably taken more as a result of the strident criticisms of the advertisers in Copenhagen in 1987 than from the lengthy ALC discussions over a period of years and the criticism from the OFT in 1984.

ITV Revenue Trends and Forms of Advertising

ITV advertising revenue statistics were not published by the IBA until 1984/85. ITCA, however, issued figures of independent television advertising revenue which were net after payment of all commissions and discounts but before the deduction of Exchequer Levy. ITV net revenue from 1980 to 1984, on this basis was as follows:

Year	£
1980	529,311,243
1981	611,222,523
1982	697,169,612
1983	824,417,275
1984	912,265,807

Source: ITCA.

A more detailed breakdown of Net Advertising Revenue from 1985 was published in the IBA/ITC annual reports:

Net Advertising Revenue (£m)

	1985	1986	1987	1988	1989	1990	1990*	1991	1992
ITV (incl. TV-am)	921	1065	1256	1423	1625	1680	1321	1418	1486
of which C4	75	113	115	213	256	268	209	250	242
of which S4C	2	2	3	4	4	4	3	3.5	3

(Years to 31 March from 1985–90)
* 1990 – 1 April to 31 December.
(Calendar years from 1991–92)

IPA/Equity Dispute

The detail of the IPA/Equity dispute on artists' fees for work on advertisements, which dragged on from 1982 to 1984, has been covered in Chapter 4. As a result of the dispute, the IBA allowed the ITV companies, whose Channel Four revenue had been severely affected, to restribute advertising minutage on ITV to gain up to two additional minutes in peak time for a period.

Sponsorship

Restrictions on television sponsorship dated back to the first Television Act 1954. Although the term 'sponsorship' was not included in the Broadcasting Act 1981, it limited sponsorship of programmes to factual portrayals of material or events which had an existence independent of television coverage. In practice this meant, for example, that there could be sponsorship for the television relay of a production in a theatre, but not for a performance in a studio or on film. In January 1982 the IBA issued its own *Guidelines for programmes funded by non-broadcasters* which permitted ITV to show, within strict rules, mainly sporting events.

In this grey period, a limited amount of sponsored programmes were allowed although the terms of the 1981 Broadcasting Act did not specifically permit sponsorship. Torin Douglas wrote in *Marketing Week* on 6 January 1984, 'no one has much of a clue as to what the rules and regulations actually permit'.

Opportunities for sponsorship were widened by the Cable and Broadcasting Act 1984 which gave the new Cable Authority the duty of drawing up 'a code governing standards and practice in advertising (including in particular the sponsoring of programmes)'.

In May 1988, the IBA, having reviewed its policy on television sponsorship, issued a statement saying that it was asking the government to consider relaxing legislation to widen sponsorship of television programmes. It regarded the present law as 'unduly restrictive' and was particularly concerned to encourage greater coverage of the arts and special projects which might not otherwise be undertaken by ITV and Channel 4. It also recognised that sponsorship as a potential source of programme funding would remain peripheral compared with advertising revenue but that it would offer 'a useful additional source of funds in the expectation of increased competition for revenue in future'. The revised television programme guidelines on sponsorship and indirect advertising, recommended by a working party chaired by Clare Mulholland (IBA's Deputy Director of TV) consisting of representatives of the IBA, Channel 4 and the ITV companies sought to clarify what was possible within the constraints of the existing legislation.

The Broadcasting Act 1990, however, was the first time in which the ITC was positively required to draw up and implement a code of sponsorship for ITV and Channel 4. After consultation, a draft code of programme sponsorship was drawn up which came into effect in 1991.

The new Code of Programme Sponsorship permitted sponsorship of all programmes except news and current affairs or programmes where there could be a conflict of interest between the sponsor and the editorial needs of the programme, such as consumer advice programmes. It did, however, forbid any influence by sponsors on the content and scheduling of programmes and limited the content and duration of sponsor credits. Product placement was also forbidden; although the appearance of branded goods in programmes where they were an essential element was allowed, there must be no promotional purposes and such appearances must not be 'unduly prominent'.

The new opportunities were rapidly taken up in 1991 by the ITV companies, first at regional level and subsequently for network programmes. Network sponsorships included the *Rugby World Cup* (Sony) (see also Chapter 3), *Rumpole* (Croft) and *Wish You Were Here* (Barclaycard). The ITC warned however, in its 1991 Annual Report, that it was

> aware that the aspirations of some potential sponsors go well beyond what the code permits, both in terms of the content and placing of credits, and involvement with programme content. Although the ITC will be reviewing the code in the light of initial experience, it does not see scope for large changes without putting at risk both the acceptability of sponsorship to viewers and editorial credibility and integrity.

Further sponsorship deals were seen on the ITV network in 1992 including the *European Football Championship* (Sega), *Inspector Morse* (Beamish Stout), *Maigret* (Kronenburg 1664), *Prime Suspect 2* (Peugeot) and *The Darling Buds of May* (Tetley Tea). On satellite channels there was also a considerable amount of activity: BSkyB's coverage of the World Cup Cricket involved four sponsors, its Movie Premier Season (Foster's lager) and MTV's Coca-Cola Report.

Nevertheless, breaches of the code began to be detected. In April 1992 the ITC published two cases where it concluded that breaches of the code in this and related areas had taken place. The first concerned BSkyB's coverage of the World Cup Cricket Championship, where there were a number of references to sponsors' products and services in the studio element of the coverage, as well as other breaches of the rules governing separation of credits from programming. The second case was ITV's coverage of the *Grand Opening of Euro Disney* where the responsible contractor was LWT. The ITC concluded that the extent and nature of material of a promotional character had been excessive.

Although sponsorship was seen in the longer term as a supplementary source of funding, when the ITC published its first return for terrestrial sponsorship income in 1992 the grand total was only £9 million – compared with a total of £1486 million Net Advertising Revenue.

Consumer Protection – Role of the AAC

The Advertising Advisory Committee (AAC), under the Broadcasting Act 1981, represented organisations concerned with standards of conduct in advertising and of the public as consumers. It gave advice to the IBA and the ITC about advertising control policy and made recommendations for code changes, the main purpose of which were to prevent misleading, harmful or offensive advertisements being transmitted. The Cable and Broadcasting Act 1984 empowered the committee to advise jointly both the IBA and the Cable Authority. The majority of AAC members had no connection with advertising interests. Although the Broadcasting Act 1990 no longer required a statutory advisory committee, the ITC took the view that it would be useful to maintain this kind of forum. The opportunity was taken to broaden the membership of the Committee to reflect a wide range of interests and expertise and in 1991 it included a trading standards officer, a bank manager, a member of the Committee for Black Anglican Concerns, and an independent producer of children's programmes, although there was no longer a permanent member from the Pharmaceutical Society of Great Britain. Unlike its predecessor, the AAC also started to consider sponsorship issues from 1990. The Committee discussed matters as diverse as humour in analgesic advertisements, the advertising of VD clinics, personal loans for paying off fuel debts and the protection of privacy. Price information about toys had generally featured on the agenda at Christmas. Academics had chaired the AAC since 1980. Aubrey Diamond, Professor of Law and Director of the Institute of Advanced Legal Studies, was appointed Chairman in August 1980; he was followed in 1988 by Professor Geoffrey Stephenson, a social psychologist, who was succeeded in 1992 by Professor Colin Seymour-Ure, Professor of Government at the University of Kent.

In December 1990, a new Code of Advertising Standards and Practice was published which came into effect on 1 January 1991. It was the first to apply to all television services under UK jurisdiction and was the first broadcast advertising code to take account of the EC Directive and Council of Europe Convention on Transfrontier Television. New provisions were included for the regulation of religious advertising, the protection of the environment and excessive health claims by food manufacturers.

Complaints

In the debate on the Broadcasting Bill in Standing Committee E (1 April 1980), Leon Brittan, Minister for Broadcasting, advised the Committee to accept an amendment that the IBA annual report should include

> an outline account of complaints received by the Authority in respect of the provision of advertisements and arrangements under section 5(2) and in respect of the sale of advertisements in those services, respectively, and an account of the general action they took in relation to those complaints.

Since then, an account of the number and nature of complaints, together with action taken, has been included in the IBA/ITC annual reports.

In considering the number of complaints received by the IBA on TV advertisements, AAC Paper 12 (81) recorded that they

> would not appear to give cause for concern and members may have gathered from the monthly reports that a large proportion of letters received express idiosyncratic views that might be construed more as comment than complaints or demands for action.

A monthly summary of complaints of TV advertisements was sent to journalists who were generally sympathetic to the IBA's duty to deal with such complaints. Bernard Barnett, writing in *Campaign* (23 September 1983), commented that 'In August, for example (a quiet month), the IBA received 50 complaints ranging from the reasonable to the absurd. Its most significant achievement in replying to them was to keep a straight face despite the kind of provocation that would have most people screaming with rage or hilarity.' He gave examples: 'One viewer objected to Collett Dickenson Pearce's Shredded Wheat commercial "Three is impossible" on the grounds that the claim was not true (the complaint might have stood a better chance if it had been directed at literacy).' The IBA replied in an admirably deadpan way. 'We do not feel,' it said, 'that the public takes this claim as seriously as that.' Thomson Local Directories was criticised for depicting Richard III calling for 'a horse ... a horse' because 'you cannot buy horses via Thomson's directory'. The IBA pointed out gently: 'We do not feel that this nonsensical treatment needs to be construed quite so seriously.'

Commenting on the complaints summary in *Marketing Week* (7 December 1984) Iain Murray also wrote: 'The first thing that strikes one is how very few complaints there are' and that 'the complaints summary ends on a note of quite understandable world weariness. "Three more correspondents" writes ATAO (Assistant Television Administrative Officer), stifling a yawn, "complained about the title of a forthcoming Channel 4 series, The Bullshitters".'

The annual number of complaints on television and radio advertisements in the early 1980s totalled about 1,000. Initially, most of the complaints were upheld on the grounds of misleading information. By the late 1980s/early 1990s the ITC was receiving 2,000 to 3,000 complaints a year on television advertisements. The IBA (annual report 87/88) also stated that 'a substantial number of the complaints received during a year are based on viewers' perceptions that the service provided by large organisations does not match the promise of their advertising campaigns' but thought that 'it would be both unfair and unrealistic to accept isolated evidence of individual disappointment as a reason for withdrawing advertising'.

Publicity on Advertising Control

In 1984, the AAC became increasingly concerned about the number of complaints on television advertising which were being redirected to the IBA from the Advertising Standards Authority (ASA). The ASA had started to operate a voluntary complaints system on behalf of the advertising industry for printed and cinema advertisements. The AAC recommended that publicity should be strengthened to heighten public awareness of the IBA's consumer protection role in television and radio advertising. Promotions for the IBA advertising control system, fronted by Sir Harry Secombe, were transmitted at the end of 1984. This campaign generated 739 letters compared with 101 in the same period in 1983.

Again, in August 1991 a survey showed that only 7 per cent of the respondents identified the ITC as the organisation which controlled and regulated programmes and advertisements on commercial television. The advertising agency Duckworth, Finn, Grubb and Waters was commissioned by the ITC to produce three thirty-second films designed to improve awareness about the ITC and its key functions of ensuring impartiality, protecting children from excessive violence and preventing misleading advertising. These were broadcast on ITV, Channel 4 and a number of UK satellite channels from April to May 1992. A survey taken after the main burst showed that the proportion of the audience able correctly to identify the ITC as the relevant regulatory authority both for programmes and advertisements more than doubled. The advertisements were reinforced by a series of regional presentations targeting consumer representatives to ensure that they were clear about the ITC's advertising control functions.

Unacceptable Products

One of the trends in the 1980s was the progressive removal or liberalisation of several products or services which had previously been banned from being advertised on television. Lord Thomson, Chairman of the IBA, described the difficulties posed by questions of taste and decency, especially in television advertisements, at a Radio Advertising Control Seminar in January 1981:

> Because commercials come up unannounced, random and often repetitive within IBA rules, and by reason of the very power which makes them valuable to the advertiser, the commercials should be produced with due regard to the sensitivities of the vast majority of ordinary families. The subject of taste and decency is probably one of the most difficult sections of the Code to deal with. Now, I know what good taste is – it's the things I like. Each of you knows what good taste is – it's the things you like! The problem comes when Parliament sets up a statutory body – in this case the IBA – and tells it that its programmes and its advertisements must be 'in good taste' and not offensive to public feeling. What a formidable mandate this is, when tastes and feelings differ so much, and when our broadcasts reach a wide spectrum of age and opinion!

Frank Willis, Controller of Advertising, outlined the difficulties the IBA faced in arbitrating on matters of taste and decency in an interview with Robin Wright, Chairman of WCRS in *Creative Review* in 1988. In response to Wright's complaint that his agency's advertisement for the Prudential showing Griff Rhys Jones throwing a cat over his shoulder had been restricted by the IBA, Willis explained:

> It's not a question of the social consequence, the risk that people would start chucking cats over their shoulders, that isn't the issue. I don't think anybody knows what the influence of advertising is. What we do know is that people assume there is far more than there probably is, but if there are enough people out there assuming it you get into the area where it's just a question of taste: you have offended people. We have a statutory duty that says you shall not offend large numbers of people with commercials.

He also pointed out that:

> the cinema medium is very different for the consumer – you pay your money, you go out of the home. If it was possible to gear the TV commercial to the target audience so that those areas of audience that do get worked up about this sort of thing didn't see it, then you'd be fine. But no campaign is that tightly targeted, you pick up your ratings around the schedule, you can't keep any commercial away from the more sensitive areas of the audience, the more elderly, the less well-educated. They are entitled to a degree of concern by statute, they are part of the overall constituency and balancing that is quite tricky. But I think it's going to ease with the proliferation of channels. The attitude to the medium is different then. All this started when there were only two channels, BBC and ITV, and

television was more of a national institution so that people felt they had almost democratic rights over what happened on it. That attitude breaks down as you get more channels ... if you don't like what you are getting on one channel then you don't have to watch it. (*Creative Review*, August 1988)

The Great 'Sanpro' Debate

The IBA, on the recommendation of the AAC, had agreed to a trial campaign for television advertising of sanitary protection in one ITV area as far back as 1970. An experiment was conducted on Thames in 1972, and research showed that 30 per cent of London viewers said that they would object to the advertising of sanitary protection in principle. Consequently, the Authority decided not to allow any further advertising of sanitary towels or tampons on television. At the request of ITCA, the AAC again recommended an experiment in two or three regions in 1978. These were tested in 1979 and resulted in 335 letters of complaint. The research sample showed that one in five were strongly opposed to such advertising. However, the AAC was critical of the research and, again at ITCA's request, recommended that there should be a further six months' experiment with more stringently structured research. After advertisments had been transmitted in fourteen regions, the IBA had received more than 1,000 complaints and the AAC recommended to the Authority that the category should not be accepted on television.

By 1984 further IBA research showed that 55 per cent of the population now considered that advertisements for sanitary protection were acceptable for television advertising, so the AAC recommended, and the Authority accepted, that a further experiment should be run on Channel 4 only, subject to more detailed content guidelines. Transmissions on Channel 4, without formal timing restrictions, started in 1985.

In 1986, the IBA received 614 complaints; the majority who were 'against' were opposed because of embarrassment caused by viewing in mixed company. The AAC, in 1987, recommended to the Authority that no firm case had been made for the cessation of the two-year experiment and this view was accepted. Nevertheless, complaints continued to arrive, totalling 889 in the year to March 1988. Further research by the ITV companies and by the IBA in 1988 showed that there had been a significant decline in the numbers who found the category unacceptable. This time, the AAC recommended that sanpro products should be an acceptable category for advertising on Channel 4 and that permission should be extended to include ITV, subject to the imposition of suitable timing restrictions. Nevertheless, in March 1992, a commercial for Vespre Silhouette featuring a forthright product presentation by Claire Rayner attracted over 500 complaints since it began transmissions at the start of the year. The response of both the AAC and ITC in May 1992 was to align timing restrictions on ITV and Channel 4 to reduce the likelihood of sanpro advertising being seen in family viewing time.

Family Planning and Contraception

Another sensitive area which the AAC had to deal with was television advertising of contraceptives. Although the IBA code had allowed the advertising of official or officially sponsored family planning services since 1970, contraceptives – as a product – had been banned. In June 1979 the Brook Advisory Centre had sent Lady Plowden a copy of their publication *The case for the condom*. Caroline Woodroofe, Chairman of Brook Advisory Centres, in an accompanying letter, asked the Authority to reconsider its decision not to accept the advertising of branded contraceptives because it was concerned at the number of teenage couples risking pregnancy. The author, Dilys Cossey, had wryly commented that 'Sex in advertising is acceptable, of course, if the product has nothing to do with sex. So sexual innuendo and titillation are approved for the selling of cars, chocolates, cosmetics, garden furniture – of everything, it seems, except healthy, normal sexual activity.'

Another letter was received from the organisation 'The Responsible Society' opposing the advertising of branded contraceptives; this was endorsed by an extensive correspondence in the Catholic publication *The Universe*. In a dilemma, an AAC paper (November 1979) stated that

> The Authority has to maintain a balance between the undue avoidance of, and interference with, programme content and the exclusion of matter which will cause offence to the public. Almost anything is capable of causing offence to at least some members of the public so requirements have to be interpreted in a sensible fashion.

Striking a reasonable compromise, the AAC recommended to the Authority that the code should be amended to allow the advertising of branded contraceptives on an experimental basis; qualitative research should be carried out by the IBA to establish parameters of acceptability and draft guidelines should be prepared which should contain an element of educational information. In 1980, however, the IBA issued a press release (25 November 1980) saying that although the Authority had reconsidered this issue, research showed that a large majority (61 per cent) was opposed to such advertising and that the Authority had decided not to permit it on the grounds that it could cause widespread offence. The question of advertising of contraceptives should be deferred for another three years.

In February 1983 the IBA 'blocked' the first public service announcement (PSA) to encourage boys to use contraceptives because it appeared to condone premarital sex. The film, featuring Adam Faith and filmed by LWT's community information unit, carried the message 'If you're not man enough to use birth control, you're not old enough to make love.' A press furore followed. Lord Thomson took the unusual step of publishing an explanatory letter on 16 June 1983, saying that the IBA was not opposed to the concept of a PSA on contraception but the film was unacceptable because it might be appearing to 'condone promiscuity'.

However by the end of the year the script was modified; it omitted the phrase 'up the spout' and transmission was allowed with Adam Faith saying: 'Any idiot can get a girl into trouble, do not let it be you.'

On 12 November 1986, Lord Thomson in a letter to William Whitelaw, Chairman of the Cabinet Committee considering whether the broadcast media could be used to create a public awareness of the dangers of Aids, admitted that 'an official campaign, because of the nature of the problem, may need to be more explicit than we would be prepared to allow a commercial advertisement'. The ban on the advertising of branded contraceptives was still operating but research indicated that there had been a swing in favour of such advertisements. This, too, was probably exacerbated by the explicitness of the government's Aids commercials. In March 1987, the Authority decided that, subject to consultation with the Secretary of State, the ban should be removed and guidelines, including a compliance with British Standard 3704, were drafted in April 1987.

An IBA research paper 'Informing the public about Aids' (February 1987) had also shown that 75 per cent of those interviewed thought that the television advertisements or government announcements warning about the danger of Aids should be allowed at all times, and 50 per cent thought that there was too little coverage. Home Office approval was necessary for the removal of any banned products. This was given in July 1987 and the first approved Durex advertisement was transmitted, ending with a wide shot of a couple embracing with the superimposed line 'Together we're safer with Durex'. An advertisement for Mates condoms in November 1987 resulted in 700 complaints, including a petition of over 400 signatures on the grounds that it encouraged promiscuity. In 1988 the year of experimental transmissions ended; although there had been a further 500 complaints the Authority decided that advertisements should continue, subject to regular review. By 1991 the number of complaints had been reduced to a trickle but Frank Willis attributed this partly to the fact that in the event there had been very little advertising of branded condoms by manufacturers.

Charities

One area in which the views of the IBA were well ahead of public opinion was advertising by charities. A joint working party of representatives of the IBA, ITV, ILR and charities recommended in 1978 that the Code should be relaxed to allow charities greater freedom for television advertising. Although this recommendation was accepted by IBA Members, the government thought the time was not yet right. In April 1986, the IBA undertook a further review and in October 1988, it published proposals for relaxing the thirty-three-year-old bar on paid-for advertising by charities. The views of charities were enlisted before making recommendations to the Home Secretary. The IBA's consultative document 'Broadcast advertising by charities: a framework for liberalisation' was sent to over 1,000 charities. Frank Willis, Controller of Advertising, commented that

Charity advertising seems acceptable to the general public in all other media and we think that there would have to be compelling reasons for continuing to exclude it from the broadcast media. These proposals have been developed to illustrate how potential problems which have been identified in the past might be tackled. Now it's for the charities themselves to tell us what they think.

A clear majority of the charities which responded expressed general support for the proposals and the Authority, in March 1989, decided to recommend to the Home Secretary that they should be adopted. The Home Office accepted the IBA recommendation to lift the restrictions on charity advertising. The IBA published detailed guidelines for the handling of such advertising and established an informal contact group to help monitor developments and discuss issues. Charities were able to promote their aims and objectives and solicit funds on television from September 1989. A number of charities such as Marie Curie Cancer Care, Oxfam, the RSPCA and the NSPCC were among the first to take advantage of the new opportunity.

Financial Services

Another area which was progressively liberalised was financial services. In 1980/81 the IBA considered how to take account in the advertising code of the provisions of the Banking Act 1979. By 1983, amendments had been introduced which, subject to safeguards to protect consumer interest, would allow more flexibility for financial advertisers wanting to use television and radio. These included the greater promotion of company prospectuses; more financial information in corporate advertising by companies; the advertising of the results of Stock-Exchange listed companies and of savings facilities. This relaxation was marked in May 1983 when Kenneth Kendal, a retired newsreader, traced the financial progress of the grocers, Sainsbury.

The Financial Services Act 1986, whose main purpose was to provide an effective investor protection regulatory regime, also led to code changes in 1988 which allowed that anybody entitled to carry out investment advertising, in the sense of the Financial Services Act, should not be debarred by status from doing so on television or radio.

Matrimonial and Introduction Agencies

Possibly the more liberal approach to products and services on cable and satellite led to the relaxation of banned items in the IBA's advertising code. Television advertising of matrimonial and introduction agencies had already been allowed on the new services; in December 1991, the ITC decided that these services should also be allowed on ITV and Channel 4. In 1992, following the transmission of an advertisement for Dateline, the IBA received two complaints from viewers who had been disappointed with their acquaintances.

Religious Advertising

Religious advertising had been prohibited by all Broadcasting Acts before the Broadcasting Act 1990 except by the Cable and Broadcasting Act 1984 in respect of advertising on cable and satellite services (including satellite services, retransmitted on cable). The 1990 Act, however, did not include a specific prohibition.

Before consulting widely on proposals for new rules governing the broadcasting of religious advertisements the IBA sent a questionnaire in May 1990 to organisations representing major faiths and denominations in the UK, as well as equivalent or alternative beliefs (such as humanism). The IBA also commissioned a full-scale research study of public attitudes.

Both exercises revealed a very wide span of views. These ranged from a strongly-expressed desire mainly by evangelical churches for a minimum of restrictions on the ability to proclaim, in spot advertising, a particular faith and actively to recruit for it, to (at the opposite end of the spectrum) a considerable degree of unease about divisive effects, about increasing the influence of what were regarded as 'strange' sects and the risk of any fund-raising facility being abused.

Majority opinion, however, was cautiously in favour of allowing religious advertising, subject to strict safeguards. The rules which were published in December 1990 on behalf of the ITC reflected this consensus. The new rules permitted advertising by religious organisations which publicised events, services and so on, or described the organisation and how it might be contacted, or offered publications or merchandise. There were certain categories of organisation which were not permitted to advertise.

Fund-raising other than for bona fide charitable purposes was not allowed. Proselytising and direct attempts at recruitment were prohibited and there were restrictions on the extent to which reference might be made to claims and beliefs.

Controversial Products – Alcohol ...

Although the 1980s witnessed the progressive liberalisation of television advertising of certain banned products or services, the portrayal of others was subject to increasingly active lobbying by individual pressure or interest groups.

In January 1988 a Home Office working party was set up to examine the depiction of alcohol in television advertisements. An earlier report, the Masham Report on alcohol abuse, published in November 1987, had given rise to rumours of a total ban on alcohol advertising. Although this proved unfounded, the AAC was asked to review the alcohol rules of the advertising code and to make recommendations. In September 1988, these were amended to clarify and reinforce the rules that television advertisements should only be associated with people of at least twenty-five years old; no advertisements should feature a personality whose example people under eighteen were likely to follow; and advertisements should not imply that drinking was essential to successful social or sexual success and should not foster immoderate drinking.

... Sugar-based Products ...

A debate on the advertising of sugar-based products stemmed from a report published in December 1989 which claimed to confirm an association between excessive sugar consumption and dental caries by AIS (Action and Information on Sugars). The IBA was petitioned to revise the code provisions on the advertising of sugar-based products. A delegation, led by Joan Lestor MP, met the Director General of the IBA in May 1990. The view was that the content and weight of television advertising for sugar-based products, particularly that directed at children, were at odds with some of the recommendations of a report published by the Department of Health in 1989 drawn up by the Panel of Dietary Sugars of the Committee on the Medical Aspects of food policy (COMA).

Further pressure came from the National Consumer Council (NCC) in November 1992 following their report *Your food: whose choice?* The Council recommended that the ITC should update its guidance on the advertising of foods, particularly food with high sugar and/or fat content, targeted at children. Replying in a letter to Lady Wilcox, Chairman of the NCC, Sir George Russell pointed out in November 1992 that

> the criticism expressed by some of the single issue campaigning groups does not highlight, as is alleged, inadequacies in the procedures for code enforcement but a more fundamental difference of view on the legitimacy of marketing certain types of food product at all.

In 1991, AIS challenged the longstanding claim for Mars bars that 'A Mars a day helps you work, rest and play' as a health claim which could not be supported by sound medical evidence, the qualifying measure implied by the code. The resulting investigation was comprehensive, with Mars submitting its medical and consumer research to the Commission. The 'rest' element of the slogan was the most contentious. Finally in 1992, the ITC decided that to uphold the complaint would carry literalism beyond any reasonable bounds justified by the needs of consumer protection and the complaint was not upheld.

... and Toys

In 1984, Janey Buchan MEP fought a spirited campaign on the 'intolerable pressure' put upon shoppers, but especially the parents of young children, by toy advertising. Harry Theobalds, IBA Controller of Advertising, was robust in response:

Nobody denies the existence of a lot of television advertising for toys and games at this time of the year, but bearing in mind that this is the time at which the toy industry and retail outlets are principally marketing their products, and when people are looking for presents to buy, this is not surprising. There is no general case for shielding children from responsible advertising. Indeed, children have to live in a world in which advertising plays an important role. They also have to learn that they cannot have, nor should expect to have, everything which is on offer. Parents can still say 'no'. (*Sunday Telegraph*, 25 November 1984)

By 1986, the issue of toy advertising was more concerned with the separation of advertisements and programmes. A new development on television was the creation of commercials promoting sales of toys based on the programme characters or which were very similar in style and theme to the programmes. The IBA dealt with this issue by recommending that such advertisements should not be transmitted on the same day as the programmes and should not be too closely linked with programme material.

The question of the requirement for price indication of toys in advertisements kept the AAC busy for several meetings in the late 1980s. In 1988, some toy manufacturers and retailers had requested that the requirement to indicate prices should be repealed. In June 1989, IBA Members decided not to accept the recommendation of the AAC (which had been opposed by its consumer representatives), that the price requirement should be suspended experimentally for two years. A compromise was eventually reached in October 1989, to limit the pricing requirement to 'expensive' products which were defined at the time as those not generally available at under £15. The trigger price was raised to £18 in March 1991. Frank Willis philosophically remarked that

> The ITC believes that it is beyond dispute that there is *some* benefit to consumers from the provision of the information and *some* disbenefit to the toy trade. Unfortunately neither the benefit nor the disbenefit can be precisely quantified and the trade-off between the two must ultimately therefore be a matter of political judgement. (AAC Paper (5)91, 27 May 1991)

Controversial Issues – Comparative Advertising ...

A vicious battle erupted in 1983, with copious press coverage, between Qualcast and Flymo, two leading lawnmower manufacturers – the former selling traditional grass-cutting machines and the latter promoting a new horizontal design, the blades of which acted as a fan allowing the machine to hover just off the ground while also cutting the grass. Flymo claimed that this required less effort; Qualcast argued to the contrary. The difficulty arose from the relaxation of the rules governing comparative advertising in the 1970s. Before then, 'knocking copy' was not allowed. The Qualcast slogan for its advertising campaign was 'It's a lot less bovver than a hover'.

Flymo disputed Qualcast's claims and made a formal objection to the IBA. *Broadcast* magazine (25 April 1983) reported that Harry Theobalds was highly displeased with Qualcast PR attempts to draw the IBA into an 'official' comparison of the two machines' performances which were carried out in a blaze of publicity. Even *The Economist* (16 April 1983) saw fit to devote a full page to the row. When the matter was discussed in AAC, the chairman stressed the need to reaffirm that denigration was unacceptable and that comparisons must be fair and not unduly selective. The problem was dealt with by a revised ITCA Note of Guidance 'Special problem areas – comparative advertising' which was circulated to advertisers and agencies.

... Environmental Claims ...

In 1990, another source of pressure on misleading advertising came from the green lobby about environmental claims of television advertising. A number of misleading claims led the Copy Clearance Department of the ITV Association to publish in June 1990 the first comprehensive guidelines for environmental claims in television and radio advertisements. Despite these guidelines, a £3.3 million television advertising campaign which made false claims that Andrex toilet rolls helped counter the greenhouse effect was later withdrawn on the instructions of the IBA. Friends of the Earth and other environmentalists had complained that the advertisement was grossly misleading.

... Stereotyping of Women ...

In the early 1980s, the IBA received occasional complaints on the portrayal of women in television advertisements on the grounds that stereotypes held back equal opportunities and belittled women's status in society. The IBA staff and the AAC generally did not feel that the number or content of the complaints in such a subjective area justified special code rules. The AAC agreed that the code rules needed neither change nor any action by the IBA, although Mr P. Scruton, an AAC member, did express a reservation about the Russell Hobbs coffee maker's claim, 'Now there is intelligent life in the kitchen'.

In 1982 the Equal Opportunities Commission published a report called *Adman and Eve – a study of the portrayal of women in advertisements* which was followed by an ASA study *Herself appraised – the treatment of women in advertisements*. The IBA merely noted in its 1982/83 annual report that the former indicated that modern, liberated roles were more effective than the traditional roles played by women in advertisements and thought that the report contained a message for those who created advertisements. It noted, too, that the latter report indicated that very few of the advertisements in magazines read by women were seen by them as portraying women in an offensive manner.

Five years later, in its 1988/89 annual report, the IBA, more defensively, stated that it was not able to extend its regulatory action beyond the avoidance of offence into the area of social engineering, while welcoming the fact that advertisers were increasingly finding that consumers were rejecting stereotypes of female roles with which they refused to identify and that many of the more successful campaigns for household brands reflected a subtler and more complex understanding of current social attitudes.

... and Political Advertising

All Television and Broadcasting Acts had forbidden television advertising which was directed towards political ends. In October 1983, the IBA banned the GLC's slogan 'Working for London' on the grounds that since the government was proposing to abolish the GLC this had turned the slogan into a political statement. The situation was 'rescued' by substituting the phrase 'Working in London'. This did not cut any ice with Michael Ivens, Director of the Aims of Industry:

> I have complained to the IBA about these GLC advertisements. To my astonishment their Chairman, Lord Thomson of Monifieth, has answered that he does not believe that they are political because they do not carry the phrase 'GLC working *for* London' but the apparently acceptable 'GLC working *in* London'. The semantics of this I find baffling. Quite clearly many people see these advertisements as part of the GLC campaign to maintain its existence and that the GLC is '*working* in London', ie., being useful and successful. Even more objectionable is the fact that the IBA regard government and local government as being exonerated from the definition of a 'political organisation'. As local authorities now have more money to spend on political propaganda than anyone else, this is a dangerous situation. (*The Times*, 18 May 1984)

During the miners' dispute in 1984 the IBA also stepped in to ban a then current television advertisement for Madame Tussaud's which showed a woman roundly abusing a waxwork model of the miners' union leader, Arthur Scargill, because it was judged to be politically tendentious during the miners' strike.

A month later the *Spectator* (26 May 1984) wrote:

> The Head of Advertising Control at the Independent Broadcasting Authority, Mr Harry Theobalds, once achieved fame in these columns for saying, in an offhand way, that the *Spectator* would not be allowed to advertise on television. We therefore sent a representative to the Advertising Conference held by the IBA last week, to check the current position. The Conference itself was devoted to the control of commercial advertising, but during morning coffee Mr Theobalds

reminisced with engaging candour about the political side of his work. When he started reading the *Spectator* he realised he had been wrong. 'I got hooked on it. I buy it every week. I think it's a very good magazine. I like Taki'. Of course we could advertise. He remembered writing to 'Geoffrey Chandler' to invite an application. The only papers the IBA had ever banned were the *Daily Worker, Morning Star* and *Tribune*: they were committed to particular parties, and were therefore judged to fall foul of the (extraordinarily vague) provision in the IBA code that 'no advertisement may be inserted by or on behalf of any body, the objects whereof are wholly or mainly of a political nature, and no advertisement may be directed towards any political end'. Asked whether he would ban *Marxism Today*, he said that as far as he could tell without seeing a copy it would certainly be turned down: the title alone showed what sort of paper it was.

The IBA itself raised another political dimension to advertising in one of its Annual Reports:

An important question which arose during the year was advertising relating to various aspects of nuclear energy. The IBA considered proposals by British Nuclear Fuels PLC. The IBA decided that no advertisement would be allowed which discussed controversial aspects of nuclear energy such as the discharge of radioactive waste, safety and any other matter in a way which did not show impartiality as respects matters of political or industrial controversy. In the event, over the past 12 months, it has been possible to accept three television advertisements for British Nuclear Fuels which were in accordance with these decisions and met the requirements of the IBA Code of Advertising Standards and Practice and the provisions of the legislation. At the beginning of the first advertising campaign, the environmental group 'Greenpeace' submitted to the IBA a proposed television commercial which introduced the disaster at Chernobyl in order to take issue about the safety aspects of nuclear energy. The proposal was not in accord with the provisions of the legislation and the IBA Code and had to be rejected. (IBA Annual Report, 1986/87)

An article by Brian Rotman in *The Listener* was more sceptical.

The difference between the BNFL and Greenpeace advertisements is not, as the IBA would have us believe, that one is political and the other isn't. The difference is that the Greenpeace advertisement is *frankly* political whereas the BNFL one is only implicitly so. What one implies and insinuates – that paying a visit to a complex high-technology factory will demonstrate that it is safe and benign – the other explicitly questions. Why should insinuation be less *'political'* than outright assertion? (*The Listener*, 11 September 1986)

In 1988 political debate and press comment focused on the volume and content of television advertising by government departments, which was alleged by some critics (notably, Tony Blair MP) to be at variance with the rules in the IBA Code forbidding political advertising. Letters exchanged between Tony Blair and Lord Thomson on advertising by government departments were published on 12 April 1988. Blair had expressed his 'deep concern about the Government's use of television advertising to promote various aspects of the Government's policies and programmes'. He pointed out in a letter dated 28 March 1988 that the budget of the Central Office of Information (COI), the government's publicity unit, had more than doubled and was now running at over £150million p.a. In particular, the publicity of the Department of Trade and Industry (DTI) was set to increase almost six-fold to some £13 million p.a. Many of these campaigns to be run by the DTI covered areas of high political controversy such as the Enterprise Initiative, campaigns on inner cities and the internal market, and the privatisation advertisements. Although Tony Blair, when opposition spokesman on Energy in 1989, pursued the issue with a dossier of complaints, the IBA stuck firmly to the line that although all advertisements were carefully checked, the volume of such advertising and expenditure on it were matters for Parliament, not for the IBA.

In 1989, the IBA ruled that it could not show a film advertising the campaign to free British hostages in Beirut. The film had been made by the advertising agency Bartle Bogle Hegarty as a donation to the Friends of John McCarthy, the group formed to keep the public aware of the plight of the WTN journalist who had been kidnapped. Although the advertisement was being shown on cable television, the IBA, after taking counsel's advice, claimed that it was directed to a political end in that it sought to persuade the British government to do more to secure the release of the hostages. Further attempts to show the advertisements on ITV and Channel 4 were made in 1990 and 1991 but were turned down on the same grounds.

The difficulty of defining 'a political end' was highlighted by the different judgements by different legal counsels applied to cable and terrestrial advertisements. A divergence of standards was emerging.

SECTION II: OWNERSHIP

IBA REJECTS 'UNACCEPTABLE' CARLTON BID FOR THAMES

The IBA announced in a statement that Carlton's proposal, 'which would lead to a major change in the nature and characteristics of a viable programme company, is not acceptable having regard to the IBA's responsibilities under the Broadcasting Act'.

(*The Times*, 11 October 1985)

I liked Michael Green and I thought he'd be a breath of fresh air actually at that time. I was not at all ill-disposed to the idea of him being the owner of a television franchise, even a big one like Thames, provided he won it through the normal procedures. But I think because I rather liked him he thought this meant that I would go along with cutting the corner, and he was very dismayed when I wouldn't and he's never quite forgiven me. (Interview with Lord Thomson, Chairman of the IBA)

A thirty-seven-year-old entrepreneur and the Chairman of the Independent Broadcasting Authority in conflict over the interpretation of the Authority's duties carried echoes of the Authority's imperious past. Rupert Murdoch had only been thirty-nine when he bought into LWT and began his struggles with the Authority. But whereas Murdoch was known to the IBA, Green came with no reputation. But this did not, in the event, stand him in any better stead than if he had had a bad one.

During a period when the enterprise economy was a jungle where corporate structures seemed to swallow one another daily, the ITV companies appeared to lead a charmed life. Outsiders found this difficult to understand. The companies were very profitable and the IBA had required them to become public companies – in the market, apparently like any other.

Michael Green was perhaps the brightest – and certainly the most persuasive – young entrepreneur in the penumbra of television facilities businesses that glowed ever brighter outside the circle of the established broadcasters. This growth was the result of the explosion of independent producers working for channels new and old which expanded enormously the demands for facilities other than those belonging to the broadcasters. It was not a world the IBA knew a lot about. In 1985 their main concern in relation to independent production was to hold the ring between the independents and the companies in relation to the introduction of the government-required 25 per cent quota of independent production. The television facilities business only came into the equation later as part of the lobby against 'sweetheart' deals – deals with independents where the compulsory use of the ITV companies' own facilities in the making of the programmes concerned was entailed in the contract.

Green seems to have been born with the full set of business instincts. That was not uncommon in the north-west London Jewish milieu in which he grew up:

I think I knew at a very early age that I was going to be a businessman ... There was nothing in my background or my family that suggested that was not a good thing to do. My father was very much a businessman, ... a man who would open up the factory at 7 a.m. So you would see your father leave very early, you would see him come home late, you knew about the work ethic, and the conversation at dinner would be about business and making money. (Michael Green, quoted in *Greenfinger: The Rise of Michael Green and Carlton Communications* by Raymond Snoddy, Faber & Faber, 1996)

His friends as he reached adulthood included the the younger generation of the Wolfson family (owners of Great Universal Stores), the Saatchi brothers, and Gerald Ratner and they tended to put business each other's way. They were, of course, to become fashionable – almost heroes – in government circles (particularly in Downing Street) during the 1980s.

In 1965, at the age of seventeen, Michael Green, with his older brother David, who was nineteen, had set up an office supplies and printing business. The company was called Tangent Systems and in the following five years it expanded into direct mail advertising.

One of the most significant names amongst the companies that became available to the Greens was as a result of a social contact. The Wolfson family, whose daughter Janet was to become Michael Green's first wife, owned in their vast business grouping a photographic business which provided most of the pictures for the catalogues that were at the heart of the GUS mail-order business. The Greens were offered the chance to manage and operate the business, with an option to purchase if all went well. It was called Carlton Studios Limited.

The Green's Tangent company did purchase Carlton, as it did three other companies related to printing, in the next ten years. By 1981 the group's turnover had reached just under £20 million. Profits were not high but assets amounted to some £5 million. Michael Green had emerged as the driving force of the enterprise and it was he who followed up a lead that was to take the company into television.

The following year Tangent bought a small company, called Transvideo, which owned a mobile control room with cameras and editing facilities and used them on contract to cover sport or make videos, eventually renting a disused church in St John's Wood to use as a drive-in studio. Green renamed it Carlton Television. By a reverse takeover of a small company with shares quoted on the Unlisted Securities Market, Green was able to float a grouping of Tangent's non-printing businesses on the Stock Exchange on 25 February 1983 as Carlton Communications plc.

The flotation was a success, with the value of the company nearly doubling on the first day's trading. But, although the newcomer was clearly welcome in financial circles, he was not widely known. One other person in the television facilities business, however, did take notice. Mike Luckwell, who owned and ran the Moving Picture Company, a technically advanced, and profitable, special effects and editing facility in Soho, had met Green as a competitor for the purchase of Transvideo. Green had been impressed with Luckwell's technical and facilities management abilities and had sometimes sought his advice. Now Luckwell – himself interested in making the financial structure of Moving Picture more secure – was impressed with Green's business skills.

As a result of further advice-taking by Green, he and Luckwell bought the UK arm of the company making the first reliable automatic time-base corrector for television. 'Genlock' – the locking of one television source's frame-timing to another to prevent the picture 'rolling' on viewers' sets when a cut was made from one source to another – had been a manual and somewhat unreliable process. IVC UK had developed a PAL system version of a Silicon Valley digital solution to the problem.

Within a year a friendly takeover of the Moving Picture Company by Carlton Communications had been arranged. The new company was worth £43.5 million, of which Luckwell had 20 per cent. He became Carlton's managing director with Michael Green as chairman and chief executive. (David Green remained a major shareholder but was running the photographic side of the business at this time.) Together, Michael Green and Luckwell set about acquiring television-related businesses, ranging from electronic equipment manufacturers (including one in America), through other facilities businesses to a television and film 'props' (furniture and design detail) hire company. Green believed that Carlton was now positioned in the right place at the right time to consider a move into the broadcasting business.

To Luckwell, who also owned a programme production company (run by Nigel Stafford-Clark), such a move offered the business benefits of vertical integration with broadcasting. Green's motivation appears to have been more complex. Commercial television, though threatened by competition, was still mightily profitable and was likely to remain so in the medium term. Carlton had grown its assets hugely but its profits were not yet what all its investors would have liked to see. Perhaps also there was the matter of personal growth. Green had left Haberdashers' Aske's at seventeen with only three 'O' Levels (English Language, English Literature and History), but was welcomed as witty, perceptive and able not just amongst his peer group but also in political and city circles. However, he had no public prominence. He had built a financial power base, with net assets of £18.5 million in the accounts published in September 1984 and a market value of £200 million, inside twenty years, but it was not a base from which he could achieve broader influence. Broadcasting would involve a more public role – as advertising had done for his friends the Saatchi brothers, for instance.

Early in 1985 Green and Luckwell started to buy shares in LWT. By May they were approaching the 5 per cent threshold at which they would have to declare their holding under the Stock Exchange rules at the time. Should they, could they, go further? Green recalls that he'd 'got a feel for the legal minefield it might represent' (Interview). He decided on an informal approach to the IBA as a first step. Through one of his colleagues who knew David Glencross, the Director of Television, Green arranged a lunch to explore the possibilities.

Glencross, a product of Salford Grammar School and Trinity College Cambridge, had gone on to be one of those high flyers selected by the BBC to be a General Trainee. As a consequence he had a strong public service broadcasting background, which included time as a producer with the BBC World Service, the BBC Regions and Television Current Affairs programmes. A significant part of his role at the IBA was to ensure the maintenance of public service programme standards on independent television in the face of commercial pressures. Green was an extremely successful creature of commerce who saw any difficulties that might stand in his way in legal, rather than cultural, terms. In a way their positions were a paradigm of the forces that were to clash so fiercely in the later years of the Eighties. Not surprisingly they talked somewhat at cross purposes. Glencross believed that he had explained very clearly why it was not possible to take over an ITV company in mid-contract, unless it was in such financial difficulty that it had breached its contractual terms of service. After the Glencross lunch and a meeting with John Whitney, the Director General (held, because of a bomb scare, in Whitney's Rolls-Royce in a dark corner of the underground car park at the IBA's HQ in Brompton Road), Green believed merely that the IBA had to be satisfied as to the bona fides of the purchasing company and that the owners of the company being bought had to be agreeable to the takeover.

He and Luckwell went to see the Chairman, Managing Director and Programme Controller of LWT to seek acceptance as buyers of the company. The Chairman, Christopher Bland, was someone whom Green knew from the world of printing as the chairman of Sir Joseph Causton and Sons. At thirty-four Bland had also been the youngest Deputy Chairman ever appointed to the IBA. (In 1996, as Sir Christopher, Bland was to be appointed Chairman of the BBC.) Bland is not a man inclined to beat about the bush:

> I remember vividly Christopher Bland saying, 'Michael would you work for me?' I said 'No.' He said 'I think you've got your answer.' I said 'What do you mean, Christopher?' He said 'I think you've got the answer.' (Interview with Michael Green)

Negotiations continued in a desultory fashion for a while but it became clear that Carlton would have to find another route into ITV.

The two shareholders of Thames Television, BET and Thorn EMI, who had inherited and acquired respectively, the component parts of Thames – Rediffusion and ABC – in the aftermath of the 1968 contract round had, quite separately, developed new business strategies that made their Thames holdings redundant. Both had put out discreet 'feelers' in the market in 1984. By the middle of the following year – the year of the *Dallas* debacle that laid low Thames' Managing Director, Bryan Cowgill – Green's merchant bank, Hambros, had sounded out the potential sellers and Green himself was dealing with Colin Southgate, Chairman of Thorn EMI, and Nicholas Wills, Chief Executive of BET:

> There was no question that the relations between the two shareholders and their subsidiary were not what they should have been. And they were both keen to sell. If shareholders want to sell to a willing buyer the Board's attitude is relevant but not paramount. Initial emotional reactions are not important in the long term. (Interview with Michael Green)

And emotional reactions there certainly were. On Cowgill's departure in July, Thames' Chairman, Hugh Dundas, had turned to Richard Dunn, the man who as Director of Production had faced down the unions with a management service the previous autumn, to take over as Chief Executive.

Dunn was in the midst of personal trauma. His five-year-old son had been badly injured only four days earlier, as a result of being run over by a car outside their house. Dunn and his wife were still taking it in turns to watch over the child in hospital when Dundas rang. No mention of a possible change of ownership was made. Dunn, after talking to Cowgill, accepted the job.

It was not until eight weeks later, in mid-September, that a chance remark at lunch with Gary Dartnell, one of the Thames' directors who was also on the Thorn EMI Board, led Dunn to challenge his chairman on the subject when he returned from America at the end of September. Dundas admitted that Thorn and BET had already signed to sell their 95 per cent of the share capital of Thames. It was a shock and it also posed an ethical dilemma for Dunn:

... my two shareholders had become share sellers, and this put me as Chief Executive in an extremely difficult position, because I had duties to my two shareholders, but I also had duties under the (Broadcasting) Act, to the IBA, for the stewardship of a public contract. No precedent. What do you do? A very difficult conundrum.

I was introduced, that same day (30 September), to Michael Green, whom I had never met, and had hardly heard of before. In 1985 I think very few people had heard of Carlton. And Michael Green asked me to accompany him to the IBA, effectively to go hand-in-hand to the IBA saying that I supported this takeover and that I welcomed Carlton as a new owner. I declined to do that on the grounds that I didn't know him from Adam, I didn't know anything about his company, I didn't know anything about his intentions, and in any event, to my knowledge, IBA television contracts couldn't be bought or sold. (Interview with Richard Dunn)

Dunn saw Green again, with Mike Luckwell this time, on Tuesday 2 October, but with no greater meeting of minds than before. Faced with this impasse both sides separately turned to John Whitney at the IBA for advice.

Later that day Dunn arranged to meet Whitney over tea. Because of the need for secrecy this took place in a bedroom at the Inn on the Park hotel. It was the first anyone at the IBA had heard of the specific bid for Thames – Green's soundings with Glencross and others at the IBA were thought to refer to his interest in LWT. Whitney's first reaction was to doubt whether such a bid in mid-contract was allowable.

On Thursday, having consulted with Bryan Rook, the Secretary to the Authority and the IBA's in-house source of legal advice, Whitney agreed to see Hugh Dundas, who as well as being Chairman of Thames was Deputy Chairman of BET, and Sir John Read, his Deputy Chairman at Thames who represented Thorn EMI on the

Board. They confirmed their companies' willingness to sell, if the IBA agreed. Whitney pointed out that such a change of ownership was subject to a clause in the Broadcasting Act which did indeed give the Authority power to decide whether to allow such a substantial change in ownership or whether the contract should be readvertised. He thought the latter more likely but would discuss further – including with his Chairman, Lord Thomson, who was returning from abroad that weekend. Dundas and Whitney agreed not to respond to any press enquiries that might arise.

Green, aware that the story was about to break in the business pages of a Sunday paper, asked for a breakfast meeting with Whitney on Friday 4 October. He and Luckwell pressed for a quick decision by the Authority. They agreed to send a formal notification of the details of Carlton's purchase by hand to the Director General that day.

When it arrived the letter referred to the purchase as a merger and proposed setting up a new holding company, Carlton-Thames plc, in which Thames would be the principal subsidiary. In a careful allusion to the IBA's known requirement for a public flotation of Thames, he stated:

> The shares which will be issued to BET and Thorn-EMI as consideration for their shareholdings in Thames will be offered to the public, thus achieving the stated wish of the IBA at the time Thames' last contract was granted that – 'means of achieving wider share ownership should be investigated'. (Letter from Michael Green to John Whitney, 4 October 1985)

The letter went on to say that existing Carlton shareholders would be offered four million shares, institutional shareholders five million and the general public one million. Green offered an alternative whereby all the shares could be offered to the general public directly for subscription but pointed out that this would take some time and that Carlton had been advised that the former option avoided delay which could have a damaging effect on the financial sensitivities of the new group. He added that he and his brother David would own 12 per cent of the group and Mike Luckwell 9 per cent.

Whitney rang Green to ask for further information. This was provided in an expanded version of the original letter, sent by hand on Sunday 6 October. In this version Green added that 'Our merchant bankers, Morgan Grenfell and Hambros Bank have agreed to underwrite this offer (thus providing certainty).' He also included paragraphs repeating his agreement to retain the existing management and Board of Thames with the exception of those directors nominated by BET and Thorn EMI, and adding that, subject to consultations with the IBA and the existing management of Thames, 'it may be appropriate to invite Lord Brabourne [a widely respected film producer, who had been a director of Thames since 1978] to become Chairman of Thames', and that the existing staff shareholdings and options would be honoured. He also clarified that the shares of himself, his brother and Luckwell would not come out of the tranche of four million allotted to existing Carlton shareholders.

Finally, on the matter of possible delay he added 'you will appreciate that this ... could be unsettling for the current Thames management'.

The Thames management, and staff, were already mightily unsettled. On 6 October the *Sunday Times* business section did carry the story. Dunn hastily prepared a reassuring message to all staff at Thames and then did go to see the Chairman of the IBA, but not 'hand-in-hand' with Green. In fact he was summoned to meet the newly returned Lord Thomson as the story spread from the business section of the *Sunday Times* to the national daily papers on the morning of Monday 7 October – a week after Dunn had met Green for the first time. The conversation with Thomson, in Dunn's view, turned out to be somewhat circular in nature:

> ... he wanted to know whether I would support this takeover and whether I would be wholeheartedly in support of it. And I wanted to know whether he would countenance a change in ownership of a contract awarded to somebody else. So it wasn't an entirely conclusive conversation. But my view was that this was a matter that the IBA was able to judge and it shouldn't put the Chief Executive in the position of making the sole judgement – not least because I still had duties to my shareholders, to my staff, to the IBA and its contract, and to the viewing public ... (Interview with Richard Dunn)

The official record of this meeting, to which Dunn took the Thames Company Secretary, Ben Marr, and the IBA's Chairman and Director General were joined by Bryan Rook, the Secretary to the Authority, since there were legal issues involved, confirms Dunn's recollection but shows him as standing pretty firmly against the Carlton bid. Also, at the end of the meeting, Dunn reminded the Chairman of the Authority's stated desire to see the company reach a broader shareholding. It reads:

> Mr Dunn explained how the news of Carlton Communications' bid for Thames Television had come to his attention, the contacts he had had to date with the leading personalities involved and the position as he now saw it as Managing Director of the Company. While there had been rumours and speculation, particularly in relation to the future ownership of Thorn EMI and its Screen Entertainment Division (which held the 50 per cent interest in Thames through TTH Ltd), the news of Carlton's bid had come as a surprise and a shock. The Executive Directors had signed a statement that morning (copies of which were distributed at the meeting) expressing their concern about the bid and their confidence in their Managing Director. This was now being sent to the Chairman of the Company, Mr Hugh Dundas. A statement by the management had been posted on the company notice boards the previous day and was being sent immediately to all employees.
>
> The news had broken in great detail in the Press over the weekend and that morning. It was evident that the matter had been leaked by Carlton

Communications. Mr Dunn said that the announcement raised grave issues for the future of Thames Television. The Authority's attitude to the bid was of crucial importance. He was not persuaded at this stage that the proposals were in the best long term interests of Thames Television. So far however he had been given little information. Carlton Communications had provided him with a copy of their letter of 4th October to the Director General but there had been no discussion about the business plans for the proposed new group as a whole or about the detail of the new ownership structure. It was clear that Carlton Communications was under the control of three directors, M.P. and D.B. Green and M.S. Luckwell, through a combination of their personal holdings and their holdings in Target Ltd, (sic) and that this situation would perpetuate in the new arrangement. No mention had been made of representation for Thames on the new Board. Mr Dunn said that there had been no time so far to obtain expert professional advice on the proposals. Thames' merchant banking advisers, County Bank, now had been asked for their views and these should be available later in the week.

Mr Dunn said that he had been aware of the instability at Thorn EMI and that there were reputed to be 15 potential buyers of the Screen Entertainment Division. A price of £50 million was being quoted. It was not clear whether this included Thorn's half of Thames. Carlton's name had first cropped up in this connection in relation to Thorn at the end of July but it was not until the beginning of September that Hugh Dundas had indicated that representatives of Carlton had asked to see him also. Mr Dunn said that he believed that Hugh Dundas had had no direct knowledge of Carlton's interest up to that point. He (Mr Dunn) had been introduced to Michael Green at BET's offices shortly thereafter and he had subsequently met with Mr Green and Mr Luckwell on Tuesday 1st October. Mr Dunn said that an attempt had been made at that meeting to persuade him to support the bid on behalf of the executive management of Thames. He told Carlton that he refused to countenance the proposals until he knew the views of the Authority. At a meeting on 2nd October Hugh Dundas had held a brief meeting with the non-Executive Directors and Executive Directors of Thames and formally told them of the name of the bidder.

Mr Dunn said that it was difficult for him to discuss with Hugh Dundas what was in the best interests of Thames because Hugh Dundas, in his position as Chairman of BET, had already declared his interests in accepting Carlton's offer. The offer was understood to be worth £82.5 million reducing to £80 million if Thames' profits for the year to March 86 did not exceed £12 million. This was well above the current value of Thames and it was an offer that was therefore difficult to refuse. Mr Dunn said that time was needed to reflect coolly on the proposals. He did not wish to be hustled and he hoped that the Authority would not be rushed into taking a decision. The appointment of an independent Chairman for an interim period was desirable. He noted that Raymond Snoddy of the FT had referred to Viscount Brabourne in this context (the reference having presumably been lifted from Carlton's letter of 4th October).

Mr Dunn said that the executive management at Thames accepted that a restructuring was necessary and desirable. There was already disenchantment with Thorn EMI following that company's attempt to align with the BBC on DBS. He was glad that the Authority had taken a strong line on this. Thorn's present extreme financial instability was another cause for concern. Thames were also not happy that Granada had purchased 15 per cent of Thorn's Music Channel. So far as BET were concerned, their interest in television was not wholly compatible with their other activities but their continued presence as a shareholder was not unwelcome. Mr Dunn said that he had thought that the desire for change could be accomplished by a part flotation with the opportunity for increased participation by employees. Proposals were being developed along these lines prior to the Carlton intervention. This would have been in accordance with the proposals discussed with the Authority in 1981. It was possible that employees would be willing to acquire up to 15 per cent of the company. Employee participation was desirable in itself in negotiating with the unions on cost reduction.

Mr Dunn said that he had formed the impression that the Carlton management was young and thrusting and had achieved much in terms of growth and return on shareholders funds that was likely to appeal to the City. They had achieved a similar profit to Thames from a much smaller turnover. Whether the qualities that were attractive to the City and to shareholders were compatible with running a broadcasting service in accordance with the performance standards required by the Authority was questionable. The degree of family control of Carlton was a concern. It was reminiscent of other structures in ITV that the Authority had helped to dismantle.

Mr Dunn said that now that the two owners of Thames had openly revealed their willingness to dispose entirely of their holdings in the company, it was clear that the franchise was seriously at risk. It was appreciated that the Authority could consider terminating the franchise in mid term and offering it for readvertisement as an alternative to agreeing to the change in ownership proposed. Alternatively if the status quo was preserved because the Authority refused to sanction a change in ownership in mid term, Thorn and BET would continue as reluctant shareholders in the knowledge that the market opportunity had been lost, perhaps for all time, and that they would be unlikely to be reappointed for a further term. In this case they (and more particularly, Thorn) might wish to salvage as much as possible during the remaining four years of the contract with consequent damaging effects on the morale and integrity of the company. Staff morale would in any case be damaged if it was felt that the chance of a further contract had been forfeited.

Mr Dunn said that he could not see how the Authority could contemplate a 100 per cent acquisition of Thames or any other contractor mid-term unless there were very clear guarantees. Even so he would be very concerned about the long term stability and security of Thames within a Carlton-Thames Group. Mr Dunn said that if the Authority were to say that the bid by Carlton was not acceptable he would be ready within days to present other options and preferences.

Mr Dunn said that it would be desirable for Thames to have as broad a base of ownership as possible and for that ownership to be in voting shares. Pending further advice from the County Bank a scheme might be proposed as follows:

Thorn EMI to be encouraged to sell their interest as soon as possible under the proposals listed below. BET to retain their interest at about 47.5 per cent on enfranchisement until a flotation could be arranged (possibly in mid 1986) at which time they would agree to reduce their holding by a half with a view to disposing of the other half at the franchise renewal point.

Full opportunity to be given to staff to participate possibly up to 15 per cent (Mr Dunn said that for the equivalent investment staff would only be able to buy 2–3 per cent of the proposed joint company).

The remaining 37.5 per cent to be placed with institutions temporarily on the basis that these shares would be released in due course as part of the flotation. Mr Dunn said that he had been advised that there would be no difficulty in placing shares with institutions on this basis. If necessary he would not be against Carlton acquiring a minority interest (up to 10 per cent) on flotation.

The Chairman said that the Authority had no intention of being rushed on this very important matter. The issue had only just arisen. The Authority would wish to consider fully the options and consult with others concerned. He welcomed further information from the County Bank as soon as possible. The Director General added that the Authority was determined that its relationship would be with the Board of the Company and it would conduct the matter on that basis. He fully understood that if there was silence from the Board this did not convey acquiescence by the Board. Further consideration would be given to the need to appoint an independent Chairman for an interim period. (IBA note of meeting between the Chairman of the Authority and the Managing Director of Thames Television, 11.00 a.m., 7 October 1985)

That Monday was to see a flurry of comings and goings at 'Brompton Towers' as a consequence of the Carlton bid. A despatch rider arrived with the preliminary legal advice on the Authority's position that Bryan Rook had sought from the IBA's longstanding legal adviser, Geoffrey Sammons, the senior partner at Allen & Overy:

1. If the IBA is minded not to give its consent it is fully within its rights to do so. The contract awarded to Thames was on the basis of its then share ownership and was for a period which has several years to run.

2. If the Authority is minded to give its consent a number of constitutional and contractual matters arise in its relationship with the new owners of Thames.

The letter went on to list seven points of caution. These included the fact that it was misleading for Green to have used the term 'merger' in his letter. 'It is in effect a straightforward purchase for cash, with the cash being funded by new equity issued by Carlton.' The advice also pointed out that: 'The public shareholdings in Carlton are no more a direct investment in Thames than the public shareholdings in BET or Thorn EMI, although more materially affected in value by the performance of Thames.' The advice also pointed out that the Greens' and Luckwell's proposed shareholding would be 'approaching a *de facto* controlling interest if all the other holdings are as widely spread as Mr Green's letter seems to assume'. And:

> As the major asset in a company the size of Carlton, Thames is likely to be the main resource to support future financings of Carlton. The Authority may wish to ensure that the shareholding and assets of Thames are not used as security to support liabilities of Carlton ... (Letter from Geoffrey Sammons of Allen & Overy to Bryan Rook, the Secretary of the IBA)

Also on the morning of Monday 7 October the IBA had summoned both Green and Luckwell to a meeting with the Chairman, Director General and Secretary of the IBA, which was to take place at 6.15 that evening. However, prior to that meeting Lord Thomson sought to understand for himself the background to the Thames shareholders' agreement to sell. He asked Dundas and Read to a meeting an hour before that with Green and Luckwell. Both meetings were again very fully recorded by a member of the IBA secretariat, John Norrington:

> Neither BET nor Thorn EMI had been actively looking for a buyer. Carlton's offer of £82.5m (or £80m if Thames's profit fell below £13m according to a formula) was substantially in advance of the valuation of £50m obtained recently in connection with the plans for flotation. Heads of Agreement had been signed committing the two shareholders to sell at Carlton's offer price. This had been necessary in view of the possibility of news of the bid being leaked. Therefore, Thames were legally bound not to talk to anyone else. However, it had been made clear to Carlton that an ITV franchise was not a commodity that could be bought and sold in the normal way and that the sale was therefore conditional upon the approval of the Authority.
> The matter had originally been broached by Carlton on 6th September when Mr Dundas was about to leave for an overseas tour of three weeks. The offer price at that time was £65 million. This has been rejected outright. There was nothing to say to the IBA and to the Thames executive management at that stage. On his return from abroad Carlton had contacted him with the revised offer. Richard Dunn had been informed almost immediately. Members of the Thames Board

had been formally notified on 2nd October and Richard Dunn had been authorised to speak to Thames' merchant bank. The BET Board had not so far approved the bid. They were due to meet on 8th October. Similarly the Thorn EMI Board had not so far been officially informed. They were due to meet on 12th October.

Sir John Read said that Thorn EMI was heavily committed in managing and funding its technical operations. It was clear that there would need to be some rationalisation within the Company. The Screen Entertainment Division was the least necessary to the company's long term development. In looking for potential buyers it was understood that Thames, which for accounting purposes formed part of the Division, could not be included in the sale. But the disposal of Screen Entertainment Division would logically raise also the question of the possible disposal of Thames although no initiative had been taken on this. Mr Dundas said that BET had assessed that Thorn might wish to pull out entirely in the plans for flotation went ahead. BET was itself rationalising. The Rediffusion rental business had already been sold. As a matter of policy the Board of BET did not favour large scale minority investments. If the ownership of Thames was opened up it was unlikely that BET would want to retain more than about £2–3 million investment. Sir John Read said that 'if it was a matter of reassurance Thorn would be prepared to do something similar to BET'.

However if the Authority did not approve Carlton's bid, the shareholders would be prepared to carry on. Hugh Dundas said:

'We would be perfectly content to carry on. However it would be sensible to talk among ourselves whether some restructuring would not be preferable leading up to the next franchise. [He then explained the reasons for the delay in activating a scheme for public participation.] I would guess that even if Carlton had not come along we would have been talking about a restructuring. Thames must have shareholders who are 100 per cent enthusiastic. Things were changing. New technologies were coming along which meant that the ITV franchise was no longer so attractive.'

Sir John Read put it this way:

'There is not the same long term optimism about the franchise. Meanwhile you can rely on us to do our best with it so long as it is ours.'

Mr Dundas said that he recognised that his interests as Chairman of both Thames and BET might not be seen to be synonomous in this situation. He hoped he had persuaded Richard Dunn that he would not abandon Thames in the interests of BET. He believed that the Carlton offer could work out favourably for Thames in providing a wider ownership assuming that the preponderance of certain individuals was not too great. He suggested that the combined interest of the two Greens and Mr Luckwell of 21 per cent in the new grouping was too large and that they should be persuaded to go below this. He understood that Richard Dunn might have misgivings but he thought that there was an element of 'culture shock' about this. The possibility of appointing an independent Chairman for an interim period was discussed. Mr Dundas did not see the necessity for this at this stage although he said that he would be quite happy for Mary Baker [wife of the then Secretary of State for the Environment, Kenneth Baker, and the only truly independent director on the Thames Board] to assume this position if necessary. Sir John Read stressed that there was no conflict between the various interests on the Thames Board. It was agreed that the Board, as currently constituted, should be left to develop their views further. The Chairman said that he would rely on Mr Dundas to act honourably if there was a division of views. It was preferable for the Authority not to have to act as a broker between different factions on the Board. Mr Dundas said that he hoped to have a meeting of the Thames Board that week.

In further discussion the Chairman questioned why the shareholders thought Carlton was willing to pay £82 million for a company worth £50 million on the shareholders' own analysis. Sir John Read said that this valuation was made on the basis that 25 per cent only of the company would be floated. The shareholders had not accepted the idea of a flotation on this valuation. Carlton were prepared to pay a higher price to integrate the two businesses. They would have no difficulty in raising the money.

The Chairman said that he was concerned at this stage purely to hear the views of all the parties concerned. The proposal clearly raised major issues for the Authority. It was unparalleled in the history of ITV for anyone to be seeking to acquire a franchise half way through the franchise period. Even if the Authority disallowed it, and the status quo were to continue it would be a very uneasy status quo. Ultimately the full Authority would have to take a decision on the matter. It would need to do so on the basis of proposals put by the Board of the Company with which the Authority was in contract. (IBA note of meeting between the Chairman of the Authority and the Chairman and Deputy Chairman of Thames, 5.15 p.m., 7 October 1985)

Green and Luckwell arrived at the IBA's Brompton Road headquarters just as Dundas and Read left the Chairman's office at the back of the 8th floor. Green put the background to his company's bid to Lord Thomson:

The extension of the company into network television was the next logical step in its development. 75–80 per cent of Carlton's earnings were already television related. The Group was involved in television and photographic production facilities, design and manufacture of digital video products, programming (including commercials and productions for Channel Four) specialist publishing and exhibition contracting. The publishing activities were being disposed of. Following amalgamation with Thames 90–95 per cent of the group activity would be television related. Carlton had no debt and current cash assets of £15 million. The new group would have combined assets of £60 million of which Carlton's share would be slightly the larger.

Carlton had been looking for an ITV partner for a long time. Thames had attractions for a number of reasons. Firstly there was reason to believe that the existing shareholders would be willing to sell. The longer term development of television and, in particular, DBS did not fit logically into their activities. Carlton were enthusiastic about DBS. Next, the management was a relatively new team and might be open to change. Third, Carlton believed deeply in employee participation through share ownership. It was noted that Thames already had a share option scheme. Employees might welcome the opportunity to participate in ownership of a successful publicly-quoted company. Finally, having studied the Broadcasting Act and the IBA's contracts it was felt that the Authority might agree to a change partly because they were already on record as favouring some public participation in Thames but also because it could be argued that the existing shareholders were not contributing greatly to the company. Although the position of the Authority was crucial to the whole arrangement, Carlton had started at the shareholder end because no deal would have been possible without their agreement. An agreement had now been reached with the shareholders and discussions had been opened up with the management. Carlton were impressed by Richard Dunn. They had hoped that it would have been possible to come to the Authority with a united front. Unfortunately news of the bid had leaked to the Press and it had been necessary to come out in the open earlier than expected. Nevertheless Mr Green thought that he had Richard Dunn's support.

Mr Green said that he recognised that if Carlton had to compete with Thames for the franchise it would lose because it did not have the same studio and production resources. Carlton did however have experience of independent production and was noted for its technological innovation and good management. It also had substantial financial resources and would not starve Thames for funds. These factors would have an important bearing on the future operation of Thames.

Carlton were sensitive to the Authority's position. They were aware of fears that the new company would be dominated by three individuals. Mr Green said that none of the Carlton directors would take part in the new share issue and that the combined interest of the three individuals concerned in the new company would not exceed 21 per cent. No other individual shareholder would hold more than 5 per cent. The shareholders would not control the company. Management would be in the hands of the Board of Directors. All the shares that would be offered would be offered to institutions or to the public. This would be done by a vendor placing or by an offer for sale. In either case provision would be made for employee participation.

Carlton would like to retain the entire Thames Board (apart from the BET and Thorn representatives) and 'would follow the existing management a long way in what they were trying to do'. Mr Green would however propose that he and Mr Luckwell should join the Board.

In further discussion the following additional main points were made:

Trading in Carlton's shares had been suspended at the company's request following the disclosure in the Press. It was therefore important that the Authority gave a decision on the matter as soon as possible. The uncertainty was potentially damaging for shareholders and for employees. Also the time scale for suspension was limited by the Stock Exchange.

Carlton had tried to present a restructuring which preserved so far as possible the status quo in terms of the operation of the Board of the Company. They were open to any suggestion by the Authority to satisfy the Authority's position in the matter. However a restructuring which left either Thorn EMI or BET or both in a blocking position would not be satisfactory. Mr Green said that he recognised that the Thames executives were in a very delicate position and they perhaps would not wish to be seen to be supporting Carlton in case the Authority decided not to approve the bid because they might then feel that their own positions were vulnerable in 1989.

In responding to a question by the Chairman about whether Carlton might become a drain on the resources of Thames, Mr Green said that he had gone over this matter in detail with Thames' merchant bankers in the presence of Richard Dunn and the County Bank had given their opinion that the group would be financially healthy. Mr Green suggested that it would in fact be the healthiest television company in the country.

The Chairman said that the matter would have to go before the Authority for a decision and that this would not be before 16th October. Mr Green requested that if the conclusion was that the bid should not be allowed to succeed, he be given the opportunity to comment on the grounds on which the decision would be taken before the matter was closed. (IBA note of meeting between the Chairman of the Authority and the Chairman and Chief Executive and the Managing Director of Carlton Communications, 6.15 p.m., 7 October 1985)

Michael Green never got that opportunity:

The next conversation I had was a telephone call from John Whitney, telling me that the IBA was making an announcement as we spoke, saying that they could not accept this takeover. Nothing personal, nothing against Carlton, but under their reading of the rules this would not be acceptable. I was livid. I was absolutely livid because I knew it literally about one second before the public announcement. (Interview with Michael Green)

The share price sensitivities involved had put the IBA under pressure for a quick decision. Armed with further legal advice in relation to the Authority's responsibilities, Thomson consulted members of the Authority over the next two days. The minutes of the Authority meeting of 16 October simply refer to 'some members' having been consulted. Thomson certainly spoke to Michael Caine and Professor Cullen. Whitney talked to George Russell. Some members of the Authority who were not consulted, but who were asked to give retrospective approval of the decision, were not uncritical of the Chairman and his Director General over this.

The relevant passages in the 1981 Broadcasting Act were Section 19 and Paragraphs 4 and 5 of Section 20. Put simply, Section 19 of the Act required that franchises could not be entered into except by the due process of advertisement. However this did not exclude changes of share ownership. Therefore Section 20, which did relate to change of control, was relevant:

(4)   No contract and no interest in a contract between a programme contractor and the Authority shall be assignable in whole or in part without the previous consent in writing of the Authority.

(5)   Every contract concluded between the Authority and a programme contractor shall, where the programme contractor is a body corporate, contain all such provisions as the Authority think necessary or expedient to ensure that if any change affecting the nature or characteristics of the body corporate, or any change in the persons having control over or interests in the body corporate, takes place after the conclusion of the contract, which if it had occurred before the conclusion of the contract, would have induced the Authority to refrain from entering into the contract, the Authority may by notice in writing to the contractor, taking effect forthwith or on a date specified in the notice, determine the contract. (Broadcasting Act 1981)

The decision therefore lay with the Authority. Legal advice had warned that the proposal did involve a *de facto* change of control. The only precedent for agreeing such a change had been when an ITV company had become unviable, and even then the company taking over the contract was an ITV company with an adjacent regional contract (Wales, West and North, taken over after two years on air by TWW in 1964). The decision was, in the Authority's view, clear cut. It was made public on Thursday the 10th:

The Independent Broadcasting Authority has concluded that a proposal made by Carlton Communications which would have led to a major change in the nature and characteristics of Thames Television as a viable ITV programme company is not acceptable, having regard to the Authority's responsibilities under the Broadcasting Act. (IBA News Release, 10 October 1985)

Green consulted lawyers:

I sent to George Thomson my advice that they (the IBA) had acted wrongly and had a duty to consider our proposition. However, the internal debate at Carlton concluded that it was not the right time to confront the regulatory authority ... my business sense was not to test it. I now think that was a mistake. We should have gone ahead. At the time, I was convinced that the IBA thought they were doing the right thing. I didn't take it personally or think it was against Carlton. I don't think it was particularly for Thames. The IBA thought that was what they had to do.

But with hindsight I think we should have gone ahead with the transaction and risked disenfranchisement. The IBA would have had to take us off the air and say they were advertising the franchise. We would have applied and probably won it. The reality would not have been as terrible as everybody was fearing, not least because we would have been employing all of the people who'd worked for Thames. It's always much clearer with 20:20 hindsight. We would have succeeded in the end. (Interview with Michael Green)

Richard Dunn believes that there could have been a less apocalyptic solution:

In my opinion it was a mistake of Michael Green's not to approach me as soon as I was appointed Managing Director, and not to involve the management of Thames Television in his plans and aspirations for the London company. It came the wrong way round. It came on a sort of take-it-or-leave-it basis, and I suppose I felt that my support had been taken for granted by my shareholders and by the prospective purchaser, and I don't like being taken for granted. (Interview with Richard Dunn)

Green had contracts with Thorn EMI and BET for the sale but had negotiated an option to cancel if the IBA did not accept the proposal and he exercised that option in 1985. Four years later when the rules had changed, Green and Dunn, who was still saddled with two unwilling major shareholders, did come together more positively. But this time Carlton's price was considered too low by the sellers. Thorn EMI bought BET's shares – leaving Green to bid in the licence 'auction' that resulted from the 1990 Broadcasting Act (see Chapter 10).

There were two other, less dramatic, unsuccessful offers for Thames in 1985. In early October Andrew Skinner, a director of the merchant bankers, Hong Kong Bank Limited, sent to the IBA copies of letters the bank had sent to Thorn EMI and BET on 19 September. These outlined a scheme whereby it and its stockbrokers, James Capel (of which the HK Bank owned 30 per cent) would arrange a private placing with British institutions of 35 per cent of the Thames shares and then by putting '... a management team in place at Thames capable of imposing rigorous financial disciplines over the company, thereby improving the trading performance of all divisions ...' would raise the share price. 'BET and Thorn EMI could then realise substantially the whole of their investment in Thames or alternatively continue to hold a substantial interest in the company.'

It emerged in the letters that this bid was the initiative of one James F. Shaw – better known in ITV as Jim Shaw, the erstwhile Sales Director at Thames, who had been in that role at the time of the J. Walter Thompson complaint to the Office of Fair Trading about Thames' selling techniques (see above, Advertising, Section

I). A Member of the IBA's Secretariat noted dryly on the letter, 'Clearly, Th. EMI and BET preferred the Carlton bid' (Copy of Letter A.U. Skinner, Hong Kong Bank, to H. Morgue, Thorn EMI, 19 September 1985, and attached note).

The other proposal came from the Chairman of Anglia, Lord Buxton. When news of the Carlton bid broke, he dusted off versions of two old ideas, discarded by the Authority in earlier years. One was for the five large regional companies jointly to acquire the London weekday contract by buying out EMI and BET. The other was for 'a merger or reverse take-over by Anglia'. Buxton saw 'no great difficulty in either option in matching the finance mentioned in yesterday's press'. Like others in ITV at the time he believed Carlton was simply a non-broadcast facilities company. He ended his letter to Lord Thomson: 'Whatever happens, I implore you not to put us all in the hands of the video market. The networking performance would ultimately become a mess, and it could prove very damaging indeed' (Letter Lord Buxton to Lord Thomson, 8 October 1985).

Granada Pulls Rank

Within four months of the IBA's rejection of the Carlton bid for Thames another ITV Major was having friendly conversations with one leisure industry group, while being stalked by a predator company operating in the same field.

The years 1984/85 had not been good ones for the Granada group in the eyes of the City. The company's share price had twice fallen as low as it had been at any time since the disastrous ITV strike of 1979. The bold and successful programme making of its Television division did not compensate in financial minds for a lacklustre group performance. As *Management Today* put it:

> ... for the past ten years, Granada has been essentially a TV rental company with a significant, but in financial terms relatively minor, television franchise operation, and a few bits and pieces tacked on. (Article by Geoffrey Foster, *Management Today*, August 1986)

The fact that the 'bits and pieces' included bingo halls, motorway services and (at that time) publishing did not seem to appeal to financial commentators. However, it did appeal to other groups with similar interests which were looking to expand and, at the same time, diminish the competition. A new development director for the Granada group had been head-hunted from the Imperial group (formerly Imperial Tobacco) at the end of 1984. Derek Lewis (later to become Granada Group's Chief Executive) had bold plans for the expansion of the company into new areas. Granada's Chairman, Alex Bernstein (son of Cecil, nephew of Sidney), believed that a merger with the betting and leisure group Ladbrokes first would underpin Granada's non-television business – and its financial strength. Discussions between the two groups began in late 1985. By January the following year they had foundered – not on price, as was suggested in the press at the time, but on the question of the date at which Alex Bernstein would take over the chairmanship of the merged group from Cyril Stein, Ladbroke's Chairman.

Almost immediately another group with leisure interests, with whom Granada had also been having rather desultory merger discussions, Rank, suddenly pounced with a hostile bid worth £753 million. The interests of the two groups fitted well together – Rank had film studios and processing that would be complementary to Granada's television studios and both had cinemas and bingo and motorway service arms. Rank itself had a lacklustre record but had been kept afloat by a shrewd investment in the Sixties in the UK rights for the brand leader copying machines from the US Xerox company. Now it had hired a go-getting new Chief Executive, Michael Gifford, from Cadbury-Schweppes. Gifford and his Chairman, Sir Patrick Meaney, realised they were getting nowhere with Granada and needed to seize the initiative and they had the finance to do so. Granada turned down the bid on 19 February 1986 but shareholders looked likely to go Rank's way.

IBA agreement had to be, and was, sought by the buyer. Sir Denis Forman – now very much Granada's 'elder statesman' – lobbied Lord Thomson successfully. A special meeting of the Authority was called on 25 February. It resolved that: 'The Rank offer would lead to a major change in control of a viable ITV programme contractor which would be unacceptable to the Authority' (Minute of meeting 625 (86) of the Authority, 25 February 1986). Those words were used in the IBA News Release of that day. But shares were already changing hands fast and the Authority added:

> The IBA has been informed that Rank and persons acting in concert with Rank now own more than five per cent of the ordinary shares of the Granada Group. The IBA's approval is required to any shareholder exercising more than five per cent of the votes attributable to the ordinary shares of the Granada Group. The IBA has declined to give this approval. (IBA News Release, 25 February 1986)

Perhaps mindful of the criticism it drew for a less than full explanation of its decision on the Carlton bid for Thames, the IBA added as a note to the release the full text of Section 20(5) of the 1981 Broadcasting Act (see above). Despite that precaution Rank claimed in early March that it had received no 'satisfactory response' from the IBA as to why it was not being allowed to acquire the Granada Television franchise. Rank added that it would now seek a judicial review to ascertain if the IBA was satisfactorily carrying out its duties under the 1981 Broadcasting Act.

The Judge in High Court on 13 March, Mr Justice Mann, ruled that Rank could not be granted a judicial review. This was because the IBA had not been exercising its public law functions when it made its decision on 25 February but had been acting in accord with Granada's Articles of Association which, in common with other ITV public companies, stated that a shareholder could only vote more than 5 per cent of its stock if the IBA approved. Rank was, said the judge, refused that approval. He also rejected Rank's second ground for appeal – that the IBA had acted unfairly.

Rank appealed against this decision but the appeal was dismissed by the Lords Justices May and Lloyd and Sir John Megaw on 24 March 1986. At this point Rank dropped their bid. The underwriting costs, at nearly £1 million a week, were mounting up without prospect of victory. Despite the legal ruling, some industry observers thought the IBA decision had been harsh on Rank. The bid had been for the whole Granada group – in which its ITV contract accounted for less than a third of its business. In a free market the takeover should not have been blocked by a ruling on a minority aspect of the business – particularly, it was argued, when the contract could have been fully enforced, and would have been honoured by the new owners. Granada Television's reputation for programme quality appears to have afforded the whole group protection from market forces in this case.

By the end of 1987, with its twin strengths of a share in the winning DBS bid, BSB, and the likelihood of a boost to the Granada rentals business from satellite television in general, Granada shares were riding high again, at around the 350 pence mark. It was not until 1990 that Granada's position was to come under City scrutiny again. At that time the new BSkyB was at its most acute loss-making phase. Granada took a long view towards eventual big profits. But in the short term that and some of the more doubtful of the Granada ventures set up by Derek Lewis were putting the company's shares under pressure again.

By May 1991 shareholder criticism had forced the resignation of Derek Lewis as group Chief Executive. One of his Board colleagues said of him; 'He was a very brilliant man. Very beguiling, but ... We should have withdrawn our support a year earlier than we did and then we would not have got into those troubles.'

Lewis was replaced in October by Gerry Robinson, an able and charming Irish-born accountant who was formerly the Finance Director of Coca-Cola, before he became Chief Executive of Compass plc, a major company in the catering industry. This was the connection that gave rise to references to Robinson being 'a bean counter in every sense' but which, more seriously, was to trigger the departure from Granada television of many of the old Granada talent.

It was the turmoil arising out of the resignation of David Plowright, the Chairman of Granada Television, whose almost lifelong career with the company was seen as a talisman for quality television, that led the Chairman of the new ITC, George Russell, to summon the Chairman of Granada Group, Alex Bernstein and Gerry Robinson to meet himself and the Chief Executive of the ITC, David Glencross, on Monday 10 February 1992 for discussions. They sought assurance that the commitments in Granada's (successful) bid for a C3/ITV licence would be honoured. This was particularly important because the ITC had set aside a higher bid on programme quality grounds. (see Chapter 10). In a statement issued the following day Russell was quoted as saying:

I acknowledge the widespread concern caused by the resignation of David Plowright but I am confident that Granada Group will give Granada Television the wholehearted backing it needs to fulfil the terms of its licence (ITC News Release, 11 February 1992)

Granada's profits for the first half of 1992 exceeded those for the whole of 1991 and the company rejoined the top 100 British companies after an absence of eighteen months. Further strengthening over the next two years was to put Granada itself in a position to become a predator.

Bland Leader

1989 saw the twenty-first anniversary of London Weekend Television's first transmissions on the ITV channel. It was also the year in which its senior executives were to become part of a scheme which was to make them richer than any employees of a television company had ever been – richer by far even than the legendary earnings of LWT videotape editors in the days of union power.

These riches were the product of a simple vision on the part of the Chairman of LWT (Holdings) plc, Christopher Bland, in response to the increasing likelihood that the new licences for C3/ITV would be auctioned – but with a programme quality requirement also involved. In March of 1989 the new Chairman of the IBA/ITC had said that he would resign if there was not a quality hurdle associated with the bid.

Bland's 'scheme of arrangement', as it was called, had four key aspects: one was that in the Eighties debt had become cheaper than equity, and was likely to remain so. This would allow the company to borrow to buy back a proportion of each of the major investors' holdings (Pearl Assurance was the largest, with a holding of 5.4 per cent) while leaving them with the majority of their holding. Various schemes were offered to reduce the Capital Gains Tax involved in such a transaction.

The second aspect of the scheme was that a selected team of around forty directors and managers would exchange their existing shares and options for, or buy, a greater percentage of the capital than they held previously. This would serve to retain their services by effectively deleting any temptation to be attracted to a rival bidder.

Thirdly, the redistribution of shares to directors and staff would raise their holding in the company from less than 5 per cent to between 15 and 25 per cent, which would give them effective control of the company and be a deterrent (at least until after the licence process) to takeover attempts.

The fourth aspect was most important of all. The scheme would take cash out of the cash-rich company and force it to be a lean operation. This in turn would allow the company to bid higher than a less efficient rival. Hopefully, any newcomer's artificially low estimates would be spotted during scrutiny by the IBA (see Chapter 10).

The day before the public announcement of the scheme, LWT had arranged a boat trip on the Thames for friends in the network and at the IBA. This was to celebrate the company's anniversary. Bland had first talked to Shirley Littler, by this time the Deputy Director General at the IBA, about the scheme the previous week and she had set the Secretariat the task of producing a paper on the subject for consideration at the Authority's next meeting (which, because of pressure for decision taking was, unusually, to be held in August). Little tête à têtes in corners of the boat between IBA and LWT senior personnel during the trip aroused interest amongst those not in the know.

They were not surprised, therefore, to read about the scheme in the press, but the details did raise eyebrows. £135 million to be paid to shareholders to reduce their holdings to 85 per cent of the original, but with a 150 pence-a-share sweetener. LWT would borrow £95 million against assets of £100 million (which included a valuation of their library of programmes – always a controversial estimate – at £30 million). £50 million would be repaid by the end of the contract period, that is, by the end of 1992.

Perhaps unexpectedly, this bold move did not cause great concern when the Authority met on 17 August. This may have been because the main business of the meeting was to discuss matters concerned with the forthcoming Broadcasting Bill. It was the IBA's Finance Director, Peter Rogers, who was left to raise the need to be satisfied that financial projections would not have an adverse impact on LWT's quality and diversity of programming. By the following meeting LWT had produced a draft letter of assurance to the Authority that the programme budget would remain constant in real terms for the remainder of the contract period. The programme plan thereafter would be subject to the IBA/ITC's scrutiny at the bid process. But the IBA should not give any forward indication of what level of borrowing would be acceptable to them at that time. The Authority approved the scheme on those terms at their meeting on 19 October 1989.

The shareholders still had to be persuaded of the virtues of the scheme. 75 per cent of them had to approve. However, the combination of the confidence that Bland aroused in City circles, the verbal skills and charm of Brian Tesler, about to move up to an emeritus position within LWT, and the firecracker impact of Greg Dyke, who would take over the role of Managing Director in time to manage the bid, was ultimately unbrookable.

The incentive for the senior staff to achieve success in the bid was that if they did so a rising share price would trigger, if it reached 278 pence a share by autumn 1993 (or 327 pence by spring 1994) options worth between £130,000 and £1.5 million, at the lower of the two prices, for those involved. In fact the share price was to rise to 650 pence, when, after their licence successes, Granada was to become a predator with LWT as its prey. The realisation of these options was to more than ease the parting of the ways for the majority of the executives.

Privatisation of Transmission

A further major change of ownership during the period was one in which ITV was to lose – without compensation – an asset in which companies had been required to invest many hundreds of millions of pounds over the years since the channel's inception.

Before 1991, the IBA was responsible for transmission services for the ITV and commercial radio companies and for the fourth channel. The Engineering division which employed a majority (nearly 900) of the total IBA workforce of 1,387 (in 1988/89) had been based, since 1973, at Crawley Court – a new engineering centre built on the site of a former country house in a Hampshire village near Winchester. For efficiency, there was considerable sharing of resources, such as transmission masts and sites, between the IBA and BBC, although the transmission networks were operated separately. In the early 1980s, the main focus of the engineering division had been on achieving over 99 per cent coverage for Channel 4.

In April 1986 Dr John Forrest was recruited to succeed the current Director of Engineering, Tom Robson. Although Forrest had spent fifteen years in the academic world, much of his time had been in liaising, consulting and building up research activities within industry which led to his appointment in GEC as Technical Director of one of the Marconi companies.

When interviewed for the IBA job by John Whitney, Shirley Littler and Tom Robson, Forrest recalled that:

> I detected that they wanted somebody from industry, but somebody who had an appreciation of research and development and somebody to implement change. I don't think they were quite sure of what the change they wanted was. I think they felt that life in the Engineering Division of the IBA was probably a bit too cosy. I'm sure they had been told that by the programme companies, and they were looking for somebody to come and be somewhat incisive, probably to try to cut costs and shape the organisation into a slightly different form. (Interview with Dr John Forrest)

On joining the IBA, Forrest experienced a culture shock from the informal and flexible environment of the academic world and from his industrial career with all of the imperatives on cashflow, cost control and fairly aggressive management. Initially he found the IBA:

> Very civil service based and quite bureaucratic, and very formal in the way it operated. I'd never come across a situation where one didn't call people by their names; one called them DE or HRTP, or whatever their role was. (Interview with Dr John Forrest)

Nevertheless, he was impressed with the professionalism and quality of the people in the engineering division. Although there were tremendous abilities and project management skills in the organisation, these were not being fully used because, under the umbrella of the IBA and the current legislation, the basic remit of the Engineering division was limited to running and developing the transmission systems.

There were also tensions and conflicts between the IBA's engineering and regulatory activities. Forrest believed that staff responsible for regulation wanted to see Engineering slimmed down and put more on to a maintenance footing, whereas he fought strongly for an expansion of activities, not in terms of headcount but in the ability to start working for outside bodies. After a struggle, approval was finally given from the Authority to undertake external consultancy work.

The thrust for major change was accelerated by Margaret Thatcher and her attack on the 'comfortable duopoly' combined with the planning and construction work the Engineering division was undertaking for the development of UK Direct Broadcasting by Satellite (DBS). Forrest realised that there was a conflict in working for a new type of broadcaster, the satellite broadcaster, which was in competition with the traditional customers of the Engineering division, the terrestrial broadcasters. At this point, he could not see:

... how we could continue in a poacher and gamekeeper role and that if we were going to survive for the future we were going to have an independent or quasi-independent status which would allow us to do work for a whole series of customers in the media world. (Interview with Dr John Forrest)

The recommendation in Section 9 of the White Paper *Broadcasting in the '90s: Competition, Choice and Quality*, published in November 1988, was that there should be a regionally based, privatised transmission system designed to promote competition. The ITC would have a supervisory role but would not be responsible for transmitting these services which, in due course, would devolve to a privatised transmission system. In the short term, the ITC would appoint a number of different contractors in a particular part of the UK and monitor their performance.

Although Forrest declared (in interview) that he was 'very much pro-privatisation', he was concerned at the suggestion that the organisation should be split up since the critical mass needed for an effective organisation and research and development capability would be lost, and that individual parts of the Engineering infrastructure would have been acquired by the programme companies, thus reverting to a vertically integrated structure.

Following the commitment to privatisation in the White Paper, the Home Office and the Department of Trade and Industry jointly commissioned the management consultants Price Waterhouse to examine options for privatising the UK terrestrial transmission systems. Their report, delivered on 18 April 1989, concluded that transmission was best done as a national arrangement with each transmitter site owner-operated and maintained by a single company (*Options for Privatising the Terrestrial and Television Transmission Networks*: HMSO, Home Office/DTI, 1989).

The possibility of a management buyout was considered as an option. IBA Chairman, George Russell, and the Director of Finance, Peter Rogers, were both opposed to the idea on the grounds that it would be a risky venture. The Home Office (according to Dr Forrest) also indicated that the IBA's management team was too close to the business and might gain an unfair advantage over other bidders. Once the management buyout route was ruled out, the government decided that the company would be put up for sale, inviting bids for the company, although investment by BT and the ITV companies was limited to 20 per cent in order to encourage competition.

After the Broadcasting Act had received Royal Assent, in November 1990, the IBA's Engineering and Transmission division was established as a separate company, National Transcommunications Ltd (NTL) and started operating as a commercial company on 1 January 1991, under the temporary ownership of the government. Although Price Waterhouse sent out several copies of the information memorandum to potential bidders, the net result was that only three parties showed an interest in bidding. These included GEC, Cable and Wireless and Mercury Asset Management (MAM) (majority-owned by S.G. Warburg, the international merchant bank) who traditionally looked for ventures in which they could obtain significant returns while willing to take certain risks. In October 1991 the government accepted MAM's bid for £70 million, with the management and staff entitled to purchase 15 per cent of the equity. The purchase was financed by equity provided by MAM and NTL staff, by cash already in the company and by the issue of loan stock and debt from a syndicate of banks.

Under the Broadcasting Act 1990, the ITC retained a small team of specialist engineering staff who were responsible for technical quality regulation and, more specifically, who assessed the technical plans of the Channel 3 applicants in 1991. The ITC also retained an overall duty to ensure that effective use was made of the radio frequency spectrum in the planning of new services and extensions to new services as well as being involved in managing research and development work, through contract arrangements aimed at providing enhanced services to UK viewers.

However, under the Act, NTL became the sole provider of transmission services to all Channel 3 operators with broadcast transmission being licensed under the Telecommunications Act 1984 with economic regulation carried out by OFTEL in place of the ITC.

Initially, the level for the transmission tariff had to be calculated. Various forces were at play. The government wanted the tariff to be as high as possible because that would enhance the value of the company and provide the maximum return to the Treasury. However, it was also recognised that privatisation was supposed to bring benefits and reduce costs through increasing competition so the tariff needed to be less than the ITV companies were already paying. The major difficulty in determining the level of tariff was that there had never in the IBA been any serious attempt to separate the costs of transmission and regulation. This situation caused several disputes between Rogers and Forrest. Ultimately the level of tariff was calculated on a formula of Retail Price Index (RPI) minus 1 per cent by Price Waterhouse and the consultants, NERA, which initially resulted only in minor savings for the ITV companies although fees subsequently decreased in real terms each year.

Another problem was the business of dividing the assets, which included the freehold of Crawley Court in which the IBA Engineering and Finance divisions were located. Forrest remembered that there was in the process of privatisation:

> ... an incredibly tortuous process of classifying and accounting for all of the assets. It almost went down to every nut and bolt and picture on the wall. And when the process was over I said to Paul Wright (Assistant Secretary at the Home Office) 'You know, some of the assets were missed.' And there was a look of shock and horror on his face. And he said 'What? And I said 'The carp in the pond; they're very valuable, you know, those carp.' It's quite true. The carp were missed as an asset. (Interview with Dr John Forrest)

The requirement for a sudden complete change of culture, from the unitary revenue-led, company-supported regulatory priority of absolute reliability from studios to transmitter to a culture of cost saving and individual reponsibilities for different parts of the transmission chain, was to cause tensions. But the privatisation of transmission was seen as inevitable by the IBA. According to Peter Rogers (then Director of Finance):

> I don't think there was very much resistance in the IBA to the privatisation ... we didn't think the position was winnable ... I always felt that our transmission system was over engineered, too reliable, too gold plated. There was nothing to prevent the unconstrained maximisation of reliability. There was, of course no profit motive in the IBA, and neither at that time was there much resistance from the ITV companies to increases in the IBA's costs. There was a special tax on ITV (the Exchequer Levy) which, coupled with corporation tax, involved a marginal tax rate of 87 per cent. In other words, a cost increase of £1 incurred by the IBA would cost the ITV companies only 13 pence. Privatisation would introduce a profit motive, increase resistance to rising costs and provide the transmission function with better balanced objectives. (Interview with Peter Rogers)

The possibility of a management buyout was opposed by Rogers on the basic grounds that the philosophy of privatisation was to introduce a private sector culture of change which would not have been achieved if the Engineering division had been allowed to buy the transmission service. It would also have been unlikely to achieve as much cost saving. A management buyout would also be very highly geared. If the business started to fail, it could not be allowed to go bust and the ITV companies would have to bail it out. That would have been unreasonable and inequitable. This line of argument was also supported by the IBA Chairman, George Russell.

Once the management buyout failed to materialise and the government decided to hive the Engineering assets off with a separate unit which would be vested in the Secretary of State, Rogers recalled the problems and atmosphere generated by the splitting of costs between regulation and transmission and the difficulties of dividing the assets:

> You got this terrible tension within the division, and across divisions, of people suspecting each other of massaging figures and feelings of disloyalty ... It was a deeply unhappy period. The judicial review had nothing on this. At least you knew who was on whose side in the judicial review, and you didn't then. It was also enormously fraught because it had been telescoped down to be done in 1990 rather than 1993. Happily, once staff were assigned to one or other of the successor bodies (transmission or regulation) the atmosphere improved tremendously. Such are the evils of uncertainty and benefits of clarity. (Interview with Peter Rogers)

The division of assets and vesting scheme proved tremendously complicated. The IBA pension scheme was split between the ITC, Engineering division and the Radio Authority but the problem of where past pensioners were to be attributed remained. According to Rogers:

> We appointed our actuary and NTL appointed their actuary and the government appointed their actuary. They came to three very different conclusions: such is the science of actuaries. So much depends on the assumptions made. But the issue was crucial to the ITC. It would inherit all the accrued pension liabilities of the IBA which at one time had nearly 1500 staff. However, the ITC would itself have fewer than 200 staff making current pension contributions. The risk that the tail would wag the dog, inflicting irreparable damage to the future funding of the ITC's pension scheme, was therefore a real one. (Interview with Peter Rogers)

There were also arguments about where debts belonged, where computer systems would go and the ownership of Crawley Court. Ministers resisted apportioning to the ITC any part of the freehold value of Crawley Court, even though it had never been used wholly for transmission purposes. However, government approved and funded a medium-term business plan for the ITC and, coupled with further savings, this allowed the ITC to acquire premises of its own at Kings Worthy Court, also in Winchester. The value of that, at £2 million, was probably greater than the proportion of the Crawley Court freehold which had been in dispute. The finance, administrative, personnel, research and engineering policy staff of the ITC moved in to the new property, while the NTL engineering and transmission staff remained at Crawley Court.

Despite the tensions and problems arising from the division of assets some economies quickly became evident. The considerable supply of stores for the maintenance of transmission had for several years been a source of frustration to Peter Rogers:

> In my view we didn't need anything like the size of the central stores we were keeping ... but you simply couldn't get anything done about it. It was like walking through porridge. (Interview with Peter Rogers)

However, as soon as the move towards privatisation was underway the engineering managers' motivation was changed 'overnight' (according to Rogers) and

> ... they stripped out much of the central stores and had wagons take it away to tips somewhere ... which ... demonstrated the strength and value of privatisation. The speed and completeness with which the attitude to costs and to profits changed was absolutely breathtaking. As an economist who had lectured on the virtues of the market, to me that was all very reassuring! (Interview with Peter Rogers)

The short timescale for the transitional arrangements, although painful at the time, Rogers judged as 'well worthwhile' since it cleared the decks of long-running arguments and allowed the ITC to focus totally on the licensing round in 1991.

However, from the ITV companies' perspective they were possibly the losers since (according to Rogers in interview): 'It was the companies' money which had built the transmission operation and the whole damn lot was expropriated.'

David McCall, who had been delegated by ITV's Council to conduct on ITV's behalf in negotiations with the Home Office, Price Waterhouse and OFTEL, remembered that:

> We felt the cost base was much bigger than it ought to have been and therefore the price that was being paid for it was much lower than it should have been ... We always said that it's worth a lot more because the costs could be halved ... and we were being asked to continue to pay too high a price for the (use of the) transmitter network ... Basically, the ITV companies financed the ITC, who built the transmitters from those funds, and then the government sold it off and kept the money. (Interview with David McCall)

SECTION III: DIVERSIFICATION

TVS

As has been mentioned earlier in this volume, the fortunes of TVS described an almost perfect parabola through the period 1982–92. This rise and fall had nothing to do with failure to earn revenue – rather the reverse. James Gatward's TVS fell victim to the company's revenue success and to its founder Chief Executive's ambitions.

After recovery from the recession years of the early Eighties most ITV companies had more revenue than they could invest in their programmes and, to avoid the money falling into the Treasury coffers through tax or the Levy (see Section IV below) – and as a hedge against future industry recessions – many sought to diversify their interests. But TVS had the problem in an extreme form. Its franchise area was a particularly rich pasture, with more ABC1 viewers than any other except London. The company's profits soared from £4.5 million in 1983 to £26 million in 1988.

When Gatward was frustrated in his attempts to have his company recognised by the IBA and the major ITV companies (see Chapter 5) as a fellow Major rather than a 'middle five' regional company, he felt forced to look for growth in other directions. The only alternative market for TVS programmes at that time in the UK was Channel Four and TVS did produce a number of excellent single biographical dramas on film for the channel: on the American broadcast journalist Ed Murrow (directed by Jack Gold), Nelson Mandela and Simon Wiesenthal. It was hoped that these, along with other quality drama – like a version by Tom Stoppard of the Katayev post-revolutionary classic *Squaring the Circle* – would sell in the US and through such sales an impact would be made on the world market. They did sell in the US but the major networks there have always been an almost impossible market for British broadcasters to crack and they eventually went to a second-level broadcaster, Metromedia, which had good relationships already with UK television and did not represent the international recognition Gatward sought for his company's programmes. He turned instead to what others might call diversification but what he saw as a proper expansion of his core business.

Gatward's expansion plans were, indeed, targeted almost exclusively at television-related businesses, unlike those of most other ITV companies who were looking for investment opportunities for their growing profits in the second half of the Eighties. His first move was on target but someone else was to get closer to the bullseye on price.

In 1986 Thorn EMI, in the same rationalisation of that company's business that was to seek a buyer for their share of Thames Television, put their Screen Entertainments division on the market. Gatward saw that the old Rank library of films, the studios and cinemas would make a grouping that would be a sensible investment against a more competitive future. The IBA, whose permission was required for such a move under the terms of the contracts ITV companies had with the regulator, agreed. Gatward offered £84 million but was outbid by the Australian entreprenuer Alan Bond. Bond bought the business for £125 million but then sold it on to the Golan brothers for a £50 million profit shortly afterwards.

After this Gatward decided to focus the management of his company's investments by setting up a subsidiary – Telso. He put two of TVS's senior executives in as joint managing directors, Peter Clarke and Peter Thomas, but it was, as he described it in interview, 'a sweep-all of entrepreneurial exploration' for which he remained very much personally responsible. They invested in local commercial radio in the TVS region, cable television, a magazine publisher (they were founding partners of *Television Business International*) and a satellite receiver manufacturer, Alba. This last was sold before the take-off of Sky TV at a loss that contemporary industry estimates put at around £500,000.

Then they acquired MIDEM, the organisation that ran the major European programme markets held twice a year at Cannes, for £10 million. The more conservative ITV managing directors – never slow to take a critical view of his activities – thought that Gatward had taken leave of his senses with this move.

In fact it was to give him a better insight into European broadcasting affairs, and, importantly, its investors, than most of his ITV colleagues. Significantly TVS became involved with a bid for the newly privatised leading French television channel TF1. His group, led by the Hachette publishing conglomerate, lost but Gatward then invested in the winning rival, led by the construction group, Bouygues.

MIDEM brought in profits of around £2 million a year but in the second year of TVS's ownership Gatward was approached by the American Reed group with an offer to buy. He sold MIDEM and some associated businesses to them for £33 million. It was the most successful of Gatward's deals – but it earned him the enmity of Clarke and Thomas. The successful heart of their business had been sold over their heads. However, Gatward's next deal was to be his biggest and to lead to his and, indirectly, his company's downfall.

The American independent production company MTM had been founded by the actress Mary Tyler Moore and her producer, Arthur Price, fully to capitalise their talents, rather than allow others to make money out of them. Price's production and entrepreneurial talents led them to extend successfully to beyond *The Mary Tyler Moore Show* to *Lou Grant, Hill Street Blues, St Elsewhere* and others. In 1988, frustrated in the UK, Gatward was seeking expansion for TVS to the US market and admired the company, its talents (though Mary Tyler Moore had effectively withdrawn by this time) and its turnover – about $200 million a year, with nearly $50 million of that in profit. And it had a back library of titles valued at $310 million.

Gatward was scrupulous in his approach. It was agreed by the TVS Board; Peat Marwick, the accountants were put in to MTM to certify the figures and Gatward used his European expertise to bring two new French investors, Canal Plus and Compagnie Générale des Eaux in to take 20 per cent of TVS to strengthen the capital base from which to mount a bid. The purchase would double the size of TVS. He also ensured that Arthur Price was contracted to continue to run the company.

The purchase price was high at $325 million (£190.4 million at the then prevailing rate) but justified by MTM's previous performance. However, just as the purchase was complete, America entered a recession and, worse, US network television and the syndication market for secondary showings of series went through one of those periodic changes of fashion to which the industry there is prone. Hour-long dramas were out and half-hour comedies were in. MTM's stable consisted mostly of hours and so did its future development work.

MTM's finances went into a vicious downward spiral. All of its series were deficit financed. Like most US television production, shows were pre-sold to one of the networks for a figure less than actual cost. The deficit had to be recouped, and profits made, on subsequent syndication and overseas sales. That process could take several years. If interrupted by industry demand changes like those of 1989 losses start to accumulate. By September of that year Gatward had to issue a profits warning to the City and TVS shares lost a third of their value. Gatward also lost Arthur Price in a row over the type of new shows to develop and took charge of MTM himself – commuting back and forth to Los Angeles and heavily dependent on his TVS Chairman, Lord Boston, and his former Finance Director, Tony Brook, now Managing Director of TVS Television, to sustain relationships with Westminster, Whitehall and the ITV Network during the crucial Broadcasting White Paper and networking discussions.

Gatward tried to sell MTM but the recession in the US meant that it was not possible to achieve a realistic price. He even explored the sale of TVS to Michael Green but Gatward's price was high and Green was never totally enthusiastic about anything other than a London franchise. Also the French investors were against the deal. Relations between them and TVS were never easy but their reaction to what they saw as the mismanagement of the MTM affair – with shares that had stood as high as 362 pence reduced to 90 – was to throw TVS into its ultimate vortex of decline.

It was the French investors' successful bid to have Boston replaced by a new Chairman, Rudolph Agnew, against the wishes of Gatward, that was to lead to a confrontation between the two, Gatward's dismissal and TVS's high bid of £59 million for the South and South East licence to continue broadcasting, which led the ITC to judge that the bid jeopardised the company's business viability and award the licence to Meridian (see Chapter 10).

Greg Dyke, who as Programme Director had worked alongside Gatward for three years to try to achieve major company status for TVS but left to go to LWT before the acquisition of MTM, saw Gatward as a 'Shakespearean character':

> in the end the very spirit that had taken him from being a scene shifter to managing director of an ITV company meant that he was inevitably going to try to become a major (company). And of course in the end, it was the same thing that bought MTM and brought the company down. So as I say, in twelve years, it's a Shakespearean story. (Interview with Greg Dyke)

Although TVS/MTM was the most dramatic diversification story of the period the company was not alone in its attempts to invest outside its ITV business.

HTV and Others

Another company at which diversification and its failure was followed by boardroom upheaval was HTV. Its portfolio had been started in the era before the death of the founding Chairman Lord Harlech in a car crash in January 1985, with the purchase of an art gallery in Bristol, Frost and Reed. It was a shrewd purchase at a time before the burgeoning of prices in the art world. The gallery had good stock and its existing management and marketing were strong. It made a profit in one year of over £1million. A bid from Christie's Contemporary Arts (CCA) for Frost and Reed in March 1989 prompted HTV to buy CCA in a £15 million deal under the umbrella of a new company, Harlech Fine Art Holdings. The move was unfortunately timed. As the incoming HTV Chairman put it the following year: 'Harlech Fine Art has been hit hard by the recession. We are taking the opportunity to restructure this particular activity and significantly reduce its operating overheads. (HTV Annual Report for 1990). The Harlech Fine Art Holdings group of companies was finally sold in 1992 for only £3 million.

The company's other diversification varied from moderately successful to disastrous. Inadequate management and failure of supervision from HTV meant that a stationery company subsidiary producing high-class diaries suffered severe losses. Of a handful of other purchases only Vestron UK, renamed by HTV as First Independent, a commercial video distributor, made money.

By the end of 1990 HTV, whose share of NAR had also diminished during the period, was in deficit and on 14 March 1991, with only two months to go before the licence application and bid had to be submitted to the ITC, the Chairman of the HTV Group, Sir Melvyn Rosser, formerly a senior accountant, and the Chief Executive, Patrick Dromgoole, who had been a successful television and theatre producer and Director of Programmes at HTV, were swept away in a boardroom shake-up.

The new Chairman was Louis Sherwood, a professional businessman (he had added an MBA from Stanford University in the USA to his Oxford degree) who had risen in the supermarket world to be Chairman and Chief Executive of Gateway Foodmarkets. The Sales Director of HTV, Charles Romaine was Chief Executive for just over two years, to be replaced by a management figure recruited from outside the company to be Finance Director in May 1992, Chris Rowlands. When the 'temporary blip' of the 1990–91 recession threatened to become long term, Sherwood's first Christmas as Chairman of HTV was not a happy one:

> I certainly recall very vividly my first Christmas with HTV as Chairman, at Christmas 1991, having literally to call in the financial people every single day over the Christmas and New Year holiday to check that the cash was coming in, because we had promised the banks that we would achieve a certain cash position and we were not going to achieve it unless we took vigorous measures, at that stage we had very, very large bank borrowings and we weren't in any kind of position to repay them, and a withdrawal of bank support would have been a disaster. (Interview with Louis Sherwood)

Sherwood's measures ensured that Barclays and NatWest, who had their own financial difficulties over the next two crucial years – fortunately for HTV the two banks ran into difficulty at different times – maintained the borrowing facilities until HTV had been been successful in its bid for a licence to continue broadcasting and was back on its financial feet again.

Thames Television's success with its SES/Astra satellite investment in Europe and its less successful ventures in America and Australia have been mentioned elsewhere in this volume, as has the disposal by LWT of its publishing and travel subsidiaries. For Granada, of course, television itself had originally been a diversification.

Most other companies extended themselves less by way of diversification, having perceived that expansion away from the core business did not play on the strengths of the average ITV management. One worth mentioning was Grampian, whose canny managing directors over the years had sought only the granite-solid investment of Aberdeen property. The story that this led to the ownership of funeral premises is not apocryphal. The firm was called Bon Accord Funeral Directors – a business of consistent demand if ever there was one. In any event Grampian's diversification was always well in profit and was the exception to the general dire record of ITV companies' attempts to diversify outside their core businesses during the period.

SECTION IV: THE LEVY

The end of 1992 saw the passing of the tax, peculiar to British commercial television, that was known as the Levy. This unique tax was levied on television companies by the government on the grounds that it was through their privileged use of a scarce resource – the broadcasting spectrum – that the companies made their profits.

The Levy died with the end of the IBA contract system and the start of the ITC licences. The licence payments consist of the bid element, decided by the companies when they applied, and the Percentage of Qualifying Revenue (PQR) component, decided by the ITC (see below).

During the first half of the Eighties the Levy system was under constant review by government. From 1974 the tax had been levied at a rate of 66.7 per cent on the amount by which profit exceeded £250,000 or 2.0 per cent of advertising revenue, whichever was higher.

The Levy was charged on the profits from the companies' prime business of providing programmes and selling advertising. Any income from peripheral activities was excluded. Expenditure on rentals to the IBA, Fourth Channel Subscriptions, costs of programme sales overseas and the depreciation of fixed assets was allowed against profit. Income and expenditure relating to loan interest, the hire of facilities, merchandising and copyright royalties from book publishing were also excluded from the Levy calculation. All in all, for a company with a thoughtful approach to accounting, the Levy was a net with fairly large holes. This was something that did not escape the watchful eyes of the Treasury.

As a result, in the summer of 1981, the Home Secretary, William Whitelaw, announced that, in conjunction with the Treasury, the Home Office (which was responsible for broadcasting) was considering a system that would combine elements of the old profits-based levy with a new revenue-based component. This would have the effect of tightening the net considerably.

But in the meantime the companies were, as we have seen in Chapter 2, in some financial difficulty with the demands of the new Fourth Channel Subscription. An easement was negotiated by the IBA on the companies' behalf and in April 1982 the 'free slice' of unlevied profits was raised from 2 to 2.8 per cent or £650,000, whichever was the greater.

Because of impending changes in the television system – not just the arrival of Channel Four but the impending cable and satellite competition for ITV (which government expected to begin earlier than it did) – the IBA and the companies were successful in holding off the review of the Levy until August 1984. Then a Working party of officials from the Home Office, Treasury and the IBA was set up.

Interestingly the main emphasis of the remit of this group was '... to consider whether the high marginal rate of tax resulting from the current levy arrangements and corporation tax might be a disincentive to efficiency'. The background to this was the continuing concern of the government that ITV's tendency to buy their way out of union confrontations was forcing up artists', sports rights and purchased programme costs in a manner that was putting up the BBC's costs, and hence the cost of the Television Licence – a poll tax which the public disliked and the increase of which the Conservatives did not support or find desirable.

During the period of the Levy review two reports relating to the IBA and additional payments by the ITV companies were published. These were by the Comptroller and Auditor General (CAG) in April 1985 and by the Committee of Public Accounts in July 1985.

The main issues raised by the first report were the low levels of payments made by some companies, the need for a review of the assessment procedures and basis for calculation for payments to ensure that the interest of the Exchequer was adequately safeguarded, and the effect of the introduction of Channel Four in substantially reducing the amount levied. It also considered associated questions of accountability to Parliament. The PAC report welcomed the acceptance by the Home Office and the IBA that information and analysis of developments and trends in the amount and incidence of levy would in future be provided in the IBA annual report presented to Parliament (see also Chapter 8).

On 26 February 1986, the Home Secretary, Douglas Hurd, outlined the new levy provisions which were based on the recommendations of the review of ITV (and radio) levy structures. The necessary legislative proposals were to be included in the 1986 Finance Bill.

The main provisions of the Finance Act 1986 applied from 1 April 1986. From then the Levy was charged separately, at different rates, on the profits from two types of business. Levy on first category profits derived from the provision of ITV and fourth channel programmes (mainly from advertising revenue and the programme journal) was charged at 45 per cent (reduced from 66.7 per cent). Levy on second category profits, from the sale of programmes elsewhere, mainly overseas, was charged at 22.5 per cent. (Until 1 April 1986, income from the sale of programmes overseas was not counted as 'relevant' income, and any expenditure which was considered by the IBA to be attributable to such sales was excluded from 'relevant' expenditure in the calculation of levy. This included any expenditure incurred with the specific objective of obtaining overseas sales, and the marginal direct costs involved, such as artists' fees and dubbing. The overseas sale concession had been designed primarily as an export incentive.)

The minimum level of the 'free slice' increased from £650,000 to £800,000. Arrangements existed to permit any balance of the 'free slice' not utilised against higher rate profits to be carried across to profits charged at the lower rate. It was also possible for companies to offset trading losses in one category against profits in another category. Trading losses remaining could be set against leviable profits in future years to the end of the contract. Anti-avoidance provisions were extended containing reserve powers to prescribe a company's minimum levy bill in the event of excessive expenditure or, in the case of second category sales, at less than 'arms length'. The Levy was also charged on ITV programme contractors in respect of the relevant profits of companies 'connected' with them.

The television companies entered into agreements with the IBA to extend their programme contracts from 31 December 1989 to 31 December 1992. The extensions were made possible by the terms of the Broadcasting Act 1987 which was introduced by the government with the aim of enabling new broadcasting legislation to be in place before the new licences were advertised.

In March 1989 the government announced a new levy structure which would apply to the ITV extended contract period. From 1 January 1990 the structure of the Levy was changed by Schedule 16 of the Finance Act 1989 to a levy partly based on advertising revenue and partly on profits earned from the same business. For the period 1 January 1990 to 31 December 1991 the revenue levy was based on 10 per cent of NAR after the deduction of a free slice of £15 million and the Fourth Channel Subscription paid by each company. The profits levy was based on 25 per cent of domestic profits, that is, excluding profits from the sale of programmes outside the UK after deducting the NAR levy due and a free slice of £2 million.

There was a very steep decline in advertising revenue in 1991. After payment of the Levy based on advertising revenue, the profits of the ITV companies were greatly reduced. Other factors leading to reduced profits were the continued costs related to reorganisation and rationalisation. Consequently, the ITC lobbied the Government hard for a reduction in the Levy and for the final year, 1992, the revenue levy was reduced to 2.5 per cent of NAR (from 10 per cent) and the free slice increased to £25 million (from £15 million). The profits levy was unchanged. The annual Treasury 'take' from the ITV Levy during the period is shown in Table C.

Table C   Exchequer Levy – ITV Companies

Year ending 31 March	£m
1980	42
1981	52
1982	57
1983	38
1984	23
1985	40
1986	20
1987	75
1988	87
1989	99
1990	103
1991*	114
1992*	69

* calendar years
Source: IBA/ITC annual reports.

The 1990 Broadcasting Act established the Independent Television Commission. The Act also required that certain kinds of licences were awarded by the ITC after a process of competitive tender. Licensees appointed in this way are required to make additional payments to the ITC. The tendering system is considered to allow the 'market' to set prices for the licences through the bidding process.

These additional payments, which first became due in 1993, are more commonly known as tender payments and arise in two ways: amounts expressed as a percentage of qualifying revenue and a cash bid.

The Percentage of Qualifying Revenue is set by the ITC for each C3 licence. The cash bid is an annual sum offered by the licensee as part of its application. Neither the cash bid nor percentage of qualifying revenue can be varied during the term of the licence.

The 1990 Act does also contain provisions for the renewal of televison programme service licences for Channel 3. Licences may be renewed by the ITC at specified periods prior to the expiry of the licence. On renewal of a licence the ITC may specify a different percentage, or percentages as the case may be, of qualifying revenue from that payable during the first period of the licence. The ITC must also determine an amount equivalent to a cash bid, payable by the licensee in the first complete calendar year of the renewal period. This payment, like the initial cash bid, is a fixed sum, adjusted annually in line with the movements in the RPI.

8

POLITICAL WINDS OF CHANGE

The Peacock Inquiry

The last committee to examine the financing of the BBC, which reported in 1977, had been chaired by Lord Annan. It had recommended that, so far as possible, each broadcasting authority should have its own source or sources of revenue and should not have to compete for the same source of financing; the BBC should continue to be financed by a licence fee and proposals for financing the BBC from taxation or any form of advertising should be rejected.

The Conservative government elected in May 1979 had also supported the licensing system as the main way of financing the BBC in the publication *Two Studies Concerning the BBC*, (Home Office, 1979 p. 9 Paragraph 8 (HMSO)).

Writing in the March/April 1979 edition of *Television* Lord Whitelaw, then still Opposition Spokesman on Home Affairs but soon to be Home Secretary, had expressed the view that the first principle of broadcasting must be to defend the independence of the broadcasting authorities from government and Parliament. In this connection, a continuing licensing system for the financing of the BBC was a valuable factor and he found the arguments in the Annan Report against any other method of financing wholly convincing.

Setting Up

In December 1984, however, the BBC had applied for increases in the licence fee to £18 for monochrome television sets and £65 for colour sets. The Home Secretary, Leon Brittan, on 27 March 1985 approved the increase to £18 for monochrome but awarded a lower fee of £58 for colour sets. He also announced the establishment of a Committee under the chairmanship of Professor Alan Peacock, to consider alternative means of financing the BBC with the following terms of reference:

(1) to assess the effects of the introduction of advertising or sponsorship on the BBC's Home Services, either as an alternative or a supplement to the income now received through the licence fee, including

(a) the financial and other consequences for the BBC and for independent television and radio, prospective cable services, DBS, the press, the advertising industry and the Exchequer, and

(b) the impact on the range and quality of existing broadcasting services;

(2) to identify a range of options for the introduction, in varying amounts and on different conditions of advertising or sponsorship on some or all of the BBC's Home Services, with an assessment of the advantages and disadvantages of each option and

(3) to consider any proposals for securing income from the consumer other than through the licence fee.

Members of the Committee

The rest of the Committee members were announced on 17 May 1985. They included Samuel Brittan, principal economic commentator and Assistant Editor of the *Financial Times* who was also the brother of the Home Secretary, Leon Brittan; Judith Chalmers, a television presenter and member of the National Consumer Council; Jeremy Hardie, an accountant, economist and businessman who had been a former deputy chairman of the Monopolies and Mergers Commission; Professor Alastair Hetherington, a former editor of the *Guardian* and a former Controller of BBC Scotland who was currently a director of a small independent television production company, Scotquest, and also Research Professor of Media Studies at the University of Stirling; Lord Quinton, a philosopher and President of Trinity College, Oxford and Sir Peter Reynolds, Chairman of Rank Hovis McDougall. Dr Robert Eagle was appointed Secretary to the Committee.

The Chairman, Professor Peacock, was Research Professor at Heriot-Watt University and had held Chairs in Economics at Edinburgh, York and Buckingham Universities. He had also been Chief Economic Adviser at the Department of Trade and Industry and had written extensively on the economics of public finance, social policy and the arts.

Commenting on the appointments in the *Sunday Times* (26 May 1985) Sue Summers reported that Professor Peacock was 'unsure whether he likes the idea of advertising on all channels – "We will have to do some market research to see what the viewers feel" – and he is anxious to dispel any idea that he is the Home Secretary's hatchet man. "I wouldn't have taken the job if I was to be regarded as a hired gun."' She reported that Samuel Brittan, describing himself as a 'free-market liberal', had claimed that 'It's inconceivable that Leon (Brittan) and I would tell each other what to do' and that he admired fellow economist Peter Jay's concept that television companies should be like publishers, providing consumers with any kind of programme they cared to pay for. Judith Chalmers was seen as a 'lightweight choice'; Jeremy Hardie as 'one of the few remaining Keynesian economists'.

Summers reported that although Alastair Hetherington had been controller of BBC Scotland 'It would be wrong to assume from this that he is a BBC fan. He resigned after a row over the degree of autonomy he was promised for Scotland' but reported him as saying 'like many people, I'd probably prefer the BBC not to take advertising, though circumstances change'. Lord Quinton had also described himself as 'a battlefield of conflicting impulses' as far as changing the Corporation is concerned. 'On the one hand, I think people should get what they want; on the other, I'm infected by Reithian ideals. You have to consider the cultural arguments as well as the economic ones.' Sir Peter Reynolds, a successful businessman, had declared that 'happily' he had no connection with broadcasting other than as a consumer.

Raymond Snoddy, in the *Financial Times* (29 March 1985) had previously described Professor Peacock as 'a man of independent mind who sees himself as a classical liberal economist in the tradition of Adam Smith, sympathetic to some of the ideas of monetarism, but not to its more rigid exponents'.

Methodology

The Committee held twenty meetings; the first was on 29 May 1985 and the last on 29 May 1986. A deadline for the submission of written evidence was set for 31 August 1985. Professor Peacock had a dish aerial installed in his own home so that he could watch programmes broadcast by satellite and some of the Committee made visits to overseas countries where they felt that specific lessons might be learnt. Some of these were fleeting. In June 1985, Professor Peacock spent two days in West Germany, two days in Washington in July, and five days in Paris, Munich and Rome in November with Judith Chalmers. Sir Peter Reynolds and Lord Quinton were in New York for two days in September and the former spent a day in Japan and two days in Rome in November. The visits were, however, supplemented by research studies on broadcasting systems in France, West Germany, Italy, the USA and Australia.

Research

Consultant economists who were engaged by the Committee included Doctors Martin Cave of Brunel University, and Peter Swann of Bath University and Cento Veljanovski, a lecturer associated with the Institute of Economic Affairs, who, according to the Peacock Report, 'wrote drafts on economic questions working to well-nigh impossible deadlines. Their collection and analysis of an enormous amount of data represents a major contribution to our work.' Other research commissioned by the Committee included a market survey by NOP Market Research Ltd to gauge public opinion on the issues; by NERA to assess the effect on other media and by Leeds University, under the direction of Professor Jay Blumler, on programme range and quality. Research studies were also received as part of the Committee's evidence from the BBC, ISBA, IPA, the Newspaper Society and

ITCA who submitted a report by Alan Budd, Professor of Economics at the London Business School on 'The Impact on ITV Revenue of Extending Advertising to the BBC' which concluded that the growth in television advertising had been exceptional and that it would be dangerous to assume a similar growth in the coming years. The report also claimed that the extension of television advertising to the BBC would reduce the revenue available to ITV and that increased competition for advertising revenue would be likely to lower production standards and reduce the level of audience satisfaction with television programmes.

Evidence

Viewers

The Committee issued a consultation document listing a number of particular issues including advertising, sponsorship and alternative forms of revenue on which the Committee would like to receive views by 31 August 1985. Evidence was received from 843 individuals or organisations, with roughly half from members of the public. Since the Committee thought that 'the crucial question is whether the viewer or listener will benefit from the BBC taking advertising' (Peacock Report, Paragraph 420) they were concerned to ascertain the views of ordinary members of the public and not only from special interest groups:

> There are a number of consumer organisations which represent certain group interests within the general public who have a concern for various aspects of broadcasting. However, we recognise that, valuable as these groups are, they do not represent all consumers. Therefore, we found that the one group whose views were most difficult to determine was the viewers and listeners group. That was why we went to such lengths to invite submissions from members of the public so that we could get their views directly, and not just through an umbrella organisation. (Peacock Report, Paragraph 2.2)

Advertising Industry

The general view of the advertising industry, in their evidence, was that it would be appropriate to freeze the licence fee payment and to introduce a small amount of advertising on the BBC, initially for example at £100 million per year, which would expand on a yearly basis to meet the increasing needs of the BBC. They argued that this could be achieved by the growth trend in advertising without reducing the finances available for advertising on ITV or other media. The Committee reported that they had 'received a considerable number of complaints from individual advertisers and from ISBA which alleged that ITV companies took full advantage of the strength of their market position to hold advertisers to ransom' (Peacock Report, Paragraph 192). The IPA, in its evidence, set out six scenarios, based on the Henley Centre for Forecasting's extrapolations, which showed that if the real spending power of the ITV companies was held constant and the licence fee was pegged at its present cash level, then in nearly all cases there would be sufficient advertising revenue available to the BBC to maintain its spending power.

ITV

In addition to the analysis by Professor Alan Budd, ITCA, on behalf of the ITV companies, also submitted studies by Professor Harry Henry, Professor of Marketing and Media Policy at the International Management Centre at Buckingham, by merchant bankers Brown, Shipley and by the ITV companies' sales directors. Professor Henry's report 'Advertising on the BBC' concluded that the ITV companies' share of advertising would be reduced which implied that part of the money going to the BBC would, in effect, be funded by the Treasury in consequence of reduced levy, and that competition between the ITV companies and the BBC would, if it had any effect on rates at all, increase rather than reduce them. Brown, Shipley also calculated that the ITV network would show a loss. Overall, ITCA concluded that the arrival of TV-am and Channel 4 provided ample opportunity for new advertising but that there was no overall growth available in advertising revenue in real terms so that the advertising cake would not increase if the BBC took advertising.

IBA

The IBA evidence, submitted after the deadline, opposed the introduction of advertising on the BBC and argued that those seeking change in the system of British broadcasting should show that change would be an improvement while, according to press reports, the Director General, John Whitney claimed 'We are not adopting a dinosaur posture'. Whitney also stressed that the main issue was not only the size of the advertising cake but the range and choice of broadcasting available.

Letters to Peacock

The Listener also published a series of fourteen weekly 'Letters to Peacock' starting with David Holbrook, Director of English Studies at Downing College, Cambridge on 4 July 1985 and ending with Alasdair Milne, DG of the BBC, on 10 October 1985. The wide range of contributors included MPs Edwina Currie and Norman Buchan, programme makers such as David Plowright, David Elstein and William G. Stewart, advertising specialists such as the media consultant Harold Lind and Rodney Harris, Media Director of the advertising agency D'Arcy MacManus Masius, academics Anthony Smith and Philip Schlesinger and media correspondent, Brenda Maddox. Not surprisingly, there was no consensus on the advice they offered Peacock.

David Plowright, Chairman of ITCA and MD of Granada Television, claimed that 'there is insufficient advertising revenue in prospect to support the two institutions in the manner to which they and their customers have grown accustomed'. He also warned of the dangers of tampering with the 'regional breakthrough' which ITV had achieved. He claimed that 'ITV is not just a system of distributing programmes to the regions. It feeds back into the system the diversity of views which the regions have to offer, injecting into the mainstream of programming new ideas from new vantage-points.' He concluded:

> If I could leave a single thought with you, it is that you and your colleagues should not regard ITV as being merely the BBC with advertisements. The two organisations are different in structure, in outlook, in personality and in accomplishments. They are genuinely complementary to each other, not merely alternative versions of the same thing. Together they bring a richness to the screen which is envied throughout the world. (*The Listener*, 18 July 1985)

Brenda Maddox, then editor of *Connections*, the communications newsletter of *The Economist*, also warned Peacock (*The Listener*, 15 August 1985) that

> You should also try to catch an evening of an American public broadcasting (ie. non-commercial) station's output, preferably one of those nights they are begging for money and auctioning off the station manager's underwear to try and pull in enough dollars to keep going through the next year. Experience all that, then ponder the wise American maxim 'If it's not broke, don't fix it'.

Conflicting advice came from Bruce Fireman, head of the technology department at merchant bankers Charterhouse Japhet, who argued that 'the answer lies in breaking the mould of the two networks, and packaging channels in different ways' (*The Listener*, 25 July 1985). Edwina Currie (*The Listener*, 5 September 1985) confessed that she was 'deeply suspicious of what is meant by "public service broadcasting"' and concluded that 'The BBC's monopoly of the audience disappeared a long time ago – and with it, in my opinion, the BBC's right to the audience's hard-earned money.' Only David Elstein, then MD of Primetime Television Ltd, came close to the Committee's thinking in arguing for the replacement of the licence fee with a subscription system (*The Listener*, 11 July 1985).

Meetings

Voice of the Listener
After evidence had been submitted to the Committee at the end of August 1985, Professor Peacock addressed the annual general meeting of the Voice of the Listener, on 21 October 1985 in the Royal Festival Hall. This organisation was set up by Mrs Jocelyn Hay, initially to encourage high standards in radio, but subsequently was extended to television viewers. Professor Peacock told the audience that it was unusual for government committees, which generally kept matters close their chest, to hold public meetings at this stage. He also stressed that the Committee was there to analyse the issues rather than to reach foregone conclusions.

Church House Conference

The Peacock Committee held a one-day conference in Church House, Westminster, on 28 November 1985 with the stated purpose to disseminate information to the public so that those wishing to make submissions could do so from a more informed position. With their underlying belief in 'consumer sovereignty' and distaste for peer evaluation between broadcasters the Committee was aiming for more effective communication with the viewers and listeners whose views and preferences, they claimed, were paramount.

At the conference, Professor Peacock explained that 'the idea behind the day was to enable the main points of some principal contributors of evidence to be given a public hearing and to provide a forum for discussion around these central issues' (*Television Today*, 15 December 1985). He told the conference that the status quo and the licence fee would be assessed in their own right and the question of BBC financing would be considered in the broader context of UK economic growth and new technologies.

The conference, which was chaired by Lord (Jo) Grimond, was organised so that one representative from an invited group presented the organisation's views followed by a short discussion to which all invited groups could contribute. Only if those invited guests had run out of questions could other people in the audience participate.

Those invited to speak were ITCA, represented by David Plowright and Professor Alan Budd; ISBA, represented by its president, Donald McLure and Dick Johnson, Chairman of ISBA's executive committee; the Cable Television Association represented by Patrick Scott of Aberdeen Cable, and the Association of Independent Radio Contractors (AIRC) by Richard Findlay.

After lunch, Peter Jay, representing no one but himself, addressed the conference on his concept of electronic publishing. He was followed by Jeremy Mitchell, Director of the National Consumer Council, and by BBC Director General, Alasdair Milne, who concluded the day's proceedings. Plowright reiterated ITCA evidence that the total advertising spend would not increase if advertising was permitted on the BBC, although he admitted that the ITV federal system might not be a model of cost effectiveness in that it did duplicate manpower and resources, but it did give the regions of the UK a voice. He also criticised the tactical use of opinion polls and some of the 'humbug' which was appearing in print in the guise of commentary on the findings. He found that *The Times*, with its Murdoch connection, had particularly demonstrated 'a disturbing mastery in this field'. Professor Alan Budd expanded on points in ITCA's evidence which concentrated on the effects of extending television advertising. If this happened:

– ITV companies would lose revenue;
– the loss of revenue would cause a decline in ITV production standards;
– competition for funds would affect standards on all channels.

Since advertising time was rationed by the IBA, Budd argued, any arrangement resulting in more television advertising being sold would cause a fall in the average price. Taking a 'sensible working assumption' on the elasticity of demand for television time (that is, the response of demand to a change in price) any revenue the BBC gained from advertising would produce an equal loss of revenue from the ITV companies. In the longer term, Budd forecast, there was not going to be a 'revenue bonanza'. He questioned the 'quite extraordinary' assumption of the IPA scenarios that the real revenue of the ITV companies should be held constant at its 1987 level. He also criticised the 'indefensible assumption' by the NERA study that ITV companies only needed their current real level of revenue and that any extra could safely be given to the BBC. He said that he was not convinced by allegations of waste and that the regional pattern of ITV, which was 'inevitably expensive', would be destroyed.

Although Budd claimed that he was 'a warm supporter of competition between suppliers of goods and services' as well as of 'the maximum freedom of choice for consumers' he pointed out that consumer choice did not relate just to the size of the audience but also to the intensity of enjoyment of programmes. Under the current system, programmes were enjoyed intensively by smaller audiences. Although the system was not perfect it did produce diversity, excellence and popularity (IBA Information Paper 157, 1985).

Both ISBA and IPA stressed that they were looking for defined groups of consumers and were tapping new markets; it was thought that the ITCA case was far too pessimistic and that advertising on the BBC would open up additional specialised audiences for a new set of products and services.

Peter Jay said he had nothing to offer but an ideal based on the freedom of consumers to choose, of producers to create and of businessmen to invest. Although he conceded that, like a free press, some trash might be produced, the pre-market had 'thrown up' Milton and Shakespeare and was no 'cultural desert'. European culture did not start with the first BBC Charter. He saw the licence fee as a paternalistic system and as a regressive poll tax. Significantly he also thought that television franchises should be auctioned, not allocated, to introduce some economic reality into the situation. Defending his friend Jay, Samuel Brittan retorted that anyone who had read the early history of printing and publishing would appreciate that every argument which was being offered against electronic publishing was being offered then.

Alasdair Milne, in the closing speech of the conference, pronounced that the aim should not be to help advertisers lower costs, but for public service broadcasting to provide stimulating programmes. Wisdom, luck and decent management had created the system; politicians had helped to pilot the ship and they must now create a secure environment in which the success story could continue to unfold.

David Glencross, IBA Director of Television, claimed that the issue which the Peacock Committee needed to address itself was not about how the BBC should be financed but whether broadcasting was to be treated simply as a commodity or as a national service, with social obligations to stimulate as well as to gratify. His speech was one of the few to be received with applause from the audience.

IBA Information Paper 157(1985) concluded that 'The Committee will now have to act as arbiters of the conflicting research, evidence and beliefs. It is doubtful if any new ideas and approaches will emerge from any further evidence.'

Press comment on the conference was generally critical. Brenda Maddox wrote that:

> Conferences are like parties. Some can give them, others can't. Professor Alan Peacock's day at Church House was a flop. The venue was dismal; the guest list gave offence (trade unions and the Independent Broadcasting Authority were omitted from the list of those officially invited to speak) ... Then there was the problem of the magician hired to keep the guests in order. Lord Grimond, handsomer than ever with age, suffered from two handicaps. Not the stone-deafness for which he apologised (that was an advantage). Rather his illiberal zeal to allow only the first three rows of elite to speak, and his total ignorance of the personalities of the British television scene. Clearly unable to tell his John Birt from his elbow, he curtly ordered the controller of London Weekend Television, because he was 'a member of the general public', to confine his remarks to 30 seconds. Mr Birt was thus classified because he had been required to sit towards the back in the benches reserved for the supposed public and which included among their sparse occupants such faces from the Clapham omnibus as Paul Fox and Michael Grade. Mr Birt wisely declined the opportunity. (*The Listener*, 5 December 1985)

Phillip Whitehead, a former member of the Annan Committee, found that 'Church House, as a forum for debate, about as stimulating as a Mogadon cocktail'. He concluded that:

> ... as an exercise in open debate the day was a waste of time. My memory will be of the two ex-Head Boys of Winchester arguing out the future of our broadcasting system. The tall Jay, fluent to the point of arrogance, pouring out his vision of the 'free' world of electronic publishing, which will be upon us before you can say Bob's your Maxwell, treated some of his questioners like *The Times* sub-editor who was told that he was not one of the three people for whom the Jay articles were written. Milne, a slight figure padded out by an old-fashioned suit read out that curious mix of BBC programme gongs and political grovels which the Secretariat still think is their best case. (*New Statesman*, 6 December 1985)

David Watt of *The Times* also found the conference

> ... a pretty dismal affair. Billed as an opportunity for high-class public debate, it rapidly deteriorated into a languid exchange of hostilities between familiar

opponents who had heard, and said, it all a dozen times before. On the side of the status quo beside the BBC were the independent television companies, which fear a loss of advertising revenue if the BBC were obliged to take advertising.

On the other side were the usual motley alliance of revolutionaries: the advertising industry, which wants to widen the market for TV advertisements in order to drive down rates, the free-market ideologists, who find the present system an intolerable affront to the memory of Adam Smith, and the cultural Thatcherites who detest the BBC as the epitome of old, soggy establishment paternalism. I don't know what the members of the Peacock Committee made of all this. I thought they looked dutiful but a bit glazed. (*The Times*, 6 December 1985)

ITV Activities (November 1985–June 1986)

Shortly after the Church House Conference, *Campaign* (29 November 1985), the journal for advertisers, alleged (prompted by claims from the Henley Centre) that there had been errors in Budd's analysis and that there were serious discrepancies which had resulted in a faulty economic model. The ITV contractors, however, while admitting that there had been a 'typographical error' in the ITCA submission, claimed that 'the mistake affects ITCA's case not one jot'.

On 9 January 1986, some members – Peacock, Hetherington, Hardie and Eagle (the secretary) visited Thames TV and met Richard Dunn (MD), Muir Sutherland, Jonathan Shier and Donald Cullimore. Notes taken by Cullimore revealed that the majority view of the Peacock members present seemed to be that they did not have a high regard for the IBA, particularly over the awarding of the ITV franchises. Peacock had floated tentatively the idea of putting out the contracts to tender. When asked if they thought that Thames would have any rival bidders, Dunn had replied that although he had 'shrewd ideas', he expected that as Thames emerged from its recent period of difficulties and restricted ownership, the potential bidders would 'retire from the contest'. The Thames representatives in response to queries on costs, had also claimed that although there might have been examples of extravagance in ITV and that costs were high, 'We at Thames were facing this realistically.'

A letter (received 3 March 1986) from James Graham (MD of Border) to David Shaw (General Secretary of ITCA) confidently asserted that at a reception for William Whitelaw at Border TV, Whitelaw had reiterated his views that he was 'implacably imposed' to advertising on the BBC and that the Peacock Committee would make no clear recommendations of the sort that would win the necessary parliamentary support for implementation.

Such confidence however, was not wholeheartedly repeated in a note (1 April 1986) from David Shaw, for a special meeting of Council. He warned that ITV faced a future of:

Contradictions		Peacock, DBS
Conflicts	arising from	Levy, Superchannel
Confusions		Franchise renewal
Challenges		

Shaw did not include in his note the fifth 'C' – Competition. But a further study was commissioned by ITCA from the International Institute of Communications (IIC) on 'The Competition factors affecting ITV companies in the 1990s' to serve as an input to the ongoing debates about Peacock and the future of ITV. It concluded that:

> The ITV companies have been essentially non-competitive from 1955 until very recently. However, several factors are now introducing disequilibria into the system. Each company within the ITV system has to take decisions about its participation in (and/or the supply of programmes to) each new service opportunity. Companies will tend increasingly to evaluate these opportunities primarily according to their own corporate financial status (eg., Thames' decision not to participate in Superchannel; the Granada Group's interest in DBS) and not, as previously, primarily with regard to the likely effect on the ITV system as a whole. For 30 years the ITV companies have had a singular focus: the ITV system. Today, ITV managements have to look at a spectrum of opportunities, some within ITV, some outside. (IIC Report, 'The Competition factors affecting ITV companies in the 1990s', 3 June 1986)

General Conclusions

The *Report of the Committee on Financing the BBC* (HMSO Cmnd 9824) was published on 3 July 1986.

Underlying Assumptions
Instead of tackling the narrow question of whether or not the BBC should take advertising directly the Committee initially examined the background and values of the broadcasting market.

Consumer Sovereignty
The underlying assumption of the Committee was that a broadcasting market should be designed to promote the welfare and express the preferences of viewers and listeners. This, however, did not carry the implication that a crude system of 'commercial *laissez-faire*' should take over since it ignored an important feature of the competitive market as a 'discovery mechanism' for finding out by trial and error what the consumer might be enticed to accept (as well as the least costly method of supplying it) and for trying out new and challenging ideas. A 'commercial *laissez-faire*' system would simply require that all broadcasting channels should

be privatised and that the whole of broadcasting should be deregulated without worrying about whether channels should be financed by advertising or in other ways. Neither would it meet British standards of public accountability for the private use of public assets. They also thought that any state support should be direct and visible, and not achieved by cross-subsidisation or 'leaning' on programme makers.

Censorship
Heavily influenced by Samuel Brittan, the Committee also proclaimed the value of freedom of expression which was imbedded in the First Amendment to the US Constitution (15 December 1791) which laid down that 'Congress shall make no law ... abridging the freedom of speech or of the press' (Paragraph 548). This was compared with the history of the printing press which had been subject to many kinds of regulation and censorship in the first two-and-a-half centuries of its existence. The Report pointed out that

> The abolition of pre-publication censorship by Parliament (in 1694) was described by Macaulay as a greater contribution to liberty and civilisation than either the Magna Carta or the Bill of Rights. (Paragraph 23)

The way that the IBA had to clear programmes in advance was compared with the Index of the Council of Trent (1564) which set up conditions for the examination and licensing of books before publication and for the inspection of printing houses and bookshops.

Public Service Broadcasting
One of the questions which the Committee admitted they had found most difficult was a satisfactory definition of the term 'Public Service Broadcasting' (PSB) which had been bandied around in public debate and submissions to the Committee. Although they had received from the Broadcasting Research Unit their publication *The Public Service Idea in British Broadcasting* (1985) which analysed the principles embodied in the idea of PSB, they concluded that the best operational definition of public service was simply any major modification of purely commercial provision resulting from public policy (Paragraph 580).

They conceded, however, that:

> The BBC and the regulated ITV system have done far better, in mimicking the effects of a true consumer market, than any purely *laissez-faire* system, financed by advertising could have done under conditions of spectrum shortage. To aid them in their task they have established systematic and frequent market research, covering audience appreciation as well as ratings, of a kind that no newspaper has available on a regular basis. In addition they have provided more demanding programmes (for instance in the arts), which viewers and listeners might have

been willing to pay for in their capacity as taxpayers and voters, but not as consumers. (Paragraph 581)

Nevertheless, the Committee, while allowing that the broadcasting authorities had not only mimicked the market and provided packages of programmes to audiences at remarkably low cost, noted limitations.

There is an absence of true consumer sovereignty and of market signals, which only direct payment by viewers and listeners could establish. Because of its dependence on public finance and regulation, the system is vulnerable to political pressure, and vulnerable to trade union and other special interest groups ... and the near impossibility of the IBA to be seen to be discharging fairly its award of franchises. (Paragraph 584)

The Committee did, however, note in many of the submissions that although most people did want to be able to choose programmes which interested them most, they did not want those which talked down to them or treated them simply as 'fodder for advertisers'. The study by the University of Leeds had shown that those interviewed were predominantly of the view that British broadcasting in its existing public service mode should and did assert and reflect Britain as a community, society and culture and that it was the principal forum by which the nation as a whole was able to talk to itself. An emphasis was placed on the degree of innovation in British television, again in ITV and BBC alike, and on the readiness within the British system to allow time for new styles of programme to evolve and to become acceptable to large audiences. Emphasis was also placed on regional commitment, particularly in ITV. Yorkshire TV was cited as an example of a company seeking regional output not only from the centre of its area but from the outlying districts, with permanent crews as far apart as Ripon and Grimsby. Similar comments were made of, for example, Central as a large company and Grampian as a small one, each with commitments to remote parts of their regions.

Not totally convinced by this paean of praise, however, the Committee also incorporated in the Report some of the comments that Jeremy Mitchell, Director of the National Consumer Council, had made at the Church House conference: 'It would not be wise for broadcasters to assume that consumers think that everything is wonderful in the world of British broadcasting.' He claimed that: 'When some broadcasters talk about good programmes they mean programmes which win prizes awarded by other broadcasters.' He offered as evidence a recent MORI survey in which 46 per cent of television viewers said that they were very or fairly satisfied with the quality of television, against 45 per cent who were very or fairly dissatisfied and added 'All our experience of measuring consumers' attitudes show that you can normally expect about 75 per cent to 80 per cent to say that they are satisfied with a service, whatever it is. 46 per cent satisfaction is a very low figure' (Paragraph 198). The Committee itself registered a certain distaste and scepticism of peer group evaluation. This theme was reiterated later in the Report (Paragraph 526). 'It is clear that the BBC would place considerable weight on the annual number of Emmy and similar awards received, that is to say it would judge its "success" by its standing with its fellow-broadcasters. It is a moot point whether such an indicator would accord with the views of listeners and viewers as a measure of their degree of satisfaction.' The commissioned market research by NOP had also shown that 69 per cent had thought that the introduction of advertising would not reduce programme quality on the BBC, although the method of posing the question was queried by some opponents.

Finance and Costs
In looking at the issue of whether or not the BBC should take advertising on a broader basis, the Report claimed that the inflation of costs in broadcasting probably had its origin in the ITV side. Inevitably, the profits theoretically obtainable from a monopoly franchise in a large and prosperous region were shared between the programme contractors and the unions, with the taxpayers – the real freeholder of the franchised public asset – coming a poor third through the Levy. It was thought that even after its 1986 reform, the Levy system offered too little incentive to economise in costs, which might be inflated in order to reduce the net profit which was the tax base of the Levy.

The Committee also noted that the low yield of revenue from the Levy alongside the rapid growth of revenue of independent companies had been a matter of concern to the Public Accounts Committee. Table 2.10 of the Report showed that the yield from the Levy was £34 million in 1983 and £24 million in both 1984 and 1985 although net profits had risen from £64 million in 1983 to £82.6 million in 1985. Annual levy receipts and Net Advertising Revenue (1972–84) were depicted by a graph (fig. 4.1) showing a virtually flat line for the former and a steeply rising curve for the latter. The Committee commented that 'It is certainly true that the low yield is a consequence of the generous exemption allowed, particularly the exemption of foreign sales' (Paragraph 201). They attributed this to what they termed the 'comfortable duopoly' which was 'remarkable' in that 'it has been deliberately created as a duopoly, subject to extensive regulation, by Government itself ...' (Paragraph 185). They saw that the comfortable duopoly would be seriously threatened by the development of alternative means of programme delivery, including DBS, cable and video. They also believed that 'duopolists' do not have the same incentive, as exists among competing suppliers who serve their market directly, to be cost-conscious' (Paragraph 197). ITCA evidence had also claimed that the system of cross-subsidisation by the larger companies had added considerably to the costs of their operation and that all the ITV companies considered that they were overcharged for the cost of transmission of programmes which was an IBA monopoly (Paragraph 200). They did, however, warn that if ITV's profits were to fall as a result of the introduction of advertising on the BBC, the consequence would be reduced levy and tax receipts for the Exchequer.

However, in the longer term there were dangers that

> The past successes of IBA regulation and the ability of the authorities to maintain
> the duopoly until now may in the future create a fool's paradise ... the ability of
> the existing system to finance these programmes could wither away without any
> alternative source of provision of finance having been developed. (Paragraph 591)

Subsequently, in his preface to *Deregulation and the future of commercial television*
(The David Hume Institute 1989) Peacock claimed that the Committee saw the
BBC and the IBA as 'modern equivalents of the East India Company in the
eighteenth century on whom was conferred a state monopoly of British trade in
the East'.

Overseas Models
With a combination of visits overseas and commissioned research, the Committee
tried to ascertain whether any lessons might be learnt from broadcasting systems
in other countries. Each country presented a different picture. Australian broadcasting
consisted of three sectors: the national sector funded through government
appropriation; the commercial sector derived from advertising revenue, and the
public sector which was funded through a limited sponsorship of programmes and
government grants. In France, there was a firm trend away from public control
towards 'pluralisation'. Italy was in a 'state of confusion' mainly because of the
rapid takeover of most of the private sector television stations by Silvio Berlusconi.
The US was a fully commercial, market-dominated operation with only a small
element of public television and radio services. West Germany, based on a regional
pattern, had no purely commercial channels – although like most other European
countries, its state-owned channels were financed in part by advertising.
    Although the Committee admitted that

> In every country we encountered expressions of amazement – even from NBC
> and ABC in the United States – that the British should be thinking of changing
> their system, which is almost universally admired. (Paragraph 312)

they also warned that

> The rapidly changing scene in Western countries had impressed the Committee
> to the extent of putting considerable emphasis in its analysis and recommendations
> on a much wider range of methods of financing broadcasting with the consumer
> interest in mind than the extension of advertising alone which has been at the
> centre of British debate. (Paragraph 181)

Before reaching its more specific recommendations, the Committee outlined areas which, in the longer term, would implement its underlying beliefs in consumer sovereignty and freedom of expression.

Electronic Publishing and Subscription
The Committee claimed that the scarcity of the airwaves had contributed to maintaining the 'comfortable duopoly' but that this was only a transitional stage in the development of broadcasting which would ultimately become a form of electronic publishing. The Report noted that whereas the number of books produced was unlimited, the number of television channels had been restricted to four in the UK because of wavelength availability. These severe limits had reflected not just technology, but government policy in assigning spectrum space for other purposes and the doctrine of 'universal availability'.

Seeing unlimited electronic publishing as a desirable goal, the Report reiterated the vision delivered by Peter Jay, a close friend of Samuel Brittan, at the Church House seminar. They enthused about:

One particular form of subscription service put to us by a number of people, most notably Mr Peter Jay, was the method of pay-per-view in a deregulated system. Mr Jay called this a system of 'electronic publishing'. The argument runs that broadcasting is currently regulated because of the technical limitations of scarcity of airwaves. It is argued that if a fibre-optic national grid were installed in the country, which could be achieved either by public or private enterprise, then there would be scope for an unlimited number of channels and hence no regulation would be necessary, save that to maintain standards of taste and decency. Electronic publishing is founded on the proposition that communication is an activity which does not normally require government intervention ... Rather before the end of the century, Mr Jay argues, it would be possible using fibre-optic technology to create a grid connecting every household in the country, whereby the nation's viewers could simultaneously watch as many different programmes as the nation's readers can simultaneously read different books, magazines, newspapers etc. In other words, a television set (or radio) would be like a telephone in that the user would select for himself the connection he wanted. The number of 'channels' would become, if not infinite, at least indefinitely large – certainly as large as the number of receivers. (Paragraphs 477, 478 and 481)

Technology
This ideal of 'electronic publishing' depended, according to BT, on whether they were allowed to carry additional services, particularly cable TV, when the whole situation would change and it would be viable to use fibre-optic technology. The Committee had also been convinced by various experts that the technical problems of encoding signals had been solved.

Chapter 10 of the Report on 'Subscription', enhanced by large blue box diagrams, elaborated on the possibilities of scrambling and encryption which could be achieved by adapting the manufacture of television sets to incorporate a peritelevision socket. This was the opportunity for the Committee to realise their vision of enabling people to pay for what they wanted to see. Their dismissal of the BBC being financed by advertising rested on their basic hypothesis that, like the licence fee, it failed to provide a direct relationship between programme makers and the consumers, whereas with pay-per-view and subscription consumers could register their preferences directly. Although the BBC and IBA had acknowledged that technological developments meant that the broadcasting scene was inevitably a changing one, the emphasis, however, had been on the likely slowness and gradualism of any change. The Committee queried the timescale of such innovations and asserted that 'Governments would find that, like King Canute, they could not control the waves' (Paragraph 543).

Transitional Stages
Following the likely development of broadcasting in this context the Report outlined three stages for transition:

The Three Stages

Stage	Likely broadcasting developments	Policy regime
1	Satellite and cable develop, but most viewers continue to rely on BBC and ITV.	Indexation of BBC licence fee.
2	Proliferation of broadcasting systems, channels and payment methods.	Subscription replaces main part of licence fee.
3	Indefinite number of channels. Pay-per-programme or pay-per channel available. Technology reduces cost of multiplicity of outlets and of charging system.	Multiplicity of choice leading to full broadcasting market.

The report did, however, emphasise that a public service provision should continue through all three stages. It was also suggested that the task of monitoring developments should be undertaken by an appropriate Commons Select Committee, which could be Home Affairs or Trade and Industry.

Specific Recommendations

The Report had, it was generally agreed, provided a full, clear and original analysis of the economics of broadcasting in its first 123 pages. It had described how broadcasting had emerged and the environment in which it would continue to develop. The general problems of broadcasting finance and the specific nature of the 'comfortable duopoly' had been examined. Various options, implications and strategies had been discussed. The underlying value judgements on such issues as consumer sovereignty and freedom of expression had been explicitly stated and defended. Squeezed in between the hefty sixty-three pages of appendices which summarised the main evidence and research, the Committee delivered its recommendations. To some, they appeared almost more as an afterthought and not always directly linked or following from the more heady philosophical thought which preceded them. The eagerly awaited answer as to whether or not the Committee would recommend advertising on the BBC was, in the short term, 'No', although the carefully reasoned argument leading to this conclusion was probably lost by many commentators. As a measure of insulation of the BBC from political influence, it was recommended that, for the meantime, the licence fee should be indexed although it should be replaced by subscription in the longer term. To facilitate the introduction of a subscription system, all restrictions on pay-per-view and pay-per-programme should be removed and all new TV sets in the UK market should be required to have a peritelevision socket and associated equipment which would interface with a decoder to deal with encrypted signals (not later than 1 January 1988). Pre-publication censorship and vetting should be abolished, and broadcasting should be subject to the normal law of the land. There was also a case for a single transmission authority which would be responsible for transmitting all programmes over air and on uplinked DBS services. To increase competition and multiply sources of supply it was recommended that both the BBC and ITV should be required over a ten-year period to increase to not less than 40 per cent the proportion of programmes supplied by independent producers.

Implications for ITV
The Report which started out looking at the financing of the BBC, concluded with far more recommendations on ITV, which were to have a much greater and immediate effect on the commercial sector than on the BBC itself. However, if the Committee's analysis of the broadcasting market was accepted, it would have been impossible to have disentangled the issues arising from the funding of the BBC to those of ITV, particularly in relation to costs.

Once the Committee had established the interdependence of the cost structure of the BBC and the independent sector, the question was raised on how far improvements in the efficiency of the broadcasting system required them to look beyond the internal workings of the BBC towards the influences governing the cost structure of the independent sector.

It was admitted that the ITV companies could reasonably claim that the ITV system was regionally based, with fifteen individual regional contractors each operating as an individual company with its own premises, personnel and plant; that they spent more on local programmes than the BBC; and that they were in a risk business while the BBC had a guaranteed income and that non-renewal of a licence might mean that a large company might cease trading overnight. The Committee stated:

However, we received evidence from a number of contributors that the broadcasting industry was wasteful of resources through overmanning and self-indulgent working practices ... The BBC, it is claimed, faces a major difficulty because it is a 'price follower' of the ITV companies so far as a large part of its labour input is concerned. This is because the ITV companies, once granted the franchise, have considerable monopoly power, and make returns on capital employed, often far in excess of those in most industries. This together with the method of raising the levy does not encourage these companies to minimise costs. Their levels of remuneration are higher than is necessary to retain their professional labour force (i.e. monopoly profits are shared between employees and shareholders) and this puts pressure on the BBC to follow wage increases granted by the independent television companies. (Paragraphs 532–3)

Competitive Tendering

The biggest bombshell for ITV in the report was the recommendation that the ITV franchises should be put out to competitive tender, although this was decided on a split vote of 4:3 (with Chalmers, Hardie and Hetherington declining their support). There was a proviso that if the IBA decided to award a franchise to a contractor other than the highest bidder, it should be required to make a full, public and detailed statement of its reasons. Once bidders had satisfied the IBA that they could meet the minimum criteria, the franchise for each area should be awarded by a tendering system. The IBA could decide that a company offering a lower price was giving more 'value for money' in terms of a public service, and accordingly award a franchise to them. Thereafter the franchises should be awarded on a rolling review basis with a formal annual review of the contractor's performance by the Authority. If they were not meeting requirements, the IBA would issue a warning to this effect (the so-called 'yellow card' system); in the last resort, the franchise could be readvertised. Successful bidders would either pay the entry fee as a lump sum in advance, or in appropriate annual instalments over the franchise period. Since the monopoly rent would have been effectively eliminated there would be no further need for the Levy (see Chapter 7).

Public Service Broadcasting Council

In the longer term, the supply of 'public service' programmes (that is, those which the market might not deliver but which Peacock saw as an integral part of consumer welfare) might be provided by the setting up of a Public Service Broadcasting Council (PSBC), possibly financed by economic rents paid by ITV contractors as a result of the new tender system. The non-occupied night-time hours (1.00 a.m. to 6.00 a.m.) of both ITV and BBC television wavelengths were recommended to be sold for broadcasting purposes.

The main recommendation relating to Channel 4, which will be treated in greater detail in Volume 6 of *Independent Television in Britain*, was that it should be given the option of selling its own advertising time and no longer be funded by a subscription from the ITV companies.

Epilogue

The Committee ended the Report with an epilogue which stated that

> Although we would not claim canonical status for each and every one of our recommendations, they are designed to form part of a coherent strategy. It is not possible to pick and choose at will among them, without destroying the whole thrust.
>
> We have neither sought to 'get the BBC off the hook' nor to persecute it. If we had to summarise our conclusion by one slogan (which most of us would not want to do), it would be direct consumer choice rather than continuation of the licence fee. The arrangements we suggest for the latter, though designed to take the heat out of the subject, are designed to bridge the period before subscription becomes practicable. Eventually we hope to reach a position where the mystique is taken out of broadcasting and it becomes no more special than publishing became once the world became used to living with the printing press. (Paragraphs 710–11)

Reception of the Report

In his initial statement on the report in the House of Commons on 3 July 1986 Douglas Hurd, Home Secretary, described it as 'essentially a holding statement', while Gerald Kaufman, Shadow Home Secretary, said it 'should be put in the waste paper basket'.

Reporting on the press conference in Lancaster House, Raymond Snoddy (*Financial Times*, 4 July 1986) reported that Peacock was 'phlegmatic' about the report's ultimate fate but thought that: 'This report cannot be shelved because it raises issues that go far beyond the immediate interests of this Government.' Looking ahead, Snoddy commented that

> It may be at least a decade before it is known whether the Peacock report will become an historical curiosity – flawed by too much abstract thought undiluted by commonsense – or whether it will be seen as a visionary document that pointed towards a new age of broadcasting choice, independent of government interference.

Yorkshire TV issued a press release stating 'Leave well alone – that's the message from Yorkshire TV to the Peacock Report.' *The Economist* (5 July 1986) congratulated the Committee on doing 'a useful job because it has understood that the future of broadcasting will be decided not by committees, like itself, nor by governments, but by the galloping progress of technology'. *The Times* (3 September 1986) claimed that the genesis of the auctioning concept was 'David Owen telling the audience of "What the Papers Say" awards in February 1986 ... that the franchises should be awarded to the highest bidder'.

Peacock in Retrospective

IBA

Although Lord Thomson, IBA Chairman, had floated the idea of 'a better way' soon (see Chapter 1) after the contract awards in 1980, no 'better way' had been articulated or recommended, although a system of rolling franchises had been tentatively suggested. The view of at least one senior insider at the IBA at that time was that the Authority missed a great opportunity of seizing the high ground and staking out a future for itself. The IBA's failure to come up with a new means of awarding contracts meant that it was saddled with George Thomson's feeling that the way it had been done in 1980 was not the right way, but it had not really come up with a better one. There was a view with hindsight that the Authority might have gone for allowing takeovers. But having taken the stance that it did over Thames and Carlton, this was not an easy option. The IBA had laid itself open and lost the high ground to Peacock and government.

Although Lord Thomson was, personally as a fellow Scotsman and Chancellor of Heriot-Watt University, on friendly terms with Professor Peacock, he has attributed the concept of the auction to the political ideology of the inner Cabinet Committee and the failure of Peacock to grasp the full meaning of public service broadcasting.

> [Peacock] was fascinated by how you defined public service broadcasting. What did it really mean? Was it just a pious phrase? And that of course took him on to the fact that PSB was based on a public asset, a national asset, the frequency spectrum. It was a valuable asset and had all sorts of other possible uses. And why should so much of it be used for TV broadcasting? And shouldn't the people who want to use it for television broadcasting be forced to pay the market price for it in competition with other possible users? ... We kept trying to press that PSB was a concept in its own right and had its own value and he kept saying, what of the economics? In that sense it was a bit of a dialogue of the deaf.
>
> ... Behind the scenes, in a way that I didn't really know about, and maybe I should have known more about it, but the political barriers in this country are fairly high, but behind the Conservative scenes there was a group, for which I'm sure Alan Peacock was an academic part, Sam Brittan at the FT, Leon Brittan his brother who was the Home Office Minister for Broadcasting and Griffiths who were beavering away at an alternative concept.
>
> ... and Nigel Lawson, of course, if you look at his memoirs he claims the credit for it. He took a very simple sort of Treasury economic view about it and

regarded the public service values as being simply bogus. (Interview with Lord Thomson)

According to Shirley Littler, the IBA's contact and response to the Committee failed to persuade them that the status quo should be left unaltered:

I think George (Thomson) and John (Whitney) went and talked to them, John certainly was never very good on reporting back so one didn't really get any feedback, except when the report came it was obvious that whatever they'd said had cut no ice. Or cut very little ice. (Interview with Shirley Littler)

ITV

Like Thomson, Paul Fox (then Managing Director of Yorkshire TV) saw the power lying in the Cabinet Committee and was perhaps unwisely dismissive of Peacock himself:

You remember that report from the strange man from Scotland, the economist, Peacock. Douglas (Hurd) said Peacock was going to be put out to grass. And it wasn't. Because it was overturned inside cabinet ... In the end she [Thatcher] set up her committee and while Douglas was on it, the enemies of television sat on that, and the enemies were Lawson, Young and Tebbit. Solidly. And Douglas was outmanoeuvred and outnumbered. (Interview with Sir Paul Fox)

Christopher Bland (Chairman of LWT), however, laid the main blame for the recommendation for competitive tendering to the lack of perception and unity within the ITV companies:

I kidded myself that the government wouldn't introduce a bid process. I thought that it was a pretty loopy procedure; none of us believed they would go ahead with it. I think it was a Friday afternoon suggestion, that fitted a certain Thatcherite view of the world. It hadn't been thought through; the Peacock Committee, after all, was set up to look at the BBC, and it was ironic that it should have made its most radical changes in relation to the ITV system, changes that didn't improve programmes, and in the end did not maximise revenue. There were other ways of doing it, but I think ITV – and I must take my share of the blame for it – was not effectively led at the time. We didn't have the ear of politicians. Ian Trethowan wasn't well thought of by Mrs Thatcher. Neither was I. Neither was Granada; we didn't have much of a voice. And the IBA also wasn't taken as seriously as perhaps it should have been ... We didn't play to our strengths. We weren't united even against what one could now see as a common enemy. The threat wasn't perceived. Peacock was treated as a joke, even after he'd reported. (Interview with Sir Christopher Bland)

The complacency within ITV was also appreciated by Brian Tesler (then Managing Director of LWT) who confessed that initially:

> Of course there was shock. It seemed a crazy idea, how could it not? And we all thought, as the old regime had always done, that if we behaved well, we'd performed reasonably, produced worthwhile programmes, not frightened the horses in the street, that it made nonsense of the sole criteria for renewing a franchise or awarding a franchise being the amount of money that could be raised to apply for it, that made no sense at all. (Interview with Brian Tesler)

But with the wisdom of hindsight he admitted a decade later that:

> What Thatcher did and Peacock ... was marvellous for ITV actually because her anti-union attitude helped us break the union control of independent television. The argument that in dealing with the BBC we've got to deal with ITV first was a perfectly logical one. After all, if ITV was spending vast sums of money on this or that then the BBC had to match. So the thing to do was to reduce the cost of ITV: if you reduced the cost of ITV then the BBC doesn't have to spend so much in order to fight ITV on the same battlefield. Why were the costs of ITV so high? Well, because ITV was in the hands of the unions. There were too many people, and they were paid too much money. Get those right, get a leaner independent television with less waste and by definition we'll get a leaner, less wasteful BBC. (Ibid.)

Civil Service

Quentin Thomas, head of the broadcasting department in the Home Office, who had presided over the period of the Peacock Inquiry and was to remain until the publication of the White Paper on broadcasting in November 1988, recounted the influence of the Department of Trade and Industry, stemming from its interest in cable and satellite legislation:

> There was a very close interest in the period I was there, from the DTI and the Treasury, which was partly of institutional interest and partly reflected the personalities of the different ministers at the time. It started before I arrived because the cable legislation inevitably had a very strong telecommunications aspect and the DTI were positively evangelical in their support for the opportunities this new technology opened up and the implications it might have for the existing broadcasting system. Certainly under Nigel Lawson the Treasury took great interest, and I think you can see how this was played out was that the initial response to the Peacock Committee was one of profound disappointment from those bits of the government machine which approached the matter from an economic or free market point of view because it, in their terms, gave the wrong answer on advertising on the BBC. But when properly instructed, when Sam

Brittan got round to do a bit of lobbying, they came to see the virtues of the challenge to the ITV system. Some of this could be seen in terms of personalities of ministers. Some you could put in terms of the institutional personalities of the DTI. Probably the right way to look at it is that there was this interplay of interests. There were commercial interests; there was a view that the industrial opportunity of the country meant being at the forefront of the telecommunications developments and that if we were to be internationally competitive on these issues, we should jump on to satellites and so on. There were space industry interests, there were ideologues for free marketry all playing there. Later joined by another interest group, the independent producers who, for perhaps only a brief moment, could do no wrong because they represented at one and the same time, the attractions of the alternative society, wearing interesting shirts and so on and being at the forefront of artistic creativity as well as being prototypes for the Conservative dream of the entrepreneur starting a new business in his garage. And they combined both these things; they could do absolutely no wrong and when they said 25 per cent, of course, it was given to them on the instant ... But it always seemed to me there was a likelihood that there would be a concentration of power into fewer and fewer producers' hands and they would find it harder to sustain this double act. (Interview with Quentin Thomas)

Nevertheless, Thomas claims that such underlying trends and interplay of interests were reinforced by the coherence of the economic argument in the Peacock Report, although Peacock himself never tried to influence the outcome in public policy decisions.

You can give the Peacock Committee very full marks for intellectual coherence. When it analysed the advertising issue in relation to the BBC, it produced the answer which some of those who'd urged the thing to be set up, hadn't expected because they hadn't got as coherent a view of the economic arguments as the Peacock Committee did. At the same time it went on to give an equally coherent, but unexpected, view of what all this meant for ITV. And I think that sudden thrust towards the auctioning system (or whatever the right words for it are) was not a result of political pressure, but was unexpected and I think was almost an accident of putting Brittan and Peacock in a position where they could suddenly mount an argument which would command attention.

... I think (Peacock) made sure that they saw the point of it all and that they weren't misled by the initially disappointing dismissal of advertising on the BBC. I thought Professor Peacock adopted a rather purist and proper position and the Home Secretary was very clear about this. They then analysed the issue on the merits, in what I think was a very coherent and helpful way. Then having produced it he didn't see it as his job to go round proselytising. His job, in the public interest, was to go through the ritual of taking and analysing evidence, deliberating on it and producing an answer. And then it would be considered by the public, by government and so on. And I think he played that hand very properly. I think it's a report which will come to be seen to have made a very great contribution. Some people will disagree with the results and others will say it was right or inevitable. But I think it was a very serious piece of work. (Ibid.)

From his more objective civil service perspective Quentin Thomas also appreciated the deeper problem of reconciling the value of public service broadcasting with the realities of the new technological opportunities:

The broadcasting world's quite a fevered incestuous one. Everyone talks to everyone else and gets frightfully excited, lots of gossip and things come to acquire mythological status. My general feeling about all that is that's greatly exaggerated this incident or that meeting whatever. What was happening, I think, is that people were grappling with these underlying realities that you'd got public service broadcasting, it was a great success ... everyone saw the value of public service broadcasting, everyone wanted to sustain its qualities and its merits and its achievements, but they were grappling with a situation where all that was inevitably under pressure because of new technological and commercial opportunities. So the question is 'how do you manage a transition?' And I think that's really what was going on ... But the question is 'how can it be sustained, how long can it be sustained and how do you manage the transition?' (Ibid.)

Professor Peacock
When interviewed for the purposes of this book, ten years after the publication of his report, Professor Sir Alan Peacock recounted various aspects of the Committee. On the selection of members he said that he was 'insistent that this was a committee which was going to have to deal with economic questions and, therefore, as chairman, I would welcome people on the committee who had an interest in the economics of them'. Although he remembers Leon Brittan, brother of Samuel as being very sensitive about his brother being proposed, Peacock thought that 'he was just the sort of political economist in the classical mould that was required'.

Talking about 'The Comfortable Duopoly' and the apparent surprise of both the BBC and the independent companies in discussing changes he saw it as:

... something you often see in business where you have a duopolistic or oligopolistic situation. You don't want to have intruders, you like to have comparative peace; the quiet life. And you'd rather ignore what's going on outside. But we couldn't, as a committee, ignore that. All the evidence suggested that broadcasting was going to go through very rapid technological change. As we had made the initial judgement that broadcasting is not specifically for broadcasters, but for viewers and listeners, we had to take that into account. (Interview with Professor Sir Alan Peacock)

He did, however, stress that 'we were very careful in saying that technological forecasting is a mug's game. If there's anything, looking back, which we did underestimate it was the growth of DBS.'

Despite some fears that the Committee had been set up primarily to recommend extraction of more money for the Treasury, Peacock stated that 'We had no evidence from the Treasury, we asked them to give evidence. We wanted their views on the licence fee. I wrote a letter saying "Do you regard it as a tax?" In the end I got no reply. They were very determined – but this is a very well known Treasury strategy – to keep out of it.' But he added: 'They pounce after it's all over. As no government is obliged to accept anything that a Committee or Commission recommends anyway, they can take out of its proposals what suits them. What we were concerned about was not getting the money for the Treasury but how our financial proposals supported the consumer interest.'

Comparing the evidence and meetings with the BBC and the independent companies, Peacock recounted the BBC's 'strong propagandistic flavour which it always had and which is immediately suspect to crabby economists like myself'. He found that the BBC concentrated on the case against any kind of change in funding with the underlying message 'We want to show that people are satisfied with what we're doing. The licence fee is a wonderful thing.' He also recalls that in all their discussions with the BBC, the Committee never met the governors, except the Chairman.

The BBC had also submitted studies on advertising and broadcasting by Professor Andrew Ehrenberg and Patrick Barwise of the London Business School which he found 'interesting, but seemed to us not to be getting to the central issue'. In contrast, he found that the independent sector 'as soon as they saw what we were going to do, they said "Right. We have to offer proof of our contentions. We've got to hire good people, to give serious study to say what will happen if advertising is taken by the BBC." They were on to this very much more quickly than the BBC. They had Alan Budd as consultant who's an excellent economist and very good in his presentation ... And we had every confidence in his work.'

Speaking about the Committee's split on the recommendation for competitive tendering, Peacock said 'We didn't agree entirely about this, but it was a perfectly amicable disagreement ... At least what we'd agreed was that something ought to be done to make this a logical process.'

For those who unfairly regard Peacock as the architect of a crude auctioning system, he stressed that:

We were also agreed – and this is very important, I think – that it could not be based solely on the highest bid; there had to be a quality threshold. How that was to operate was not explored in detail. Later on, I had quite a long discussion with David Mellor about this question ... I presented a system by which there was a trade off between the bid and quality. In other words, it was how high you jumped over Becher's Brook as well as whether you jumped over it at all, and that you could have some kind of weighting system ... But in the end this proposal was rejected. The government said 'No. There's a threshold; you get over Becher's Brook; it doesn't matter how high you jump, and then after that it's the bid.' (Interview with Professor Sir Alan Peacock)

After Peacock

Although *Broadcast* (4 July 1986) had described Peacock's proposals for tendering as 'a dead duck' and the following week (11 July 1986) as 'the first Peacock to end up in a pigeon hole', the ITV companies were left with the problem of how to respond to the recommendation for the competitive tendering of the ITV contracts.

Professor Alan Budd, whose economic analysis of advertising revenue had been a major contribution to ITCA's evidence to the Committee, wrote a letter to David Shaw (General Secretary at the ITCA) accompanying a further report on 'Tendering for the ITV franchises'. He expressed his doubts on the problems facing the companies:

I must confess that I have found writing this report slightly difficult. The reason why economists would approve is that they recognise that television franchises ... are extremely valuable and it is reasonable for the government to try to extract monopoly rents. Economists also recognise that monopoly rents tend to get shared with employees ... There is thus a policy dilemma. We can keep the present system which produces excellent television and gives some of the companies rather a comfortable life or we can move to tendering which would reduce the quality of the programmes and the comfort of the companies ... The Peacock Committee wants to shake up the BBC but believes it can only do this by putting pressure on the independent companies.

His letter concluded:

It is hopelessly optimistic to believe that a single system of tendering for franchises, even if it is accompanied by detailed specifications, could at the same time increase government revenue, improve the efficient allocation of resources and maintain programme quality. (Letter from Professor Alan Budd to General Secretary, ITCA, 5 September 1986)

Meanwhile at the Edinburgh Television Festival in August 1986 the independent production companies, organised by John Woodward and assisted by Michael Darlow, had stepped up their pressure for the 25% Campaign to allow more access by independents, although the target quota was less than the 40 per cent recommended by Peacock.

Douglas Hurd, the Home Secretary, in a speech to the Royal Television Society, dispelled any ideas that he had 'shelved' the Report's recommendations. He prefaced the speech by saying: 'The Members of the Committee would I think agree that they set an agenda rather than worked out full conclusions', but then he warned:

> When I gave a cautious welcome to the Peacock Report in the House of Commons, my cautious words of appreciation were handled by the media with characteristic scepticism. When I said that we intended to study the Committee's conclusions with great care this was treated as a few polite words uttered by the graveside as the coffin was lowered out of sight. Perhaps it is now clear that that was a wrong impression and that we are now doing exactly what I undertook. We are going through the Peacock analysis and Peacock recommendations with great thoroughness precisely because they provide a starting point of the new decisions which we believe before long will be necessary. (Speech by the Home Secretary to RTS Symposium, 8 November 1986, in RTS Journal *Television*, January/February 1987)

He confirmed that the government was committed to producing a Green Paper on radio and that a technical study was being set up to establish the practical possibilities of pay-per-view to fulfil Peacock's philosophy of consumer choice which 'fits well into the general approach of this government'. In the House of Commons debate on the Peacock Report on 20 November 1986 Hurd reiterated that the days of the status quo were numbered.

At a Home Office/ITCA meeting on 22 December 1986, Hurd told the ITCA representatives that among his colleagues 'there was a desire to loosen up the system a bit' although he admitted that he was not keen on the IBA's 'yellow card' option as he thought it would be too easy to exclude outsiders and deny new talent. The meeting was attended by David Mellor (Minister of State), Wilfred Hyde (Deputy Secretary), Quentin Thomas (Under-Secretary) and Edward Bickham (political adviser to the Home Secretary who was later to work for BSB). ITCA members consisted of David McCall (Chairman of ITCA Council), Bill Brown (STV), David Plowright (Granada) and David Shaw (General Secretary, ITCA).

Paving the Way

Subscription Studies

Two studies on deregulation and the feasibility of subscription were commissioned from Communications Studies and Planning International (CSP), a consultancy specialising in telecommunications, which was subsequently acquired and incorporated into another consultancy, Booz Allen Hamilton. The first of these studies, commissioned by the DTI, was published in July 1987 (*Deregulation of the radio spectrum in the UK*, HMSO, 1987). It looked at the ways in which market forces might supplement, or replace, existing administrative procedures for radio spectrum management in the UK and recommended a measure of deregulation. This was followed by a second study, commissioned by the Home Office, which explored the recommendations of the Peacock Committee on consumer payment for television services, by a detailed assessment of the technical feasibility of and economic justification for subscription television. The final report, published in July 1987, recommended additional new pay-TV services although these should not replace public broadcast television channels financed by either the licence fee or advertising revenue (*Subscription television: a study for the Home Office*, HMSO, 1987).

Extension of ITV Contracts

To pave the way for the introduction of changes to the award of ITV contracts, and to give the government more time for consideration of the franchise system, amendment legislation to the Broadcasting Act 1981 was published on 9 April 1987. The maximum period of the current contracts between the IBA and the ITV companies was extended. Instead of expiring on 31 December 1989, the ITV contracts would now continue until 31 December 1992.

Radio Green Paper

The Peacock Report had devoted very little space to the financing of radio and, it was also rumoured, very little time in discussing the subject. The main recommendation was that the BBC should have the option to privatise Radios 1, 2 and local radio in whole or in part and that the IBA regulation of commercial radio should be replaced by a looser regime. Five members of the Committee went further by recommending that Radio 1 and Radio 2 should be privatised and financed by advertising and that, subject to the government's existing commitments to community radio, any further radio frequencies becoming available should be auctioned to the highest bidder. Judith Chalmers and Alastair Hetherington were 'unable to support this recommendation' since they believed 'that it would seriously damage the residual BBC radio services, would indirectly harm the BBC's overseas services, and would cripple a number of ILR services'. However, the two did concur with the recommendation that the IBA's regulation should be replaced by a looser regime (Paragraph 644).

Well ahead of the White Paper, published in November 1988, which was mainly concerned with television, the government published a Green Paper on radio outlining the opportunities presented by additional spectrum and technological developments, setting out the future of sound broadcasting and making a case for lighter regulation (Home Office, *Radio: choices and opportunities: a consultative document* (Cmnd 92), HMSO, 1987).

These proposals were ultimately to result in the separation of the radio and television responsibilities of the IBA which had been brought together by the Sound Broadcasting Act 1972. The Broadcasting Act 1990 implemented the main proposals of the 1987 Green Paper on radio and provided for the establishment of a Radio Authority on 1 January 1991 to replace the IBA as the regulator of commercial radio (ILR). The separation of regulation for radio and television was not wholly unwelcome to the IBA. On the financial side, Peter Rogers (IBA Director of Finance) described the commercial radio industry as having various 'feasts and famines' which, together with conflicting views on how regulatory costs should be allocated between radio and television, put 'considerable pressure' on IBA resources (Interview with Peter Rogers). Shirley Littler (then IBA Director of Administration) was also critical of the rolling contract system for ILR which

> created a huge burden of work on the Authority – all these interviews. And I'm going to be very rude about the radio interviews because I sat through one of them and I said never again will I waste my time sitting through these things ... It never looked to me to be a competent way of awarding a contract ... It was too detailed ... and a huge burden of work on everybody ... (Interview with Shirley Littler)

The Broadcasting Standards Council (BSC)
The Conservative government, under Margaret Thatcher, was returned in the General Election on 11 June 1987. Although the Conservative Election manifesto had included proposals for a new Broadcasting Bill to 'enable the broadcasters to take full advantage of the opportunities presented by technological advances and to broaden the choice of viewing and listening' it had also promised that there would be 'stronger and more effective arrangements' to reflect an alleged public concern over the portrayal of sex and violence on television, and to remove the exemption of broadcasters from the Obscene Publications Act 1959.

On 7 October 1987, Douglas Hurd (Home Secretary) announced plans for the establishment of a Broadcasting Standards Council (BSC). The BSC started operating on a non-statutory basis after the appointment of its first Chairman, Sir William Rees-Mogg, on 16 May 1988, with the possibility of the introduction of legislation to put it on a statutory basis. Its remit was to draw up a code on standards of taste, decency, and the portrayal of sex and violence in television and radio programmes received in the UK, to monitor programme standards in these areas, to consider complaints and to initiate research into public attitudes.

David Glencross (then IBA Director of Television) recalled the proposal for the BSC as:

> Very much driven by Margaret Thatcher ... she had received the message, I think, from Mary Whitehouse and others that an instrument of this kind was necessary. In fact, events show that the BSC has had no effect on any sort of decisions made by broadcasters. But it's a useful sop ... It was a political reality. (Interview with David Glencross)

Colin Shaw, who had previously been Secretary to the BBC, IBA Director of Television and Director of the ITCA Programme Planning Secretariat, was appointed

Director of the BSC in November 1988 although he remembered that after the announcement of the government's intention to set up the BSC 'I actually wrote a piece ... saying what a dreadful idea it was.' After Rees-Mogg was appointed Chairman, head-hunters approached Shaw amongst others, to apply as Director. Rees-Mogg was rather desperate to get somebody who would carry conviction with the broadcasters and Shaw told him that 'the only thing that would give it any kind of respectability would be if it had spent a lot of money on research'.

After the Broadcasting Act 1990 established the BSC as a statutory body, a code was produced in 1990 and complaints were handled from 1991. According to Shaw 'it was just a question of going softly and catching whatever monkeys you could catch'. Although the BSC received a considerable amount of flak and ridicule from certain programme makers and the media, Shaw commented, in 1995, 'I think people would like to see us out of the way but I don't think we're going to go away ... There'll be a greater emphasis on consumerism, which I would welcome anyway' (Interview with Colin Shaw).

Political Climate

The political climate at the time of the Peacock Inquiry under Margaret Thatcher's premiership has been vividly described by Andrew Marr in *Ruling Britannia – the Failure and Future of British Democracy* (Michael Joseph, 1995):

> For the first five or six years of her rule she and her supporters really did seem to be outsiders who had seized control of the system. But as the eighties progressed, the outsiders and mavericks hardened and solidified into a new establishment clique. The radical businessmen who had chafed at Wilsonian Britain became the Downing Street trusties of Thatcherite Britain. There were the advisers, informal and sometimes formal: Sir John Hoskyns of the Burton Group, Number Ten Policy Unit and the Institute of Directors; Lord (Jeffrey) Sterling of P&O and the Department of Trade and Industry; Lord (Derek) Rayner of Marks and Spencer and the Prime Minister's Efficiency Unit. Below them, the pamphleteers and ideologues of the Centre for Policy Studies, the Adam Smith Institute and the Institute of Economic Affairs found themselves enjoying unparalleled access to ministers, including the Prime Minister ... In Margaret Thatcher's famous phrase, they were all 'one of us'; but what started as a guerilla raiding-party against the corporate state eventually aged and spread into an auxiliary state, an influence-network run exclusively through Downing Street and barely connected to the official civil service or the Commons.

Cabinet Committee
The setting up of the Cabinet Committee, in response to the Peacock Report, is described by Nigel Lawson (then Chancellor of the Exchequer) in his autobiography. In the section on what he calls the 'Television Interlude', he wrote:

Faced with the need to devise a coherent Government response to both the Peacock Report and the enormous technical possibilities that were opening up, which clearly required a wholly new statutory framework, Margaret (Thatcher) set up a Cabinet Committee on broadcasting on which I served, and which she chaired. It was not the most cost-effective way of spending time. Broadcasting was a subject on which Margaret held a great many firm views and prejudices, which she would air at some length, irrespective of whether this had any bearing on the Committee's pressing need to reach decisions on a number of complex and critical issues. Indeed, her Chairmanship became so discursive, and hence indecisive, that, with her full knowledge and consent, I took to chairing smaller meetings between the meetings of the main committee, without which it was hard to see how any decisions would ever have been taken. At these smaller meetings, I would be assisted by the Treasury official who specialised in this area, but the key participants were the two Ministers with the main departmental interest in broadcasting: Douglas Hurd, then Home Secretary, and David Young, then Trade and Industry Secretary – each of them assisted by one senior official. (*The view from No. 11: the memoirs of a Tory radical*, Bantam Press, 1992)

Lawson recounts how discussion on the basis of the award of the ITV franchises occupied many hours of the Committee's time. There was general dissatisfaction with the old system of 'entirely subjective and discretionary decisions, qualified only by inertia, and a strong disposition to follow Peacock's (majority) advice and include an auction element in the process. The tricky question was precisely where and how the balance should be struck.'

Although Lawson no longer held office by the time the Broadcasting Bill was enacted he deplored the gap between the Cabinet Committee's free market beliefs and the amendments introduced into the Broadcasting Bill which he attributed to Home Office Ministers, responsible for the Bill's passage, who 'showed little disposition to resist'. He found that the 'semi-auction' of the ITV franchises 'proved to have an unusually high farce content' which 'reflected partly defects in the Bill as originally published and, to a limited extent, deficiencies in the way it was implemented by the new Independent Television Commission'.

Cambridge Convention (September 1987)

The clash between traditional public service values and the new free market beliefs was publicly aired at the biennial Cambridge Convention, organised by the Royal Television Society, which was held on 18 September 1987 three days before the Downing Street Seminar to which Margaret Thatcher had invited leading broadcasting interests.

The keynote speech was given by Douglas Hurd, Home Secretary. Paul Fox (President of the RTS) introduced Hurd by reminding him that when he addressed the Convention in 1985 Hurd had said 'precisely, not a lot' and that Fox was looking for 'improved output' on this second outing. Fox reminded the Home Secretary:

At a time when major changes are debated endlessly, it behoves us to remember that programme-making is our true business. If we lose our ability to make good programmes; if we toss out the good and tarnish our schedules with the shoddy, then we shall lose the regard of those who gave us the freedom to broadcast. It is time we got back to the essentials: making programmes for our viewers. (RTS Journal *Television,*November/December 1987)

According to *Television*, Fox's rallying introduction cut little ice with Hurd who although

confident and assured was to remain his urbane self, making no announcements, stirring no particular brew. He ventured a tentative opinion here, reviewed with discretion some aspect of affairs there. No pledges either. The reason, it transpired for this failure to embrace 'glasnost' was that the PM herself had decided to hold a seminar on the subject of television at Downing Street the following Monday. Nothing could be said on Friday that might pre-empt an announcement on the Monday after the leaders of industry and commerce had delivered of themselves in person at the feet of the Prime Minister. So another thin speech from the Home Secretary with just the odd coded message and dismissive phrase.

Hurd, however, did manage to take a swipe at the old-style public service broadcasters, epitomised by Sir Denis Forman's Dimbleby Lecture which had been broadcast on 15 July (*British Television: Who are the masters now?*, BBC Books, 1987). He thought that the lecture had been a diversion

because it led us wittily away from what I see as the main challenge now facing us: which is to strengthen the position of the viewer as the broadcasting environment changes. We need a framework which will accommodate these changes and at the same time ensure, for the viewer, high programme standards, a wide range of choice and value for money. Denis Forman answered his question – Who are the masters now? – by talking about politicians, the broadcasting authorities, international media mercenaries and television producers. There were, to be fair, references at the beginning and end, like the nub ends of a loaf, to the viewer, but am I being too unfair in saying that the lecture gave the impression that the viewer was seen as a powerless and passive recipient of what others choose to give him? To my mind this is topsy turvy.

Ironically, Hurd concluded, like Fox, that

broadcasting is about programmes, and programmes are for viewers. The job of broadcasting policy is to ensure that the individual viewer, as consumer, citizen and taxpayer, gets the best service that broadcasters are able to provide.

Looking back, eight years later, Paul Fox saw Douglas Hurd as:

Amenable, a very super guy to deal with, did his thing at Cambridge and chatted amiably and all that. But in the end Douglas was really only passing through and everyone knew he was on his way, passing through to some other job. He didn't really want the Home Office ... You really felt that his heart wasn't totally in it. What's more I think his relationship with her wasn't all that wonderful – not like Willie's (Whitelaw) was. (Interview with Sir Paul Fox)

The Downing Street Seminar
According to Lawson, it was Margaret Thatcher's decision to hold a seminar on 21 September 1987 to assist the Cabinet Committee in its deliberations and to demonstrate the government's willingness to listen and learn. It was held at Number 12, followed by a lunch at Number 10, Downing Street.

At the seminar the government was represented by Margaret Thatcher (Prime Minster), Lord Young (Secretary of State for Trade and Industry), Douglas Hurd (Home Secretary) and Tim Renton (Minister of State, Home Office).

They were boosted by advisers from 10 Downing Street, including Professor Brian Griffiths (Head of the Policy Unit), Bernard Ingham (Thatcher's press secretary), Nigel Wicks and David Norgrove, and the DTI adviser Sir Jeffrey Sterling (Chairman, P&O). Guests invited from ITV were Sir Ian Trethowan (Chairman, Thames Television), David McCall (Chief Executive, Anglia TV), Bill Brown (Chairman, STV) and David Nicholas (Editor and Chief Executive, ITN). Channel 4 was represented by Jeremy Isaacs (Chief Executive) and the IBA by John Whitney (Director General). Other interests included David Graham (Executive Producer, Diverse Production), Andy Birchall (Chief Executive, Premiere) and Michael Darlow (Head of Negotiations for the Independent Access Steering Committee) from the independents and R.W. Johnson (Marketing Services Director, Procter & Gamble) for the advertising sector. Cable and satellite were represented by Richard Hooper (Joint MD, Superchannel), Nicolas Mellersh (Director, Cable TV Association), Graham Grist (British Satellite Broadcasting) and John Jackson (Chairman, TV Services International). The BBC presence consisted of John Birt (Deputy Director General) and Michael Grade (Director of Programmes, Television). The consultant, Charles Jonscher (Vice President, Booz Allen Hamilton Int. (UK), who had been involved in the Home Office study on subscription television was also there and Michael Green (Chairman, Carlton Communications) who had failed in 1985 to take over Thames in a bid for the London weekday contract (see Chapter 7). Professor (by this time Sir) Alan Peacock was present to talk about 'The Peacock Report 14 months later'.

Margaret Thatcher introduced the seminar by saying that its purpose was to consult members of the industry and other experts with a view to the government taking informed decisions in three areas. These were the prospects for the future of broadcasting in the light of accelerating developments; what changes should be made in response to the recommendations of the Peacock Report and what new arrangements should be made in the light of public concern about indecency and violence on television.

Professor Peacock reiterated his main theme of 'consumer sovereignty' but stressed that some elements of public service broadcasting could not survive without public funding. He expressed regret that the government had not yet commented on his proposals for a Public Service Broadcasting Council (PSBC). Richard Hooper (joint MD of Superchannel) then spoke on 'The Three T's – Television, Technology and Thatcherism'. He claimed that the key issues were political, commercial and regulatory, not technological. In his view, technological constraints were often a disguise for the perpetuation of the status quo by special interest groups. He regarded spectrum scarcity as a myth. Summing up this part of the seminar, Margaret Thatcher said that she would regret it if there was a sharp division of opinion between those with vested interests and those without. If the Conservative government had not supported competition in the 1950s there would have been no ITV system.

The next slot was filled by Dr Charles Jonscher on the financing of additional programme services. He summarised the findings of his study for the Home Office on subscription television. These showed that there was a large untapped demand for new premium programme services matched by a willingness of consumers to pay. The problem was that existing methods of payment – the licence fee and advertising – were not able to provide the key funds necessary to meet the high costs of premium programming. The key was subscription technology, coupled with arrangements to allow wider entry into the broadcasting market by freeing up spectrum allocation and removing other regulatory barriers. The independent producer, David Graham, speaking on 'Increasing efficiency and competition in the duopoly' argued that increasing competition did not depend upon new technology. What was required was to loosen up the existing duopoly. There was a shortage of popular drama and entertainment programmes on BBC and ITV because they had become hidebound in their attitudes. It was important to introduce competition in programme supply, as existed in the USA, where networks bought most of their programmes from independent production houses. He also questioned the value of the regional ITV system, which he did not believe accorded with people's sense of their geographical identity, which was more locally orientated. He envisaged ITV as a national channel with more localised channels provided by the new technologies.

Summing up this part of the discussion, Margaret Thatcher said that she was concerned that the monopoly powers of the broadcasters and what were effectively subsidies from public funds, led to excessive pay demands and restrictive practices on the part of the unions. This held back new developments and acted against the interests of the consumer. These seemed to be the central reasons for seeking to increase competition within the industry. Interestingly, the official record of the seminar did not refer to the famous phrase 'television the last bastion of restrictive practices'.

The flag for the existing public service broadcasters was waved by Michael Grade (BBC), Jeremy Isaacs (Channel 4) and John Whitney (IBA). Grade argued that the existing services should not fear the future since US experience had shown that while new technology might catch about 30 per cent of the market, 70 per cent would remain with the major networks, for reasons of consumer loyalty, equipment cost and the nature of the service which the networks provided. He saw the future role of the BBC and ITV as providing British programmes for British consumers and for export. He believed that universal reception was an important criterion for the existing services, although it had no place for new services.

Isaacs tackled the controversial concept of 'Public Service Broadcasting' head-on. He agreed fully with the argument that broadcasting existed to serve the interests of its audience. In fact the arrangements for British broadcasting acted like a highly sophisticated market catering for a wide variety of needs and interests. It had a wider variety of programming than any other television service in the world. Although the Peacock Report had appeared to recognise this, it had then set about dismantling all the arrangements that brought it about, finally restoring the virtues of public service broadcasting by means of the government-funded Public Service Broadcasting Council. He could not see the logic. The issue for politicians was to add to what we already had. In particular this would meet the problem of the advertisers, which he recognised was acute. In the future the ITV companies would find themselves under pressure to go downmarket and would come to resent their public service obligations as they saw their profits squeezed by new competition. He did not think a Public Service Broadcasting Council would work since it would be swamped with applications, and a huge bureaucracy would be required to reach decisions. Only a small proportion of the finance would end up in programme making and there would be political difficulties about the funding of news and current affairs.

John Whitney concluded the presentations, speaking about the 'Regulation of programme content'. Summing up this part of the discussion, Margaret Thatcher said that television was special because it was watched in the sitting room. Some people watched so much of it that there was a danger that they would get life itself out of perspective. Standards on television had an effect on society as a whole, and therefore was a matter of proper public interest for the government (Official Record of the PM's seminar on Broadcasting, 21 September 1987).

Eyewitness Accounts
Nigel Lawson, who was a key member of the Cabinet Committee for whose benefit the Downing Street seminar had been organised, remembers the occasion as generating 'neither heat nor (despite one or two eloquent contributions) light; merely the deafening sound of axes being ground' (*The view from No. 11: the memoirs of a Tory radical,* Bantam Press, 1992).

As a first-hand spectator of the seminar, Bill Brown (Chairman, STV) remembered Thatcher's humiliating treatment of Lawson:

Lawson bustled in at one minute past nine. And Thatcher said in front of this entire group 'Always the same, Nigel, the boy who lives nearest school is always last'. And Lawson, to his credit, completely ignored her. He didn't say, sorry, Prime Minister or ho-ho-ho, he totally ignored her. Got his papers out as if to say, she always says things like that to me. I just ignore them. (Interview with Bill Brown)

But the most vivid recollection of most of the participants was the inadequacy of John Whitney's contribution and the presence of Michael Green (Chairman, Carlton Communications) despite the fact that he was not an official speaker.

John Whitney had suffered the double disadvantage of speaking last before a prime minister not renowned for her patience at formal presentations, representing a regulator for whose performance she had scant respect. The situation would have unnerved more politically robust figures. His colleagues felt the Downing Street seminar was not Whitney's finest hour. When interviewed eight years later, Bill Brown remembered that 'one of the most distressing things about the morning was John Whitney's performance'. David Nicholas (Editor and Chief Executive, ITN) also regretted the fact that although Whitney 'was a free market person he gave the mark one bureaucrat's paper. And it was after that that somebody said, "Will he get a knighthood?" And somebody said "He'll be lucky if she lets him remain a mister".' David McCall of Anglia also reckoned that Whitney 'blew it' (Interviews).

John Whitney himself agreed that it was a 'terrible' and 'disastrous' occasion but attributed his difficulties to the:

Deeply riven divides within the IBA, which simply could provide no guidance ... There was no line or brief that we were able to form together over the future of regulation ... The result was that it was a black hole as far as I was concerned. It was terrible. Not helped [that I was] nearly run over by a cyclist on my way there, which unsettled me. It did, it actually gave me a terrible shock, but that should not be in anyway used in mitigation of a disastrous occasion. (Interview with John Whitney)

Michael Green (Chairman, Carlton Communications) had already had access to government at a high policy level. He has recalled his contacts at this time:

David Wolfson (now Lord Wolfson of Sunningdale), who is a close friend of mine, was chief of staff at 10 Downing Street. And I had other contacts. I did speak to Mrs Thatcher on broadcasting, because it's a subject that I was very interested in and I had the opportunity to do so. I had meetings with Brian Griffiths and with civil servants. I gave my views directly to the Prime Minster as to what

I thought could and should happen to the television industry in the UK. I don't think that I had any significant influence. (Interview with Michael Green)

More specifically, at the seminar, he remembered that:

I did stand up and say that we have been trying to get in to mainstream broadcasting. We were larger in financial terms than any existing television station in the UK. We were a well constituted British public company with ambitions to expand. The status quo was nonsense and she recognised that very quickly. She used the analogy of British Airways wanting to build good strong British companies that could compete internationally. She wanted the rules changed to allow this to happen. (Interview with Michael Green)

Bill Brown's recollection of Michael Green's contribution to the seminar was that:

The gist of what he said was 'I have built a £600 million business related to broadcasting, but I am still an outsider. What do I have to do to become an insider?' Of course, you could see she was beaming at that; that was just exactly what she wanted to hear. I remember, after lunch, as we were leaving, I looked over and there were Michael Green and David Young in a corner, smiling to each other and chatting away and, I thought, this man has got a major inside track. So that was the occasion when she said, of course, independent television is the last bastion of restrictive practices, except of course for the Royal Opera House, Mr Isaacs. It was not a good day for the established broadcasters and for ITV in particular. But she came with entirely preconceived ideas. She wasn't open to any kind of persuasion. (Interview with Bill Brown)

In assessing the wider significance of the Downing Street seminar, Green reserved a measure of scepticism:

Mrs Thatcher had decided to take a certain line on a certain issue and that was it. I think the Downing Street meeting thing was important. There were presentations from all sorts of people. I remember Richard Hooper making an excellent presentation. He produced a piece of cable out of his pocket which was very dramatic but this reminded me that being a good presenter did not mean your thesis was right. In fact what happened to Superchannel proved he was wrong. There was no appetite for pan-European advertising. But he did present extremely well. I think the meeting mattered for taking place rather than its conclusions. It was a defining moment ... But I don't remember leaving Downing Street thinking great I've had a meeting where something very relevant has been decided and the future of broadcasting is now taking a different route. It was not. (Interview with Michael Green)

From the perspective of the ITV companies, David McCall remembers that:

There was a lot of sniping at the ITV companies. It was a series of papers, questions and answers. Margaret Thatcher being provocative and picking you up. We said bits and pieces but we weren't delivering papers. There was, of course, an anti-ITV thing from most people ... We'd no allies in there and we didn't get a set piece ... For me, Downing Street was an experience but I don't think it was a defining moment. (Interview with David McCall)

In her memoirs *The Downing Street Years* (HarperCollins, 1993) recalling the Downing Street seminar, Mrs Thatcher omits any reference to the 'Last bastion of restrictive practices' but recounts the 'dim view by some of those present' of the decision to set up a Broadcasting Standards Council and to remove the exemption of broadcasters from the provisions of the Obscene Publications Act. She recalls that 'I was entirely unrepentant. I said that they must remember that television was special because it was watched in the family's sitting-room. Standards on television had an effect on society as a whole and were therefore a matter of proper public interest for the Government.'

Political Personalities

Margaret Thatcher
Reading further into *The Downing Street Years* it is apparent that Mrs Thatcher had a distaste for the attitudes of the broadcasting sector and other professions:

Broadcasting was one of a number of areas – the professions such as teaching, medicine and the law were others – in which special pleading by powerful interest groups was disguised as high-minded commitment to some greater good ... Attempts to break the powerful duopoly which the BBC and ITV had achieved – which encouraged restrictive practices, increased costs and kept out talent – were decried as threatening the 'quality of broadcasting'.

Thatcher deplored the Home Office's alleged support of the broadcasters: 'The idea that a small clique of broadcasting professionals always knew what was best and that they should be more or less immune from criticism was not one I could accept. Unfortunately, in the Home Office, the broadcasters often found a ready advocate.' She also was sceptical about the concept of 'public service broadcasting' which 'was the kernel of what the broadcasting oligopolists claimed to be defending. Unfortunately, when subject to closer inspection that kernel began rapidly to disintegrate.' She found it a 'somewhat nebulous and increasingly outdated theory'. She also doubted whether the output matched the ideals: 'BBC1 and ITV ran programmes that were increasingly indistinguishable from commercial programming in market systems – soap operas, sport, game shows and made-for-TV films. To use Benthamite language, the public broadcasters were claiming the rights of poetry but providing us with pushpin.'

ITV's failure to understand the political realities of Thatcher's reign has been described by Andy Allan (Director of Programmes, Central):

> The reality is that ITV was an industry that came late to an understanding of what Thatcher's Britain had created. And it had to be led, I think, kicking and screaming into proper reform. And it was not a trailblazer. It actually followed the mood of the country. The claim that it was the 'last bastion of restrictive practices' may have been a bit harsh, but if it wasn't the last, it was one of the latest. (Interview with Andy Allan)

The outward expression of this tension and lack of understanding had been apparent at a much earlier meeting with Thatcher at Knighton House (ITCA's headquarters) chaired by Paul Fox in 1984 (see also Chapter 2). According to Allan:

> She came in a mood of some abrasion, I think; basically we were the chumps who weren't going to support her British Aerospace satellite. And therefore she was cross with us because she saw this as the platform on which to build some extraordinary employment policy. And because we were less than welcoming of the British Aerospace venture and realised it would have been a disaster, everything got off to a fairly bad start. She then asked us if we were the sort of men who could have run the railways back in the nineteenth century. I don't know who it was who said to her, I think it may have been David Plowright: 'But you don't like railways, Prime Minister.' She didn't really like jokes and it went from bad to worse. She eventually stood up at the end of it all, walked to the door, turned round and said 'I'm going back to Downing Street to run the country. May I suggest you stay around for half an hour or so and try and work out what it is you boys want' ... She liked nothing more than handbagging 15 middle-aged men who thought they were capitalist fat cats and behaved as if they were, and had all the superiority and arrogance that was part of ITV. So that was a black day for ITV in terms of relationships with government, or certainly with the Prime Minister. (Interview with Andy Allan)

The relationship between Thatcher and the ITV companies did not improve with time. Again, Allan recounts his meeting with her about three years after the Knighton House meeting:

> I remember when the blessed Margaret visited Nottingham, she'd shifted tack then. She was now on to the export or die phase of her policy. I remember showing her round the studio and her saying to me 'All your cameras are Japanese.' And

I said 'Well, they make very good cameras, Prime Minister.' And she said 'Well, don't you make very good programmes? Why don't you sell them to the Japanese?' So I said 'The Japanese like very violent programmes. Would you like me to make our programmes more violent for the market?' She didn't like jokes. (Interview with Andy Allan)

Ironically, Allan also recounts that the few ITV people she did champion were, eventually, to become losers in the system:

> I think the people she championed were those who were fighting the system from within. She had a soft spot for Jimmy Gatward and a soft spot for Bruce Gyngell. Bruce in taking on the unions, was doing the Eddie Shah of telly and performing some champion role. And James because he was able to characterise himself as the little guy fighting the fat cats. Extraordinary that they both became losers. (Interview with Andy Allan)

Nigel Lawson
Nigel Lawson had been a prime force in the Cabinet Committee and David Mellor, who inherited some of its main recommendations in the Broadcasting Bill after Lawson's resignation in 1989, laid much of the blame for the cruder measures at Lawson's door:

> What I objected to, I think, was what I regard as the Lawson contribution which was that you didn't need a quality threshold and a group of paint merchants could run a television company provided their successful career in paint gave them enough money to buy this as a sort of vanity purchase. And that I couldn't stomach at any price and would not accept. (Interview with David Mellor)

Leslie Hill (MD, Central), however, believed that if the implications of the 'highest bid' formula had been explained to Lawson more fully in terms of it being an unviable business proposition at the appropriate time by those managing ITV's relationship with the government, he might have been less opposed to the objections of the ITV companies:

> At the very end of the process I went with Marshall Stewart (Director of Public Affairs, Central) and had lunch with Nigel Lawson at the Garrick. I set out my objections to the licence auction, simply as it being a very bad business proposition. I have to say Nigel Lawson listened very, very carefully and he seemed very sympathetic. He understood what I was saying ... some people might argue that he was just stringing me along, but I think it was more than that ... Lawson appeared to accept the point when I explained to him how advertising revenue worked and the fact that you couldn't forecast advertising revenue for six months ahead, let alone twelve years ahead, and that in Central's case a 1 per

cent movement in the growth of advertising revenue equalled £10 million a year on the cash bid. Lawson appeared to recognise what a ridiculous thing it was from a business perspective to have to try and forecast the unforecastable so far in advance to enable you to form a sensible view of what the cash bid should be. But by this stage it was too late. The problem was, I think, that no one had put it to him this way before. They had simply made noises about the likely loss of quality programming and that just didn't wash with someone like Lawson. (Interview with Leslie Hill)

Lawson's resignation in October 1989, however, heralded a softening of the polarised position between the government and the ITV companies, and also weakened the position of Margaret Thatcher in terms of detailed intervention in broadcasting although the tendering principle was retained. According to Barry Cox (LWT):

Lawson resigning was tremendous in the short term for ITV. It took out the most articulate defender of the market position as espoused in the White Paper. After the ministerial re-shuffle Mellor came in. He was an opportunist and not wedded to the Bill. Thatcher herself was seriously weakened and when the counter attack came, she had to decide the bits of the Bill that she was really going to stick with and let other bits go. (Interview with Barry Cox)

Professor Brian Griffiths
A more low-profile person, influencing policy behind the public scene, was Professor Brian Griffiths, a former Professor of Banking and International Finance at City University who had replaced John Redwood as Head of Thatcher's Number 10 Policy Unit. Chris Scoble, one of the senior Civil Servants at the Home Office, has described Griffiths as someone with 'a lot of Peacock-type orientation in thinking'. Scoble saw him in the post-Peacock Report era as:

Extremely central. This was an area where No. 10 picked up the co-ordination of the policy, and that inevitably means that that's where the power in decision making ultimately lies ... The person advising the Prime Minister on this was Brian, I think. (Interview with Chris Scoble)

David Mellor remembered his stint at the Home Office before he became Minister of State in 1989:

Brian Griffiths was quite influential and he and I used to talk about these matters. Before I left the Home Office in 1987, Brian and I had talked about the idea of an auction. And I had always been in favour of, at a certain point, being prepared to differentiate between some equally well qualified contenders through a financial mechanism. And I was aware of the fact that governments had always failed in the past to get the levy arrangements right ... Brian and I always had quite constructive conversations. And my objection was not to there being a commercial element in what was commercial television – and a highly commercial business as far as the people were concerned. So Brian would have had quite an influence and not necessarily an unconstructive one. (Interview with David Mellor)

The independent producers' lobby also had access to Griffiths. Paul Styles, who saw him as a 'right wing but independent sort of academic thinker' remembered that:

He was slightly eccentric but I think that he did at one point in the middle period of the 1980s have a significant sway with the Thatcher back office ... We had a number of discussions with him. He was the one who kept putting up the agenda. He also gave us very political advice. (Interview with Paul Styles)

As a fellow Welshman, Huw Davies (Chief Executive, HTV Wales) probably had the closest contact of anyone in ITV with Griffiths. He remembered several meetings but the timing was, according to Davies, too late for much persuasion or influence:

The trouble was that Brian was too far down the road. I feel sure that he's sorrier now than anybody about what happened. I didn't know him that well, at that point, when the whole thing was being set in place. And it was then set in concrete, by the time that Brian started to change his mind ... Brian at the beginning was very much a hawk, a market purist. But by the end he certainly wasn't ... Brian was an evangelical Christian. I was saying 'What are you doing?' and I was taking the very opposite view. I used to tease him saying 'You're in bed with the Great Satan himself, you're in bed with Murdoch, you do anything that he tells you.' 'I don't. I'm doing this because of principle.' I said 'No. Everything you're doing is suiting Murdoch. You're destroying a system so that Murdoch can come into the vacuum.' And he was always worried about that because I was saying, 'Well what are Murdoch's intentions? Look at the *Sun*. I mean, the man's got no morals, no principles, nothing. He's the Great 'Satan, and you the evangelical Christian, you are letting him in to all this.' And I think he would take the point. (Interview with Huw Davies)

Nevertheless, like Lawson, Griffiths' influence tended to diminish once the Broadcasting Bill had been enacted and the political climate changed.

Lord Young
Lord Young, brother of Stuart Young (Chairman of the BBC), cousin by marriage to Michael Green of Carlton Communications, businessman, and Secretary of

State for Trade and Industry, was one of the triumvirate on the Cabinet Committee who was pushing hard for technological change and free competition and was backing the interests of the advertisers. On 10 June 1988 it was announced out of the blue that Lord Young was proposing that BBC2 and Channel 4, the two minority channels, should be broadcast on satellite, phasing out their terrestrial transmissions, the frequencies of which would be released for more commercial channels, thus providing more scope for the advertisers and encouraging viewers to buy satellite dishes. Shirley Littler remembered that:

> Apparently there was some meeting at which Young just came in and threw this bombshell and the Home Office wasn't strong enough and had got so many other problems on their plate and they let him do it although I don't think they thought it was possible. (Interview with Shirley Littler)

The plan, however, was withdrawn almost as swiftly as it appeared. According to Peter Fiddick in the *Guardian* (8 August 1988) this 'simultaneously lunatic and sinister' idea which was formally withdrawn six weeks later 'amidst a load of blather about its having been examined by the experts and so forth, should not diminish our alarm that it was ever put in the first place'.

Sir Jeffrey Sterling
Professor Peacock, when interviewed, had described Sir Jeffrey Sterling as 'a mysterious figure who suddenly emerged'. He was Chairman of P&O and a special adviser to the DTI and had presided over earlier meetings with the 'Club of 21' which had tried, and failed, to accelerate the development of a UK DBS initiative in 1985. According to Andrew Dickson (*Sunday Telegraph*, 23 October 1988) he was 'the most radical of free marketeers' and was 'unperturbed about the quality of programmes in a free market. Millions of people read the *Sun* and who are we to stop them? runs his argument. If the public chooses the television equivalent of tabloid newspapers, that is their affair.' One of his so-called 'contributions' to Thatcher's thinking was to host a series of 'broadcasting breakfasts'. Guests (according to *Campaign*, 15 July 1988) had included Rupert Murdoch, Robert Maxwell and Michael Green. The Home Office was notable for its absence.

Bill Brown remembered them as follows:

> They were in Brook Street, his offices. We went there for breakfast at 8.30 a.m. and we had to go through a National Union of Seamen picket line, because the P&O ferries were on strike. Sterling was late. Terribly sorry. And I thought God this is outrageous that this man should be sitting in judgement on the future of our industry. And he clearly knows nothing about it. (Interview with Bill Brown)

ITV Response
Looking back, with the wisdom of hindsight, key figures in ITV in the mid-1980s later admitted ITV's failure in not engaging with or responding effectively to the

new set of ideas which were being generated and expounded by the Cabinet
Committee and its advisers.

John Birt, then at LWT, but who was later, as BBC Director General, to develop
a sharp political acumen to deal with the current political climate remembered that:

> We did not see the free market coming in ITV. Although I was familiar with the
> ideas in general, like so many other people, I didn't see their relevance to what
> I was doing myself. And I don't think any of us did really. When you're in a
> cosy monopolistic situation you don't. It's like being in prison. You work in that
> world and you have the perspectives of that world and we didn't see it coming.
> (Interview with John Birt)

Barry Cox of LWT also saw the failure of ITV's tactics in clinging to the status quo:

> We clung to attitudes and statements which absolutely sent the wrong signals
> to Thatcher and the rest of them, particularly in the way we droned on about
> 'public service'. However much it meant to people, it was just tactically stupid
> to do this because it was interpreted as 'preserve the status quo'. ITV's hostility
> to the independent producers was ridiculous and it put a bunch of people who
> ought to have been on our side into the other camp. The advertisers ... were up
> in arms. So you suddenly got this enormous coalition building against ITV which
> ITV could do nothing about. In fact, some ITV people exacerbated it. Paul Fox's
> 'over my dead body' stuff at Edinburgh was a disaster. It was like open warfare.
> (Interview with Barry Cox)

A newcomer to ITV, Leslie Hill of Central, took a more detached view of the industry
and saw its shortcomings in responding to Thatcher's government:

> These people in ITV were either not hearing what the politicians were saying
> or were misconstruing it in some way, or were just getting it wrong. They
> seemed to hear what they wanted to believe they should be hearing. They
> weren't really hearing what was being said so they were very naive about the
> real threats to them. I think we should have been much more prepared to have
> been positive and been prepared to change some things. I think the Broadcasting
> Act came out as bad as it did because the attitude on the part of ITV was 'We
> won't be moved. We can have the status quo. We'll fight it all the way.' So ITV
> at the time was foolish not to recognise that change was coming and therefore
> it would have made more sense to have been a bit more positive and constructive
> about the changes. (Interview with Leslie Hill)

The person who was most in accord with the government's thinking, who had been
waiting in the wings for an opportunity to gain access to ITV and whose aspirations
were able to be fulfilled by his acquisition of the London weekday licence in 1991,

after the highest bid/competitive tendering system had been introduced, was Michael Green, Chairman of Carlton Communications, whose views perfectly matched those of Mrs Thatcher:

> Compared to the old system of nods and winks and whether your face fitted, this was a far more transparent system. And that's what Mrs Thatcher wanted ... I applauded that and I think it worked. The people who passed the quality threshold and made the highest bid won. (Interview with Michael Green)

Home Affairs Committee

IBA Policy Statement
In December 1987, the government announced that it was setting up a House of Commons Inquiry into the implications of satellite broadcasting and the future of public service broadcasting in an increasingly deregulated broadcasting industry by the all-party Home Affairs Committee, chaired by John Wheeler, Conservative MP.

Meanwhile, since the publication of the Peacock Report, the IBA had failed to devise a clear formula for a 'better way' of awarding the ITV franchises. Colette Bowe had joined the IBA in December 1986 as Controller of Information Services, having previously been Director of Information at the Department of Trade and Industry at the time of the high-profile 'Westland' affair. She had prepared a paper for IBA Members (Paper 109, 1987) on 'The IBA approach to communication' warning that 'it is no exaggeration to say that the functioning and indeed the existence of the IBA itself is being called into question'. Her conclusion was that the whole broadcasting industry was already involved in a debate, which would change the industry and its institutions radically. The ITV system was also showing signs of strain – in the sense of reluctance to act cooperatively – as outside pressures intensified. Her recommendation was that the top communications priority of the IBA should be to secure a better understanding of what the IBA did, and why, at Westminster, since most politicians had little or no knowledge of the structure of broadcasting.

Two versions of the IBA's policy statement *Independent Television in the 90s* were published on 14 April 1988, one a simplified 'pop' version with a glossy cover showing a family on a sofa watching television and the other a more formal and detailed edition. The purpose of the policy statement was, according to the foreword, 'to make a contribution to the public debate. It describes the main features of the independent television system as it is now and looks ahead to some of the changes that might come.' The document outlined ways of paying for ITV contracts and favoured a method of choosing companies on the basis of a judgement about ability to make good and diverse programmes and then making them pay a special tax that would fluctuate with their business success.

Although the IBA remained vague on a possible method for the award, Littler considered that Colette Bowe 'did a lot to improve the quality of the Authority's public presentation and she also knew how to lobby' (Interview with Shirley Littler). According to her predecessor, Barbara Hosking, who left the IBA to become political adviser to Yorkshire TV, 'She is Liverpool Irish and she is a fighter and all that education is accessible. She's not an ivory tower' (Interview with Barbara Hosking).

Colette Bowe, however, left the IBA on 1 November 1988 to join the Securities and Investment Board (SIB), just before the publication of the White Paper on broadcasting. According to Lord Thomson (IBA Chairman) 'We only got her because of the extraordinary melodrama in Whitehall that she'd been part of. We got her on the bounce back, but she bounced off fairly quickly' (Interview with Lord Thomson).

Bowe was succeeded, in March 1989, by the appointment of Sarah Thane as IBA Controller of Public Affairs. Described by Hosking as 'First class, a safe pair of hands', she had worked her way up the IBA hierarchy as an IBA regional officer in the Midlands and East of England and was to consolidate and reinforce the IBA's links with MPs, special interest groups and lobbies in the passage of the Broadcasting Bill.

Home Affairs Committee

Evidence
The IBA evidence to the Committee gave a detailed account of the development of independent television and its current method of operation but was cautious in making any specific recommendations for the future other than to warn that the 'regulatory framework should be used positively, rather than as a prohibitive heavy hand to bring new opportunities forward'. On the timescale for any changes, the IBA considered that 'the regulation needed to sustain commercially financed public service broadcasting television can be maintained through the 1990s and perhaps longer' (Paragraph 33, Home Affairs Committee, Third Report, *The Future of Broadcasting*, Volume II, Minutes of Evidence and Appendices, 22 June 1988).

In retrospect, Shirley Littler commented:

I don't think the IBA oral evidence went down particularly well but it was partly that which made Colette (Bowe), Peter (Rogers) and me feel that we really must start doing something to help ourselves. (Interview with Shirley Littler)

On 17 February 1988, the Independent Television Association (ITVA), represented by Richard Dunn (Chairman of Council), David Shaw (Director) and Ivor Stolliday (Secretary) were examined by the Committee as witnesses. In their written evidence on 'The Way Ahead' ITVA had, in very broad terms, recommended that the ITV contracts should continue to be awarded on the basis of programme quality, and service to the public, and not sold to the highest bidder. On being questioned by the Chairman John Wheeler on the future role of the IBA, Dunn replied that ITVA envisaged the IBA remaining as the regulatory authority and that there was no reason for substantially altering the regulatory environment within which the ITV companies operated. Questioned by Roger Gale MP, Dunn also thought that a specific quota for independent productions would be 'inadvisable'.

Recommendations
The Home Affairs report on *The Future of Broadcasting* was published on 4 July 1988 (House of Commons, *Home Affairs Committee: Third Report: The Future of Broadcasting* (1987–88 HC 262–1, 262–11), HMSO, 1988). The main recommendations were that a new Commercial Television Authority should replace the IBA as sole regulatory body for all commercial television, however transmitted, including a new fifth channel, which would operate a system of competitive tendering for ITV franchises. Although the Committee paid tribute to the IBA and the ITV companies and acknowledged that 'ITV programmes have been indistinguishable in quality and distinction from those of the BBC' it also stated that 'if the independent sector does not change, the market place may well enforce changes'. Although the Committee recommended that the contracting arrangements for the ITV franchises taking effect from 1993 should continue to be regionally-based, the tendering competition for the franchises should be based on the ability to meet programme requirements and a bid based on a profit formula. The IBA's successor body should support 'principled sponsorship' and examine the structure of advisory bodies. In relation to commercial television, it recommended that when the ITV franchises were next awarded, the night-time hours from midnight to 6.00 a.m. should be let as a separate franchise. Other recommendations included an end to the monopoly of television programme listings by the *TV Times* and *Radio Times*, and an obligation for broadcasters to negotiate with cable and satellite companies over 'listed' sporting events such as test matches, Wimbledon and the Cup Final. Taking up the Peacock Committee's recommendation, they confirmed that every television set bought in the UK by 1990 should include a standard peritelevision socket which would make subscription possible. The Committee also supported the target of 25 per cent of programmes made by independent producers shown on the BBC and ITV should be achieved by 1992. However, despite such changes, the report also concluded that the principles of public service broadcasting should be an integral part of the new broadcasting environment.

Responses
The IBA, while publicly not appearing too disconcerted about the proposal for its abolition, praised the Committee's support for public service broadcasting but stated that it would need to study proposals for a new authority. An internal paper to IBA Members (Paper 116, 1988) was swiftly prepared by Shirley Littler recommending that the IBA should establish its claim to be the nucleus of the proposed single authority for all commercial financed services and that the method of contract award should be reviewed, with advice from Rothschilds. Perhaps rather surprisingly in

the context of the IBA's death-knell, Littler concluded that 'We believe that the form of the Committee's recommendation has been helpful rather than otherwise.'

Elaborating on her reasons for this qualified optimism, seven years later, Shirley Littler explained:

> The Report recommended the introduction of a system of regulated tendering, although it didn't say anything about what the system was. But as far as I was concerned, the thing that absolutely ended the debate was that it was an All-Party Report. And if the Labour Party is now saying they didn't like competitive tender, they jolly went along with that ... It was a very influential report. A lot must have gone on behind the scenes between Wheeler and Home Office Ministers. It had got a lot of PSB flavour which you could latch on to, and it did open up quite a bit of debate. It had got the concept of the technology-neutral regulator and it was obviously sensible that terrestrial TV, cable and satellite should come together at some stage. Although it said firmly the end of the IBA, which undoubtedly pleased Mrs T., I think it said something about building on the skills of IBA staff, so that you could develop a message if the IBA was prepared to change. (Interview with Shirley Littler)

The ITV Association responded with a qualified welcome to the parts of the report which emphasised that the principle of public service broadcasting should continue but was worried by the rather vague proposals for the tendering process. Like the IBA, the ITV companies had not proposed their own formula, although they had continued to retain the services of the economic consultants, NERA, who had produced a report, commissioned in June 1987, for ITVA on '1992 and beyond ... options for ITV' in March 1988. NERA had been asked to assess the implications for the ITV companies of potentially fundamental changes in broadcasting regulation and competition. Various scenarios were drawn and possible 'blueprints' for an ITV model. This had been followed by a report in April 1988 by another consultancy, Booz Allen Hamilton, *The Economics of Television Advertising in the UK* (Economist Publications, 1988) under the guidance of Dr Charles Jonscher, who had previously worked on the subscription study for the Home Office and had been present at the Downing Street seminar in 1987. This report was particularly critical about the costs of ITV and was followed by a further report by NERA in June 1988 assessing the validity of the analysis and conclusions presented. NERA's review of the Booz Allen Hamilton report alleged to uncover a series of problems with the report's data and analysis which undermined Booz Allen Hamilton's conclusions and the policy implications drawn from them. The advertisers generally welcomed the Home Affairs Committee report, particularly the recommendation for a speedy introduction of a fifth commercial television channel, with its increased opportunities for advertising and for the proposed relaxation of programme sponsorship.

Samuel Brittan, an influential member of the Peacock Committee, received the Home Affairs report with mixed feelings. Writing in the Lombard column of the

Financial Times (11 July 1988) in an article 'Guard us from the Guardians' he welcomed many of its individual ideas as 'excellent' and 'much the best comprehensive update on developments since the 1986 Peacock Report'. These included the endorsement for the peritelevision socket on TV sets; the idea of competitive tendering; and that when telecommunications was reviewed the advantages involved in the introduction of optical fibre as a means of transmission might become a common carrier for an indefinite number of broadcasting signals, thus creating conditions for a fully competitive customer-driven broadcasting market.

Nevertheless, he saw the report as 'fatally flawed' by a concept of public service broadcasting designed not to simulate or supplement but to distort, the market as well as protectionist ideas about a 'proper proportion' of British and EC content. He also deplored the Committee's proposal for a fifth terrestrial channel financed by advertising when it provided the cheapest opportunity of introducing direct viewer payment by pay-TV or subscription.

By the end of July 1988, Raymond Snoddy, who had already detected the potential significance of the Peacock Inquiry, reported in his article 'The rehabilitation of a much-maligned report' (*Financial Times*, 30 July 1988) Professor Peacock as commenting that 'I think we have had a very good run for our money. We have stirred the pot a bit and given a point of reference and departure.' Snoddy reckoned that there had been 'a strike rate of about two-thirds on recommendations that are either already accepted or are very likely to appear in next year's Broadcasting Bill' and that they 'will form the basic template for the most dramatic changes in British Broadcasting since the introduction of commercial television more than 30 years ago'.

The White Paper

After months of speculation and leaks, the White Paper *Broadcasting in the '90s: competition, choice and quality. The Government's plans for broadcasting legislation* (HMSO Cm 517) was published on 7 November 1988.

Its appearance was unusual. Described as a White Paper with green edges, the glossy cover showed a grey and white hand on a zapper beaming into red lettering. In the centre were coloured photos of cable, microwave, D-Mac and satellite systems ending with a large picture of a lion from the BBC's children's drama *Chronicles of Narnia*.

Although sponsored by the Home Office, Richard Brooks in the *Observer* (13 November 1988) detected the hands of various government departments: 'You can spot the vested interests at work: scrapping the IBA (the Prime Minister), auctioning franchises (Professor Brian Griffiths, head of Mrs Thatcher's think tank), subscription for the BBC (the Treasury), more advertising-funded channels (the Department of Trade and Industry), Channel 4 maintaining its programme remit (the Home Office), Channel 3, for this is how we must call the deliberately down-rated ITV, keeping schools programmes (Education Secretary, Kenneth Baker). And so the list goes on.'

Recommendations

The government claimed that the purpose of the proposals was to place 'the viewer and listener at the centre of broadcasting policy', and to enable the individual to exercise much wider choice. Specific proposals for the independent television sector included the authorisation of a new national fifth channel, and, if technically feasible, a sixth channel. The present ITV system would be replaced by a regionally-based Channel 3 with positive programme obligations (the term 'public service broadcasting' was avoided) but also greater freedom to match its programming to market conditions. The statutory positive programme requirements would include regional programming, high quality national and international news and current affairs, a diverse programme service, a minimum of 25 per cent of original programming from independent producers and a proper proportion of programme material of EC origin. There would be provision for at least one body which would be effectively equipped to provide high quality news programmes on Channel 3. A new agency, the Independent Television Commission (ITC) would be established in place of both the Independent Broadcasting Authority (IBA) and the Cable Authority, to licence and supervise all parts of a liberalised commercial television sector. It would have tough sanctions but would operate with a lighter touch than the IBA. A tendering process should be introduced to replace the present 'arbitrary and opaque' arrangements for the award of the ITV franchises by which the ITC should operate a two-stage procedure. In the first stage applicants would have to pass a quality threshold and satisfy the ITC that they would meet specified programming requirements. At the second stage, the ITC would be required to select the applicant for each licence who had submitted the highest tender. The Broadcasting Standards Council, which had been established to reinforce standards on taste and decency and the portrayal of sex and violence, would be placed on a statutory footing. The exemption of broadcasting from obscenity legislation would be removed. There would be a major reform of the transmission arrangements, giving scope for greater private sector involvement. Meanwhile, the BBC would continue to be the 'cornerstone of public service broadcasting' although the government looked forward to the eventual replacement of the licence fee.

The deadline for comments on these proposals was sixteen weeks later, 28 February 1989.

ITV Response

An initial draft response to the White Paper in November 1988, prepared by ITVA Chairman's Committee, although laying down the guideline that the 'tone should be measured, thoughtful, confident' was that 'ITV is against auctions' since they would discriminate against incumbents and destabilise ITV. The draft claimed that

Auctions may please the Treasury, but bidding is only objective as a means of determining price on a given day, not programme quality over an 8-year contract ... The price should be set first and bidding to be about programme quality, not money. The ITV companies are small. The market capitalisation of Thames, LWT, Central and Yorkshire totals £563m (31/10/88) compared to, for example, Warner Bros at £1,700m.

There was opposition also to a statutory quota for independent productions since ITV was already aiming, on a voluntary basis, for 25 per cent as a 1992 target. Privatisation of transmission was not rejected, although it was thought that current cross subsidies should continue. The generally hard-line tone of this draft was subsequently softened.But the anti-auction stance was maintained.

An ITVA brief was prepared for the debate on the White Paper in the House of Lords. It was prefaced by a welcome for the general thrust of the White Paper in its encouragement of competition, choice and quality but the overriding message was that it was 'flawed in several key respects', with 'auctioning' being 'the most damaging and inappropriate proposal'. It was pointed out that Peacock had only recommended auctioning the ITV contracts on a split vote, and with the reserved right for the IBA to prefer a lower to a higher bid. It continued

The ITV companies cannot understand why government rejects the right for the ITC to accept a lower financial bid if quality of service is a key government objective. The planned auction will place present contractors at a severe disadvantage, owning as they do the very considerable studio and staff resources for which they were contracted. Not only will publisher contractors seek to replace the existing programme production centres but to do so they will only need to bid the highest sum. As outlined in the White Paper, the 'quality threshold' will be very easy to cross. The outcome will have much more to do with the maximum possible return to the Treasury than the provision of a quality service to viewers.

On 10 March 1989, over a week after the official deadline, a press conference was held in the St Ermine's Hotel, London to explain the ITV companies' submission to the Home Office on the White Paper. The event has been vividly described by Raymond Snoddy of the *Financial Times* in his personal column in *Media Week* (17 March 1989):

A small miracle occurred at the St Ermine's Hotel on Friday morning. Three ITV managing directors managed to agree with each other on the future of broadcasting. They were even given in writing the authority to say that the other 13 ITV managing directors agreed too. 'This is the consensus', Richard Dunn, Chairman of the ITV Association and Managing Director of Thames Television announced – of course, no one believed him. Could the body of men notorious for being unable to agree on what time to have lunch really have reached consensus on anything? Surely only the naive would believe such a suggestion. Somewhere they must be cleaning up the blood and sewing the ears back on again. The unexpected truth is that, faced with the prospect of possible extinction, the ITV companies were able to summon up enough wisdom to stop squabbling at least long enough to get a sensible document to the Home Office.

Some areas of potential disagreement included the future map of ITV and the number and size of ITV companies; the status of the Breakfast franchise, and the ownership control of licences, but all were unanimously opposed to the government proposal to award the new licences to the highest bidder.

The appendices to the submission summarised seven pieces of research ITVA had commissioned from independent consultants including NERA, Professor Andrew Ehrenberg of the London Business School and Leeds University, all of which – from different stances – were critical of the proposal to auction the franchises to the highest bidder. On the basis of the research, ITVA put forward four options to meet the need for competitive tendering while protecting quality. Broadly these were:

– the Peacock Committee recommendation whereby the ITC would have the discretion not to accept the highest bid if a lower one offered the opportunity of a higher quality service.
– the free market option proposed by Dr Cento Veljanovski of the Institute of Economic Affairs whereby the Treasury would set a price for each licence which would then be awarded in perpetuity to the existing contractors. Efficiency would be encouraged by lifting restrictions on takeovers.
– the frequency rental option whereby a price would be set for the contract with regular reviews and contracts awarded on the basis of programme plans and performance.
– the fixed price option whereby the ITC would set a price for the contract based on profit potential and then assess if applicants could meet its requirements and decide which contender offered the best programme proposals.

IBA Response
The IBA's response to the White Paper was published even later than ITVA's on 21 March 1989.

Shirley Littler has described her initial personal reactions to the White paper:

The White Paper, I thought, was very poor quality. In many ways I think it was both incompetent and spiteful. You could see bits that had been written by Ministers. All this rubbish about over-arching, that was a Douglas Hurd sort of phraseology. The bit about transmission I thought was a disgrace. That was obviously a dispute between the Home Office and the DTI. In a sense the best thing the Home Office could do was to leave it in a mess and hope to try to pull it back ... Everybody had put little bits into the White Paper. The Treasury had been allowed to put in stuff about a competitive tender *and* a levy, the DTI had got all sorts of rubbish about competition. There was stuff in it about educational broadcasting. Nobody had really thought about where you ended up. So it was a total mess. And that gave an immense opportunity to the IBA to adopt the line, we know what you're trying to achieve but let us suggest that you won't actually achieve it if you use some of these particular methods. And we will give you good professional advice about what it is that you want to achieve. (Interview with Shirley Littler)

Meanwhile, Lord Thomson, who had, at the start of his term of office as IBA Chairman, advocated a 'better way', but failed to find it, was preparing his valedictory address with the Robert Fraser Lecture at the Banqueting House in Whitehall on 24 November 1988. Reporting the event, Maggie Brown in the *Independent* (25 November 1988) thought that 'this lecture amounted to a rebuttal of the underlying principles' of the White Paper when he claimed that Britain's public service broadcasting was 'more likely to be damaged by zealots in Whitehall than by satellites from outer space'.

Looking back, Lord Thomson referred to the last 'Franchise Affair' in 1980 which had 'left such a mark on me that I recklessly committed myself to the view that there must be a "better way"'. He explained that he would have abolished the concept of a single franchise round, and compulsory readvertisement, and would have allowed the IBA to roll forward contracts if programme making was satisfactory, but would have permitted newcomers to take over contractors subject to IBA approval. He regretted that 'such ideas proved badly and sadly out of tune with the times' but was afraid that 'we may now end up with a worse way in terms of the quality of programmes for viewers'. He expressed his opposition to the proposed auctioning of the ITV franchises and thought that the government was running the risk, in Oscar Wilde's words, 'of knowing the price of everything and the value of nothing'. The government's approach, based on the proposition that broadcasting and telecommunications were merging, failed to recognise that broadcasting was more than an economic or business activity but

a creative activity, (with) perhaps the major influence on our society's capacity to be informed, to provide enhancing ways for increasing leisure, to nurture a sense of identity, to preserve and enhance the rich diversity of its cultural life.

Splendid as this eloquent defence of the basic values of traditional public service broadcasting may have been, the speech caused consternation within the IBA, partly because there had been no consultation with other Authority members and partly because it appeared to ignore the realities of political power.

Lord Thomson's deputy at the IBA, Sir Donald Maitland, a man of wide diplomatic and political experience, which had included a period as Chief Press Secretary at Downing Street, was one of those who felt that it was a mistake for George Thomson to take the line he did:

> It was a pity that in his last year as chairman of the Authority George Thomson should have been so publicly at odds with the government. More important issues had to be settled, but not in his time. (*Diverse Times, Sundry Places* by Donald Maitland, Alpha Press, 1996)

Shirley Littler, who had seen a draft of the speech, also regretted the occasion:

> He'd shown us a draft. It was a very low ebb for the Authority. And we tried to say to George, please don't destroy the IBA's credibility and willingness to adjust. Could he make clear that it was a personal view ... He couldn't change his views because he held them very genuinely. (Interview with Shirley Littler)

On 3 December 1988, however, George Russell, a businessman who had been an IBA Member from 1979–86, was appointed IBA Chairman and ITC Chairman designate. In preparing the IBA's formal response to the challenges of the White Paper, a series of papers to the Members recommended a change of tack involving a more flexible approach to the inevitable changes, instead of a stout defence of the 'old' values. IBA Paper 1 (1989), 5 January, concluded that the IBA should not challenge the broad aim of the government's proposals but there was a need to strengthen the commitment to 'quality'. The principle of a competitive tendering process should not be opposed but substantial improvements might be suggested on the methods involved in the two stages of the process. Programme requirements should be strengthened by placing weight also on the quality of applicant money and the support and continuation of a network.

An internal working party was set up to consider how the regulatory activities and staffing of the IBA might need to be reorganised if it were to form the core of the future ITC. Advice was taken from Sir Christopher Foster of Coopers & Lybrand about what might be involved in a licensing approach to broadcasting. The assessment of the 'quality of money', advocated by George Russell, was to be reinforced by merchant bank advisers who would be invited to supply detailed assessments of applicants. Hill Samuel were later appointed to this role. Particular emphasis was to be placed on how realistic were the expected income streams from the programme proposals and the way in which the resources so generated would be used within the applicant company to meet each requirement of the licence.

On 21 March 1989, the IBA faced the press, armed with its response to the White Paper. While following the general thrust of the government's proposals, George Russell questioned whether particular proposals were workable in the form in which they were put forward and would achieve the desired objectives. The IBA's proposal for a form of competitive tendering was to place considerable weight on the quality of both the applicants' money and their programmes. In practical terms this meant that after a minimum lease price for each licence had been set in the form of specific percentages of an applicant's Net Advertising Revenue, applicants would have to submit a sealed bid, together with an open dossier available for public inspection, complete with details of their organisation and programme plans. The IBA considered that the applicant with the soundest business plan would yield the highest value to the ITC and to the Exchequer in terms of the tender and corporation tax over time and also would sustain a programme service of the requisite quality serving viewers' interests. Russell also confirmed that although he was prepared to allow friendly takeovers of ITV companies from 1990 he wanted to see a moratorium on hostile takeovers after the start of the new licences.

When asked by Raymond Snoddy, media correspondent of the *Financial Times*, what his reaction would be if the government limited the award to the highest bid, he replied 'If I am faced with a straight envelope tender, which I cannot believe in, if that actually happens, I do not think I could continue in the job.'

This 'ultimatum to quit' was well received by the press the following morning. The Home Office, taken off guard by Russell's remark and attempting to forestall the impression of a breach between the IBA and the government, hurriedly called a press briefing at which Timothy Renton, Broadcasting Minister, praised the IBA submission as 'ingenuous' and 'extremely constructive'. John Wheeler, Chairman of the Home Affairs Committee, was also reported (*Guardian*, 27 March 1989) as saying 'What George Russell has done is fill in the pot-holes in the Government's proposals. He has done a first-class job in setting out practical plans while marching in tune with the Government's views. I think he's cracked it.'

A week later, when the dust had settled, Georgina Henry wrote in the *Guardian*:

When the Government hand-picks its lieutenants in public institutions, it comes as a nasty shock to find them threatening to resign over key points of policy ... No one really believes Russell will be forced to leave after just three months. The 53-year-old Geordie is central to the successful implementation of the government plans for commercial television in the 1990s, and was chosen for combining impeccable business credentials with a sound understanding of Britain's commercial television sector ... The stage is set for a substantial revision of the most attacked proposal. At least it is if the Home Office gets its way. What is unknown is the reaction to the furore of the Cabinet Committee which approved the White Paper, the mysteriously named MISC128. Home Secretary, Douglas Hurd, has made it clear that quality (of money and programme plans) should be the central issue in awarding the franchises, but he still has to convince his more gung-ho colleagues that the IBA has come up with a winning formula. (*Guardian*, 27 March 1989)

Raymond Snoddy, who had sparked off the publicity on the IBA's submission by his direct question to Russell, signed off his Comment Column in *Media Week* (31 March 1989) with an optimistic note on the White Paper:

I am by nature an optimist. That is probably why, against all reason, history or common sense, I have come to the quite preposterous conclusion that the politicians will, in the end, get the Broadcasting Bill about right. Not perfect, but much less damaging than would have appeared possible a few months ago. If you look very carefully you can see the outlines of a deal beginning to take shape. It will, in the end, look remarkably like the document submitted to the Home Office by George Russell and the Independent Broadcasting Authority. There is no need to continue wading through the rest of the 2,800 submissions looking for the one wheeze that might take the Government's fancy. It is simply time to award the prize for ingenuity to Russell and be relieved he was in the right place at the right time. The clear challenge, you will remember, was to find a mechanism that would give the Government the 'objective' method of awarding franchises it wanted without devastating the TV system, and a regime that would encourage more choice and competition without undermining the best aspects of quality television. The IBA has found the compromise by going with the Government's thinking while pointing to the bits of the White Paper that simply would not work. It has, for instance, offered up a privatised transmission system, provided it is national and not regional and, despite the opposition of the ITV companies, the separate selling of Channel 4's airtime. Most important of all, it has found a competitive tender mechanism that appears to be capable of satisfying everyone. The Treasury share is more than protected, the quality of both the programmes and the money offered by applicants is properly scrutinised and there is still the element of bidding, although with percentages of advertising revenue rather than with crude lump sums of cash. Such a system, with payments spread over the lifetime of the franchise, will give the existing ITV companies a reasonable chance of survival. More important, it will protect the Government from the acute embarrassment of seeing virtually all the franchises going to new tenants with no guarantees on the sort of service they might offer. In all this, Russell has emerged as the key figure – the man who can sell a compromise to the Government with the tacit backing of both the Home Office and the Department of Trade and Industry. (*Media Week*, 31 March 1989)

Implementation of Government Plans

In the interlude of March to December 1989 between responses to the White Paper and the publication of the Broadcasting Bill, the government made more specific moves. In April, it was announced that plans for the introduction of a sixth national television channel, proposed in the White Paper, had been abandoned. Lord Young, Trade and Industry Secretary, had decided that technical studies on a sixth channel should be discontinued since coverage would be so limited. However, plans for the privatisation of transmission progressed (see Chapter 7). Following a report in April, 'Study of privatisation options for the Terrestrial Broadcasting Transmission Networks' by Price Waterhouse, the Home Office announced on 4 July that the government intended to privatise the transmission networks owned and operated by the IBA and the BBC as soon as it was in a position to do so. In October, the Home Office advertised for financial advisers to provide preliminary financial advice on the privatisation of the IBA's terrestrial radio and television transmission system and also to assess the feasibility of privatising the IBA's Experimental and Development Department. Price Waterhouse was, again, appointed.

The major announcement, however, was the Home Secretary's measures to strengthen the quality requirements for the award of the ITV contracts.

Hurd's Statement

On 13 June 1989 Douglas Hurd, the Home Secretary, announced a substantial strengthening of the quality threshold which every applicant would have to pass. They would have to provide a reasonable proportion of programmes (in addition to news and current affairs) of high quality and would have to provide a diverse programme service calculated to appeal to a wide variety of tastes and interests. Channel 3 would also be required to provide teletext subtitling on some programmes for the deaf and hard of hearing.

Although ITV franchises would normally be allocated to the highest bidder passing the quality threshold, the ITC could, in exceptional circumstances, select a lower bid, giving its reasons for doing so. The bid was to be based on a predetermined fixed percentage of Net Advertising Revenue as the minimum sale price plus a lump sum which would provide the competitive part of the bid. The ITV companies would not have to pay the current Exchequer Levy. There would be no moratorium on takeovers at the beginning of 1993, the start of the new licences. The networking arrangements would be a matter for the Channel 3 companies to decide for themselves.

In her memoirs *The Downing Street Years* Mrs Thatcher saw Hurd's statement as the first of a series of concessions made in response to lobbying by the broadcasters, and by the Home Office team who argued that there would be 'great parliamentary difficulties otherwise'. She thought that these 'unfortunately muddied the transparency which I had hoped to achieve and produced a compromise which turned out to be less than satisfactory when the ITC bestowed the franchises ... in the old-fashioned way'.

Hurd's statement, however, did nothing to appease ITV's opposition to the auctioning of the contracts. In a long letter to the *Financial Times* (22 June 1989), Richard Dunn (in his role as Chairman of the ITVA) argued that

The one policy to which we are implacably and unanimously opposed is the Government's determination, despite remarkably widespread opposition, to go ahead with the auctioning of commercial broadcast licences to the bidder, not of the highest quality service, but of the biggest amount of cash ... This is a policy that looks to be driven by Treasury greed ... The case against auctioning is that big money can outbid good quality; it catastrophically destabilises a £1.5bn industry for at least two years before and two years after the auction; there are plenty of pressures acting against any resumption of inefficiency; the auction outcome is unpredictable; it is impossible to define conditions like programme 'quality' in terms valid for a sale contract or acceptable in judicial review; and the likelihood of overbidding will impact adversely on the investment needed for quality programmes.

He was not impressed with Hurd's claimed strengthening of the 'quality threshold': 'These "safeguards" smack of the locks going on after the quality has bolted with the auction proceeds.'

Christopher Dunkley, named broadcast journalist of the year at the TV-am awards of 1989, in the *Financial Times* (14 June 1989) the day after Hurd's statement in an article 'The End of an Epoch' forecast that 'franchise blight looks set to ruin our chances of high risk, high cost, high quality programming from ITV for the next three years ... History will see Margaret Thatcher as the destroyer of an extraordinary golden age in British television.'

9

THE BATTLE OF THE BILL

Preparation for the Broadcasting Bill (March to December 1989)

The Independent Broadcasting Authority

After the IBA's response to the White Paper in March 1989, there was a continuing process of discussion and negotiation, led by Shirley Littler who had previously been Assistant Under Secretary at the Broadcasting Department of the Home Office and was now the IBA's Acting Director General, while her former colleagues at the Home Office, Chris Scoble and Paul Wright, were the senior civil servants involved in preparing the Bill.

Regarding the White Paper as a 'total mess' she saw the Bill as:

> an immense opportunity to the IBA to adopt the line, we know what you're trying to achieve but let us suggest that you won't achieve it if you use some of these particular methods ... And we will give you good professional advice about what it is you want to achieve ... Government trusted George Russell, whereas of course they didn't by the end trust George Thomson. (Interview with Shirley Littler)

Anticipating publication of the Broadcasting Bill at the end of 1989, Shirley Littler prepared a Paper (107 (89)) in June for IBA Members which summarised progress since March and warned that 'we need to watch that any concessions are not eroded in the Bill itself and should aim to widen any chinks which are favourable to us'.

The IBA's main aims, at this stage, were to abandon efforts to persuade the Government that the ITC should be able to require Channel 3 licensees to share in a network but to ensure an orderly transition; to pursue efforts to secure a place for ITN as the Channel 3 news provider; to ensure that the BSC did not regulate programmes while maintaining the IBA's opposition to preview; to pursue the outcome of the privatised transmission system following the report for government by consultants Price Waterhouse and to secure a future for engineering research and development in independent broadcasting.

381

Peter Rogers, IBA's Director of Finance, in IBA Paper 135(89) in August stressed the need 'to avoid ... the problem of conflict and mistrust within ITV during the extended contract period'.

More specifically he recommended that the IBA should accept common ownership of two Channel 3 licensees, other than two large licences, but should argue for a limit on cross-shareholdings; the IBA should continue to argue against the non-contiguity rules and if there was a tied bid the IBA should award the licence on the basis of the proposal which offered a better service to viewers.

David Glencross, Director of Programmes, outlined his perception of future ITC Programme Regulation in a separate IBA Paper. He thought that the new pattern of regulation envisaged in the White Paper and in subsequent ministerial statements lurched awkwardly between encouraging programme quality and imposing programme penalties. He wrote:

> It has a commitment of a kind to quality and diversity on Channel 3 but lays much greater emphasis on penalties for non-compliance and for breaches of standards. If this is a stick and carrot approach then the stick is a pretty hefty deterrent and the carrot is a puny incentive. Nonetheless, the word 'quality' is in the White Paper's title, even if some indications of government thinking suggest that quality needs little more than an absence of offence or controversy. (IBA Paper 134(89))

Glencross foresaw regulation after 1992 as more arm's length and more post hoc. The government also intended regulation to be lighter, more objective and subject to judicial review. He recommended that the general aim should be to enable the ITC to distance itself from day-to-day programme matters, to transfer editorial responsibility to the licensees and to leave the ITC free to impose appropriate sanctions without the previous involvement in the editorial process. The ITC should not be reluctant to use sanctions and would need to demonstrate generally that it had not succumbed to 'agency capture', by identifying with the interests of those it regulated rather than those of viewers. He was adamant that the ITC should not preview programmes. Positive programme requirements and licensees' programme undertakings should be specified where possible in measurable form as licence conditions. Although consumer protection requirements should be covered in the programme code there should continue to be a large degree of subjective judgement in matters of taste and decency. The companies needed to have appropriate procedures in place for self-regulation and for investigating breaches of programme requirements and assume more responsibility for handling complaints. The ITC should undertake annual performance reviews and set up regional Viewer Consultative Councils (VCCs) to monitor viewers' responses and tastes.

A more detailed scrutiny of the selection process for Channel 3 followed in October with an IBA Paper (153(89) prepared in October by Michael Redley, an economist who had been seconded from the Treasury to be Shirley Littler's Chief Assistant.

He argued that the quality threshold should be set as high as the Act and economic prospects would allow and that the ITC should test for 'high quality' as an aspect of diversity. The ITC should avoid a 'shopping list' of programme types to be required but should endorse the government's proposal that applicants should be invited to propose the service they wished to offer, drawing on illustrative guidelines as to what the ITC would consider acceptable. Applicants should also explain the cost of proposed programmes and their source of supply. Specific financial information should be available for the assessment of business plans. Regional aspects of the quality threshold should be reinforced by the provision of separate regional services in subregions in some areas and a minimum number of hours of regional interest programming. There should also be a genuine regional presence and identity. A further definition of the 'exceptional circumstances' provision was discouraged in case it might qualify and reduce the way in which it might be applied, particularly in circumstances where financial tenders were close but there was a wide discrepancy in programme quality, financial or business capability. It was also suggested that the existing map and the clock on Channel 3 might bear more radical examination since a smaller number of regions more equal in size might become inevitable for a mixture of political and economic reasons. This had already been suggested by the IBA's financial modelling which indicated that at least some of the smaller regions might not be viable in the 1990s.

In relation to the Home Office, the recommendation was to continue 'sticking to our present approach of quiet and persistent diplomacy, at least until the Bill is published, coupled with the adoption of a further set of objectives against which to judge proposals as they come forward'. The government's basic objectives were seen as a more 'transparent' selection process where the applicants knew the basis on which they were judged than was applied in the previous contract awards; a due return to the Exchequer for the private use of a public asset and a greater opportunity for viewers, as the consumers of television, to influence the content of services offered by applicants.

By the end of October, the issue of networking had not been resolved in discussions with the Home Office. In a progress report (IBA Paper 164(89)) Shirley Littler reported to the Authority that

> There is no further progress on the network, though we have left the Home Office in no doubt that we do not ourselves see how, without the shape of the network being clear in advance, applicants can offer to provide a programme service and the ITC judge their offers in a meaningful way.

She also, rather tartly, reported that 'We have pressed on officials the need to enable the ITC to advertise dual-region services, which has so far escaped their notice.' However, she also reported that 'We understand that Ministers have agreed to drop the contentious proposal to take powers to control advertising minutage. As we advocated in the IBA response this is to be left with the ITC.'

The privatisation of the IBA's Engineering function had progressed with an IBA team, led by Peter Rogers (IBA Director of Finance), with John Forrest (Director of Engineering) having a first meeting with Price Waterhouse in October 1989. It was clear that the government was eager to press on with the transfer to the Home Secretary and with privatisation speedily after the Bill was enacted, if possible before the end of 1990.

At the end of October, following the resignation of Nigel Lawson, the Chancellor of the Exchequer, Margaret Thatcher appointed David Waddington, formerly the Chief Whip, as Home Secretary and David Mellor as Minister of State in place of Douglas Hurd and Timothy Renton respectively. Both had previous Home Office experience. Waddington had been Minister of State at the Home Office from 1983–87, and Mellor, as Minister of State, had handled broadcast matters for nine months before the 1987 General Election when he had been involved in the implementation of the government's intention for a quota of independent producers. Although IBA Paper 171(89) reported that 'The new Home Office Ministers have expressed a continued readiness to listen to reasoned criticism of the approach to be taken in the Bill', it warned that

> We are doubtful that there is much 'give' in Government's approach at present ... Officials have warned us not to read too much into recent suggestions, by Mr Mellor in particular, that policy remains fluid, or to assume that any major re-think is possible. The agreement between senior Ministers reached in the Cabinet Committee which devised the approach to the Bill still underpins policy. Mr Waddington and Mr Mellor will be bound by it through the passage of the Bill, and will still have to obtain their colleagues' assent for any departure from it.

The Government
David Mellor's view of the preparation for the Bill was that:

> ... the gestation arrangements were inappropriate ... in the run-up to the publication of the Broadcasting Bill the small high-powered committee (reflected), of course, the then Prime Minister's interest in broadcasting and not always frankly constructive approach to broadcasting. And so she sat with the Chancellor, Nigel Lawson, her Trade and Industry Secretary, David Young, and her Home Secretary, Douglas Hurd, and they really prepared the Bill in these discussions in which I was not present. But one doesn't require Mystic Meg's insights to know that Douglas Hurd found himself quite often in a minority of one and the Bill was fairly ideologically driven, and that one of the strongest influences on it was Nigel Lawson. History will show that his determination to involve himself in other people's departments was at an all-time high. And there's no doubt that the Bill, as it emerged from those conclaves, was always going to be difficult to get through because it had been starved of the oxygen of a wider public opinion.

So it was a poor undernourished thing with some good and necessary ideas that I would always defend ... I always felt that the ITV system did need opening up ... The Bill, therefore, that emerged reflected an ideological majority against the then Home Secretary and his Minister for broadcasting, Tim Renton. The interesting question is what they would have done had history not taken its course. It was the resignation of Lawson in '89 that took John Major from the Foreign Office to the Treasury; took Douglas Hurd from the Home Office to the Foreign Office; brought David Waddington to the Home Office; sent Renton to be Chief Whip and left a gap at the Minister of State. David Waddington had been Minister of State responsible for immigration matters when I'd been doing the Criminal Justice, Broadcasting and other things. He came over to see me one Friday morning in the House of Commons when I was doing a debate and said 'I want to explain to you something that otherwise might not please you very much, which is that you're going to be asked to go back to be Minister of State at the Home Office. The reason is not because anybody wants to get you out of Health ... but because I find myself thrown in at the deep end. I've never done broadcasting, we've got a big Bill going. I've asked for you and I assume you'll have real control of the Bill. I'll back you 100%.' Which, indeed, he did. 'But I'm really saying to you it's all hands to the pump.' I was quite touched by that.

Kenneth Clarke didn't want it, and there was quite a row about it and it was news that was treated quite badly by the media who tried to suggest one was being removed from Health because Clarke and I were bovver boys and it needed fragrant Virginia (Bottomley) to come in and she took over as Minister of State. So I was not best pleased ... I was then presented with this wretched Bill. And it's interesting to know what Hurd and Renton would have done with it. It might have been weakness or Machiavellian tendencies that let it get to the stage it was. It could have been weakness that they just didn't want to make waves, or it could have been that a shrewd man like Douglas might well have thought as soon as this comes out in the open all hell will be let loose and I'll be able to gently redecorate the premises without too much hassle and aggravation.

As soon as I looked at the Bill, I was quite clear in my own mind that I was not going to be anyone's creature on this. That I was going to do what was the right thing to do and I was going to use the fact that I had been asked to come back as a sign of favour in that limited context as someone who knew about broadcasting. I would use that to the nth degree. (Interview with David Mellor)

Chris Scoble, head of the Broadcasting Department, has described the preparation of the Bill and the working relationship between the IBA and David Mellor from the Civil Service perspective as follows:

It was all done extremely quickly, of course, and there was an enormous amount to do ... Often each area was a subject in itself. But I think on introduction all the main parts were there ... There may or may not have been contradictions in it and things that needed to be worked out, but that was because of the complexity of the material. To have worked all these things out in detail might well have taken another year, and there was a sort of dynamic in terms of getting decisions as you went along ... Whenever we were shaping policy in relation to the ITV system as a whole, we relied very much on the IBA as our sort of second arm, because they were the experts in terms of the relationship between the IBA and regulation and the individual companies ... It was particularly useful that Shirley (Littler), having been the Head of the Broadcasting Department ten years before, that she had good relationships with us and knew how the Ministerial and Parliamentary machine worked, so she was in a position to understand what might be possible and what might not be possible. And that obviously was quite helpful ...

Mellor's involvement was very strong ... so there was continuous dialogue between us as officials and him ... he had a very clear grasp of what the policy issues were and what he wanted to do ... Although he supported broadcasting and maintaining the quality, he also had a bit of scepticism about people who said everything was wonderful and couldn't be touched ... When Waddington came in a sense it made it easier, because Waddington, in terms of his approach was seen very much as a Thatcherite ... he was somebody whom Number 10 would know that they had complete confidence in him and not need to hold him on a tight string... He didn't know a lot about the detail, so he was entirely dependent upon Mellor ... So Waddington relied upon Mellor's judgement, which indeed was all he could do in the sense that he wasn't grasping the detail, and he hadn't been in, as Hurd had been, on all the initial policy developments, so he didn't know the background to it ... David Mellor had to explain what he was proposing ... but once Waddington had accepted that this was alright he could go to the Prime Minister and actually do business and things would go through that in other circumstances might actually have been difficult ... simply because she trusted him. (Interview with Chris Scoble)

The ITV Association (ITVA)
After the publication of the White Paper, the ITV Association prepared a report on 'Strategy for Action' in November 1988, stressing that the ITV companies must present a coherent view of alternatives to the White Paper and needed to speak through ITVA with one voice on major issues. It warned that 'The ITV companies must hang together on the future of British broadcasting or they will most surely be hanged separately.' The main issues were seen as the proposed tendering process, the level of the quality threshold, the constitution of Channel 4 and the transitional period before 1993. The strategy was divided into three phases. In Phase 1 (December 1988 to February 1989) ITVA would make official representations to the Home Office. Phase 2 (February 1989 to November 1989) would involve continuing lobbying of government, reinforced by third-party endorsement of ITVA objectives. Hill and Knowlton, the parliamentary lobbyists engaged by ITV,

would design the tactics. Phase 3, the passage of the Bill, would target specific clauses and prepare briefs for MPs and Lords. A number of research projects were also commissioned from various consultants including Patrick Barwise and Andrew Ehrenberg of the London Business School, Cento Veljanovski of the Institute of Economic Affairs, two economists, Gordon Hughes (University of Edinburgh) and David Vines (University of Glasgow and also a director of Channel 4), and from the economics consultancy, NERA.

In January 1989, a conference on the White Paper was arranged entitled 'What is the ITV Association doing about it?' Richard Dunn, Chairman of the ITVA, told the conference that there was 'no need to panic'. He reported that Council had agreed to create a small Chairman's Committee, including Peter Battle (Chairman of the Marketing Committee), Bill Brown (MD of STV), Greg Dyke (Director of Programmes, LWT), Dick Emery (Director of Sales at Central) and Andrew Quinn (MD, Granada TV) to help devise and co-ordinate the ITV companies' strategy. Hill and Knowlton had been retained as lobby advisers and J. Walter Thompson would prepare advertising material on behalf of ITV. Dunn reported that since the publication of the White Paper, ITVA had held three meetings with the Home Office and had set out fifty-five questions. Although he conceded that ITV could not be expected to speak with one voice on every issue, he claimed that there was universal opposition to the auctioning of the franchises. He also stressed the importance of the current system of substantial subsidies for the smaller ITV companies. In Grampian's area, for instance, there were seventy-five transmitters but only one in the Thames area. Thames, however, paid more to the IBA for the use of transmitters. The operation of the networking system and the financing of Channel 4 also bore more heavily on the larger companies. If such cross-subsidies disappeared, some other form of financial support would have to be found if regional television was to survive. He referred to Mrs Thatcher's description of ITV as the 'last bastion of restrictive practices' as damaging, but hoped that the pending Monopolies and Mergers Commission inquiry would find no restrictive practices in relation to staff unions in ITV.

The conference was also addressed by Alan Sapper, General Secretary of ACTT, Jim Horrocks, a member of ACTT National Negotiating Committee and Tony Hearn, General Secretary of BETA. The final speaker Harry Conroy, General Secretary of NUJ, however, was critical of ITV and said he 'could not agree with the rather gentle tactics pursued by the ITV Association in seeking to change the views of government'.

The ITVA meetings with the Home Office before the publication of the Broadcasting Bill proved to be rather inconclusive. The initial meeting after the publication of the White Paper was held on 30 November 1988 to discuss the fifty-five questions which had been sent by ITVA to the Home Office. Civil servants present included Chris Scoble, Elliot Grant and Simon Hickson; ITVA was represented by Richard Dunn, Bill Brown and David Shaw, Director of ITVA. ITVA's opposition to the highest financial tender was based on the argument that although

Peacock had recommended the auctioning of the ITV franchises this had only been favoured on a split 4:3 vote and with the reserved right for the IBA to prefer a lower bid to a higher bid. Dunn pressed the argument that if quality of the ITV service was the government's key objective it should be prepared to allow the IBA to accept a lower financial bid. The Home Office response was that the objective was to determine a market price and to obtain an economic rent. It was also stressed that the regional system would be expected to operate without cross-subsidies. The response to several of the fifty-five questions was that many answers were 'still to be determined' although ITV's views would be welcome. Notes on the meeting record that the civil servants were 'unmoved by the opposition in principle to quotas' (for independent production) and that there was 'no recognition of major improvements made in ITV efficiency over the last few years'.

The next meeting with the Home Office on 7 December 1988 also included Timothy Renton, Minister of State for Broadcasting and Andrew Quinn of Granada. Renton firmly told ITVA that 'the Government was not to be shifted on auctioning' but ITV was welcome to offer suggestions on ways of constructing competitive tendering on more acceptable lines. He also warned that 'You shouldn't waste too much time on your own proposal' since 'the Cabinet Committee was unanimous in support of competitive tendering'. The government's rationale was that there was a need for an objective method of franchise allocation, the establishment of a fair rent for future licensees and the ability for newcomers to enter the field.

The polarisation of views on the auctioning of the franchises continued with further Home Office ITVA meetings from February to December 1989. On 14 February, Richard Dunn pointed out the difficulty of obtaining total unanimity of fifteen plcs on the issue of competitive tendering. Douglas Hurd (Home Secretary) replied that 'a sharp presentation was better than trying to be all things to all men'.

By November 1989, David Mellor, the newly appointed Minister of State, was attending the meetings with ITVA. He was in robust form. At a meeting on 22 November, Richard Dunn suggested that a form of competitive tendering might be that once the quality threshold had been passed and the bids opened, an overall judgement by the ITC could be made by reassessing the business and quality aspects of the application. He also stressed the dangers of non-broadcasters overbidding. These points stimulated a sceptical response from Mellor who said 'Aren't you creating a totally false vision of the other bidders? If they're as awful as you say, they won't get in. Are you aiming at the right barn door? After all, you had to start somewhere.' He also reminded ITVA of Southern TV's loss of franchise in 1980 by asking if it had not been 'ITV's Admiral Byng' last time round and how that decision could be defended. He said 'I still see this as a longing to go back to past security.'

The acrimonious debate on competitive tendering continued at a further meeting with Mellor on 4 December 1989. When Dunn pointed out the threats of non-broadcasters to the present contractors and the networking system, Mellor retorted 'Your interests and ours part company when we are in the area of "non-broadcasters";

if they can do it [i.e. make a success of television] what's wrong?' He also argued that 'exceptional circumstances' could be applied 'If the Chairman of the ITC and its Members were to determine that the scale of change constituted "exceptional circumstances", then they could take that on board.' Mellor claimed that George Russell 'believes that he has powers to achieve what is expected. The undesirables will be weeded out; not all will be left to the bid.'

Mellor also told ITVA that he hoped that it would be possible for the networking plans to be finalised early in 1990 since George Russell needed 'a credible arrangement against a framework which will ensure continuity'. His parting shot was that 'If you sort it out you will have done a great service to broadcasting and it will do you no harm at all', but he warned, 'a period of fumbling around is just not on'.

Lobbies/Campaigns

One of the most influential campaigns established in response to the government's proposals was the Campaign for Quality Television.

The genesis of the campaign has been described by David Plowright:

> I used to have programme committee meetings where they were forced to sit around and talk and then have a dinner and exchange ideas, which seemed important to me to try and knit them all together. I remember going into one ... Madame Thatcher was doing things, and I looked at this assembled company and I said 'You ought to be bloody well ashamed of yourselves, the lot of you. You've been castrated by her.' They didn't say anything. I said 'in my day', risking a trip down memory lane, 'Isaacs, Fox and myself we'd have been writing to *The Times*. We'd have been demonstrating that the people in the industry, not just hacks like Chairmen and Managing Directors and Finance Directors, cared about it.' They listened. I went back to my office and Mr Prebble shuffled in. He said 'We all think you've got a point. So we want to form a little group.' So I said 'Oh good.' 'Will you give us some money?' I said: 'Yes, of course, I will, but it'll be a bad idea if it's seen to be Granada. Can't you do it collectively through ITVA or something? I'll give you £5000 and if you want we can second Simon [Albury]': [He] demonstrated a terrific ability as a lobbyist. (Interview with David Plowright)

Stuart Prebble described the development of the Campaign as follows:

> I called the *Independent* and booked a quarter page of advertising space ... We decided to write an open letter to Mrs Thatcher about British Television and have it signed by a range of respected people from different areas of the industry. And immediately I contacted some *World in Action* people in London, because I was the Editor of *World in Action* at the time, to canvass who we might call ... We wanted somebody from the independent sector, somebody from the BBC,

somebody from Channel 4, and two or three people from ITV. [We] formed ourselves into a sort of unofficial steering group and had discussions about how we ought to proceed. And plainly I think we benefited from the fact that we were all in the factual programmes business and (were) fairly close to how politics works. [We] worked out very quickly that the trick was to be very focused, very targeted ... The person who was utterly central was Simon Albury. Simon was right on the case from day one and the busiest single individual from day one ... We moved the operation to 20/20 (an independent company) [which] gave us an office that was not an ITV company ... We went to see Renton after the White Paper ... The first meeting with Renton was utterly depressing ... We all sat round with these civil servants and Renton said 'Just before you start, let me tell you the way I see things happening.' He then spoke for twenty minutes, I would think, on their approach: 'how reasonable, taking consultation, competition, maintenance of quality, certainly nothing set in stone', You know, all the stuff. He went on and on and on and on and when it came to an end we attempted a couple of points and he said 'Well I'm sorry, I've got another meeting now, but my civil servants are very happy. Please keep in touch with us. Write to my civil servants, here they are.' It was as kind a brush off as you could possibly get. He was then changed and Mellor came along and we asked to see him and I can't remember who came to the first of those, but exactly the same thing happened. He said 'Just before you start, let me tell you the way I see it.' And Simon said 'No. We really have to tell you why we're here, because if we don't I fear our time will be up.' And it was great. I think from the word go, Mellor found it a refreshing exercise. In fairness to him, I think he did enjoy the debate. He is a man who does enjoy debate and hearing points of view that he'd not heard. He was very candid and reported in the press that he basically wasn't going to take any notice of the ITV companies, and, frankly, couldn't be seen to be doing so. In one way I think that for producers to be representing some of the same points gave an excuse for them to submit on some points that they wouldn't have been able to submit on had it only been ITV companies. I think at the second meeting there was a call to Simon from Paul Wright or one of Mellor's civil servants, asking whether there was any chance of some well-known faces coming along to this meeting? It might well be that's better. So we said 'Sure'. And we took Rowan Atkinson and I think Terry (Jones) as well.

Michael Palin helped. He certainly was on the case and put his name to things very readily. But Rowan (Atkinson) was obviously a big star and we certainly got more time. I do have a clear memory that at one of these meetings where Terry Jones was there, as we were all trooping out, Mellor and Rowan got together and made a date to have lunch. I think David Mellor certainly enjoyed the thought that he was meeting all these stars. But I don't know how many meetings we had. We had several in the office and we had several over dinner, and we discussed every aspect of the Bill as it went through. He listened and took our points on board. It would be very difficult to count or quantify our influence because a lot of it was in nuance or dispelling misunderstandings that they had about how things would work. But it was quite clear that I think Mellor's heart was in the right place. I think for him it was the art of the possible. He made it absolutely clear from the very early stage that the only thing that was not negotiable was the auction itself. One could talk about quality thresholds and things of that kind, but at the end of the day the auction was going to remain in place and that was because Mrs Thatcher wanted it. He was talking to David Waddington. He had to persuade Waddington of the detail. She was never going to be interested in the detail. She was only going to be interested in the big picture and the big picture included the auction. So whatever else they might be able to get through, we were never going to get any change on that. For us, because plainly that was the most dreadful aspect of it, I think we were not clear about what position we were in the end going to take, because while they were taking on board a lot of what we were suggesting, we were obviously not going to achieve our objective of scrapping the auction. The quality threshold, it might not be wrong to say that we invented it. There was a lot of detailed discussions about what categories should be in and what should be out. But I think Mellor said 'If we deliver on all of these things, will you say so?' And we put our heads together in an American football players way and came out and said 'Yes. If you deliver on these things, we will say so.' So it was a sort of exercise in *realpolitik*. I'm not ashamed of that, I do believe to this day that his heart was in the right place. He wanted to get something sensible ... Having the line into Mellor was our key contact. (Interview with Stuart Prebble)

Whereas the Campaign for Quality Television was concerned mainly with the creative side of television, especially drama and current affairs, the Broadcasting Consortium umbrella organisation represented voluntary organisations and the 'caring' professions. They worked to defend the social role of public service television. There were fears that Public Service Announcements and continuing education and social action programmes would be threatened, together with the Community Education Officers who were employed by the ITV companies to provide information and support to such programmes. There were links with Community Service Volunteers (CSV), the National Council for Voluntary Organisations (NCVO) and the media project at the Volunteer Centre.

The Voice of the Listener (later the Voice of the Listener and Viewer) organised by Jocelyn Hay, which was concerned, on a broader basis, with the effects of the changes from the perspective of viewers, also ran a vigorous lobbying campaign and organised a number of conferences with top-level speakers.

Standing Committee (January to March 1990)

The Broadcasting Bill was published on 7 December 1989. According to Shirley Littler:

the draftsmen hadn't anything like completed it. They were told that they'd got to publish it before Christmas, so they published it as it was, thinking they would pick up various bits. It was better to publish it incomplete in December than to have done a bit more work on it and publish it in January, because that would have given everybody else less time to do anything. However it made it very difficult for the IBA, because a lot of what we were concerned with was the detail of the Bill, not just the principles. We were also immensely concerned about what was going to happen to the Authority and its staff, which nobody else worried too much about, and most of the stuff in the annexes on that didn't come in till much later and one was given about two days to have a look at it and turn it back and hope that it was all right. (Interview with Shirley Littler)

Following its second reading in the House of Commons on 18 December 1989, Standing Committee F had the first of its thirty-eight sittings on 9 January 1990. Robin Corbett, a former journalist, was lead speaker for the Labour Party backed by Mark Fisher (Shadow Arts Minister); other Labour representatives included Scotsmen Alistair Darling, John McAllion, and Norman Buchan together with Welsh MPs Ted Rowlands and Llin Golding. Gwyneth Dunwoody lobbied hard for the mandatory status of children's programmes and Tony Banks, representing the broadcasting union BETA, struck up a rapport with Mellor, a fellow Chelsea football supporter.

Although David Mellor, as Minister of State for Broadcasting and former barrister, dominated the debate, other prominent Conservatives included Roger Gale (nicknamed 'Blue Peter' because of his previous connection with the children's programme), Emma Nicholson (who had a particular interest in subtitling since she was partially deaf) and John Greenway, a former policeman, and member of the Home Affairs Committee, who made several points on behalf of Yorkshire TV and the ITV Association. Robert Maclennan, another lawyer who had a mastery of the details of the legislation, was spokesman for the Liberal Democrats and the Welsh input was reinforced by Dr Dafydd Elis Thomas of Plaid Cymru.

David Mellor said the intention of the Bill was to establish

a different sort of regulatory framework that is far from being entirely permissive, but recognises some contemporary realities such as the increasingly competitive framework in which commercial television must operate in the 1990s and the significance in this era of viewer power. (Column 183, Standing Committee F, 18 January 1990)

When asked about his Sunday evening viewing, Mellor compared ITV's schedule with an 'entrancing' programme on Ravel whereas

Channel 3 gave us *The Two of Us*. The episode called *The Telephone Only Rings Twice* and was described as the return of a new series about Mr and Mrs Average in which 'Ashley finds a portable telephone on the way home' – now there's an intriguing idea – and when it rings, the young couple find themselves caught in crime'. I am really sorry that I missed that! Then there was the news, and at 9.05p.m. there was '*Agatha Christie's Poirot*' – so called to distinguish it from Norman Buchan's Poirot. Then we had *The New Statesman*, loosely based on the career of the hon. Member for Birmingham, Erdington (Mr Corbett). Those were the rival attractions that were offered. To be fair to the hon. Gentleman, the *South Bank Show* had been on the week before. It was about Boris Pasternak, and ran from 10.35pm to 12.15am. I am sure that it was a good programme, and I am genuinely sorry that I missed it. Interestingly, it was not shown in peak-time, although it was a worthwhile programme – the kind of programme that I hope and believe will continue to be made for Channel 3 consumption. (Ibid.)

In the first article of what was to be a weekly commentary in *The Listener* on the Committee Stage of the Broadcasting Bill Barry Cox, Director of Corporate Affairs at LWT, commented that:

> By and large, the debates were good-humoured, and had a fair share of good jokes. The best came from the Home Office Minister of State piloting the Bill, David Mellor, and Labour's Tony Banks. Mr Mellor's wit is smoothly cerebral. Mr Banks, on the other hand, looking like an updated teddy boy, has a wonderful line in rough-edged outrageousness. Last week he was standing in as the Labour Whip – the 'only privatised Whip in the parliamentary Labour Party, or Instant Whip', as he called himself. (*The Listener*, 18 January 1990)

The opposition won a concession on the composition of the Independent Television Commission; as drafted, there was no requirement for a national member from each of Scotland, Wales and Ireland but Mellor accepted Labour's amendment for the current requirement to be retained, although Labour's attempts to make Parliament more involved in the appointment of the Chairman and members of the ITC, the 'glasnost' amendments introduced by Robin Corbett, failed. Opposition amendments to Clause 2, which laid out the functions of the ITC, provoked a debate about basic principles.

According to Barry Cox:

> in a series of amendments, Robin Corbett and Robert Maclennan sought to preserve the interventionist and public service ethos of the existing IBA/ITV system. In reply David Mellor developed a vision of a popular Channel 3 of the 1990s that was, I am ashamed to say, more eloquent and convincing than anything said in public by any ITV executive or programme-maker in the past two years.
>
> Pointing out that there would be three terrestrial channels with clear public service remits (BBC and Channel 4) he rejected requests for ITV's current public service obligations to be continued at the same level after 1992: 'let us not piously create a service that has every conceivable merit except that of being watched'. (*The Listener*, 25 January 1990)

The issue of the ITV network was raised early in the debate. Mellor's stance was that:

> The networking arrangements emerged in the 1950s when there was some doubt in the people's minds about whether the ITV system was sustainable. Thereafter, it became a source of controversy, as many larger companies such as HTV and TVS found themselves outside the magic circle ... Hence, further discussions have been taking place with a view to arriving at fresh networking arrangements within weeks.
>
> We seek to express the hope and belief that the companies involved will be able to arrive at networking arrangements between themselves. That would obviously be the best solution. That is certainly the view of George Russell ... If we are dealing with top-of-the-range programmes costing £500,000 an hour, they obviously cannot be done on a regional basis. There has to be a network. Equally obvious is the fact that a networking arrangement is of enormous benefit in ensuring continuity of the system, but one hopes that any networking arrangement that emerges will not be perpetuated, without anyone being able to challenge it, for 30 years, but that it will allow for change at sensible intervals. Circumstances and the capability of companies change. (Columns 200–1, Standing Committee F, 18 January 1990)

On 23 January 1990 Ivor Stanbrook noted that 'In the third week of our consideration of a Bill with more than 160 clauses, we are still debating clause 2'. The discussion then turned to the controversial topic of takeovers and ownership changes. Mellor made his position clear:

> The absence of the possibility of takeovers in any industry is often conducive to inefficiency ... I am opposed in principle to restrictions on takeovers that appear to imply that there is some magic about a particular company having responsibilities ... Once the public interest is protected, there is no compelling case for a moratorium. Existing companies have been largely protected by the IBA's refusal to agree to the transfer of shares in several cases that would have led to a change in control. Mr Russell has already announced that the IBA intends to allow takeovers of existing companies pre-1993, so there may be some takeovers of existing franchise holders pre-1993. That is a further reason why it would be artificial to reintroduce a moratorium at the award of a new franchise. (Columns 230–45, Standing Committee F, 23 January 1990)

By mid-February, Shirley Littler in a progress report to the Members on the Broadcasting Bill summed up developments in the Standing Committee as follows:

> Mr Mellor has set the tone of the debate by listening carefully to points made to him from all sides, and by being ready to make concessions where the case

is strong. Government has introduced a few of its own amendments. Eleven changes covering the powers of the ITC and operation of the selection process as well as some key features of the new regime have already been agreed in detail. But almost more important have been the numerous issues on which Mr Mellor has promised further thought, with the possibility, amounting to certainty in some cases, of an amendment at the Report Stage. (IBA Paper 20(90))

Agreed amendments, at this stage, related to the programme quality threshold which included powers for the ITC to ensure competition and high quality in the provision of services and of the award of licences only to 'fit and proper' persons. The ITC would publish 'illustrative guidelines' including an indication of a range of programmes and the independent production quota would be required to have a range and diversity in terms of cost of acquisition and types of programmes. Applicants would also have to provide information on what would be offered in terms of facilities as well as programmes. Despite the Minister's and the IBA's reluctance to compile a 'shopping list' of mandatory programmes it was promised (after heavy lobbying) that children's and religious programmes would be added to the statutory requirements in Clause 16. Throughout the Standing Committee the IBA had prepared a series of briefs 'Notes for MPs', which were often referred to by speakers in the debates. Shirley Littler commented that:

> the value of the IBA's views has been enhanced by Mr Mellor's readiness to invoke the endorsement of the Chairman and senior staff of the IBA for his own points wherever this is possible. The Opposition has been quick to quote IBA views back at the Minister where, as is often the case, our briefs have been critical of the provisions in the Bill.

By the end of the Standing Committee, thirty-eight briefs, ranging from the importance of networking in Channel 3, schools programmes, subtitling for the deaf, teletext, the preservation of due impartiality, the map and the clock had been delivered to the Committee, often moments before the opening of the debate. David Mellor paid tribute to the quality of these briefings.

According to Shirley Littler again:

> Our briefing was comparable in quality to the sort of briefing of Ministers that goes on from the Department ... [although she recalled that]: We overplayed it at one point ... I remember Edwina Currie being furious about this and coming up to me and saying she thought it was an abuse of parliamentary privilege that MPs were bringing in these notes. So we held off a bit after that. But it was nonsense that it was an abuse of parliamentary privilege, although I could understand that the Conservative backbenchers resented this, because one object of the Whips is to tell their own backbenchers to shut up so that they can get through things on time, and the fact that there were some rather good briefings

going round about some of these clauses was extending things and they weren't allowed to say anything. But apart from Edwina Currie, who in any case disliked the IBA and was a difficult lady, I don't think we did overplay our briefing at all. (Interview with Shirley Littler)

Barry Cox noted that:

The IBA seems to be getting every amendment it asks for ... Mr Mellor's willingness to help Mr Russell as much as possible is understandable – after all, as chairman of the ITC, Mr Russell will have to make this vast piece of legislation actually work – the Minister is getting increasing warnings from his own side about 'not recreating the IBA'. (*The Listener*, 15 February 1990)

The following week Cox reckoned that:

The best debate of the week was over the Channel 3 news service. As Mr Mellor admitted, the Government's proposals to oblige the ITC to nominate one or more news providers for the Channel (and to prevent the Channel 3 licensees from owning a majority of the shares in any such provider) did create a conflict between their wish to avoid monopoly supply and their wish to see a news service capable of taking on the BBC.

   He was prepared to leave it to the ITC to sort out this dilemma, though he accepted amendments from Robert Maclennan which would require the Commission to conduct a more open contest for the news supply contracts than the Bill at present proposes. None the less, Mr Maclennan's account of the widespread anxieties about the news proposals that existed among the ITV companies and inside the IBA – anxieties about loss of editorial control and potential conflicts of interest between broadcasters and news suppliers – suggested that this issue was unlikely to go away that easily. (*The Listener*, 22 February 1990)

In an earlier column Cox had noted that:

Mr Maclennan also speaks often, but then he is the official Liberal spokesman, and sponsors many amendments. His dull delivery irritates his audience in a different way to Mr Buchan, but it usually pays to attend to what he says, certainly Mr Mellor treats him with respect. (*The Listener*, 8 February 1990)

As a spectator of the Committee, Cox found that:

It was noticeable that, now the committee had finished with the contentious ITV auction clauses, an atmosphere of anti-climax did begin to pervade its deliberations. Half the professional lobbyists (including the quality campaigners with their string of showbiz supporters) had gone – as had the cameras, though we did have the Deaf lobby in their place. At least those of us that remained didn't have to queue to get in any more. (*The Listener*, 22 February 1990)

Having achieved concessions on subtitling, the issue of teletext united both Conservative and Labour MPs to challenge the government's proposal to allow the spare lines capacity of the existing channels to be sold off to the highest bidders. Most speakers wanted some capacity guaranteed on Channels 3 and 4 and, under pressure, the Minister agreed to consider the matter further. Opposition to the establishment of the Broadcasting Standards Council, as an unnecessary duplication of the activities of the IBA/ITC and the BBC, was overruled by Mellor although Cox noted:

Watching David Mellor on the subject was like watching Chris Patten on the poll tax: you get a highly professional defence but you suspect they don't really agree with any of it. (*The Listener*, 8 March 1990)

Similarly, in response to the provision in the Bill for extending the Obscene Publications Act to broadcasting, Cox observed that:

Mr Mellor clearly didn't believe the Obscene Publications Act had any relevance to broadcasting, since the broadcasters' own codes were far more restrictive, but as the broadcasters had evidently annoyed a significant section of the population by their behaviour they were just going to have to live with this new restraint. None the less he did remove most of the objectionable police powers of search and seizure from these clauses. (*The Listener*, 15 March 1990)

The Standing Committee had ended its 38th sitting on 15 March, and many agreed with Cox (*The Listener*, 15 March 1990) that 'this does seem to have been an unusually effective committee, and a model of how our law-making is supposed to work'.

Even Tony Banks, Labour MP, admitted (Column 1519, Standing Committee F, 15 March 1990) that 'The Minister has pulled many rabbits out of many hats and got out of many tight corners. In some respects, he has made Houdini look positively leaden-footed.'

This was confirmed by the Chairman, Sir Michael Shaw who, in his closing remarks observed (Column 1520, Standing Committee F, 15 March 1990) that

The Committee has worked hard to improve the Bill. Having sat in this chair many times, I can say that is not always the case with all Committees. There has been very little partisanship but a genuine attempt to get it right, or at any rate to get it better. This is an example that many Committees could follow.

By the end of the Standing Committee many promises had been made although the amendments were still not finalised. Shirley Littler commented:

> Mellor was given a fairly free hand on a lot of things, and I think he was very clever because he went through the Committee Stage not making much in the way of amendments but promising to consider things, and then that did give the Home Office the opportunity to put a lot of change together as a whole and introduce it into the report stage. And the Bill was very different by the time it went into Report. Partly because extra bits were being added and partly because a lot of sensible points had been introduced as a result of amendments discussed at Committee Stage. (Interview with Shirley Littler)

Houses of Commons/Lords Stages (May to October 1990)

By early April, the IBA was taking stock of changes in the Standing Committee in preparation for the House of Commons Report Stage in May and for the House of Lords debates in June and July. They had been advised by their Parliamentary Consultants, MAI, to circulate a note to all MPs before the Report Stage started, summarising the IBA's main points on the Bill as amended, supplemented by additional briefs on particular topics. Outstanding topics were seen as news provision, on which the government had confirmed its intention to maintain the ownership provisions for the nominated news provider (51 per cent outside ownership and 49 per cent licensee ownership after the specified period). A report on the progress of the Bill by Shirley Littler (IBA Paper 27(90) in March) indicated that

> we are lying low on this at present and considering what would be involved in the way of additional powers for the ITC if the Government's underlying intention, that ITN should be the Channel 3 news provider, is to be achieved, other than with the agreement of ITN's present owners.

As Shirley Littler later concluded:

> There was no room for manoeuvre on ITN. Alastair Burnet had got Mrs Thatcher's ear and nothing we said or did could persuade him ... I think we got a bit of a change in the clause but not a real change. (Interview with Shirley Littler)

David Mellor was also realistic about his scope for manoeuvre on the structure of the news provider:

> Burnet had gone to her and there was some sort of emotional overlay to the meeting which meant that it could never be. And I took the view that they'd got themselves

into this hole, why should I pull them out of it? I would have done if I could. But it was not a bottom-line issue. (Interview with David Mellor)

ITVA had distributed a brief for MPs in May 1990 expressing concern for the implications for ITV news provision. Although ITV lobbying was further reinforced by letters to David Waddington from Richard Dunn on the ownership provisions and from David Nicholas expressing concern at the 'cash call' (in October 1990) on ITN describing the McKinsey review and five-year business plan (see Chapter 6) the government refused to shift on the news issue.

A schism was developing within ITV on networking (see Chapter 5). Although the companies had presented the Shadow ITC with a draft of agreed principles, the detail needed to be worked out before the ITC could finally approve it as acceptable for the extended contract period and regard it as the basis for the transitional network which might be adopted by Channel 3 licensees. Shirley Littler commented (IBA Paper 27(90)) that

> The companies are also playing hard to get, since they want to sell their agreement to a revised network scheme in return for concessions from Government on the selection process itself including perhaps a Government decision to prevent multiple bidding. Staff are presently considering whether and how we can get all the various horses to the water, *and* then persuade them to drink together.

Conceptually, Shirley Littler found the network one of the most difficult areas in the Bill:

> The difficulty was that if you really explained the significance of the network, it became practically impossible to see how individual contractors could put forward proper proposals. I always found this intellectually very difficult to grasp, and I don't think MPs grasped it, and the DTI with its anti-uncompetitive ITV pro-independent producer lobby stance was determined not to grasp it. (Interview with Shirley Littler)

Final agreement by government was also awaited in relation to the issues of a limited moratorium on takeovers, ownership, control, cross-holdings and the definition of exceptional circumstances. A further concern also remained on the issue of impartiality which it was anticipated in the debate in the Lords, partly inspired by the longstanding campaign of Norris McWhirter and the Freedom Association, might focus on the desirability of even tighter statutory definitions.

Religious matters in the Broadcasting Bill were another controversial area which was still unresolved. David Glencross, in IBA Paper 45(90) in April reported to members that in the course of a recent meeting with the Home Office officials it had become clear that Ministers were looking to the IBA for help on two questions, in particular, firstly, ownership of stations by religious groups, and secondly, a definition of 'undue prominence' in relation to specific churches or religious groups. As it stood, the Bill disqualified bodies whose aims were wholly or mainly religious from holding an ITC licence. Owners of ITC licences would not be able to use them to express their own views and opinions on religious matters. However, the Minister had indicated that he intended to amend the Bill to allow the regulatory body to licence Christian (and other religious groups) on cable and satellite TV channels whose programming was responsible. Although the 1981 Broadcasting Act prohibited advertising 'by or on behalf of any body whose objects are wholly or mainly of a religious nature' and 'which is directed towards any religious end', this had not been repeated in the Bill. In the light of reservations from the Central Religious Advisory Committee (CRAC) and the likelihood that any consensus on acceptable rules for religious advertising was likely to be difficult to achieve, Glencross recommended wide consultation before rules were formulated.

Bill in the House of Commons (May/June 1990)

> The Bill has emerged with much wider acceptance for many of its key requirements than was the case before the Committee Stage, and that is a tribute to the work of the Standing Committee ... Although it is true that we have a formidable task in front of us, with some 700 amendments, to consider, of which more than 500 are Government amendments ... those amendments reflect the hard work of the Committee and are a sign of the success of parliamentary procedures, not a criticism of them. (David Mellor opening the House of Commons Report Stage of the Bill on 8 May 1990. Broadcasting Bill, House of Commons, Column 50)

The Report Stage of the Bill was debated in the House of Commons on 8/9 May 1990. Many of the amendments fulfilled pledges to change the Bill which had been made by David Mellor at Committee Stage. Non-government amendments included those tabled by John Greenway for the ITV Association concerning exceptional circumstances and networking. There was also substantial political interest in the amendment by Michael Alison, a Church Commissioner, calling for broadcasting to be predominantly Christian in character, and for religious interests not to be bound by the 'no editorialising' requirement of Clause 6 in the Bill.

The IBA had not sponsored any amendments at this stage but had maintained a close dialogue with the Home Office and shown them IBA briefing in key areas in advance of wider distribution so that the approach was generally understood. They had, however, sought counsel's opinion from William Blackburne QC on the amendments the government had tabled for the Report Stage on the application of exceptional circumstances in Section 17(3) of the Bill. The Home Office had issued a press release on 18 April 1990 stating that the Minister would table an amendment to 'provide that the exceptional circumstances provision applied to quality'. Blackburne's interpretation was that the government's intention was that all the applicant's proposals should be 'outstanding' although he admitted that 'the use of the word "exceptionally" is one which is, in my view, capable of causing difficulty'.

When Mellor opened the debate in the House of Commons on 8 May 1990, he reported that the ITV companies were aware of the deficiencies of the present networking arrangements and proposed to make changes although these were still in the process of negotiation. Clarification, however, was still needed on how far the ITC, as the regulator, should regulate competition issues and at what point it should hand over to the Office of Fair Trading (OFT) and those charged with the responsibility of more broadly-based jurisdiction over competition issues.

George Walden, MP for Buckingham, who had spoken eloquently in the opening debate of the Bill in December 1989, warned of a 'grave danger of a dilution of standards' and pointed out 'that there was still some uncertainty about how many notches down the new arrangements will be' (Broadcasting Bill, Column 99, House of Commons debate, 8 May 1990). The question of how long a moratorium on takeovers should be was raised yet again. Michael Alison, who had been lobbying in association with the Evangelical Alliance and Christian Standards in Society, expressed concern that Christian and other religious bodies were being restricted in a way unprecedented in previous broadcasting legislation but welcomed the amendment which allowed religious bodies to hold television service licences for both non-domestic satellite and cable services. Mellor reminded him that the government's aim was to strike a fair balance between ensuring that responsible Christian broadcasters had the opportunity to participate in the expanded services while maintaining adequate protection against the exploitative religious programming that might be provided by religious cults – or by the American evangelists 'who have almost brought our religious broadcasting into dispute' (Column 158). He proposed to remove the 'no undue prominence' and 'no editorialising' arrangements from religious broadcasting and to replace them with 'a concept yet to be fully worked out' (Column 158).

By the third reading in the House of Commons on 10 May 1990 the Bill contained over 170 Clauses and 12 Schedules. Mellor summarised the major improvements in the Bill, endorsed on Report as:

> a thickening of the quality threshold ... by the addition of the requirements for children's and religious programming and for high quality regional news, and of the power for the ITC to publish an illustrative specification of the elements of programming which it would expect to see in a diverse programme service. (Column 416)

He also pointed out the enhancement of the regional content of Channel 3 services by the statutory introduction of the concept of dual regions with distinct regional programming and the power for the ITC to require applicants to specify what regional resources and facilities they would plan to use, as well as the requirement that Scotland should not be a single franchise area. He also hoped that amendments to the exceptional circumstances provision would make it clear that high quality could displace the highest money bid and that 'the overt striking of a fair balance between quality and price' had been 'one of the major achievements of the Committee' (Column 417).

Alistair Darling, Labour MP, however, expressed doubt on the claimed triumph of the exceptional circumstances provision and warned that 'Notwithstanding the amendment and the Minister's sentiments, the Bill means that the highest bidder will win unless the lower bidder is exceptionally better.' He saw this as 'difficult to assess or to establish' (Column 446). He also doubted that, unless a three-year moratorium on takeovers was introduced, the safeguards for regional television would be swept away if there was a flurry of takeover bids after the auction by those who had not passed the quality threshold.

David Mellor, however, saw the progress of the Bill from a different perspective:

We have given Channel 3 the elbow room that it will need to be competitive, while ensuring that no one can get a Channel 3 franchise who is not properly qualified or has not surmounted a rigorous quality test. (Column 448)

Bill in the House of Lords (June/July/October 1990)

Religious Broadcasting and Impartiality
Discussion on the Bill continued in the House of Lords on 5 June 1990 (Second Reading) and at Committee Stage for seven days in July. The issues, which had not provoked detailed debate in Standing Committee, but now dominated the proceedings, were the status of Christianity in religious broadcasting, the role of the BBC/ITV Central Religious Advisory Committee (CRAC) and the key matter of impartiality in broadcasting as a whole. Lord Orr-Ewing, the Earl of Halsbury and Baroness Cox were the main speakers on religious broadcasting; they were joined by Lord Wyatt of Weeford on impartiality.

Lord Orr-Ewing hoped that:

when we see the amendments which have now been promised we shall remember that the established Church in this country is the Church of England and also that our monarch is defender of the faith. I should not have to say this in front of bishops but we sometimes forget that that faith is Christianity. It is not a mish-mash of various faiths; it is Christianity of which the monarch bears the defence. We back her and the Church in their efforts. (House of Lords, Second Reading, 5 June 1990, Column 1278)

This led later to his more specific attack on CRAC which 'has not proved to be imaginative or conscientious. Too much power has fallen into the hands of the officials' (House of Lords, 9 July 1990, Column 54).

Barry Cox saw the debate as partly tilting at windmills and partly reflecting a deeper division within the Church itself:

CRAC ... turns out to be an organ of censorship as reprehensible as any of those going out of favour in Eastern Europe. I had always thought CRAC's most effective action in recent years was preventing LWT shifting *Highway* out of peak-time to make way for a current affairs show, which was deeply irritating to LWT but scarcely something which put CRAC alongside the Stasi or the Securitate.

However, listening to the Earl of Halsbury, Lord Orr-Ewing and Baroness Cox you had the clear sense that CRAC not only kept good Christians off the screen but was actually working to weaken the position of Christianity in Britain. This was strong stuff, given that the past and present chairmen of CRAC – the Bishops of London and Liverpool – were sitting a couple of benches away. At one point Baroness Cox described the many prayer groups praying at that moment for the defeat of CRAC which provoked the dignified response from the Bishop of Liverpool, David Sheppard, that he was grateful they were praying, but he wondered what they had been told to make them think Christianity was in such dire straits.

Decoded, this proved to be part of the wider tussle going on between the evangelicals and the mainstream religious establishment. As Earl Ferrers, the Home Office Minister in charge of the Bill in the Lords implied, it was pretty tangential to the Bill itself, whose freeing up of religious broadcasting was, in fact, highly welcome to the evangelical camp. (As the Bishop of Liverpool pointed out it was highly unlikely that the cash-strapped Church of England was going to be able to take advantage of the new freedom to bid for a cable licence or radio station.) (*The Listener*, 9 July 1990)

In her progress report in June on the Broadcasting Bill Shirley Littler warned members that:

We are expecting a lot of trouble on impartiality. Although the main attack has been on BBC programmes, the IBA has not escaped criticism. We are vulnerable on certain programmes and series (notably on Channel 4 and *World in Action*) to charges that our own guidelines have not been fully enforced. I believe that the Home Office will have to give something to pressure in the Lords and the least damaging concession would be to remove the word 'current' from the phrase 'matters of current controversy'.

Two particular changes have to be addressed as a result of the Lords Second Reading. The first is that impartiality requirements are not adequate as they appear in the Bill. The second is that whatever legislation and codes as applied by the ITC say, the broadcaster will go his own sweet way as in the past.

On the first, the Home Office are likely to say that while requirements have in the past lacked the force of law and the criteria used have not been stated in detail, the statutory requirement to have an enforceable code in which the criteria must be fully stated will be more vigorous. I think that in our briefing we shall have to take the same line ... I hope that if we can offer some clear and sensible guidelines about how the ITC should define a series, it would help to convince the doubters that experienced regulators can adapt to new requirements and new systems. (IBA Paper 74(90))

Lord Wyatt had introduced, in the Lords Committee Stage, amendments to incorporate the impartiality code itself as a statutory requirement in the Bill. His amendment was withdrawn after the promise by Earl Ferrers that the government would consider the matter further. Lord Chalfont, Deputy Chairman of the IBA, although he had previously been active in the Media Monitoring Unit which had alleged partiality, notably in *World in Action*, in a series of monitoring reports, expressed his belief that 'due impartiality or true impartiality lie at the heart of responsible broadcast journalism' but conceded that 'I believe that this can best be achieved by giving effective powers to the regulatory authorities and leaving them to exercise those powers rather than by attempting to prescribe these extremely complicated matters on the face of a Bill' (House of Lords, 11 July 1990, Column 379). He advised that the ITC should publish a draft code and invite comments from all interested parties.

The issue remained to be thrashed out at the Report Stage in the House of Lords, starting on 9 October 1990. Legal opinions were quoted profusely, including advice from Professor John Finnis (Professor of Law at Oxford), Lord Goodman (of Goodman, Derrick & Co., the ITVA's solicitors), Anthony Scrivener QC and Christopher Beaumont, the leading counsel advising ITN. Lord Annan, former Chairman of the Committee on the Future of Broadcasting, offered a broader perspective on the issue :

Some noble Lords, with great sincerity, believe that broadcasting as it stands is entirely impartial. But the noble Viscount, Lord Whitelaw, was entirely right when he said that although there is an injunction to be impartial, television is usually biased simply because many broadcasters like to tilt against the establishment, and every government, whether Labour or Conservative, find themselves up against that tilt ... Our Committee found that then, as today, there was concern that broadcasters were not taking due impartiality seriously enough. But that did not deter us from saying that there must be programmes that took a biased and a personal point of view. Without such programmes television would not fulfil its role of stimulating public discussion ... The question is not whether the BBC and IBA codes on impartiality are adequate. Of course they are. The question is not even whether they are applied. The question is whether the inevitable tilt ... has gone too far. (House of Lords, 22 October 1990, Columns 1160–2)

The outcome was that the government agreed that although there would be a general statutory requirement for due impartiality the definitions of what constituted a series and the interpretation of 'major matters' would be left to the discretion of the ITC.

According to Barry Cox:

The problem for the Home Office was that they erroneously thought they had got it all sorted out with the Independent Broadcasting Authority in the week before the Bill came back to the Lords for the Report Stage ... Unfortunately for the Home Office, its normally surefooted relationship with Brompton Road went awry. On the Friday before the Lords reassembled, George Russell, the IBA's Chairman, broke free from his minders, Lord Chalfont and Lady Littler, and to the consternation of the Government, declared the amendment unworkable. (Internal disagreement at the IBA, together with the speed with which the whole business was being bounced along, seems to have misled the Home Office about the IBA's likely response) ...

The day before the debate, Lord Whitelaw, a pivotal figure on the Conservative benches, told a packed meeting in the Lords that he might vote against the Government. David Mellor, peeved, decided they would have to compromise.

... Procedural confusion was now complicating political uncertainty and Earl Ferrers offered to withdraw the amendment and bring it back at Third Reading in its sanitised form, rather to the dismay of the massed troops on both sides who had been dragooned into attendance in the expectation of an exciting vote. (*The Listener*, 18 October 1990)

Shirley Littler's account of this confused communication and alleged failure to inform the Home Office what the IBA's stance on impartiality was that:

I think ... it was the only time we said that something was unworkable as it stood. We didn't warn the Home Office and this created a real furore, and that was the point that Willie Whitelaw came in. We had told him on odd occasions about some of our problems. He came to dinner on one occasion and George (Russell) and I went to see him at the House of Lords, and I think after this note we may have gone to see him and explained what the problem was ... He thought the line we were taking was very sensible and he did say ... if you run into real trouble let me know ... We threw out a little bombshell; Mellor got very agitato and the Home Office realised that they'd have to do something about this, they couldn't just let it go with deciding that Woodrow Wyatt was the lesser of two evils ... We did obviously accept a certain amount of change in the impartiality provisions, but not as much as he wanted. (Interview with Shirley Littler)

When the Lords amendments returned to the House of Commons on 25 October 1990, Mellor introduced the debate by clarifying the amendment on impartiality:

I want to restate the principle with as much clarity as I can muster that it is the right of Parliament – it has been so for four decades – to insist that there is due impartiality on matters of current political or industrial controversy and so on. However, it is not for us to usurp the function of the regulators and state exactly what the detailed rules should be. We are not doing that in the amendments. (House of Commons, 25 October 1990, Column 522)

Looking back at the impartiality issue, Mellor saw it as:

... a very bad business really. And that showed that Mrs Thatcher who always used to complain about disloyalty had a somewhat flexible concept of loyalty herself. Because I discovered, to my dismay, that there was this group of peers, Woodrow, Ewing, and so on, who were very concerned about impartiality. And I was astonished to discover that having got the Bill through the Commons and put it in good shape in the Lords, she, without telling either the Home Secretary or myself, had had a private dinner with these characters. And although it was never made clear to me exactly what was said at that meeting, one had the impression that she had encouraged them to cause quite a lot of trouble on this issue in the House of Lords, which I thought was an extraordinarily underhand thing to do. It did cause a lot of trouble and the last thing one wanted was a bloody great row and everything coming apart and Michael Grade having a cardiac arrest just when we thought everything was sorted. (Interview with David Mellor)

The Map and the Clock

Overshadowed by the more high-profile debates on religious broadcasting and impartiality in the Lords, the IBA still had to consider further the map and the clock for Channel 3. Shirley Littler reported on developments to Members on 5 July 1990 in IBA Paper 77(90). The IBA's finance division had constructed a model indicating the viability of the current regions. A letter was being prepared for the Chairman, George Russell, to send to David Mellor, which would alert the government to the questions raised by potentially non-viable regions in considering whether or not to retain the present map. This also raised questions of regionalism and contiguity. The conclusions based on the financial modelling of dual and triple regions were summarised by Peter Rogers, Finance Director, in Annexe 'A' to IBA Paper 77(90). Hill Samuel, in an assessment of the work, also agreed that the four smallest areas, Ulster, Grampian, Border and Channel were unlikely to be financially viable, even under more favourable assumptions. By the end of August 1990, Members were asked to take a final decision on the Channel 3 map and clock with a view to a public announcement as soon as possible. Staff recommended in IBA Paper 93(90) that all the sixteen existing ITV contracts as at present should be advertised as Channel 3 licences; the existing clock should be retained but licensees must be required to broadcast during all the hours made available to them, and that the financial risks of the smaller licences must be made clear in public. In order to sustain the smaller licence areas and to guarantee continuity of programme service to viewers in the event of financial collapse, a number of undertakings had been sought from government. These included powers for the ITC to arrange a substitute service if no licence could be awarded for an area or if a licence collapsed; the contiguity rules could be relaxed, possibly after the end of the moratorium on takeovers and that there would be assurance from government that assistance would be provided, if required, for the Northern Ireland licence.

Although the paper, presented by David Glencross, Director of Television, conceded that on the basis of forecasting, the financial strength of the federal Channel 3 system would be improved in the 1990s by reducing the number of companies, there was limited room for manoeuvre at this stage. This view was reinforced by George Russell's judgement that in a period of restructuring and of possible disruption, the rate of change should be managed gradually to allow the system to stabilise although, in the longer term, he realised the need for larger economic units.

Looking back at the question of how many Channel 3 licences to advertise, Peter Rogers (then Director of Finance) recounts the process as follows:

There was a real question about whether we should advertise as many as 15 licences. And in the end we did, but we gave a fair bit of thought to advertising only perhaps seven or eight ... One of the options I was quite interested in was whether we could advertise a smaller number of bigger licences but still preserve the local distinctiveness of them by making them dual or triple regions, because the notion of a dual region had been pioneered and shown to work ... You could still preserve what was valued by the viewers but you could do it within a more economically viable enterprise. The difficulty with this approach was twofold.

First, some of the areas that you would put together were fairly obvious, but some were very difficult. So you could have put, using the terminology of the time, Scottish in with Grampian, you could have put Yorkshire in with Tyne Tees, you could have put Border in with Granada, you could have put TSW with either HTV or TVS, and if you wanted to go further you might have put Anglia in with Central or something of that kind. But in those days of bombs going off and the sensitivity of Ulster, what on earth were you going to do with Ulster? Because it was not at all clear that anyone on the mainland would actually want Ulster. They would be buying into something which was of great sensitivity and not easy to comprehend if you weren't born and brought up there. And what about Channel, with its different political system?

Secondly, if you put two areas together and advertised only a single larger licence then one of the incumbents, usually the smaller one, would have no prospect of continuity. The shareholder value built up over the years would be wiped out. You could be hard-nosed about that and argue that the IBA's contractors had always known that their contracts were leasehold and not freehold and that was the risk they had taken. But I think that particularly George [Russell] felt badly about that, coming from the business end, and had said 'Well, why don't we let them try and if they can't survive let them come together by acquisition and merger.' At least in that way the shareholders would get something back for their investment. (Interview with Peter Rogers)

Educational Programmes

Another area in which pressure was being exerted on the IBA by educational interests, including the IBA's Educational Advisory Council (EAC), was to support an enlarged programme shopping list which would include documentaries, educational and social action programmes and the requirement that all programmes in the shopping list (including regional, religious and children's programmes) should be shown at appropriate times of the day and the week. Although the Lords led by Baroness David succeeded in adding educational programming to the shopping list, the amendment was overturned when the Bill was finally reconsidered by the House of Commons at the end of October.

Engineering Privatisation

The future of the Engineering division of the IBA had been arranged before Royal Assent to the Bill (see Chapter 7). Numerous amendments had been rushed through the Commons Report Stage tying up the division of assets and privatisation of the engineering resource. Initially the IBA engineers had proposed a management buy-out but this idea had been firmly discouraged by the Chairman, George Russell, who had had considerable experience of management buyouts. Shirley Littler recalled the process of privatisation, which was overseen from the IBA by Peter Rogers, Director of Finance:

> The Home Office were adamant that the change had got to happen by the end of '90, which when it came to the point was sensible, because prolonging the change wouldn't have worked. The IBA had got to be replaced and you'd got to work it out. But Peter [Rogers] was very good about this because he'd collected a little nest egg to ease the transition, and those rotters from the Treasury tried to pinch it from him ... I think he'd started to collect a bit of a surplus and the theory was that if the IBA had a surplus the Treasury could send a direction to remove the surplus. This was to stop it overspending. But he'd got the auditors to say that we had to keep the surplus because we might be making a lot of redundancy payments. The other thing that was absolutely crucial was that we had to cope properly with the pensions because there was a long string of IBA pensioners ... The engineers, backed up by their own lawyers, Treasury or Home Office appointed lawyers and solicitors and consultants and so on, I thought, had a tendency to be extremely greedy about the share of assets they should get. But it did eventually work out and, quite frankly, when I think that

our transmission system was simply nationalised without compensation and cut down to size with the IBA paying the pensions, the Treasury did damn well. I mean bad luck on the ITV companies. (Interview with Shirley Littler)

The outcome of the privatisation plans was that the sale of National Transcommunications Ltd, which had been owned by the Crown since its formal vesting on 1 January 1991 was launched on 2 May 1991 and sold for £70 million to Mercury Asset Management in October 1991.

Finalisation of the Bill

A few weeks before the Bill received Royal Assent, Richard Dunn addressed a *Financial Times* conference on 9 October 1990 on 'The new shape of independent broadcasting'. Summarising, from his perspective, the events and issues from the publication of the White Paper to the passage of the Bill through Parliament, he attributed the improvements made in the Bill to David Mellor but generally saw the position as one of compromise and re-regulation rather than deregulation. He recollected that:

When the White Paper 'Competition, choice and quality' was published wise heads in the industry said it was all over. The Philistine tendency had beaten the One Nation Conservatives and ITV was to go to the auction block for the heresy of monopoly. Public Service Broadcasting was dead. Regulation would go, the market would decide. I and my colleagues in ITV decided nevertheless to take up the invitation of the then Home Secretary, Douglas Hurd, and the then Broadcasting Minister, Tim Renton, to enter into a period of dialogue and debate before the White Paper was developed into a Bill. We spent most of last year talking and talking with Ministers and officials, debating hurdles and thresholds and Bechers Brooks.

We did not lose heart when we found Douglas Hurd replaced by David Waddington and Tim Renton replaced by David Mellor. Many at the time saw it as a couple of cultured and concerned Etonians being replaced by a pair of grasping and uncaring lawyers. I was reminded of this on Sunday when I went to a press conference for our new series of *Minder*, in which Terry McCann will be replaced by a new minder for Arthur Daley, his young nephew, Ray. George Cole was asked what was the difference between the old minder and the new one, 'Well' he said, 'this new boy's got ... what's the stuff you find when cheese goes bad?... culture, that's it, he's got culture'.

Well David Mellor, our new minder ... er, Minister, proved eager to show the more cultural and sensitive side of his nature. So successful was he that within a year he found himself as Arts Minister. Fortunately, however, he has remained responsible for the Broadcasting Bill.

I say fortunately because David Mellor has, throughout the passage of the Bill, shown himself a willing listener without ever putting himself in the pocket of any lobby or interest group. The result has been that the Bill has been changing almost week by week throughout its long passage through Parliament, so that it reaches its final stages a very different beast from the market forces White Paper. Instead, what we have is a more competitive, but still heavily regulated system. Not deregulation, just re-regulation. It is a compromise. A peculiarly British compromise – and not necessarily a great British compromise.

Whatever change eventually results from the new Act, the pressure for change has already had a big effect. As far as ITV is concerned, no one can seriously sustain the two most famous charges levelled against us. We are not the last bastion of restrictive practices. The industry is lean, fit and supremely cost conscious ...

Neither are we the owners of a licence to print money. The new levy is penal ... Even the advertisers who accused us in the past of abuse of our monopoly position now recognise that Channel 3 will be fighting for its share of the advertising cake in a very crowded market place. The old monopoly is dead and I feel no nostalgia for it ... though I am proud of its record. (Speech by Richard Dunn to *Financial Times* conference, 9 October 1990)

Although Dunn issued warnings on the risk to ITV news provision, the difficulties arising from the pending amendment on the impartiality code and the competitive aspects of the networking arrangements, he concluded that:

The Act will be better than the Bill, which was better than the really shoddy White Paper. The Act is a mass of compromises mostly for the better ... A very great deal will depend on the way the ITC interprets its powers. (Ibid.)

Nearly a year after its introduction, the Bill received Royal Assent on 1 November 1990. It had expanded from 167 to 204 Sections and from 12 to 22 Schedules. In his final column on the subject in *The Listener*, Barry Cox signed off with the following comment:

The 1990 Broadcasting Act remains faithful to the neo-liberal spirit of the 1988 White Paper but has been made workable by the hundreds of detailed changes which, I suspect, few other Conservative ministers would have attempted. David Mellor has done the state – and broadcasting – some service. I hope he gets some benefit from it. (*The Listener*, 1 November 1990)

Major Changes in the Bill

Some of the major changes achieved in the passage of the Bill through Parliament included a strengthening of the quality threshold by the statutory requirement for a suitable amount of children's and religious programmes to be included in the schedules; for regional news to be of high quality and for the power of the ITC to publish illustrative guidelines of the elements of programming which would be expected in a diverse programme service. The 'highest bid' auction concept was modified by the possible application of 'exceptional circumstances' which could include the circumstance where the quality of programmes was exceptionally higher rather than that of the applicant offering the highest bid. The teletext services on Channels 3 and 4 were to have some public service provisions and at least half of all programmes, within five years of the start of the licences, would have to be subtitled for deaf viewers. A limited moratorium on takeovers was introduced from the point of licence award to one year after the start of broadcasting. Increased market access to non-broadcasters was facilitated by a 25 per cent quota for independent producers and for the provision for religious groups to own cable and non-domestic satellite licences. The restrictions on religious advertising were lifted, although religious programmes had to avoid 'improper exploitation' of their audience and 'abusive treatment' of other religious views. The monopoly on programme listings was ended and the ringfencing for the BBC and ITV of 'listed' sporting events was reduced. A disciplined framework on ITV networking arrangements was imposed by the statutory requirement for a network, with power for the ITC to impose a networking agreement if the licensees had not implemented a voluntary arrangement. Competitive aspects of the networking arrangements had also to be scrutinised and agreed by the Office of Fair Trading (OFT).

Supplementary Legislation

Details of rules on ownership and independent production were introduced as orders under the Broadcasting Act by Kenneth Baker who was appointed Home Secretary in November 1990. The rules on ownership, announced in December 1990, allowed anyone to hold a controlling interest in two regional Channel 3 licences as long as both were not large. 'Large' was defined as the nine companies with the highest Net Advertising Revenue (NAR), and 'small' as the six companies with the lowest NAR. These were known as the penny farthing rules. Initially, it was not possible until the end of 1992 for a single person to control two licence areas which were contiguous (that is, if they were adjacent with a significant land border between them). Further provisions were introduced in a supplementary order in March 1991 which limited broadcasters to a 15 per cent shareholding in an independent producer which was defined in detail. In April 1991, the scope of listed sported events which were not permitted to be shown on pay-per-view terms was reduced from twelve to eight.

Influences on the Bill

The Government
The influence of David Mellor in modifying, and it was generally agreed, in improving the crude White Paper to a manageable Act which preserved some of

the public service aspects of independent television has already been documented in this chapter. His previous experience of broadcasting, his clear-cut relationship with the Home Secretary David Waddington, who gave him a comparatively free rein while ensuring Mrs Thatcher did not intervene directly in detail because of the basic preservation of the 'auction' principle, and his ability to keep an open mind on policy issues which might be possible to change but his political awareness of areas such as news provision where he had little scope for influence, are evident from interviews with both civil servants, journalists, the ITC and the ITV companies.

ITC

Shirley Littler has attributed George Russell's appointment as ITC Chairman designate in December 1988 as the start of a new era when the government began to trust and work with the ITC in a way that they had not previously with the IBA, especially in the wake of *Death on the Rock*.

> The thing that changed the atmosphere completely was George Russell's appointment ... He knew the system, people liked him, and he made it clear right from the start that he wanted to use the staff ... He contributed intellectually into the thinking of the whole contract procedure, because he quite clearly felt that the 1980 system had been very badly handled in terms of identifying what you wanted. And, of course, once it was a question of judging financial bids you had got to be clear what you wanted and how you were going to judge them and be judicial review proof ... It really gave the whole system a chance to work, because with George really leading the Authority, but at the same time making sure that he kept the Authority on his side, which he did a lot of, they were never taken by surprise, as they were over *Death on the Rock*. (Interview with Shirley Littler)

Chris Scoble (head of the Broadcasting Department at the Home Office) also confirmed ministers' trust in Russell:

> A lot of things that made the Bill work were in quite technical areas which it was a matter of the people who knew what was going on sitting down and getting round the table and sorting it all out ... when you got into semi-technical areas, like questions of map and clock, and George [Russell] was pushing it very hard, then I think Ministers happily deferred to him in relation to that, because they felt the strength of the conviction there and obviously they wanted him very much on their side. (Interview with Chris Scoble)

Mellor himself also describes the respect he felt for Russell in the following terms:

I felt that George was a man I should listen to, should influence my thinking and the relationship between George and I would be the cornerstone of the success of this. (Interview with David Mellor)

The ITV companies also identified more closely with Russell as an experienced businessman who had a good track record in the management of change and who was clear about the changes which he needed to make the new system work:

Russell's appointment was crucial because having appointed him the Government had to listen to him and he was very pragmatic and shrewd about the nature of what was coming. That transformed the position of the IBA. From then on they were taken seriously by the Government as opposed to being totally ignored in anything they said – and they began to say much more sensible things too which was a help. (Interview with Barry Cox)

Senior staff at the ITC also attributed the strength of the Commission to the calibre of the members during this period and in the subsequent selection of the Channel 3 licensees. These included Lady Popplewell (wife of Judge Popplewell and educationalist), Professor Jim Ring (Professor of Physics at Imperial College), the Earl of Dalkeith (Member for Scotland), Mrs Eleri Wynne Jones (Member for Wales and a former Director of Channel 4), Roy Goddard (a head-hunter) and Pauline Mathias (former headmistress of More House, a Catholic School) and Pranlal Sheth (a barrister and businessman). Professor Sean Fulton, the Member for Northern Ireland, was described by Shirley Littler (in interview) as having a 'first class mind' and as being 'the outstanding intellectual on the Authority ... but he was certainly prepared to think in terms of change when it was obvious that change was in the air'.

On the departure of Lord Chalfont to be Chairman of the Radio Authority, Jocelyn Stevens, Rector of the Royal College of Art, who had been Managing Director of Express Newspapers became the ITC's Deputy Chairman in 1991.

Outside views did not always endorse the view of the Commission members taken inside the ITC. John Dugdale, writing in the *Guardian* (13 May 1991) detected that the Commission members had

a definite political complexion. Although the imbalance has been corrected by the resignation of Lord Chalfont, no attempt has been made to offset the bias in the usual way by appointing a safe trade unionist. The ITC conforms not to the familiar pattern of 'Butskellite' committee chemistry, but to that of patronage in the Thatcher era.

Above all, however, it was Russell who had inspired the loyalty of IBA/ITC staff when he accepted his appointment as Chairman only on the condition that most of the IBA staff, to whom he paid tribute, would be retained in the ITC. His public pronouncement at the IBA press conference, in March 1989, on the IBA's response to the White Paper, that he would resign if the licence awards were to be determined solely by the highest bid – in response to a leading question by Raymond Snoddy of the *Financial Times* – and his christening of the quality threshold, in racing terms, as the 'Becher's Brook', contributed to his popularity with the press, who had previously been generally critical of and hostile to the IBA.

Russell himself saw his firm stand with the government on the need for quality in terms of both programmes and money in the following terms:

> I had only met the Prime Minister a few times but I did have access to Downing Street. This was a help when it came to the fundamental clash on the quality standard to be used in judging the ITV franchise (C3 Licence) round. I had to crack the concept of a simple cash auction in favour of a mixture of cash plus quality standards. The former route would have permitted anyone with money to put on anything they liked on television. The latter would provide some control.
>
> The access permitted me enough support to carry the concept on standards. My efforts coincided with a mood swing in the Conservative party against solely the monetary argument. Although Nigel Lawson was probably still pro the simple auction and that it didn't matter a row of beans what was on television, I stressed that what was to be on TV had to be the first criterion and the quantity of money the second. I also believed at the time that there was no way of getting rid of an auction concept. That had been agreed by Cabinet long before I became Chairman of the IBA. (Interview with Sir George Russell)

His verdict on the operation of the powers in the Act was, typically, pragmatic and practical:

> Neither Mrs Thatcher nor I wished to be known as people who did not care what was shown on TV. I was able to weld the quality of programmes and the quality of money in such a way that we were able to run the franchise system in a way that surprised many people. We did turn down ten of the highest bidders. The debate was really about: could we be given the powers to create a structure that would survive into the future rather than risk the destruction of a successful commercial TV system?
>
> Whilst I'm aware that certain companies are very sore about the results of the franchise decisions, an awful lot of others could have been upset. It is hard for those (then) incumbents who have been hurt to realise that there was a limit under the law under which you could properly act. And as far as I'm concerned we stretched it to the limit. (Ibid.)

Stephen Redfarn, a merchant banker newcomer to ITV after the licence awards, when his group won the South West licence, endorsed the view that the previously unworkable had become more workable by saying that the ITC '... made a comparative silk purse out of a sow's ear of legislation' (Interview with Stephen Redfarn).

Russell, himself, also has paid tribute to the role Shirley Littler played in dealing with the complex Bill especially by her knowledge of and experience in the Home Office:

> We had the period of the writing of the Broadcasting Bill. It was a period where the IBA was expected by a variety of interests to attack, defend, re-draft clauses. In short help improve the law and definition under which the ITC would act.
>
> Nobody was better able than she [Shirley Littler] to fill that role. She left, and was well able to leave, the question of programming to David Glencross. This was slap bang in the middle of his skill area. In each of these phases I tried to pick the sort of person I thought fitted the special task at that time.
>
> The Shirley Littler appointment ... was received well by the Home Office, who trusted her ability to provide this sort of information and I think it was received well in the industry because they knew she wasn't going to be driving hard in terms of programmes; she'd leave it to David (Glencross) and Clare (Mulholland). That's how it worked in fact. (Interview with Sir George Russell)

Shirley Littler also acknowledges the role played by her relationship and communication with the Home Office and also to her independence in relation to the fact that she planned to retire after the Bill was enacted:

> Chris (Scoble, of the Broadcasting Department) had worked for me in two jobs – I think in the Broadcasting and Immigration Departments – so I knew him quite well and had the greatest respect for him. One never presumed on an old friendship. It was a proper professional relationship. If we disagreed, we disagreed. But I think over quite a number of things the Home Office was basically sympathetic because ... Chris had never spoken to me about the White Paper ... but I'm quite sure he thought bits of it were absolutely unacceptable and there's no advantage for them in having something that's just a mess at the end of it.
>
> Enormously helpful was the fact ... that I made it clear that I wanted to call it a day when the IBA came to an end. This meant that while other people were jockeying for position in successor authorities, I could hold the ring to some extent, just as I could over rows about the assets. Because I'd got no personal axe to grind. (Interview with Shirley Littler)

ITV

The ITV companies, co-ordinated by the ITV Association in their response to the White Paper and their lobbying during the passage of the Bill, faced difficulties in presenting a united front in that they had to represent the views of fifteen individual companies. With varying interests and needs, ITVA lobbying, under the chairmanship of Richard Dunn, aimed to shift the government away from the principle of the 'highest bidder wins' and made little headway in their meetings with the Home Office civil servants and ministers. But Russell and the ITC were realistic in seeing that the basic principle of the auction, already decided upon by the Cabinet Committee, would not be susceptible to radical change. They concentrated on chiselling away at some of the more unsatisfactory provisions and in reinforcing the quality threshold. Russell was trusted and cooperated with Mellor in helping make the Bill more workable in a series of targeted briefs and amendments, whereas the ITVA tended to chip away at the concept of the auction without suggesting an acceptable alternative to competitive tendering.

The division within the industry was described by Barry Cox in the following terms:

> ITV was split. There was Richard Dunn and some of the others who were much more pro public service ... Thank God for Central ... That stuff about re-drawing the map was never on politically but quite useful to have someone out there saying it because you could make what some of the rest of us were saying look reasonable, as between the public service die-hards on the one hand and Leslie [Hill] out there on the other looking for a much bigger shake up. (Interview with Barry Cox)

Individual ITV companies continued to lobby for their own interests alongside the ITVA initiative, and tended to provide confusing messages to the government. Possibly one of the most effective initiatives was by the Scottish ITV companies, Grampian and STV, who briefed the Scottish MPs on the Standing Committee on major issues. One of the results was that the possibility of reducing Scotland to a single licence area was resisted, and that government funds were made available for Gaelic programmes (see also Chapter 3, Section IV, 'ITV's Regional Programmes').

The lobbying of Scottish MPs and the Scottish Minister, Malcolm Rifkind, led to the provision of £9.5 million a year of Treasury funds for Gaelic programmes and the establishment of the Gaelic Television Committee. The 1980 Broadcasting Act had set up the Welsh language service S4C in Wales financed by 20 per cent of the Fourth Channel Subscription, but no similar resource was available to Gaelic speakers in Scotland.

According to Gus Macdonald:

> I had been campaigning to have Scotland pay less for the S4C levy ... My argument was that the native Celtic language of Scotland, Gaelic was not being subsidised by the Government but the Scottish companies were being forced to subsidise Welsh by a couple of million a year and this was clearly wrong. Where I remember feeling I'd made a direct impact with Rifkind was when I told him that Willie Whitelaw had done a very sophisticated piece of political statecraft with S4C because Gwynfor Evans (the former leader of Plaid Cymru) had

recently been quoted as bewailing the fact that his language activists had vanished. There was now something, he said, called independent producers, and they spent more in a night with these American Express cards they'd all got than they'd ever given to Plaid Cymru in a year ... Willie by putting £40 million this way had utterly diverted the whole Welsh language cause and while it was quite an expensive way of doing things, it was less troublesome than chasing people for burning cottages ... I think that Rifkind took the point since there was growing agitation among the Gaels. Here was something he could achieve for Gaelic and Scotland to right what was clearly a bit of injustice between one Celtic language and another. In the end, strongly lobbied by Gaelic language groups, who also won the ear of Tim Renton, he gave it a pro rata with Welsh and that's why it ended up with £8 million for 80,000 Gaelic speakers against the almost £50 million for 500,000 Welsh speakers. (Interview with Gus Macdonald)

The difficulties of lobbying on an individual basis were summarised by Harry Turner, the then Managing Director of TSW, as follows:

I think we'd have got more changes if we'd had more co-ordination at the Centre, if we'd had a much more united front ... One of David Mellor's aides said 'The trouble is we're being lobbied by all the companies as well as the Centre. You're not always saying the same thing. It's a bit confusing to a busy Minister when Grampian come in and say one thing, and you come in and say something marginally different, then Central come in and say something else, then the Centre comes in and says we speak on behalf of the industry.' (Interview with Harry Turner)

Since the ITVA appeared to have no major figure with the detailed understanding of the workings of government and the psychology of ministers of the type available to the IBA in Shirley Littler, individual companies made their own approaches with their own agenda – which served to underline the impression amongst ministers of a fragmented ITV. These efforts ranged from very effective to disastrous. Professional help was not always a guarantee of success either. Harry Turner vividly recalled his one encounter with Mrs Thatcher at this time, arranged through a lobbyist:

I was introduced to her, I had an audience, it was like Queen Victoria. I went to the Carlton Club after the Cabinet dinner one evening. It was 11.30 at night and they all filed in looking exhausted, except her, who was looking superb. Groomed and not a hair out of place. I was taken into a private room upstairs in the Carlton Club, introduced to her by a man call Michael Stephen who's now an MP ... he wasn't then, he was a lobbyist ... and he said 'Oh, this is Mr Turner of one of the smaller regional stations. He wants to talk to you about the Broadcasting Bill.' 'Oh yes?' she said, 'There's one or two aspects, Prime Minister, I'm concerned about.' She said 'Not afraid of competition are you, Mr Turner?' And she then proceeded to verbally handbag me. I couldn't get a word in edgeways. I was tempted at the end to say 'I suppose a fuck's out of the question, Prime Minister.' But I didn't. And I really got handbagged, and when I said 'Well, Prime Minister, surely there must be some area for debate' she said 'If you've got anything else to say, say it to Lord Young. I've got to go now,' and she swept out and left me truly handbagged. (Interview with Harry Turner)

The longer-term impact of the Bill on ITV companies was, ironically, seen by some of the companies as leading to re-regulation rather than deregulation: Central, led by Leslie Hill, was one who saw it that way:

In the end what we got was, in my view, a typical British fudge. We got a considerable degree of deregulation – and I would include the auctioning of the licences in that – but a great deal of re-regulation. There's more regulation in many ways than there was before. Of course the ITC latched on to that and has gone on doing its job to the utmost. So the whole idea that British television was being deregulated got lost as it went through the House of Commons. I think one of the reasons for that was the changing of ministers and having David Mellor at the crucial time. He recognised I think quite correctly, that British television was in some danger, but I think a lot of the problem stemmed from the fact that Margaret Thatcher herself took a personal interest in television but never really knew that much about it. (Interview with Leslie Hill)

Nevertheless, on the wider front, Hill conceded that markets require regulation:

I'm always amazed at the extent to which people believe, or the right-wing Conservatives, believe that markets will solve it all ... Unless you're going to allow people to be duped and robbed and swindled, you've got to have regulation of various kinds. And that applies to television as much as to anything else, and more so because of the taste and decency aspects and the previous shortage of spectrum. So the idea of swinging from one sort of extreme to the other was probably never right anyway. My own personal view still is that we ended up with too much regulation ... ITV is the most regulated of all channels, and yet is meant to be a largely commercial channel based on the sale of advertising revenue. There are still people who think ITV is a public service broadcaster, and others who think it's a commercial animal ... The truth is we got a hybrid which is neither one thing or the other, but it is ironic that it is the most regulated of all the terrestrial channels when you would expect it, as the most commercial of the terrestrial channels, to be the least regulated. (Interview with Leslie Hill)

Looking back five years later, Barry Cox of LWT, that special correspondent on the Broadcasting Bill for *The Listener*, thought that, despite the unwavering opposition of ITVA to the highest bid principle, 'The auction system obliged everybody to attack their cost base.'

The Campaign for Quality Television

How much the Campaign for Quality Television contributed directly to changes in the Bill is a matter for conjecture but David Mellor attributes the following impact from them:

> I think they were very influential ... First of all, they were interesting people because they were practical people involved in television and I found it interesting to talk to them. And they were people who were interested in the product and not really interested in what the fat cats of the business were interested in. Secondly, they were vocal and therefore politically, even if I hadn't enjoyed their company, it would have been necessary to have had dealings with them. But thirdly, they provided the pressure that gave me the ability to tell my elders and betters that changes had to be made, because these people were in a position to cause the Government severe embarrassment. (Interview with David Mellor)

The empathy which was struck up with Mellor, particularly by the Campaign organiser Simon Albury, ensured that the Campaign achieved direct access to Mellor and senior civil servants such as Paul Wright to argue about issues of programme quality, a moratorium on takeovers and the refinement of the exceptional circumstances provision. Whether the reasons for this empathy were valid or not, they did ultimately prove to be effective.

The *Telegraph*'s media correspondent, Jane Thynne, commented that 'whether or not the Campaign turned up at just the right time, it was far more effective at lobbying than the anxious-eyed ITV executives, whose attempts could not help but appear as special pleading' (*Sunday Telegraph*, 10 June 1990).

Barry Cox, LWT, also thought that the Campaign had:

> a very important symbolic value. I think Mellor was a star fucker and loved all that stuff ... Also these weren't the ITV establishment. Not only did Mellor enjoy dealing with them, but he could use them. If arguments came from them it was slightly easier for the Government to accept them than if it was a straight ITV lobby. And that was important. (Interview with Barry Cox)

10

WINNERS AND LOSERS: THE LICENCE PROCESS AND BIDS

Applications for the fifteen regional Channel 3 licences were due at the ITC by noon, 15 May 1991. There were thirty-seven applications. The awards were announced by the ITC on 16 October 1991:

– Border, Central and Scottish TV were uncontested winners.
– Incumbent contractors, Thames TV, TSW and TVS lost respectively to Carlton, Westcountry and Meridian.
– Tyne Tees, Yorkshire and HTV retained their licences, although their business plans had been initially judged 'marginal' by the ITC.
– Other existing contractors who won despite making the lowest bid included Channel, Grampian, Granada, LWT and Ulster while Anglia won with the highest bid.
– Newcomer losers were CPV-TV who had bid for London weekday, East of England and South/South East England, LIB (London weekend), Three-East (East of England), CI3 (Channel Islands) and TeleWest (South West England). Losers for Wales and the West of England were C3W, C3WW and Merlin; for the North of Scotland were C3 Caledonia and North of Scotland, and for Northern Ireland were TVNi and Lagan.

The London weekday licence was perhaps the most controversial and vulnerable area. There was speculation that if Thames, the largest contributor to the weekday peak-time network, failed to make the highest bid, would the ITC be willing to make use of the 'exceptional circumstances' section of the Act which might allow them to award the licence to Thames.

Incumbent Losers

Thames' Loss of Licence
Two months before the publication of the White Paper *Broadcasting in the '90s: Competition, Choice and Quality* in November 1988, Richard Dunn, Chief Executive

of Thames Television, was appointed Chairman of the ITV Association (ITVA). There were difficulties in achieving a coherent ITVA response on the method of competitive tendering proposed in the White Paper since the fifteen companies comprising ITV failed to agree. Greg Dyke, who succeeded Dunn as Chairman in 1991, comparing his style with that of Dunn, said

> Richard was the last of the grandees. His role as Chairman of Council was to try to get consensus. My role wasn't that at all. I saw myself as banging them on the head. Try to do it with some humour, but bang them on the head. (Interview with Greg Dyke)

The following summer the quality requirements in the White Paper were strengthened when Douglas Hurd, then Home Secretary, announced on 13 June 1989 that although the licences would normally be allocated to the highest bidder passing the quality threshold the ITC could, in exceptional circumstances, select a lower bid giving its reasons for doing so. After the publication of the Broadcasting Bill on 7 December 1989 David Mellor, Broadcasting Minister, gave further guidance when he stated on 18 April 1990 that exceptional circumstances could include the circumstance where the quality of programmes was exceptionally higher than that of the applicant offering the highest bid.

During the passage of the Bill, David Mellor and George Russell, ITC Chairman, worked closely together but Mellor's relationship with Dunn was not so close.

> I formed the view early on that the ITV Association, chaired as it was by Richard Dunn, who never seemed to be raising his game enough, nor having the flexibility of mind for reaching the kind of sensible compromises that are the essence of these processes. I just felt that he didn't have the flexibility of mind to do that and so soon started to talk on an individual basis to certain key figures in the industry including, of course, Christopher Bland, as to what was bearable and what wasn't. (Interview with David Mellor)

Thames' initial response to the Bill was summarised by the Chairman, Sir Ian Trethowan:

> The Bill does not in any way guarantee Thames a licence from the new ITC. We expect to fight for it against stiff competition. But at least we know that proper weight will now be given to our proven track record as a provider of a remarkably wide range of high quality programming. (Thames' Annual Report, 1990)

Such confidence in their programming record, however, as a means of winning the licence was not allied to any specific power in the Bill to allow the ITC to take track record into account.

There was also continuing uncertainty about the ownership of Thames. The two major shareholders Thorn EMI and BET, each controlling 28 per cent of Thames, announced in March 1990 that they would seek offers together for their shareholdings. The disposal was 'in line with both companies' stated strategies to concentrate their resources on their core businesses'. However, after failing to find outside buyers, it was agreed in February 1991, just before the licence applications were due, that Thorn EMI would acquire BET's stake.

In 1991, after sharp rises in Exchequer Levy and redundancy costs, Thames reported that group profit before tax was £10 million, which was substantially down on the previous year. This was compounded by losses on investments including the purchase of Reeves, an American distribution company, which was resulting in heavy loan interest repayments and in Northern Star, an Australian broadcaster, which went into receivership in 1991.

Despite the pioneering management service organised by Dunn in 1984, by the late 1980s 'the situation had worsened. Its main shareholders wanted out. Its executives were hopelessly divided on strategy. Its employees were demoralised by round after round of staff cuts' (*Under the Hammer* by Andrew Davidson, Heinemann, 1992).

Some managers in ITV also questioned whether Thames had implemented their cost reduction programme far enough. Andy Allan, Programme Controller of Central, compared Central's reductions with those at Thames:

> We went from 2800 to 1800. And we knew that there was still more to come the way television was changing. Although I know there were voices in Thames urging them to do that, they nevertheless believed they were at the right staffing level. And they were wrong ... they miscalculated what they could have done two to three years ahead of the franchise round in order to get their business in a better shape. (Interview with Andy Allan)

There were others who disagreed with Dunn's belief that Thames had dealt with their cost problems, including his London Weekend colleagues. But both Central and LWT, with shareholding limits ensuring a breadth of ownership, were in a very different position from Thames with – by March 1991 – a single controlling shareholder in Thorn EMI which wanted to sell and which was not prepared to make the necessary investment to cover staff redundancies beyond a certain point. This shareholder also ultimately controlled the level of bid Thames could make.

Dunn described the preparation of the bid for the London weekday licence as follows:

> The Thames bid was decided by a committee of the Chairman of Thames, Lord Brabourne, myself, the Finance Director, Derek Hunt, and Mike Metcalfe, who was Thorn EMI's representative on the Board. Those were the four people appointed by the Board to conduct the highly secretive business of determining

finally the bid. And I think that there was virtually no disagreement about the eventual bid of £30 million plus inflation. We thought that was a very full bid for the likely value to the shareholders of Thames for the tenure of the ten-year licence, given the extreme uncertainty of the second five years of that ten-year licence. And looked at another way, there were, to simplify, two broad ways of determining a bid. You could either say what do we have to bid to win, having a view to the competition, and then that's what we bid. Or what do we think this licence is worth and go to the full value that you think that it is worth and maybe a little bit more. It's like going into the auction room and looking at a painting. I want that painting but this is the maximum I'm prepared to pay for it, and that's that, and I won't bid any more. Or, I'm going to bid what it takes to get it. Now, history will show, and maybe your book will show, that there were other licensees that took the view that they had to bid whatever it took to win. Some of them lost as a result, some of them retained as a result and got into God awful problems. The board of Thames unanimously took the view that we would value this licence at the full value that we thought it was worth, and that's what we would bid. Our judgement was that if we were to take the alternative course, we would have to bid in excess of £50 million a year to be sure of winning. No one on the board of Thames was prepared to do that. We just did not believe that it was worth it. We thought that we would get the company into terrible problems, and we also had a very, very fully worked out model of the alternative business that we would run if we didn't get the broadcast bid. (Interview with Richard Dunn)

On programming, Thames' application stressed the importance of the London weekday licensee to the network as a whole. Its own proposals would make it the largest single supplier by a considerable margin, with offers of over 450 hours of programming a year across all categories listed in the ITC's *Invitation to Apply*. Thames claimed that currently it was generating up to a third of ITV's weekday peak time with a wide range of network series ranging from *The Bill* and *This is Your Life* to *This Week* and *Wish You Were Here*. It argued that quality across all strands of programmes was most likely to emerge from a dedicated producer-broadcaster with teams of talented people working together in an environment where excellence was positively encouraged.

The Assessment Procedure

The assessment procedure was rigorous in all its dimensions. Security within the old IBA building at Brompton Road had been tightened and an especially secure area within that was created for the licensing group and Secretariat staff. Both Members and staff had also been in what was called 'purdah'. This meant that they were required to decline offers of hospitality and entertainment from the ITV companies from November 1990 until after the awards in October 1991.

ITC staff set to work on examining the programming, engineering and financial proposals in relation to the requirements of the Act and the *Invitation to Apply*. Programme proposals were assessed in terms of Section 16(1)(a) of the Act which required the service to give 'sufficient amount of time' to high quality news and current affairs programmes on both national and international matters and to a suitable range of regional programmes which would be of particular interest to people living within the area for which the service was provided. The service also had to include religious and children's programmes; programmes appealing to a wide variety of tastes and interests; a 'proper proportion' must be of European origin and 25 per cent of the total output had to be allocated to a range and diversity of independent productions. Section 16(1)(b) of the Broadcasting Act specified that the applicant should be able to maintain the service throughout the licence period.

The programme proposals were assessed by six staff teams led by an experienced ITC staff member and relevant national or regional officer. In addition, specialist officers submitted written notes on each application on the sections dealing with children's, religious and education programmes, audience research, subtitling for the deaf, VBI line use, training and equal opportunities. These teams had access to Sections A and B on programmes of the applications and confidential side letters, detailing proposed staff appointments and use of independent producers but not to the business plan (Section C). The assessments were prepared against a checklist based on the *Invitation to Apply*. When drafted, they were discussed in detail with Clare Mulholland (Director of Programmes) and Mike Johnson (Chief Assistant, Policy) who also did their own assessments. Recommendations then followed on whether the applicants had failed or passed the quality threshold in terms of satisfying the minimum requirements of the *Invitation to Apply*. There also had to be enough convincing evidence that the proposals could and would be delivered.

The financial plans were assessed by two teams in the ITC's Finance Division, each of two people, in the light of whether the applicant could maintain the service. These teams reported to Sheila Cassells (Chief Assistant, Finance) who prepared her own analysis and conclusions which were then sent to Peter Rogers (Director of Finance) and to Richard Meddings (Hill Samuel) who advised on the funding of applicants. The assessments were then discussed at Management Board and at a meeting with the designated ITC Member for the area who, in the case of the London weekday licence, was Pranlal Sheth, an Asian lawyer and businessman.

The first overview (ITC Paper 70(91)) which included eight of the sixteen licences, was presented to ITC Members at their meeting on 18/19 July 1991. There were three contenders for the London weekday licence. The initial staff assessments were contained in ITC Papers (91) for Carlton (73), Greater London TV, also known as CPV-TV, (74) and Thames (75). Any decisions at this meeting were to be provisional, pending final decisions on all areas in September/October. At this stage, staff recommended that Thames and Carlton had passed the quality threshold and, on the basis of their business plans, could maintain the service. Additionally, it was proposed that Thames should be a possible candidate for the consideration of exceptional circumstances. CPV-TV was, however, judged to have failed the quality threshold in terms of their programme proposals. Thames' business plan, however, was not seen in such glowing terms. The conclusion was that

> There can be no real doubt that Thames could maintain the service throughout the licence period, but the business plan is a disappointing document. The profitability is poor, for what should be a particularly attractive licence, perhaps because of a reluctance to adjust to the changing environment of the 1990s. (ITC Paper 75(91))

Thames' application was next discussed at the ITC meeting on 18/19 September when the cash bids were revealed to Members (ITC Paper 145(91)). Until then, these had only been seen on the afternoon of 16 May by the ITC Chairman (George Russell), Deputy Chairman (Jocelyn Stevens), Chief Executive (David Glencross) and Secretary (Kenneth Blyth). Afterwards they had been lodged in a safe box in their sealed brown envelopes. Thames had bid £32.79 million compared with Carlton's £43.17 million and CPV-TV's £45.32 million. ITC Paper 143(91) summarised the staff's initial recommendations on which applicants had passed the quality threshold in relation to programmes, finance and engineering. There was also a general consideration that, on the basis of the knowledge of the bid by each applicant, whether 'exceptional circumstances' could be applied in any instance in order to award the licence to other than the highest bidder. Thames' application was considered in relation to Carlton. The staff had identified:

> ... several strands of programming in which the quality of the service proposed by Thames would be exceptionally high, including drama series of wide appeal such as *Minder* and *Rumpole of the Bailey*. Thames' proposals for religion, arts performances, social action, and some editions of its current affairs output, both network and regional, also offer exceptionally high quality. Thames has an impressive line-up of senior staff. Programme heads for entertainment, drama, factual programming, education and children's, and arts and features are respected throughout the industry as among the leaders in their respective fields.
>
> It is as the workhorse of the network, regularly producing up to a third of its peaktime ratings, that Thames should be considered to be exceptional. Against this, it may fairly be argued that the application is short on innovation. *Nevertheless we consider that Thames' proposals for the service are in themselves of exceptional quality.* (ITC Paper 143 (91))

In considering whether the service proposed by Thames would be of a substantially higher quality than Carlton's, a comparison had to be made between a producer-licensee and a publisher-licensee which would commission all of its network offerings from the independent sector.

The ITC's staff had concerns about this:

> ... whether Carlton can deliver its proposals for high quality programming will depend on the quality of the independent producers it engages to provide programmes. In the drama and entertainment strands, firm arrangements have been made with an impressive line-up of companies, though the programme proposals themselves are not particularly original. This may be partly explained by the fact that Carlton has yet to appoint a Controller of Drama, though the appointment of a person of the highest calibre is promised in the application. Nevertheless, on the basis of what the two applicants actually offer, we conclude that overall, Thames' proposals in this critical area for the network are at this stage of higher quality than those put forward by Carlton. Whether they are of substantially higher quality is a fine – and ultimately subjective – judgement. The basis for comparison is further complicated by the fact that one is an established broadcaster and the other is an outsider whose resources and talent can only be brought fully to bear after the award of the licence. On this basis, Carlton has contracts with independent companies which are known to have the ability to produce high quality programmes as well as the commitment to nurture them. We cannot therefore conclude with any certainty that over the period of the licence the difference in the quality of the two companies' output in this area would be substantial. (ITC Paper 118(91))

In the same paper staff expressed concern about Carlton's proposal for commissioning a peak-time current affairs programme for the network from a single independent producer:

> Based on their track record, the quality of Thames's current affairs proposals would appear to be higher. However, since the current affairs strand under the new network arrangements will depend more on decisions taken by the central scheduler than on the offers put forward by individual licensees, we cannot conclude that the difference between the two proposals would result in a substantially higher quality of programmes actually being broadcast.
>
> Staff conclude that some aspects of Thames' proposals, covering arts and religious programming proposals for example, are of a substantially higher quality than Carlton's, as are some aspects of its regional and social action output. However, these are limited areas. We do not consider that Thames' proposals are of higher quality overall in a substantial sense.
>
> In spite of the weakness in some areas of Carlton's proposed service and higher quality proposed in several programme strands by Thames, *we do not believe that this application would justify invoking the 'exceptional circumstances'*

provision of S.17(3)-(4). We should emphasise that this judgement is a fine one. (ITC Paper 143(91))

At the last ITC meeting on 10/11 October 1991 before the announcement of the licence awards on 16 October, there was a final run-through of whether exceptional circumstances might be used where more than one application for each area had passed the quality threshold. Thames was again considered in relation to Carlton and staff still recommended that although Thames' proposals for the service were in themselves of exceptional quality, the use of exceptional circumstances was not justified. Although at the September meeting it was agreed (in ITC Paper 143(91)) that no factors other than matters of programme quality would give rise to the consideration of the exceptional circumstances provisions of the Act, it was noted in October that benefit to Channel 3 as a whole could be a legitimate reason for an award on the grounds of 'exceptional circumstances'. George Russell, ITC Chairman, emphasised that in taking their final decision Members must form their own independent judgements on the basis of all relevant evidence and should not feel bound to accept the staff recommendations (ITC Minutes 10(91)). Nevertheless the Members, like the staff, concluded that 'exceptional circumstances' should not apply to Thames' application.

The delivery by fax to Thames of the ITC decision on 16 October 1991 did not come as a complete shock. According to David Elstein, Thames Director of Programmes:

I think everyone from the four Ts had more or less worked out their fates from the leak to the *Financial Times* ... where Ray Snoddy confidently predicted that TVS, TV-am, TSW and Thames would lose ... He was guessing odd things but his information was good. (Interview with David Elstein)

Elstein's description of that morning was as follows:

Richard came in with the fax. He was ashen. Absolutely ashen. And it was extremely painful, hard to take. Hard to think through it. And I think Richard was also desperately upset that George [Russell] didn't ring him after the outcome. He'd got a kind of brief call from David Glencross but he was really deeply upset, and I think made quite ill by all of that. And of course the worst thing was we had to then go down within half an hour to meet the assembled staff and talk to them. Now, Barrie Sales and I had spent the previous three months preparing the contingency plans, because you know it was fairly obvious that we were heavily at risk. So, fortunately we had a whole range of contingency plans ready so that when I held my staff meeting at the end of the week for the programming people, they were better able to cope because I had something definite to say. This is what we're gonna do, we're gonna get you onto the job market early, we're gonna get your cheques in your hands early, there's no point in hanging around, we're gonna reduce our cost base in order to increase your redundancy cheques. This is the only way to do it. We've thought it through, I guarantee it is the right way. And virtually everyone accepted it. And as you know, we also had our plans in hand for the network, immediately after, where Thames put forward a proposal to reduce costs and do a whole range of things, which eventually the rest of the network took on board. People were in many ways sympathetic, although Thames had been a bit of a bully at the network table. I mean, regularly flexing its muscles and throwing its weight around and being pretty unpopular as a result. But I think on an individual basis and even on a company to company basis, there was a good deal of understanding. (Interview with David Elstein)

Dunn described the event in the following terms:

We were completely planned for what we were going to do if we lost the licence, as well as knowing what we were going to do if we won the licence. And that meant that on the day that we lost, I was able to – I don't mean to make it sound terribly calm because it was ghastly – but I was able to take the fax into my Board, tell them that we lost, deal with the shock of that, because however prepared we were for it, and we were prepared, it was still deeply unpleasant, shocking. I told my wife a week later that my teeth hurt, and she said, that's because you haven't stopped clenching your teeth in the last week. It was tough. But I was able to go out to the staff and to the press an hour later and deliver a two and a half page printed off text of what we were going to do now that we'd lost our broadcast arm. And it was all there. (Interview with Richard Dunn)

In the aftermath of the licence awards, there was much speculation as to why Thames lost its licence. The saga of *Death on the Rock* has been described in detail in Chapter 3. Rumours were to persist that the showing of the programme followed by the government's hostility and refusal to accept the findings of the Windlesham Report led to Thames' downfall. The ITC procedure of awarding the London weekday licence, however, showed an independence from government and a scrupulous interpretation of the Broadcasting Act in which process the earlier transmission of *Death on the Rock* had no apparent bearing on the outcome.

Richard Dunn, however, believed that the programme may have had an indirect effect on the government's actions in relation to independent television:

It had no direct influence on the ITC's decision in 1991 to award the franchise to Carlton rather than to Thames. On the other hand, I think it had a significant influence on the government's decisions in 1988/89, to harden up the auction proposal, because it had so lost confidence in the IBA in particular and wanted to disband the IBA and remove discretionary powers from the IBA which it now mistrusted. So it firmed up an auction process which, because money was going to be the major determinant, was disadvantageous particularly to the large contractors and in particular, I think, to Thames Television, because shareholders who really want to sell are hardly likely to go to the top of the bidding tree. And it is true that the auction was strengthened in the government's mind by *Death on the Rock*. And it is true that the ITC was affected by the clamour over *Death on the Rock*, and whether or not it had been a good judgement by the IBA to transmit *Death on the Rock*. It is true to say that the IBA was the transmitter and the IBA made the decision to transmit it, but it was George Thomson's IBA not George Russell's ITC. That's different, and the members were different, and they took very different views. And even George Thomson's IBA Members of the Authority, including Lord Chalfont, had different views. And it was an incredibly contentious issue. I don't say it split the country because I think the country was about 80 per cent in favour of banning the transmission, but it certainly split opinion formers and broadcasters very substantially. So *Death on the Rock* had an effect. It didn't make Mrs Thatcher or Douglas Hurd or anybody else pick up a rifle and aim it at the heart of Thames and shoot and therefore dismiss us, that's silly, but it was part of a chain of things. (Interview with Richard Dunn)

There was a view in some quarters that Thames had relied too heavily on the possibility of the ITC preserving their licence by the application of exceptional circumstances whereas the reality was that the ITC had never intended to use this power, especially if it might have to give reasons for doing so. The scale of the Thames bid (at just under £33 million) would not seem to indicate a reliance on 'exceptional circumstances'.

It is worth examining the concept of 'exceptional circumstances' from the ministerial point of view. When queried about the genesis of the idea of exceptional circumstances, David Mellor said:

I was always keen to say to George [Russell] what do you need to make this work? My job was to give him what he needed. I was saying to George what do you guys need to be able to do this job? The great thing about George he was never a flapper and never a panicker. He was a practical man and he'd say if we've got this we can get by. He would never say to you well if I'd been doing this I would have done X, Y & Z. He'd always say well, within this context, if you give us this, that'll be fine. We can make it work ... It was slightly belt and braces. I know there was a view that the exceptional circumstances clause could not have been used. I remember George saying, off the record, ages after, musing over the fate of Thames that if Thames had put all the money into programming that might have then been a trigger of exceptional circumstances. And it might have been a better defence than trying to get involved in a bidding game with Carlton. I don't know. (Interview with David Mellor)

As far as the ITC staff and solicitors (Allen & Overy) were concerned, the selection procedure gave scope for the application of exceptional circumstances. John Wotton, partner in Allen & Overy, who advised the ITC on legal matters, believed that the power could have been used:

> I think it was usable, yes. The Thames/Carlton case, you've seen the papers which show that it was considered at least, and in two or three cases as well. It was obviously considered in each case where they got more than one qualified bidder. My recollection is that the Members thought that Carlton had made a pretty good programme offer. I don't think anybody's ever taken the view it's inoperable. Just by the process of assessment that the Commission used, a lot of fairly unsatisfactory proposals were weeded out and in most cases there wasn't that judgement to make. (Interview with John Wotton, Allen & Overy)

Senior staff at the ITC at the time recall that the use of 'exceptional circumstances' was very seriously considered. David Glencross, then ITC Director General, confirmed that the possible use of exceptional circumstances was 'firmly explored' but:

> At the end of the day we felt that we couldn't apply it, we didn't have sufficient justification. Not that we couldn't, we didn't have sufficient justification for applying exceptional circumstances for Thames or indeed for anybody else. But there's no doubt the Thames one was probably the most difficult judgement to make in terms of exceptional circumstances. (Interview with David Glencross)

Reflecting on the possible use of exceptional circumstances David Elstein, however, saw the provision as a possible hindrance to Thames' chance to retain the licence:

> In many ways I think Thames would have been better off if that clause had not been there. It would have forced us, absolutely compelled us, to decide did we want the licence or didn't we? And there was this fatal flaw whereby I think we basically rationalised to the point where okay, we were going to be outbid by someone whose cost base was zero compared with our very high cost base, but we would make a virtue of all our merits, we would put in a high bid, as high as we could get, so that nobody could say that we were trying to fiddle our way through on exceptionality and then wait for exceptionality to save us. And you know, if we'd talked to Allen & Overy beforehand we might have been disabused of the notion that exceptionality was a viable proposition. It was evident somewhat later that the ITC was advised that it was such a frail piece of drafting that it would be susceptible to challenge, and did they want a challenge? So instead of demolishing our cost base, closing our studio division, reducing down to 200 staff before putting in our licence bid, we waited till we lost the licence and then

we reduced the staff down to 200, having lost it. So you know, in retrospect all the effort that was put into improving the Bill only increased our lack of realism. (Interview with David Elstein)

Opinions vary on whether Thames' bid strategy was at fault. Andy Allan, at that time Programme Controller of Central, claimed that Thames could have bid higher:

I think it was a sheer underestimation of the strength of the Carlton bid, which was a very well put together piece of work, put together by a lot of seasoned television professionals who knew what they were doing. There was no doubt that Michael Green was known by then, he'd already made his pre-emptive strike against Thames. It possibly could have all been settled then. But I think Thames had the opportunity to bid higher, had convinced themselves that there were no more savings to be had. (Interview with Andy Allan)

The dilemma of how to bid was described by David Elstein:

The alternative was extremely unpalatable, which was to turn it into a green field site. You'd have to start doing it in 1990–91 in order to be convincing that you'd be there by the end of '92, otherwise how do you make a bid based on your historic cost base? So we were stuck with at least £10 million of costs that we didn't need, which was of course all the difference. And it was a bit like slow motion walking towards the edge, and the whole Board kind of edged its way – in fact, I was arguing for, if this was the strategy, don't bid as high as £30 million. Or certainly don't bid much higher. But of course, bizarrely I could see that if we lost we would have, with a 200-person cost base, a £15 million plus profitable business per annum without a licence. So it didn't seem to me wise to bid high with the cost base, to the point whether you'd be worse off than losing and still having a profitable business. It was lunacy, in retrospect, or just a failure to see clearly. And again a lack of ruthless analysis and sheer bloody mindedness. (Interview with David Elstein)

A further consideration on whether Thames' bid strategy was debilitated by Richard Dunn's diversion as Chairman of ITVA has been firmly rejected by Dunn himself:

In answer to the question of whether I was dallying on the poop of the flagship, ITV, I plead absolutely not guilty. I was in the thick of the politics of ITV. I suppose I would confess to being a little arrogant in feeling, whether it was justified or not, when the chairmanship of ITV came up, in 1988, and knowing that the Broadcasting Bill was about to go through the House, and the government was going to hit ITV for six, and we were the lead company with the most to lose, I was the best person to lead Council, in that scenario. Had there been somebody else on Council whom I thought would really have done a good job of trying to change that Bill, in a way that would have been favourable to my company, I might have taken a different decision and let somebody else do that. My view was that I was best placed to do that job and that it was more important to Thames Television than to any of the other Majors that the job was done well. That's the truth of the matter and I still believe that was right. It's true that my advocacy didn't get rid of the auction, but I think it was not get riddable of. (Interview with Richard Dunn)

Subsequent events showed that there could be life after death for Thames, despite the loss of their licence. Thames returned pre-tax profits to its shareholders of £44 million in 1992, its last year as a broadcaster. The company then continued to be a major supplier to the ITV network as an independent producer. Having been bought by Pearson in June 1993 for £99 million, the company provided its new owners with profits of £13 million for calendar year 1993.

However, another disappointment was in store for its plan to acquire the Channel 5 licence when the ITC announced on 18 December 1992 that, after a series of missed deadlines to clarify the financial backing, the Channel 5 licence would not be awarded to Channel 5 Holdings, in which Thames was a major shareholder, even though it was the sole bidder.

TVS and TSW
According to Peter Rogers, then Director of Finance,

> The most difficult decisions for me were of course the existing licensees that we rejected on the financial sustainability test, namely TVS and TSW. The key executives involved were industry colleagues, frequently of long standing, and some were friends. We had to conclude that in our view – and rightly or wrongly, that is what counted – the amount they had bid at tender was a fatal error of judgement. We did not shirk our responsibility, but it wasn't much fun. (Interview with Peter Rogers)

TSW – Failed Business Plan
Sir Brian Bailey, then Chairman, described TSW's bid strategy:

> First of all, the Board took a decision. We knew we'd got competitors. We'd got one competitor who, candidly, we didn't take too seriously because we thought they would not clear the quality hurdle. We'd got another competitor which we thought almost certainly would clear the quality hurdle, and that was Westcountry Television. And we were also aware of the fact that they had vast resources behind them. And that spelled trouble to us. And so the Board took a decision that we really can't mess about with this and try some sort of finesse, we're going to bid the highest figure that we believe the traffic will allow, and that was our approach from start to finish ... Everybody'd agreed on the principle, we go high,

and when all the number crunching was finished, everybody agreed on the figure that the numbers produced. And we knew it was a high bid, but we were quite confident it would be the highest bid and that was what we were about. (Interview with Sir Brian Bailey)

Harry Turner, TSW Managing Director, justified the high bid in the following terms:

From day one we said, 'Look, don't worry about our programmes. We need to lay out clearly what our intentions are for the future, but as far as the track record is concerned we have nothing to fear.' Because we'd won awards, we won business awards to industry, sponsorship, all sorts of awards, and I'd received a huge and ugly bowl from the Duchess of York for our business programmes and so on, and sponsorship of the arts in the south-west. We'd done all sorts of worthy things which we knew were fine. So we majored on the bid, we majored on that, because we thought that was where the battle ground would be. I believed we could survive in a much leaner form, almost as a publisher contractor, without carrying the baggage of unnecessary departments, and we could survive with a high bid. But how high the bid could be, we didn't know. We had to be certain, because we all believed that the auction was what it was about, this was what was imposed upon us, therefore highest bid wins. This seemed to me amazing logic. So we set about making a judgement about where the company would be two to three years from the start of the new franchise. We knew if our bid was accepted, £16.1 million, that we would not be in profit for at least two years, but we were cash rich, we had a lot of fat to draw upon, we had many millions in the bank, we had supportive shareholders, and we had a plan to reduce our overheads very dramatically. In fact over a three to five year programme we would probably reduce costs by as much as 35 per cent, which is pretty dramatic. That would have been reducing staff, commissioning out nearly everything, catering, everything, and the last thing to go would have been the sales department which was my pet, but I think in the end we would have probably had to go to a sales house, against the grain for me personally, but in order to get the company down to about a hundred people on the pay roll, or maybe less, you could still run a regional station and produce eight hours of programming a week with a staff – you'd have a newsroom and you'd have an accounts department, maybe you wouldn't even have that, certainly you'd have a newsroom, and you'd have a Director of Programmes who'd be also the commissioning editor for the company, and you'd have a sales operation. And then you'd just get rid of all the rest. You'd sell the studio and you'd work out of a much smaller premise – we had a huge studio in Plymouth which really could have done twenty hours a week, two vast studios, so that was the plan, and we approached the bid with that in mind. (Interview with Harry Turner)

The ITC, however, was not convinced that the business plan was viable. Staff recommended that TSW had satisfied the programme test, but ITC Paper 112(91) stated that TSW's revenue assumptions were 'extremely optimistic particularly in the earlier years. The projections show average trading surpluses of £19.9 million which is very much higher than anything that the company has been able to achieve in the recent past. On the basis of profit projections, TSW has made a very high cash bid ... this adds to an already high burden of fixed costs and there is only limited strength in the balance sheet.' At their meeting on 18/19 September, ITC Members agreed with the staff verdict that TSW had failed to satisfy the requirements of Section 16(1)(b) of the Act.

Commenting four years later on TSW's bid, Peter Rogers explained that:

Everything turned really, I think, in the TSW case, on two propositions. First that we said their forecast of the revenue that they would earn was incredibly high. And secondly we said, if they earn as much revenue as that and make as much pre-tax profit as that, there is no way on earth that the network will agree to leave them with their subsidised contribution to the network. And those were our two arguments. Firstly, they won't be able to get it in the first place. And secondly, if they do it will be taken off them. The profit margin they said they could make put them right towards the top end of the largest of the business plans coming in. And we were saying there's no way that is compatible with other licensees with lower profitability agreeing to give them a substantial network subsidy. And if they don't get the network subsidy they won't have the money to support that bid. (Interview with Peter Rogers)

Looking back at the ITC's decision to reject the bid, Turner conceded that the details of the proposed business plan had not been fully explained to the ITC:

We hadn't revealed the long-term strategy of the company, but we did indicate that we believed that the revenue would grow at a higher rate in the regions than the ITC were prepared to believe, and a lot of the argument subsequently, when we went to judicial review, was over the different forecasts, the interpretation of the way revenue would grow, it majored on that. The ITC also appeared not to believe – didn't say so, but they appeared not to believe that we could reduce the costs in the way that we said. We perhaps weren't specific enough in the way we'd reduce costs. I didn't give them chapter and verse and name the people who'd go because it would have been premature. So I think they probably weren't convinced. They thought we were paying lip service to cost reduction. We were advised by Rothschilds and by NERA, so we weren't making an irresponsible bid, we actually believed, high though that bid was, and £16.1 million was very high bid, it would have been uncomfortable. If I'd won I would have had an uncomfortable two or three years, no question about that. (Interview with Harry Turner)

Robin Foster, senior consultant at NERA at the time (now working at the BBC), claimed that:

> the problem for TSW was, with the benefit of hindsight, that they placed too much reliance on a single forecast, which came initially from the NERA model. They upped it to reflect the fact that they felt they knew the market and could do better than the consultants were suggesting. They had a good sales force, they knew the region, the West Country was performing better than the economy as a whole and would do, and they took quite a robust approach to the efficiency gains they were going to be able to make over the period. So really the assumptions they were making, each of those sounded reasonable on its own and could be justified. The problem was that adding them all together produced what the ITC chose to view as too tight a bid. The four successful bidders which also used the NERA forecasts built in a much larger contingency into their bids to allow for uncertainties, and hence were able to satisfy the ITC that they would be able to cope with market shortfalls in the event of a market downturn. (Interview with Robin Foster)

TVS – Failed Business Plan

TVS's track record as a programme maker had been qualified in the IBA's mid-term review in 1986 when it was judged that the company still had 'some way to go before reaching its full potential and fulfilling the high expectations which accompanies the award of its contract'. Subsequently, the company's long-term strategy was to expand beyond its ITV franchise (see Chapter 7, Section III, 'Diversification'). In 1988, TVS, under the leadership of James Gatward, decided to buy MTM, the US studio named after its actress founder Mary Tyler Moore, with which it had already co-produced joint ventures. Two new investors were brought in, Canal Plus and Générale des Eaux, the French utility with media interests. The company was also restructured with TVS TV as a subsidiary of the group TVS Entertainment. By 1989, Gatward had been appointed Chairman of MTM when the American programme market had collapsed. In September 1989, Gatward had issued a profits warning to the City, cutting predicted profits by one-third of their value on the London Stock Exchange, and MTM became 'locked into a horrendous loss-making spiral' (*Under the Hammer* by Andrew Davidson). In 1990, Rudolph Agnew from Consgold was appointed Chairman of the group. Gatward was removed from the main Board but remained as Executive Chairman of TVS TV, with Tony Brook as Managing Director and Alan Boyd as Programme Director, with the remit to work on TVS's licence application. Gatward, however, left the company on 11 February 1991. Agnew's strategy was to submit the highest possible bid. To sustain its bid to offset the heavy losses made by MTM, TVS shares were restructured by bringing in two new shareholders to underwrite the bid: Home Box Office and Associated Newspapers' Daily Mail and General Trust. The Stock Exchange insisted that TVS should reveal in a circular to shareholders the size of its bid and the details of its licence application before the new shareholders and the decision to raise an extra £30 million could be implemented. On 30 August 1991, at an EGM for TVS shareholders, Agnew confirmed publicly that TVS had submitted a bid of £59.758 million. This bid proved to be more than double those of the two other contenders, Carlton (£18.080 million) and CPV-TV (South of England) (£22.105 million) and nearly twice as much as Meridian (£36.523 million), the eventual winner.

The ITC's initial reaction in ITC Paper 81(91) was that TVS's application proposals were 'clear and full' and that 'TVS has gone to extraordinary lengths to provide information and much of what has been written is thoughtful and interesting albeit repetitive.' Programme Division, however, did express concern at the proposed reduction of staff to 566 which was:

> ... only 72 more than Carlton which intends to be a publisher licensee. Even allowing for an increase in the amount of programmes made by independents, the staff reduction is nonetheless of concern and is bound to have an impact on the quality of output, especially bearing in mind the significant increase in regional programmes. (ITC Paper 81(91))

Doubts on the viability of the business plan, however, led to a recommendation that TVS should fail the sustainability test.

> Other applicants have made their revenue projections on much the same basis as the ITC adopted in its own modelling ... However, TVS rejects this approach and opts instead for an analysis of the revenue generated by 75 product groups. It then predicts future revenue on the basis of product life cycles and competitive behaviour. We are not aware of any forecasting tradition of this kind, and this makes analysis difficult to judge on its own terms. (Ibid.)

Although the use of a different methodology was not, per se, seen as a problem if the resulting projections were plausible, doubts were expressed about the staff numbers at 633 which were about 600 less than in 1990 and left room for doubt whether the company could fulfil its plans with such a large reduction.

The paper concluded:

> There are three main reasons for doubting the viability of the business plan, and the strength of the commitment to the programme service. First, we believe that the revenue projections are very optimistic, and the very high bid serves to make the applicant dependent upon achieving these results. Secondly, we believe that the provision which has been made for the cost of network programmes and sport will prove to be inadequate. Moreover, the company proposes to make only a very modest contribution, in relation to its size, to the production or commissioning for sale to the network. Thirdly, the business plan creates the impression that the holding company's desire to extricate itself from major financial difficulties

in relation to MTM has had an important influence on its strategy for TVS. There must be a risk that further problems with MTM would have adverse consequences for the TVS programme service. (Ibid.)

Although the paper on TVS was issued in a revised format (ITC Paper 126(91)) for further discussion by Members at their meeting on 18/19 September, the staff recommendations were upheld.

Looking back, James Gatward who had left TVS before the bid had been finalised, agreed that the bid had been too high:

> There's no way I'd have gone up to the odd £50 million; and that was literally the guys with no experience at all sitting round tables saying, 'Well, you know, let's put in a lot of money, we can claim it back later.' (Interview with James Gatward)

Robin Foster, senior consultant to NERA, commenting on the bids, thought that:

> The one that actually was interesting in terms of its disqualification was TVS, which probably was underwritten sufficiently to ride out the rough patch. (Interview with Robin Foster)

Unlike TSW, the assessment of TVS's bid was not scrutinised by the process of judicial review, because their leave to apply was judged to have been lodged too late and so was dismissed.

Marginal Incumbents – HTV, Tyne Tees and YTV

Three incumbent contractors were initially judged by the ITC to be on the borderline in terms of their business plans.

HTV – Marginal Pass

In preparing their bid, HTV engaged the consultants Booz Allen Hamilton to help with the industry analysis. Huw Davies, Chief Executive, HTV Wales, thought that the only option was to bid high: 'In the end we decided that we had to be the highest. None of the other kinds of winning was open to us' (Interview with Huw Davies).

The ITC, however, in Paper 101(91), had reservations. It found that the application on programmes was 'pragmatic and convincing on quality' but there were a number of significant concerns on the business plans:

> The provision for network costs is below that implied by the ITC's indicative range; the overall level of staffing looks too low to the proposed programme output; some of the provision for overhead expenditure looks light; the response to the sensitivity tests create an unease about the strength of the company's commitment to the Channel 3 service ... These are significant shortcomings which

makes us uneasy about this application and the prospects for a satisfactory relationship with the ITC or with other regional Channel 3 licences. However we believe on balance that HTV should be able to sustain the service for the full ten year term of the licence. (ITC Paper 101(91))

Looking back, Louis Sherwood, who was appointed Chairman in March 1991, just before the applications were due, admitted that 'We greatly overestimated the revenue prospects ... We also overestimated the share of ITV NAR that we in HTV would have' (Interview with Louis Sherwood). However, HTV's bid was successful and they regained their licence for Wales and the West of England. Two of HTV's rivals failed to pass the programme quality threshold. C3WW, headed by Lord Morris, did not convince the ITC that the service would include sufficient programmes of high quality. The application by Merlin, the group with Lord Richard as Chairman and Lady Harlech as Deputy Chairman, was also queried on the quality of its regional programmes. C3W, whose Chairman was Sir David Nicholas from ITN, managed to pass the programme quality test with the ITC's assessment of a 'commitment to a lively and effective regional service', but its bid was £2.7 million below that of HTV.

Yorkshire TV – Marginal Decision
Like HTV, Yorkshire's philosophy on bidding was that they would have to bid high:

> Yorkshire's approach was pretty simple really. We wanted to retain the franchise. And as long as there was still a business, at the end of the day we were prepared to do whatever was necessary, including the assessing of a hefty bid. In other words, we accepted that this was going to be an auction process, or a bidding, you know, highest bid was likely ... it was the only way you were most likely to win. (Interview with John Fairley)

The ITC, however, again expressed doubts on the size of the bid. Although Yorkshire's programme plans were judged to have passed the quality threshold by a clear margin:

> Our chief concern is with the size of the bid which is very high in absolute terms, and as a percentage of both revenue and profit. But as the applicant has an established track record as a broadcaster and programme maker, and the holding company has a strong balance sheet, we are prepared to conclude it could maintain the service but the judgement is a fine one and the going will probably be difficult at times. (ITC Paper 84(91))

One of Yorkshire TV's rival bidders was Viking, with Chairman designate Sir Trevor Holdsworth and MD Hilary Lawson. The ITC (Paper 82(91)) found a 'lack of clarity and detail in the majority of programme strands' and the Programme

Division did not 'share the applicant's confidence in the quality of the proposals' and so failed Viking on the programme test. White Rose TV, headed by Lord Lewisham with Chairman Richard Hanwell and Nicholas Fraser as Director of Programmes, was more problematic. The ITC (Paper 83(91)) approved their programme plans: 'a convincing application particularly in terms of the range and relevance of the regional elements of the proposed service' but initially, the staff recommended that White Rose should fail the business test because although the 'cash bid is low in relation to revenue' it was judged to be 'very high in relation to profit'. Evidence of funding was also thought 'scant'. However, by September a revised staff paper 128(91) reported that the total funding of £59.2 million was now fully committed and would give White Rose 'sufficient resources to cope with significant variations in revenues and costs'. The original decision was reversed at the Members' meeting on 18/19 September but the size of White Rose's bid was still £20m less than YTV's which had been cleared, albeit reluctantly.

Tyne Tees – reversed decision
The IBA had decided in the previous 1980 contract awards to split Trident TV into two separate areas, Yorkshire and Tyne Tees, and to find major local investors. At the time of the 1991 licence applications according to Sir Ralph Carr-Ellison (later Deputy Chairman of Yorkshire-Tyne Tees Television) Tyne Tees and Yorkshire still wanted a joint (dual) region. George Russell was said to be keen on this idea in principle but the proposal was postponed due to his belief that the management of change required as much stability as possible. In the face of so many unknown outcomes resulting from the 1990 Broadcasting Act, it had been decided that the map and the clock should remain the same and that the Tyne Tees Yorkshire dual region should not proceed any further at this stage.

   Ward Thomas, the man who had led the old joint Yorkshire-Tyne Tees company, Trident, as Chairman and Managing Director, from 1976 to its IBA-enforced separation in 1981 and is now again Chairman and Chief Executive of the new Yorkshire-Tyne Tees company, remembers the remerger having been agreed by the IBA just prior to the 1991 application and then:

   Some 48 hours before the merger was to be announced publicly, the IBA changed its mind and asked us to delay the merger for another three months, while it was decided whether the map should be changed to provide inter alia for a single Yorkshire-Tyne Tees region. In the event they decided to leave them as two separate regions and asked the two companies to defer the merger until the contracts had been separately awarded ... we were all very angry at the time, as were the merchant banks, as was the then Managing Director (Clive Leach), whose contract was terminated at the time of the first agreed but frustrated remerger date. (Letter G.E. Ward Thomas to author, 16 July 1997)

The Tyne Tees Board decided that a high bid would be required for the North East licence because of a known competitive bid from a consortium which included Granada, Border TV and the *Newcastle Chronicle* led by two well-known broadcasters form the north-east, Stuart Prebble and Paul Corley. This, Sir Ralph Carr-Ellison believed, had to be taken 'very seriously indeed'. (Interview with Sir Ralph Carr-Ellison). The consortium had developed from Granada's strategy to strengthen its foothold in the north. Initially Granada was uncertain whether they would be able to bid for another area until the rules on contiguity (that is, takeovers on adjoining areas) had been clarified. Yorkshire was ruled out, but a bid for Tyne Tees was permissible.

Unlike HTV and Yorkshire TV, who both scraped through the business test with reservations, Tyne Tees was initially judged by the ITC staff to have failed the business plan, although it was offering an impressive range of programmes for the region:

The cash bid is very high and cash flow is very tight. We doubt that the profit projections can be achieved. The principal difficulty with the application is the size of the bid. It could only be sustained by a significant improvement in the second half of the licence period. The bid adds substantially to the already high fixed costs which are inevitable from a licence of this size. With already low dividends and overheads, the only recourse would be to obtain additional funding or to reduce programme expenditure if trading turned out to be worse than expected ... We consider that there is a real risk of this outcome ... We believe that there would be an unacceptable persistent tension for the available resources between the claims of the shareholders on the one hand and the claims of the programme service on the other. (ITC Paper 110(91))

Faced with the staff's recommendation that Tyne Tees should fail the business test, ITC Minutes 9(91) of the Commission meeting on 18/19 September recorded that assessment of Tyne Tees should be held over for further consideration. Staff were also asked to carry out a further review to check the consistency of their analysis with those they had carried out for the business plans of TVS, TSW, TVNi and Yorkshire.

A further paper (ITC Paper 168(91)) for the Commission meeting on 10/11 October modified the initial recommendation and concluded that Tyne Tees' business plan might pass 'by the finest of margins'. The Paper stated that:

Even in the first half of the licence period the size of the bid and its impact on fixed costs means that the applicant would have very little room for manoeuvre if trading conditions turned out worse than expected. However, an existing ITV company avoids the risks which are inherent in a start-up situation, and if it is accepted that there are good prospects of a further injection of funds from 1997, should the outlook for the second half turn out worse than Tyne Tees expect, then it could be concluded, though by the finest of margins, that this applicant could maintain the service over the licence term. (ITC Paper 168(91))

Although North-East TV's application also passed the quality threshold on all counts, it had only bid £5 million in contrast to Tyne Tees £15 million. Later, in 1992, Yorkshire and Tyne Tees were allowed to merge to form the holding company Yorkshire-Tyne Tees. Although the separate licence commitment for each area had to be honoured, the merger, with its consequent economies, strengthened the finances of both companies which had been judged insecure at the time of the licence application assessments.

Uncontested Winners

Three incumbent contractors were unopposed, although each one experienced varying degrees of uncertainty on whether they would face competition.

Border
Jim Graham, MD of Border, has recounted how Border's bid was prepared in a situation in which he was not totally convinced that theirs was the sole bid.

> We had a report from Lancashire that someone was interested in a small north-west regional franchise. We understood that an engineer had been asked to prepare an engineering plan. We made enquiries and we thought that somebody might have been in the brush. Now we had to calculate, or guess if you like: we did have this rumour. Border had allied itself with Granada and caused great affront by bidding for Tyne Tees which disturbed, I guess, relationships with Yorkshire. Now it's a matter of record that Yorkshire were affronted and bid for the Granada contract involving Phil Redmond and *Brookside* – so those are the facts. Putting the two together that someone had been asked to look at the possibilities of a small north-west franchise, everybody was cross at everybody all the way round, we would not have been surprised if someone from Liverpool had just had a punt. So as against that, instead of bidding £2,000, which was possible, we had to think of a figure, and we thought that since Border's been advised by TSMS that it's not really viable, and at that point we had not enacted the cuts that we did have in mind although we'd planned for them, we'd better think of a figure that is not an economic figure. It just had to be a kind of symbolic figure. So we thought well, okay, let's make it £50,000: and then we did what Greg Dyke and others have done since, we rubbed our chins and we thought that if there is somebody – we've made it £50,000 and not £2,000 because there may be another bidder; supposing they're just taking punt and they make it £50,000? Why don't we make it £52,000 – a thousand a week. And we honestly did it for that reason in case someone else had come in at £50,000. (Interview with Jim Graham)

Melvyn Bragg, director of Border, also thought that since Yorkshire Television 'had been stung badly' by Border's involvement with Granada in a bid for the North East area, that Yorkshire might

> at the last minute spring a surprise bid for us. As it turned out this was groundless. But I thought if we put in a bid for £52,000 a year, which is not a great deal of money given our income level at the time, it wasn't a stupid bid. And so I'm glad that we did that rather than £2,000. So we spent £50,000 a year, but I think it was worth it for the sort of comfort it gave to us at that particular time. (Interview with Melvyn Bragg)

The ITC was not overenthusiastic with Border's application (ITC Paper 87(91)); the programme proposals were seen as 'limited and disappointingly cautious' and the business plan 'a trifle optimistic in parts but not sufficient to cast doubt on the viability of the business' and the application was passed.

Central

Central's approach was more confident. Leslie Hill, former boss of EMI Records UK and EMI Music, Europe, who had joined Central as MD in 1987, took deliberate and positive steps to clear the path for an uncontested bid for the Midlands area. According to Hill, who had started preparation for the bid in 1989, the nature of the licence area itself was a basic advantage:

> Central ... geographically had 25 per cent of England ... in terms of square miles, which is a huge piece of England: right across into the north-east to Lincolnshire, and then Leicester, Derby, Nottingham, down to Milton Keynes and across through Swindon, Cheltenham and Gloucester, Hereford and Worcester, and then all the way round up to Stoke. It's a colossal area. Interestingly enough we are the only licensed area, even though it's so big, that is landlocked. There is no sea on any of our boundaries, and everybody else has got sea. And the point about that therefore is that we've got six other licensees around our borders and so there were a lot of people going to the IBA saying we could do better with that piece of the Midlands than Central can. So there's great sensitivity here about serving the whole region ... In 1988, we'd had research done which showed that we'd been incredibly successful throughout most of the area and that people in the fringe areas, on the periphery, didn't want Granada really, and they didn't want Anglia, and they didn't want Yorkshire. There was one major exception which was in the south. The people of Gloucester and Cheltenham were saying 'we don't want news of muggings from Birmingham. We'd rather have our news from Bristol (HTV) please.' (Interview with Leslie Hill)

Hill, as a Bristolian himself had 'total sympathy' with this view and anticipating a campaign from HTV, which covered the West of England as well as Wales, to take away Central's southern areas, decided to provide a separate and third sub-regional news service called Central South at a cost of £3 million a year (see Chapter 3, Section IV, 'The Levy'). The implication of this move was that 'anyone applying for the licence in the Midlands would have to supply the three news services'. Hill also attributed the lack of contenders to the effectiveness of a special licence campaign under Central's corporate strategy director Marshall Stewart, who was 'close to politicians', and briefed local opinion formers and publicised Central's claimed strengths. One potential bidder, the East Midlands Electricity Board, withdrew six weeks before the bids were due. According to Hill, he met the Chairman, John Harris, who told him that they had carried out research which had shown that Central was so strong and well-liked that they did not believe that they could oust Central and, being newly privatised, they did not want to be seen to be a loser (Interview with Leslie Hill).

Hill was also convinced about the loyalty of the independents which Central worked with. Confident that he had eliminated potential bidders, Hill had to decide on the size of the bid. After comparing notes with Bill Brown at Scottish TV, and not totally convinced by the advice of Laurence Ward, legal adviser to Scottish TV, that a multiple of £1,000 could not be £1,000, the bid at £2,000 was finally settled.

Andy Allan, Central's Programme Director, also stressed the significance of creating the additional third area well ahead of the licence applications and the meticulous planning which was carried out over a long period:

We'd always assumed there would be rival bidders. And we took some pretty major preventative steps, like creating Central South 18 months ahead of the bid process, just because we needed to be there. We had the choice, we could have offered it as a licence promise or do it. My argument was to do it now and have it up there and, in part create such a strength in regional service that (a) it would be very offputting to everybody else, but (b) it would be extremely expensive for somebody else to replicate. (Interview with Andy Allan)

Although Allan admitted he could not be absolutely certain whether there would be contenders, he also was confident:

I think you could make some pretty fine judgements about what the quality of a rival application must be like if none of your own staff had been approached, no planning application made. This is a leaky business. I just don't believe you could have kept quiet given the number of people you'd have had to approach to put in your brown envelopes and all of that. I just don't believe you could have kept a bid quiet. And in the event I don't think there was a single surprise bid in the whole bidding process. (Interview with Andy Allan)

The ITC (Paper 85(91)) found Central's application 'impressive and thorough' and judged that it had passed the quality threshold in all respects.

Scottish TV

Although Scottish TV had faced strong opposition for the Central Scotland contract in 1980, no obvious competitor was observed in 1990. The late Bill Brown, then Chairman of STV, remembered that:

> We didn't actually detect that there was a strong, well-founded, determined group ahead of us, about to challenge us. I did get some straws in the wind from friends of mine who were approached to go on the Board or to find the money and so on. But as I said to our non-executive directors, when the process was about to begin, I said, well, you're now going to earn your fee, because you're all here for the main reason that if you lot don't know what the hell's going on in Scotland, nobody does. You're Scotland's foremost corporate lawyer, Scotland's foremost trade union leader, Scotland's foremost merchant banker you should damned well know what's going on. (Interview with Bill Brown)

Although a fledgling group advised by Hambros Bank had been formed, Gus Macdonald (MD), reacted defensively by tying Scottish TV key personnel in with post-franchise bonuses and doing deals with all known independent producers.

Once convinced that there was no opposition, STV's Chairman's Committee which included Bill Brown (Chairman), Gus Macdonald (MD), Charlie Fraser and Angus Grossart decided to bid as low as possible at £1,000. Laurence Ward, STV's lawyer, expressed concern that £1,000 was not a multiple of £1,000, as specified in the ITC's *Invitation to Apply*. On the basis of this advice, STV decided to bid £2,000. As mentioned earlier, Brown passed this advice on to Leslie Hill of Central.

Gus Macdonald's account of STV's bid strategy has a different emphasis:

> I think we had six or eight independents who had signed up to supply us. In fact there were two or three dozen in Scotland and a number of people that we had no deal with ended up running against Grampian. We had associations with people that I felt were talented, but none of them were big in a sense that they had a dominant position inside the Scottish market and a number of them were just old colleagues of mine ... Ours was a high risk strategy. It depended not just on setting a high quality threshold but also on a belief that exceptionality would come into play, which it didn't in the end for Thames. We declared well in advance that our plans for Scotland were to make a greater range and diversity of programmes as befitted a nation with so many national dimensions that we felt were undercovered. By declaring in advance that expansion programming, it was clear that we couldn't win the highest bid but the commitment to quality won allies in the creative community and deterred all potential rivals. (Interview with Gus Macdonald)

There was, however, a last-minute shock on the day of the awards when STV's brokers rang to say that there was a competing bid for Scottish TV. The bidder claimed to have a machine for bleeping out swear words on televison. His bid, however, arrived after the ITC's noon deadline and the application was disqualified.

The ITC warmly approved Scottish TV's application. ITC Paper 86(91) commented that on programmes it was 'a most impressive and fully rounded application which provides satisfactory responses in all areas. It reflects an acute awareness of Scotland as a separate nation and the audience expectations that ensue. The application easily passes the quality threshold in all respects.' The business plan was seen as 'unexciting but solid' but 'with no foreseeable financial problems'.

Incumbent Winners

Granada
Granada TV, one of the network 'Big Five' and subsidiary of the Granada Group, had experienced a decline in both Group and Television profits. Derek Lewis, Chief Executive, had been replaced by Gerry Robinson, former Chief Executive of the Compass Catering Group, who arrived after the Granada application had been submitted but not yet awarded.

Andrew Quinn, who had returned as Managing Director to Granada Television from their Cable and Satellite division in 1987, described how the bid strategy was devised:

> Until about six weeks before the closing date, we believed that we were going to be substantially unchallenged, and we would have done the Central Scottish £2,000 bid. But then, at that very late point, it came to our knowledge that Phil Redmond was in a relationship with Yorkshire to bid against us, and we thought that was really serious ... And so it was back to the drawing board. We were always determined that we weren't going to bid the profits away, we weren't going to be in ITV at any price ... At the end of the day, we actually had three bids in the envelopes that we sent to London with the Company Secretary. And the night before, Derek Lewis, Alex Bernstein, David Plowright and I sat down to talk about it and we chose the middle one (£9 million). I think we persuaded ourselves that we might rely on exceptional circumstances ... We thought we had a really top-class editorial bid. We had credibility as management. We had the *Street*. And if we were going to rely on exceptional circumstances we thought we'd better not be too cheeky, we shouldn't put in a bid which was so low as to make it difficult for that principle to be applied, and we shouldn't put in a bid so high that we were seriously bidding the profits away. So we put in the lowest respectable figure we could come up with. And in the event, we could have bid £2,000 because Phil Redmond's application didn't pass the quality threshold. But I think we were entitled to believe that it would have been stronger than it

was, given the input that they had (from Yorkshire), albeit at very short notice. (Interview with Andrew Quinn)

The initial ITC staff assessment in July on the application was that it proposed 'an impressive supply of programmes to the network' and contained 'strong elements of high quality'. Although the revenue projections were seen as 'entirely credible' the cash bid was 'low in relation to both profit and revenue'. The main risk to Granada TV was seen to be that 'the Group might become over dependent on high dividends from the television company so that at some stage the television company became starved of funds' (ITC Paper 71(91)).

A revised staff paper in September (ITC Paper 116(91)) confirmed the 'high calibre individuals in key posts' and claimed that 'the pattern of training, promotion and recruitment from outside have built a cohesive company identity which forms a strong organisational base for high quality programme making'. There were still reservations on the business plan in relation to possible weakness at Group level, but the Commission had by this time received a letter from the Group Chairman stating that dividends paid by the TV company would be such as to maintain adequate capital in the TV business. The Paper found that his letter 'gives as much comfort as we can expect'.

The Group balance sheet had also been strengthened recently by a rights issue for £163 million and the sale of bingo clubs to Bass for £147 million.

In contrast, the programme plans for the competitive bidder, North-West TV, whose major backers were Mersey TV, and Yorkshire TV and Tyne Tees whose Chief Executive was Phil Redmond, were described in disparaging terms in the initial ITC staff assessment paper in July, which found:

> ... programme plans very thin in places. Although the proposed service includes a very significant increase in the amount of regional programming these would involve the use of sub-broadcast standard equipment and semi-professional or non-professional programme makers, provided with a very low level of funding by the applicant. Programme Division has serious doubts about whether this material would be of a satisfactory standard and appeal to viewers. There is a lack of supporting evidence in respect of most of NWT's programme plans. It is also over dependent on Mersey TV. The application is not one in which we can feel much confidence. (ITC Paper 72(91))

These doubts were reinforced in a further paper in September where it was stated that concerns had been:

> strengthened as a result of follow-up correspondence from the applicant that NWT will lean heavily for management production and technical expertise on Mersey TV. Programme Division believes that it is not a sufficiently secure arrangement for a major Channel 3 licensee to be so dependent upon a single independent

producer in respect of so many of its core organisational functions. There are also worrying gaps in key appointments. (ITC Paper 117(91))

Since North West TV failed the quality threshold on programmes, Granada regained its licence despite bidding £9 million against North West TV's £35.3 million.

Nevertheless, Granada did not achieve all its objectives in its longer-term strategy to strengthen its influence in the North. As David Plowright recounted:

We decided we'd bid for Tyne Tees. And once we'd announced that we were going to bid for that, then Yorkshire decided they'd bid for the north west, and the pack of cards fell about. (Interview with David Plowright)

Stuart Prebble, Programme Director of Granada, backed by Border and the *Newcastle Chronicle* headed the competitive bid for Tyne Tees and persuaded Paul Corley from Border to become Director of Programmes. Despite passing the quality threshold on both programmes and business plan, once the ITC made the difficult decision to pass Tyne Tees 'marginal' business plan and bid, Tyne Tees as the highest bidder at £15 million exceeded the £5 million bid by North-East TV and so was awarded the licence.

LWT

Like Thames, the London weekday contractor, LWT, the London weekend contractor, put in the lowest bid for their area (that is, £7.585 million compared with the £35.406 million bid by the other contender, London Independent Broadcasting (LIB)). LWT's bid, unlike Thames', succeeded because LIB failed the programme quality threshold and so their high bid was not even considered. The LIB consortium included Polygram, Working Title, Palace Group and Mentorn Enterprises headed by Tom Gutteridge and Andy Birchall.

The initial staff assessment paper in July found that on programmes:

There are many inconsistencies throughout the application. A particular difficulty exists with local news where three different plans are provided at various points ... It is difficult to regard LIB's local news plans as credible. ((ITC Paper 76(91))

There were also serious reservations about LIB's proposals for using independents, and information about key postholders indicated 'a serious deficiency with only one individual in the entire structure so far having programme-making or commissioning experience'. ITC Members did not depart from the staff recommendation.

Chairman, Christopher Bland, described LWT's preparations for the bid process:

We started to plan hard when it became clear that there was going to be a bid process ... It was based on the simple financial premise which is broadly true of most businesses which is that debt is cheaper than equity ... So, if you can sensibly gear yourself up to reduce your level of equity, then you have additional money free with which to bid. So the first argument was about the most efficient balance between debt and equity. The second was that ... a company awash with cash is less likely to be really efficient than a company with a big burden of debt which has got to work really hard to pay back. Finally we were, I suppose pre the reconstruction capitalised at about £180 million, after reconstruction at about £70 million – the balance was money given back to the shareholders. As a result they were risking £110 million less on the outcome of the franchise process. (Interview with Sir Christopher Bland)

The specific calculation on what to bid, according to Greg Dyke (Interview) was 'we knew there was a higher bid. We would have bid £2,000 if we thought there wasn't a higher bid', but he was highly sceptical of LIB's ability to pass the quality threshold. Ultimately, the Board decided to submit a 'respectable' bid. There was a strong belief was that LIB might not pass the quality threshold and that LWT programme quality could be considered exceptional. According to Brian Tesler:

We didn't think exceptional circumstances came into it, we were not like Thames, in other words. Polygram, LIB were not offering the same as we were offering, and what they were offering we believed we demonstrated was not only unsubstantiated but insubstantial. (Interview with Brian Tesler)

Ulster

Ulster TV was another incumbent contractor which won with the lowest bid. Its two rivals failed the quality threshold; Lagan on programmes and TVNi on the business plan.

Desmond Smyth (MD of Ulster) has described his two rivals:

One (i.e. TVNi) was very serious, very professional, they produced a professional business plan and good programme plans. The other [Lagan TV], in which Bryan Cowgill had been involved ... we felt would have difficulty in even meeting the programme specification which the ITC had set out ... We felt even with the name of the company, Lagan Television, there was a big degree of naivety because the River Lagan would be closely associated with Belfast and there's a great sensitivity in Northern Ireland about the west and the east and about Derry, Londonderry ... And we had gone to great lengths ... to position ourselves in the public mind here as a broadcaster that was interested in the whole of Northern Ireland ... Then this consortium coming up calling themselves Lagan Television, we just sort of felt that will be a red rag to a bull in the west of the province. (Interview with Desmond Smyth)

The Ulster bid was settled on the basis of a viable business plan derived from a conservative model of growth.

> We decided to be realistic. We decided it would be entirely wrong to go in with a low bid, and depend upon us being the only ones to get through the quality threshold. But we felt we'd go in with a realistic bid, but nevertheless one that we felt would be a sustainable one for the business during the licence period. And we felt very strongly that we didn't want to go in with a bid that would embarrass the ITC. We'd pitch the bid at such a level that the ITC would have to go through a careful thought process. It wouldn't be easy to discard it on the basis that it had been a very low or frivolous bid. And indeed I read afterwards that Granada had a similar sort of thought process, and LWT to some extent as well. So I think that LWT, Granada, Grampian and Ulster seemed to have a very similar approach, even though we were working obviously totally independently and didn't know about the strategies that they were adopting. (Interview with Desmond Smyth)

The UTV bid was settled at £1.027 million. The ITC response to Lagan's application was similar to that of Smyth. It found that

> the application overall fails to demonstrate a genuine commitment to serve, and a sound knowledge of, the region. This is crucial in any prospective provider of a programme service for Northern Ireland ... The programme proposals do not reflect the detailed knowledge and experience required to provide an effective service for the Province. (ITC Paper 96(91))

The assessment of TVNi's application was more qualified. The group consisted of successful local businessmen and shareholders including Tayto (NI) Ltd, W&G Baird and Thomson Regional Newspapers. ITC staff regarded the programme proposals as 'ambitious and well thought-out' despite the 'occasional failure to convince on specific ideas'. The business plan, however, raised:

> a number of substantial concerns about optimistic revenues and inadequate provision for costs which lead us to conclude that the projected average trading surplus of £7.2 million a year is very optimistic ... We have serious doubts about whether the regional programme service and the high cash bid can be sustained. (ITC Paper 97(91))

ITC Minutes 8(91) record that at their meeting on 5 September, ITC Members asked the staff to prepare a revised financial assessment and to reconsider their recommendation that TVNi should fail the business test.

At the meeting on 10/11 October, Peter Rogers, ITC Finance Director, presented a Paper 203(91) on 'Channel 3 licences: an overview of key financial assessments'.

It reviewed the findings of the financial assessments for TVS, TSW, TVNi, Tyne Tees and Yorkshire, and checked these for consistency using a series of graphs and charts to compare projections for advertising revenue, costs, profits and tender payments. Members agreed with staff that the first three, including TVNi, should fail and the latter two pass, although marginally.

Channel
John Henwood (MD of Channel TV) described how:

> We worked on the basis, from day one, that there would be opposition, because we feared that if we went into it believing that we were the only applicant it would breed complacency and our application may not be very good. And we were right to do that, because in the event there was a rival, a consortium made up very largely of local former Channel Television staff who had left for various reasons ... They formed a consortium which they called CI3, and they set about writing an application. And in the event, of course, they outbid us by a very substantial sum. (Interview with John Henwood)

On similar lines to Ulster TV, Channel TV decided to concentrate on quality and to bid the minimum sustainable. Initially the CI3 bid was headed by the *Bergerac* actor John Nettles who later withdrew his independent company's association with CI3. CI3's application was received critically by the ITC staff who found:

> The description of the programme plans and information provided in support of these plans is very thin throughout, and in many places either incomplete or showing a lack of understanding of what is required. (ITC Paper 114(91))

The financial plans were also severely criticised:

> The revenue analysis is confused and almost incomprehensible ... The business plan is a very poor low quality document, and there is not a letter from a firm of accountants stating that the projections have been properly compiled. The plan does not persuade us that CI3 could establish and operate a television company. (Ibid.)

The ITC liked Channel TV's programme proposals, particularly:

> some interesting ideas for the network including a children's drama called *Children's Ward* which represents a programme of potentially high quality. The animated strand *Bertie the Bat* represents another production of marked creative individuality. (ITC Paper 115(91)

When preserving the ITV map the ITC had always been aware of the marginal profitability when advertising the smaller regions but it was thought that Channel TV's business plans highlighted the risks, particularly the effects of the cessation of the current fourth channel funding arrangements. Nevertheless they concluded that although the licence was close to the limits of commercial viability, they were satisfied that Channel TV could maintain the service over the licence period.

Grampian
Grampian, following a similar strategy to Ulster and Channel were convinced that there would be higher rival bids for the North of Scotland licence. According to Donald Waters, Chief Executive of Grampian:

> We realised fairly early on that we were going to have competition because it was a good area of Britain. We were prospering mightily. The oil industry was doing well ... And because the whole of Scotland is really a very small community, the rumours began to filter back quickly. (Interview with Donald Waters)

The most serious contender was thought to be North of Scotland TV whose Chairman was Anne Duguid who had once been a continuity announcer in Scotland and conducted a series of roadshows all round the licence area criticising Grampian TV. Grampian responded with their own series of roadshows and enlisted support from local authorities and MPs. Donald Waters recalled (in interview) meetings when North of Scotland TV revealed their ignorance of the area – one in Fort William, which they mistakenly thought was in the Grampian area but was, in fact, in the STV area, and the other was a promise to cover Highland League football in Gaelic in areas where Gaelic was not spoken.

C3 Caledonia's application was dismissed by the ITC in Paper 93(91) which stated that 'the application provides only limited evidence of any arrangements for programme provision, either in-house or from independent producers'. The business plan, too, was suspect (ITC Paper 148(91)) in that 'it reveals confusion and muddle, and a lack of any proper professional grasp of the issues and skills involved in providing a licensed broadcast service'.

At the Commission meeting on 19 September, the staff paper 95(91) recommended that North of Scotland TV should pass the programme test. ITC Minutes 8(91), however, record that the staff were asked by the Commission to prepare a revised programme assessment to take account of the Members' views of the ability and local knowledge of the company's proposed management ... and to bring out more clearly the factors in the financial assessment which led to the staff's recommendation.

At the next meeting in October, the staff's initial recommendation was reversed. ITC Paper 166(91) concluded 'It is not apparent that the tastes and interests of the viewers in the region will be adequately provided for overall (and also in relation to Gaelic programmes).'

Grampian's application, assessed in ITC Papers 94(91) and 149(91) passed both tests. It was judged that Grampian had made a good case for showing that the region could be viable and that the low cash bid helped to contain the costs, together with a strong balance sheet which gave added resilience. And so yet another incumbent contractor had regained its licence while submitting the lowest bid.

Anglia

Anglia was an incumbent contested contractor to win with the highest bid.

Competition was anticipated by David McCall, Chief Executive of Anglia:

> We had two competitors and we thought they were both serious competitors. One was Virgin (CPV-TV) and the other one was the Jeremy Fox EMAP-led consortium and we were always concerned about them because they also had a regional dimension, EMAP being based in Peterborough. So we treated the opposition as credible players. We didn't bargain for Virgin writing a weak application for a regional company. By that I mean they just changed the words from their London application. But nonetheless we weren't to know that until after we read it. (Interview with David McCall)

Confident that Anglia 'knew the ropes' and that the 'cost base wasn't out of kilter' David McCall described how Anglia settled on the size of its bid:

> The key issue was the level of the bid. That was a tough, tough call and however you looked at it, the final bid was: at what stage are our shareholders better off or worse off with this contract? We did quite a lot of sophisticated modelling ... In the end we decided the value was something around £15 million; that over £15 million or £16 million you'd almost be better selling off the assets and handing it all back to shareholders ... So we pitched it at the high end. (Interview with David McCall)

The CPV-TV operation, which was backed by Virgin, had also applied for the South/South East and London weekday licences. In each case it failed the programme quality test. In relation to the East of England area application it was found that 'Hill Samuel have some concerns whether Virgin would be able to make the necessary investment. The licence would not be granted unless funds were irrevocably committed' (ITC Paper 107(91)).

The Three-East group's application with Lord Prior as Chairman, Jeremy Fox (Chief Executive) and Linda Agran (Director of Programmes) and shareholders including EMAP and the *Daily Telegraph*, sailed through both programme and business tests. On programmes, ITC Paper 108(91) applauded the 'management team of high calibre, most of whom have been associated with past productions of considerable merit' and the proposed schedule was seen as 'interesting and varied

... The trading projections are sound; the funding is fully committed.' A further Paper 158(91) in October confirmed that the 'application demonstrates that it is well aware of the complexity of the region' and approved plans for a main studio in Cambridge, with opt-out studios in Norwich and Colchester. The business plan was again approved. 'The trading projections are basically sound. The revenue projections are cautious.'

Anglia had been wise to pitch their bid at £17.8 million since their strong rival, Three-East, was not so far behind with a bid of £14.078 million.

Newcomer Winners

Meridian

The failure of two rival applicants to pass the quality threshold helped pave the way for a newcomer – Meridian, a publisher broadcaster, in the South/South East licence area. TVS had failed on its business plan and CPV-TV, as in other regions, on the programme test. Carlton TV, despite reservations expressed in ITC Paper 78(91) that 'there were some worries about proposed staffing' and that the application 'does not give the impression that it has a particular attachment to the region and it is not offering much more than the minimum in terms of regional programmes', passed the quality threshold but it had only bid £18 million compared with Meridian's bid of £36.5 million.

Lord Hollick, Chairman of MAI Group, who had failed to win the ITV breakfast contract in 1980 as a shareholder in Harold Lever's group, had decided in the late 1980s that although MAI had built a powerful position in cinema screen and outdoor advertising, they had, for various monopoly reasons, little scope for further expansion. In his words:

> We decided to make a portfolio move ... to sell outdoor advertising. We sold out of that for around £200 million with a view to investing it in broadcasting. The decision to go for the South and South East was a relatively simple one, because that's where I come from. We also took the decision right at the outset that we were only going to concentrate on one region. And my old and dear friend, Simon Albury, had been very much involved in quality television, he led the Campaign for Quality Television. So I spoke to Simon, who was still working for the Campaign at the time, and said look, I would like to build a quality broadcasting business. At MAI we've taken the view we have the resources and some of the management skills to do it. We know about advertising revenue. So would he be interested in working to form a consortium? And he said 'Yes' and we then went to see a good mutual friend of ours, Michael Palin, and so the three of us sat down and mapped out what we though would be the key ingredients of a bid. (Interview with Lord Hollick)

Roger Laughton, an experienced BBC broadcaster, was recruited as project director. Laughton had been Assistant Editor of *Pebble Mill at One* from the Midlands before becoming Editor of Features Programmes at BBC Manchester. He then moved to London as Head of Network Features and Head of Daytime Programmes before he took over the running of Co-Productions at BBC Enterprises. This portfolio of regional and network programming and scheduling, combined with commercial judgement, was to make Laughton one of the limited number of successful transfers from the BBC to ITV at a senior level – and an asset to the Meridian stable. He was made Chief Executive in 1991. Later his calm and thoughtful approach to the complexities of ITV was to prove an asset at Council and other forums of the network.

Meanwhile there was a need to have a broadcasting ally who would bring the inside knowledge of how ITV works. Initial discussions with Granada were unfruitful but Hollick was then approached by Leslie Hill (MD of Central) and his Finance Director, Kevin Betts. They proved helpful, and Central came in with a 20 per cent shareholding. Since the group intended to be a publisher broadcaster, using Laughton's contacts, about a dozen independents were signed up including Select TV. There was no shortage of fund managers and venture capitalists who were willing to back the group but their support was not needed in the event.

The size of the bid had to be based on a minimum rate of return over the licence period. TVS was judged to have a very high cost base and the Meridian team thought that they were likely to bid in the low thirties. Finally Meridian settled for £36.5 million which they thought had a good chance of exceeding TVS. Although the Carlton and Virgin potential bids had to be taken into account, the area was not the first choice for either of them. It was also decided to incorporate something different from what anyone else might offer and this was to create a triple region, since Hollick took the view that:

> ... it was clear from all the research that we'd done that people wanted more local news. We also believed that there was an opportunity to create a new region around Newbury which would give us over the period of the licence an attractive proposition for advertisers. (Ibid.)

Hollick also thought 'in the event that the ITC was faced with roughly matching bids it would be just enough to give us exceptional quality' (ibid.).

The link with Central proved extremely effective in that they had been operating a tripartite region successfully in the Midlands, and so were able to advise Meridian on their three different newsrooms in Maidstone, Southampton and Newbury.

The ITC staff (Paper 80(91)) commended Meridian's application as clear, very well presented and internally consistent. 'The way in which the statistical information is laid out ... is admirable.' The staff were so impressed with the high quality of the programme plans that they initially recommended that Meridian might be considered as a candidate for exceptional circumstances. Thames was the only other application singled out in this way but as TVS's high bid had been disqualified there were no grounds for the use of exceptional circumstances since Meridian emerged as the highest bidder.

Westcountry
Of the three contenders for the South West England licence, TSW was disqualified in terms of its unrealistic bid, and TeleWest on its programme plans, which meant that Westcountry was the clear winner.

TeleWest's application was headed by Malory Maltby (MD) but the ITC were sceptical about his programme-making record and management experience. ITC Paper 111(91) also pointed out that no Chairman for the group had been selected. Equal scepticism was expressed about TeleWest's business plan which, TeleWest claimed, had been 'tested vigorously for business and financial feasibility'. The ITC did not accept this and remarked 'Given the error and discrepancies we cannot agree with this statement ... virtually none of the equity is committed.'

Westcountry had received substantial backing from its shareholders, Brittany Ferries, Associated Newspapers and South West Water. Stephen Redfarn, a banker who had advised TVS for the 1980 contracts, had started to form the group in April 1990, together with Frank Copplestone, the former Managing Director of Southern which had been replaced by TVS in 1980. In addition to enlisting core investors through Redfarn's city connections, John Banham (DG of the CBI) was recruited as Chairman and John Prescott Thomas, a BBC executive, as Managing Director. Although, when interviewed, Redfarn 'as a poker player' declined to say how he played his cards in formulating the bid, the Westcountry application was received favourably by the ITC. Paper 113(91) recorded that 'the strength of this application in its commitment to high quality rests a good deal on the combined editorial and managerial experience of the senior staff team which is considerable. A novel feature of this application is the proposed mobile studio (the dome).' The business plan was also approved. 'Overall the trading projections are ambitious but credible. The funding package is satisfactory and most of it is committed.'

Carlton
Although Carlton had been prevented by the IBA from taking over Thames in 1985, Michael Green (Chairman) had entered into further discussions with Thames about a possible takeover in the late 1980s. Richard Dunn (Chief Executive, Thames) was becoming increasingly concerned about Thames' ability to retain its franchise, particularly in relation to its shareholding base of two major unwilling shareholders, BET and Thorn. Although the discussions continued until January 1991, talks finally foundered on the question of price. Looking back, Michael Green admitted:

I definitely think we should have bought Thames second time round ... I think it's the biggest single mistake I've made in business – so far. (Interview with Michael Green)

Since the option of buying Thames was now ruled out, Green was faced with the question of whom to bid for. He already had a 20 per cent stake in Central and owned Zenith, the largest UK independent producer. Although several other groups had approached him to join their bids, he finally plumped for the London weekday licence knowing that Thames was the largest and more vulnerable, and for the South/South East licence. His first choice was London since he was 'a Londoner through and through' (Interview with Michael Green).

Nigel Walmsley (Chief Executive of Carlton Communications) was responsible for preparing most of the application which the ITC (Paper 73(91)) appraised as 'clear and lucid,' although 'the overall feel is that of a competent, well-reasoned but unimaginative application put together by a facilities house rather than a broadcaster with a commitment to original creative ideas'. A further Paper (159 (91)) commented that Carlton 'already has an impressive line-up for drama and entertainment strands. These include Zenith, Noel Gay, Humphrey Barclay, Hat Trick Productions and Chrysalis TV. Clear arrangements have been reached with programme suppliers.'

Since CPV-TV had failed to pass the programme quality threshold and the ITC was unwilling to apply 'exceptional circumstances' to Thames' application, Carlton won the London weekday licence with a bid of £43.17 million.

Brian Tesler (Chairman, LWT) summed up the situation in the following terms:

> Carlton's ingenuity was to offer Thames' programme schedule, in effect, and at more money. The difference between what they were offering could not be said to be exceptional. The most you could say with Thames was ... that they'd done it, but that's no guarantee they're going to be able to continue to do it. The worst you could say about Carlton is that they hadn't done it. But they haven't done it because you haven't let them do it, there's no reason why Carlton's offering should be any worse than Thames'. Thames' is not so much better than Carlton's that we have got to give it to them for that reason. (Interview with Brian Tesler)

Public Teletext Licence

The single public Teletext Service licence for Channels 3 and 4 was awarded by competitive tender six months later in April 1992 to Teletext UK Ltd (owned by Associated Newspapers and later renamed Teletext Ltd). Although there were four other applicants, including Oracle (the incumbent), Teletext UK Ltd submitted the highest bid of £8.2 million. This marked the end of an era in this small but important corner of independent television. Oracle, which was owned by the ITV companies, had provided teletext services on ITV (and later part of the service on Channel Four) since the service started in 1975. The market had opened up to yet another newcomer.

Table D   Channel 3 Licences – Winners and Losers

LICENCE	AWARDED TO	FIRST PART OF TENDER % see note below	CASH BID IN 1993 PRICES	OTHER APPLICANTS	CASH BID IN 1993 PRICES
Borders & Isle of Man	**Border Television plc**	0	£52,000		
Central Scotland	**Scottish Television plc**	2	£2,000		
Channel Islands	**Channel Television Ltd**	0	£1,000	† CI3 Group	£102,000
East, West & South Midlands	**Central Independent Television plc**	11	£2,000		
East of England	**Anglia Television Ltd**	7	£17,804,000	† CPV-TV Ltd (East of England TV)	£10,125,000
				• Three-East TV Ltd	£14,078,000
London Weekday	**Carlton Television Ltd**	11	£43,170,000	† CPV-TV Ltd (Greater London TV)	£45,319,000
				• Thames TV plc	£32,794,000
London Weekend	**LWT (Holdings) plc**	11	£7,585,000	† Consortium for Independent Broadcasting Ltd	£35,406,000
North of Scotland	**Grampian Television plc**	0	£720,000	† C3 Caledonia plc	£1,125,000
				† North of Scotland TV Ltd	£2,709,000
North East England	**Tyne Tees Television Ltd**	2	£15,057,000	• North East TV Ltd	£5,010,000
North West England	**Granada Television Ltd**	11	£9,000,000	† North West TV Ltd	£35,303,000
Northern Ireland	**Ulster Television plc**	0	£1,027,000	* TVNi Ltd	£3,100,000
				† Lagan TV Ltd	£2,712,000
South & South East England	**Meridian Broadcasting Ltd**	11	£36,523,000	• Carlton TV Ltd	£18,080,000
				† CPV-TV Ltd (South of England TV)	£22,105,000
				* TVS TV Ltd	£59,758,000
South West England	**Westcountry Television Ltd**	0	£7,815,000	† TeleWest Ltd	£7,266,000
				* TSW Broadcasting Ltd	£16,117,000
Wales & The West of England	**HTV Group plc**	2	£20,530,000	• C3W Ltd	£17,760,000
				† Channel 3 Wales & The West Ltd	£18,289,000
				† Merlin TV Ltd	£19,367,000
Yorkshire	**Yorkshire Television Ltd**	7	£37,700,000	† Viking TV Ltd	£30,116,000
				• White Rose Ltd	£17,403,000
National Breakfast-time	**Sunrise Television Ltd** (renamed GMTV)	15	£34,610,000	§ Daybreak TV Ltd	£33,261,000
				§ TV-am plc	£14,125,000

† Applicant did not satisfy requirements specified in Section 16(2) (that is, the programme quality threshold for Channel 3 regional licences) of the Broadcasting Act 1990.
• Applicant satisfied requirements specified in Section 16(2) but did not submit highest bid.
* Applicant satisfied requirements specified in Section 16(2) and submitted highest bid, but did not satisfy ITC that it would be able to maintain proposed service throughout licence period (Section 16(1)9b)).
§ Applicant satisfied requirements specified in Section 16(3) (that is, the programme quality threshold for the Channel 3 national breakfast-time licence) but did not submit highest bid.
Note: Tender payments for each licence are in two parts. The first part is a percentage of annual qualifying revenue which was set in advance by the ITC. The second is the cash bid, the annual sum bid by the licensee, which will be index-linked. Neither part of the tender can be varied during the term of the licence.

Source: ITC.

11

THE AFTERMATH –
FOR THE ITC: JUDICIAL REVIEW –
FOR ITV: THE MONOPOLIES AND
MERGERS COMMISSION

IBA Experience of Judicial Review

The IBA had been subject to a judicial review in relation to the programme *Scum* broadcast on Channel 4 on 10 June 1983, which had previously been banned by the BBC. Mary Whitehouse, President of the National Viewers and Listeners Association (NVALA), had been granted leave by the High Court to seek a judicial declaration that the IBA had breached its statutory duty in allowing *Scum*, a programme about conditions inside a Borstal for young offenders, to be broadcast. On 13 April 1984 the High Court ruled that although the programme was highly controversial and at the borders of tolerance allowed by Section 4(1)(a) on taste and decency and offence of the 1981 Broadcasting Act, the decision to show the programme was not perverse. But it ruled that the IBA Director General, John Whitney, had committed a grave error of judgement by failing, initially, to refer *Scum* to Members of the Authority. However, following an appeal by the IBA against the High Court declaration, the Appeal Court, on 3 April 1985, under Sir John Donaldson, ruled that the IBA (unlike the NVALA) had been set up to make qualitative judgements about programmes and that the Divisional Court was wrong to criticise the Director General. Mrs Whitehouse's considerable costs, estimated at £30,000, were paid by an unnamed donor.

In July 1985 Norris McWhirter, of the Freedom Association, filed a summons at a magistrate's court which alleged that subliminal images of his head on a naked woman's body had been shown in the satirical programme on ITV, *Spitting Image*. The basis of the application was that the IBA had a statutory duty under Section 4(3) of the 1981 Broadcasting Act not to show images (of brief duration) in programmes and that by breach of statute the IBA was guilty of a criminal offence. The IBA sought a judicial review on the grounds that, if there had been a breach of the Act (which it denied), this did not constitute a criminal offence. The Divisional Court's findings were in favour of the IBA.

No applications for judicial review had been made as a result of the 1980 franchise awards despite some criticisms of alleged Byzantine processes and arbitrary decisions. Although the 1990 Broadcasting Act had laid down a general framework for the award of Channel 3 licences, the ITC had no statutory duty to give reasons for their decisions, unless they chose to apply the 'exceptional circumstances' power in the context of a lower bidder being substantially better qualified than a higher bidder.

Before work started on the assessment of the Channel 3 applications in 1991, ITC staff were briefed on possible grounds for judicial review and were warned to document their decisions clearly with supporting arguments and not to resort to 'back of the envelope' comments.

Judicial review would not allow dissatisfied applicants to query the Commission's decisions directly, but decisions might be reversed if discretionary powers had been abused, if relevant considerations had failed to be taken into account or if there had been a breach of natural justice or a denial of a fair hearing (*International Media Law*: 'The Trumper Out Trumped? The ITC and judicial review', October 1991, Volume 9, No. 10).

Application by TSW

On 1 November 1991, a statement was issued by Citigate Communications on behalf of TSW, saying that TSW would be seeking a judicial review of the decision announced on 16 October 1991 by the ITC that it did not appear that TSW could maintain its service throughout the ten-year licence period, despite the fact that it had passed the programme quality threshold and submitted a higher bid than Westcountry, who had been awarded the licence for the South West region. The ITC, in response, issued a press release claiming that TSW's statement was 'inaccurate and misleading' since, while passing the programme quality threshold, it had failed the financial sustainability test and so could not have its bid considered under Section 17 of the Act.

According to Sir Brian Bailey (Chairman, TSW):

> We knew there was such a thing as judicial review. Everything we heard about it was discouraging, but we took the view that we owed it to everybody, our employees most of all, but also to our shareholders, at least to explore it. We went to our London solicitors and they in turn produced counsel, and there were one or two aspects to it which suggested there was at least an argument. And in the end we took the view, that we must challenge it. (Interview with Sir Brian Bailey)

Initially, TSW had to satisfy a judge that it had an arguable case before permission to challenge the ITC would be granted. On 13 November 1991, Justice Simon Brown in the High Court refused TSW permission to seek a judicial review of the ITC decision and claimed that its argument was 'doomed to inevitable failure'.

Court of Appeal

Feeling that they had been unfairly treated TSW decided to renew their application. Lord Donaldson, Master of the Rolls, decided to hear the appeal himself together with Lords Justices McCowan and Nolan. TSW had engaged Gordon Pollock QC, who according to Harry Turner (Managing Director of TSW) was a 'splendid lawyer with the build and stance of a rugby scrum half', (RTS Journal *Television*, April 1992) and by Stephen Redfarn (in interview) as 'a very, very good counsel'. The ITC engaged Patrick Elias QC who was a well-respected academic judicial review lawyer, supported by junior counsel, David Pannick.

At the start of the Court of Appeal proceedings on 28 November 1991 Lord Donaldson made it clear that the court saw the main issue as that of alleged irrationality. In the absence of any account of the ITC's reasons, Lord Donaldson said that the court was 'groping in the dark' since there might have been irrationality or there might not. He asked Patrick Elias whether the ITC would be prepared to indicate what reasons it had had in mind. According to an ITC Information Paper prepared by the Secretary Kenneth Blyth:

> At a consultation with Counsel the previous evening, we had discussed different courses that the hearing of the appeal might take. A request from the Court for an indication of the ITC's reasons had been seen as one possibility. In the event, it seemed apparent that a refusal to give reasons (which would have been a legitimate course to hold to) would lead to the appeal being successful and an application for judicial review being granted. The most convenient (and compelling) way of giving some account of the Commission's reasons appeared to be to disclose the assessment paper, ITC Paper 179(91). This was done. (ITC Paper 123(91))

After adjournment, six copies of the nine-page assessment paper were made and TSW's counsel asked for additional time in which to study the paper.

The Staff Paper

The staff assessment paper (one of the two 'secret papers' referred to in court) questioned whether TSW would be able to obtain a £10 million loan from Barclays Bank and compared TSW's projected 5.3 per cent p.a. real increase in advertising revenue unfavourably with the 4 per cent average of the other bids. Questions were also raised about whether TSW could cut their costs as promised. The document concluded that: 'It would appear that TSW would be unable to maintain the service proposed throughout the ten-year period for which the licence is in force' (ITC Paper 179(91)).

According to John Wotton, a partner of Allen & Overy, the ITC's solicitors, who was in court when the document was handed over:

> The internal document wasn't volunteered in a spirit of generosity. The situation was that Lord Donaldson had evidently taken the view that there was a serious issue here. He was not happy with what had happened to TSW. And therefore he was clearly going to give leave. The Commission obviously thought they'd done quite well to have leave refused in the lower court. But it was quite clear that leave would be granted unless an indication of the reasons were given in court that morning. No statement of reasons had ever been prepared by the Commission. This paper was available and the judgement was taken by counsel that it was a strong paper, a sound explanation and it should be made available to the court. But when the judges reviewed it they felt it did raise serious questions. And they related to the basis of the financial assessment, particularly the concerns about TSW's projections on which they relied in framing their bid. In retrospect, the only alternative would have been to say well 'We're not giving any reasons at all' and the case would have proceeded in basically the same way. One of the judges in the House of Lords said the Counsel had acted quite properly in making that paper available to the court at that stage. I think it was a sensible decision. What it did mean was that paper assumed a prominence in the court above and beyond anything else. The court of appeal was actually acting as a fact-finding tribunal as well as an appeal tribunal. (Interview with John Wotton)

Peter Rogers (ITC Director of Finance), who had taken the decision in court that the paper should be disclosed, had reservations about the appropriateness of the document, which was only the final culmination of a much more detailed decision-making process by Members and was not designed to be a free-standing document explaining the reasons why TSW's application had been rejected.

> The problem was that the process had been that firstly the Members had seen in full all the applications. Secondly, for each of the licences on offer there had been two or three Members designated to take a special interest in the applications. These Members would, as it were, lead the discussion at the relevant Commission meeting. All the Commission were equally responsible. But the designated Members would meet with the staff and they would know the staff deliberations at first hand. And so in relation to each case, at the staff level and at that Member level, we had the benefit of extensive discusssion and a large amount of documentation. At the end, that was distilled down into the staff summary and the recommendations, which set out the main strengths and weaknesses as the staff saw them at the end of this process. What that summary didn't purport to do was to summarise, at all, let alone in any fair and balanced way, the original

case put by the applicant. That was in the application itself, and in the summary which applicants were required to provide. (Interview with Peter Rogers)

Subsequently the 'secret' staff paper 203(91) which had been considered at the final meeting of the ITC on 10/11 October 1991 was also made available at the second substantive hearing presided over by Lord Donaldson. This paper tested the case for consistency in rejecting five unrealistic or marginal bidders. Comparative charts showed that the TSW forecasts were the most optimistic and their financial position was the most vulnerable.

On 2 December 1991, TSW, after scrutinising the staff papers, announced that they wished to continue with the Appeal. This was resumed on 5 December. Before the hearing, TSW had submitted an amended application with affidavits from their Finance Director and from Robin Foster, a director of NERA, the economic consultancy which had helped TSW to prepare their advertising revenue forecasts. The main elements of TSW's argument in the amended application were that the ITC could not reasonably have considered the assumptions underlying TSW's forecasts not to be credible; and that the ITC was irrational in the view it took of the letter from Barclays Bank about loan facilities. Without hearing from TSW's counsel, Lord Donaldson said that, having read the documents, the Court had formed the view that the matter should go to judicial review. It had decided also that the case should stay in the Court of Appeal. The ITC was asked to submit its evidence for a hearing as early as could be arranged in the New Year (ITC Information Paper 125(91)).

Affidavits

ITC evidence for the forthcoming hearing was contained in affidavits, prepared in December 1991, by George Russell (ITC Chairman) and Peter Rogers (ITC Director of Finance).

George Russell's affidavit (ITC Information Paper 2(92)) dealt with ITC procedures and the Commission's view of TSW's application and Rogers' with the details of TSW's financial assessment. Russell stated that he had spent the whole of his working life from 1958 in major businesses and that 'the assessment of business plans has been one of my principal tasks throughout this period of over 30 years'. He stressed that the Broadcasting Act had shown that it was Parliament's intention that applicants for Channel 3 licences should have the financial resources to provide what was promised. There had to be 'quality of money' as well as quality of programmes.

Russell was unequivocal about TSW's business plan which he described as 'grossly optimistic' and a 'very risky venture'. He found the TSW forecast of average profit margins of 38 per cent over the licence period 'remarkable' when compared with their profit margins of 12–15 per cent achieved during the 1980s. He claimed that it was 'stretching credulity to believe that the same management could suddenly increase TSW's profit margins by such a dramatic figure in what they accept will be a more competitive environment'. TSW's revenue forecasting showed that they had actually added to the NERA forecast, which was already considered high. There was also the question of subsidy. The South West as one of the small ITV regions had been subsidised by the larger regions in the prices paid for network programmes over the current franchise period. The value of the subsidy in TSW's business plan was substantial (that is, £7 million p.a.) and Russell added that it was 'inconceivable that larger licensees would agree to providing such a network subsidy to TSW'.

Rogers' affidavit (ITC Information Paper 3(92)) spelled out his qualifications as an economist rather than an accountant. He had graduated with first-class honours in Economics from the University of Manchester and had received an MSc in Economics from LSE. Subsequently he had been employed as an economic adviser by HM Treasury, the Cabinet Office and the Department of Environment. Before joining the IBA in 1982 he had been Deputy Chief Executive of the Housing Corporation.

He saw the TSW business plan as 'a clear and very serious case of overbidding' which was based on the unrealistic expectation that the very rapid growth of advertising revenue experienced in the 1980s would continue in the next decade. IBA staff had constructed a mathematical model of the broadcasting economy up to the end of the Channel 3 licence term in 2002. In the course of this modelling work, an opinion had been sought from Professor Alan Budd, then Economic Adviser to Barclays Bank, on the estimated 4 per cent p.a. for growth of television advertising revenue in real terms. Budd had found this assumption 'perfectly sensible'.

NERA's projections were considered to be optimistic. Although NERA had been commissioned by several applicants there had been considerable variation in the extent to which applicants relied on the forecasts. TSW, however, had taken NERA's revenue projections and added a premium to them. TSW was the only applicant using NERA who had done this. However, it was TSW's 'irrevocable' cash bid which had caused most concern since it anticipated an average profitability over the ten-year licence period which was some 40 per cent higher than the profits which TSW had been able to earn from its ITV operations in the recent past.

On 20 January 1992, TSW's case returned to the Court of Appeal presided over by Lord Donaldson and Lords Justices Nolan and Steyn. TSW claimed that it had been a victim of an unfair and irrational decision by the ITC. Gordon Pollock QC, TSW's counsel, said that the crucial issue concerned TSW's forecast of Net Advertising Revenue (NAR) for the period of the licence. He claimed that the ITC had applied more stringent criteria to its bid than was anticipated in the *Invitation to Apply* and that TSW had a legitimate expectation that that would not occur and that its bid was based upon that expectation. TSW's secondary complaint was that staff paper 179(91) which was one basis of the ITC's decision was flawed on account of its failure to assess the TSW bid fairly or accurately (*Guardian* Law Reports, 12 February 1992).

Had TSW known in advance that ITC would choose the 4 per cent forecast as the test then its bid and business plan would have been different. Pollock also claimed that the ITC approach had been 'thoroughly shoddy, incompetent and unprofessional' and that TSW's forecasts were 'well considered, consistent and credible'.

Lord Donaldson paraphrased Russell's affidavit as saying 'Cor, these people are out of their tiny minds.' The question of Sheila Cassell's qualifications was also raised. As Head of ITC's external finance department, her work in TSW's financial assessment had been referred to in Rogers' affidavit. Pollock queried whether she was fit for the job. After her very considerable CV was produced, which included an MA (Hons) in Economics from Edinburgh University, an MBA in finance from the City University Business School and, more surprisingly, an MPhil in Town Planning, the court proceeded. Although Rogers (in interview) characterised Donaldson's remarks as 'snide', Nick Higham (*Marketing Week*, 6 December 1991) took the view that 'The Master of the Rolls' ability to cut through the crap was impressive.'

George Russell's memories of this time were as follows:

It was like being roped up on a cross and you either waited for the nails to be put in or the ropes to be cut down. That's what it felt like. You talk to Peter Rogers, whose whole career was at stake. Talk to Sheila Cassells, who was impugned by the court: 'Who is this woman who's done this work?' Meaning, is it a clerk? It's a woman, it's got to be a clerk. You read the transcript. It was nasty. 'Has she got qualifications?' says the judge. So it was read out; the whole gamut that said if anybody's better qualified to do this job find them. But there she was, she was there. She had to take it. It was not easy for them. (Interview with Sir George Russell)

Donaldson's Judgment

On 5 February 1992, the Court of Appeal dismissed TSW's application for judicial review in a 2:1 majority decision of the court, with Lord Donaldson dissenting. All three judges concluded that the ITC's *Invitation to Apply* was not misleading and agreed unanimously that TSW's primary case failed.

However, Lord Donaldson, in his judgment, criticised in detail the staff assessment paper 179(91) on TSW's application. While admitting that his previous description of it as a 'hatchet job' might have been an exaggeration, he concluded that there were reasonable grounds for considering that TSW's bid did not receive the fair evaluation to which it was entitled. He would have preferred to set aside the decision to award the licence to Westcountry, thereby enabling the ITC to take a fresh look at both Westcountry's and TSW's application.

Although Lord Justice Steyn criticised certain aspects of the staff paper he concluded that in the light of the information previously before the Commission, the ITC Members would probably not have been misled by the staff paper and that this challenge to the decision therefore failed.

Lord Justice Nolan agreed with Lord Donaldson that the staff assessment paper could be criticised as failing in a number of respects to provide a balanced picture of the TSW bid, but the ITC's decision had been fully explained in their affidavits and, thus explained, it was plainly one which the ITC was entitled to make (Summary of Judgment, Allen & Overy, 5 February 1992).

Leave, however, was granted for TSW to appeal to the House of Lords.

Appeal to the House of Lords

At the end of a five-day hearing before the Law Lords Keith, Templeman, Ackner, Goff and Lowry, TSW's appeal, in which it had argued that the ITC had been 'unfair and irrational' in rejecting its £16.1 million bid, was unanimously dismissed on 25 February 1992. Reasons for the dismissal were given at a later date.

Lord Templeman, delivering his judgment on 26 March 1992, said that the 1990 Act inevitably created a number of problems for the ITC and its applicants. He concluded that there was no scope, however, for the court to intervene. There was no doubt that the ITC had considered fully the application from TSW but felt bound to reject it. He said that Parliament might by virtue of statute confer powers and discretions and impose duties on the decision maker who might be an individual, a body of persons or a corporation. It might or might not provide machinery for an appeal against the decision which might be concerned with fact or law or both and might or might not involve the courts of law. Where Parliament had not provided for an appeal from a decision maker, the courts were not empowered to invent an appeal machinery. In this case Parliament had conferred powers and discretion and had imposed duties on the ITC. It had not however provided an appeal mechanism. It would therefore follow that even if the ITC had made a mistake in fact or law there was no appeal from that decision. The courts had invented the remedy of judicial review not to provide an appeal machinery but to ensure that the decision maker did not exceed or abuse his powers. It was made clear that natural justice did not render the decision invalid because the decision maker or his advisers had made a mistake of fact or law. The procedure for judicial review could operate only if it was disclosed that the ITC had acted illegally, irrationally or procedurally improperly. It was held that the procedure adopted by the ITC had in this case been admirable. The papers in evidence disclosed that the qualified staff and the experienced members of the ITC had carried out their duties properly, TSW's criticisms could not be substantiated and the court could not consider TSW's licence application. It was made abundantly clear that judicial review was not intended to cover the situation where the decision maker had made a mistake but merely to ensure that administration was properly carried out. Where the decision was made in good faith following proper procedure the application for judicial review must fail (*Journal of Media Law & Practice*, June 1992, p. 204).

Other Applicants

TSW, however, was not the only disappointed applicant to ask for reasons for their rejection by the ITC and to seek leave for judicial review. In December 1991, TVNi and TVS's applications were turned down by the Appeal Court on grounds of delay. White Rose's application was also dismissed in January 1992, on grounds of delay. The fact that licences had already been granted to Ulster and Meridian was also a factor in influencing the court's decision.

Since Thames was one of the more controversial losers who might have considered the possibility of judicial review, Richard Dunn (Chief Executive, Thames) said, when interviewed, that it was not seriously considered:

> Legal advice that we had taken in advance of the decision confirmed what any sensible intelligent person reading the Broadcasting Act would see, that the dice was so heavily loaded in favour of the ITC as to make challenge almost irrelevant. The judge would just turn around and say, 'Well, who's the competent authority to judge this matter. The ITC, what did they judge?' So unlike other losers who said 'Either, our successor will be bankrupt within two years, or we're immediately taking judicial action and we will reverse this decision,' the Board of Thames simply, in a measured, written statement said, 'We reserve our position.' We had decided there was no way in which we were going to take this to judicial review. (Interview with Richard Dunn)

Reasons for Giving Reasons

The general perception of the IBA had been that it was a secretive body with strong discretionary powers which was not statutorily obliged to give reasons for its decisions and, culturally, was disinclined to do so.

When asked about the reason for not giving reasons, John Wotton (one of the IBA/ITC's senior legal advisers) said:

> The consensus was that the Commission, in those circumstances, had nothing to gain by giving reasons where it wasn't required by the statute to do so. The Act had said that the only circumstance where the Commission had to give reasons was where they invoked exceptional circumstances. And it seemed clear that it wasn't intended they should be obliged to do so. Any reasons given clearly could form the subject of an application for judicial review and given the difficulty and complexity of the case, awarding fifteen licences simultaneously, with a real problem arising if the whole thing fell apart through challenge, it would just be giving hostages to fortune to give reasons. Now what I can't recall is when the final decision not to give reasons was taken. I think it was always assumed from the start that there wouldn't be a detailed statement of reasons published. In 1980, when the IBA announced the last re-award of ITV, there was a little paragraph

of explanation in relation to each of the awards. Nothing of any detail, but just something very brief. It may have been quite late in the day that it was decided to limit the press statement very much to precisely the statutory criteria and that there wouldn't be any gloss put on it. But I'm not certain of how the ITC reached that position. But it was reached with the agreement of both the Commission itself and by all the legal advisers. (Interview with John Wotton)

There was, however, a difference in opinion among senior ITC staff on the wisdom of withholding reasons. It is possible to argue that if the ITC had voluntarily given reasons for rejecting TSW's application, Lord Donaldson might not have granted leave for judicial review.

Peter Rogers (ITC Director of Finance) who was in the direct firing line in the Court of Appeal and whose professional credibility was at stake thought that reasons should have been given:

At an early stage the question came up of whether, when we announced our decisions, we should give reasons. I thought we should, and so did David Glencross, but some of our senior colleagues were either more doubtful or were opposed to this approach. The decisive consideration however, was that both our solicitors and our senior counsel advised strongly that we should not give reasons. I believe the argument was that we were not obliged to give reasons and if we did so opposing counsel would have more material to work on and to find fault with. When you face judicial review for the first time in relation to the implementation of a major new piece of legislation it is quite difficult to reject the firm advice of experienced lawyers. We should have done, but we did not.

We paid quite a high price for this decision in terms of the uncertainty and tension of two major court hearings, the second one before the House of Lords. No one can be certain that if we had given reasons these hearings would have been avoided, but in my view there was a real prospect that virtue would have reaped its reward.

What happened was that TSW applied for leave to bring a judicial review and Judge Simon Brown rejected it. TSW appealed and Lord Donaldson, then Master of the Rolls, presided in the Court of Appeal. Lord Donaldson accepted that the ITC was within its legal rights to refuse to give reasons, but none the less he invited us to do so. It seemed pretty clear to me, as the ITC's senior representative in court, that if we did not give reasons the court would uphold TSW's appeal and the case would go forward for a full substantive judicial review. If we gave reasons however, the Court of Appeal might uphold the decision of the lower court and reject the application for full review.

The only existing document which was in any way suitable for this purpose was the summary paper which set out the staff's recommendations and which had been subsequently endorsed by the Commission itself. I decided to release this to the court. But after a short adjournment the court allowed TSW's appeal and sent the case for full judicial review. The gambit had failed, and I returned to the office to tell George Russell what I had done.

The problem was, of course, that had we decided from the outset to give reasons for our decision then those reasons would have been incorporated in a document which had been designed from the outset to be read as a self-standing document. The document I put into court was not drawn up in this way. It was the culmination of a long process; the tip of the iceberg as it were. Consequently, read in isolation it raised as many questions as it answered. The prospect of hearing those answers attracted the court and so the case went for a full hearing.

The ITC was successful in the Court of Appeal but by a 2 to 1 majority, with Lord Donaldson dissenting. I am sure it was this split verdict which encouraged TSW to appeal to the House of Lords. Again the ITC was successful, with all five Law Lords rejecting TSW's case. The terms of the written judgment were generally very satisfactory and supportive from the ITC's standpoint, but along the way Lord Templeman said he thought that TSW should have had an explanation.

That did it. The ITC's policy was reversed and since then we have always accepted that we should publish reasons for our decisions. Indeed, in the spirit of the age, I think we are now much more open about our affairs generally and take some pride in it. (Interview with Peter Rogers)

The press sat on the sidelines revelling in the fact that the ITC was being forced to be more open and accountable than was customary. Commenting in *Broadcast* (22 November 1991) Peter Goodwin said 'nobody is going to judicial review to get a licence. What they want is an explanation from the ITC' and 'some insight into the ITC's thought processes'. The day after the staff paper was wrestled reluctantly from the ITC, Raymond Snoddy (*Financial Times*, 29 November 1991) wrote 'it is believed to be the first time that the regulatory body for commercial television has provided reasons for the awarding or removal of a franchise'. Nick Higham (*Marketing Week*, 6 December 1991) thought that 'Perhaps a greater degree of *glasnost* on the ITC's part would have paid dividends: TSW and others would still have protested, but a public debate about the fairness or otherwise of the system might have served as a safety valve, and the case might never have come to court.' After the Master of the Rolls' judgment was delivered, an editorial in *Broadcast* (6 December 1991) declared that 'broadcasting history had been made by forcing the ITC to participate in the democratic process ... TSW should be commended for its courage and persistence. It has been the only casualty of the franchise round to have publicly demanded answers from the ITC ... The Master of the Rolls has forced the ITC to take a few faltering steps on the road to an open system of regulation.' Harry Turner (RTS Journal *Television*, April 1992) also thought that 'like most quangos the ITC prefers to conduct its affairs in a blaze of secrecy. By diligent argument our QC, Gordon Pollock, was able to peel away several layers of this administrative onion.'

Impact on Westcountry

Although Westcountry was granted the South West licence after the House of Lords rejected TSW's appeal, the new Channel 3 licensees had only just over a year to prepare for the start of broadcasting on 1 January 1993. Due to the TSW judicial review, Westcountry had had to put their operational plans on hold.

The late Frank Copplestone (Deputy Chairman of Westcountry, who died in 1996) remembered that:

> The judicial review was a nightmare ... Lord Donaldson was the fly in the ointment. Without him it would have been over very much more quickly ... The effect of it was, of course, we could do nothing for five months. We'd estimated that fourteen months was short enough time to get from scratch to on air. And to be cut down to nine months, unbelievable. (Interview with Frank Copplestone)

Stephen Redfarn (MD) reckoned that the judicial review cost Westcountry between £500,000 and £750,000 and involved several cancelled contracts.

Demise of TSW

The first wave of redundancies at TSW took place in spring 1992. After announcing a sharp drop in pre-tax profits in June 1992, Harry Turner left the company. The TSW Film and Video Archive was created in October 1992 as a charitable trust with material dating back to 1961 when TSW's predecessor, Westward, had first broadcast. By the autumn, TSW was in talks with a private Bristol-based shoe manufacturer, UK Safety Group, formed in 1988 by a management buyout of the footwear business of the Ward White Group. In April 1993 a £9.5 million reverse takeover deal was announced. TSW's name was to be changed to UK Safety.

According to the *Western Morning News* (27 May 1993) bidders from all over the world poured into Plymouth for the auction of broadcasting equipment in rain-battered marquees at TSW's Derry Cross studios.

Turner Perspective

When interviewed over four years later, Harry Turner remembered that 'We approached the Judicial Review with a sense of naive optimism. We believed we could turn that decision round because we thought right was on our side.' Later, after the appeal was rejected by the House of Lords, the political realities began to sink in. He remembered that:

> I had a meeting after the House of Lords, when we finally got blown out and knew the game was up, with an ex-Cabinet Minister who asked not to be named, and he said to me, 'Harry, it's almost impossible to contemplate a regional company

of your size overturning an ITC decision, for two reasons: one is they do cross the t's and dot the i's; they know precisely what their legal position is, they were indeed appointed by the government with the authority to make those judgements, and they are judgement decisions, they had the discretion to make them. The second thing is this, you don't think that there weren't conversations in the Garrick or in the United Services Club or White's, between the Lord Chancellor and a few other people, saying 'Of course I can't influence the Lords of Appeal, I wouldn't even dream of doing that, but think of the embarrassment to the government if a decision is overturned, it would undermine the whole concept ...' And he said those sort of conversations were taking place. In other words, they could not tell the three Lords of Appeal at the judicial review to throw our application out. What they could do is indicate to them unofficially, over the port and the stilton, the implications of what would happen to the credibility of the government, the Home Office, the ITC and all the other companies who'd lost or who had made applications – they said 'The flood gates will open.' The Minister told me, 'You'd be naive to think that the government just sat back. You could be certain that officials at the Home Office, as soon as you went for judicial review, phoned the ITC and said, "Are you sure of your ground?", and George almost certainly said, "Yes, we can see this off".' I think they were a bit worried because of popular feeling, you know, a little one, a sort of David and Goliath syndrome which the press was building. But the ex-Cabinet Minister believed that we were doomed and he said 'if I'd have been around I would have advised you to save your money'.

Turner still thinks that at the time it was right to seek judicial review but his last memories of the legal process were that:

By the time we got to the House of Lords it became a kind of fantasy. I remember arriving at the House of Lords with Gordon (Pollock QC), who then had to put on a long wig, and we arrived and a man in black uniform with knee britches and buckles and big stick came up, and I said, 'Who are you?' He said, 'I am the principal door keeper.' And I said, 'Who's he?' He said, 'He is the principal under-door keeper.' All these people. And then I knew I was living in a kind of insane world of fantasy. (Interview with Harry Turner)

Sweeping up after the OFT: ITV and ITC, the Independents and the MMC

The new ITV companies – Carlton, Meridian and, despite the law's delays, Westcountry – all arrived on screen in good order as New Year's Eve turned to New Year's Day 1993. Westcountry did have to find and fit out a newsroom and studio on a Plymouth industrial estate (they subcontracted their transmission and presentation to HTV in Cardiff) in the short time left to them after the judicial review.

It required hard work and ingenuity but they managed it. There had not been a repeat of the instability of 1968.

However, for ITV as a whole the key date of the start of the newly licensed existence of the companies on 1 January 1993 was clouded by unfinished networking business. The network was sailing under a 'jury rig' of transitional networking arrangements towards a permanent system for the scheduling and commissioning of programmes from the new Network Centre that would have to be unpicked if the OFT's adverse findings (see Chapter 5) were accepted.

The OFT report was published on 3 December 1992. ITV's Council meeting four days later decided it must seek the ITC's agreement to a referral of the findings to the Monopolies and Mergers Commission (MMC), which under the Broadcasting Act was the appeal body. Such a referral had to be lodged with the MMC within a month.

ITV had to move faster than was its wont – the full legal and documentary submission had to be compiled in two months, part of which lay across the holiday period. This was to be one Christmas and New Year when few senior figures in ITV would go skiing.

The ITC had registered its concerns over the OFT report at a meeting between David Glencross and Peter Rogers and Sir Bryan Carsberg on 20 November. At its December meeting the Commission noted ITV's intention to submit a referral to the MMC, to which it agreed that the ITC would make a parallel referral submission.

A Special Council meeting was held eleven days later, with legal advisers present, to agree the terms of referral and to decide strategy for ITV's submission. ITV's referral document – 'the reference' – was taken by hand to the MMC's offices in Carey Street on 22 December and the ITC's followed on 30 December. (The Carey Street address was the source of some ITV 'gallows' humour. It had been the site of the Bankruptcy Court in Chancery in the nineteenth century.)

Leslie Hill, Central's Chief Executive, had been critical of the ITV team's performance at the OFT hearings, as he recalls:

> When I read the transcript ... I was absolutely shocked. I mean it read so badly. Our own people were contradicting each other, and I just felt we handled it very badly, simply through lack of preparation. There had been no preparation as I understand it; it was all shoot from the hip stuff. (Interview with Leslie Hill)

Greg Dyke, as Chairman of Council, had led the ITV delegation to the OFT but he recognised the validity of Hill's criticism and believed that Hill's type of approach, with its thoughtful, almost pedantic, attention to detail might pay off this time. Council agreed that Hill should lead the MMC submission team, supported by the equally diligent Andrew Quinn, who, as Chief Executive of the new Network Centre was responsible for its operation and for any redrafting of the key networking documents. It was the original versions of these documents – derived from the A.11 meetings (see Chapter 5) – at which the OFT had levelled much of its criticism.

Hill believed that one of the failings of the OFT submission was that it had not drawn on the expertise that lay in the companies. He therefore summoned a meeting of the companies' in-house legal and contractual experts to go through the networking arrangements documents and modify them in the light of the OFT's comments and to ensure that they were both clear and correct. The documents then went forward to a reference group of managing directors for approval.

By the following week, on 5 January 1993, Hill had assembled his team, 'the MMC submission group', which now included the competition lawyer Nicholas Green QC as well as the legal adviser to the ITVA, Patrick Swaffer of Goodman, Derrick. Other members of the group were Dr Cento Veljanovski, an advocate of free-market economics being applied to broadcasting, who brought with him an academic economist who was also an expert on competition law, Professor Basil Yamey of the University of London, who had actually served on the MMC. Together they were commissioned through Veljanovski's consultancy firm, Lexecon, to produce an economic analysis of ITV's networking arrangements for submission to the MMC.

The ITV members included several from Hill's own company, Central. These were the Director of Programmes, Andy Allan, the Controller of News and Current Affairs, Bob Southgate and Central's Head of Legal Affairs, Rod Henwood. All these could speak from personal experience on the subject of programme commissioning and compliance. Also on call was Hill's Public Affairs adviser, Marshall Stewart. The author, who as chairman of the now defunct Controllers Group and Quinn's Director of Secretariat was responsible for the transitional networking arrangements, was also one of Hill's team.

An important new factor in ITV's post-1992 networking system was the existence of a new form of ITV company – 'the publisher contractor' – which commissioned programmes (other than news) rather than making them in-house. These – Carlton, Meridian and Westcountry – were in fact, of course, licensees rather than contractors but the description derived from pre-1990 Act terminology.

It was agreed that Nigel Walmsley, then Managing Director of Carlton Television, would represent the new breed. All in all, the submission group was a formidable body of expertise, but now it had to convince the MMC, an organisation with a reputation for great rigour in its examinations, of the errors of the OFT's conclusions.

There were complex jurisdictional issues to be addressed but while discussions about those took place on the ITV side and at the ITC, Hill and Quinn sought an informal 'getting to know you' meeting between some members of Council and the MMC group who would be responsible for the report.

As well as his other qualifications for the leadership of the submission team, Hill knew the Chairman of the MMC, Sir Sydney Lipworth, socially (he played cricket with him) and was able, with Greg Dyke's agreement, to show the MMC team of Lipworth, Sir Ronald Halstead, Dr Morris, Mr Odgers and Mr Owens, round

LWT's Television Centre on the South Bank and let them see a presentation by Andrew Quinn on the basics of the ITV network system, its business and its economics. This took place on 20 January 1993 – a fortnight before the submission date of 5 February.

In this way ITV was able to give the MMC the sort of insight into its business that the Independent Producers (PACT) had achieved with the OFT. Anybody reading the two reports will notice the understanding in the OFT's summary of PACT's views and the business situation of the independent producer (Paragraphs 10.33–10.56, OFT Report, *Channel 3 Networking Arrangements*, OFT, 3 December 1992) as compared to the rather less focused view of PACT's objectives in the MMC's summary (Paragraphs 6.1–6.40, MMC Report, *Channel 3 Networking arrangements*, HMSO, April 1993).

Conversely, the understanding of the ITV licensees' business and concerns are very clear throughout the MMC Report, and although the views of the Independent Television Association were coherently represented in the OFT Report, no great understanding of the business of British commercial television is evident from the Report's findings. Both bodies seem to have been clear about the ITC's views, though the OFT had been inclined to discount some of its key responsibilities.

Logic demanded that the MMC examined ITV's submissions on the jurisdictional questions with the group before it heard the evidence in support of the networking aspects of the submission. The ITV group first went before the MMC on Friday 19 February 1993 for the legal discussions and then returned on 2 March for the examination of the operational, contractual and business aspects of the ITV proposals for networking arrangements. An ITC group, consisting of David Glencross and Peter Rogers, with John Wotton the ITC's legal adviser from Allen & Overy, attended the Commission on the same days, in each case immediately after ITV.

The jurisdictional approach employed the sort of finesse beloved of lawyers, but it somewhat unnerved some in ITV who were not members of the experts group, in that it appeared to question the competence of the OFT (and by implication the MMC) to deal with the networking arrangements at all. However the key question was whether the OFT's findings on the competition test had been wrong in law.

One of the five parts of the jurisdictional aspect of the submission argued that for the purposes of Section 39 of the Broadcasting Act the networking arrangements only dealt with finished programmes and that in relation to the competition test that the OFT had applied:

Agreements between licensees and independent producers relating to programme proposals, production or the provision of services or financing did not relate to finished products and were excluded. To the extent that the DGFT had misapplied the test, his report was *ultra vires*. (Paragraph 5.4, MMC Report, ibid.)

Other key jurisdictional questions included those relating to the ITC's role. The ITC had issued the ground rules for networking in the *Invitation to Apply* and had checked them, as it was required to do under the Act, with the Director General of the OFT. ITV had submitted its arrangements to the ITC and had them approved. How, then, could they now not be acceptable?

There was a further question as to whether the OFT had given due weight to one purpose of Section 39 (networking) of the Broadcasting Act, which was to enable the licensees through the networking arrangements to compete on a nationwide basis with other broadcasting channels.

Finally there were two legal points about whether the OFT had applied the proper jurisprudence when considering those parts of the competition tests that were subject to European law. Several of these questions were also raised in the ITC's submission.

The ITC was critical of the OFT's judgements on the Network Centre's role in relation to competition:

> In the ITC's view, the competition test does not require the network arrangements to be designed with a view to overcoming structural weaknesses in the independent production sector ... i.e., a large number of small firms which are lightly capitalised and with poor access to project finance on a commercial basis ... Particularly when other solutions are possible, it is not reasonable for the DGFT to require the Network Centre to take a much wider role which involves the provision of deficit funding in connection with the exploitation of non-broadcasting rights in commissioned programmes, and meeting the working capital requirements of independent programme production by funding cash flow through a series of progress payments. If the Network Centre is compelled to undertake additional, unnecessary and unwanted duties of this kind it will add considerably to its administrative and managerial workload. (Paragraph 87, ITC document, *Reference to the Monopolies and Mergers Commission, Channel 3 Networking Arrangements, Statement of Position by the Independent Television Commission*, 1 February 1993)

When its Report was published on 6 April 1993, it showed that the MMC had found, in twenty paragraphs of careful legal argument (Paragraphs 8.1–8.20), that the OFT had been correct in law on all the points raised.

The MMC also concluded that by precluding direct contracting between the Network Centre and independent producers the networking arrangements did not satisfy the competition test. They further concluded that the arrangements provisions for dealing with the acquisition of rights in the programmes did not do so either (Paragraph 9.59).

On the compliance issue, the MMC did accept the ITC's argument that it could only be exercised by the regulator through a licenced broadcaster and to ITV's considerable relief the MMC set aside the OFT's unworkable four-fold programme contract requirements for all programmes (Paragraph. 9.61) (see also Chapter 5) and replaced them with a tripartite contract – solely for independent productions – in which the licensee was conjoined for compliance purposes only. The MMC did require that compliance was carried out by the licensee's broadcasting, rather than production, staff.

On finance from the Centre, the MMC ruled that the Centre must produce a Code of Practice in relation to confidentiality of programme proposals and arrangements to provide Letters of Intent and Deal Letters to allow independent producers to raise development money and programme cash flow arrangements for themselves commercially.

On the matter of programme rights, the OFT had ruled that ITV's licence period of ten years for exclusive use of a finished programme with an option of a further five must be reduced to five years' initial licence with a further two as an option. This too was set aside by the MMC, which said that any period of licence must be agreed between the parties in negotiation. However ITV must not acquire any rights other than:

UK broadcasting rights,
non-UK simultaneous transmission rights, and
options to acquire Further Programmes (including where appropriate the licensing of Format Rights); and
there must be no restriction on the power of producers to seek to reacquire rights granted to ITV under the licence. (Paragraph 10.11)

ITV had argued very strongly on the 'further programmes' issue that its competitiveness would be crippled if series, having proven successful on ITV, could be offered by the producer to other UK broadcasters. The MMC clearly had understood the business context in which ITV was now competing.

Finally, amongst various changes of documentation the MMC required that ITV produce a Code of Practice to specify its procedures for commissioning programmes and to demonstrate its evenhandedness between independent and in-house productions (Paragraph 10.16).

When the MMC Report appeared on 6 April 1993, it offered some sense of success to all the parties. John Woodward, the Chief Executive of PACT, claimed victory in interviews in *Broadcast* magazine and *Television Today*. In *Broadcast* Andrew Quinn welcomed the report as showing 'a very shrewd understanding of the business we are in'. The *Financial Times*, however, in an editorial, managed to have its cake and eat it by pronouncing the Report: 'an elegant solution to an intractable dispute' but also that 'the exercise smells unmistakably of fudge'.

The MMC having reported, the modified documents and procedures then had to be submitted to the OFT for agreement. The deadline for this was set for the end of June. Once again ITV had to move fast. Andrew Quinn, who was by now also in the midst of preparations for the move of the embryonic Network Centre and the remaining elements of the ITVA from Knighton House to the new ITN building in Gray's Inn Road by 1 June, was already in consultation with lawyers (and with PACT) about the redrafting of the documents well before he was formally set the task by the first Council after publication of the Report. The Council minutes for May note:

> The Chairman and members of Council expressed thanks to Mr Hill and his team on the successful outcome of the MMC report. (Minutes of ITVA Council, 10 May 1993)

Hill had earned those words. The submission had been clear and well supported with relevant documentation. Above all, at the hearings at the MMC the contributions from the ITV team had been organised and disciplined:

> ... everybody knew what their subject was and what their questions were likely to be, and they were chosen on the basis of their ability ... to answer and deal with follow-up points. (Interview with Leslie Hill)

All that had required Hill to dedicate time and effort on behalf of the network:

> I spent three or four months on it, probably two-thirds of my time during that period ... in fact I was very tired at the end of that, almost as tired as I was at the end of the licence application. (Ibid.)

After a further failure by ITV in July 1993 to get its arguments properly understood – as a result of the leaking of a proposal, made at a Broadcast Board Strategy Meeting, to review the scheduling of *News at Ten* – Hill's efforts were to have a lasting effect on the way that ITV approached policy issues and its relations with outside bodies.

An important debate took place at Council on 1 November 1993, in which a proposal by Meridian that Council should have an independent chairman was discussed. There was some support for the idea from HTV and Channel Television, but it became clear that the majority view was against such a move. After Roger Laughton, Meridian's Chief Executive, withdrew the proposal, the outgoing Chairman, Greg Dyke, proposed Hill as his successor. Though Hill's approach was in some ways the very opposite of his own, Dyke had come to see its virtues in a world where political and regulatory criticism of ITV could have an effect on its competitiveness.

Characteristically, Hill laid down conditions for his chairmanship. He was not prepared to serve unless the ITV companies were willing to reach 'common cause':

> Mr Hill said a debate was needed to establish what ITV stood for, what ITV wanted and where ITV was going. ITV needed to explain its environment and articulate its longer term aims. It needed to create confidence and promote good

news about itself. The positive aspects of ITV needed to be publicised in addition to the companies' achievements. (Minutes of ITVA Council, 1 November 1993)

Hill also sought to 'bond' Council with the new Centre, with the Chairman's Committee extending to embrace the Chief Executive and relevant Directors there. Hill's ideas were agreed in principle and he was elected unanimously to the Chairmanship that he was to hold for far longer than any of his predecessors. He presided over a period during which the new ITV was to be tested in many ways but throughout which it maintained a stability that was in marked contrast with the network's traumas of the late Eighties and the start of the Nineties.

Conclusion – Consolidation and its Consequences – Regulation by Licence

Much of the change in ITV after the the start of the first licence period was related to ownership. When it was announced by the then Secretary of State for National Heritage, Peter Brooke (note: the responsibility for broadcasting was transferred from the Home Office to the Department of National Heritage when it was formed in April 1992), on 22 November 1993 that the moratorium on takeovers was to be lifted on 1 January 1994, it acted like a starting gun for those like Michael Green who believed that greater stability and cost-effectiveness lay in the acquisition of a larger broadcaster base.

Green moved fast and he had acquired a further 19 per cent of Central Independent Television to add to his previous 20 per cent. The 39 per cent brought him effective control of Central by 29 November, with, after they had briefly considered a defence plan which would have involved a Central bid for Anglia, the agreement of Central's Board and senior executives. The deal valued Central at £758 million. But in moving so fast Green had in fact jumped the gun and there was more than a remote possibility that Labour might have blocked the enabling legislation when it went before the House of Commons on 8 December. However, the measure passed by 144 votes to 106. Michael Green then became the most powerful figure in Independent Television.

Others were not far behind. Within a year Gerry Robinson, the new Chief Executive of Granada Group, had launched a hostile takeover for LWT. It was a bruising battle that carried certain ironies – given the history of antagonism between the two companies within the ITV network. However, Robinson's motivation for the acquisition was in essence the same as Green's – an increase of strength and stability for his Group.

Ultimately he was successful, though at a price (740 pence per LWT share for those who chose the option of one 'new' Granada share plus 100 pence cash or otherwise 686 pence cash) that many thought at the time to be too high.

The vigorous defenders, Chairman Christopher Bland and Chief Executive Greg Dyke, departed. As a result of the LWT 'share arrangement' (see Chapter 7, Section II, 'Ownership') at the price offered they were rich men. Both were soon to reappear on the broadcast scene. Dyke became Chief Executive of Pearson Television and Bland ascended to the ultimate peak position in British broadcasting, as Chairman of the BBC. Robinson took over as Chairman at LWT, which like Central had to be maintained as a separate broadcaster entity to honour the terms of its ITC licence. Until a change in the legislation occurs there are limits to the cost benefits of consolidation. Even the increased revenue stream engendered by conjoining ITV companies was initially limited by rules that specified that no one grouping of broadcasters could broadcast to more than 15 per cent of the UK audience or control more than 25 per cent of total terrestrial television advertising. Nevertheless no serious player could afford to be left behind.

A third consolidated force grew around Lord Hollick's MAI group of diverse financial interests of which Meridian, the holder of the licence for the South and South East, was the original broadcasting component. Hollick broadened his grouping to take in United Newspapers and Anglia Television. It was renamed United News and Media. He also made a play for the company with the licence adjoining that of Meridian, Westcountry Television. However his bid was beaten by that of Michael Green.

Scottish Television has aquired Grampian, producing a Scottish national broadcaster prepared for devolution, and Yorkshire Television and HTV have been taken over by Granada and United respectively.

Significantly, in the late 1990s, the three major owners, Green, Robinson and Hollick, are reported to be exploring the possibility of joint ownership of an ITV Ltd to run the ITV Network Centre – a proposal which was one of the options offered originally by Paragraph 118 in the ITC's *Invitation to Apply for Regional Channel 3 Licences* (1991).

Granada's takeover of Yorkshire has made Granada the largest supplier of programmes to the network. Is it possible to assess how the licence system and consolidation have affected programming? The mid-Nineties is too early a point perhaps at which to do so but it is worth reflecting upon the impact of the new form of programme regulation brought in by the 1990 Broadcasting Act. The prime change is that the regulation has become *post facto*. There is no previewing of programmes by the regulator as there was under the previous Act. The ITC maintains guidelines on programme standards to which the companies must adhere. Where the old IBA was once the legally accountable broadcaster the companies now fulfil that role. They must depend on their own judgement – a responsibility many senior executives in ITV had long sought.

Compliance with licence requirements, the issue that caused so much difficulty with the independent sector at the time of the new networking discussions, is now routine. The ITC each year issues a commentary arising from its monitoring of the programme performance of the network and the individual companies in the previous year. The ITC's assessment takes account of audience research findings and of reports from the eleven Viewer Consultative Councils spread across the

UK – each containing a cross-section of people reflecting a range of tastes and interests. Draft assessments on programme quality and diversity are prepared by the ITC's National and Regional Officers and the staff of the Programmes and Engineering divisions.

After a difficulty with the first Annual Report under the new system, which was held by some companies to have contained unfair comment and some factually erroneous material, these drafts are now discussed with companies thoroughly and comments and corrections noted or accepted before publication.

The system does have teeth. Ultimately the ITC can remove a company's licence to broadcast for persistent offences. In the contentious first annual ITC Performance Review Carlton Television was publicly rebuked for a lack of programme quality in some areas. The acquisition of Central allowed Carlton to respond to the ITC's criticism by bringing some of that company's programme management expertise across to bolster its own. Since then Granada has been fined £500,000 for a 'product placement' offence (a form of advertising within a programme instead of in the designated commercial breaks). And LWT received a severe public warning for the behaviour of a performer on a live programme.

If there is a downside to the new system it would appear to be that *post facto* regulation carries with it the danger that the regulator is more out of touch with the industry it controls. In a business where new technical developments take place regularly and generate new artistic and editorial techniques that impact on programme quality this can lead to an ignorance of judgement that reflects badly on the regulator. A case in point was the Carlton-commissioned documentary series *Hollywood Women*. This series was criticised as being 'glib and superficial'. In fact, whatever judgement may be made on its content, the series was made with what was then an innovative technique – previously only used in commercial advertisement making – called non-linear editing. The series owed to that technique its breathtaking pace and appropriate style of wit, which appealed sufficiently to viewers for three further series in a similar vein to be commissioned. The ITC might have been more respected by the industry had the report acknowleged this innovative use of a new technique (and perhaps encouraged its further use on more serious subjects) in a judgement of content balanced by recognition of the new form.

It is impossible to judge whether the much vaunted 'golden age' of television passed during the period covered by this book. An audience like that in the UK, brought up to expect high-quality broadcasting, sets high standards for what it wants to see. The regulator is important for the retention of diversity of programming and the control of violence and other anti-social content. It cannot guarantee programme quality. Quality in programmes can only be achieved by producers and broadcasters determined to strive for it. Television viewing time was reducing by the end of the Eighties but that can be attributed to social factors rather than any decline in the quality of programmes. But there have long been signs that viewers want more control of what they want to see and when. The increasing number of channels ('The New Competitors' of the next volume in this series), more sophisticated transmission techniques and advances in viewing and recording technology at home are beginning to give them that control. In the name of media choice and democracy that cannot be a bad development. But it is one that faces broadcasters with a whole new set of challenges for the future.

APPENDIX A   IBA MEMBERS (1981–90)

Chairmen
Lord Thomson of Monifieth	1981–88
George Russell	1989–90

Deputy Chairmen
Sir John Riddell	1981–85
Sir Donald Maitland	1986–89
Lord Chalfont	1989–90

Members for Scotland
Rev. William Morris	1979–84
John Purvis	1985–89
The Earl of Dalkeith	1990

Members for Wales
Professor Huw Morris Jones	1976–82
Gwilym Peregrine	1982–89
Eleri Wynne Jones	1990

Members for Northern Ireland
Jill McIvor	1980–86
Professor John Fulton	1987–90

Other Members
Mary Warnock	1973–81
Professor James Ring	1974–81
The Marchioness of Anglesey	1976–82
Anthony Purssell	1976–81
Anthony Christopher	1978–83
George Russell	1979–86
Sir Denis Hamilton	1981–83
Juliet Jowitt	1981–86
Yvonne Conolly	1982–86
Paula Ridley	1982–88
Professor Alexander Cullen	1982–89
Roy Grantham	1984–90
Sir Michael Caine	1984–89
Sir Anthony Jolliffe	1987–89
Ranjit Sondhi	1987–90
Lady Popplewell	1987–90
Pauline Mathias	1989–90
Pranlal Sheth	1990
Roy Goddard	1990

APPENDIX B   ITC MEMBERS (1991–92)

Chairman
Sir George Russell

Deputy Chairman
Jocelyn Stevens

Member for Scotland
The Earl of Dalkeith

Member for Wales
Eleri Wynne Jones

Member for Northern Ireland
Professor John Fulton

Other Members
Roy Goddard
Pauline Mathias
Lady Popplewell
Professor James Ring
Pranlal Sheth

APPENDIX C   GOVERNMENT MINISTERS RESPONSIBLE FOR BROADCASTING, 1979–92

This table lists the Cabinet Ministers with overall responsibility for broadcasting, and the Ministers of State and Parliamentary Under-Secretaries of State who had specific departmental responsibility for broadcasting and acted as spokesmen on the topic in Parliament. The government department with primary responsibility for broadcasting policy changed from the Home Office to the newly created Department of National Heritage in April 1992.

HOME OFFICE (–1992)

Home Secretary	Dates	Minister of State	Dates	Parliamentary Under-Secretary of State	Dates
William Whitelaw	1979–83	Leon Brittan	1979–81	Lord Belstead	1979–82
Leon Brittan	1983–85	Timothy Raison	1979–83	Lord Elton	1982–84
Douglas Hurd	1985–89	Patrick Mayhew	1981–83	David Mellor	1983–86
David Waddington	1989–90	Douglas Hurd	1983–84	Lord Glenarthur	1985–86
Kenneth Baker	1990–92	Lord Elton	1984–85	Peter Lloyd	1989–92
		Giles Shaw	1984–86		
		Earl of Caithness	1986–88		
		David Mellor	1986–87		
		Timothy Renton	1987–89		
		Earl Ferrers	1988–94		
		David Mellor	1989–90		

DEPARTMENT OF NATIONAL HERITAGE (1992–)

Secretary of State for National Heritage	Dates	Minister of State	Dates	Government Spokesman	Dates
David Mellor	1992	Robert Key	1992–93	Viscount Astor	1992–93
Peter Brooke	1992–94				

APPENDIX D   FOURTH CHANNEL SUBSCRIPTIONS (£000)

Contractor	1983/84	1984/85	1985/86	1986/87	1987/88	1988/89	1989/90	1990/91	1991/92
Anglia	7,569	9,324	10,461	10,890	12,459	14,335	17,390	19,094	19,003
Border	114	144	159	165	160	170	190	190	190
Central	16,470	21,024	24,336	26,928	29,134	34,469	38,911	41,289	40,812
Channel	5	54	54	66	90	99	115	115	115
Grampian	485	582	588	555	395	385	375	375	375
Granada	18,945	22,506	22,089	22,383	23,658	25,136	28,704	30,841	30,670
HTV	7,880	9,897	11,628	12,492	13,756	15,144	17,174	17,853	17,624
London Weekend	15,785	18,690	20,067	20,352	24,097	26,942	31,432	32,801	32,943
Scottish	6,582	8,355	9,756	11,631	12,631	13,199	14,609	15,511	15,606
Television South	14,956	17,340	17,259	19,674	22,514	25,952	30,756	32,595	32,134
Television South West	2,013	2,553	2,877	3,300	3,437	3,769	4,372	4,885	4,865
Thames	20,844	26,547	27,366	28,641	33,255	36,747	41,045	44,962	43,110
Tyne Tees	7,933	9,246	8,712	8,193	8,065	8,758	9,352	9,052	8,281
Ulster	215	255	426	672	460	442	503	541	526
Yorkshire	12,986	16,284	18,720	17,310	19,289	21,717	23,763	24,294	24,405
Total (£000)	132,782	162,801	174,498	183,252	203,400	227,264	258,691	274,398	270,659

Source: IBA Annual Reports and IBA/ITC News Releases

Note: In 1982, subscriptions were limited to £49 million with additional borrowings of £49 million.

APPENDIX E   ITV RENTALS (£000)

Contractor	1982/83	1983/84	1984/85	1985/86	1986/87	1987/88	1988/89	1990	1991	1992
Thames	8,572	8,928	9,498	10,115	10,775	11,006	no	11,452	3,221	2,899
LWT	4,977	5,183	5,514	5,873	6,256	7,482	increase	8,304	2,335	2,102
Central	6,635	6,911	7,353	7,830	8,341	9,898		10,706	3,011	2,710
Granada	7,189	7,488	7,966	8,484	9,038	7,795		7,640	2,149	1,934
Yorkshire	5,529	5,759	6,127	6,525	6,996	6,068		6,002	1,688	1,519
TVS	5,392	5,616	5,975	6,578	7,232	7,248		8,159	2,295	2,066
HTV	1,776	3,311	3,523	3,751	3,996	4,140		4,056	1,141	1,027
Scottish	2,281	2,375	2,527	2,691	2,867	3,429		3,301	928	835
Anglia	2,281	2,375	2,527	2,691	2,867	3,429		4,160	1,170	1,053
Tyne Tees	2,212	2,303	2,451	2,394	2,327	2,153		1,819	512	461
TSW	548	504	605	673	868	903		957	269	242
Ulster	414	431	459	386	304	316		320	90	81
Grampian	69	72	76	185	304	316		275	77	69
Border	55	58	61	65	69	73		69	20	18
Channel	14	14	15	16	17	26		27	8	7
TV-am	115	690	766	805	847	1,300		2,232	628	565
Oracle	–	–	–	–	–	–		30	8	7
Total*	48,059	52,018	55,443	59,062	63,104	65,582		69,509	19,550	17,595

* 1981–89 are financial years; 1990–92 are calendar years.

Source: IBA Annual Reports and IBA/ITC News Releases.

BIBLIOGRAPHY

10. Programmes

    (a) General
    (b) News, current affairs and documentaries
    (c) Drama programmes
    (d) Comedy and light entertainment
    (e) Children's and educational programmes
    (f) Religious broadcasting
    (g) Arts programmes
    (h) Sports on television

11. Personalities: biographies, autobiographies and memoirs

Volume 4 of *Independent Television in Britain* contained a list of selected contemporary publications covering (or published in) the period 1962 to 1980. This bibliography covers the next stage of the history of Independent Television, from 1981 to 1992. It contains the key government and parliamentary publications, and selected books on broadcasting and society, the television industry, the political background, regulation, ITV and its companies, Channel 4, advertising, broadcasting research, programmes, and the personalities of the period.

Books specifically and solely about the BBC are not included. They can be found listed in *British broadcasting 1922–1982: a selected bibliography* (London: BBC Data Publications, 1983), and *The history of broadcasting in the United Kingdom*, by Asa Briggs (Volumes 1–5. Oxford: Oxford University Press, 1961–95).

1.   GOVERNMENT AND PARLIAMENTARY PUBLICATIONS

(a)   Acts of Parliament

Broadcasting Act 1980.
Broadcasting Act 1981. (Consolidating Act)
Cable and Broadcasting Act 1984.
Telecommunications Act 1984.
Video Recordings Act 1984.
Copyright, Designs and Patents Act 1988.
Broadcasting Act 1987.
Broadcasting Act 1990.

(b)   Government White Papers

HOME OFFICE/DEPARTMENT OF TRADE AND INDUSTRY. *The development of cable systems and services.* (Cmnd 8866) London: HMSO, 1983.

HOME OFFICE. *Broadcasting in the '90s: competition, choice and quality. The Government's plans for broadcasting legislation.* (Cm 517) London: HMSO, 1988.
DEPARTMENT OF TRADE AND INDUSTRY. *Competition and choice: telecommunications policy for the 1990s.* (Cm 1461) London: HMSO, 1991.

(c)   Government Committee of Inquiry Reports

Report of the Committee on the Future of Broadcasting. (Chairman: Lord Annan) (Cmnd 6753) London: HMSO, 1977.
Report of the Inquiry into Cable Expansion and Broadcasting Policy. (Chairman: Lord Hunt of Tanworth) (Cmnd 8679) London: HMSO, 1982.
Report of the Committee on Financing the BBC. (Chairman: Professor Alan Peacock) (Cmnd 9824) London: HMSO, 1986.
Enquiry into Standards of Cross Media Promotion. Report to the Secretary of State for Trade and Industry. (Chairman: John Sadler) (Cm 1436) London: HMSO, 1991.

(d)   Parliamentary Select Committee Reports

HOUSE OF COMMONS. *Fifth report from the Committee of Public Accounts, together with the proceedings of the Committee and the minutes of evidence. Independent Broadcasting Authority: additional payments by programme contractors.* (Session 1979–80: HC 445) London: HMSO, 1980.
HOUSE OF COMMONS. *Second report from the Committee on Welsh Affairs, together with proceedings of the Committee thereon, the minutes of evidence and appendices. Broadcasting in the Welsh language and the implications for Welsh and non-Welsh speaking viewers and listeners.* (Session 1980–81: HC 448–I, HC 448–II) London: HMSO, 1981.
HOUSE OF COMMONS. *First report from the Defence Committee. The handling of press and public information during the Falklands conflict.* (Session 1982–83: HC 17–I, 17–II) London: HMSO, 1982.
HOUSE OF COMMONS. *Fourth report from the Select Committee on European Legislation, together with the proceedings of the Committee.* (EC Green Paper: *Television without frontiers*) (Session 1984–85: HC 5–iv) London: HMSO, 1984.
HOUSE OF COMMONS. *Thirtieth report from the Select Committee on European Legislation, together with the proceedings of the Committee.* (Session 1984–85: HC 5–xxx) (*Transmission standards for Direct Broadcasting via Satellite*) London: HMSO, 1985.
HOUSE OF COMMONS. *Twenty-ninth report from the Committee of Public Accounts. Independent Broadcasting Authority: additional payments by programme contractors.* (Session 1984–85: HC 400) London: HMSO, 1985.

HOUSE OF LORDS. *Select Committee on the European Communities. Fourth report. Television without frontiers. With evidence.* (Session 1985–86: HL 43) London: HMSO, 1985.

HOUSE OF COMMONS. *Fifteenth report from the Select Committee on European Legislation, together with the proceedings of the Committee.* (*Transmission standards for Direct Broadcasting via Satellite*) (Sessions 1985–86: HC 21–xv) London: HMSO, 1986.

HOUSE OF LORDS. *Select Committee on the European Communities. Fourth Report. European broadcasting.* (EC draft Directive on broadcasting (6739/86 COR 1 COM (86) 146) (Session 1986–87: HL 67) London: HMSO, 1987.

HOUSE OF COMMONS. *Home Affairs Committee. Third report. The future of broadcasting.* (Session 1987–88: HC 262–I, HC 262–II) London: HMSO, 1988.

HOUSE OF COMMONS. *Forty-third report from the Committee of Public Accounts. Independent Broadcasting Authority: additional payments by programme contractors.* (Session 1987–88: HC 317) London: HMSO, 1988.

HOUSE OF COMMONS. *Select Committee on European Legislation. Seventeenth report, together with the proceedings of the Committee on 5 April 1989.* (Draft EC Directive on broadcasting (5574/88 COM (88) 554) (Session 1988–89: HC 15–xvii) London: HMSO, 1989.

HOUSE OF COMMONS. *Select Committee on European Legislation. Twenty-first report, together with proceedings of the Committee on 10 May 1989.* (Session 1988–89: HC 15–xxi) London: HMSO, 1989.

HOUSE OF COMMONS. *Select Committee on European Legislation. Twenty-fourth report, together with the proceedings of the Committee on 7 June 1989.* (Session 1988–89: HC 15–xxiv) London: HMSO, 1989.

HOUSE OF COMMONS. *First report from the Select Committee on Televising of Proceedings of the House.* (Session 1988–89: HC 141–I, HC 141–II) London: HMSO, 1989.

HOUSE OF COMMONS. *Home Affairs Committee. Second Report. The financing of Channel 4.* (Session 1988–89: HC 185) London: HMSO, 1989.

HOUSE OF COMMONS. *First report from the Select Committee on Televising of Proceedings of the House. Review of the experiment in televising the proceedings of the House, together with the proceedings of Committee, relating to the report, minutes of evidence and appendices.* (Session 1989–90: HC 265–I, HC 265–II) London: HMSO, 1990.

HOUSE OF LORDS. *Select Committee on Broadcasting. Future arrangements for televising the proceedings of the House of Lords.* (Session 1990–91: HL 31) London: HMSO, 1991.

HOUSE OF COMMONS. *First report from the Select Committee on Broadcasting. The arrangements for the permanent televising of the proceedings of the House.* (Session 1990–91: HC 11) London: HMSO, 1991.

HOUSE OF COMMONS. *National Heritage Committee. Fourth report. Privacy and media intrusion.* (Session 1992–93: HC 294–I, HC 294–II, HC 294–III) London: HMSO, 1993.

HOUSE OF COMMONS: *National Heritage Committee. Sixth report. News at Ten.* (Session 1992–93: HC 799) London: HMSO, 1993.

(e) Advisory Committee Reports

CABINET OFFICE: INFORMATION TECHNOLOGY ADVISORY PANEL. *Report on cable systems.* London: HMSO, 1982.

HOME OFFICE. *Independent Review of the Radio Spectrum (30–960 MHz). Interim report. The future use of the television bands I and III.* (Chairman: Dr J.H.H. Merriman) (Cmnd 8666) London: HMSO, 1982.

HOME OFFICE and DEPARTMENT OF INDUSTRY. *Direct Broadcasting by Satellite. Report of the Advisory Panel on Technical Transmission Standards.* (Chairman: Sir Antony Part) (Cmnd 8751) London: HMSO, 1982.

MINISTRY OF DEFENCE. *The protection of military information. Report of the Study Group on Censorship.* (Chairman: General Sir Hugh Beach) (Cmnd 9112) London: HMSO, 1983.

(f) Government Departmental Reports and Studies

HOME OFFICE. *Two studies concerning the British Broadcasting Corporation: 1. The BBC's forward planning; 2. Methods of payment of the television licence fee.* London: HMSO, 1979.

HOME OFFICE. *Direct Broadcasting by Satellite.* London: HMSO, 1981.

NATIONAL AUDIT OFFICE. *Report by the Comptroller and Auditor General. Independent Broadcasting Authority: additional payments by programme contractors.* (Session 1984–85: HC 358) London: HMSO, 1985.

DEPARTMENT OF TRADE AND INDUSTRY. *Deregulation of the radio spectrum in the UK.* (CSP International) London: HMSO, 1987.

HOME OFFICE. *Radio: choices and opportunities: a consultative document.* (Cm 92) London: HMSO, 1987.

HOME OFFICE. *Subscription television: a study for the Home Office.* (CSP International) London: HMSO, 1987.

HOME OFFICE/DEPARTMENT OF TRADE AND INDUSTRY. *Options for privatising the terrestrial television and radio transmission networks.* (Price Waterhouse) London: HMSO, 1989.

DEPARTMENT OF TRADE AND INDUSTRY. *High Definition Television (HDTV): the potential for non-broadcast applications.* London: HMSO, 1990. 31pp.

HOME OFFICE. *Television licence fee: a study for the Home Office.* (Price Waterhouse) London: HMSO, 1991.

(g) Licences to Broadcast Granted to the IBA/ITC

Terms   *Licence*

1979–81   *Broadcasting*. (Cmnd 7616) London: HMSO, 1979.
1982–96   *Broadcasting*. (Cmnd 8467) London: HMSO, 1982.

(h) European Directives and Convention

COMMISSION OF THE EUROPEAN COMMUNITIES. *Television without frontiers. Green paper on the establishment of the Common Market for broadcasting, especially by satellite and cable.* (COM (84) 300) Final. Brussels: The Commission, 1984.
COUNCIL OF THE EUROPEAN COMMUNITIES. *Council Directive of 3 October 1989 on the co-ordination of certain provisions laid down by law, regulation or administrative action in Member States concerning the pursuit of television broadcasting activities.* (89/552/EEC). *Official Journal.* L298, 17 October 1989.
COUNCIL OF EUROPE. *European Convention on transfrontier television.* Strasbourg: Council of Europe, 1989.

2.   GENERAL MASS MEDIA, BROADCASTING AND SOCIETY

ANNAN, Lord. *The politics of a broadcasting enquiry.* (1981 Ulster Television Lecture) Belfast: Ulster Television, 1981. 19pp.
BOULTON, David. *The third age of broadcasting.* London: Institute for Public Policy Research, 1991.16pp. (IPPR social policy paper, 3)
BRIGGS, Asa. *The history of broadcasting in the United Kingdom.* London: Oxford University Press, 1961–95.
    Volume 1: *The birth of broadcasting.* (1896–1927). 1961. xiii, 425pp.
    Volume 2: *The golden age of wireless.* (1927–1939). 1965. xvi, 688pp.
    Volume 3: *The war of the words.* (1939–1945). 1970. xviii, 766pp.
    Volume 4: *Sound and vision.* (1945–1955). 1979. xiv, 1082pp.
    Volume 5: *Competition.* (1955–1974) 1995. xxvi, 1133pp.
BUCHAN, Norman, and SUMMER, Tricia. (eds) *Glasnost in Britain?: against censorship and in defence of the word.* London: Macmillan, 1989. xiv, 190pp.
CONSUMERS' ASSOCIATION. *Broadcasting in the 1990s: the policy issues from a consumer perspective.* London: Consumers' Association, 1991. 35pp.
CONSUMERS' ASSOCIATION. *Broadcasting policy: listening to the consumer.* London: Consumers' Association, 1992. 52pp.
CURRAN, James, and GUREVITCH, Michael. *Mass media in society.* 2nd edition. London: Edward Arnold, 1996. 378pp.

CURRAN, James, and SEATON, Jean. *Power without responsibility: the press and broadcasting in Britain.* 4th edition. London: Routledge, 1991. xi, 429pp.

HART, Andrew. *Understanding the media: a practical guide.* London: Routledge, 1991. xvi, 267pp.

HOGGART, Richard, and MORGAN, Janet. (eds) *The future of broadcasting.* London: Methuen, 1982. viii, 166pp.

HOOD, Stuart, and O'LEARY, Garret. *Questions of broadcasting.* London: Methuen, 1990. xviii, 237pp.

HOOD, Stuart, and TABARY-PETERSEN, Thalia. *On television.* 4th edition. London: Pluto Press, 1997. x, 111pp.

MACDONALD, Barrie. *Broadcasting in the United Kingdom: a guide to information sources.* 2nd edition. London: Mansell, 1993. xvii, 316pp.

McQUAIL, Denis. *Communication.* 2nd edition. London: Longman, 1984. xiii, 266pp.

SMITH, Anthony. *Television: an international history.* Oxford: Oxford University Press, 1995. x, 419pp.

WARNOCK, Mary. *The social responsibility of the broadcasting media.* Liverpool: Liverpool University Press, 1985. 17pp. (Eleanor Rathbone Memorial Lecture)

WENHAM, Brian. (ed.) *The third age of broadcasting.* London: Faber & Faber, 1982. 139pp.

WHALE, John. *Politics of the media.* 2nd edition, London: Fontana, 1980. 176pp.

WINDLESHAM, Lord. *Broadcasting in a free society.* Oxford: Basil Blackwell, 1980. 172pp.

3.   TELEVISION INDUSTRY: REGULATION, OWNERSHIP AND FINANCING

BARENDT, Eric. *Broadcasting law: a comparative study.* Oxford: Clarendon Press, 1993. xxiii, 249pp.

BLUMLER, Jay G., and NOSSITER, T.J. (eds) *Broadcasting finance in transition: a comparative handbook.* Oxford: Oxford University Press, 1991. vi, 443pp.

BOOZ ALLEN HAMILTON. *The changing environment for UK broadcasters and its economic implications.* London: ITV Association, 1993. 23pp.

BROADCASTING RESEARCH UNIT. *The public service idea in British broadcasting: main principles.* London: BRU, 1985. 27pp.

CENTRE FOR TELEVISION RESEARCH, UNIVERSITY OF LEEDS. *Research on the range and quality of broadcasting services: a report for the Committee on Financing the BBC, by the West Yorkshire Media Group, Centre for Television Research, University of Leeds.* London: HMSO, 1986. 180pp.

CHIPPINDALE, Peter, and FRANKS, Suzanne. *Dished!: the rise and fall of British Satellite Broadcasting.* London: Simon & Schuster, 1991. xviii, 329pp.

COLLINS, Richard. *Television: policy and culture.* London: Unwin Hyman, 1990. xii, 276pp.

COLLINS, Richard, GARNHAM, Nicholas, and LOCKSLEY, Gareth. *The economics of UK television*. London: London Centre for Information and Communications Policy Studies of the Polytechnic of Central London, 1986. 174pp.

COLLINS, Richard, and MURRONI, Cristina. *New media, new policies: media and communications strategies for the future*. Cambridge: Polity Press, 1996. ix, 243pp.

CONGDON, Tim, et al. *Paying for broadcasting: the handbook*. London: Routledge, 1992. xxxvii, 226pp.

COOPERS & LYBRAND. *Licensing approach to broadcasting regulation in the 1990s*. London: Coopers & Lybrand, 1988. 38pp.

COOPERS & LYBRAND. *Regulatory functions of an Independent Television Commission*. London: Coopers & Lybrand, n.d. 23pp.

DAY-LEWIS, Sean. *One day in the life of television*. London: Grafton Books, 1989. xv, 413pp.

DUNN, Richard. *The 1990 Broadcasting Act: a benefit or a disaster?* (Speech to the Royal Society of Arts, 16 November 1994) London: Royal Society of Arts, 1994. 29pp

EHRENBERG, A.S.C. *Advertisers or viewers paying?* London: Admap, 1986. 37pp.

EHRENBERG, A.S.C., and BARWISE, T.P. *How much does UK television cost?: a position paper*. London: London Business School, 1982.

FORMAN, Denis. *British television: who are the masters now?* London: BBC Books, 1987. 15pp. (The Richard Dimbleby Lecture, 1987)

FOSTER, Robin. *Public broadcasters: accountability and efficiency*. Edinburgh: Edinburgh University Press, 1992. xiii, 66pp. (The David Hume Institute paper, 18)

HOOD, Stuart. (ed.) *Behind the scenes: the structure of British broadcasting in the nineties*. London: Lawrence & Wishart, 1994. x, 214pp.

HUGHES, Gordon, and VINES, David. (eds) *Deregulation and the future of commercial television*. Aberdeen: Aberdeen University Press, 1989. viii, 139pp. (The David Hume Institute paper, 12)

INDEPENDENT BROADCASTING AUTHORITY. *Deregulation of TV in the UK: the public's view*, by Michael Svennevig. London: IBA, 1989. 18pp. (IBA research)

INDEPENDENT TELEVISION ASSOCIATION. *ITV: a response to the Government's White Paper. Broadcasting in the 90s: competition, choice and quality*. London: ITV Association, 1989. vi, 104pp.

INDEPENDENT TELEVISION COMPANIES ASSOCIATION. *ITV evidence to the Peacock Committee*. London: ITCA, 1985. 84pp.

McDONNELL, James. *Public service broadcasting: a reader*. London: Routledge, 1991. vii, 127pp.

MILLER, Nod, and NORRIS, Cresta. (eds) *Life after the Broadcasting Bill. Proceedings of the 20th University of Manchester Broadcasting Symposium*. Manchester: Manchester Monographs, 1989. 157pp.

MULGAN, Geoff. (ed.) *The question of quality*. London: British Film Institute, 1990. 72pp. (The Broadcasting Debate, 6)

MURDOCH, Rupert. *Freedom in broadcasting*. London: News International, 1989. 11pp. (MacTaggart Lecture at the Edinburgh International Television Festival, 1989)

PATERSON, Richard. (ed.) *Organising for change*. London: British Film Institute, 1990. 64pp. (The Broadcasting Debate, 1)

PAULU, Burton. *Television and radio in the United Kingdom*. London: Macmillan, 1981. xiv, 476pp.

REVILLE, Nicholas. *Broadcasting: the new law*. London: Butterworths, 1991. xi, 214pp.

SEYMOUR-URE, Colin. *The British press and broadcasting since 1945*. 2nd edition. Oxford: Blackwell, 1996. xiii, 289pp.

SMITH, Anthony. *Licences and liberty: the future of public service broadcasting*. London: Acton Society Trust, 1985. (John Logie Baird Lecture, 1985)

STARKS, Michael. *Paying for broadcasting: public funds for a private service*. London: Political Quarterly, 1985. (Reprinted from *Political Quarterly*, Vol. 56, No. 4, October– December 1985, pp.374–85)

STEVENSON, Wilf, and SMEDLEY, Nick. (eds) *Responses to the White Paper*. London: British Film Institute, 1989. 85pp. (The Broadcasting Debate, 3)

THOMPSON, Kenneth. (ed.) *Media and cultural regulation*. London: Sage (in association with the Open University), 1997. 248pp.

TUNSTALL, Jeremy. *The media in Britain*. London: Constable, 1983. 304pp.

TUNSTALL, Jeremy, and PALMER, Michael. *Media moguls*. London: Routledge, 1991. 258pp.

VELJANOVSKI, Cento. *Commercial broadcasting in the UK – over-regulation and misregulation?* London: Centre for Economic Policy Research, 1987. 27pp.

VELJANOVSKI, Cento. (ed.) *Freedom in broadcasting*. London: Institute of Economic Affairs, 1989. xv, 262pp.

VELJANOVSKI, Cento. *The future of industry regulation in the UK: a report of an independent inquiry*. London: European Policy Forum, 1993. 92pp.

VELJANOVSKI, Cento. *Regulation and the market: an assessment of the growth of regulation in the UK*. London: Institute of Economic Affairs, 1991. xi, 243pp.

VOICE OF THE LISTENER AND VIEWER. *What is public service broadcasting and how should it be funded*. Gravesend, Kent: Voice of the Listener and Viewer, 1985. 68pp.

4.   POLITICS AND GOVERNMENT

BAKER, Kenneth. *The turbulent years: my life in politics*. London: Faber & Faber, 1993. 498pp.

HOWE, Geoffrey. *Conflict of loyalty*. London: Macmillan, 1994. xxii, 736pp.

LAWSON, Nigel. *The view from No. 11: the memoirs of a Tory radical*. London: Bantam Press, 1992.

MARR, Andrew. *Ruling Britannia: the failure and future of British democracy*. London: Michael Joseph, 1995. 372pp.

SAMPSON, Anthony. *The changing anatomy of Britain*. London: Hodder & Stoughton, 1982. xv, 476pp.

SAMPSON, Anthony. *The essential anatomy of Britain: democracy in crisis*. London: Hodder & Stoughton, 1992. xi, 172pp.

THATCHER, Margaret. *The Downing Street years*. London: HarperCollins, 1993. xiv, 914pp.

WHITELAW, William. *The Whitelaw memoirs*. London: Aurum Press, 1989. vii, 280pp.

WIGG, Lord. *George Wigg*. London: Michael Joseph, 1972. 384pp.

WILSON, Harold. *Final term: the Labour Government 1974–1976*. London: Weidenfeld and Nicolson, 1979. viii, 322pp.

YOUNG, Lord. *The enterprise years: a businessman in the Cabinet*. London: Headline, 1990. 338pp.

5.   INDEPENDENT BROADCASTING AUTHORITY/INDEPENDENT TELEVISION COMMISSION

A full account of the activities and finances of the IBA, then the ITC appears each year in the *IBA annual report and accounts* (1955–90), and the *ITC annual report and accounts* (1991–). Summaries of the Annual Performance Reviews of the Channel 3, Channel 4, Channel 5 and Teletext services conducted by the ITC appear in the *ITC annual report and accounts*. Publications of the IBA were listed in the *IBA annual report and accounts*, the IBA's Yearbook *Television and radio* (1963–88), and *IBA factfile* (1988–89, 1989–90); those of the ITC are listed in *ITC factfile* (1991–). A selection of IBA and ITC publications for the period are listed below.

(a)   Independent Broadcasting Authority

Additional payments by programme contractors: statement of principles under the Broadcasting Act 1981. London: IBA, various editions.

Airwaves. Quarterly. London: IBA, 1984–90.

Attitudes to broadcasting. London: ITA/IBA, 1970–91. (Formerly *Attitudes to television*)

Broadcasting in the 90s: competition, choice and quality. The IBA's response to the White Paper. London: IBA, 1989. 68pp.

Evidence to the Inquiry into Cable Expansion and Broadcasting. London: IBA, 1982. 15pp.

IBA code of teletext transmissions. London: IBA, 1984.

IBA code of advertising standards and practice. London: ITA/IBA, 1964-90. (Regular revisions and reprints)

IBA evidence to the Committee on Financing the BBC. London: IBA, 1985. 44pp

IBA Technical Review. Issues 1-24. Crawley Court, Hampshire: IBA, 1972-88.

Independent Broadcasting. Quarterly. London: IBA, 1974-84.

Independent Television in the 1990s. London: IBA, 1988. 51pp.

Independent Television now - and in the 90s. London: IBA, 1988. 15pp.

TV Take-up. London: IBA. (Regular booklets giving advance information on learning resources for adults on ITV and Channel 4)

Television and radio (formerly *ITV*) Annual. London: IBA, 1963-88.

Television programme guidelines. London: IBA, 1978-90. (Regular revisions and reprints)

(b)   Independent Television Commission

Factfile. Annual. London: 1991-.

The ITC code of advertising standards and practice. London: ITC, 1991-. (Regular revisions and reprints)

The ITC code of programme sponsorship. London: 1991-. (Regular revisions and reprints)

The ITC programme code. London: ITC, 1991-. (Regular revisions and reprints)

ITC rules on advertising breaks. London: ITC, 1992-. (Regular revisions and reprints)

Invitation to apply for the national Channel 3 breakfast-time licence. London: ITC, 1991. 75pp.

Invitation to apply for regional Channel 3 licences. London: ITC, 1991. 100pp.

Memorandum to the National Heritage Select Committee on the operation of the Broadcasting Act 1990. London: ITC, 1993.

Qualifying revenue: statement of principles under the Broadcasting Act 1990. 1st edition. London: ITC, 1993.

Spectrum. Quarterly. London: ITC, 1991-97.

Television: the public's view. Annual. London: John Libbey, 1992-4; London: ITC, 1995-. (Formerly *Attitudes to television*, then *Attitudes to broadcasting.* London: IBA, 1970 -90)

6.   INDEPENDENT TELEVISION (ITV)

(a)   ITV/Channel 3

BRIGGS, Asa, and SPICER, Joanna. *The franchise affair: creating fortunes and failures in Independent Television.* London: Century Hutchinson, 1986. 226pp.

DAVIDSON, Andrew. *Under the hammer: the inside story of the 1991 ITV franchise battle.* London: Heinemann, 1992. xvi, 318pp.

ITV ASSOCIATION. *Channel 3 networking arrangements: statements of principles as approved by the Independent Television Commission*. London: ITVA, 1992. 7pp.

INTERNATIONAL BUSINESS COMMUNICATIONS. *Whither ITV?: politicians, pundits and practitioners debate the issues*. London: IBC, 1988.

MONOPOLIES AND MERGERS COMMISSION. *Channel 3 networking arrangements: a report on whether the arrangements satisfy the competition test contained in the Broadcasting Act 1990*. London: HMSO, 1993.

OFFICE OF FAIR TRADING. *Channel 3 networking arrangements: a consultative paper by the Office of Fair Trading*. London: OFT, 1992. 25pp.

OFFICE OF FAIR TRADING. *Channel 3 networking arrangements: a report by the Director General of Fair Trading*. London: OFT, 1992. 139pp.

NATIONAL ECONOMIC RESEARCH ASSOCIATES. *1992 and beyond ... options for ITV: an assessment for the ITV Association*. London: NERA, 1988. 193pp.

POTTER, Jeremy. *Independent Television in Britain*. Volume 3: *Politics and control, 1968–80*. London: Macmillan, 1989. ix, 352pp.

POTTER, Jeremy. *Independent Television in Britain*. Volume 4: *Companies and programmes, 1968–80*. London: Macmillan, 1990. xi, 428pp.

ROTHSCHILD, N.M., & Sons. *Report on competitive tendering for the award of ITV licences to members of the Independent Broadcasting Authority from N.M. Rothschild & Sons Ltd*. London: N.M. Rothschild & Sons, 1989. 38pp.

SENDALL, Bernard. *Independent Television in Britain*. Volume 1: *Origin and foundation, 1946–62*. London: Macmillan, 1982. xviii, 418pp.

SENDALL, Bernard. *Independent Television in Britain*. Volume 2: *Expansion and change, 1958–68*. London: Macmillan, 1983. xvii, 429pp.

(b) ITV Companies

ANGLIA TELEVISION. ... *the first twenty-one years*. Norwich: Anglia Television, 1980. 128pp.

BRITISH FILM INSTITUTE. *Granada: the first 25 years*. London: BFI, 1981. 132pp.

CHANNEL TELEVISION. *CTV21: a special [21st] anniversary publication*. St Helier, Jersey: Channel Islands Communications (Television) Ltd, 1983. 62pp.

DOCHERTY, David. *Running the show: 21 years of London Weekend Television*. London: Boxtree, 1990. vi, 218pp.

GRANADA TELEVISION. *As others see us*. Manchester: Granada Television, 1981. 69pp.

HENDERSON, Brum. *A musing on the lighter side of Ulster Television and its first 25 years*. Belfast: Ulster Television, 1984. 80pp.

LEAPMAN, Michael. *Treachery?: the power struggle at TV-am*. London: Allen & Unwin, 1984. xi, 211pp.

OFFICE OF FAIR TRADING. *Thames Television Ltd*. London: OFT, 1984. 87pp.

PANDIT, S.A. *From making to music: the history of Thorn-EMI.* London: Hodder & Stoughton, 1996. xv, 270pp. (Major shareholder in Thames Television until 1993)

TAYLOR, Edward Durham. *The great TV book: 21 years of LWT.* London: Sidgwick & Jackson, 1989. 96pp.

THAMES TELEVISION. *Twenty-one years: a celebration of twenty-one years of broadcasting by Thames Television.* London: Thames Television, 1989. 68pp.

WINTER, Gordon. *Here we were.* London: Granada Group, 1984. 119pp. (History of the Granada Group from 1934 to 1984)

7. CHANNEL 4

BLANCHARD, Simon, and MORLEY, David. (eds) *What's this Channel Fo(u)r?: an alternative report.* London: Comedia, 1982. 186pp.

DOCHERTY, David, MORRISON, David M., and TRACEY, Michael. *Keeping faith?: Channel Four and its audience.* London: John Libbey, 1988. 184pp.

INDEPENDENT BROADCASTING AUTHORITY. *Channel 4: the audience's response,* by Jacob Wakshlag. London: IBA, 1985. 54pp. (IBA Research Department)

ISAACS, Jeremy. *Storm over 4: a personal account.* London: Weidenfeld & Nicolson, 1989. viii, 215pp.

KUSTOW, Michael. *One in Four: a year in the life of a Channel Four Commissioning Editor.* London: Chatto & Windus, 1987. viii, 248pp.

LAMBERT, Stephen. *Channel Four: television with a difference.* London: British Film Institute, 1982. vi, 178pp.

8. TELEVISION ADVERTISING

ADVERTISING ASSOCIATION. *Advertising and the freedom of communication.* (Peterhouse Seminar on 15–16 July 1988) London: Advertising Association, 1983. 54pp.

BOOZ ALLEN & HAMILTON. *The economics of television advertising in the UK.* London: Economist, 1988.

BULLMORE, J.J.D., and WATERSON, M.J. (eds) *The Advertising Association handbook.* London: Holt, Rinehart & Winston, 1983. xi, 378pp.

CAMPAIGN/ADMAP. *ITV and the advertisers – must there be conflict?* (Seminar on 24 September 1987) London: Campaign/Admap Seminars, 1987. 59pp.

CAVE, Martin, and SWANN, Peter. *The effects on advertising revenues of allowing advertising on BBC Television: a report for the Committee on Financing the BBC.* London: HMSO, 1985. 46pp.

GABLE, Jo. *The tuppenny Punch and Judy show: 25 years of TV commercials.* London: Michael Joseph, 1980. 192pp.

HENRY, Brian. (ed.) *British television advertising: the first 30 years.* London: Century Benham, 1986. 528pp.

HENRY, Harry. *Towards a better understanding of the economics of television advertising.* London: ITV Association, 1988. 48pp.

INTERNATIONAL BUSINESS COMMUNICATIONS. *Advertising regulations: new controls and more to come!* (Seminar on 8 July 1988) London: IBC, 1988.

NATIONAL ECONOMIC RESEARCH ASSOCIATES. *The economics of television advertising: a review by NERA for the ITV Association.* London: NERA, 1988. 47pp.

9.   BROADCASTING RESEARCH

(a)   General Audience Studies

ANG, Ien. *Desperately seeking the audience.* London: Routledge, 1991. xii, 203pp.

BARWISE, Patrick, and EHRENBERG, Andrew. *Television and its audience.* London: Sage, 1988. xii, 206pp.

DRUMMOND, Phillip, and PATERSON, Richard. (eds) *Television and its audience*: *international research perspectives.* London: British Film Institute, 1988. x, 334pp.

GOODHARDT, G.J., EHRENBERG, A.S.C., and COLLINS, M.A. *The television audience: patterns of viewing: an update.* Aldershot, Hampshire: Gower, 1987. xv, 134pp.

INDEPENDENT BROADCASTING AUTHORITY. *An audience for daytime television,* by Barrie Gunter. London: IBA, 1984. 32pp. (IBA Research Department research paper)

INDEPENDENT BROADCASTING AUTHORITY. *Attitudes to broadcasting over the years,* by Barrie Gunter and Michael Svennevig. London: John Libbey, 1988. 77pp. (Television research monograph)

INDEPENDENT BROADCASTING AUTHORITY. *The audience and breakfast television,* by Barrie Gunter. London: IBA, 1984. 17pp. (IBA Research Department research paper)

INDEPENDENT BROADCASTING AUTHORITY. *The effects of subtitles on appreciation of TV programmes among the hearing audience,* by Barrie Gunter. London: IBA, 1982. 32pp. (IBA Audience Research Department special report)

INDEPENDENT BROADCASTING AUTHORITY. *Mapping regional views: a report on viewer's preferences for regional television in the UK.* London: IBA, 1990. 27pp.

INDEPENDENT BROADCASTING AUTHORITY. *A portrait of the IBA,* by J. Mallory Wober. London: IBA, 1983. 15pp. (IBA Audience Research Department special report)

INDEPENDENT BROADCASTING AUTHORITY. *The psychological and economic value of TV: a pointer from Peter Tavy*, by J. Mallory Wober. London: IBA, 1984. 19pp. (IBA Research Department research paper)

INDEPENDENT BROADCASTING AUTHORITY. *The quality of language on television: listener-viewer's perception and attitudes to what they hear*, by J. Mallory Wober. London: IBA, 1987. 18pp. (IBA Research Department research paper)

INDEPENDENT BROADCASTING AUTHORITY. *Viewers' reactions to breakfast television*, by Barrie Gunter. London: IBA, 1985. 94pp. (IBA Research Department research paper)

INDEPENDENT TELEVISION COMMISSION. *The qualities of channels and the amounts they are viewed*, by J. Mallory Wober. London: ITC, 1992. 27pp. (ITC Research research paper)

INDEPENDENT TELEVISION COMMISSION. *The reactive viewer: a review of research on Audience Reaction Measurement*. London: John Libbey, 1992. 119pp. (Television research mongraph)

MORLEY, David. *Television, audiences and cultural studies*. London: Routledge, 1992. viii, 325pp.

TAYLOR, Laurie, and MULLAN, Bob. *Uninvited guests: the intimate secrets of television and radio*. London: Chatto & Windus, 1986. 218pp.

WILLIS, Janet, and WOLLEN, Tana. *The neglected audience*. London: British Film Institute, 1990. 111pp. (The Broadcasting Debate, 5)

WOBER, J.Mallory. *The use and abuse of television: a social psychological analysis of the changing screen*. Hillsdale, New Jersey: Lawrence Erlbaum, 1988. vii, 252pp.

(b)   Effects of Television

BROADCASTING STANDARDS COUNCIL. *A measure of uncertainty: the effects of the mass media*, by Guy Cumberbatch and Dennis Howitt. London: John Libbey, 1989. vii, 88pp. (Research monograph series, 1)

PHILO, Greg. *Seeing is believing: the influence of television*. London: Routledge, 1990. vii, 244pp.

(c)   Violence on Television

BARLOW, Geoffrey, and HILL, Alison. (eds) *Video violence and children*. London: Hodder and Stoughton, 1985. x, 182pp.

BELSON, William A., *Television violence and the adolescent boy*. Farnborough, Hampshire: Saxon House, 1978. x, 529pp.

BRITISH BROADCASTING CORPORATION. *The portrayal of violence in television programmes: suggestions for a revised note of guidance*. London: BBC, 1979. 36pp.

BRITISH BROADCASTING CORPORATION *The portrayal of violence on British television: a content analysis*, by Guy Cumberbatch, et al. London: BBC, 1987. x, 60pp.

BRITISH BROADCASTING CORPORATION. *Violence on television: the report of the Wyatt Committee*. London: BBC, 1987. 23pp.

BRITISH BROADCASTING CORPORATION/INDEPENDENT BROAD-CASTING AUTHORITY *The portrayal of violence on television: BBC & IBA guidelines*. London: BBC/IBA, 1980. 52pp.

BROADCASTING STANDARDS COUNCIL. *Violence in factual television*, by Andrea Millwood Hargrave. London: John Libbey, 1993. viii, 151pp. (Public opinion and broadcasting standards, 4)

BROADCASTING STANDARDS COUNCIL. *Violence in television fiction*, by David Docherty. London: John Libbey, 1990. 39pp. (Public opinion and broadcasting standards, 1)

DAVIES, Tom. *The man of lawlessness: the effect of the media on violence*. London: Hodder & Stoughton, 1989. 266pp.

FOX, Julian. *Violence in the news*. Hove: Wayland, 1983. 64pp.

GUNTER, Barrie. *Dimensions of television violence*. Aldershot, Hampshire: Gower, 1985. ix, 282pp.

INDEPENDENT BROADCASTING AUTHORITY. *Television and the fear of crime*, by Barrie Gunter. London: John Libbey, 1987. 104pp. (Television research monograph)

INDEPENDENT BROADCASTING AUTHORITY. *Television and violence*, by Robert Towler. London: IBA, 1983. 3pp. (IBA Research Department research paper)

INDEPENDENT BROADCASTING AUTHORITY. *Television violence*, by Barrie Gunter. London: IBA, 1986. 33pp. (IBA Research Department reference paper)

INDEPENDENT BROADCASTING AUTHORITY. *Violence on television: what the viewers think*, by Barrie Gunter and J. Mallory Wober. London: John Libbey, 1988. xiii, 73pp. (Television research mongraph)

NEWSON, Elizabeth. *Video violence and the protection of children*. Nottingham: University of Nottingham, 1994. 8pp.

PARLIAMENTARY GROUP VIDEO ENQUIRY. *Video violence and children*. Part I: *Children's viewing patterns in England and Wales*. Part II: *Children's viewing patterns and parental attitudes in England and Wales*. Part III: *Effects of video violence upon children*. London: Oasis Projects, 1984. 19pp., 49pp., n.a.

SCHLESINGER, Philip, MURDOCK, Graham, and ELLIOTT, Philip. *Televising terrorism: political violence in popular culture*. London: Comedia, 1983. vii, 181pp.

(d)   Taste and Decency Issues

BROADCASTING STANDARDS COUNCIL. *A matter of manners?: the limits of broadcasting language*, edited by Andrea Millwood Hargrave. London: John Libbey, 1991. 105pp. (Research monograph series, 3)

BROADCASTING STANDARDS COUNCIL. *Sex and sexuality in broadcasting*, by Andrea Millwood Hargrave. London: John Libbey, 1992. 146pp. (Public opinion and broadcasting standards, 3)

BROADCASTING STANDARDS COUNCIL. *Survivors and the media*, by Ann Shearer. London: John Libbey, 1991. 73pp. (Research monograph series, 2)

BROADCASTING STANDARDS COUNCIL. *Taste and decency in broadcasting*, by Andrea Millwood Hargrave. London: John Libbey, 1991. 53pp. (Public opinion and broadcasting standards, 2)

INDEPENDENT BROADCASTING AUTHORITY. *Taste and decency: the main findings from recent research*, by Robert Towler. London: IBA, 1984. 31pp. (IBA Research Department working paper)

INDEPENDENT BROADCASTING AUTHORITY. *Why we broadcast 'V'*. London: IBA, 1988. 23pp.

(e)   Women, Gender and Race on Television

ANWAR, Muhammad. *Ethnic minority broadcasting: a research report*. London: Commission for Racial Equality, 1983. 80pp.

ANWAR, Muhammad, and SHANG, Anthony. *Television in a multi-racial society: a research report*. London: Commission for Racial Equality, 1982. 84pp.

BAEHR, Helen and DYER, Gillian. (eds). *Boxed in: women and television*. London: Pandora Press, 1987. xi, 233pp.

BAEHR, Helen. *Women and media*. Oxford: Pergamon Press, 1980. viii, 137pp.

COHEN, Phil, and GARDNER, Carl. *It ain't half racist, mum: fighting racism in the media*. London: Comedia, 1982. 120pp.

DAVIES, Kath, and others. *Out of focus: writings on women in the media*. London: The Women's Press, 1987. x, 230pp.

HAMILTON, Robert, HAWORTH, Brian and SARDAR, Nazli. *Adman and Eve: a study of the portrayal of women in advertising*. Manchester: Equal Opportunities Commission, 1982. 41pp.

HOLLAND, Patricia. *Women and the media*. Hove, East Sussex: Wayland, 1991. 48pp.

INDEPENDENT BROADCASTING AUTHORITY. *Television and sex role stereotyping*. London: John Libbey, 1986. 89pp. (Television research monograph)

ROOT, Jane. *Pictures of women: sexuality*. London: Pandora Press, 1984. 128pp. (Based on a Channel 4 series)

SCHLESINGER, Philip, et al. *Women viewing violence*. London: British Film Institute, 1992. xii, 210pp.

SCREEN. *The sexual subject: a Screen reader in sexuality*. London: Routledge, 1992. viii, 339pp.

TRADES UNION CONGRESS. *Images of inequality: the portrayal of women in the media and advertising*. London: TUC, 1984. 28pp.

WATNEY, Simon. *Policing desire: pornography, AIDS and the media*. London: Methuen, 1987.

(f)   Children and Television

BAZALGETTE, Cary, and BUCKINGHAM, David. (eds) *In front of the children: screen entertainment and young audiences*. London: British Film Institute, 1995. xii, 220pp.

BROADCASTING STANDARDS COUNCIL. *The future of children's television in Britain: an enquiry for the Broadcasting Standards Council*, by Jay G. Blumler. London: BSC, 1992. 70pp. (Research working paper, VIII)

BROWN, Ray. (ed.) *Children and television*. London: Collier Macmillan, 1976. 368pp.

DAVIES, Maire Messenger. *Television is good for your kids*. London: Hilary Shipman, 1989. viii, 232pp.

GUNTER, Barrie, and McALEER, Jill. *Children and television: the one-eyed monster?* London: Routledge, 1990.

INDEPENDENT BROADCASTING AUTHORITY. *Children's views on advertising*, by Bradley S. Greenberg, Shehina Fazal and J. Mallory Wober. London: IBA, 1986. 15pp.

INDEPENDENT BROADCASTING AUTHORITY. *How much television children view: measurement problems and some results*, by J.Mallory Wober. London: IBA, 1988.10pp. (IBA Research Department research paper)

INDEPENDENT BROADCASTING AUTHORITY. *Parental control of children's viewing*, by J. Mallory Wober, Shehina Fazal and Geoff Reardon. London: IBA, 1986. 20pp. (IBA Research Department research paper)

LARGE, Martin. *Who's bringing them up? Television and child development: how to break the TV habit*. 2nd edition. Stroud, Gloucestershire: Hawthorn Press, 1990. xii, 176pp.

YOUNG, Brian M. *Television advertising and children*. Oxford: Clarendon Press, 1990. viii, 360pp.

10.   PROGRAMMES

(a)   General

BROADCASTING RESEARCH UNIT. *Quality in programmes: programmes, programme-makers, systems*. London: John Libbey, 1989. 32pp.

EVANS, Jeff. *The Guinness television encyclopedia*. London: Guinness Publishing, 1995. 592pp.

GAMBACCINI, Paul, and TAYLOR, Rod. *Television's greatest hits: every hit television since 1960*. London: Network Books, 1993. 544pp.

HALLIWELL, Leslie, and PURSER, Philip. *Halliwell's television companion.* 3rd edition. London: Grafton Books, 1986. xv, 941pp.

HARBORD, Jane, and WRIGHT, Jeff. *40 years of British television.* London: Boxtree, 1992. 160pp.

INDEPENDENT BROADCASTING AUTHORITY. *The assessment of television quality*, by J. Mallory Wober. London: IBA, 1990. 35pp. (IBA Research department research paper)

KINGSLEY, Hilary, and TIBBALLS, Geoff. *Box of delights: the golden years of television.* London: Macmillan, 1989. 314pp.

MILLER, Nod, NORRIS, Cresta, and HUGHES, Janice. (eds) *Broadcasting standards: quality or control? Proceedings of the 21st University of Manchester Broadcasting Symposium.* Manchester: Manchester Monographs, 1990. 157pp.

VAHIMAGI, Tise. *British television: an illustrated guide.* London: Oxford University Press, 1994. ix, 364pp.

(b)   News, Current Affairs and Documentaries

ADAMS, Valerie. *The media and the Falklands campaign.* London: Macmillan, 1986. x, 224pp.

BBC/INDEPENDENT BROADCASTING AUTHORITY. *Television coverage of the 1983 General Election*, by Barrie Gunter, Michael Svennevig and J. Mallory Wober. London: BBC/IBA, 1984. 21pp.

BELL, Alan. *The language of the news media.* Oxford: Blackwell, 1991. xv, 277pp.

BOLTON, Roger. *Death on the Rock and other stories.* London: W.H. Allen, 1990. x, 318pp.

Coast to Coast, 1982–1992. Westerham, Kent: Froglet Publications, 1992. 112pp. (TVS local news magazine programme for the ITV South and South East of England region)

COX, Geoffrey. *See it happen: the making of ITN.* London: Bodley Head, 1983. 248pp.

DAY, Robin. *... but with respect: memorable television interviews with statesmen and parliamentarians.* London: Weidenfeld & Nicolson, 1993. xi, 349pp.

GLASGOW UNIVERSITY MEDIA GROUP. *Bad news.* London: Routledge & Kegan Paul, 1976. xvi, 310pp.

GLASGOW UNIVERSITY MEDIA GROUP. *More bad news.* London: Routledge & Kegan Paul, 1980. xviii, 483pp.

GLASGOW UNIVERSITY MEDIA GROUP. *Really bad news.* London: Writers and Readers, 1982. xi, 170pp.

GLASGOW UNIVERSITY MEDIA GROUP. *War and peace news.* Milton Keynes: Open University Press, 1985. 355pp.

GRANADA TELEVISION. *World in Action: the first twenty-one years.* Manchester, Granada Television, 1984. 16pp.

HARRIS, Robert. *Gotcha!: the media, the Government and the Falklands crisis.* London: Faber & Faber, 1983. 158pp.

HARRISON, Martin. *TV news: whose bias?: a casebook analysis of strikes, television and media studies.* Hermitage, Berkshire: Policy Journals, 1985. 408pp.

HETHERINGTON, Alastair, WEAVER, Kay, and RYLE, Michael. *Cameras in the Commons: the study for the Hansard Society on the televising of the House of Commons.* London: The Hansard Society, 1990. viii, 96pp.

HETHERINGTON, Alastair. *News in the regions: Plymouth Sound to Moray Firth.* London: Macmillan, 1989. xv, 263pp.

HETHERINGTON, Alastair. *News, newspapers and television.* London: Macmillan, 1985. ix, 329pp.

INDEPENDENT BROADCASTING AUTHORITY. *Consultation on television coverage of industry, 9 December 1983.* London: IBA, 1983. 83pp.

INDEPENDENT BROADCASTING AUTHORITY. *Consultation on television coverage of industry and economic affairs, The Runnymede Hotel, Egham, Surrey on 16–18 April 1982.* London: IBA. 1982. 170pp.

INDEPENDENT BROADCASTING AUTHORITY. *Court on camera?: views on the possibilities of television broadcasts from the courts,* by J. Mallory Wober. London: IBA, 1990. 22pp. (IBA Research Department reference paper)

INDEPENDENT BROADCASTING AUTHORITY. *Evaluating the broadcast campaign on AIDS,* by J. Mallory Wober. London: IBA, 1987. 77pp.

INDEPENDENT BROADCASTING AUTHORITY. *The Falklands conflict: further analysis of viewers' behaviour and attitudes,* by J. Mallory Wober. London: IBA, 1982. 27pp. (IBA Research Department special report)

INDEPENDENT BROADCASTING AUTHORITY. *From House to House: bringing the Commons home to British viewers,* by J. Mallory Wober. London: IBA, 1990. 25pp. (IBA Research Department reference paper)

INDEPENDENT BROADCASTING AUTHORITY. *The House on the screen: public knowledge and attitudes over six months television of the House of Lords,* by J. Mallory Wober. London: IBA, 1985. 38pp. (IBA Research Department research paper)

INDEPENDENT BROADCASTING AUTHORITY. *Informing the public about AIDS.* London: IBA, 1987. 32pp.

INDEPENDENT BROADCASTING AUTHORITY. *Learning from television news: effects of presentation and knowledge on comprehension and memory,* by Colin Berry and Brian R. Clifford. London: IBA, 1985. 50pp.

INDEPENDENT BROADCASTING AUTHORITY. *News and current affairs on Independent Television: a report of an IBA Consultation held in Gosforth Park, October 1982.* London: IBA, 1983. 63pp.

INDEPENDENT BROADCASTING AUTHORITY. *Patterns of network TV news viewing in Britain,* by Barrie Gunter. London: IBA, 1984. 13pp. (IBA Research Department working paper)

INDEPENDENT BROADCASTING AUTHORITY. *Television coverage of the 1983 General Election*, by Barrie Gunter. London: IBA, 1983. 19pp. (IBA Research Department research paper)

INDEPENDENT BROADCASTING AUTHORITY. *Television in the Houses of Parliament: education for democracy?*, by J. Mallory Wober. London: IBA, 1989. 26pp. (IBA Research Department research paper)

INDEPENDENT BROADCASTING AUTHORITY. *Three months into the conflict with Iraq: television and viewers reactions*, by J. Mallory Wober. London: IBA, 1990. 17pp. (IBA Research Department reference paper)

INDEPENDENT TELEVISION COMMISSION. *Dimensions of quality in news*, J. Mallory Wober. London: ITC, 1991. (ITC Research reference paper)

INDEPENDENT TELEVISION COMMISSION. *The outbreak of war: public perceptions and feelings related to television news coverage*, by J. Mallory Wober. London: ITC, 1991. 33pp. (ITC Research reference paper)

INDEPENDENT TELEVISION COMMISSION. *Television and the tension of war*, by J. Mallory Wober. London: ITC, 1991. 16pp. (ITC Research reference paper)

INDEPENDENT TELEVISION COMMISSION. *Television news coverage of the Gulf War*, by Jane Aldridge. London: ITC, 1991. 42pp. (ITC Research reference paper)

INDEPENDENT TELEVISION COMMISSION. *Television tries the law: public opinion on televising the court*, by J. Mallory Wober. London: ITC, 1991. 29pp. (ITC Research reference paper)

JONES, Nicholas. *Strikes and the media: communication and conflict.* Oxford: Basil Blackwell, 1986. iv, 220pp.

KAY, Richard. *Desert warrior: reporting from the Gulf.* London: Penumbra Books, 1992. viii, 150pp.

McNAIR, Brian. *Images of the enemy: reporting the new cold war.* London: Routledge, 1988. vii, 216pp.

MORRISON, David E. *Television and the Gulf War.* London: John Libbey, 1992. (Acamedia Research Monograph 7)

MORRISON, David E., and TUMBER, Howard. *Journalists at war: the dynamics of news reporting during the Falklands conflict.* London: Sage, 1988. xiv, 370pp.

PEDRICK, Martyn. *In the front line.* London: Robson Books, 1983. 238pp. (Account of fifteen years' foreign news coverage by ITN)

ROLSTON, Bill. (ed.) *The media and Northern Ireland: covering the troubles.* London: Macmillan, 1991. xi, 227pp.

SCHLESINGER, Philip. *Putting 'reality' together: BBC news.* London: Constable, 1978; reprinted London: Routledge, 1992. xlvi, 303pp.

SUCHET, John. *TV news: the inside story.* London: Collins, 1989. 64pp.

TAYLOR, Philip M. *War and the media: propaganda and persuasion in the Gulf War.* Manchester: Manchester University Press, 1992. xiv, 338pp.

THOMSON, Alex. *Smokescreen: the media, the censor, the Gulf.* Tunbridge Wells, Kent: Laburnham Books, 1992. xi, 277pp.

TRACEY, Michael. *In the culture of the eye: ten years of 'Weekend World'*. London: Hutchinson, 1983. 157pp.

TUMBER, Howard. *Television and the riots*. London: British Film Institute, 1982. viii, 54pp.

WINDLESHAM, Lord, and RAMPTON, Richard. *The Windlesham/Rampton report on 'Death on the Rock'*. London: Faber & Faber, 1989. viii, 145pp.

YORKE, Ivor. *The technique of television news*. London: Focal Press, 2nd edition 1987. xi, 258pp.

(c) Drama Programmes

ANG, Ien. *Watching Dallas: soap opera and the melodramatic imagination*. London: Methuen, 1985. viii, 148pp.

ALAVARADO, Manuel, and STEWART, John. *Made for television: Euston Films Limited:* London: British Film Institute, 1985. xii, 228pp.

BRANDT, George W. *British television drama in the 1980s*. Cambridge: Cambridge University Press, 1993. xix, 283pp.

BUCKINGHAM, David. *Public secrets: EastEnders and its audience*. London: British Film Institute, 1987. 212pp.

BUCKMAN, Peter. *All for love: a study in soap opera*. London: Secker & Warburg, 1984. 226pp.

BURKE, John. *The Bill*. London: Methuen, 1985. iv, 203pp.

BUXTON, David. *From Avengers to Miami Vice: form and ideology in television series*. Manchester: Manchester University Press, 1990. 170pp.

CURTEIS, Ian. *The Falklands play*. London: Hutchinson, 1987. 192pp.

ELDER, Michael. *10 years of Take the High Road*. London: Boxtree, 1990. 96pp.

FERGUSON, James. *Emmerdale Farm: the official companion*. London: Weidenfeld and Nicolson, 1988. 117pp.

GRANADA TELEVISION. *The making of The Jewel in the Crown*. London: Granada Publishing, 1983. 146pp.

HILL, Bill, and HEATLEY, Michael. *Emmerdale: the first twenty years*. London: Boxtree, 1992. 128pp.

HOBSON, Dorothy. *Crossroads: the drama of a soap opera*. London: Methuen, 1982. 176pp.

INDEPENDENT BROADCASTING AUTHORITY. *Audiences for major drama series, The Thornbirds, The Far Pavilions, and Kennedy*, by Barrie Gunter. London: IBA, 1984. 18pp. (IBA Research Department research paper)

INDEPENDENT BROADCASTING AUTHORITY. *Brideshead Revisited: a flawed and final masterpiece of major TV series production?*, by J. Mallory Wober. London: IBA, 1982. 32pp. (IBA Audience Research Department special report).

INDEPENDENT BROADCASTING AUTHORITY. *Drama-documentary seminar: a report of the seminar held at the Museum of the Moving Image on 15 October 1990*. London: IBA, 1990. 23pp.

INDEPENDENT BROADCASTING AUTHORITY. *The Winds of War: audiences, appreciation and opinions for television's most heavily promoted series*, by J. Mallory Wober and Barrie Gunter. London: IBA, 1984. 26pp. (IBA Research Department research paper)

INDEPENDENT TELEVISION COMMISSION. *Coronation Street: an anatomy of its appreciation*, by J. Mallory Wober. London: ITC, 1992. 18pp. (ITC Research reference paper)

INDEPENDENT TELEVISION COMMISSION. *Neighbours at Home and Away: viewers, perceptions of soap operas in Britain*, by J. Mallory Wober. London: ITC, 1992. 17pp.

KAY, Graeme. *Coronation Street: celebrating 30 years*. London: Boxtree, 1990. 160pp.

KERSHAW, H.V. *The Street where I live*. London: Granada, 1981. 192pp.

KINGSLEY, Hilary. *The Bill: the first ten years*. London: Boxtree, 1994. 128pp.

KINGSLEY, Hilary. *Prisoner on Cell Block H: the inside story*. London: Boxtree, 1990. 96pp.

KINGSLEY, Hilary. *Soap box: the Papermac guide to soap opera*. London: Papermac, 1988. 453pp.

LITTLE, Daran. *The Coronation Street story: celebrating thirty-five years of the street*. London: Boxtree, 1995. 288pp.

LYNCH, Tony. *The Bill: the inside story of British television's most successful police series*. London: Boxtree, 1991. 127pp.

PODMORE, Bill, and REECE, Peter. *Coronation Street: the inside story*. London: Macdonald, 1990. 184pp.

POOLE, Mike, and WYVER, John. *Powerplays: Trevor Griffiths in television*. London: British Film Institute, 1984. 203pp.

REDMOND, Phil. *Brookside: the official companion*. London: Weidenfeld & Nicolson, 1987. 114pp.

ROGERS, Dave. *The complete Avengers*. London: Boxtree, 1989. 285pp.

ROGERS, Dave. *The Prisoner and Danger Man*. London: Boxtree, 1989. 254pp.

ROSSINGTON, Jane, *The Crossroads years: the official album*. London: Weidenfeld & Nicolson, 1988. 73pp.

SANDERSON, Mark. *The making of Inspector Morse*. London: Macmillan, 1995. 128pp.

SELF, David. *Television drama: an introduction*. London: Macmillan, 1984. xiii, 173pp.

SILJ, Alessandro. *East of Dallas: the European challenge to American television*. London: British Film Institute, 1988. 224pp.

STACEY, Chris, and SULLIVAN, Davey. *Supersoaps*. London: Boxtree, 1988. 140pp.

STEAD, Peter. *Dennis Potter*. Bridgend: Seren Books, 1993. 147pp.

SUTTON, Shaun. *The largest theatre in the world: thirty years of television drama*. London: BBC, 1982. 160pp.

TIBBALLS, Geoff. *Brookside: the first ten years*. London: Boxtree, 1992. 128pp.

TIBBALLS, Geoff. *London's Burning*. London: Boxtree, 1992. 127pp.

TIBBALLS, Geoff. *Soldier, Soldier*. London: Boxtree, 1993. 128pp.

TIBBALLS, Geoff. *Taggart casebook*. London: Boxtree, 1994. 128pp.

(d)   Comedy and Light Entertainment

CHESTER, Lewis. *Tooth and claw: the inside story of Spitting Image*. London: Faber & Faber, 1986. xi, 146pp.

CROWTHER, Bruce, and PINFOLD, Mike. *Bring me laughter: four decades of TV comedy*. London: Columbus Books, 1987. 192pp.

DAVIS, Anthony. *The laughtermakers: the story of TV comedy*. London: Boxtree/Independent Television Books, 1989.

INDEPENDENT BROADCASTING AUTHORITY. *Attitudes towards TV quiz and game shows*, by Barrie Gunter. London: IBA, 1986.

INDEPENDENT BROADCASTING AUTHORITY. *Entertainment programmes: a report of an IBA Consultation held in Cheltenham, February 1986*. London: IBA, 1986. 89pp.

LLOYD, Jeremy. *Listen very carefully, I shall say this only once: an autobiography*. London: BBC Books, 1992. 170pp.

NEALE, Steve, and KRUTNIK, Frank. *Popular film and television comedy*. London: Routledge, 1990. 291pp.

SNOAD, Harold. *Directing situation comedy*. Borehamwood, Hertfordshire: BBC Television Training, 1988. 56pp.

STRINATI, Dominic, and WAGG, Stephen. *Come on down?: popular media culture in post-war Britain*. London: Routledge, 1992. xi, 391pp. (Chapter 7: 'The price is right but the moments are sticky: television, quiz and game shows, and popular culture', by Garry Whannel)

WILMUT, Roger, and ROSENGARD, Peter. *Didn't you kill my Mother-in-law?: the story of alternative comedy in Britain from the Comedy Store to Saturday Live*. London: Methuen, 1989. xvii, 284pp.

(e)   Children's and Educational Programmes

CHOAT, Ernest, et al. *Teachers and television*. London: Croom Helm, 1987. xii, 162pp.

CHOAT, Ernest, and GRIFFIN, Harry. *Using television in the primary school*. London: Routledge, 1989. ix, 104pp.

CORRIE, Andrew, and McCREADY, John. *Phil Redmond's Grange Hill: the official companion*. London: Weidenfeld & Nicolson, 1988. 96pp.

DUNCAN, Judith. (ed.) *Broadcasting and school education in Scotland*. Edinburgh: HMSO, 1989. 150pp.

FINCH, Christopher. *Of muppets and men: the making of The Muppet Show.* London: Michael Joseph, 1982. 180pp.

HARTLEY, Ian. *Goodnight children ... everywhere: an informal history of children's broadcasting.* Southborough, Kent: Midas Books, 1983. 165pp.

HAWKRIDGE, David, and ROBINSON, John. *Organizing educational broadcasting.* London: Croom Helm, 1982. 302pp.

HOME, Anna. *Into the box of delights: a history of children's television.* London: BBC Books, 1993. 176pp.

LANGHAM, Josephine. *Teachers and television: a history of the IBA's Educational Fellowship Scheme.* London: John Libbey, 1990. vii, 328pp.

MOSS, Robin et al. *Television in schools.* London: John Libbey, 1991. 62pp.

TIBBALLS, Geoff. *The golden age of children's television.* London: Titan Books, 1991. 159pp.

(f)   Religious Broadcasting

ARTHUR, Chris. (ed.) *Religion and the media: an introductory reader.* Cardiff: University of Wales Press, 1993. xii, 302pp.

INDEPENDENT BROADCASTING AUTHORITY. *Audiences for religious broadcasts on television: 1983–84,* by Barrie Gunter and Shehina Fazal. London: IBA, 1984. 16pp. (IBA Research Department working paper)

INDEPENDENT BROADCASTING AUTHORITY. *Broadcasting and the community: a report on a Consultation held at the Kilbirnie Hotel, Newquay, 14–16 November 1983.* London: IBA, 1983. 47pp.

INDEPENDENT BROADCASTING AUTHORITY. *The end of the road?: report of the seventh IBA Religious Consultation, Grange-over-Sands, 13–15 April 1983.* London: IBA, 1983. 96pp.

INDEPENDENT BROADCASTING AUTHORITY. *Godwatching: viewers, religion and Television,* by Michael Svennevig et al. London: John Libbey, 1988. 67pp. (IBA Television research monograph)

INDEPENDENT BROADCASTING AUTHORITY. *Morning Worship: viewer's reactions to the Sunday morning religious service,* by Shehina Fazal. London: IBA, 1990. 8pp. (IBA Research Department research paper)

INDEPENDENT BROADCASTING AUTHORITY. *Religious broadcasting in the 1990s. Report of the Consultation: 2–4 November 1988, Newcastle, County Down.* London: IBA, 1988. 84pp.

INDEPENDENT TELEVISION COMMISSION. *Seeing is believing: religion and television in the 1990s,* by Barrie Gunter and Rachel Viney. London: John Libbey, 1994. vi, 134pp. (Television research monograph)

MORRIS, Colin. *God-in-a-box: Christian strategy in the television age.* London: Hodder & Stoughton, 1984. 238pp.

QUICKE, Andrew, and QUICKE, Juliet. *Hidden agendas: the politics of religious Broadcasting in Britain 1987–1991.* Virginia Beach, Virginia: Dominion Kings Grant Publications, 1992. 276pp.

(g) Arts and Science Programmes

CARVER, Robert. (ed.) *Ariel at bay: reflections on broadcasting and the arts: a festschrift for Philip French.* Manchester: Carcanet, 1990. 212pp.

HAYWARD, Philip. (ed.) *Picture this: media representations of visual art and artists.* London: John Libbey, 1988. viii, 200pp. (Arts Council series)

INDEPENDENT BROADCASTING AUTHORITY. *A report of the IBA/Arts Council Consultation on arts programmes.* (15 June 1988 at Granada Television) London: IBA, 1988. 56pp.

INDEPENDENT BROADCASTING AUTHORITY. *Report of the Consultation on Science. The Royal Society,* 12 October 1988. London: IBA, 1988. 82pp.

INDEPENDENT BROADCASTING AUTHORITY. *The art of television: arts programming and its audience.* London: IBA, 1989. 24pp.

INDEPENDENT BROADCASTING AUTHORITY. *The television audience for the arts,* by D.S. Kerr. London: IBA, 1983. 17pp.

INDEPENDENT TELEVISION COMMISSION. *Science and technology on television: patterns of viewing and perception,* by J. Mallory Wober. London: ITC, 1992. 33pp. (ITC Research reference paper)

JORDAN, Stephanie, and ALLEN, Dave. (eds) *Parallel lines: media representations of dance.* London: John Libbey, 1993. 241pp. (Arts Council series)

TAMBLING, Jeremy. (ed.) *A night at the opera: media representations of opera.* London: John Libbey, 1994. iii, 310pp. (Arts Council series)

WALKER, John A. *Arts TV: a history of arts television in Britain.* London: John Libbey, 1993. x, 245pp. (Arts Council series)

(h) Sport on Television

BARNETT, Steven. *Games and sets: the changing face of sport on television.* London: British Film Institute, 1990. 214pp.

BLAIN, Neil, BOYLE, Raymond, and O'DONNELL, Hugh. *Sport and national identity in the European media.* Leicester: Leicester University Press, 1993. vii, 209pp.

INDEPENDENT BROADCASTING AUTHORITY. *Anyone for tennis?,* by Shehina Fazal. London: IBA, 1983. 7pp. (IBA Research Department research paper)

INDEPENDENT BROADCASTING AUTHORITY. *Attitudes concerning television sport,* by Barrie Gunter. London: IBA, 1985. 24pp. (IBA Research Department research paper)

INDEPENDENT BROADCASTING AUTHORITY. *Television's coverage of the 1986 World Cup*, by Barrie Gunter. London: IBA, 1986. 34pp. (IBA Research Department research paper)

WHANNEL, Garry. *Fields in vision: television sport and cultural transformation.* London: Routledge, 1992. xii, 243pp.

11. PERSONALITIES: BIOGRAPHIES, AUTOBIOGRAPHIES AND MEMOIRS

BOSE, Mihir. *Michael Grade: screening the image.* London: Virgin Publishing, 1992. viii, 296pp.

COOK, John R. *Dennis Potter: a life on screen.* Manchester: Manchester University Press, 1995. x, 368pp.

DAVIES, Hunter. *The Grades: the first family of British entertainment.* London: Weidenfeld & Nicolson, 1981. xv, 268pp.

DAY, Robin. *Grand inquisitor: memoirs.* London: Weidenfeld & Nicolson,1989. xv, 296pp.

FALK, Quentin, and PRINCE, Dominic. *Last of a kind: the sinking of Lew Grade.* London: Quartet Books, 1987. viii, 183pp.

FERRIS, Paul. *Sir Huge: the life of Huw Wheldon.* London: Michael Joseph, 1990. x, 307pp.

FORMAN, Denis. *Persona Granada: some memories of Sidney Bernstein and the early days of Independent Television.* London: Andre Deutsch, 1997. 320pp.

FROST, David. *An autobiography: Part One – From congregations to audiences.* London: HarperCollins, 1993. xiii, 542pp.

GRADE, Lew. *Still dancing: my story.* London: Collins, 1987. 314pp.

MAITLAND, Donald. *Diverse times, sundry places.* Brighton: Alpha Press, 1996. x, 310pp.

MOOREHEAD, Caroline. *Sidney Bernstein: a biography.* London: Jonathan Cape, 1984. xiv, 329pp.

NEIL, Andrew. *Full disclosure.* London: Macmillan, 1996. 481pp.

POTTER, Dennis. *Potter on Potter*, edited by Graham Fuller. London: Faber & Faber, 1993. xviii, 171pp.

SHAWCROSS, William. *Rupert Murdoch: ringmaster of the information circus.* London: Chatto & Windus, 1992. xiv, 616pp.

SMITH, Gus. *Eamonn Andrews: his life.* London: W.H. Allen, 1988. xi, 241pp.

SNODDY, Raymond. *Greenfinger: the rise of Michael Green and Carlton Communications.* London: Faber & Faber, 1996. xiv, 306pp.

TINKER, Jack. *The television barons.* London: Quartet Books, 1980. xii, 222pp.

TUCCILLE, Jerome. *Murdoch: a biography.* London: Piatkus, 1989. xvi, 284pp.

WHITEHOUSE, Mary. *Quite contrary: an autobiography by Mary Whitehouse.* London: Sidgwick & Jackson, 1993. vii, 239pp.

INDEX